THE KNIGHT AND CHIVALRY

The Knight and Chivalry

REVISED EDITION

Richard Barber

THE BOYDELL PRESS

First published 1970
First published by The Boydell Press, Woodbridge, 1974
Revised edition 1995
Reprinted with revised bibliography 2000

ISBN 0 85115 627 4 (hardback)
ISBN 0 85115 663 0 (paperback)

A catalogue record for this book is available
from the British Library

Library of Congress Cataloging-in-Publication Data applied for

The Boydell Press is an imprint of Boydell & Brewer Ltd
P O Box 9, Woodbridge, Suffolk IP12 3DF, UK
and of Boydell & Brewer Inc.
P O Box 41026, Rochester, N Y 14604-4126, U S A

This publication is printed on acid-free paper

Printed in Slovenia

Contents

LIST OF ILLUSTRATIONS

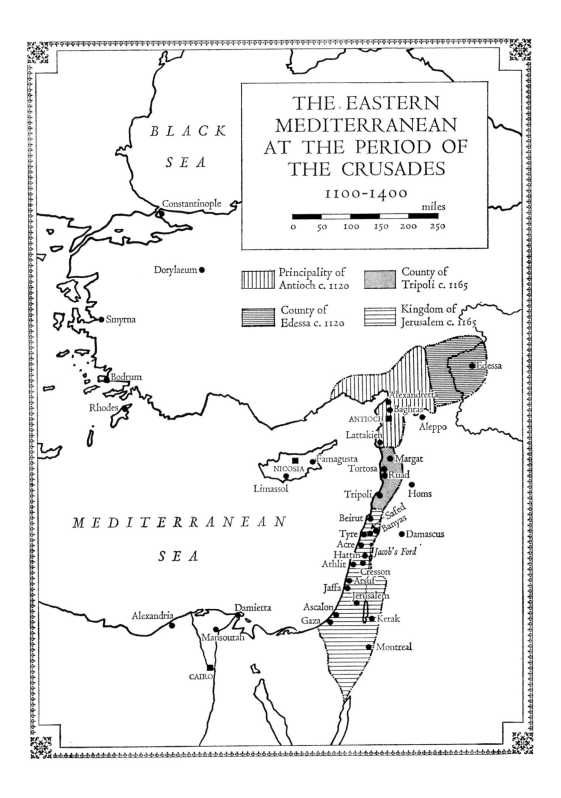

THE EASTERN
MEDITERRANEAN
AT THE PERIOD OF
THE CRUSADES
1100-1400

miles

0   50   100   150   200   250

Principality of
Antioch c. 1120

County of
Tripoli c. 1165

County of
Edessa c. 1120

Kingdom of
Jerusalem c. 1165

BLACK
SEA

Constantinople

Dorylaeum

Smyrna

Bodrum

Rhodes

MEDITERRANEAN

SEA

Edessa

Alexandretta

Baghras

ANTIOCH

Aleppo

Lattakieh

Famagusta

Margat

NICOSIA

Tortosa

Ruad

Limassol

Homs

Tripoli

Beirut

Safed

Banyas

Tyre

Damascus

Acre

Hattin

Jacob's Ford

Athlit

Cresson

Arsuf

Jaffa

Jerusalem

Ascalon

Gaza

Kerak

Alexandria

Damietta

Montreal

Mansourah

CAIRO

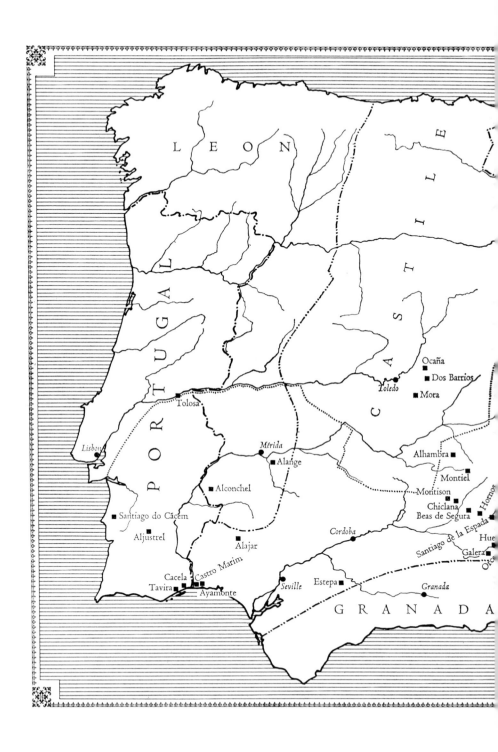

LEON

PORTUGAL

CASTILE

GRANADA

Ocaña
Dos Barrios
Toledo
Mora

Tolosa

Lisbon

Mérida
Alange

Alhambra

Montiel
Montison
Chiclana
Beas de Segura
Hornos

Alconchel

Santiago de la Espada
Hue

Cordoba

Galera

Santiago do Cácem

Otc

Aljustrel

Alajar

Cacela Castro Marim
Tavira
Ayamonte

Seville

Estepa

Granada

G R A N A D A

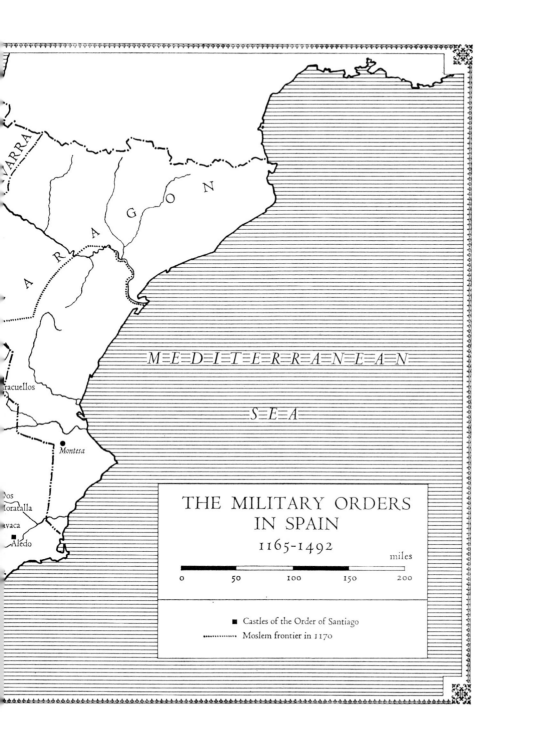

ARAGON

NAVARRA

MEDITERRANEAN

SEA

THE MILITARY ORDERS
IN SPAIN
1165-1492

miles

| 0 | 50 | 100 | 150 | 200 |

■ Castles of the Order of Santiago
·········· Moslem frontier in 1170

racuellos

Montesa

os
Moratalla

avaca

Aledo

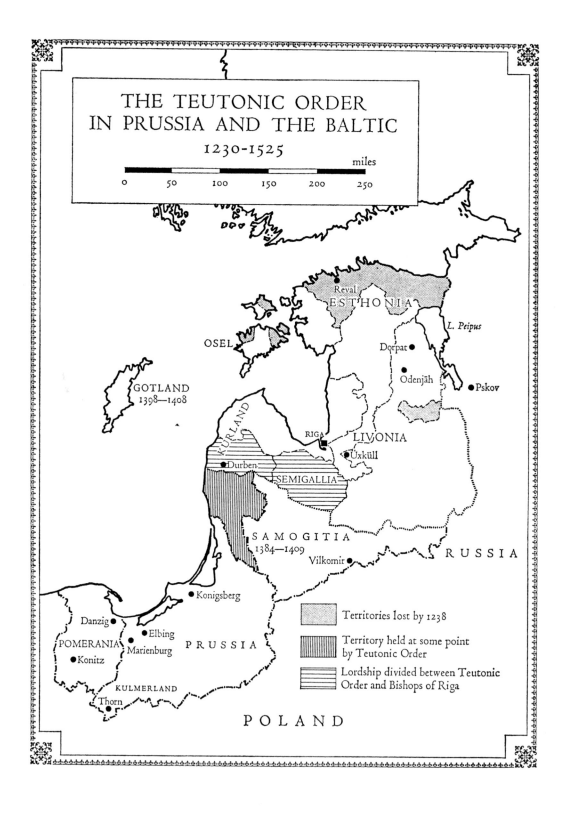

THE TEUTONIC ORDER
IN PRUSSIA AND THE BALTIC
1230–1525

miles

0   50   100   150   200   250

Reval
ESTHONIA

OSEL

L. Peipus

Dorpat

Odenjäh

Pskov

GOTLAND
1398—1408

KURLAND

RIGA
LIVONIA

Üxküll

Durben

SEMIGALLIA

SAMOGITIA
1384—1409

Vilkomir

RUSSIA

Konigsberg

Danzig

Elbing

POMERANIA

Marienburg

PRUSSIA

Konitz

KULMERLAND

Thorn

POLAND

Territories lost by 1238

Territory held at some point
by Teutonic Order

Lordship divided between Teutonic
Order and Bishops of Riga

Preface to the 1995 edition

When the first version of this book appeared, in 1970, chivalry was a neglected subject; there had been relatively little written on the subject in this century, and the critical literature was modest. In recent years, there has been a veritable flood of publications in the field, and revising the text has been a considerable undertaking.

I hope that the original concept of the book has survived intact, and even improved: my aim - perhaps rashly - was to provide an overview of knighthood and chivalry from the beginnings to the Renaissance, covering not only the historical sources but also the literature of courtly love and chivalry. In an introductory work of this kind, there are inevitably simplifications and generalisations: to provide references for every fact and statement would hopelessly overburden the book, and I have concentrated on giving pointers to sources and to recent scholarship, with a select bibliography as a guide to further reading.

My debts in the work of revision are considerable; I have benefitted from conversations and suggestions over a number of years, and a list of those who have contributed will inevitably fail to record all my debts. First and foremost, I am most grateful to those who have been kind enough to read the book in its final draft and to make valuable suggestions, as well as saving me from my more egregious errors: Harry Jackson, John Gillingham, Matthew Bennett, Jonathan Boulton, Tony Hunt, and Matthew Strickland have all contributed in this way. On a wider front, I have benefitted greatly from discussions with the participants at the Medieval Knighthood conferences at Strawberry Hill, and at the Harlaxton conferences, as well as the more wide-ranging occasions at Kalamazoo and Leeds.

I owe a particular debt to Juliet Barker, who has kindly allowed me to rework and summarise our joint book on *Tournaments* as chapters 9 - 11 of the present book; in so doing, some of her *ipsissima verba* may have been incorporated into the text, and I can only plead that if this has happened, it was not done intentionally.

In terms of reference material and unpublished articles, my thanks are due particularly to John Gillingham, Matthew Strickland and Elspeth Kennedy, and to Marina Smyth for a copy of the American Bar Association translation of the *Siete Partidas*.

Finally, the responsibility for all errors, omissions (and outdated opinions!) is of course my own, including those of typesetting.

While a great deal of the text in the current edition is completely new, substantial parts of the original remain, and I am grateful for the advice given at the time of the first edition by Professor Edward Miller and Miss Madeline Blaess, then of the

University of Sheffield, and Professor R. J. Taylor, then of the University of Sussex, by Sir Roy Strong and by Kevin Crossley-Holland.

Neither edition would have been possible without the unfailing assistance of the staff of the London Library, the British Library and Cambridge University Library.

Finally, I must record a special debt to the late John MacCallum Scott for his enthusiasm for the idea of this book and for encouragement in the wider world of publishing. And in the twenty-five years since the book first appeared, I have incurred a larger, private debt which a mere acknowledgement could never repay.

A Note on Terms

In a wide-ranging book such as this, the problem of naming concepts, ranks and periods of time is always a difficulty. The very word 'knight' is the largest problem of all. In order not to confuse the reader, it is probably best to pre-empt some of my argument, and to say at the outset that I use the term 'mounted warrior' to describe the predecessor of the knight, up to the point in the early twelfth century when – so I believe – we can distinguish the first emergence of an idealised view of 'knighthood'. The 'knight' is therefore a mounted warrior who enjoys a specific social status and a distinct ethos, which eventually blossoms into the wider culture of chivalry. I am primarily interested in the history of classic knighthood; the complex and uncertain image of the 'proto-knight' deserves a study of its own.

Secondly, I have used the terms 'middle ages' and 'medieval' in a way which is perhaps unfashionable today, to refer to the period from c.800 to 1500. For a discussion of the origin and problems of the concept of the middle ages, the reader is referred to Fred C. Robinson, 'Medieval, The Middle Ages', *Speculum* 59, 1984, 745-756, and Toby Burrows, 'Unmaking 'the middle ages'', *Journal of Medieval History* 7, 1981, 127-134.

PART ONE

From Mounted Warrior to Knight

I

The Mounted Warrior

IT IS A GREY WINDSWEPT DAY in September 1991. On a bleak field overlooking a river on the east coast of England, two newly-dug pits lie open to the sky, revealing for the first time in a thousand years the burial of a young chieftain and his horse, interred a few feet from each other, each with their provisions for the journey to the next world. Here at Sutton Hoo, a seafaring people raised a great mound over the treasure-ship in which they sent their dead lord into the unknown. Yet when they came to bury the younger man, they chose to set beside him his weapons and his steed. From the very outset of the middle ages, the man on horseback was set apart from the rest of society: the horse was a sign of rank, of wealth. But there was no other mystique attached to horsemanship: the warriors of Sutton Hoo fought on foot, riding to battle and then dismounting, and the burial of a horse beside the young warrior was designed to enable him to reach the otherworld quickly, just as his lord would journey there swiftly in his ship.

Contrast with this a passage from one of the greatest twelfth-century French romances, Chrétien de Troyes' *Perceval*, which was to become the story of the Holy Grail. The hero, whose father and uncles have all been killed in battle, is brought up by his mother remote from the world which has proved so fatal to those she loved, deep in the forest. One day he hears riders crashing through the thickets towards him, and is confronted by dazzling beings in white and red, gold and blue and silver. Overcome with awe, he replies to their leader's greeting with the simple question: 'Are you God?'

Perceval's question arises out of the physical splendour of the knights, but it has a further resonance once we turn to look at the history of knighthood and chivalry. For what distinguishes the mounted warrior from the knight, and in turn knighthood from chivalry, is an ethical and spiritual content. The mounted warrior, up to the late eleventh century, is no more than a proto-knight, an embryonic version of the knight of the high middle ages; and twelfth-century knighthood is only a precursor of chivalry proper. To use the word knight, with the overtones that it now carries, of mounted warriors of the ninth or tenth century, makes it difficult for us to see them as they really are: it may be a convenience for the historian, but in tracing the rise of an institution and an idea, it confuses the issue. The man on horseback may have a mystique — the

3

Roman emperor immortalised in equestrian bronze, the Norse god Odin on the eight-legged Sleipnir – but it was a vaguer and wider aura than the concepts which we shall try to explore. The 'knight' is a mounted warrior who enjoys a specific social status and a distinct ethos, *ésprit de corps*, mentality – call it what we will – which eventually blossoms into the wider culture of chivalry, and draws on literary and spiritual ideals, until we begin to wonder whether Perceval's question does not go to the heart of the matter: were these indeed the gods of a possible religion? But we must first turn to the mounted warriors, the proto-knights and humble precursors of the high priests of chivalry.

Cavalry in the early middle ages

The figure of the knight at once dominates the mediaeval world and distinguishes it from the classical era. The knight inherited both the lands and status of the magnate of the Roman world in his luxurious villa and the political power of the infantry soldier of the Praetorian Guard. His roots were barbarian; his ideals, born of the three turbulent centuries between the end of the western Empire and the accession of Charlemagne, were in sharp contrast to the Roman order. Above all, two characteristics stand out: in war, he fought on horseback where the Roman legions had fought on foot; in peace, he held his land because he was a skilled fighter.

In the Roman wars of conquest and defence, the legions had occasionally encountered light horsemen armed with javelins. Such horsemen were not unusual among the Germanic tribes, but rarely caused any great reverses of fortune; they were little esteemed as auxiliary troops when the Romans did think fit to hire them. They were mounted bareback, with a loose cloth as saddle and a very primitive bit, and lacking stirrups, their light javelins were difficult to use accurately, and they were too easily unseated to make a really effective charge. As mounted archers, the German horsemen did not compare with the Parthian troops who overwhelmed Crassus at Carrhae in 53 BC. It was only with the advent of the Goths that cavalry began to count. The new enemies, nomads whose life was lived on horseback, were at first raiders and plunderers; for this they needed the horseman's speed and mobility. Initially, they used horses as means of transport, and dismounted on the battlefield; however, by the late fourth century, they considered it more honourable to fight on horseback. At Adrianople in 378, for example, the cavalry of the Goths played an important part in an admittedly confused battle, which resulted in a serious Roman defeat.

However, even with the advent of the Huns (who were so inseparable from their horses that a Roman writer called them shaggy centaurs) the new style of cavalry warfare found favour only in the eastern Empire. Under Belisarius, in the sixth century, the heavy cavalry or cataphracts were developed into an effective force, using javelins and bows in imitation of the eastern horsemen whom they faced in battle. By contrast, armed riders were scarce in the west. Of the Germanic tribes, only the Visigoths, Franks, and to a lesser extent the Lombards, were successful horsemen; and the Franks and Anglo-Saxons remained skilled in infantry tactics as late as the eleventh century. It was probably the Frankish infantry that broke the onslaught of the Arab cavalry at Poitiers in 732: 'The men of the north remained as motionless as a wall, and frozen together like a block of ice, they put the Arabs to the sword.'[1] But the Franks had already experimented with horses in the field, and perhaps learned from their Arab adversaries.

A slight superiority in mobility and striking power would not have been enough to ensure that the horseman would supersede the foot-soldier. At this point, however, technical developments vastly increased his usefulness. The most important was the use of stirrups.[2] These made it much easier for the rider to stay securely in the saddle and to wield weapons without losing his balance. The stirrup first appears in China at the end of the fifth century, and may have come originally from nomadic tribes on the eastern borders. In the simple form of two iron rings suspended on thongs, they were adopted by the Chinese, but the idea did not spread further until late in the seventh century; contacts between east and west were slow, and the fashion was by no means universal in China itself until considerably later. At the end of the seventh century it appeared in Iran just before the Arab conquest, and in Hungary, where Avar tribes from central Asia had settled. Its progress continued to western Europe, though exactly how it came to Carolingian France remains a mystery. Stirrups are found in burials in Frisia and Saxony in the eighth century, but do not appear among the Vikings until the next century, though the evidence is scanty. They were not used in Byzantium until the ninth century.

The emergence of cavalry in the eighth and ninth centuries as an important part of Frankish armies is difficult to document, and arises from a complex interplay of changes in society and in the objectives of warfare. In the chaotic centuries in which the Roman empire in the west disintegrated, to be replaced eventually by the rise of Frankish power, the nature of warfare was disorganised, spasmodic, and largely between nomadic marauders as the aggressors and an ill-organised native population defending their homes. There was some primitive siege-warfare, but pitched battles were rare;

---

1   *MGH, Auctores Antiqui* xi.361.

2   On the stirrup, see A.D.H.Bivar, 'The stirrup and its origin', *Oriental Art*, NS I, 1955, 61-5; Lynn White, *Medieval Technology and Social Change*, Oxford 1962; Bernard S. Bachrach, 'Charles Martel, Mounted Shock Combat, the Stirrup and Feudalism', *Studies in Medieval and Renaissance History* VII, 1970, 47-75; D.A.Bullough, '*Europae Pater*; Charlemagne and his achievement in the light of recent scholarship', *EHR* 85, 1970, 84-89; Wolfgang Braunfels (ed.) *Charlemagne: Oeuvre, Rayonnement, Survivances* (Aix-la-Chapelle 1965) 63-4 .

skirmishes against would-be raiders were the typical pattern. The defenders were local levies, fighting on foot, and because they were rarely far from home, they did not need horses for transport. Indeed, they probably could not have afforded them; and it was only with the gradual reorganisation of civilian society that the economic situation improved sufficiently to allow a class of semi-professional soldiers to re-emerge, towards the end of the sixth century, who could afford to fight a long distance from home, because slaves or serfs worked their lands. A century later, we find organised garrisons in the major cities, under the direction of the central administration, combined with forces led by the local magnates.

It is with the establishment of effective central control under Pepin and Charlemagne that we find a military structure re-emerging which is not *ad hoc* and dependent on local levies. Charlemagne needed troops who would serve anywhere, and who could be rewarded or dismissed at his pleasure. War for the Franks was no longer local or defensive, but was a matter of massively-planned long-range wars of conquest, across the Pyrenees, beyond the Rhine, among the forests of Brittany or over the Alps into Italy. The men who went on those expeditions were now an elite and in military terms, a largely successful elite. Experience, training and confidence counted for much, but we need to look for other factors as well. The Byzantine cataphracts had all these qualities, yet they never achieved the status of the medieval knight.

Warfare rapidly became a duel between cavalry with infantry support, and the spectacle of two armies meeting in a full-scale charge was soon to become the classic climax of a battle. Even in the heyday of the knight, however, cavalry were not always used as mounted troops. There are numerous examples of battles won by cavalry dismounted for the actual battle, and just as many where rash action by mounted troops against infantry over unfavourable ground proved fatal. For the knight was not simply a good horseman; his efficiency in the field depended also on his skill in all kinds of fighting. The superiority of cavalry forces, whether mounted or dismounted, depended on other factors; they were more likely to have received proper training, for example, and mounted troops usually arrived in better condition on the battlefield than footsoldiers. The quality and condition of mounted forces was at least as important as the brute power of the cavalry charge.

However, the stirrup alone was not enough to ensure the predominance of the mounted warrior. It was not until after AD 1000, and possibly as late as 1100, that the cavalry charge with lances held in rest became common.[3] In the epic *Chanson de Roland*, Roland unseats his foes, and thrusts them 'pleine sa hanste', the length of his

---

[3] See D.J.A.Ross, 'L'originalité de "Turoldus": le maniement de la lance', *Cahiers de civilisation medievale*, 6, 1963, 127-138, and R.Allen Brown, 'The Battle of Hastings', *Proceedings of the Battle Conference on Anglo-Norman Studies* iii, 1981, 12-15.

lance, from the saddle, which would only be possible with a lance held in rest. The poem, as it has come down to us, is usually dated to the second half of the twelfth century; and the use of this technique is confirmed by the Bayeux Tapestry, which shows heavy lances used in rest, and smaller javelin-lances thrown overarm and used underarm against infantry. The Normans seem to have been pioneers of the technique; artistic evidence from Catalonia, for example, would imply that the couched lance was little used there before 1140.[4] The technique of using a lance in rest at close quarters needed changes in armour, notably a long pointed shield as protection while the rider was unable to use a sword in his own defence, and in harness: a saddle with a high pommel which provided support at the moment of impact was evolved. It seems to have been at this time that horses were shod for the first time in western Europe, enabling them to negotiate rougher terrain and longer distances. This gave cavalry a new degree of mobility, while the use of the lance in rest transformed their effectiveness. Anna Comnena, daughter of Alexius Comnenus, who saw the Franks at Byzantium on the First Crusade in 1096-7, said that a Frank on horseback 'would make a hole in the walls of Babylon', and spoke of their 'irresistible first shock'.[5] The sheer force of the new cavalry seemed awesome, even when set against the sophisticated military resources of Byzantium. The new pattern of warfare had arrived.

Social and economic status of warriors

The military power of the new mounted warriors explained only part of their pre-eminence. They were powerful figures in peacetime as well as in wartime, and had begun to emerge as such in the great transition from classical to mediaeval society during the centuries once known as the Dark Ages. This period was marked by violence and anarchy such as even pre-Roman Europe had scarcely known. The internecine wars of the Merovingians in France, the heathen domination of Germany, the wars of Visigoth and Saracen in Spain, Goth and Lombard in Italy, in their various and separate times and theatres, made the birth of the new society a harsh one. The marks of this ordeal by fire and the sword can be traced in many mediaeval attitudes of mind, from the great concept of the sanctity of the established order down to small superstitions stemming from the terror the invaders had once inspired.

The period of transition falls into two great phases, the watershed being the reign of Charlemagne and the breathing-space of civilisation which the military victories of

---

4   Victoria Cirlot, 'Techniques guerrières en Catalogne féodale: le maniement de la lance', *Cahiers de civilisation médiévale*, 28, 1985, 35-43

5   Anna Comnena, *The Alexiad*, tr. Elizabeth A.S. Dawes (London 1967) 122-3, 342.

his house made possible. Up to this point, men had looked back to the Roman Empire as the great example of peace and prosperity, even if it was an inheritance largely misunderstood. Charlemagne's reign was the new starting-point for laws and social institutions. In the earlier period, the veneer of Roman customs was clearer, if weak in practice when tested against the realities of a barbarian world. The Romans had relied on the imperial administration to provide those elements of order which were now so conspicuously lacking: the great legions of the Empire encamped on the German frontier guaranteed the peace of the pro-consul in retirement at his Gaulish villa, the safety of the merchant trafficking in Spain. The men who held power or wealth in the Roman empire had no need for more immediate protection, and little contact with, or respect for, the realities of military life. The glorious ancient days of the Republic, the conquering forays of the early Empire, had faded in men's memories, and military service was seen only as a burden fit only for hired menials. Let barbarian fight barbarian, one under the Roman eagles, the other in his rustic skins; if peace could be bought by hiring soldiers, it was worth the price. How the price became more than the Empire could raise, and the other causes of Rome's decline, are not part of our present theme; but when the barbarians overran Gaul and Spain, the heart of the Roman Empire in the west, there was no tradition of military service among the local magnates which might have inspired a stouter, individual resistance. The Roman *equester ordo* (equestrian order), descended from the cavalry troops of the Republic, had largely become a class of wealthy financiers and administrators who had no military connections whatsoever. It was not in the Roman world that the mediaeval knight had his origins, though many medieval writers tried to make the connection, out of veneration for the Classical past.

The barbarian invaders, on the other hand, were a nomadic society for whom war was commonplace, necessary and almost a welcome alternative to their pastoral life. Their incessant movement in search of new pastures meant that they grouped naturally into close-knit tribes, never more than a few thousand strong, and personal bonds were much more important than in a more settled society. They relied only on each other for security in face of danger, and the hierarchy was of the simplest: a chief and a few chosen companions-in-arms were their leaders. This structure of the tribe remained unchanged until the era of settlements began; and Tacitus' picture of it as it was in the late first century AD remained true until as late as the Carolingian wars with the Saxons in north Germany:

> No business, public or private, is transacted except in arms. But it is the rule that no one shall take up his arms until the State has attested that he is likely to make good. When that time comes, one of the chiefs or the father or a kinsman equips the young warrior with shield and spear in the public council. This with the Germans is the equivalent of our *toga* – the first public distinction of youth. They cease to rank merely as members of the household and are now members of the state. Conspicuous ancestry or great services

8

rendered by their fathers can win the rank of chief for boys still in their teens. They are attached to the other chiefs, who are more mature and approved, and no one blushes to be seen thus in the ranks of the companions. This order of companions has even its different grades, as determined by the leader, and there is intense rivalry among the companions for the first place beside the chief, among the chiefs for the most numerous and enthusiastic companions. Dignity and power alike consist in being continually attended by a corps of chosen youths. This gives you consideration in peacetime and security in war. Nor is it only in a man's own nation that he can win name and fame by the superior number and quality of his companions, but in neighbouring states as well. Chiefs are courted by embassies and complimented by gifts, and they often virtually decide wars by the mere weight of their reputation. On the field of battle it is a disgrace to the chief to be surpassed in valour by his companions, to the companions not to come up to the valour of their chiefs. As for leaving a battle alive after your chief has fallen, *that* means life-long infamy and shame. To defend and protect him, to put down one's own acts of heroism to his credit that is what they really mean by 'allegiance'. The chiefs fight for victory, the companions for their chief. Many noble youths, if the land of their birth is stagnating in a protracted peace, deliberately seek out other tribes, where some war is afoot. The Germans have no taste for peace; renown is easier won among perils, and you cannot maintain a large body of companions except by violence and war.[6]

The emphasis on companionship and the investing of arms in public ceremony are commonplaces of primitive societies in many parts of the world. Yet they were in sharp contrast with Roman practice and thought, not only by reason of the uncouthness of one and the civilisation of the other. The toga which marked the Roman's coming of age was a legal, almost administrative distinction; the German's shield and spear were practical. The companions of the chief were chosen for strength and skill in fighting, not for their subtlety or political acumen: and yet they were the chief councillors of the tribe by virtue of their position.

This war-based organisation remained appropriate long after the nomadic existence, which in itself entailed so much fighting, had been exchanged for a settled life as farmers. Wars which had been fought for booty were now fought for political reasons, to gain control of land. War remained 'the normal thread of every leader's career and the *raison d'être* of every position of authority.'[7] In the troubles of the dying Empire, when the *pax romana* failed, the magnates looked to their own security in face of the collapse of public order and acquired hired soldiers. The *bucellarii*, as they were called, were in a position of power only because of ever-present danger; they were a nuisance to be tolerated, not companions of equal rank. Although apparently similar

6   Tacitus, *On Britain and Germany*, tr. H.Mattingly (London & Baltimore 1948) III-II2.
7   Marc Bloch, *La société féodale* (Paris 1939-40) tr as *Feudal Society* (2nd edn, London 1962) 151.

to the *bucellarii*, the small group around the Merovingian chieftains in France known as *gasindi*, and a similar band around the kings called *antrustiones*, derived from Germanic predecessors; the name *gasindi* implies fellowship, the comradeship of Tacitus' *'comites'*. The royal warriors were also bound by an oath to their leader. To the *antrustiones* were given the great positions of state, as *comes* meaning comrade in classical Latin, count in mediaeval Latin or as duke (*dux*, leader) with more specifically military duties.

Until the seventh century, the bond between leader and follower consisted of nothing more than an oath of personal loyalty. However, another form of personal dependence had been developing in this turbulent society, a tie arising out of the need for protection. Under the late Roman empire, magnates had provided themselves with a bodyguard by accepting the service of clients, a practice with political rather than military obligations which had now become a form of mutual defence and a source of security for both parties; the client was under the magnate's protection, and in turn furthered the latter's interests. Roman poets often wrote satires about clients and their patrons, showing the client as downtrodden and reduced to flattery; but this form of service was not servile, that is, free men did not regard it a tainted with slavery, but as a basically honourable contract.

In the chaos of the sixth and seventh centuries, this institution, under the name of 'commendation', became much more widespread. The most usual case was that in which a very poor man, simply in order to survive, bound himself completely to a magnate in return for sustenance. The benefits and services changed all the way up the scale. It was a very flexible institution, whose strength derived from one chief characteristic of those troubled times: that loyalty was at a premium, whether from slave or boon-companion. The Merovingian kingship has been tersely described as 'despotism tempered by assassination'. A follower of King Guntram in the sixth century could remind him: 'We know where the axe is which cut off your brothers' heads, and its edge is still sharp; soon it will cut off your head too.' So it became just as important to have some kind of formal tie between king and lord, and lord and warrior, as between starving peasant and provider.

Commendation, as a solemn contract in an age when the legal niceties were rarely observed, was soon symbolised in the ceremony of homage, an outward and visible sign of the relationship of the two parties. The suppliant placed his hands between those of his lord, in token of his obedience and the lord's protection. Later, the formula grew more complex; the would-be vassal knelt bareheaded and weaponless before his lord, and declared his intention aloud: 'Sire, I become your man.' This was followed by an affirmation of loyalty, and finally by an oath of loyalty, usually sworn on a relic. But the basic relationship of lord and vassal remained almost unchanged from the eighth century to the fourteenth. Homage coloured men's unconscious thought, and was reflected in other liaisons: lovers swore fealty to their beloved, their more serious companions did spiritual homage to Our Lady.

If loyalty was to flourish, more tangible bonds than those of oaths were needed. Just as the poor man who virtually enslaved himself expected his sustenance in return, so the great lords had their price. In theory, the grants made after homage had been paid were for maintenance, but a lord did not have to support his vassal as well as protect him unless this was a specific condition of the agreement. The benefice was a simple means of maintaining the vassal by giving him sufficient land to feed himself. Vassalage and benefices had originally been all-embracing institutions, capable of providing for the household servants of a lesser vassal (for example the cook, who would be granted a small corner of the benefice his employer had received from a higher lord) as well as for the *vassi dominici*, the great magnates who were the king's direct vassals and who received estates which were almost principalities.

By the end of the eighth century, the system of vassalage was operating from the highest to the lowest levels of society.[8] The earliest instances of full and formal contracts of vassalage that have come down to us involve the German princes who formed alliances with the rising Carolingian dynasty, such as duke Tassilo III of Bavaria in 757. The principal political use of the idea at this time was to ensure the loyalty of the great officers of state, the counts and magnates. At the other end of the scale, the Carolingian kings rewarded their servants and stewards by granting them estates, and men who were little more than serfs could hope to rise in the world by hard work in the royal service. Between these two groups came the freemen, a yeoman class owning small holdings without any tie, and the new mounted warriors who owed military service to the king. The combination of military service and landholding was a new one, and to see how it arose, we must retrace our steps, to the early days of the Frankish kingdom.

The Franks, unlike the majority of the Germanic tribes, were accustomed to fighting on horseback. In the latter days of the Roman empire, they provided a number of mounted units, and under the Merovingian king Clovis, we find an edict about taking food and water for horses on a campaign in 507. Other units in Clovis' army were drawn from tribes which had traditionally provided horsemen for the Romans, such as the Alans of Brittany and the Alamans. Clovis' principal enemies, the Visigoths, were also horsemen, and the combats between them were dominated by cavalry action.

But the support of large and well-organised troops of cavalry required an efficient government and a central authority capable of raising large sums of money. With the

8   The basic work on early feudalism is still F.L.Ganshof, *Qu'est-ce que la feodalité?* (Paris 1944; 5th edn Paris 1982), translated as *Feudalism* (London 1966); recent scholarship has modified some of his conclusions.

degeneration of the Frankish kingdom into a web of small principalities continually at war with each other at the end of the sixth century, it was increasingly difficult to organise cavalry on a large scale. Instead, the military scene was dominated by small marauding war bands and by more or less defensive local levies based on the towns. The men who served in them were expected to provide their own equipment and provisions which meant that the poorer citizens were excluded. With the return of central authority under Pepin and Charles Martel, the war bands and the levies began to merge into one. The war band, supported by the magnate, was unreliable, since one man's gold was as good as another's; and an oath was at best uncertain assurance of loyalty in an age of anarchy. Pepin seems to have formalised the arrangement whereby warriors were paid not in gold, but in lands or benefices, which had originally had no military significance, and which had grown up under the Merovingian kings. In order to do this, both they and Pepin and his successors were reputed to have seized church lands, which confirms the idea that this was a novel approach, since they needed a new supply of land to carry it out. At the same time, the towns, which had been the basis of the earlier local levies and the focal points of warfare under the first Merovingian kings, were now declining in importance, and the economic basis of government was transferred to the countryside. With the return of a strong ruler, the independent magnates and their personal war bands were integrated into a formal structure of government, and used as the new source of local levies. From these varied and often obscure developments grew the military fief which was to become the cornerstone of later mediaeval society.

At first, warrior service applied to a relatively small number of estates, and it seems to have grown only gradually throughout the period of Charlemagne's rule. But the troubles that followed the disintegration of the over-ambitious structure of the empire built by Charlemagne bore heaviest on the remaining freemen, who owed no such service. Until now, only the poorest among them had been forced to take refuge in the protection of vassalage, and agreements with private lords were only at this humble level. But now that the royal vassals had begun to show that the condition was neither dishonourable nor onerous, small landowners found that there were many advantages to be gained by doing homage and holding land from a lord who offered some hope of protection from Saracen, Dane or Hun. Hence in the early eleventh century, there emerged a radically different pattern of society. The royal vassals predominated, and the former freemen who had belatedly joined their ranks or become vassals of other lords were generally at a disadvantage, possibly because their protectors had driven a hard bargain in hard times. The various kinds of service by which the benefice was held became a single type: warrior-service. The vassal was the owner of the warrior's equipment, and he held his fief in return for his readiness to fight. As a German law-code, the *Sachsenspiegel*, put it in the thirteenth century, 'the fief is the pay of the knight'.[9] And he certainly needed his pay: the mounted warrior had to spend a considerable amount on his equipment. Even in the ninth century a horse cost six times as much as a cow and armour possibly as much again. The only detailed summons to one of Charlemagne's vassals to survive, from *c.* 806, specifies shield, lance, sword, dagger, a bow and a quiver, besides all 'warlike equipment of clothing and victuals'. In thirteenth-century Spain, an ordinary cavalryman's horse — not a knight's warhorse — was worth 40 cows.[10]

The cost of equipping a warrior remained high throughout the Middle Ages. In the twelfth century, the basic equipment was still relatively simple: a shirt of mail, helmet, sword and lance. Mail consisted merely of interlinked metal rings forming a tough but pliable garment proof against cuts and stabs, and made up as a hauberk; it only covered the upper part of the body, with a coif over the head and neck. The conical helmet of four flat plates riveted together and shaped with a projecting nasel was also a very simple piece of armour, within the average blacksmith's skill. The shield and sword were plain and practical. Yet the painstaking work required to make a shirt of mail took many hours, and the cost of steel of reasonable quality was a considerable factor; as in Charlemagne's day, such equipment was only for those who could afford it.

The warrior of the late thirteenth century cut a very different figure. The helm had replaced the helmet, covering the head completely, and was later to be equipped with a vizor to protect the eyes: the wearer was unrecognisable, and elaborate crests were worn to distinguish him from other fighting men in similar attire. The whole body was now encased in armour of varying degrees of flexibility. A series of plates attached to the basic mail armour protected the arms, legs, chest and back, and a quilted garment was worn beneath to lessen the discomfort. Besides this, the warhorse would bear a mail or cloth trapper, often both, and a chamfron on its head, as protection.[11]

All this was extremely expensive, and not easy to obtain. In a strongly governed and peaceful country like England, only a man who intended to make fighting his career, and to go in person to do his service rather than paying scutage (shield-tax) and other dues, was likely to regard the outlay as worthwhile. It was these professional warriors who continued to foster the traditions of their class as a whole. Their personal

9   Quoted in Bloch, *Feudal Society*, 168

10   *MGH Leges* Sectio 2.i, 168; Carmela Pescador, 'La caballeria popular en León y Castilla', *Cuadernos de Historia de España*, XXXIII-XL, 1960-64 (XXXV, 108).

11   See the two articles by Ian Pierce, 'The Knight, his Arms and Armour in the Eleventh and Twelfth Centuries', in *The Ideals and Practice of Medieval Knighthood*, ed. Christopher Harper-Bill and Ruth Harvey (Woodbridge & Dover, N.H., 1986) 152-164 (see p.155 for a discussion of length of time required to make weapons and armour); and 'The Knight, his Arms and Armour, c.1150-1250', in *Anglo-Norman Studies XV*, ed. Marjorie Chibnall (Woodbridge & Rochester, N.Y., 1993) 251-274.

prestige stemmed from their achievements in the field, not from their financial or social standing, and they acquired something of the aura that sportsmen have today, while retaining their role as the focal point of the army. Men like these could not be raised by mere royal command, as Edward I's experience in the feudal levy of 1282 showed; he had to excuse those who did not possess a horse, and allow them to pay a fine, even though they were possessors of land worth £20 a year. It was much easier to rely on paid troops, who might well be the same men as the feudal levy, but were at least likely to be properly turned out. In 1297 Edward specifically stated that he was only summoning a small number of knights in order that they should be better mounted and equipped.

The status of the warrior

We can trace the rise of the warrior through the use of the word *miles* in legal documents; it is not perhaps as precise a measure of the warrior's status as some writers would have us believe. However, we can see a general pattern, which indicates that the earliest region to make this distinction was central France, the lands where Carolingian traditions were strongest. In the area around Mâcon, the *miles* seems to emerge as a distinct figure before 1000; by the early eleventh century the title was in use elsewhere in France, but the pattern varied from region to region, especially along the borders of the Empire. Namur has been closely studied: here in the eleventh century a group of about twenty noble families predominated, and freemen scarcely appeared outside these families. Towards 1150 a small group of *milites* appeared among the unfree vassals, and by 1200 had grown numerous, while about half the noble families had disappeared. On the other hand, in twelfth-century Burgundy all except two of a group of forty-three knights in the lands around Cluny were related to old noble families, and the number of knightly families remained remarkably constant.[12] In Germany it was another fifty years before the usage became common. The vernacular equivalent, *ritter*, appears for the first time in a text of 1060–5, a new word for a new phenomenon, perhaps.[13] Thereafter, the distinction between the mounted warrior, as a man with a specific status and function, and the older nobility, whose status as free lords of ancient lineage was initially superior, was gradually eroded.

---

12   Georges Duby, *The Chivalrous Society*, tr. C. Postan (London 1977) 94-111.
13   W.H.Jackson, *Chivalry in Twelfth Century Germany: the Works of Hartmann von Aue* (Woodbridge & Rochester, N.Y., 1994) 41-43.

It was not until the thirteenth century that warriors acquired a social rather than practical status: as we shall see, this was largely due to the emergence of knighthood as an order within society, replacing its original specialist military nature. In Normandy, the descendants of Rollo's freebooting companions of the early tenth century were William the Conqueror's warriors of the mid-eleventh century. In Spain, *miles* had come to mean 'light horseman' instead of merely 'soldier' by the early eleventh century.[14] Because horses were relatively cheaper and easier to obtain in Spain, the sharp financial distinction between the mounted warrior and the footsoldier did not apply, and we find a class of 'peasant-warriors', farmers with relatively small holdings who were nonetheless equipped for military service. (In 1034, a helmet was valued at 60 solidos, the same price as a horse.) At the other end of the scale were the *infanzones*, descended from the Visigoth nobles of the days before the Arab invasions, who served in return for *prestamos* or *atondos*, the Spanish equivalents of the benefice. But as the *reconquista* proceeded, and the frontier warfare with the Arabs grew ever more distant, a different kind of service was needed, less reliant on local levies anxious to get back to their day-to-day business; and the 'estate cavalry' was replaced by a 'vassal cavalry' by the late tenth century. There was a long tradition of money payments for military service, going back to the Gothic kings in the seventh century who made grants for taking part in the 'public expedition'. As a result, the mounted warrior was never a figure set apart by a particular mystique, but remained a military figure within society, with a specific function.

In Spain, the freemen of the early eleventh century in Castile and León had become mounted warriors a hundred years later, if they were rich enough to equip themselves. In these western kingdoms of Spain the feudal system failed to take real root. Furthermore, the social status of the freemen had no connection with bearing arms. A social hierarchy based on the monarchy appeared, but it was founded on the extent of free-holdings and not on personal allegiances. Warfare was constant in Spain until the beginning of the thirteenth century, and a militia was needed, formed of the broader class of armed warrior produced by enforcing the old general duty of freemen to bear arms. The towns were deliberately fostered by successive kings as a source of military support independent of the great lords, whether secular or religious, and in particular new foundations on the frontier with the Arab kingdoms were often given privileges designed to encourage such town militias, or civic cavalry, as in the *fueros* or privileges of Castrojeriz, granted in 954. We also find men whose horse and armour are the property of the town, and are to be returned on the user's death.[15] The town privileges could also contain

14   Claudio Sanchez-Albornoz, 'El ejercito y la guerra en el reino asturleonés 718-1037', in *Ordinamenti militari in occidente nell'alto medioevo* (Settimane di studio del centro italiano di studi sull'alto medioevo) (Spoleto 1968) 293-428.

very detailed military regulations, amounting to a virtual military code, as in the case of Cuenca in c. 1180-90. The quality of the horses and arms to be supplied was specified in detail in some of the regulations. The encouragement of civic cavalry reached its peak under Alfonso X of Castile in the mid-thirteenth century, and is reflected in the military sections of his *Siete Partidas*. Indeed, in frontier towns, possession of a horse and arms, and hence membership of the cavalry militia, was often compulsory for all except the poorest inhabitants.[16]

The transition from warrior to knight

We can only trace the emergence of the knight indistinctly; historical records are rare, and literary works scarcer still. The best indicators are actually changes in vocabulary, in the words used in legal documents. The key word is *miles*, the simple Roman name for a soldier. In the tenth and eleventh century it is used variously to mean warrior, vassal and armed retainer; note that it is not yet a term of distinction, implying a sought-after social status. We also find the word *caballarius*, horseman, used interchangeably for *miles* as the name for a warrior, emphasizing the superiority of mounted troops. The problem is to distinguish the rise of the knight, who has a specific social status but whose chief characteristic is that he pursues the profession of arms, from the early medieval concepts of nobility, and much scholarly ink has been spilt in trying to do so.[17] For the knight was not merely the soldier of an earlier age in a new guise. If he had been nothing more than that, he would have formed a much larger class. Equipment for mounted warfare was expensive, and only those who were prosperous could afford it. Hence the new class was a compound of men whose families were well-established without being noble, and of newcomers whose wealth had been won by adventure or ambition: but in both cases landed property was a pre-requisite, in order to finance the equipment needed for warfare. The distinction between them and the older nobility, whose roots go back to Merovingian and even Germanic princely families, was quickly blurred. The nobility had claimed special status by virtue of their descent; but at the moment in time at which pressure from the warrior class was strongest, the rules by which descent was traced were changing. The emphasis on the standing of the mother's and the father's family had been equal in early Germanic

15   Pescador, 'La caballeria popular', XXXIII-XXXIV, 144, 136.
16   Pescador, 'La caballeria popular', XXXV-XXXVI, 67 ff.
17   For a good summary see Tony Hunt, ' The emergence of the knight in France and England 1000-1200', in *Knighthood in Medieval Literature*, ed. W.H.Jackson (Woodbridge 1981) 1-22. See also G. Duby, 'The origins of knighthood' in *The Chivalrous Society*, 158-170.

society, where land tenure was less important. Once the problem of landed inheritance came to the fore, the dominance of the eldest son and descent in the father's line became paramount. This meant that the mounted warriors were less sharply isolated by their lack of high birth than might have been the case if noble descent had been determined by a rigid set of rules.

By the mid-twelfth century, the freemen with no military function had almost entirely disappeared, and their place had been taken by the new warriors. Political power was based almost entirely on force of arms, both at a national and local level; and the economic monopoly of agriculture had not yet been challenged by the towns. After the threads of common political institutions which had bound Carolingian France and Germany into one loosely connected state had snapped, the status of the knightly vassal evolved differently in each country. In France the relative weakness of royal authority until the twelfth century meant that the royal vassals were conveniently able to forget the royal claims to their land, and to set themselves up as free nobles, or nobles whose land was largely free with a few small fief-holdings, as in central France in the eleventh century. In Germany, on the other hand, the Ottonian emperors were able to enforce their title, and the new type of vassalage did not spread so quickly or widely on the east bank of the Rhine. As a result, the typical German warrior was not a freeman, but the descendant of the old royal vassal, bound in person as well as land, even if he often had a small freehold besides his fief.

The power of the mounted warriors had been increased by the weakening of the central authority after Charlemagne, caused partly by external circumstances, but also by the weakening of the king's hold over his vassals. The vassal felt that he could easily provide the necessary service for two or more benefices, either by creating his own vassals, or by keeping men trained in the arts of war as household warriors, vassals who were supported as part of his household instead of receiving land. By the tenth century, vassalage had become less a tie between man and man than a strictly commercial arrangement: if a man held several fiefs, the lord who gave most land had the greatest claim. The old personal link had had a passionate loyalty derived from the Germanic warrior tradition, reflected in the Anglo-Saxon *Battle of Maldon* as well as the *Chanson de Roland*. The lady Dhuoda might instruct her son in these high precepts in the ninth century as follows: 'Since God, as I believe, and your father Bernard have chosen you, in the flower of your youth, to serve Charles as your lord, I urge you ever to remember the record of your family, illustrious on both sides, and not to serve your master simply to satisfy him outwardly, but to maintain towards him and his service in all things a devoted and certain fealty both of body and soul.'[18] Thereafter, as property became

---

18   Ganshof, *Feudalism*, 33

the predominant element in the relationship of lord and vassal, the personal side receded. The fief could be inherited, divided, and joined to other fiefs, despite the lawyers' insistence that the contract was from man to man: homage had to be renewed on the death of the lord or vassal, when the fief was technically returned to the lord; the ceremony itself was a personal one; and only personal wrongs allowed the contract to be repudiated. As a result of the conflicting claims which the holding of several fiefs involved, a man with two lords all too often had to choose between them in times when local feuds were common, and the vassal's oath came to be taken more and more lightly.

To counteract this problem, the solution of liege homage was devised. A vassal holding several fiefs would choose one (again, usually the lord from whom he held most land) as his especial lord, and swear a specific oath to serve him in preference to the others. The liege lord and his liegemen were bound in the same exclusive way as the earliest lords and vassals. The personal tie was revived, the vassal again being bound to defend his lord against all others. Though the idea of the special nature of liege homage persisted throughout the Middle Ages, it was soon debased in much the same way as simple vassalage before it. A man could become the liege vassal of a second lord with the consent of the original liege lord, and by the beginning of the thirteenth century this was generally accepted. England and the Kingdom of Jerusalem were exceptions, since liege homage there was the fealty sworn to the king irrespective of other feudal ties; elsewhere almost every lord was liege to his vassal, and ordinary vassalage was merely a less usual and less exacting form of the feudal contract.

The direct personal tie became less important as a more ordered society developed. In this society, the warrior added to his role as landowner that of administrator. Justice, in early mediaeval society, was no theoretical abstraction, a high ideal that had to be translated into reality, but an eminently practical affair, concerned with personal and community relationships. As lord of his small and often self-contained world, he became dispenser of justice and keeper of the peace; at the same time, the structure of society became more hierarchical and the freemen less numerous. The rise of a legal system based on the grass-roots manor court is difficult to chart. To some extent, these rights had been usurped from the king during the anarchy of the ninth and tenth centuries; but as central authority was re-asserted, so the warriors became the acknowledged administrators of justice at this local level, save in those matters reserved to the crown, controlling rather than replacing the old village assembly. This 'low justice' covered all manner of civil disputes, which would usually be questions of landholding, and some minor crimes; major offences were 'high justice' and hence within the exclusive scope of the royal courts. Even 'high justice' came into the hands of local lords in France by 1200. However, all such rights of justice stemmed from property-owning, and it was only the warrior's position as lord that gave him these powers: there was no connection as of right between bearing arms and jurisdiction.

Yet within this new order, there were broad variations in personal circumstances. The castellans and their superiors were important figures, while many of the ordinary mounted warriors were no more than farmers, living directly off the land, even if closely related to greater lords. The real difference between them and the richer peasants was the intermittent summons to warfare, whether their lord's private feud or a greater royal quarrel, which took them into a wider and different world, and gave them a broader outlook. The need to avoid division of the fief if they were to maintain their status led them to send sons into the Church, and some inkling of the new intellectual ferment reached them through these contacts. Until the rural economy gave way to a money system, the lesser knight retained his close and practical contact with the land, which restricted his part in tournaments, court life and the developing ideas of knighthood. Even in the later period the northern European nobility remained predominantly rural in background, rarely moving into the towns; in the south, however, town-knights were common, building the fortified houses which can still be seen at Regensburg and San Gimignano.

Other warriors were to be found in the *familia* or household of great lords, or in the garrisons of major castles, where they might be maintained out of the lord's own resources rather than being given lands. Such men might have no ties to the land at all, and were thus free to move around as their lord required. They might also take administrative posts with a salary within the household, such as marshal, chamberlain or butler, and would act as the lord's advisers in peace as well as fighting for him in wartime.

So far we have looked at the warrior within a relatively settled context, as possessor of a fief and therefore tied to a particular place. But there was another, often neglected aspect to the early medieval warrior's existence, which was in many ways more glamorous and spectacular, and which lent itself to the creation of heroes and legends, despite its eminently practical origins and purpose. For every warrior who held a settled estate, there was probably one who was an entrepreneur: not a mercenary, though these existed from the eleventh century onwards, but a man who used his skills to make his fortune, often in distant lands. It was a tradition which went back to the viking ancestors of the Normans, who had provided men for the Varangian guard in Byzantium, and who had raided and eventually settled widely in northern Europe, farmers who became fighters and eventually landowners again. Similarly, we can find Norman warriors, grandsons of the viking raiders, pursuing the main chance in Spain or Sicily, Benevento or Byzantium. There were Normans in the near East before the First Crusade, like Roussel of Bailleul who carved out a principality for himself in the centre of Turkey in the 1070s. At the other end of the Mediterranean, Roger of Tosny was fighting in

Spain in the service of the countess of Barcelona, and winning a fortune which helped him to found the abbey of Conches on his return home.[19]

The Norman conquest of England was an organised, political enterprise; but the equally dramatic conquest of southern Italy and Sicily at about the same period was entirely a matter of private enterprise. The Norman leaders were a loosely organised group of like-minded fighters, bound by family ties and prone to internecine feuds. Chief among them were the Hauteville brothers, Robert Guiscard ('the Wily') and Roger, his younger brother and conqueror of Sicily, were the most remarkable of the five sons of Tancred of Hauteville who made their way south. Roger was the central figure of Geoffrey Malaterra's chronicle, written while he was still alive; and Geoffrey had no doubt what Roger and his kin were up to – *per diversa loca militanter lucrum quaerentes,* 'seeking wealth through feats of arms in many places'.[20] So warriors became heroes of literature; Roger, prince of Capua, was the hero, along with Robert Guiscard, of the chronicle of Amatus of Monte Cassino, written about the same time.

Some of the wanderers were political exiles, but for the most part these were younger sons, for whom their father could not provide. Younger sons were to continue to play an important part in the history of knighthood and chivalry. They had to make their own way in the world, and their careers could be dramatic; but we must remember that for every Roger of Sicily there were thousands who set out hopefully but came to an obscure and impoverished end. We shall meet them again as the *iuvenes* or young men of northern France and England among whom the tournament flourished in the late twelfth century, and as the ambitious squires of later medieval society: it was among these men that the dreams and ideals of knighthood grew and were cherished.

---

19   Alan Fletcher, *The Quest for El Cid* (London 1989) 78-9.
20   Quoted in R. Allen Brown, *The Normans* (Woodbridge and New York 1984) 79.

2

The Order of Knighthood

THE KNIGHT IS an elusive, chameleon-like figure; the moment we try to define him, he appears in a different guise. His forerunners first appear against the background of the anarchy of ninth and tenth century society. They are little more than simple fighting men, skilled in horsemanship and the use of arms, valued for their function as defenders and feared as potential disturbers of the peace. Their role is enigmatic, their purpose determined by chance and circumstance. The identity of the knight has not been made any clearer by historians who have happily used the term to describe any mounted warrior of the post-Carolingian era, translating *miles* and *chevalier* as knight, without regard to the context. It may seem that we are chasing a chimaera; but in that case, why do we find the nobility from the thirteenth century onwards describing themselves proudly by precisely these names, humble though they are in comparison with their honorific titles? There is a concept of something greater than the mere strength of arm of a fighting man, transcending feudal and economic hierarchies. Having looked at the world of the post-Carolingian warrior, it is this wider concept that we need to explore.

At the outset, the knight was a warrior who served a lord by fighting for him. The degree by which he was bound by this service varied; the *ministeriales* in Germany were technically not merely servants, but in some ways more akin to serfs, bound by law to their lord's ownership. This was very different from that of their French counterparts, who might, in the south at least, be free of all feudal ties. 'Whereas French knights were free men constrained by the contractual nature of vassalage, German *ministeriales* were not free men, and their service was an ineluctable hereditary duty to the lord upon whose patrimony and into whose ownership they had been born.'[1] In practice, the *ministerialis* was much less closely bound to his lord than the serf whose unfree status he shared. But it is interesting to note that 'service' is nonetheless an essential element of knighthood: *ministerialis* was usually translated as *dienestman*, servant, just as the

---

[1]   Benjamin Arnold, *German Knighthood 1050-1300* (Oxford 1985) 18.

Anglo-Saxon word *cniht*, meaning servant, is the root of the English word knight. To a modern mind, it is difficult to reconcile this emphasis on tied service with the fact that the ministerialis was also regarded as a noble.

The concept of service is nonetheless central to knighthood; only a handful of men in medieval Christendom would have regarded themselves as truly free. Even the king of England owed feudal service for Normandy and Aquitaine to the king of France; and the Pope, claiming to be overlord of all temporal rulers, styled himself 'servant of the servants of God'. Service is in no wise demeaning when conceived in these terms. The question of when the idea of knight-service as such emerged has not perhaps been given sufficient weight by scholars. As we have said, it is easy to assume that mounted warriors with shield, spear and sword, helm and hauberk, are knights; but are we applying retrospectively an identification that they themselves would not have acknowledged? The earliest systematic lists of fiefs date from the mid-twelfth century, and are exclusively Norman in origin: from Norman Sicily in 1149–50, revised in 1167–8, and from England (1166) and Normandy six years later.[2] Henry II's survey asked 'How many knights did you have enfeoffed before 1135?'; given that there is no question of knight-service as such in Domesday Book in 1087, the concept of such service is likely to have evolved in the first quarter of the twelfth century.

That *miles* meant something more than warrior to Henry II's officials can be shown by reference to the *Dialogue of the Exchequer*, [3] which speaks in this context of 'anyone who had ever possessed the knightly belt'. It is perhaps excessive to claim that 'the extent of Henry II's lands, the number of his vassals and his fame as a hirer of knights make it credible that the 1166 enquiry ... contributed to the change to life knighthood reflected in the chansons two decades later.'[4] Rather, the 1166 inquest is symptomatic of a change already in process: even though only four men can be found before 1181 described as knights (*miles*) when witnessing English charters,[5] the concept of knighthood as a distinctive status is confirmed by the *Dialogue of the Exchequer*, with its clear distinction between the social rank of knight and the knight as professional

---

2   R.H.C.Davis, 'Domesday Book: Continental Parallels' in *Domesday Studies* ed. J.C.Holt (Woodbridge & Wolfeboro, N.H., 1987) 24.

3   *Dialogus de Scaccario*, ed. Charles Johnson (Edinburgh, London & New York 1950) 111: 'militie cingulum semel optinuerit'.

4   Jean Scammell, 'The Formation of the English Social Structure: Freedom, Knights and Gentry, 1066-1300', *Speculum* 68 (1993) 591-618.

5   D.F.Fleming, 'Milites as Attestors to Charters in England, 1101-1300', *Albion* 22 1990,186-7. I would argue that the figures of 16% and 23% for witnesses to charters in the Maconnais between 970-1000 and 1000-1300 given by G.Duby, *The Chivalrous Society* (London 1977) 77, relates to a milieu where *miles* means nothing more than soldier, but much more work on the soldier/knight distinction is needed.

soldier. If such a person is unable to pay his debts, he may retain his horse, as befits his rank; but if he is an active warrior, he is to keep all his personal armour and the necessary horses, so that he can pursue his profession.[6] What is striking is the coincidence in time of the emergence of knight-service with the first development of romance: the world of Chrétien de Troyes is the world of a new, *arriviste* group, not of a tradition-bound, established class.

As we have seen, the Latin and vernacular words for 'knight' and 'soldier' are often identical; even *caballarius* merely qualifies the meaning to 'mounted soldier'. The vernacular equivalents of *caballarius* in French and German, *chevalier* and *ritter* mean at different periods 'knight' and 'mounted warrior'. It is therefore extremely difficult to know when a distinction between soldiers and knights arises, but this is the crucial moment for historians of knighthood, because we can only say that there was a concept of 'knighthood' as such when this distinction can be documented. The commonest mistake is to assume that the use of *miles* in Latin charters is an indicator of knighthood, but it does not carry this distinction: *Guido miles* is distinguished from *Guido clericus* by his occupation as a soldier. Nor do the grand phrases about 'taking up arms' or 'girding on the soldier's belt' found in the chronicles necessarily imply anything more than membership of the military profession. What we are looking for goes beyond merely professional status; it is exclusive, in the way that a guild might be exclusive, but it also carries idealistic overtones.

The point at which we can be reasonably sure that such attitudes are being invoked is when we first encounter the phrase 'to make a knight'.[7] This implies both ritual and a non-military status; the phrase becomes meaningless when we translate it as 'to make a soldier'. If we admit this as the crucial test for knighthood as opposed to soldiering, and given that the earliest traces of 'making knights' date from the last quarter of the eleventh century, then we must abandon the image of the 'Norman knight' at Hastings, and see the tenth and eleventh century 'knights' as mounted warriors and nothing more, earning the right to their lands by the use of their swords. There is nothing that leads us to see them as any different from the warriors of Catalonia, who were deemed to have ceased to be *milites* if they disposed of their horse and armour, no longer held a warrior's fee, or ceased to serve in the host or on chevauchées.[8]

6   *Dialogus de Scaccario*, ed. cit., III-12
7   See Jean Flori, 'Les origines de l'adoubement chevaleresque; étude des remises d'armes et du vocabulaire qui les exprime dans les sources historiques latines jusqu'au début du xiie siècle', *Traditio*, 35, 1979, 209-272, esp. table IV, p.269; and J.M. van Winter, 'Cingulum militiae. Schwertleite en *miles-* terminologie als spiegel van veranderend menselijk gedrad', *Tijdschrift voor Rechtsgeschiedenis*, 44, 1976, I-92.
8   Winter, 'Cingulum militiae', 60

But what about all the instances of a ritual in which a young prince or great lord is at the centre, and which involve the presentation of arms or a symbolic sword-belt, the *cingulum* of Pallas which Turnus wears as a trophy in Book XII of the *Aeneid* and which leads to his death at the hands of Pallas' friend Aeneas? Investiture with such a badge appears to imply a concept of a separate order. Is this perhaps the mark of knighthood? It is obviously in the tradition of both Rome and the German tribes described by Tacitus; but it is precisely because it has parallels in both societies that we can identify it for what it is: a ceremony that marks the arrival of the prince at adult status, and celebrates his coming of age with a presentation of the weapons of a full-grown man. Most of the instances from the ninth and tenth century mention the adoption or presentation of arms only in connection with some other event or ceremony. Thus Louis the Pious, Charlemagne's son, was girded with the sword at Regensburg in 791, before going with his father on a campaign against the Avars. Both Charles the Bald and Louis the German were given arms – *armis virilibus cinxit, cingulo decorauit* – when they were crowned;[9] Otto I took his sword from the altar at his consecration in 936, and the archbishop of Mainz admonished him to use it aright.[10] Just as sword and sword-belt were symbols of assumption of power, so they could mark its renunciation, as at the deposition of Louis the Pious in 833, when he took off his sword-belt and placed it on the altar as evidence of his surrender of authority.

This, as Jean Flori has demonstrated, is the context of the early orders of service for the consecration of arms; and it only extended downwards as far as the nobles who acted as 'advocates' for the great monasteries, in other words, their military protectors. The often-cited *ordo* used by the bishops of Cambrai in the later eleventh century is concerned not with warriors in general, but specifically with *defensores ecclesiae*, men of standing who are powerful enough to take up such a role.[11]

The phrases about 'girding on the swordbelt' and 'taking up arms' are also found at a much humbler level, where they simply indicate that someone has become a soldier – or ceased to be one, when they laid aside their weapons of war to become a monk – *cingulum militiae solvens*, as Leotbaldus declared in a charter in favour of the abbey of Cluny to mark his entry into the monastery.[12] To be a soldier was indeed a mark of distinction; it generally earned you the disapproval of the Church and the suspicion of your neighbours; but there was no concept of a separate order involved. It has been

---

9   Winter, '*Cingulum militiae*', 51
10 Winter, '*Cingulum militiae*',53-54
11 Jean Flori, *L'Essor de la Chevalerie VIe – XIIe siècles*, Travaux d'histoire éthno-politiques xlvi (Geneva 1986) 97-111
12 Winter, '*Cingulum militiae*',53

24

suggested that there are knightly ideals implicit in Nithard's account of the deeds of Charles the Bald, but Nithard is concerned to show Charles as a man suited to the leadership of armies, who can wield the symbolic sword of power, not as a member of a group with a distinctive ethos.[13] In the eleventh century, as records multiplied, lesser princes were described as being 'girded with the sword', a phrase which is used almost invariably until the early thirteenth century. The Norman kings introduced the custom to England; from William I's knighting by the French king onwards, we have a record of the knighting of each heir to the throne in turn. The point is that this marks their coming of age; and I believe that we should read the declarations in the preambles to charters in the same way: contrast *Ego itaque Rotrocus, militari balteo accinctus atque castri Mauritanie comes* – i.e. a nobleman who has come of age – with *Ecbertus marchio Turingorum, puer adhuc infra militares annos,* a mere stripling despite his first title.[14] To gird on the swordbelt is a question of age, not an additional sign of honour.

A more convincing first stage in the transformation of the mounted warrior into the knight is the recognition that by giving certain weapons to a footsoldier, he can be 'made' into a mounted warrior. This usage is found in late tenth century France,[15] and writers such as Fulcher of Chartres, recording the exploits of the First Crusade, use 'making a knight' to mark promotion from squire or footsoldier to mounted warrior, specifying that the new knight was 'made' by providing him with the necessary equipment.[16] Some of the earliest evidence for 'making' knights comes from England. An entry in the Peterborough version of the Anglo-Saxon Chronicle written no later than the 1120s tells us that at Whitsun 1086 William I 'dubbed his son Henry to knight' (*dubbade his sunu Henric to ridere thaere*),[17] William Rufus having already been knighted. The implication is that the ritual may have been new and unfamiliar to the monk who made the entry, but that he nonetheless recognised the ceremony as conferring a distinct status. Henry was not given arms, or otherwise declared of age: he was specifically *dubbed* a knight; *dub* is a word whose origins are obscure, but by using it the writer implies a special ceremony attached to the simple presentation of arms. That this was a relatively new idea, but one which was very much in the air in England at that time, is confirmed by other evidence. In 1102, the council of London enacted that abbots should not make knights, a decree echoed

13   Janet Nelson, 'Ninth-century Knighthood: the evidence of Nithard', in *Studies in Medieval History presented to R.Allen Brown*, ed. Christopher Harper-Bill *et al.* (Woodbridge & Wolfeboro, N.H., 1989) 255-66.

14   Winter, 'Cingulum militiae', 62

15   Flori, *Traditio* 241

16   *Ibid.*, 233-5.

17   *The Peterborough Chronicle 1070-1154,* ed. Cecily Clark (Oxford 1958) 9.

in modified form in the foundation charter of Reading Abbey in 1125, which stipulates that the abbot may not make knights 'except in the holy clothing of Christ'.[18] The Latin *Gesta Herwardi*, written in the thirteenth century, but drawing on Ely traditions, shows the Saxon rebel Hereward seeking out the abbot of Burgh in order to be knighted 'in the English fashion', declaring that although the Normans claimed that only a knight could make a knight, he preferred men who had been knighted by a priest, because they would use their power only in a just cause, as they had promised at their initiation.[19]

It is of course vital to read the chronicles which record the making of knights as indicating attitudes at the time they were written, not as evidence of the past: once the concept of knighthood had come into being, noble ancestors were of course admitted into the order, rather as the Mormons baptise their forebears. (The same problem bedevils the history of the tournament, though the fifteenth century writers who describe in detail the great events put on by Henry the Fowler in the ninth century are carrying their enthusiasm beyond the bounds of belief.) This is very noticeable in the history of the counts of Anjou; around 1100, Fulk le Réchin, in an autobiographical fragment, uses the current phrase *militem facere* to describe his coming of age forty years earlier,[20] and John of Marmoutier in the 1180s describes the knighting of Geoffrey of Anjou in 1128 in terms of a lavish late twelfth-century ceremony.[21]

If the specific terminology of the knighting ceremony does not enable us to draw firm conclusions as to when 'knighthood' emerged as a distinctive concept, we need to look further afield. We can point to a number of crucial changes in attitude in the late eleventh and twelfth century. In warfare, it was no longer regarded as praiseworthy to put to death defeated rivals, as had been the custom in the Anglo-Saxon and Norse world, and indeed, in the turbulence of the ninth and tenth centuries, throughout Europe. William the Conqueror's biographers, writing during his lifetime, praised him for his clemency towards his defeated enemies, in terms which imply that although

---

18   William of Malmesbury, *Gesta Pontificum*, RS 52 (London 1870) i,170: 'Ne abbates fatiant [sic] milites et ut in eadem domo cum monachis suis dormiant et comedant nisi aliqua necessitate prohibuit.' *Reading Abbey Cartularies* ed. B.R.Kemp, Camden Society Fourth Series 31 (London 1986) I, 34: 'Terra censuales non ad foedum donet nec faciat milites nisi in sacra veste Christi in qua parvulos suscipere modeste caveat, maturos autem seu discretos tam clericos quam laicos provide suscipiat.'

19   Elsbet Orth, 'Formen und Funktion der höfischen Rittererhebung' in Joseph Fleckenstein (ed.) *Curialitas: Studien zu Grundfragen der höfisch-ritterlichen Kultur* (Veröffentlichungen des Max-Planck-Instituts für Geschichte 100 (Göttingen 1990) 153.

20   *Chroniques des comtes d'Anjou et des seigneurs d'Amboise* ed. Louis Halphen et René Poupardin (Paris 1913) 235

21   See p.31 below

such attitudes were unusual when he first came to power, they were now the accepted norm. Similarly, Orderic Vitalis portrays William Rufus as going beyond the bounds of political prudence in his magnanimity towards his enemies.[22] We may perhaps see in this the influence of movements such as the Truce of God, which attempted to regulate warfare: if so, the church's efforts to bring about a reform of warrior mores met with some success. In a different way, the status of the soldier, particularly those in the service of local lords, may have been enhanced by the emergence of the castle, which gave them new security and a visible focal point for their authority.[23] The emergence of the tournament as a sport in the early twelfth century also points to a more restrained attitude towards fighting, a tendency to see it as an activity which did not necessarily involve maximum bloodshed, but which could become a skilled exercise. Another key may be in the First Crusade itself, with its vision of a secular militia engaged in the service of the Church, bringing together the concept of soldiering as part of the order of society with the concept of orders in a religious sense. St Bernard's first biographer wrote of the saint's father that he was 'a man of ancient and legitimate *militiae*', which implies exactly the distinctive qualities of 'knighthood' in the sense of a separate social order for which we are looking.[24] The same is true of Geoffrey Gaimar's *L'estoire des Engleis*, written for the wife of a Lincolnshire landowner in the 1130s, in which the *chevaliers* in his audience are regaled with the exploits of the *chevaliers* of the previous century, and in which William Rufus appears as a chivalrous king who presides over the mass dubbing of thirty knights.[25]

It is at this period, rather than in the depths of the ninth century or earlier, that we should place the emergence of knighthood. The idea that distinguishes knighthood from the mounted warrior is that of an élite, selected group, with a formal ceremony of admission. To explore this, we must turn to the way in which medieval men looked at the world. One of the most powerful images in medieval romance is that of the castle surrounded by wide, wild forests. Within the castle all is order and harmony; and the inhabitants of the castle seek to impose that order on the denizens of the forest, replacing natural disorder with civilisation. The fear of disorder was rooted in medieval attitudes, haunted by memories of Viking raids, civil war and the famine and destruction which these brought. The ideal vision of medieval society was of a perfect hierarchy, where all men worked together for the common wealth, each fulfilling his appointed role. For the Church, whose philosophers shaped men's thoughts, the

22 See John Gillingham, 'Conquering the Barbarians', *The Haskins Society Journal*, 4, 1992, 74-84.
23 Flori, *Essor de la Chevalerie*, 266
24 Flori, *Essor de la Chevalerie*, 209
25 John Gillingham, 'Thegns and knights in eleventh century England: who was then the gentleman?', *Transactions of the Royal Historical Society*, 1995, forthcoming.

spiritual destiny of man could only be accomplished in the context of a stable society. From the fathers of the Church onwards, the ordering of society was a common theme; and the usual framework was that of mankind divided into three orders, following the biblical precedents of Noah, Daniel and Job as exemplars of righteousness (Ezekiel 14.14) or of Shem, Ham and Japhet as progenitors of the respective divisions, which gave such an image of society weight and authority.

The triple division was at first clergy, monks and laity; secular commentators thought in judicial terms, of nobles, freemen and slaves.[26] The two images were first combined in king Alfred's translation of Boethius' book *On consolation*, one of the classics of medieval thought. When Boethius discusses the administration of the state, Alfred adds that to govern well a king must have a well-populated land containing men of prayer, men of war, men who work – in Anglo-Saxon *'gebedmen and fyrdmen and weorcmen'*.[27] The theme was taken up by Latin writers, and by the eleventh century it had become a commonplace: furthermore, with the revival of classical learning in the twelfth century, the warriors became identified with the classical *ordo equestris*. When Arnold of Brescia tried to revive the senate at Rome, together with the *ordo equestris* or knightly order, claiming that it would redound to the greater glory of the emperor, Frederick Barbarossa replied that if he wanted to know about the glories of ancient Rome and 'the virtue and discipline of its knightly class, he had only to look at the imperial entourage.'[28]

The important point here is not that all medieval thinkers saw a triple division of society into orders, for this was not the case. What matters is that fighting men are frequently seen as a separate and important order in society, contrasted with churchmen and peasants, yet linked in an interdependent trinity. Once this concept begins to form, so the knights acquire the social function and moral authority they had hitherto lacked. Furthermore, the church, which had once been implacably opposed to all forms of warfare, had gradually developed a very different attitude: war could, in certain circumstances, be regarded as just, and the pantheon of saints had widened to include, besides St Michael, leader of the heavenly hosts, such figures as St James 'the Moor-slayer', and St George.[29] The image of the Christian as 'soldier of Christ' was put forward in the lives of holy men: Odo of Cluny in the 930s used the term 'miles Christi' of a lay noble. The church's increasing involvement in secular affairs, and the

26 Georges Duby, *The Three Orders: Feudal Society Imagined*, tr. Arthur Goldhammer (Chicago and London 1980) 92, citing Nithard.
27 *King Alfred's Old English Version of Boethius' De Consolatione Philosophiae*, ed. W.J.Sedgefield (Oxford 1899) 40.
28 Joachim Bumke, *The Concept of Knighthood in the Middle Ages*, tr.W.T.H. & Erika Jackson (New York 1982) 111, 246, quoting Otto of Freising, *Gesta Friderici*, II, 30.
29 Franco Cardini, *Alle radice della cavalleria* (Firenze 1981) 227 ff.

papal claim, from the eleventh century onwards, to be the supreme authority in both this world and the next meant that the old hostility towards the warrior could not be maintained. Instead, his energy was to be channelled into the maintenance of peace and the defence of the weaker members of society. First, however, the lust for war had to be restrained. The earliest attempts to protect society from its supposed defenders appeared in central France in the late tenth century, when Wido, bishop of Le Puy, persuaded the knights and peasants of his bishopric to swear an oath to respect church property. This movement grew rapidly, and by the mid-eleventh century the protection offered under such 'truces of God' was to be found throughout southern France, and as far afield as Catalonia and Burgundy. It was extended to the persons of clergy, women and children, and warfare was prohibited on all except some eighty days in the year, by the time all the days of peace – church festivals and the period from Thursday to Sunday each week – were taken into account. In practice, the realities of warfare meant that the church's rules were frequently breached, but the 'peace of God' was nonetheless a powerful statement of intent.

Beside the regulation of war in general, the Church also turned its attention to the individual warrior, beginning with the princes and leaders of armies, devising appropriate rituals for blessing their endeavours at the start of their career or at the outset of a campaign. The roots of such ceremonies lay in the initiation ritual by which primitive societies marked the coming of age of adolescents. In Roman and Germanic society, the tokens of maturity were common to all free men; there was no idea of entry into an exclusive class restricted to the privileged few. The Roman's white toga and the German's spear and shield set the free man apart from the slave, but nothing more. Tacitus remarks of the German ceremony that 'no one shall take up his arms until the state has attested that he is likely to make good . . . . when that time comes, one of the chiefs or the father or a kinsman equips the young warrior with shield and spear in the public council,'[30] but he does not imply that the privilege is ever withheld, only that it can be delayed if the candidate is not yet ready for the field. In the eighth century, a very similar ceremony reappeared, as we learn from the meagre chronicles of the period. There seems little doubt that it related to the earlier German custom, as its form was specifically that of equipping with arms. It was now the sword that was the symbolic weapon, and it is either this (*ensis, gladius*) or the sword-belt (*cingulum militiae*) that is at the centre of the ceremony. The ritual, however, is not a general custom, but, as we have seen, specifically concerns the Carolingian emperors, usually as part of their coronation rites. The Church was thus taking a part in the consecration of rulers as leaders of armies, and it is in this context that we need to consider the appearance in

30   Tacitus, *On Britain and Germany*, 111-112.1

the Pontifical of St Alban of Mainz of what at first appears to be a prayer for a newly-made knight; in fact it was probably used at the investiture of an *advocatus*, a lay lord who undertook to defend a monastery or church from secular enemies. This order of service for the blessing of the sword was drawn up in the mid-tenth century, and it implies that the sword is laid for a moment on the altar just before the gospel is read at Mass. The usual form of prayer said over it ran:

> Hearken, we beseech Thee, O Lord, to our prayers, and deign to bless with the right hand of thy majesty this sword with which this Thy servant desires to be girded, that it may be a defence of churches, widows, orphans and all Thy servants against the scourge of the pagans, that it may be the terror and dread of other evildoers, and that it may be just both in attack and defence.[31]

The sword was then girded on by attendants; Matthew Paris's illustration to the *Lives of the Two Offas* is exactly apposite, showing a young prince undergoing this ceremony.

The Church's concern with the ethics of knighthood increased during the following century, and there was an attempt to adopt knighthood as an order of a quasireligious nature, of similar status to that of clerks in minor orders. The institution of the religious orders of knighthood proper in the early twelfth century, and the rise of the crusading ideal, both lent colour to the argument that knighthood was intended as the secular arm of the Church, for its protection and for the defence of the weak. A later prayer for the new knight underlined this: 'O Lord, who after the fall didst ordain three ranks of men to be in the whole world that Thy faithful people might dwell in safety and quietness secure from evil, hearken to our prayer. . . .'[32]

This princely ceremony of investiture was quite distinct, however, from the actual creation of a knight. Although, as we have seen, the Church attempted to claim the power to make knights, it never established its jurisdiction in this sphere; and just as the authority of the Church rested on the concept of the apostolic succession, so the status of knight depended on the handing on of the tradition from knight to knight: only a knight could make a knight. It was, however, from the Church that the ideals of knighthood stemmed: what had once been the Church's precept for kings and emperors, came, as power was fragmented and devolved in the eleventh century, to be applied to the local lords and those who enforced their authority. The existence of military power was permitted by God only if it was used to defend the weak and sustain society at large.

31   Flori, *Essor de la Chevalerie*, 90-2 for discussion; text, 379.
32   H.A.Wilson, *The Pontifical of Magdalen College*, Henry Bradshaw Society XXXIX (London 1910) 255.

If the ancient German custom of a ritual marking the coming of age of the warrior lingered in the imperial coronation ceremonies of the ninth century, it also seems to have survived in secular form at a much humbler level; but the lack of records of everyday life means that we can only guess at how it came to be handed down, to re-emerge in the twelfth century. The fact that the earliest use of the word to 'dub' is Anglo-Saxon, in the *Anglo-Saxon Chronicle* entry already cited, hints at a continuity in the Germanic world rather than among the Franks. Such evidence as we have is literary rather than historical, and occasionally, in the thirteenth century and later, visual. Dubbing was a blow struck with the hand or the sword, called in French the *colée* or *paumée*, later regarded as the one essential act in the ceremony, is shrouded in mystery. It may be related to the obscure Germanic custom of striking the witnesses to a legal act to make them remember it, or to the blow which freed slaves in the act of manumission. Before 1350 it is only found in France and England, and even there is not universal. Raimon Llull's *Book of the Order of Chivalry*, written in Spain in 1265, and perhaps the most influential of all such treatises, knows nothing of it, and none of the many later translations of his book add it to the text. On the other hand, Geoffroi de Charny, writing about 1352, sees it as an essential part of the ceremony:

> And then that knight must give them the *colée*, as a sign that they must always bear in mind the order of chivalry which they have received, and do those deeds which appertain to the said order; and thus knights are made, and ought to be made.[33]

When we hear of knights being created *en masse* it is usually in the context of the knighting of a great lord's son, and the occasional apparently early record of a knighting ceremony in chronicles is often an attempt to rewrite family history in chivalric terms: the best example of this is John of Marmoutier's life of Geoffrey of Anjou, written in the 1180s, where a knighting ceremony ostensibly performed by Henry I at Rouen in 1128 is described as follows:

> On the great day, as was required by the custom for making knights, baths were prepared for use. The king had learned from his chamberlains that the Angevin and those who came with him had come from the purification ceremony. He commanded that they be summoned before him. After having cleansed his body, and come from the purification of bathing, the noble offspring of the count of Anjou dressed in a linen undershirt, putting on a robe woven with gold and a surcoat of a rich purple hue: his stockings were of silk, and on his feet he wore shoes with little gold lions on them. His companions, who were to be knighted with him, were all clothed in linen and purple. He left his privy

33   Geoffroi de Charny, *Le livre de chevalerie*, in Kervyn de Lettenhove (ed.) *Oeuvres de Froissart: Chroniques* (Brussels 1873) I, pt.iii,515.

chamber and paraded in public, accompanied by his noble retinue. Their horses were led, arms carried to be distributed to each in turn, according to their need. The Angevin led a wonderfully ornamented Spanish horse, whose speed was said to be so great that birds in flight were far slower. He wore a matching hauberk made of double mail, in which no hole had been pierced by spear or dart. He was shod in iron shoes, also made from double mail. To his ankles were fastened golden spurs. A shield hung from his neck, on which were golden images of lioncels. On his head was placed a helmet, reflecting the lights of many precious gems, tempered in such a way that no sword could break or pierce it. He carried an ash spear with a point of Poitevin iron, and finally a sword from the royal treasure, bearing an ancient inscription over which the superlative Wayland had sweated with much labour and application in the forge of the smiths.[34]

From the mid-twelfth century onwards, the ceremony of knighting became the central moment in a knight's life, whether it was the simplest of ceremonies or a great extravaganza belonging to the most elaborate kind of chivalry. At this point we can be reasonably sure that there was a formal concept of 'making a knight', even if the specific evidence is elusive. John of Salisbury, in his *Policraticus* (*Statesman's Book*) of 1159 describes *militiae* as a profession, which would imply an equation with soldiering, but he does suggest that there was now a widespread custom of formal, secular admission. When a man has been knighted - and we have to note that he uses the old expression 'girt with the belt of a soldier' - he goes solemnly to church and offers his sword on the altar, dedicating both his weapon and himself to the service of God. There is, first, a secular ceremony, and only then is there a religious service. John makes much of the girding on of the sword, and implies that it has classical origins; in this he is a true disciple of the renaissance of learning in the twelfth century, which looked back to a classical golden age. Guibert de Nogent half a century earlier had tried to link the *ordo equestris* of republican Rome with the crusaders, and this was to be a popular theme until the sixteenth century; but it was a rhetorical flourish, with no grounding in reality.

We begin to have firm evidence of a ceremony at a relatively humble level in the early thirteenth century. In 1204, king John ordered the sheriff of Southampton to provide 'a scarlet robe with a hood of deerskin, another green or brown robe, a saddle, a harness, a rain-cape, a mattress and a pair of linen shirts' for the occasion of the knighting of a squire.[35] The mattress and sheets would have been for the ritual vigil. Entries of this kind become increasingly frequent in the royal records of the thirteenth century, marking occasions when ordinary squires of the royal household came to take

---

34 Halphen & Poupardin, *Chroniques des comtes d'Anjou*, 179, tr. Jim Bradbury, 'Geoffrey V of Anjou, count and knight', in *The Ideals and Practice of Medieval Knighthood III*, ed. Christopher Harper-Bill and Ruth Harvey (Woodbridge & Rochester, N.Y., 1990) 32.

35 *Rotuli Litterarum Clausarum ... 1204-27* ed. T.D.Hardy (London 1833-44) I, 3.

up knighthood. For example, in September 1248 William de Plessetis is told to send 'one silk robe, two linen robes, a cape and a bed and other things necessary to the making of a knight' to Marlborough in time for Christmas.[36]

It is reasonable to assume that the ceremony on such occasions might have been something like that described in *L'Ordene de Chevalerie*, .[37] an anonymous poem dating from 1220-1225. This sets out to explain the symbolism behind the ritual, using a fictional episoded in the life of Saladin, who had a reputation for chivalrous behaviour, but, as a heathen, could not be expected to know the ceremonies of knighthood. Hue de Tabarie, a Christian knight, has been captured by Saladin, who offers him his freedom if he will explain the mysteries of knighthood to him, and make him a knight. Hue is reluctant to do so, but realises that he has no choice, even though Saladin can never be a true knight, because he disdains the 'law of good, of baptism, of faith'. He begins by trimming Saladin's hair and beard, and leads him to a bath, explaining that it symbolises the cleansing of sins by baptism in water. A splendid bed is prepared, foreshadowing the place in paradise which each knight should win for himself. When Saladin has rested, he is dressed (like Geoffrey of Anjou) in white linen and a scarlet robe, with a white belt. Hue girds on Saladin's sword, but refuses to give him the actual blow or *colée*, alleging that he cannot do so because he is Saladin's prisoner. The narrative details the symbolism of each stage, but in a somewhat unusual way: the scarlet robe is said to represent the readiness to shed blood, while the image of the bed as a precursor of paradise is mildly eccentric, to say the least. What is important for our present purpose is the way in which rituals developed originally for great lords by the Church are now seen as appertaining purely to knighthood, and how the secular ritual of the *colée* has become part of them.

So the order of knighthood as it evolved in the later middle ages derived both from the Church's conception of the order inherent in society and from much older *rites de passage* marking the warrior's acceptance by his peers as a member of the war-band. The Church was concerned to bring warriors within its orbit, but knighthood evaded its efforts and remained a secular institution. Investiture, an ecclesiastical and princely occasion, and dubbing, the much more modest secular moment of the making of an ordinary knight, continue side by side.[38]

Examples of investiture are relatively easy to find, because the knighting of a prince found its way into the chronicles, and the not inconsiderable expenses featured in administrative records. Indeed, the knighting of an eldest son was one of the occasions

36   *Calendar of Close Rolls Henry III 6: 1247-51* (London 1922) 84.
37   *L'Ordene de Chevalerie* in Raoul Houdenc, *Le Roman des Eles* and *The Anonymous Ordene de Chevalerie* ed. Keith Busby (Amsterdam & Philadelphia 1983)
38   Flori, *Essor de la Chevalerie*, 115

for which a feudal lord was entitled to levy 'aid' from his vassals, on a par with the marriage of a daughter. Apart from feasting, the celebration often included a self-contained church ritual specific to the occasion. Frederick II of Austria was knighted by the bishop of Passau at Vienna in 1232 after Candlemas in what seems to have been such a ceremony; and at the turn of the century counts Otto and Stefan of Bavaria were knighted by the archbishop of Salzburg with 200 companions. The mass knighting of the prince's companions was held to make the ceremony more magnificent. It might also take place on the occasion of a marriage: Ulrich von Lichtenstein tells us that he was among 250 new knights made at the wedding of the daughter of duke Leopold of Austria in 1222.[39]

A fuller order of service appears in the late thirteenth century, in the pontifical of Guillaume Durand, Bishop of Mende, written about 1295. Here the sword is first blessed, followed by any other pieces of armour, a prayer is said, and the naked sword is given to the knight. It is sheathed and girded on; the knight then takes it out and brandishes it three times. The kiss of peace is exchanged, and the bishop gives him a light blow, saying 'Awake from evil dreams and keep watch, faithful in Christ and praiseworthy in fame'. The nobles standing by then put on his spurs, and if he is entitled to a banner, this is presented with a final blessing. The phrases of the service repeat the idea of protection: 'O Lord. . . who didst wish to institute the order of knighthood for the safeguard of Thy people. . .'; and there is a warning against the misuse of power: 'that he may not unjustly harm anyone with this sword or any other'.[40]

A ritual such as this was for use only on great occasions such as the knighting of Edward II in 1306, when 276 squires accompanied the twenty-two-year-old prince. Because the royal palace was too small, the grounds of the London Temple were commandeered, and tents pitched there. All expenses, save those of horses and armour, were paid, and the richest garments provided. The night before Whitsun the prince and a few chosen companions kept vigil at Westminster, the remainder at the Temple; the prince was then knighted at the palace by his father, and returned to Westminster to knight the other candidates. In the press of the crowd, two knights were killed, several fainted, and fighting broke out; only when the disturbance had been settled could the prince proceed with the ceremony.

Such an occasion was by no means exceptional, save that Edward had political reasons (the renewed war with Scotland) for requiring so many knights at once. For splendour, the knighting of Louis d'Anjou and his brother Charles by Charles VI at

---

39 Bumke, *Knighthoood*, 94; Ulrich von Liechtenstein, *Service of Ladies*, tr. J.W.Thomas, University of North Carolina Studies in the Germanic Languages and Literatures 63(Chapel Hill, N.C.) 1969, stanzas 40-1.

40 Flori, *Essor de la Chevalerie*, 385.

Saint Denis at Easter 1389 easily matched it. Once again a religious establishment (the monastery of Saint Denis) was taken over in order to provide enough room, and even so a temporary great hall, decorated within like a temple, had to be erected in the main courtyard. The proceedings began on the Sunday, when at Mass the king administered 'the usual oath, [and] then bound on their swords and ordered M. de Chauvigny to put on their spurs'. Three tournaments, one for knights, one for squires, and a general one, followed, with dances and other festivities each night; festivities which seemed to have disturbed the monks somewhat, as the chronicler of Saint Denis records that 'the lords, in making day of night and giving themselves up to all the excesses of the table, were driven by drunkenness to all such disorders, that, without respect for the king's presence, several of them sullied the sanctity of the religious house, and abandoned themselves to libertinage and adultery'.[41]

Knighting, from the twelfth century onwards, became the ceremony that marked the coming of age of the warrior and the completion of his military apprenticeship. Until a squire was knighted he was technically not able to lead troops in battle. Hence there were occasions when knighthood was associated with the opening of a campaign or an imminent battle. At a princely level, Louis' girding on of a sword in 791 before the Avar campaign, and the giving of arms to Geisa II in 1146 before a battle are the forerunners of numerous occasions on which knighthood was conferred on the field. In such circumstances it may not always have been possible to carry out the full ritual, and the very brief formula of a blow and the words 'Be thou a knight' may well have originated on such an occasion. When battle was expected at Vironfosse in 1338 between the armies of France and England, a hasty knighting took place by accident:

> The day passed until near twelve o'clock in disputes and debates. About noon a hare was started in the plain, and ran among the French army, who began to make a great shouting and noise, which caused those in the rear to imagine the combat was begun in the front, and many put on their helmets and made ready their swords. Several new knights were made, especially by the earl of Hainault, who knighted fourteen and they were ever after called *Knights of the Hare*.[42]

Against this, most of the examples of knighting before a battle date from the fourteenth and fifteenth century, and seem to be inspired by slightly less theoretical ideas than fitness to bear arms. It was, first, one of the few occasions when the ceremony did not entail vast costs, and hence a poor squire would seek such an excuse wherever possible.

41   Réligieux de Saint-Denys, *Chronique du réligieux de Saint Denys*, ed. L. Bellagut (Paris 1839) I, 599.
42   Jean Froissart, *Chroniques*, ed. Lettenhove, III, 44-5; tr Thomas Johnes, (London 1839) I, 57.

Secondly, the knight was paid more for fighting per day than the squire. And finally, a knight was less likely to have difficulty in raising a ransom, and was certainly in little danger of being killed out of hand instead of being taken prisoner.

The period of the Hundred Years' War provides numerous examples of the ceremony on the field of battle. In a foray into Scotland in 1335, Edward had made knights when expecting action at Annandale on 20 July; and in 1346, at the outset of the Crécy campaign, the Black Prince was knighted when the English army landed in France, with a number of young noblemen; he in turn made a number of other knights. A particular act of valour might be honoured by knighthood. On the crossing of the Scheldt in September 1339, Henry Eam was thus honoured, and being a poor squire was given lands worth £200 a year to support his new estate; and similarly Nigel Loring was knighted and given lands for his part in the sea fight off Sluys. Before a great battle, the numbers might be considerable: at Aljubarrota, in 1385, Froissart claims a total of 140 newly made Spanish knights, naming nine, and says that there were sixty created on the Portuguese side, who were placed in the front of the battalion to do honour to their new status. Knighting as a method of improving morale and making men eager for the fray is also mentioned at an attack on a stronghold near Ardres in 1380, when ten knights were dubbed and 'eager to do honour to their new knighthood, surrounded the tower of Folant, and immediately began the attack'.[43] The most scrupulous would-be knights, however, waited until they had in some way distinguished themselves, 'won their spurs', before their knighting. The phrase originated with those men such as Henry Eam and Nigel Loring who owed their knighthood to a specific feat of arms; we find du Guesclin knighted after he had foiled an ambush by Hugh Calverley at Montmauron in 1354; and Pero Niño, 'the unconquered knight', was only knighted when he had seen thirteen years in the service of arms, aged twenty-eight.

There were other special occasions when knighting might be part of the proceedings. The journeys to Rome of the German emperors for their coronation by the Pope were frequently occasions for mass knightings: seven examples occur, though the ceremony was exploited for other ends, such as propaganda for imperial rights in Italy and the sale of titles to help the imperial treasury. From such a journey, the first contemporary record of dubbing by accolade occurs, when, on 31 December 1354, Charles IV knighted Francesco Carrara; the Emperor sat on horseback, and striking Francesco on the neck with the flat of his hand said, 'Be a good knight and true to the Empire.' Spurs were then put on by two of Charles's attendant nobles. This tradition survived beyond the middle ages; the young Goethe witnessed the knighting ceremony at the coronation of a German emperor in 1765. The crusading visits to Prussia made

---

43   Froissart, *Chroniques*, ed. Lettenhove, IX, 246; tr. Johnes, I, 605.

by many western European knights and squires were another occasion for knighting, as when the Grand Master of the Teutonic Order knighted visiting squires in Prussia in 1377. Knighting could also take place in the Holy Land, where the tradition of knighting pilgrims to the Holy Sepulchre continued until the eighteenth century.

The idea of knighthood as a special estate had been further strengthened by the royal and imperial ordinances which decreed that only sons of knights should be made knights. Originally little more than a restriction on the entry to the profession of arms, this now served to strengthen the feeling that knighthood was a corporation or fraternity. Indeed, to represent it as a kind of guild of soldiers aptly describes one of its aspects. Yet this and the Church's efforts to make it an order within its own view of secular society are not quite enough to explain all its characteristics. The missing element, which begins to appear towards the end of the twelfth century, is a particular pride in descent, a kind of inherited glory, and a restriction on entry into the ranks of knights.

Hitherto, knights had been distinguished from the rest of society merely by their qualification in arms, which in turn had brought them relative wealth. Entry into knighthood and the attendant ceremony had been a simple formality that could be carried out by any knight for anyone's benefit. Nonetheless, it was acknowledged at a very early date that it was not advisable to knight men of low birth, and legal restrictions appear in Germany and Sicily in the twelfth century. In 1152 and 1179 German peasants had been forbidden to bear knightly arms on pain of a fine, and this purely practical measure was followed in 1186 by an order that sons of priests, as being illegitimate, and sons of peasants, as being unfree, were not to be knighted.[44] Equally, Otto of Freising pours scorn on the Italians for knighting tradesmen and apprentices; but he refers to the towns of the north, because the Sicilian kingdom had preceded the Empire in imposing restrictions. Roger II in 1140 had forbidden the knighting of men who might disturb the peace, a move designed to prevent the raising of a rebellious force by wholesale dubbing and equipping of merchants or rich peasants. Though these measures were designed to counter civil disorder, both in Sicily and Germany, the implication that the king could control the practice of knighting remained; and the old right of any knight to make a knight of whomsoever he pleased, by which knighthood was a kind of apostolic succession, was replaced by the idea of hierarchy

---

44   See Eberhard Otto, 'Von der Abschliessung des Ritterstandes', *Historische Zeitschrift* 162, 1940, 19-39 (rptd in Arno Borst, *Das Rittertum im Mittelalter*, Wege der Forschung 394, (Darmstadt 1976) 106-129, and Josef Fleckenstein, 'Zum Problem der Abschliessung der Ritterstandes' in *Ordnungen und formende Kräfte des Mittelalters: ausgewählte Beiträge* (Göttingen 1989) 266-267, and references cited there.

in which the king, as fount of all honour, had sole jurisdiction as to the making of knights.

The process by which the status of knight became a hereditary right is an obscure one. It was partly based on the old Frankish law that only freemen might bear arms and serve in the national levies; as knight and freeman became more and more closely identified in the tenth and eleventh centuries, so the right to bear full arms was restricted to the knight only. Since personal freedom was hereditary, so the knightly title too passed from father to son. In 1186 Frederick I implied in the edict already quoted that knighthood was to be restricted to the sons of knights. In 1188, Alfonso IX of Léon decreed that sons of peasants (*rusticos*) who pretended to be knights were to be fined heavily. [45]In 1231 Frederick II laid this down as law, both in his Sicilian and German domains: 'No one shall acquire the standing of a knight who is not of knightly family unless by grace of our special licence and mandate.' In 1235 the Cortes of Catalonia, in session at Tarragona, echoed his words: 'We decree that no one shall be knighted unless he is a knight's son.' By the mid-thirteenth century, both the law of Anjou and St Louis' legal collections insisted that both parents must be noble, though under certain conditions a peasant whose forebears had inherited a knight's fief four generations earlier could be knighted.[46] The restrictions were similar to those which applied to holy orders – Alexander III had told the bishop of Tours in the mid-twelfth century that neither bastards nor serfs should be ordained – and the Church broadly supported any effort to close the ranks of the knights and increase their standing.

From this period onwards the exclusive nature of the knightly caste was unquestioned, save in England. Those who contrived to join its ranks from below did so only by exercise of the royal prerogative; those who tried to do so under false pretences were duly punished. In France, under the regency of Blanche of Castile in the early thirteenth century, Robert de Beaumont, a bourgeois, was fined £100 for having himself knighted. Exceptionally, knighthood was the reward for great deeds of arms, in particular on the battlefield: more usually, it became another of the privileges put up for sale by a hard-pressed royal exchequer. After the defeat at Courtrai in 1302, Philip the Fair advertised his readiness to grant it for a fee. In France this could make sound financial sense to a rich merchant, as the knights had begun to acquire those exemptions from taxation which were to become one of the great abuses of the *ancien régime* in the eighteenth century, and the purchase of knighthood soon became a kind of quittance for future taxes by payment of a single lump sum. For an imprudent king, it was an easy way of raising money at the expense of future income, and similar schemes were used by Charles IV and his successors in Germany. Likewise, in the early

45   Pescador, 'La caballeria popular', XXXV-XXXVI, 58.
46   Otto, 'Von der Abschliessung des Ritterstandes', 118, 119.

fourteenth century those fiefs which by their extent conferred nobility on their holder, could only be purchased by a non-noble on payment of a heavy tax, which made the fief 'free'; and this remained a possible means of entry into the French nobility until 1579, when titles acquired by the sale of a specific piece of land were abolished.

Despite these privileges, and the evident anxiety of wealthy non-nobles to make their way up the social ladder, the majority of the nobles, and particularly simple knights, grew steadily poorer during the thirteenth and fourteenth centuries. The new economic order was less favourable to agriculture as coinage was increasingly used, and the towns and new merchant classes stood outside the old hierarchy. The rise in prices throughout the next two centuries was not matched by an appreciable increase in the knight's income from his lands: no agricultural revolution came to the aid of the old kind of estate, with its small strip fields where the lord's land was hopelessly jumbled with the serfs' holdings, comparable to that in the wool industry in England, where the East Anglian churches stand as evidence of the farmers' and wool-dealers' wealth. Not only were the lucrative rewards of trade forbidden to the knight by social convention, but the merchants themselves were hostile interlopers. And just when the one hope seemed to be alliance with this new moneyed class, the instinctive reaction of a threatened order prevailed: knighthood became more sharply self-conscious and exclusive in this period.

Knights did, however, enjoy some economic privileges. The freedom from ordinary taxes in France was more than offset by the expenses of feudal service and the heavy 'relief' payable on inheritance of a fief; Philippe de Beaumanoir in the 1280s reckoned a knight's lands to be worth one-sixth less than those of a non-noble. In England the exemptions were non-existent, and the feudal dues added to an already heavy burden of taxation. Conditions in Germany were unfavourable for other reasons, the chief being the incessant private wars and lack of political stability. The poor knight was a common figure throughout the Middle Ages, ranging from the younger son making his fortune in tournament and the old knight fallen on harsh days who could not find a dowry for his daughter (like the touching portrait of Enide's father in Chrétien de Troyes' *Erec et Enide* [47]) to the mercenaries and men of the 'great companies' fighting and plundering for a living or the robber knights turned to evil ways. Knighthood and wealth were by no means synonymous.

The special status of knighthood survived the mercenary instincts of the kings who were supposed to be its protectors. Initiation into knighthood became a costly ceremonial process, which the poorer nobles were unwilling to undertake; and knighthood and nobility once again became separate concepts, having briefly converged

47   Chrétien de Troyes, *Erec et Enide*, ed. Mario Roques, Classiques Français du Moyen Age (Paris 1955) ll.373-546.

during the late twelfth and early thirteenth centuries. Nobility took on once more its hereditary form, requiring no formal admission or acknowledgment; knighthood became entirely a matter of membership of an order with a specific ceremony as its distinguishing mark. At the period in the mid-thirteenth century when the rulers of western Europe began to try to restrict the numbers of those who were exempted from taxes by reason of nobility, the old rule that a noble was a knight was no longer true. Hence nobility, once rarer than knighthood, now became dependent on it: to prove nobility, a man had to have a knight in his family. In Provence, grandsons of knights were regarded as having knightly privileges, but had to be knighted by the time they were thirty if they were to continue to claim these rights; in 1275 at Oppenheim in Germany a similar custom without the need for knighting at a specified age prevailed. By the early fourteenth century it was quite common for nobles to die as unknighted 'donzeaux' in France; of a group of fifty-six potential knights in the rebellion at Forez in 1314–15, only thirty-five were knighted before they were forty, and eleven died without being knighted at all.[48]

This leads us to a problem which was never satisfactorily resolved, that of the relationship between the fief and the standing of the knight. It was all very well for Philip Augustus to try to enforce knighthood on fief-holders; but the fiefs were often split up, and a rich man might hold several parts of fiefs and still not fall under the terms of the enforcement. It is not uncommon to find fractions as small as one-tenth of a knight's fief in charters. Henry II had attempted a solution to the problem as early as 1180, when all who held land yielding more than £100 Angevin in his French domains were obliged to equip themselves as knights, although nothing was said about actual knighthood. From 1224 onwards, when all laymen holding one or more knight's fees were required to arm themselves and be knighted, the 'distraint' of knighthood becomes a regular feature.[49] This measure was undoubtedly aimed at increasing the numbers of titular knights, since as a class they had important administrative duties; though it was also a revenue measure, as fines payable for not taking up knighthood had been levied since the beginning of the century. There had been a vast decline from Henry II's day, when there were 5,000 landholders who could have been knights. By the end of the thirteenth century, when the greatest possible pressure was exerted by the king and new knights were even given arms at royal expense, the total of English knights was unlikely to exceed 1,500, and only about 500 were capable of fighting. There were, however, still a number of landless knights: the Dictum of Kenilworth in 1266 includes provisions for dealing with those of Simon de Montfort's supporters who came from this class. The same proportion of knights to the whole population,

48   Duby, *The Chivalrous Society*, 111.
49   Peter Coss, *The Knight in Medieval England 1000–1400* (Stroud & Dover, N.H., 1993) 60ff.

estimated at one in 500 of all able-bodied men of full age, probably applies to France and Germany as well.

As knighthood became a matter of legal status, so the warlike character of the English knights was eclipsed by their duties in peacetime. The 'knights of the shire' became key figures in both local and central government. At the local level they were responsible for providing juries for the grand assize, and thus dealt with royal justice as well as their own manorial courts. By 1258 evasions and exemptions, and the persistent decline in numbers, meant that the grand assize could not be held in some counties because there were not enough knights available. And yet despite this the Provisions of Oxford, instigated by the barons in the same year, and probably supported by most of the knights themselves, gave the knights of the shire even greater responsibility in the sphere of local justice, a responsibility soon extended into what was in effect a complete review of all local administration. Quite apart from this, ordinary jury duty itself was not simply a matter of listening to skilled pleaders and assessing their prepared case; it often involved actual inspection of lands in dispute, administrative work connected with the court's decision, and police duties in criminal cases.

In central affairs, it was the knights of the shire who were the original members of the House of Commons. The four knights of the shire who brought their reports to Westminster in October 1258 were the forerunners of the most active part of the mediaeval parliament, though they quickly became public figures first and foremost, and knights only incidentally. In the country their standing as knights was a clear distinguishing mark; as members of parliament, they would have regarded 'knight of the shire' as a title having little to do with nobility or knighthood, and much to do with administrative duties. For this reason, parliament never became a class pressure group in the way that the estates of France did, and the knights as a body conscious of their identity did not appear in England. Indeed, within parliament they combined with their social rivals from city and borough, and became representatives of one part of the whole community.

In France the same development took place in rather different circumstances. The English kings, being relatively poorer, relied largely on partly paid men to do the work of local administration and the purely professional civil service remained small, the rewards slight except for the great officers. In France the king's service was better paid and became a means of livelihood for many French knights who found themselves in financial straits, and knighthood was often the key to a political rather than military career. In Germany, the *ministeriales* were above all administrators, as their name implies, and filled the important court offices, both in the households of minor counts and in that of the emperor himself, where they were to be found as marshal, butler, chamberlain or seneschal. They were also entrusted with financial offices, and were put in charge of such sources of revenue as tolls, mints and markets, as well as dispensing justice and maintaining law and order. Like their English and French counterparts, however, they were also expected to be versed in military skills, whether in the field or garrisoning a castle.[50]

Hence by the early fourteenth century the old feudal basis of knighthood had virtually disappeared. The summons to the feudal levy for forty days' service was a technical obligation, and the last two attempts at raising an English army by this method were in 1327 and 1385,[51] though it persisted elsewhere: in Liège an unsuccessful effort was made as late as 1435. Instead, a system of taxation based on landed wealth had become the means of raising revenue to pay a mercenary army. The distinction between the knight and the paid soldier after the late thirteenth century was merely one of name; both served of their own free will, though the knight had other financial means and was therefore not entirely dependent on warfare for his bread and butter. Furthermore the knight was also in many cases paid on a different basis, that of the *fief-rente*, whereby his military service was part of a feudal contract. Instead of land, however, he received a specified income in money. In an era which still thought in feudal terms this was a more natural arrangement than a straightforward salary and had the additional advantage of ensuring that men were easily available, since otherwise mercenaries had to be found for each separate expedition. Such arrangements could be made with either land-owning knights or household knights: as witness the agreement between the count of Flanders and Jean Traiment de Noyelles in 1338. In return for £60 Paris per annum, John was to serve the count in all wars and tournaments, and was to receive in addition wages and maintenance in kind.

Spain, where warfare against the Muslims was still endemic, even if there were long intervals between campaigns, was, as always, something of an exception. Membership of the civic cavalry became a hereditary status by the early fourteenth century, and membership conferred certain exemptions from taxes, both in kind and in cash. In the late fourteenth century the civic militia moved even close to knighthood; they were allowed to take part in a form of tournament, the *bohort*.[52] In 1388, Juan I ennobled all those who had served him with horse and arms in his wars against John of Gaunt, declaring them to be *hidalgos*. Enrique IV and Ferdinand and Isabella issued secular privileges for their cavalry, but stipulated a minimum service of four months and two months respectively.[53]

50   Arnold, *German Knighthood 1050-1200* 184.
51   May McKisack, *The Fourteenth Century* (Oxford 1959) 234.
52   Pescador, 'La caballeria popular', XXXVII-XXXVIII, 235.
53   Pescador, 'La caballeria popular', XXXIII-XXXIV, 145.

From the mid-fourteenth century, nobility became a question of legal definitions, an almost artificial institution quite divorced from its knightly and warrior overtones. A clever lawyer could argue his way into it; the Pastons did so in England, rising from yeomen (or possibly serfs) via the law to knighthood in three or four generations, and in France maître Jean Boutaud did much the same in 1475, producing witnesses to swear that his family had always lived in a noble fashion, and had served in the king's armies. Another advocate, Jean Barbin, argued that his father was 'descended of a noble line, and as such held and reputed publicly and to the knowledge of all'.[54] Both cases succeeded; and it was the style of living and general esteem in which the family was held that decided the matter, rather than any question of formal knighthood. The two ideas had completely separated, even though the nobleman's alleged duty to fight was no more than a vestige of his former glories as a warrior.

This change had largely come about with the development of an economy in which money was more important to the knight than landed wealth. The lesser nobles depended not so much on landed fiefs as on the pensions, or 'fief-rentes', the reward of military allegiance or service at court, whether the king's court or some greater noble's. Even for the magnates, the outward and visible signs of their social standing were no longer the family castle, perhaps already a ruin, but their town house and country manor, neither necessarily fortified in any way. The old relationship between lord and peasant inherent in the older system had dissolved as well, partly because the state had taken over the knight's role as protector.

What now mattered was inherited status, pride in descent, which found its most visible expression in heraldry. By the late twelfth century, nobles are knights, and knights are the highest social class, though the last traces of the dividing line only disappear in the late fourteenth century, when the descendants of the knights had fully adopted the nobles' insistence on birth as the great criterion. The way in which the fief was inherited had had considerable influence on the attitude of the nobles to ancestry. There is some evidence that the old way of tracing the family through the mother's line had survived into the tenth century. Now not only was this superseded, but the patriarchal side was heavily emphasised. The eldest son would normally inherit the fief; while the younger sons would have to go out and seek their fortune, as part of that society of *iuvenes*, men between knighthood and marriage, who are most distinct in northern France in the twelfth and thirteenth centuries. The best recommendation in such circles, until a knight had earned his own reputation, was his father's name as a warrior.

It was probably for this reason that heraldic devices, originally personal, became hereditary, and the herald's interest in genealogy developed, an interest furthered by

---

54   P.S.Lewis, *Later Medieval France* (London 1968) 174.

the exclusion from tournaments of men who were not qualified to become knights, again towards the end of the twelfth century. The original function of heralds had been to conduct tournaments, first proclaiming their place and date, and on the occasion announcing the combatants to the spectators, adding their own commentary on the deeds and renown of each. As the question of arms became more involved and more important, they kept records of armorial bearings, and from their knowledge of the conduct of business became officials with a recognised standing by the mid-thirteenth century. A hundred years later they appeared as diplomatic messengers, under the authority of the two chief officers of war, the marshal and the constable, doubtless because of their experience in proclaiming tournaments abroad.

The heralds had originally been involved with arms simply as a means of identifying combatants, a task which would have become increasingly difficult as armour covered the entire head and body. The first tournament shields were very simple, of a single colour with a simple device: the three leopards of Anjou, the three lions of England, the fleurs-de-lis of France, are examples. As the claims to use these individual devices were inherited by several sons, the practice grew of quartering the arms, taking those of both parents, especially since French law insisted that both parents had to be noble if a man was to be knighted. By the fourteenth century, only those who could lay claim to four noble grandparents were qualified to take part in tournaments, and the German 'tournament societies' could be even stricter. *Turnierfähigkeit*, the ability to take part in tournaments, was a jealously guarded privilege.

The rules of these societies were carefully framed to exclude 'robber knights', and as these might easily be nobles fallen on evil day, a moral censorship was also exercised. In 1434 Albrecht III of Bavaria was refused entry to a tournament because of his scandalous relationship with Agnes Bernauer; and in René d'Anjou's *Le Livre des Tournois* written in the 1450s, three main cases for exclusion are listed: perjurers and those who have broken their word of honour, usurers, and those who have married beneath their station. Thus secular knighthood adopted some of the characteristics which the Church had proposed for it some two centuries earlier.

The particular mystique of the word of honour, however, cannot be explained by religious influence. It was this, perhaps more than any other single feature, that distinguished the way of thought of the knight. If, as Francis I's motto after his Italian defeat ran, 'Tout est perdu fors l'honneur' (All is lost save honour), little was lost. Honour was the shrine at which the knight worshipped: it implied renown, good conduct, and the world's approval. The 'word of honour' was the most solemn oath the knight knew, and this alone became the reason for the most extravagant exploits, fruit of a rash word spoken in the heat of the moment. Walter Manny's expedition into France in 1338 with a small band of forty horsemen was the result of his vow to be the first to strike a blow in the newly declared war. The whole world of romance depends for its incidents on the convention that a knight's word once given can never be retracted, and only the knight's lord could absolve such oaths. Usually they took a relatively harmless form: the holding of tournaments which outdid even those of romance – Moriz von Craûn's exploit of arriving in a ship on wheels at the tournament he had arranged outside his lady's castle pales beside the real splendours of the Burgundian festivals. On the other hand a vow could be overridden by ducal or royal command; the duke of Burgundy in 1454 annulled a vow by one of his knights to wear a piece of armour until he had found an opponent prepared to fight, and never to turn his horse's head back until he had killed an infidel.

René d'Anjou's second prohibition, that against knights who were usurers taking part in tournaments, marked another way in which knights were set apart. This was partly due to the rigid order of mediaeval society; if a merchant could not be a knight, then neither should a knight be a merchant. But there were deeper roots than this, in civil law. For the lawyer, working from late classical texts, *miles* meant soldier in general, as it had done in Roman days; but the same text could equally well seem to mean knight in particular. Thus when Giovanni da Legnano gathered the opinions of ancient authorities in his *Tractatus de Bello* used Justinian and the Roman lawbooks when he said that soldiers *(milites)* 'ought to abstain from the cultivation of the land, from the care of animals, from trade in commodities. They should not manage the business of other people; nor engage in civil duties.'[55] Towards the end of the fourteenth century, Honoré Bonet in *The Tree of Battles*, a work on the conduct of war, used this passage as the basis of his passage on the duties of a good knight and translated *miles* as knight, making the obligations of a Roman legionary part of a knight's way of life. Likewise, the romances about Alexander and Troy, which appeared in the twelfth century, and which describe classical heroes as though they were contemporary knights, gave knighthood a false classical pedigree, much on the lines of the eponymous Trojan founders of France and Britain. Knighthood was seen as an ancient institution, and proper pride was taken in its venerable age.

The realities of war, the ideals of the Church, the pride of noble families, the records of the heralds, and the researches of the lawyers all contributed to give the cult of knighthood an ardent following. Without the splendour of secular ceremonies and the flights of fancy of the romances, however, its flame would never have been so bright. The moment when a young prince came to take up knighthood was one of the occasions when the mediaeval love of pageant could be exploited to the full.

Even if romantic ideas gained wide enough currency for a preacher to say that 'no knight can be brave unless he is in love; love gives the knight his courage',[56] the older,

55   Giovanni da Legnano, *Tractatus de bello, de represaliis et de duello* ed.T.E.Holland (London & Washington 1917) 235.

simpler view of knighthood persists in the following century. In the prose romance of *Lancelot*, the Lady of the Lake can lecture Lancelot on knightly duties and virtues without once mentioning love. *L'Ordene de Chevalerie* depicts the actual knighting in great detail, has only a brief list of things a knight should never do: never give false judgment; never give evil counsel to ladies, but help them; fast on Fridays; hear Mass every day and make an offering. In contrast to this simple advice, great attention is paid in both works to the symbolic meaning of each part of the knight's armour. As the hauberk safeguards the body so the knight safeguards the Church; as the helm defends the head so the knight defends the Church; as the fear of the lance drives back the unarmed so the knight drives back the Church's enemies. The two edges of the sword show that the knight serves both God and the people, and its point shows that all people must obey him. The horse that carries him represents the people, whom the knight must lead, but who must support him and give him the wherewithal for an honourable life.

This idea of knighthood as the bulwark of society against disorder runs right through the manuals on the subject, and is partly a justification of the knight's right to lead, partly a sanctification of the feudal warrior. It is not enough to bear arms; the power given to the knight must be used rightly if he is to be worthy of his knighthood. In the late fourteenth century, Geoffroi de Charny, one of the foremost knights of France, wrote of brigands as 'those armed men who are far from being men-at-arms'. He also saw the dangers of those who, in an age when knighthood was becoming a rare title, sought knighthood for the wrong reasons. The enthusiastic young knight was welcome, as long as he realised that knighthood was hard work; the middle-aged man had to be sure that he wanted the duties as well as the honour; and as for the old men who would have liked to have ended their days as knights, let them be sensible about it.

Knighthood becomes inextricably bound up with the ideals of chivalry after the mid-thirteenth century, and the later manuals on it belong to the ethics of chivalrous behaviour. Knighthood begins as a personal status which does not depend on the holding of land on the one hand, nor on belief in a certain code of behaviour on the other. Its distinctive character is supported by the Church's ideas of it as an order with moral obligations towards the society which supports it, combined with the adoption of knightly descent as a test of nobility. It is a warrior caste such as can be found in many societies, both feudal and non-feudal; and it is no more than the basis for chivalry. Here the knight is soldier and lord; later we will find him as knight-errant, lover and crusader: but we must still remember that chivalry and all its glories are only an extension of the original, simple institution of the recognised bearer of knightly arms.

56   A. Lecoy de la Marche, *La Chaire Française au Moyen Age* (Paris 1886) 392.

3

Heroes and Warriors: the *Chansons de Geste* and Twelfth Century Warfare

CHIVALRY INVOLVES certain attitudes of mind, and in order to understand it, we need to look not only at literature contemporary with knighthood and centred on chivalry, but also on earlier poems which evoke the more primitive attitudes of their predecessors. The warriors of the tenth century, preoccupied with survival in a hostile world, had little time or thought for literature; their songs and stories, like those in the camps of Troy during the historical Trojan wars, have not come down to us. The picture of those heroic days, both of chivalry and of the Greek epic, depends on later witnesses, both for its details and for the ideals which men held dear. Homer in his day preserved some of the real feelings of the men who fought these already legendary battles, and in the same way the old French poems known as the *chansons de geste* (*geste* being a deed or exploit) brought to life the battles of Charlemagne and preserved them in a literary form.

The *chansons de geste*, as far as they have survived, comprise a fragment and a complete poem from the late eleventh century, a group of fairly primitive poems of the twelfth century, and poems which gradually merge into the common stock of romance in the following years. Besides these we may place as both a yardstick and as another branch of the same literary form the Spanish *Cantar de Mio Cid* (Song of the Cid), and the German heroic tale, the *Nibelungenlied* (Song of the Nibelungs). The latter, written in the early thirteenth century, reflects a much older society, some of its episodes belonging to sixth-century history. The early thirteenth-century *Cantar de Mio Cid* is set in the eleventh century, and the twelfth-century *chansons de geste* deal with the Carolingian period, from the eighth century onwards.

The three great themes of the *chansons de geste* remained static from an early period. The defeat of Roland at Roncevaux, the deeds of Guillaume d'Orange, count of Toulouse, and the rebelliousness of the northern French barons under Charlemagne's successors, became established as the accepted subjects for such poems. Both authentic independent episodes and invented scenes were attached to them until they formed three great cycles, tenuously connected by a series of common figures. The chief characters largely belong to Charlemagne's family and two great clans: that descended from Garin de Montglane, the fearless, righteous heroes, and that of Doon de Mayence, the corrupted traitors. There is scarcely a single character who does not find a place in this scheme, though the general traits of the clan may not appear in each of its members: for example, Charlemagne is a grandiose, heroic figure, but his son Louis is presented as a simple, weak and indecisive character who has to be rescued from his own folly, and is far from a worthy descendant of the great emperor.

In the form in which these poems have come down to us they date from the early twelfth century or later, with the exception of the great *Chanson de Roland* and the fragment *Gormont et Isembart*. Hence they largely belong to an age when knighthood was becoming an established institution, and when the crusading movement had already achieved its first triumphs. The attitudes they reflect are only a decade or two earlier than those of the romances, as are their expressions and turns of phrase; and there is a literary element, however crude they may seem beside the romances, which nonetheless brings them close to the calculated inventions of the latter. Even in the *Chanson de Roland*, the earliest complete poem, the story is treated as a triptych in which the death of Roland, Charlemagne's victory, and the avenging of Ganelon's treachery balance and complement each other. The very fact that almost all the tales have been cast in the form of cycles is another mark of a conscious idea of literary method.

Yet the material of the *chansons de geste* belongs to a much less sophisticated world than the enchantments of romance. For this reason it is easy to be deceived by the stories into taking the actual poems to be the original raw material of epic. In that case one would have to account for a remarkable burst of literary activity in France about the year 1100, centring on events which had happened two or three centuries earlier, for all the historical events which these poems celebrate belong to the years 716-943. Furthermore, the records of this period are never detailed enough in style to enable a poet, however scholarly and assiduous in his research, and with access to a multitude of lost sources, to provide such lifelike accounts. Above all, there are certain details in many of the poems which are too much at variance with the story to have been invented, and yet ring true as history.

There is only one convincing explanation for this mixture of literature and history in the *chansons de geste*: that the versions we possess are descendants of a tradition which goes back to contemporary poems on the events of Charlemagne's time. This is supported by studies of modern societies where the epic still flourished in recent times, notably in Serbia. Long poems composed on recent political events were recited by local bards; their methods, notably of variation at each telling and repetition of stanzas for emphasis, are echoed in the old French epics. And beside these recent works, this traditional poetry dealt with the events of five centuries ago with some degree of historical accuracy. Indeed, it has been argued that variation (which the surviving

1   Warrior, tenth century
(BL MS Add. 11695 f. 194)

2   Making a knight (BL MS Nero D. i. f. 3; mid-thirteenth century)

3   Accolade on the field of battle, fourteenth century
(Bibliothèque Nationale MS fr. 343 f. 79)

4   Knighting ceremony showing dubbing, girding on of swords and spurs,
fifteenth century (BL MS Add. 15469 f. 28v)

5   Roland fights the Saracen Ferragut

(Capital on ducal palace at Estella; photo MAS, Barcelona)

6   Charlemagne sets out against the Saracens

(Santiago, Archivo de la Catedral. Codex Calixtinus f. 162 v., twelfth century. Photo MAS, Barcelona)

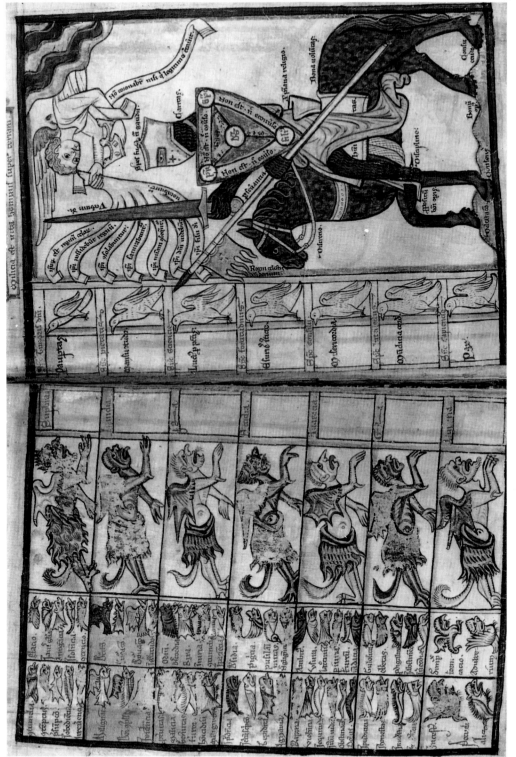

7 The virtues of the knight, thirteenth century (BL MS Harley 3244 ff. 27v–28r)

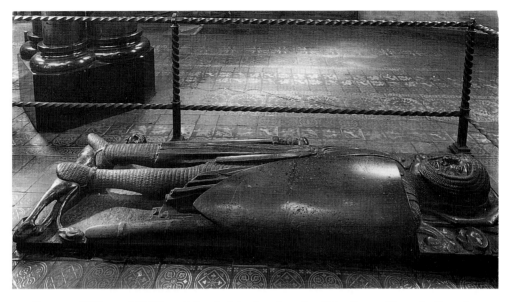

8   Effigy of William Marshal in the church of the Inner Temple, London
(Taken before the bombing of 1940. Photo Walter Scott, Bradford)

9   Effigy of the Black Prince in Canterbury Cathedral.
(National Monuments Record)

10 Du Guesclin is appointed Constable of France; early fifteenth century (BL MS Sloane 2433a, f. 220v)

11 The knight in full array: Sir Geoffrey Luttrell (BL MS Add. 42130, f. 202v)

12   Marshal Boucicaut as St George

(Musée Jacquemart-André, Heures du maréchal Boucicaut. Photo Giraudon)

13   Minnesinger: Walther von der Vogelweide

14   Minnesinger: Hartmann von Aue

15   Minnesinger: Der von Kürenberc

16   Minnesinger: Walther von Klingen

(Universitätsbibliothek, Heidelberg, MS pal.germ 848)

17   The adventures of Lancelot at Castle Perilous: he crosses the sword bridge, fights three lions and jousts with Meleagant in order to rescue Guinevere (BN MS fr. 122, f. Ir)

18   The appearance of the Grail at Arthur's court (BN MS Arsenal 5218 f. 88)

19   Lovers in conversation
(Ivory mirror case, Victoria and Albert Museum 220-1867, fourteenth century)

20   Riding to a tournament, early fourteenth century
(BM MS Royal 19 C i. f. 204)

21   A tournament; Italy, fourteenth century (BL MS Add. 12228 f. 182v-183r)

22   Joust; England, fourteenth century (BL MS Royal 10 E IV, f. 65v)

23   Practising: tilting at the quintain (BL MS Facs. 237, pl.XIX)

24   The start of a tournament, fifteenth century (BN MS fr. 2692 f. 62v-63)

25   The dukes of Brittany and Bourbon armed for jousting (BN MS fr. 2692 f. 32v.-33: fifteenth century)

26   Distribution of prizes after a tournament (BN MS fr. 2692 f. 50)

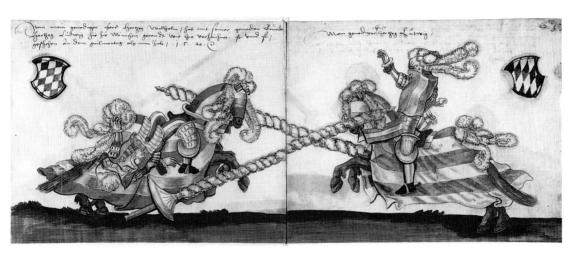

27   Duke Wilhelm IV of Bavaria is unhorsed by his brother Ludwig at a joust in Munich in July 1520 (Munich, Bayerische Staatsbibliothek MS Cgm 1929 ff. 22v-23)

28   Combat with halberds on foot, Smithfield 1466
(BL MS Cotton Julius E IV art (6) f. 7v)

29   Marx Walther is unhorsed in a civic joust in 1518
(Munich, Bayerische Staatsbibliothek MS Cgm 1930 ff. 3v-4)

30   Flemish parade shield (British Museum)

manuscripts of the *chansons de geste* provide to a remarkable degree) was essential to keep the oral poetic tradition alive; no audience wanted to hear exactly the same version told again, and the older version would be forgotten as the poet learnt or invented some new phrase, metaphor or even episode. Finally, there is the parallel of the twelfth-century German *Nibelungenlied* already mentioned, where events of the sixth and seventh century (again a period in which the style of historical works was terse and not given to great detail) are described in terms which imply the use of material handed down by tradition and including details unknown to orthodox historians.

Thus the *chansons de geste* reflect in varying degrees the whole formative period of knighthood. The historical background of the eighth century and the emerging knightly attitudes of the early twelfth century predominate respectively in the matter and the point of view. Two of the cycles, those based on the *Chanson de Roland* and the *Chanson de Guillaume*, share a common theme: the struggle between Frank and Muslim in southern France and Spain in the eighth century. Despite Charles Martel's great victory at Poitiers in 732, the Muslims continued to threaten the safety of the south, through their presence in Spain and their raids from the sea and from their bases on the Mediterranean coast. Charlemagne's aggressive imperial policy, which consisted of reducing hostile enemies on his frontier to client-states, was bound to bring him into conflict with the Moorish kingdoms beyond the Pyrenees. Only the Saxons on his German borders caused him more anxiety; but from 777 onwards the Muslims ranked as a problem of the same order, and expeditions of varying sizes set out almost every year until 814.

In 778, in response to an appeal from Spain – though it was not because Charlemagne was 'moved by the cries and complaints of the Christians under the heavy yoke of the Saracens', as a contemporary chronicler has it, for the appeal came from Muslim emirs engaged in a feud with others of their religion – Charlemagne moved into Spain, hoping to establish his influence over his allies and thus secure the frontier. The *Chanson de Roland* celebrates this, the first and greatest of his forays into Spain. Pamplona and Gerona fell, but Saragossa was resisting him successfully when news came from Germany of fresh Saxon attacks. As the Spanish expedition had engaged most of his military resources, this meant retreat, and as he recrossed the Pyrenees his rearguard was ambushed in the narrow pass of Roncevaux, on the Spanish side of the mountains, by the Basques or Gascons (probably with Muslim assistance, though the early chroniclers know nothing of this). Among those who fell were the king's seneschal and count of the palace, as well as 'Roland, duke of the Breton march, and many others'. There were at most 1,000 horsemen involved in the encounter; trapped in the steep-sided defile, they must have been an easy prey, unable to manoeuvre. Charlemagne was unable to avenge the disaster, not so much because the enemy had disappeared into their native mountains, but because of the more urgent threat from Germany.

Guillaume d'Orange belongs to the same era; his prototype was probably William, count of Toulouse, the first of a series of powerful magnates to bear that title, who defeated a renewed Muslim onslaught on the banks of the Orbieu, between Carcassonne and Narbonne, in 793. Both he and Roland remain shadowy figures in history, and the only early chronicle to relate their deeds at length is that ascribed to Turpin, archbishop of Rheims and Roland's supposed companion at Roncevaux, which is really a twelfth-century confabulation.

The third cycle, of the rebellious barons, is a more diffuse group. *Gormont et Isembart* is not strictly part of it, dealing with a victory of Charles III over the Northmen in 881: the tradition that all great battles were fought against the southern infidels is so strong that the traitor Isembart's allies have become Muslims. The real cycle is centred on Raoul de Cambrai, to whom the *Geste des Lorrains* was connected by thirteenth-century writers using a tenuous genealogy. Here again historical notices are very sparse. In 943, the chronicler records, after the death of count Hubert II of Vermandois, there was war between his sons and Raoul, son of Raoul de Gouy; and the only other detailed record draws on a literary source akin to the *chanson de geste*. Likewise, Garin de Lorrain and Girart de Roussillon or de Vienne are shadowy figures, and it is only with difficulty that their historical counterparts can be identified.

If the historical facts behind the *chansons de geste* are obscure, so are their literary antecedents. If we accept the idea of oral tradition as the missing link between the actual events and their written versions, there still remains the problem of who wrote the poems we now have. We have possible authors' names: the enigmatic Turoldus appears at the end of the *Chanson de Roland*, and in *Raoul de Cambrai*, Bertolai is presented as the original author, but we know nothing about them. If the writers, or even the recorders – who would have refashioned the poems somewhat – were clerics, we must make due allowance for clerical attitudes; while if they were *jongleurs* themselves, the poems are more valuable to us as witnesses of warrior society and its ethics.

We start with poems 'born on the spot relating notable contemporary dates or facts'.[1] This is the foundation of all our poems: the main course of action and the main traits of the characters belong to this period. The elaboration and connection of this material was the work of *jongleurs* in the following centuries, who omitted details, invented new ones, and welded earlier unconnected pieces into longer works. Of these poems nothing survives, but we can infer their existence from the versions that have come down to us, which are clearly not literary reworkings of chronicles and historical records. The *Chanson de Roland*, first and also finest of the surviving poems, comes from the last phase when the literate men who wrote the legends down probably gave them a

---

1   Ramon Menéndez Pidal, *La Chanson de Roland y el Neotradicionalismo (Origenes de la épica romanica)* , (Madrid 1959) 428.

more polished style and borrowed literary turns of phrase in order to gloss over the weaknesses which repetition had introduced; and made from crude recital, elegant reading. Hence the *chansons de geste* were the product of a society still not fully literate, but which had moved beyond the most primitive stage of oral records. They were probably shaped in their original form largely by their immediate surroundings, the great baronial halls where the *jongleur* recited them to a simple musical cadence. The rapport between an audience of fighting men, capable of appreciating the subtleties of their descriptions of battles, and the minstrel was an essential part of their ambience.

The themes and heroes which held the rough fighters spellbound were close to their own enthusiasms and way of life. Warfare is central to all of them: the hero is a good fighter in battle. And as in warfare loyalty to the leader is paramount, so fidelity and treachery are the twin poles of virtue and vice for these warriors. The *Chanson de Roland* is the masterpiece among the *chansons de geste*. It is built on two great episodes: Charlemagne's retreat from Spain and Roland's death, and Charlemagne's revenge on Baligant and Ganelon. Roland's death is the key to the action. It is encompassed by Ganelon, who, sent on an embassy to Spain after Roland has insulted him, arranges that the Saracens[2] shall fall on the emperor's rearguard. He will see that Roland is in command of it; for not only is Roland his enemy, but he is also the implacable foe of peace; Charles will never weary of going to the wars 'while Roland still bears sword'. Ganelon favours peace, and has said so at the council with which the poem opens: thus there is a subtle equation between the pacifists and the traitors. Ganelon's scheme succeeds: Roland is named leader of the rearguard, and with him go Oliver, his friend and companion, and the warlike archbishop Turpin. The trap is set, and when Oliver sees that not one but five armies confront them he begs Roland to summon Charlemagne by blowing his ivory horn. In a famous scene, Roland refuses and Oliver insists:

> *'Roland, my friend, blow your ivory horn*
> *For Charles to hear as he rides through the gates*
> *Of Spain. Be sure, the Franks will soon return.'*
> *'Let it please God,' Roland quickly replied,*
> *'No man on earth shall ever say of me*
> *I blew my horn for fear of pagan troops;*
> *My kin shall never be reproached for that.*
> *When in the battle's heat I take my stand,*
> *I'll deal even hundred — no, a thousand — strokes*
> *And Durendal's bright blade shall run with blood.*

---

2   In the poems, the Muslims are always called Saracens.

51

The French are brave, they'll do as vassals should;
Our Spanish foes come only to their graves.[3]

'Roland is valiant, Oliver is wise'; but the hero is Roland, not Oliver, and it is his boast that he will destroy the entire heathen army, despite its evident folly that wins the poet's admiration, rather than Oliver's practical caution. The last hint of fear must be shunned: 'And damn the man whose heart admits despair'.[4] Bravery is what a baron's reputation and position depend on: 'If the King loves us it's for our valour's sake.'[5]

So Roland goes willingly to his almost certain death, because of an ideal courage and trust. To object that it is not in the emperor's best interest that he should do so, is to make the argument too subtle. Roland has been given a task to do: when he was given command of the rearguard, he declares that Charles shall not lose even a mule unless it is bought with the sword.[6] This is all that counts: the task he has been entrusted with by his lord. When, having destroyed four of the pagan armies, he is overwhelmed by the last attack, and Oliver rebukes him for his foolhardiness, he cannot see what he has done wrong, nor why he should not now summon help, since his resources are at an end. And as he dies, his last thoughts before he commends himself to heaven are that his emperor should see that he had carried out his charge well, now that the Saracens have fled:

He turned his head to face the pagan host;
For he desired that Charles, and all the men
Of France, should see his dying glance and say
That he died as he lived, a conqueror.[7]

If faithfulness is the subject's great virtue, justice is that of the lord. Charlemagne must do justice to his dead vassal by avenging him; first on the Saracens, second on the traitor. The battle against Baligant, Marsile's new ally, is a huge set piece, as emir rides against peer, Frank against paynim, culminating in the duel between Charlemagne and Baligant. Once the heathen are defeated, their leaders slain, and the idols down, Charlemagne can return to France, and deal with Ganelon. For one terrible moment it seems as though the traitor will be forgiven: there are many of Ganelon's kin to

---

3   *Chanson de Roland* ll.1070-81 (author's translation). The line references are to *La Chanson de Roland* ed. Joseph Bédier (Paris 1921). A good modern verse translation is that of D.D.R.Owen, *The Song of Roland* (Woodbridge & Wolfeboro, N.H. 1990) which has a useful introduction.

4   *Chanson de Roland*, ll.1107

5   *Chanson de Roland*, l.1093.

6   *Chanson de Roland*, ll.755-8.

7   *Chanson de Roland*, ll.2360-3.

declare that it is better that he should live to serve the king. But a champion comes forward to support the king's angry reply, 'False traitors are ye all', and Ganelon's supporters are vanquished. With their death, 'the Emperor's debt of vengeance now is paid';[8] though the business of empire goes on, and a new summons to war ends the poem, perhaps leaving the way open for a continuation.

Of the central characters of the poem, Roland, Oliver and Ganelon are the most individual; Charlemagne and Turpin represent ideals rather than personalities. Roland, too, has a large measure of the ideal hero in him. His courage is unsurpassed — 'There's none so valiant beneath the heavens broad' — and his appearance handsome and gay:

> Now Roland rides through passes into Spain
> On Veillantif, his swift and sturdy horse,
> Bearing such arms as well become his ways.
> Fearless the baron goes, grasping his spear —
> Its head so proudly pointed at the sky,
> And to its tip a snow-white pennon laced.
> The golden fringes reach down to his hands.
> His heart is bold, his face is clear and gay.[9]

This proud appearance betrays a proud heart within: when at the beginning of the poem he offers to go as messenger to the Saracens, Oliver retorts:

> You're fierce in mood and proud in your heart,
> I fear you'll start some dangerous argument . . .'[10]

It is this ferocity and tenacity that makes him a superb fighter; only at the turn of the battle at Roncevaux does his heart fail him, and then it is from grief at the sight of so many good men slain, not from fear. Oliver is the foil to the hero's impulsive bravery, and is one of the few characters on the French side for whom no historical roots have been found. His country, the 'Vale of Runers', is mythical; yet his name is found linked with Roland's from the beginning of the tenth century. If he is an entirely invented character, he belongs to the *jongleur's* inventions, not the later literary refashioning. But he was probably brought in less as a foil than as the type of the perfect companion. It is mistaken to see only the contrast between his wisdom and calculation and Roland's headstrong, berserker ways, and forget the close links that bind them. The poignant

8   *Chanson de Roland*, 1.3975.
9   *Chanson de Roland*, ll.1151-8.
10   *Chanson de Roland*, ll.256-7.

moment when Oliver, dazed and blinded by his wounds, strikes Roland in his confusion, and Roland answers him gently, reveals the depth of the bond:

> *The blow strikes home; then Roland stares at him*
> *And asks, his voice as always soft and mild:*
> *'My friend, can you have meant to strike that blow?*
> *Look, I am Roland, look, your dearest friend*
> *And, Oliver, you did not challenge me.'*[11]

Oliver is second only to Roland in battle once the fray begins; but he lacks the high zeal of his companion. If he is a more attractive character, his example does not fire the spirit as Roland's does.

Ganelon is likewise a more complex being than Roland. Roland cannot understand his stepfather's devious mind, which sees threats everywhere. He sees Roland's recommendation of him as ambassador as a plot to encompass his death (the last envoys were killed) and Roland makes matters worse by laughing outright at his fears; but he responds courageously enough that it is better than he should die on the embassy than that many knights should be killed on the battlefield. Being cunning himself, he expects others to be equally cunning: hence his success with the Saracens, when he at first defies them and then waits for his treacherous conversation with their envoy to bear fruit. But cunning is not a virtue in this heroic world, and treason against one's lord is the foulest of crimes: so Ganelon meets his gruesome end, dragged apart by four stallions. If he had his good points – he has served Charlemagne well, and is as fine a figure of a man as any of the barons – they are all marred by his betrayal: 'A man right noble he'd seem, were he not false.' Yet there are still human touches to his conduct: his first thought, when he is faced with almost certain death, is of his wife and son: and his kinsmen's loyalty to him costs them their lives. Roland and Oliver have no such ties, and Roland's cause finds but one lone champion besides the Emperor.

Charlemagne himself dominates the poem. He is an ideal figure to the extent that he never gives orders himself but always asks his barons their advice. Even in the duel with Baligant, the two rulers of Christendom and Islam seem gigantic allegorical figures, isolated and apart from the throng of the general battle. He is a focus for men's reverence: the dying Oliver thinks of him and 'la douce France' which he rules, as much as of Roland, and Roland's last earthly thought is of 'Charles his lord.'

Roland serves Charles as warrior first, as a Christian second; Turpin, the representative of religion, is a warrior as well. His war-like ways are more in evidence

---

11   *Chanson de Roland*, ll.1999-2004.

than Roland's Christianity. He breaks canonical laws about bloodshed, and he does not even trouble to observe the letter of the law by using a mace, that standard weapon of warrior-bishops. Indeed, he shines more as a fighter than as an archbishop: an ideal cleric from the fighting man's point of view, he belongs entirely to the world of the barons. His exhortation to the troops is brief and to the point: by the sword one can win a martyr's reward in heaven.[12] Yet he has an aura of real Christianity, soothing the quarrel between the two champions, and dying as he goes to fetch Roland some water, though he himself is more in need of help than the count.

The other *chansons de geste* do not present us with such sharp characters, polished manners, and subtle motives. Even the cycle of Guillaume d'Orange, which opens with a debate on the theme of the merits of peace and war, and contains some fine scenes, tends to portray everything in black and white, and only Guillaume and his wife stand out vividly. Whereas Roland has his moments of weakness, and Ganelon his moments of humanity, Guillaume and the treacherous barons whom he opposes are contrasted in the crudest terms. We are merely told that Erneis d'Orléans is a traitor; ample justification for Guillaume to stride up to him at Louis' coronation, and to kill him in the church, not with a sword, for that would mean bloodshed on hallowed ground, but with a blow of his fist.

This very simplicity is at times more revealing than the *Chanson de Roland*'s subtleties. Guillaume goes to reproach the king for giving fiefs to his favourites, and finds no satisfaction in promises of other men's lands or indeed of a quarter of the kingdom. Guillaume wants not simply a reward for his services, but the fair and proper reward. For his story is above all that of a great warrior, but of a warrior who is also just, faithful to his wife and family, and a wise counsellor: he is, in a word, the ideal baron rather than a heroic figure on the scale of Roland. In the competition for glory, he is always in the forefront: So much so that his nephew Bertrand complains: 'You get everything – all the battles and all the glory. Your prowess makes ours appear as nothing.' He has conquered Provence, Champagne and Burgundy and overthrown most of the king's enemies almost singlehanded; and when he finally claims his reward, he asks for lands held by the Saracens, which he will have to conquer.

The main part of the poems about Guillaume d'Orange is concerned with his war with the heathen. He takes Orange, and makes it his chief residence: and here he weds the lovely Saracen princess Orable, christening her as Guibourc. It is for her sake that the Saracens make war on Guillaume; there is little religious element in the count's wars, though the maxim put forward in the *Chanson de Roland* that 'pagans are wrong and Christians are right' still holds good. If there were monsters among Roland's foes, such as

12   This is a distinctly twelfth-century idea, and almost certainly postdates the First Crusade.

Chernubles of Munigre, whose hair sweeps the ground, and whose home is a desert land, sunless and black, there are apparitions as strange among Desramé's men: 'What is this strange army of beasts who come at us?' Guillaume demands as King Agrapax is killed, 'a squat creature two feet high, with hairy face, shining eyes and sharp claws like a griffin's'. Yet Rainouart, who kills this nightmarish creature, is a Saracen by birth, like his aunt Guibourc and cousin Vivien; and these converted heathen are the heroes of the Christian side.

In the *Chanson de Roland*, Marsile, the heathen king, and Charlemagne are both described in council, at the beginning of the poem, in very similar terms: both are imposing figures with a noble and valiant following and wise counsellors. Nor is the attraction of the heathen as people denied in either poem: there is Margaris of Seville on the one hand:

> *His handsome face wins all the ladies' love*
> *And every girl that looks at him grows gay;*
> *She cannot keep from smiling for pure joy.*
> *No pagan knight can match his chivalry.*[13]

And on the other there is Orable-Guibourc, a second Helen, whose beauty is at the root of Guillaume's war with the Saracens. It is only the errors of their faith, the laws of the three idols that they worship, that makes them treacherous and deceitful. No attempt is made to understand the Muslim religion; the three images which the Saracens are supposed to worship are absurdities, with no counterpart in the real Islam, a monotheistic religion which abhors idolatry. There is sympathy on a human level, but no intellectual contact.

Guibourc, Guillaume's wife, is a very individual character. Her counterpart does not occur anywhere else in the *chansons de geste*, nor in the later romances. For she is an eminently practical figure, yet dearly loved by Guillaume. The exotic princess becomes a woman who can welcome her defeated husband home in his blackest hour, and find the means to comfort him. This scene, when Guillaume returns alone after the great defeat at Aliscans, having lost his nephew Vivien and 15,000 men, is more poignant than all Roland's heroics: Guillaume seated at the lowest place in the hall, because he cannot bear to sit at the high table as he used to do with his men around him; Guibourc's tender care mingled with courage, which makes her send him on his way again into the darkness in search of help. But its poignancy is because it is homely, familiar, and down-to-earth; it is a scene from the Scandinavian epics or from the *Nibelungenlied*, where

---

13   *Chanson de Roland*, ll.958-62.

woman is a helpmeet and equal. 'La belle Aude' in the *Chanson de Roland* is much more fitted to this world of heroic knighthood; she appears only to die of grief at the news of Roland's death, expressing the blind devotion that such a figure inspires.

As a warrior, Guillaume can be brutal as well as fierce: in a macabre scene at the battle of Aliscans, he fights with Aerofle and cuts off his leg and thigh, then proceeds to mock him, saying that he should get a crutch now, and everyone will see that he is one of the Count of Orange's victims. He seizes Aerofle's splendid horse, Folatise, and gallops round as Aerofle watches in despair and agony before Guillaume returns to give him his death blow; and for the sake of Folatise he abandons his faithful steed Baucent to be hewn apart by the Saracens.

If a mixture of idealism and vivid reality is typical of the legends of Guillaume d'Orange, there is almost no idealism at all in *Raoul de Cambrai*. Raoul is scarcely a hero at all. He is a fine warrior, it is true, but all is ruined by lack of self-restraint: 'a man who cannot hold himself in check is good for nothing,' his chronicler declares. His career is almost an exemplary tale, a warning. He slowly alienates all his best followers, until only a like throng of evildoers accompanies him: Bernier, his faithful companion, bastard son of the man Raoul has killed, puts up with his misdeeds for as long as he can. In the culminating horror, Raoul attacks a nunnery at Origny, and orders his tent to be pitched in the church, his bed to be made up against the altar, and his hawks to be mewed to the crucifix. This is too much even for his followers, and he gives way with a bad grace. Later, despite the pleas of the abbess, he takes offence at an imagined slight, and burns the nuns alive in their nunnery, including the abbess, who is Bernier's mother. Even now, Bernier comes to Raoul to reproach him, rather than rebelling at once, and only when Raoul actually strikes him does he turn and utter a *défi*, the formula by which a wronged vassal disowned his lord. Bernier becomes his deadliest enemy; and when Raoul's pride leads him into fresh battle, and into a blasphemous declaration that no power on heaven and earth, not even God and all the saints, can prevent him from killing a man whom he has at his mercy, it is Bernier who appears as an avenging angel and who, when he refuses to stay his hand, strikes him down.

If the relationship between Guillaume and King Louis showed how a vassal should not be rewarded, that between Raoul and Bernier shows how a vassal should not be treated. Bernier asks for no more than that his lord should not wrong him, and serves him until there can be no question of making amends. In both cases, the central part played by the feudal bond in the plot reflects its importance in real life, and the familiarity of the listeners with the correct procedure in such relationships, and the occasions on which a vassal could lawfully 'defy' his lord. The true working of the relationship between vassal and lord is shown in Roland's loyalty to the trust which Charlemagne has placed in him, and in Charlemagne's deep grief for his dead warriors, whom he carefully bears away with him for burial in 'la douce France' as custom demands.

Lastly, there is the relationship between warriors on equal terms and between the family, 'compagnonnage' and the ties of blood. The high regard for the kinship of uncle and nephew, particularly when the latter is a sister's son, which can be traced back to Germanic society, is remarkable throughout the *chansons de geste*. Roland is Charlemagne's nephew; Guillaume has two nephews, Bertrand and Vivien, both of whom prove worthy of him. Sons, on the other hand, are less highly regarded: indeed, Charlemagne's son Louis drives his father to despair in the *Couronnement Louis*, the opening of the story of Guillaume d'Orange. 'Compagnonnage', blood-brotherhood from childhood, which was to find its epitome in the romance of Amis et Amiloun, the classical mediaeval example of friendship, is at its most poignant in the *Chanson de Roland*, but it is best summed up in the famous words from *Garin le Loherains*:

> There is no worth in mantles or furs
> Nor wealth in coins, in mules or asses
> But riches lie in friends and kindred;
> One man's heart's worth a country's gold.[14]

As are, the poet might have added, a swift horse and a well-tempered blade. Throughout the *chansons de geste*, these essential parts of a warrior's equipment play a special part, and almost acquire a life of their own. Roland tries to destroy his sword Durendal lest it falls into heathen hands: Charlemagne's sword Joyeuse is almost magical in its properties. Elsewhere, it is the horses that are highly prized: Guillaume's Baucent is almost capable of understanding speech.

If we compare the *chansons de geste* with the Scandinavian epics, we will find many points of similarity, and the Anglo-Saxon heroic poems reflect the same qualities. Only the context varies: the *chansons de geste* are firmly Christian, the northern poems heathen or converted in name only. What is perhaps missing in the northern poets is the sense of a 'grand design', a right order of society, in which the warrior, like everyone else, has his pre-ordained place: he is different only in that he is the chief glory of his nation. In the northern poems, we are in a narrower, more personal world, which does not look outwards beyond the confines of the warband, the chosen few comrades-in-arms: in *The Battle of Maldon* Byrthwold sums up this attitude in the famous lines at the end of the poem:

14   Quoted in Jessie Crosland, *The Old French Epic* (Oxford 1951) 289; author's translation.

Mind must be the firmer, heart the more fierce.
Courage the greater, as our strength diminishes.
Here lies our leader, dead,
An heroic man in the dust.
He who now longs to escape will lament for ever.
I am old. I will not go from here,
But I mean to lie by the side of my lord,
Lie in the dust with the man I loved so dearly.[15]

There is only one fierce virtue here, that of loyalty. Roland holds to the same ideal but in a more complex world, where loyalty is concerned with not only a warrior's lord, but with the emperor and with Christ. The feudal warrior has to bear in mind more demands on his allegiance than the heroic simplicity of Byrthwold's creed.

The *chansons de geste* and their ideals arise directly out of the nature of feudal society. There is no alien magic in them, no high concepts of love or abstract notions of duty. Roland and Guillaume obey the ordinary rules of feudal conduct; because they move on an heroic plane, with heroic tasks to accomplish, what in mere mortals would be simple obedience to duty becomes heroic. And in this lies the code of honour of the *chansons de geste*. *Chevalier* by itself means no more than mounted warrior; but the poet never speaks of a bad *chevalier* – it is always a matter of a good, courageous, valiant or bold *chevalier*, and the adjective *chevalerus* denotes a quality of strength and boldness combined. *Chevalerie* itself means the state of being a *chevalier*. It also means prowess, but it turns up in unexpected places and Ganelon can call the idea of killing Roland *gente chevalerie* – a fine deed of arms. There is a rudimentary idea of fair play, but it is scarcely more advanced than that of the *Nibelungenlied*: to kill a man from behind, or with a thrown javelin, is regarded as cowardly, but to fight two against one is by no means bad conduct. Before attacking, it is usual to issue a challenge, and in the *Chanson de Roland* the duels within the battles take on a formal and slightly unreal air. A defiant threat is followed by a course with lance in rest, and the fight is continued on horseback with swords until one or both are dismounted. If there is a pause, both sides call on each other to surrender but all the fights continue to the death, whereupon the victor insults his vanquished foe. Part of this is poetic stylisation, part an epic tradition with parallels in Homer; but there remains the beginning of a formal set of rules for warfare, the rudiments of chivalry proper.

---

15   Tr. Kevin Crossley-Holland, *The Anglo-Saxon World* (Woodbridge 1982) 17.

For the realities of war, we must turn to the pages of the Anglo-Norman chroniclers of the twelfth century, particularly Orderic Vitalis, who portrays a kind of brotherhood in arms in the internecine wars of the French and Norman barons and kings. Of the battle of Brémule he says that the knights 'were clad in mail and spared each other on both sides, out of fear of God and fellowship in arms; they wished rather to capture than to kill those they had routed.'[16] This seems to have been a largely unwritten and individual code, though the commanders may have given orders to the effect that deaths were to be avoided if possible. The basis was as much self-interest as any code of honour which forbade the slaying of enemy knights; it was a question of professional conduct and practicality rather than idealism. Yet the very fact that it was possible to fight battles and undertake skirmishes and sieges with relatively little loss of life was a novelty in itself, and opened up the possibility of limitations on the behaviour of knight in combat.[17]

In this atmosphere, the deeds of Roland and Oliver could be emulated, not in heroic desperation, but with a good chance of surviving to fight another day. The Norman warrior could more easily win honour in his lifetime. But this was knightly honour, the respect accorded to a doughty fighter, rather than the more complex chivalric honour, the questions of loyalty and promises kept. and the shame attached to even minor breaches of the code. In Orderic Vitalis' world, the realities of war were still very much to the forefront; condemnation was reserved for the real-life equivalents of Ganelon, or, if we are to believe William of Newburgh's story, for a blatant breach of a sworn truce such as that perpetrated by Louis VII at Rouen in 1174.[18] Chivalric honour, pursued to the extreme, could be quixotic or downright impractical; the nearest we perhaps come to it in the early twelfth century is the case of William de Grandcourt, who released Amaury de Montfort when he captured him at Bourgthéroulde in 1124, because he knew that his master, Henry I, would never release him from prison; he himself became an exile to avoid Henry's wrath.[19]

Across the Pyrenees, the first fruits of Spanish secular literature took a form not unlike the *chansons de geste*. The *joglars*, like their French counterparts, were wandering minstrels,

---

16   *The Ecclesiastical History of Ordericus Vitalis*, ed. Marjorie Chibnall (Oxford 1968-80) VI 240-1

17   John Gillingham has argued that 'chivalry in the sense of a secular code of values' was introduced into England after the conquest, and that ransoming and the treatment of prisoners were an important element. See his '1066 and the introduction of chivalry into England' in *Law and Government in medieval England and Normandy: essays in honour of Sir James Holt*, ed. George Garnett and John Hudson (Cambridge 1994). I am most grateful to him for providing a proof copy before publication.

18   William of Newburgh, *Historia rerum anglicarum* in *Chronicles of the reign of Stephen, Henry II, and Richard I*, ed. Richard Howlett, RS 82 (London 1884) I, 192-4.

19   *Ordericus Vitalis* V, I 350-3

purveyors of news as well as entertainment, and the ballads they composed on the events of the day formed the basis for the Spanish *cantares de gesta*. The contemporary 'news poems' have not survived, and the earliest of the works that have come down to us is, like the *Chanson de Roland*, a distinctly polished work. Indeed, the *Cantar de mio Cid* owes something to the French *chansons de geste*, for in its earliest form it is at least forty years later than the *Chanson de Roland*; elsewhere the same phrases, the same metres recur in both French and Spanish works.

French and Spanish society were in very different stages of development, however, when the *chansons de geste* appeared. In France the Saracens had ceased to be a serious threat and warfare was internecine rather than national. Royal authority was at a low ebb, and there were strong memories of the Carolingian age. The Spaniards, and more particularly the men of Castile, to whom the Cid belonged, were faced with a continuous campaign against the Muslim kingdoms of the south, whom they had gradually forced back in the preceding centuries from a position of almost total control of the peninsula. The intensity of the struggle might wax and wane; alliance might even be made with the Muslim kings against Christian rivals; but it was an ever-present and therefore accepted part of life. This had produced a rather different society from that of France. In Castile, anyone could own horse and armour, and all those who could afford to buy such equipment usually did so. There was no mystique to the profession of arms, and it was seen in an entirely practical light. The social hierarchy depended on wealth and political power instead. At the highest level were the *ricos hombres*, the immediate counsellors of the king; they and the *infanzones* or barons made up the royal court. Outside the royal circle were small landowners who were not necessarily vassals but fought on horseback either for the king or in their own interest. These *caballeros villanos* played a major part in the military history of medieval Spain, particularly in the period from 1085, when Toledo was recaptured from the Muslims, to the fall of Seville to a Christian army in 1248.[20]

The historical figure of the Cid is deeply rooted in these circumstances.[21] Unlike the heroes of French epic, whose fame reached its height two or three centuries after their death, the Cid was celebrated almost at once, in the *Historia Roderici*, a Latin narrative compiled not long after his death. Rodrigo Diaz de Vivar was the son of a small landowner, born about 1043. Brought up at the court of the heir of Castile, he became a leading figure in Sancho's entourage when the latter became king, only to find himself out of favour when Sancho was murdered by his brother Alfonso in 1072, in the course of a civil war. In 1081 he was sent into exile, despite his great reputation

20 Elena Lourie, 'A Society Organized for War: Medieval Spain', *Past and Present* 35, 1966, 54-76; and Pescador, 'La caballeria popular'.
21 Fletcher, *The Quest for El Cid*, is the best general study of the historical figure of the Cid.

as a warrior. By equal skill in the murky waters of frontier politics he succeeded in making himself master of Valencia in 1089 in alliance with a Muslim party, and later as sole lord from 1093 until his death in 1099. His relations with both Christians and Muslims were equally variable; at times he regained Alfonso's favour at times he was allied to his bitter enemies. He fought the count of Barcelona and the king of Aragon as well as the Almoravide emperor and numerous petty Muslim kings, though his personal following was largely drawn from Castile.

Towards the end of the twelfth century, this complex history of intrigue and counter-intrigue was reworked by a poet as a relatively simple tale in three main episodes: the exile of the Cid, his exploits and pardon, and the story of the marriage of his daughters.[22] Although the author seems to have been aware of the French *chansons de geste*, his style is generally much more realistic, though he is no more respectful of history than his counterparts on the other side of the Pyrenees.

The Cid, or 'My Cid,' as he is usually called, owed his title to the Arabic word, *sidi*, lord, which he may have earned because of his position as an adventurer, without official standing either in Castile or elsewhere. He is a very different kind of hero from Roland. His modest birth is acknowledged: an enemy can taunt him by saying:

> *Since when might we receive honour   from my Cid of Vivar!*
> *Let him go now to the River Ubierna   and look after his mills*
> *And be paid in corn   as he used to do?*[23]

The Cid was typical of the Castilian landowner, a small freeholder ready to take up arms when occasion demanded. Much of the interest of the poem lies in the contrast between the great deeds of the Cid and the great pride of his noble enemies of Carrión, and when the Cid's daughters, whom the lords of Carrión have wedded and then abandoned, are claimed in marriage by the kings of Aragon and Navarre, the Cid's triumph is complete. Yet he accepts the order of society as he finds it; his quarrel is only with pride unmatched by deeds.

He is conscious of his obedience to the king, even though Alfonso has wronged him, and makes several efforts to regain favour by sending him part of the spoils he has won; but he does not sentimentalise over his duty or take anything except a very down-to-earth view of the situation. If it serves his purposes to treat the Moors well, he does so; if he needs their wealth he will take it, for that is why he fights them. When he gazes on the Moorish host that has come to besiege Valencia, and which so terrifies his wife and daughters, he calmly remarks that the more of the enemy there are, the greater will be the booty:

22   See Fletcher, *Quest for El Cid.*, 192-3, for date.
23   *Cantar de Mio Cid (The Poem of the Cid)* tr W.S.Merwin (London 1959) 219, stanza 148.

This is great and marvellous wealth   to be added unto us:
You have barely arrived here   and they send you gifts,
They bring the marriage portion   for the wedding of your daughters.[24]

Pride in his family is a central theme in the poem, and with it that of vengeance. Doña Jimena, his wife, and his daughters, Doña Elvira and Doña Sol, are never far from his thoughts. One of the loveliest passages in the poem is the Cid's farewell to Doña Jimena as he goes into exile, leaving her behind; a scene which even Guillaume and Guibourc could never have acted:

My Cid went and embraced   Doña Jimena;
Doña Jimena   kissed my Cid's hand,
weeping   she could not hold back the tears.
He turned and looked   upon his daughter
'To God I commend you and to the heavenly Father:
Now we part; God knows   when we shall come together.'
Weeping from his eyes   you have never seen such grief
Thus parted the one from the others   as the nail from the flesh.[25]

Such emotion is only matched in the French epics by Charlemagne's grief for Roland or Guillaume's lament for Vivien. And the vengeance of the insult offered by the Cid's enemies, the lords of Carrión, to his daughters to whom they are betrothed occupies the last part of the poem. The lords of Carrión (who appear, despite their lineage, as cowardly and somewhat comic figures) decide to make off with their dowries and abandon their brides in the depths of the forest once they have left the Cid's court at Valencia; they beat the girls and leave them for dead, but the crime is revealed. In a magnificent scene, the Cid obtains justice of the king. At first he demands the swords he has given them, the precious weapons Colada and Tison; they yield, glad to escape so lightly. But he then demands the dowry, which they have already spent, and they have to borrow to repay him. Lastly, he claims reparation for the insult, and a battle of words begins. Three of his followers challenge those of Carrión, and in the ensuing combat the two lords and another of their clan are overthrown. With the brilliant marriages of his daughters the poem closes:

See how he grows in honour   who was born in a good hour
His daughters are wives of the Kings   of Navarre and Aragon
Now the Kings of Spain are his kinsmen
And all advance in honour   through my Cid the Campeador.[26]

24   *Cantar de mio Cid*, ed.cit., 110, stanza 90.
25   *Cantar de mio Cid*, ed.cit., 27, stanza 18.

The Cid's other title, 'Campeador', appears in the Latin poems as 'Campidoctor', learned in battle. Battle, however, takes up less of the poem than in the French epics. There are no heroic duels, and the Cid kills the Moorish king Bucar not in the thick of the fray, but in ignominious pursuit; he does not hurl insults, but offers friendship. Only when this is spurned does the race between the two become earnest; the Cid's horse Babieca proves the swifter, and his master slays Bucar with a mightly blow. Realism prevails: we find Pedro Bermudez disobeying the Cid's instruction to wait for the signal before charging with the standard, and having to be rescued from the result of his rashness. Even the ease with which the Cid wins his battles might be regarded as realistic, given his record in real life.

In this practical world there is no place for the monstrous enemies of French epic; no giants or witches bar the Cid's path. His wars are not even tinged with the idea of a battle for higher ideals, for 'la douce France' against the Saracens, for God against the heathen. There is no sense of nationality, nor even scarcely of Christian versus heathen, though he is blindly loyal to his lord, king Alfonso, despite the latter's unjust banishment of him. He treats the Moors as human beings, and we hear of the ransoming of captives, and even of their release if no ransom was forthcoming. He shares his booty with those Moors who are loyal to him, and his subjects regard him with affection. His contest with the lords of Carríon reflects another element in Spanish society, that insistence on the prestige conferred by high birth, which was to colour the view of knighthood in Spain down to the present day.

If there is much that is historical and realistic in the *Cantar de mio Cid*, and if it records historical details not mentioned elsewhere, it is nonetheless a work of fiction, which tells us more about the attitudes of the court of Castile in the late twelfth century than about the real mentality of the Cid. The fiction consists in the Cid's unwavering heroism,and loyalty to his family and followers, and in the struggle between him and the lords of Carrión. His place as sole leader is also imagined, since his second-in-command, Minaya Alvar Fáñez, was really an independent leader who sometimes made common cause with him. The Cid is thus a romanticised character in a setting which is realistic; his great virtues are a combination of courage and *mesure*, moderation. But his real attraction to the first audience of the poem about him was his example as a successful warrior-adventurer; his exploits were the dream of many a lesser knight in an age when it was still possible to carve out a domain by sheer force of arms. Even as his story was shaped into literature, such feats became increasingly remote; the heroic reshaping of Europe in the eleventh century gave way to the more settled society of twelfth century, and knighthood yielded its place to chivalry.

26   *Cantar de mio Cid*, ed. cit., 240, stanza 152.

PART TWO

Chivalry and Literature

4

From Courtesy to Chivalry

K NIGHTHOOD GAVE the warrior an honoured place in society, acknowledged by the Church despite its fundamental distaste for all things warlike. The knight enjoyed the mystique of power, both civil and military; this might have been the limit of his cultural ambition, a more up-to-date version of the men of the mead-hall in *Beowulf*, loyal to their lord, but laying no claim to social graces or cultural achievements. The evolution of knighthood into chivalry is remarkable in that it brings together unexpected elements, and transforms the rude warrior into an idealistic figure.

If the knight had belonged only to a military context, this civilising process would not have happened. But his civil ambitions and status brought him into contact with the very different world of government, administered by well-educated clerics whose norms, even in secular circumstances, were shaped by their religious background and literary education. The meeting-place of knight and cleric was the royal or princely court, where both had their place in the prince's service. In the Latin west, the concept of the court first emerged in the Frankish kingdom, and flourished under Charlemagne, who attracted to his entourage scholars and artists from all over Europe. This idea of the prince's household as a place where scholars and artists might find patronage was revived under his successors in what became the German empire.

In tenth century Germany we begin to see certain ideals of courtly life and courtly behaviour emerging.[1] The first evidence is a change in the style of biographies of bishops, who were rapidly becoming temporal lords in their own right. Earlier lives of religious men had looked to a monastic-ascetic tradition, in which restraint and devotion to religion at the expense of worldly vanities were the highest merits. Around the year 1000, we find a change of attitude: such men are praised instead for their learning and personal gifts. Hincmar of Rheims at the end of the ninth century had already declared that royal ministers should be 'noble in heart and body', and the bishops' schools, where future administrators received their training, devised a system of education aimed at producing such men. The virtues which are praised can be

---

1   For what follows see C. Stephen Jaeger, *The Origins of Courtliness: Civilizing Trends and the Formation of Courtly Ideals 939-1210* (Philadelphia 1985).

summed up in the phrase *elegantia morum*, a sophistication of both manners and morals. The individual virtues to which a courtier should aspire are affability, friendliness, a benign countenance; moderation and measured conduct; gentleness, temperate moods, and reticence about his accomplishments.

The evidence for this new concept comes from Latin literature, usually produced in religious circles; it is written by and for clerics. But clerical tastes could also extend into the secular world of storytelling and poetry: the tradition of Latin lyric poetry, kept alive by monks and bishops and travelling scholars[2] is one aspect of the contact between clerical and secular, to which we shall return. Less familiar, but perhaps more striking, is the earliest surviving 'courtly' narrative, *Ruodlieb*, probably written at the Bavarian monastery of Tegernsee in the mid-eleventh century. It is courtly to the extent that its eponymous hero is a member of the royal court, and a distinguished figure who takes part in diplomatic negotiations for his master; the latter is portrayed as a great and wise king. Ruodlieb's adventures take him on journeys among ordinary people, and some of the episodes echo folktales, despite the author's evident intimacy with, and admiration for, the writers of classical Rome. It is a *Bildungsroman*, showing Ruodlieb's path to maturity and it is evidently intended to set an example for young men in a similar situation.

Because we have only fragments – three thousand lines representing perhaps half to two-thirds of the whole – it is not always easy to follow the story, but it is plain that it is not a 'romance' in the later sense of the word, set in an unreal, charmed world. It offers a remarkably clear-sighted view of normal life. To take only two examples, Ruodlieb's companion on his travels (called simply 'the red-haired man') seduces the young wife of his elderly host; the pair are discovered and the old man is murdered. The woman shows true repentance, is pardoned, and leads a life of penitence, while the red-haired man is condemned to death.[3] This contrasts sharply with the following episode, in which Ruodlieb's nephew, whom he has rescued from an entanglement with a woman of ill-repute, woos and wins the daughter of the widowed lady of a nearby castle. We watch Ruodlieb in the world of the court, displaying (like Tristan in later romances) his skill on the harp, or conversing in the garden while the ladies feed their tame birds.

The portrayal of the love-match between Ruodlieb's nephew and the girl is both spirited and idyllic at the same time. The poet shows us a marriage based not on convention or dynastic considerations, but on 'mutual frankness and trust'.[4] The lovers

---

2   And recreated, delightfully, in this century by Helen Waddell in *Medieval Latin Lyrics* (London 1929) and *The Wandering Scholars* (London 1927).

3   Although the text is lost, there is agreement among scholars that such an outcome is implied.

4   Peter Dronke, *Poetic Individuality in the Middle Ages: New Departures in Poetry 1000-1150* (Oxford 1970) 59.

play dice: the young man loses to the girl, who in turn loses to him and lightly throws him her ring. She knows that he has misbehaved in the past, and at the wedding, refers to the game in which she had won him to make the point that she will love him in proportion to his devotion to her. When he tries to insist that she must be bound to him without conditions, just as the ring encircles the finger, or suffer the extreme penalty, she answers:

> It's only fair that both be judged by the same standard.
> Why should I be more faithful to you, tell me,
> than you to me? Tell me, could you justify it
> if Adam had a wench as well as Eve,
> though God made but one rib into a woman?
> The young man said: 'Beloved, it's as you say.
> If ever I deceive you, let me lose all I give you –
> And you shall have the right to cut off my head!'
> Laughing gently, she turned to him again:
> 'This then shall be our marriage-bargain – no deceit.'[5]

For all the courtly games, this has the ring of truth and experience, acutely observed and portrayed; here is a realism all too often missing in the romances of chivalry. The darker side of this reality is brought to the fore when Ruodlieb himself, encouraged by his mother, becomes engaged; but his fiancée is secretly the mistress of a cleric, and when Ruodlieb discovers this, he sends her a sealed box as a gift. Expecting an engagement present, she opens it, only to find her veil and laces which she had lost at a rendez-vous with the cleric. Ruodlieb's love proves to be the reverse image of his nephew's wooing, even though he has followed the advice of his royal master and found a girl of whom his mother approved.

Ruodlieb is told in a polished Latin, though the novelty of the form sometimes leads the writer into difficulties. He is writing for an audience with the same background and education, a narrow but ultimately influential circle. Yet his hero is *not* a cleric like himself, but a soldier, and a man of considerable accomplishments beyond his military skills; the latter are taken for granted, and form no part of the story. Equally important, Ruodlieb, although nobly born, is not a prince, and has little in the way of lands of his own: his career is in the royal service.[6] The courtesy of the clerics has begun to invade the world of the warriors; just as the church had begun to mould the spiritual attitudes of the warrior about this time, so the secular culture which derived from the

5   *Ibid.*, 58-9
6   Joachim Bumke, *Courtly Culture: Literature and Society in the Middle Ages*, tr. Thomas Dunlap (Berkeley, Los Angeles & Oxford 1991) 292.

Church came to shape his social life as well. *Ruodlieb* stands alone in literary terms, but it is precious evidence of the moment in time when the court began to be more than an administrative or military centre, and to develop a culture of its own.

Another tiny fragment of this pre-chivalric world survives in the Tegernsee letters of the mid-twelfth century, a collection of model epistles intended to serve for copy when needed. In a Latin love-letter supposed to be written by a girl, the author inserted a verse in German:

> *You are mine, I am yours;*
> *Of this you should rest assured.*
> *You lie hidden*
> *In my heart's prison*
> *And, now the little key is lost,*
> *There, for ever, you are locked.*[7]

One more glimpse of this world is provided by a poem in German, written by a cleric in the Rhineland at about the same time, which sets out a series of commandments for knightly behaviour.[8] The knight is to use wealth carefully, choose his companions well, go frequently to church. Courage and readiness for battle are praised; he should not care too much for hunting, and 'should be interested in noble horses, and also his sister's honour', avenging insults to himself as well. Above all, he should practise knightly deeds and 'seek whole victories'. The writer gives us a homely vignette of a knightly courtship: 'A young knight should woo a noble woman, one who can be recognised as such by her noble bearing. He knocks at her door until she opens. He talks with her by the fireside; she wants to talk the sorrow away from her heart. Whoever becomes too deeply in love and cannot tear himself away, loses his soul.' Yet despite the relative simplicity of approach, this is still a manual for behaviour in courtly circles, and the poet aims to instruct a newcomer in the ways of court and castle.

We are in a world where the knight is a novice, and the clerk is his teacher. A poem from the *Carmina Burana* nicely sums up the relationship:

> *All that's rich in Venus' realm*
> *And the treasures of the god of love,*
> *Were first discovered by a clerk*
> *And he it was who taught my lover.*

7   *Poets of the Minnesang*, ed. Olive Sayce (Oxford 1967) 4; author's translation.

8   H. Menhardt, 'Rittersitte: ein rheinfränkisches Lehrgedicht des 12. Jahrhunderts', *Zeitschrift für deutsches Altertum*, 68 (NS 56), 1931, 153-63.

It is through the lesson that he gave
    That the knight has learnt to serve Venus.[9]

Courtly manners are the essential prelude to courtly love; the word courtly, *curialis*, first emerges in the period around 1060-80, at the same time as the concept of knighthood begins to appear.[10] But the kind of straightforward love praised in *Ruodlieb* and the poem from the Rhineland belongs to the real world; courtly love is literary, stylised and immensely complex. Just as courtly manners became theatrical and affected, and courtly fashions extravagant and exaggerated, so this early and simple approach to the affairs of the heart in literature is quickly superseded.

'The knight in love is a literary invention of the clerk.'[11] Knighthood began as a stranger to the world of courtesy; masculine, aggressive, it was a battle with rules and limits, but its ethos was that of do as you would be done by. Its heroes and feats of arms were those of the *Iliad* as much as of the *Chanson de Roland*. The distinctive touch of chivalry was missing; the play lacked its heroine. When the knight's lady first appears in the literature of the mid-twelfth century, she is unlike anything before or since, unrivalled in her command over men's hearts, a remote, almost divine being.

From the time of the first romances, chivalry and the worship of fair ladies are so intimately bound up as to become almost indistinguishable; the knight who aspires to chivalric glory does not yearn to lead armies in Alexander's footsteps, does not dream of the gold of power, but longs to shine for his prowess as an individual, that he may earn the silver of his lady's love. It is the world of those early Renaissance portraits, where the close physical presence of the subject yields in one corner of the canvas to a sudden ethereal vista. So the knights saw their ladies, real and physical presences in an idealised setting; the honest lady of some grey-stoned castle held the keys to their paradise. Once her love was won they would be sure against their opponent's spears, in tournament and battle, and from her all spiritual wealth would flow.

With the appearance of the romances, the lady becomes the inspiration behind knightly deeds. The subtle ideas of the Provençal troubadours, who envisaged love as a kind of moral and spiritual education through emotion are simplified in the less sophisticated writers of northern France and Germany into the idea that the thought of his loved one will lend strength to a knight's arm, skill to his riding, and accuracy to his aim: to us, a commonplace, but unknown to the Roman or old French heroes,

9   *Carmina Burana*, ed. A.Hilka and O.Schumann (Heidelberg 1930-41) 92, stanza 41; author's translation
10   Jaeger, *Origins of Courtliness*, 158
11   Edmond Faral, quoted in Jaeger, *Origins of Courtliness*, 209

who thought of fatherland or friend – *dulce et decorum est pro patria mori*, Roland's dying vision of *la douce France* and Charlemagne.

This change in attitude marks the watershed between the old warrior ideals and the arrival of chivalry, the softening, civilising element in a rough and ready world. The central philosophy of chivalry my have in it a certain contradiction, in that the knight does not achieve his lady's love and his feats of arms by the same means: the most polished lover is not necessarily likely to be the finest jouster. But this contradiction is essential to the nature of chivalry, for if we judge chivalry by skill in arms and valour, the introduction of the worship of ladies may seem to mark a decline. To take this view, as some writers have done, and to see the *chansons de geste* and the Provençal poets as the twin peaks of chivalry's achievement is to misunderstand the entire nature of it, which lies in the humanising of the fighting man: what the Church had sought to do through religious precepts, the clerks achieved through secular exemplars.

The origins of chivalry have therefore much to do with the history of love and of the relationship between the sexes. Twelfth century society derived its attitudes, by and large, from two great intellectual inheritances from the past: classical Rome and the Viking north. The Roman legacy was predominant in literature and philosophy; the northern past was reflected in the everyday world, but was in retreat before the anti-feminism of the contemporary church. The Roman poets wrote against the background of a society where women were minders of children, not to be seen in public unless high birth or notoriety brought them into prominence. Ovid, whose *Art of Love* was well-known to medieval writers, treated love in a realistic, often cynical fashion. His effect on medieval ideas of love is one of the problems we shall return to; but in his original context, there is no difficulty of interpretation. He is writing verse for the amusement of the public, satirising more serious manuals in verse on other subjects, in a style designed to entertain and occasionally to shock, spiced by the acuteness of his observation. If he is outspoken – for instance when he talks boldly of the best positions for intercourse – it reflects the freedom of Roman morals rather than the poet's own stance. Less well known to medieval writers was the poetry of Catullus, with its searing depiction of passionate love and its dark obverse, bitter hatred. The tortured world of 'Odi et amo' is too personal to be freely imitated; no troubadour ever cursed his mistress in later years as bitingly as Catullus cursed Clodia – indeed, they hardly dared whisper that all was not perfect, lest the whole carefully contrived edifice should crumble on top of them. Even when Raimon de Miraval declaims against his lady, he does so in anger at the betrayal of a precious ideal rather than in the process of pouring out the bitter dregs of love. But love is not a central, all-consuming concern for the Roman poets, who had other concerns: the pastoral and the epic were more important than love-poetry. Lucretius neatly puts love in its place: 'a pretty face or a pleasing complexion gives the body nothing to enjoy but insubstantial images, which all too often fond hope scatters to the winds'.

Yet if the Roman poets rejected the idea of woman as goddess, or at least made of her an idol with feet of clay, the religions of the later Roman empire went to the opposite extreme. The Empire was the great period of the importation of foreign cults to Rome, Eastern fertility cults which were in strong contrast to the Roman state religion, with its ideals of manliness and patriotism. In the Eastern myths, the male protagonists were subordinate to the mother-figure of the goddess, a psychological attitude foreign to the native Roman ideals. Christian tradition, on the other hand, was strongly biased against women. In its theology, the cult of Mary only began to grow in the sixth and seventh centuries, and scarcely appears in the imperial Christian period.[12] In the circle around Charlemagne's court it had made some headway, as the *Carmen dogmaticum ad Beatam Virginem Mariam* of Hincmar shows; and the lovely *Ave Maris Stella* is a popular hymn of the ninth century. But the worship of the Virgin is little more than a variant of the cults of the individual saints, and holds no special significance until the early eleventh century. Its flowering coincides with the emergence of chivalry, and is evidence of the great sea-change in society in the late eleventh and early twelfth century. Mariolatry runs parallel to the chivalric idealisation of women; the two are complementary rather than competing ideals, even if Mariolatry eventually takes over many of the secular expressions of chivalric love. What the worship of Mary represents is a new attitude within the Church towards women. The early fathers regarded woman as the serpent's ally in her relations with the opposite sex, sent to lure man from the paths of purity as Eve had once lured Adam; and chastity was at a premium, following St Paul's teaching. On the other hand, women as individuals were highly regarded by the Church; the pagan role of women as priestesses was transmuted into something more humane and practical. By the eighth and ninth centuries, the tradition of patronage and pious works which became the expected function of the mediaeval princess and noblewoman had become established; if it owed something to the classical idea of the mistress of the house as guardian of the domestic deities, there was a much more constructive force evident in the works of Radegunde of Tours, saint and queen, and of her successors in France.

Beside the classical and Christian views on women's place in society, there was a very different influence at work on twelfth-century attitudes: the heroic tradition of the Northmen and Germans. From Ireland and England in Charlemagne's day had come the Celtic and Saxon teachers who led the Christian world in learning, and their ways of thought harked back to ideals that owed much to the pagan past. Women,

---

12   Marina Warner, *Alone of all her sex: the myth and the cult of the Virgin Mary*, London 1976.

whether because they were endowed with magic powers, like Deirdre in Irish myth, or because they were a match for warriors as in the *Nibelungenlied* of German legend, enjoyed a very different standing in the north. They were treated with the respect due to equals, even if their influence in high affairs of state might be less. Very little actual love poetry has survived in any of these languages; the remaining fragments of Anglo-Saxon love poems are enigmatic, and there is nothing in Norse literature, so we know little of how the most cultured of these races set about their wooing. The legal status of women was certainly high; they could inherit and rule much in the same way as a man. The Germanic attitude was honest and practical; unlike the Celtic world, it ascribed little special magic to women, though they do appear as mystical priestesses in Norse religion; but the lack of awe is balanced by a greater respect. Women can actively help men to greater deeds and valour by their solace and comfort. It is an unpassionate view; but it is much more positive than the classical and early Christian ideas.

The Northmen who came to France in the tenth century were pagans when they settled there. Their religion was unusual in that it was dominated to an even greater extent than the Roman worship by its gods. Even the dominating female fertility goddess was absent, and the twin deities of Freyr and Freyja ruled instead. Of the pair, Freyr, who had absorbed the characteristics of a large number of minor fertility gods, was the dominant partner and was worshipped as the god of plenty; Freyja was largely concerned with the hearth and home, though there was a darker, magical side to her worship in soothsaying and witchcraft. The myths do not centre on her, but on the heroic struggle between the gods and the powers of darkness, which will only end at the day of Ragnarok, when the gods are overthrown. This active but pessimistic religion has no Venus, no Diana, and none of the lesser goddesses who decorate Olympus: it reflects a society with little time for the contemplation of beauty and an obsessive concern with the struggle for existence.

It was this world that was inherited by the authors of the *chansons de geste*, thinly veneered with Christianity. Four or five generations separate the invading pagan Norseman from the Anglo-Norman clerk who wrote or copied the *Chanson de Roland*. This is an epic world, not concerned with women. High matters of state and the heroes who determine their outcome, politics and war, inspire their muse. We have seen how Roland's loyalties are to France and to Oliver, and how the fair Aude is a shadowy figure, whose only moment at the centre of the stage is when she dies of grief on hearing of the heroic end of her betrothed. Likewise, we have seen how Guibourc is a central character in the cycle of Guillaume d'Orange; her beauty, and the affection between Guillaume and herself are warmly depicted. But she has something of the Valkyrie in her, and their relationship is as much that of companions in arms as of husband and wife. It is for her heroism in the defence of Orange as much as her beauty that the poet admires her. Likewise in the other rare appearances of women in the *chansons de geste*, it is the ideal of the helpmeet, in the Norse tradition, that prevails; if the fight is no longer one for mere existence, but a war fought for God and the Emperor, the struggle is as paramount as ever.

The *chansons de geste* are a specialised form of literature, addressed to the newly-emerging warrior class. They deal with a fairly narrow set of circumstances, and represent only one facet of the immense variety of the eleventh and twelfth century world. The love lyric is much closer to being a universal phenomenon, written by all sorts and conditions of men and women. It is easy to divide the medieval literary tradition into its main components and to see, in this harsh world of fire and bloodshed, the monasteries as the islands of refuge where not only Christianity but also the scattered relics of pagan learning survived. The love poems which they preserved are in that scholarly tradition of poems in praise of women which runs from the late Latin poets down to the Renaissance, essentially exercises on a theme, though at their best they can be delightful. In the sixth century, Fortunatus addresses Radegunde of Tours in lines scented with flowers but tempered with the deep respect due to a queen and a saint.[13] In the twelfth century the Parisian scholar Serlo of Wilton produces extraordinary word-plays, of which the most fantastical Elizabethan lover would have been proud. But by and large this tradition is formal, the coin of homage paid to the great; and intimacies are out of place.

There is a much stronger undercurrent, less stylistically accomplished, but belonging to the real world, the tradition of lyric verse written by the wandering scholars in both Latin and vernacular. Some of it may even be the work of educated laymen, but given that education was almost entirely religious, and the surviving texts all come from religious sources, it is difficult to tell. The mood is realistic and cheerful, pleading and urging for sweet solace. From this it is a short step to the *Carmina Burana*, the most famous collection of the genre, set down in the thirteenth century; the poems are earlier, and among their anonymous, exquisite lines may be disguised one of the love songs Abelard wrote for Héloise. The freshness of these poems is their most astonishing virtue; they cannot be other than the first fruits of learning laid light-heartedly on pagan altars before more serious cares befell their authors.

Their sources are wide-ranging, and the themes that they treat have parallels as far afield in time and place as ancient Egypt and medieval Georgia. They cannot match in sophistication their ninth-century predecessors in the resplendent Islamic civilisation of the Abbassid empire; if we detect common themes, it is worth remembering that even in the darkest years of Viking and Muslim invasions, there was an extraordinary

13   Helen Waddell, *Medieval Latin Lyrics*, 60.

range of contact between east and west, north and south, on a peaceful level: Irish monks in Switzerland, Byzantine embassies in Germany, traders working round the coast of Europe, clerics and pilgrims travelling to Rome, Compostela and Jerusalem. With Latin as a *lingua franca*, there was no reason why a striking set of verses should not make its way by word of mouth from one end of Europe to another. It is not always easy to say which theme is 'universal', common to all human experience, and which is simply the fashionable phrase of the moment.

The earliest poems in the *Carmina Burana* are roughly contemporary with the first troubadour songs, though many of them are later. But they give us a very good idea of attitudes to love outside the world of the courts, at a more popular level where literary style and courtly modishness are not involved. Here, the poet pays court directly and love is physical rather than spiritual. Praise is a means to an end, a weapon in the lover's armoury in persuading the object of his desire to yield to him. We are in a world where passion reigns, more powerful than ever, the world of the student-singers, impoverished and tipsy, but always with an eye for a girl. The girl may only be a serving-wench in a tavern, but her beauty earns her extravagant titles. There is a sense of urgency, 'Come live with me and be my love' on a sensual plane, which contrasts with the oblique approach of the troubadours, who sing of their own feelings, into which their lady's beauty enters only as a cause. The lyric poets, too, are always conscious that their love is undoubtedly illicit, no more than a peccadillo perhaps, yet still a sin of sorts. They have half an eye on their clerical superiors even in their most abandoned moment, and the founts of love are all the tastier for it:

Loving's no crime, for if to love were to go astray
God would never have made of love so divine a joy.

This is not the troubadour's way of thinking; love was far too serious a subject to be treated as a diversion en route for the higher callings of scholarship and the religious life. There, even poets who turned cleric, such as Folquet de Marseille, who was to become a zealous bishop of Toulouse, never betray by the least flicker of their features that they are not in deadly earnest: here among the poets of the schools and taverns, and even perhaps of the manor house and marketplace, love is a pastime, not a high calling.

The origins of chivalric ideas of love are to be found in eleventh century Provence, a world in many ways outside the conventions of the rest of Christian Europe. The lands to the south of the Dordogne lay outside the immediate power of the great rulers of the north, the kings of France and the emperors of Germany, and there was no great local ruler. The dukes of Aquitaine and the counts of Barcelona and Toulouse all claimed varying degrees of overlordship, but even Henry II of England, whose title to the duchy of Aquitaine stemmed from his marriage to Eleanor, was unable to hold the unruly local lords in check: nor was his son Richard much more successful as count of Poitou. The rigid feudal hierarchies of the Norman world and the established tradition of vassal-knights in the Holy Roman Empire were not part of the pattern of Provençal society. Instead of a centralised, powerful and government-orientated court, the courts of Provence were small-scale, but, because of the natural riches of the country, wealthy out of proportion to their size. Spasmodic warfare was a feature of Provençal life, but the impression left by its chroniclers and poets is of a largely peaceful society, where the courtly virtues of imperial Germany broadened out into a culture where social intercourse came to be valued for its own sake, unlike the northern courts where ambitious clerics who formed the backbone of the administration set the tone of the royal entourage. Because the members of the Provençal courts were less steeped in the Latin curriculum of the medieval schools, they were also more at liberty to develop their own vernacular culture.

For peace and prosperity alone do not explain the appearance of such a singular culture as that of Provence. The northern Italian towns were equally flourishing; yet until the latter part of the Middle Ages Italy never displayed any great enthusiasm for either the courtly ideal in its original form, or the ideal of chivalry itself. Italy had mercantile prosperity and peace; her merchants were busier than ever; Provence had aristocratic peace, and her nobles were leisured as they had rarely been before. Attitudes to money were also important. The Italian merchants traded with it, increasing their power: cities were the cultural centres, rather than princely courts. To the lords of the south, power was a matter of politics; their estates were defined, not by wealth, but by personal ties, and to a lesser extent, feudal bonds. Once the prosperity derived from their lands had been hoarded in coffers. But by the early twelfth century, the income from lands was being used to buy luxuries and to hold great feasts.

We shall find generosity enthroned as one of the troubadours' principal virtues: for it was on the free-spending lords that not only their own existence depended, but the whole way of life that they championed. This transformation in habits begins at almost exactly the same moment that the troubadours first appear: Orderic Vitalis, observing the northern courts, sees a decline in morals from about 1085. He writes of the Angevin court under Fulk Nerra:

> But now laymen in their pride seize upon a fashion typical of their corrupt morals. What honourable men once thought shameful and utterly rejected as filth, the men of this age consider sweet as honey, and flaunt abroad as though it were a special grace.
> They rejected the traditions of honest men, ridiculed the counsel of priests, and persisted in their barbarous way of life and style of dress. They parted their hair from the crown of the head to the forehead, and grew long and luxurious locks like women, and loved

to deck themselves in long, over-tight shirts and tunics.... Now almost all our fellow countrymen are crazy and wear little beards, openly proclaiming by such a token that they revel in filthy lusts like stinking goats.[14]

Courtliness had escaped from its clerical origins, and was beginning to run riot. Geoffrey, prior of Vigeois near Limoges, writing about 1175, describes even more extravagant fashions than those Orderic decried. Contrasting the simplicity of olden days with the new flamboyance, he says:

> Nowadays the meanest would blush to wear such clothes. Rich and precious stuffs are woven, whose colours suit each man's mood; the borders of the clothes are cut into little balls and pointed tongues, until their wearers look like the devils in a painting.[15]

But it is his description of the festivities at Beaucaire near Avignon in 1177 that shows the fashion for extravagance at its height:

> That summer, a multitude of local princes and celebrities held a foolish festival at the castle of Beaucaire. It was apparently to commemorate the reconciliation brought about by the King of England [Henry II] between Raymond of Narbonne and Alfonso of Aragon. But the King was for some reason absent, and the princes held this inane feast in his name. The count of Toulouse gave a knight, one Raymond Dagout, a hundred thousand shillings, which he immediately divided into a hundred times a thousand and gave a hundred knights each a thousand shillings. Bertrand Raiembaus had twelve yoke of oxen plough the streets of the castle and sowed them with thirty thousand shillings. William Gros de Martel, who had three hundred knights with him (there were about ten thousand knights at that court), had all their food cooked in the kitchen with wax candles and torches. The Countess Sorgest sent a crown valued at 40,000 shillings; they appointed William Mita as king of the jongleurs, unless he was absent for any reason. Raymond of Venoul had thirty horses burnt there in front of everyone for a boast.[16]

One reason for the easier morals of the south was the relative weakness of the Church; the bishops of the province of Narbonne, which included much of Aquitaine, were much less influential than their northern counterparts, and the mainstay of religion was the abbeys which proliferated in the mid-twelfth century in the region. These conspicuously wealthy establishments played little part in secular life, but aroused envy and anti-clerical feeling by their presence. There was an independence of thought in

14   *Ordericus Vitalis*, IV, 187.
15   *RHGF*, xii, 450.
16   *Ibid.*, 444.

the south which was to lead in due course to the spread of the Cathar heresy. Its suppression in the thirteenth century was disastrous for the whole of Provençal society.

Legal and social attitudes to women in the south gave them much more freedom than their northern counterparts, and we find them as great landowners: in the twelfth century, Ermengarde of Narbonne and Eleanor of Aquitaine wielded as much power as their male counterparts in times of peace. The sons of lesser lords and knights came crowding into their courts to make their way in the social world; and even where the lady of the castle was not a ruler in her own right, she was at once the centre of that social world and yet inaccessible. Her favour was important, but mere ordinary approaches were unrewarding or dangerous, so the man who could entertain and flatter her was at a distinct advantage. The poems of the *chansons de geste*, sung in long episodes to the monotonous sound of a crude string instrument, woke no echoes of glory in the hearts of women such as these; nor were the barons of the south as wholeheartedly warlike as their northern counterparts.

The new knights were only occasionally required to fight, and had no great estates to preoccupy them:[17] they and the ladies of the court had time on their hands and hence there was an audience for a new kind of song, a song to while away an idle hour. It could not be in Latin, for few women were educated in that language; and its spontaneous nature meant that it was not to be epic, but short and poignant, a verse that could equally be turned easily enough by nobles with more artistic talent than scholastic learning. The poetry that resulted could only be personal, immediate and concerned with the actual world rather than flights of fantasy or rhetoric: it was emotional rather than intellectual from the beginning and reflected the feelings of the poets themselves. Its roots were aristocratic, its metaphors feudal, but its problems within anyone's experience.

The remarkable thing about the poems that resulted is their subtlety; it is part of a process of increasing civilisation that can be observed elsewhere in France, in the new scholastic arguments of the philosophers, in the artistic revival leading to the architectural triumphs of the twelfth and thirteenth centuries. Just as the philosophers sharpened their theses in debate, so the troubadours honed their style in competiont with each other, producing formal variations on their chosen themes. Hence there is no need to search too hard for the forerunners of the troubadours; their great good fortune was that they were working free of the burden of tradition for an audience ready to appreciate novelty. The pattern of their work was shaped by the demands of this audience, rather than by a conscious harking-back to earlier poets and thinkers.

17   Erich Köhler, 'Die Rolle des niederen Rittertums bei der Entstehung der Trobadorlyrik', in Borst, *Das Rittertum im Mittelalter*, 306-310.

Guilhem IX of Aquitaine (1071–1127) is the earliest poet of the new tradition whose name and work has survived. He was not the first to work in the common tongue: fragments of popular language had been mixed into Latin verse since the eighth century, and the *kharjas*, Arabic songs with a refrain in Spanish, appeared in Andalusia in the tenth century. But there was no long tradition of written verse in the vernacular at the end of the eleventh century, when Guilhem was writing, on which he could draw. If verse there was, it was sung and stored in the memories of *joglars*, minstrels who wandered from castle to castle, performing at dinner, reciting stories, singing verses and bringing gossip from the outside world. The network of their profession was wide enough to spread the Breton tales of Arthur as far as Italy by the early twelfth century. Those who could compose their own songs, instead of merely performing the compositions of others, must have attained some degree of social respectability for a man of Guilhem's standing to have joined their ranks. The troubadour poems undoubtedly belong to this tradition, for they were written to be sung in public, and reading them on the page, divorced from their often haunting music, fails to do them justice; the demands of music, as with all song lyrics, affect the form of the verse.

Guilhem's poems, and those of the other early troubadours, contain no small number of surprises if we expect them to be entirely courtly and polite. The first group of Guilhem's poems are highly obscene; they can only have been intended for drunken evenings among friends, written, like Peire d'Auvergne's satire on his fellow-troubadours, 'to the sound of pipes, amid gaming and laughter'. The view of women is coarser and bawdier, and more masculine, than anything that has survived in the *Carmina Burana*; they are erotic fantasies on the physical level. It is tempting to regard these as Guilhem's first work, and there are signs of a development, both in technique and attitude, which would make his 'courtly' poems later. If so, the astonishing lyric 'Farai un vers de dreyt nien' marks the transition. It is a nonsense-rhyme on the surface, first of a long line of such verses; to write such an enigmatic, sophisticated and yet world-weary poem at all is a radical departure. If it owes something to the mediaeval fondness for riddles, it is not a riddle that demands an answer. Guilhem is expressing his boredom with the conventional subjects for poetry, and with sensual love he has so far experienced; the sly humour is there to sugar the pill for his audience:

> *I'll write a song about nothing at all,*
> *Not about myself, nor about anyone else.*
> *Not about love, nor about the joys of youth,*
> > *Nor anything else.*
> *I wrote it just now as I slept*
> > *In the saddle.*
> *I do not know at which hour I was born;*

I am not joyful and yet not sad;
I am neither reserved nor intimate
   And can do nothing about it:
I was put under a spell one night
   on a high hill.[18]

He goes on to describe his listlessness, and fears he will die of an unknown disease. He has a lady whom he has never seen, and to whom he is indifferent; indeed, he knows another much fairer and more gentle. Finally he declares his poem finished; he will send it to beyond Anjou, and the receiver will send the 'counter-key' back in return.

From this we come to the first 'courtly' poems. They do not contain the 'code of courtly love' fully fledged: indeed, to speak of such a code is to fall into a dangerous trap. The men of the Middle Ages loved to codify and classify, as witness the tradition of the encyclopedists from Isidore of Seville to Vincent of Beauvais. The writers who inherited the ideas propounded by the troubadours turned them into Latin treatises, to which we shall return; but this systematic approach is a difficult yoke to impose on the unruly subject of love, and was not the troubadours' intention. They recognised certain virtues, taught certain morals, and sought certain ends; but each singer followed his own vision, and the ideals waxed and waned in each new poet's work. So Guilhem's poems merely contain the first phrasing of some of the ideas that later became common stock.

Guilhem's ideal of love is centred on the knightly class; he roundly declares that a lady 'commits a great and mortal sin if she does not love a loyal knight; but if it is a monk or cleric, she is wrong; by rights she should be burnt to death', implying that the smooth-tongued clerk (who, as we have seen, had taught the knight his manners) was already a rival. His terms of praise for his lady, too, show that he was familiar with religious literature; but if some of the turns of phrase echo this familiarity, he appeals for the physical consolations of love. The novelty here is the intensity of the feeling. He cannot live without his lady, whom he worships, 'for her I shiver and tremble, because I love her so deeply'. We are not quite at 'Vénus toute entière à sa proie attachée', but the hunt has begun. Guilhem sees 'joy d'amour' as the salvation of mortal man:

No man can ever dream what that joy
Is like, neither by wishing or desiring it
Nor by thinking of it nor imagining it
Such a joy can never find its match
And he who would praise it worthily
Would not succeed in the space of a year.[19]

18   *Les Chansons de Guillaume IX, duc d'Aquitaine (1071-1127)*, ed. A.Jeanroy (Paris 1913) 6-8.
19   *Ibid.*, 22, ll.13-18; author's translations.

Guilhem stands alone, without contemporary rivals; if there were such singers, time has used them harshly, for there is no record of them left. The troubadours who succeed him are numerous enough for two general trends to appear. One refines the abstract idealising mood of Guilhem's later poems until the rarefied atmosphere leaves the reader breathless in the fantasies of *trobar clus*, deliberately obscure verbal feats; the other takes Guilhem's realistic side, which had been a mere ploughshare of obscenity, and beats it into a sword of social criticism. The aesthetic school was centred on the court of Ventadorn and Eble II, its viscount, seems to have been its leader. Unfortunately his verses, written shortly after Guilhem's, have not survived; his poetic heir was Bernart de Ventadorn, whose delicate verses probably reflect his master's ideas. Bernart, wrongly famous as the lover of Eleanor of Aquitaine, wife of Henry II of England, pays homage to his lady in a feudal relationship where the poet becomes the lady's vassal, an idea which re-echoes down to *The Faerie Queene* and persists as a poetic image beyond the demise of chivalry itself. (The *vidas*, or lives of the troubadours, which precede their works in most manuscripts, are thirteenth-century embroiderings on the content of the poems; so, because Bernart addresses a panegyric to Eleanor, the author of his *vida* makes him her lover.) The relationship is not a rewarding one; all Bernart's poems reflect a personal world where suffering predominates over recompense. Yet he draws comfort from his pangs, and shows how *joy d'amour*, the lover's ecstasy, feeds on frustration and despair. The object of his desire remains explicitly the carnal possession of his beloved; yet the desire comes to outstrips its end in importance, and we are face to face with the particular twist of troubadour love, its self-denying, contradictory longing.

Rilke's *mot*, that the troubadours feared nothing so much as the attainment of what they longed for, seems even closer to the mark with Jaufre Rudel, renowned for his apocryphal love of the countess of Tripoli, to whom he sent sweet love songs, without having seen her, and finally went himself, only to die in her arms a moment after glimpsing her fabled beauty. (The story – once again from the *vidas* – has gained such force that one is tempted to believe it against the evidence; but history says no.) Jaufre was not quite so unworldly, if his own story of being caught in bed with his mistress is true. It may be that the shame of this exposure led him to seek a higher love, and this he found in the idea of *amor de lonh*, love from afar. The first verse of his most famous lyric, 'Lanquan li jorn son lonc en mai', enshrines the essence of his mood:

> *When the days grow long in May*
> *I love to hear the distant bird;*
> *When I have left off listening*
> *It reminds me of my distant love*
> *And I go dull and bent with longing*

So that song, flower and hawthorn
Might as well be winter frosts for me.[20]

He and his lady are separated by space as well as the lady's resistance, hope is dead and only desire remains. 'He speaks truly who says that I am hungry for my distant love, because no joy pleases me as much as the enjoyment of my distant love.' This is the nearest to a mystical or philosophical approach that the troubadours were to come until the declining days of their art. Once again, it is a personal, introspective world, where the poet himself occupies the foreground. Of his lady we learn nothing; she is a shadowy divinity, to be worshipped unquestioningly. But in the end Jaufre is writing about passionate love, not a mystical ideal.[21] His 'distant love' is an elaboration of the idea that absence intensifies love, a theme common to lovelorn poets throughout the ages.

At the opposite extreme to Jaufre, we find the pungent attacks of Marcabru. In deliberately obscure but razor-edged poems, he sets about the exponents of false love, calling down the wrath of Heaven on an impious generation like some stern prophet. But he is not a religious prophet; his idol is pure love, the undefined opposite to the garish world he paints. He brands the love current among his fellows as promiscuous, disturbing the peace of honest men. The only difficulty is that he names the exponents of this coarse and sensual love as the school of Ventadorn; and such poems as survive from this source are far from licentious. His attack is perhaps two-pronged: against his rivals as a poet, and against the practices of the courts he had visited. So his poems became tirades against the nobility and their lax morals — he himself was probably of humble birth — and if his often coarse language reflects reality, it is a reality distorted by jealousy and the moral attitude he adopts. What he attacks is not adultery but licence, adultery being at worst a venial sin, and in these circles scarcely a sin at all. His rejection of the grossness of carnal love does not necessarily mean that a decline in morals was taking place, but is rather a measure of the increasing civilisation of his surroundings.

To see Marcabru as an early representative of some popular resentment against the nobility, a forerunner of Wat Tyler, is to ignore his use of the most refined poetic devices, current only within the very circles he is supposed to despise. His search for rich images, the technique of 'mixing' words – *entrebescar les mots* – regardless of immediate sense, foreshadow the later thickets of this *trobar clus*, poems so full of allusions that they become crossword puzzles in rhyme; it seems doubtful whether their authors really understood them.

20 René Nelli and René Lavaud, *Les Troubadours* (Bruges 1966) II, 52; author's translation
21 Moshé Lazar, *Amour courtois et 'fin amors' dans la littérature du XIIe siècle*, Bibliothèque française et romane série C: Etudes littéraires VIII (Paris 1964) 86-102

If Marcabru is in some ways a split personality as a result of his refinement of the ultimate ideal on one hand and his description of reality on the other, troubadour poetry was not a movement with a single stream. While there are poets who live entirely in Venus' realm, others come to prefer the arts of Mars. Bertran de Born's political squibs, such as his *sirventes* to Henry II's sons, are in the realistic manner; while in the thirteenth century the Italian Sordello singing of the ecstasy of unfulfilled love, until his friend Bertran d'Alamanon feared that he was mad, is the heir of Jaufre Rudel. And between the two extremes the joys of physical love, casual or passionate, are reflected throughout the troubadours' poetry. If we concentrate here on the more high-flown fancies, it is because these are the most original of their ideas, and the most influential for later chivalry; though if it seems that the poets moved in a rarefied atmosphere where the chief tenet was that the least carnal desire was 'th'expense of spirit in a waste of shame', there were many aspects of their poetry which were well grounded in reality. Equally it is a mistake to make of this exaltation of restraint a paean to purity and hence to connect them with the contemporary Cathar heresy, whose *perfecti* abstained from all carnal pleasures. They suggested rather that sexual pleasure could be increased and prolonged beyond the act of love itself by means of restraint.

The later troubadours move further into the realms of what was later to be known as 'platonic' love, and the movement that had a sensual beginning draws to a spiritual end. The search for technical improvements that had led to *trobar clus* continued with Peire d'Auvergne, who says of himself 'he would be master to all troubadours if only he would make his words a little clearer; people can scarcely understand them,' and meaning has almost as little place in the rich language and complex verse forms of *trobar ric* as it had in the parallel obscurities of *trobar clus*. The artificiality of the verses was matched by a slavish following of the 'formula' of courtly love: Elias Cairel admits to his lady: 'If I have sung of your worth and wisdom, it was not because I loved you; I did it to gain honour and profit, as *joglars* addressing a noble lady do.'[22] Raimbaut of Orange, even more original in technique, mixes prose into his poems; while Arnaut Daniel, his brilliant and wide-ranging successor, who produced one of the most unprintable as well as some of the most dazzling troubadour poems, sums up the artificiality of *trobar ric* in a wry self-portrait:

> *I am Arnaut, who gathers the air into sacks*
> *Who uses oxen from the yoke to hunt the hare*
> *Who swims in swift rivers against the current.*[23]

---

22   Hilde Jaeschke, *Der Trobador Elias Cairel,* Romanische Studien 20 (Berlin 1921) 134.
23   A.Berry, *Florilège des troubadours* (Paris 1930) 190; author's translation.

The end of the twelfth century was possibly the richest and most productive period for the troubadour poets. Yet no great figures emerge; competent poets there are by the dozen, some with considerable claims to our attention, such as Peire Vidal, Raimon de Miraval and Uc de Saint Circ. The reaction against *trobar ric* after the *ne plus ultra* of Raimbaut d'Orange's efforts failed to produce the real new impetus which was needed; the formulae begin to grow a little stereotyped. Raimon de Miraval, whom a later poet, Elias de Barjols, was to call the greatest singer of all, is nonetheless systematic, almost didactic in his approach to love. His anger is reserved for those who have betrayed his ideal rather than wronged him personally; it is in this mood that he reproaches his lady for her infidelity. And he esteems *pretz*, worthiness won through love's service, above *joy d'amour*. His lesser contemporaries, more concerned with form and expression, tended to work over the familiar themes in increasingly eccentric imagery, replacing obscure language by tortuous ideas. The figures of lover and lady in the *chansons* of the thirteenth century have been neatly described as 'puppets refashioned by the dozen'.[24]

The troubadours were very dependent on the whim of their masters: one count might heap them with honours, and his successor chase them out of the gate. Yet certain courts were particular havens for them; and the decline of their art is directly connected with the rise and fall of these. Poitiers, capital of the county of Poitou, had been one of the greatest centres in the south throughout the twelfth century; at its most brilliant under Guilhem IX, Guilhem X and Eleanor, it became less important after the latter's marriage to Henry II of England, though Richard I was acclaimed count in 1172 and always preferred the southern parts of his domain. Richard wrote a few verses himself, elegant enough of their kind; but the Plantagenets were not the best of patrons. Ventadorn and Narbonne, Orange and Limoges all had their moments of popularity; and Barcelona and Castile across the Pyrenees were for long periods places where the troubadours were welcome. Yet the real strength of the movement was with the minor lords, castellans who could barely have maintained a court in harsher times, who were amateurs themselves: men such as Blacatz d'Aups in Provence, a fierce partisan of the old modes and styles. The ladies of the court, too, remained ardent supporters of the poets to the end; in the declining days of the troubadours in Provence the court of Aix had several patronesses of their art, the most notable being Guida de Rodez, whose praises were sung by Blacatz, Sordello and others. Once their patronage disappeared, and the troubadours had to seek favour in the more preoccupied courts of greater princes, their livelihood became much harder to find.

24   A. Jeanroy, *La poésie lyrique des troubadours* (Toulouse & Paris 1934) 102.

With the horrors of the crusade against the Cathars, the civilisation of Provence which had flourished in the same easy atmosphere and rich soil was to wither and die. In the fifty years after 1200 the fair land the poets had known and loved was to pay dearly for its independence. If the Cathars were a thorn in the flesh of the Church, the unruly nobles of the south, who had owed neither political nor cultural allegiance to the north, had aroused the enmity of the kings of France. Church and State in formidable alliance were too much for the lords of the south, with no central figure or organisation on which to base their resistance. The violence and atrocity of the attack on the Cathars and their political allies at Béziers and elsewhere, and the terrors of the Inquisition, aroused passionate resistance, but it was uncoordinated and spontaneous, and the prolonged sieges of the Cathars in their mountain fortresses at Montségur and elsewhere increased the damage to Provence as a whole; Languedoc was heavily ravaged after the abortive revolt of 1242. The poetic tradition needed patrons and peace for the writing of verses; the wars which Bertran de Born had celebrated were mere child's play compared with the crusade.

The troubadours of this last era come mainly from Provence and northern Italy. Their efforts are more carefully orthodox, and platonic love in Guillem de Montanhagnol becomes pure adoration of the Virgin for Guiraut Riquier, though the transition from profane to sacred had come as early as the last decade of the twelfth century, with Folquet de Marseille's lovely dawn hymn and its refrain:

> The shadows flee, the light draws near;
> The sky is calm and clear.
> The dawn no longer hesitates,
> The day in fair perfection waits.[25]

But the later poets address Our Lady as their *domna*: thus Guiraut Riquier:

> God, in whose power it lies, had made me standard bearer
> For my Lady, Lady of the Pure, in Love's high kingdom.[26]

And on this note, the last of the major poets of the south ends his swan-song. The tradition lingers for another half-century; the last troubadours moved to Italy, where their inheritance was handed on to the poets of the Sicilian court and of the *dolce stil novo*, Guinizelli and Cavalcanti; so through Petrarch it finally returns to Renaissance France by way of the Lyons poets, Scève and Louise Labé, finding renewed life as a theme for royal pageants.

---

25 A.Berry, *Florilège des Troubadours*, 336; author's translation.
26 Joseph Anglade, *Anthologie des Troubadours* (Paris 1927) 177.

The fame of the troubadours did not need such cataclysms to spread it abroad; they had long ago found imitators in Italy and, more important for our present purpose, in northern France. The *trouvères*, working while the original ideas were still developing, remained on a more down-to-earth level. But it was through them that the ideas of the troubadours entered the active world of chivalry, and were subtly metamorphosed from the abstract to the concrete. The knight wearing his lady's favour in a sixteenth-century tournament was still subscribing to the troubadour idea that love is an improving force: instead of moral prowess, however, he wore the favour so that the thought of his lady would lend physical strength to his arm, a notion which came about in the more literal schools of northern France.

Courtly and chivalric love

The troubadours' real innovation is to make love the central topic of literary discussion, to analyse feelings and their consequences instead of simply expressing them, however elegantly.[27] From this discussion, they arrived at one generally accepted conclusion: that man could become more noble through love. Personality and love are connected for the first time. From enthroning the lady as a superhuman creature, it was a short step to endowing her with the power of granting gifts, albeit in an indirect way, through the effect of the love she inspired. Troubadour poetry is not about women, their beauty or charms; it is about the lover and his longings. The highest praise is measured in terms of the lady's influence on the admirer, and so the qualities of the lover loom large in their philosophy. But the literature about love is a continuing dialogue between the poets, in which the emphasis moves from lover to lady, from secular to religious, and back again. It is possible, nonetheless, to outline some common ideals, which run like a golden thread through troubadour lyrics, *minnesang* and chivalric romances.

We start with the lover and the lady. It was assumed that they were both noble; nothing is said of their attachment, whether they were married to others or were both unmarried. The lover may have adored his lady from childhood up, a common theme; or equally, passion may have struck suddenly, at the meeting of two pairs of eyes. The love which resulted was not designed to lead to marriage, so whether they had partners was incidental; but it was exclusive within the conventions. Marcabru is particularly scornful of these who entertain more than one lover at a time, and only in very lax circles was it permitted.

27   One of the best recent discussions of courtly love is Rüdiger Schnell, 'Die 'höfische' Liebe als 'höfischer' Diskurs über die Liebe', in Fleckenstein, *Curialitas*, 231-301.

It becomes a lady well
If she should love a knight;
But woe betide her, if she chooses
Companions in love for him.[28]

It was not an equal relationship: the beloved was always regarded as a superior being. Much of the vocabulary, despite feudalism's relatively weak hold in Provence, is drawn from the legal language of homage and vassalage, and the commonest description of the lover is as the vassal of his lady, serving her in hope of reward. This applies from the earliest poems onwards; Guilhem IX declares that he will deliver himself to his lady, so that he can be written into her charters, and it is a completely new trait in love-poetry, without parallel in the Latin lyrics. The lover attempted to win his lady's favour by noble acts. In the Provençal tradition these do not seem to have included deeds of arms; more civilised ways of paying court, such as the composing of songs, and the cultivation of wit and good manners were preferred. If a lover was adept at pleasing his lady, she might in due course recognise his suit, and grant him some token of his favour, perhaps after several years. After a similar period of waiting, she might admit him to more physical joys, and it was not unknown for her to surrender herself completely.

On a higher plane, it was the harmony between lover and beloved that was all-important: 'Any lover who rebukes his beloved for not giving him what he desires, or who asks things which she should not grant, is indeed a fool.' Love had to be both reciprocal and freely granted on both sides, underlining the contrast between such affairs of the heart and the dynastic, calculating nature of feudal marriage. It could also be withdrawn if circumstances changed: in the late twelfth century romance of *Ille et Galeron*, Ille is disfigured in battle, and flees from Galeron, because he assumes - wrongly, as it turns out - that she will no longer accept him as her lover. Jaufre Rudel renounces all hope of consummation: 'Since there is never a chance of my seeing her, no wonder I long for her so.'[29]

Despite the implied though remote possibility of union with the beloved, and despite the solace of harmony of minds, the usual state of the troubadour was represented as one of ceaseless inner turmoil. It was through this turmoil that the lover was supposed to acquire the qualities which brought him nearer to the heights on which the beloved moved. Tension is the mainspring of much of the poetic action, in varying forms: hesitation versus boldness, the power of love versus the individual's desire of happiness, the possibility of consummation versus the long service expected of the lover. Waiting and delay were a recognised part of the ritual: Folquet de Marseille, in

28   Cadenet, quoted in Schnell, 'Die 'höfische' Liebe', 239; author's translation.
29   Berry, *Florilège des Troubadours*, 96.

an early poem, attacks this idea and inveighs against those who 'through foolish waiting, do their penance before they sin'. There is also a tension between the lovers and society at large. The Church frowned on such affairs, of course, but secrecy was regarded as *de rigueur*. It underlined the special status of the love-relationship, added to the excitement and offered dramatic possibilities for concealment, suspicion and watchfulness for the *losangiers*, the jealous rivals who would betray everything to the world.

The virtues and merits of the lover, in contrast to the values involved in feudal marriage, were entirely personal. Whereas a match between knightly or noble families involved questions of status and wealth above all else, the lover was judged by his own achievements. The poets declared these standards as superior to those of the world outside; they subverted the norms of society, and created a realm where mundane considerations were deliberately excluded: this separate set of values is a crucial feature of the love-stories of the later romances. The virtues which the poets proclaimed derived from the tradition of courtly behaviour and courtesy which we discussed at the beginning of this chapter. As Gaucelm Faidit puts it:

All those who love true worth
Must know that from love stem
Much largesse and lively solace
Frank manners and humility
Valour in love, service of honour,
Noble conduct, joy, and courtesy.[30]

Any lover worth his salt was at once *cortes*, a word that meant both courteous and courtly, and implied a knowledge of the conventions. Certain things were not *cortes* — falsehood in love, miserliness, infidelity and lack of restraint or secrecy. These were the vices which the courtly code was designed to suppress: and their strange mixture only makes sense when we take love, and the effect of each on love, as the criterion. *Cortesia* was a vital aspect of troubadour love, but it was a negative virtue. The lover's *cortesia* consisted in not being miserly, but not necessarily in indulging in lavish exhibitions; in not being boastful, but not necessarily in keeping total secrecy; in not being too forward, but not in waiting on his mistress' every word — the term used is *mezura*, the golden mean.

However, more positive virtues were admired in a lover: *pretz* and *jovens*. A lover was *pretz* when he had earned esteem through his love; the word is akin to prowess, and

---

30   *Les poèmes de Gaucelm Faidit*, ed. Jean Mouzat (Paris 1965) 524.

implies accomplishment, a stage beyond mere keeping of rules. The lover had learned to please his lady, and had earned admiration for his skill in correct behaviour. *Jovens*, literally youth, was a more complex word, embracing generosity and lightness of heart, and it was linked with the *joy d'amour* which is the lover's prize. A lover who is *jovens* was not only accomplished, but had attained the state of mind which rewards that accomplishment. Generosity came into the catalogue of virtues for altogether more practical reasons. The troubadours depended on their audience for a living, and gifts to them counted in the service of love much as alms did in the church. It is the last and subtlest twist to a long tradition of skilled writers reminding their patrons of their needs. But the outcome of this insistence on the lover's accomplishments and self-improvement in his lady's service went beyond the merely courtly, and ultimately the troubadour ideal is the lover's moral improvement through the spiritual love he bears his lady.

Finally, there is the question of *joy d'amour*. This embraced so wide a range of emotions, from physical satisfaction to an almost mystical ecstasy that it can only be defined in reverse as 'the one true end of love'. Much troubadour poetry is highly erotic on a physical plane. Bernart de Ventadorn has been accused of having a single obsession: the naked body of his lady.[31] In its purest sense *joy d'amour* was associated with the restraint and yearning of *fin' amors* and unconnected with an ultimate reward. The striving towards and the achievement of harmony between lover and beloved were both part of it; and very often it was the wounds of love that produced it. The masochistic attitude is made explicit in one of the last troubadours, Hugo Brunec, lamenting its passing:

> *And now I see with its own fulfilment*
> *That love dying which once wounded sweetly.*[32]

This is the key to the apparent chastity of some of the troubadours' desires: they do not fear the attainment of their goal, they prefer the sweet torment of hope to an uncertain joy which leaves no further conquests, no new horizons, once it has been tasted.

But such exalted pinnacles of pleasure were not for all and sundry: and out of this arises the debate over *fin' amors* and *amars*, as Marcabru would have it. For pure love was too high an ideal for the ordinary courtier of the castle where the troubadours sang; seeing this new fashion in love all the rage, he might try to imitate it, and the result would probably be what the later writers called mixed love and what the Church called adultery. Marcabru might call down heaven's wrath in fierce invective, but a necessary by-product of his high visions was their corrupted reflection in lesser men.

31   Lazar, *Amour courtois*, 70.
32   Quoted in Alexander Denomy, *The Heresy of Courtly Love* (New York 1947) 24-5.

It can be argued that it is precisely in this debate that the concept of courtly love lies: as a German scholar recently wrote: 'In the heart of the poet two possibilities struggle with each other: should he diminish the high worth of the lady he is wooing by achieving consummation, or should he preserve her reputation by foregoing the enjoyment of love's favours. Both situations are painful for him. He neither wishes to harm his lady's honour, nor to completely abandon hope of consummation. It is exactly this 'neither-nor' which is the conceptual kernel of courtly love.'[33] Another writer sees the essential feature of courtly love as 'the coexistence, or rather, to use a theological term, the consubstantiality of erotic desire and its sublimation.'[34] The troubadours' concept of love is not implicitly adulterous; and Marcabru's condemnation has no Christian overtones: *amars* is faithless love, which breaches the unswerving fidelity of *fin' amors*. Love, in the troubadour poetry, is simply outside the business of marrying and giving in marriage. It never pretended to be the means of wooing a bride, and never could be in a feudal world where marriages were political or financial alliances; rather, it provided an outlet for feelings that society thus ignored. *Amars* may have been what happened, but it happens in any society: *fin' amors* was not affected as an ideal, and we shall find the paradox repeated in other branches of chivalry.

We have looked at the possible reasons for the appearance of a new attitude towards women; the more difficult question of why it took this direction remains. There are almost as many theories about 'the origins of courtly love' as there are scholars who have studied it, and the answers can only be very tentative. A great many elements in the troubadour songs can be found elsewhere, and explained as borrowings; but no consistent pattern appears, and to admit them all would be to make Provence the centre of a far-ranging network of intellectual activity, which is hardly justified by any other evidence. Again, even if all the other ideas are ascribed to outside sources, one central theme, that of the lover's yearning and suffering, of what we know as passion, remains obstinately original.

Broadly, the possible influences on the shaping of the ideals of courtly love are three: mysticism and philosophy, Latin poetry and Arabic literature. The mystical and philosophical systems such as that propounded by St Bernard are on another plane altogether. St Bernard, writing just after the first generation of troubadour poets, treats carnal love more sympathetically than the early fathers had done: though it is purely selfish, 'that love by which man loves himself, for his own sake and before all else'[35]; it is a step on the road to that divine love in which God is loved for his own sake. St

33   Schnell, 'Die 'höfische' Liebe', 252.

34   Jean Frappier, 'Sur un procès fait à l'amour courtois', *Romania* 93, 1972, 166.

35   Quoted in Etienne Gilson, *The Mystical Theology of St Bernard*, tr. A.H.C.Downes (London 1940) 14.

Bernard's divine love is echoed by phrases in the troubadours, but they never move beyond an erudite simile: usually their invocations of heaven are forerunners of the popular song lyrics of the 1930s:

> *A smile from your eyes*
> *Is my Paradise*

to translate the *trouvère* Thibaut de Champagne somewhat freely. And if we look closely at the ecstasy of the troubadours, it is not a mystical ecstasy: Etienne Gilson neatly describes it as 'a paralysis induced by passion'.[36] It is a temporary escape from the pangs of love into a numbed awe before the splendours of the beloved's spiritual and physical beauty, which has little relation to the beloved's attitude, to any spiritual union, or indeed to any spiritual achievement at all. The troubadours used the idea of ascetic renunciation to achieve more intensity of feeling by creating a tension between this restraint and the urgency of their desire. The result is not a kind of love-religion: mysticism and religious poetry lend formulae and phrases, but not the essence of their thought, to the troubadours.

None of the early Provençal poets, and few of the later ones, are likely to have read any non-Christian philosophy. However, the Christian philosophers had inherited a great deal from the ancient world, and much of their work is almost agnostic in attitude. They discuss the relations of body and soul in similar terms to those of Plotinus, the Alexandrian writer of the third century AD, and the tradition known as neoplatonism was still predominant. In the system proposed by Plotinus and his successors, all things ascend towards the One, a progress helped or hindered by the proportion of finite being and of essential good in each individual. The attraction to sensible beauty is one step on the ascent towards the contemplation of innate, ideal beauty, which is for Plotinus the highest state to be attained in this existence. The idea of yearning as the driving force behind spiritual growth is essential to this view of life, and this does offer a close parallel with the lover's attitude to his lady, which may begin with a carnal desire, but ends in spiritual improvement. As with mysticism, however, the parallel is more a result of the general nature of human love, another facet of a universal truth, than of direct borrowing.[37] The same applies to any parallels with the Augustinian tradition as expressed in works such as Alcher of Clairvaux's *De spiritu et anima*, where a systematic analysis of love in similar terms to that of the troubadours appears. The Church's doctrines on love, though admittedly part of the general cultural background of the time, were unlikely to come to the troubadours in such a way as to

---

36   *Ibid.*, 37.

37   See Peter Dronke, *Medieval Latin and the Rise of European Love-Lyric* (Oxford 1965) 1-46, for a general survey of 'courtly' motifs in a wide range of literatures.

influence them over details.[38] Again, the troubadours were consciously exploring love in non-philosophical but intelligent an serious terms; though love is seen from a different angle, its essence remains the same, and some of the results must therefore be related.

One neighbouring civilisation which had approached love in a similar way was the Arabic culture, particularly in Spain. Arab theology did not regard love as a link between the human and divine: man was not created to love God, but only to praise him. Hence the Arab view of love was not complicated by religious dogmas, and human love was the only type of love for writers such as Ibn Dawoud of Bagdad. Ibn Sina, or Avicenna (987–1030), was working within the terms of his own philosophical system, Neoplatonic in its basis, when he came to write his *Risala fi'l-'Isq* (*Treatise on Love*), and it was attacked in the east for unorthodoxy. In eleventh-century Spain a more liberal atmosphere meant that his writings were studied with interest, and from here they passed on to Latin Christendom. The *Treatise on Love* sees restraint in love-making as essential if the animal side of man's nature is not to have the upper hand; but, although the first Latin translations of Avicenna were made about 1130, this work does not seem to have been among them, either then or in later years.

Arab writings on love are refinements of sensual love, and if they arrive at a type of spiritual love, it is not connected with a higher religious love. In the ninth century, Ibn Dawoud sees chaste love as the highest type, not because the flesh is evil, and such a love will be purely spiritual, but because renunciation perpetuates desire. His successors could not elaborate further on these ideals without treading the paths of heresy, and the Andalusian poets are much readier to sing of the pleasures of the flesh. Lip-service is still paid to the supremacy of spiritual love; but the lover does not grow more noble in his lady's service (she is as often as not a young slave-girl anyway), and the yearnings are quickly satisfied or drowned in wine. It is a more realistic, easygoing world; *pretz*, fame in the world's eye, would have found no seekers among the Arab poets, and *cortesia* would have seemed an exaggerated fantasy.

At a more practical level, contacts between Arab culture in Spain and the courts of Provence were by no means impossible. Ramon Berenguer III of Catalonia married the heiress of Provence in 1112, and his realms extended from the border with the Moorish kingdom of Valencia as far east as Nice, with his capital at Barcelona. There were many *mudejars*, as the Muslims under Christian rule were called, in his Spanish domains. There are common factors in terms of the use of rhyme – an Arabic innovation - and in the borrowings from Arab music by the troubadours, even if we

38   See Rüdiger Schnell, *Causa Amoris: Liebeskonzeption und Liebesdarstellung in der mittelalterlichen Literatur* Bibliotheca Germanica 27, (Bern & München 1985) 169-179 for a discussion of the relationship between Christian ethics and courtly love.

cannot point to cases of direct translation.[39] An alternative point of contact could have been the Latin kingdoms of the east. A frequent complaint of newcomers to the Holy Land from the early twelfth century onwards was the extent to which the Frankish lords had adopted Arab ways. But, again, there is no direct evidence; we have no troubadour songs from the Christian states in the east, so the intellectual and cultural ideas would have had to travel a long way before coming to fruition.

Given the circumstances of increased leisure and greater education, and the new status of women which we have outlined above, the lyric poetry of the troubadours was essentially a spontaneous growth. The seed may have come from any of of the established traditions we have outlined: what finally grew out of it was something entirely original, compounded from any ideas that may have been to hand. To see courtly love as something adopted from elsewhere is to misunderstand it entirely. It reflects closely the life of the courts of southern France: the eternal fidelity of the lover, the superiority of the loved one, mirror the relationship of lord and vassal; the love for a woman who cannot be attained within the norms of society is the result of a world where courting and love matches were almost unknown, and marriage was a political and procreative institution only. As to the means of attaining one's goal, the quest for *cortesia* and *pretz* is an echo in peacetime of the feudal virtues sought in war: courage and loyalty are the equivalent of *cortesia*, fame is the spur for both warrior and lover. Other characteristic themes are discoveries about the psychology of love which remain true for most civilisations: the danger that a love affair will wane after its consummation, the pleasure that can be found in the pangs of love, the lover's hesitation before his mistress. Even the complex idea of *pretz*, and the lover's gain in moral worth is only an elaboration of Housman's:

> *O when I was in love with you*
> *Then I was clean and brave*
> *And miles around the wonder grew*
> *How well did I behave.*

---

39   Roger Boase, *The Origin and Meaning of Courtly Love: a critical survey of European scholarship* (Manchester & Totowa, N.J., 1977) 62-3.

Successors to the troubadours: the Minnesingers

The striking and attractive songs of the troubadours found an appreciative audience wherever the southern language was readily understood; and it was not long before the more difficult transplantation of their art to northern France and to Germany began. Even without the barrier of language, conditions were less favourable: the social world of the north was more practical, less inclined to the easy southern ways. Eleanor of Aquitaine was said to have exclaimed impatiently of her first husband, Louis VII of France: 'I have married a monk, not a king!', and her habits more than once shocked the French court. Both in northern France and across the Rhine, the lesser lords could not keep court in the style of their Provençal counterparts. King and Emperor were the centres of society, and only when they or a powerful magnate deigned to take an interest did the arts flourish. Fortunately such men did exist: courts such as Champagne, Thuringia and Austria all provided such patronage at various times, and we find the bishops too, the protectors of the wandering scholars, offering their hospitality to poets and artists.

The first imitators of the troubadours were a group of northern French poets known by the northern version of the word, *trouvères*. These poets worked in an area of France already notable for its devotion to the knightly arts, Champagne and the Flemish borders. We shall return to the court of Champagne as a home of knightly romance, and to Flanders as an especial haunt of the tourneyers: here was the audience, here the rich reward. Yet the purely troubadour element appears only in the first generation of trouvères, among poets such as Chrétien de Troyes, Gace Brulé, Conon de Béthune. By the early thirteenth century, the older traditional forms native to the region, the *pastourelle* and *chansons de toile*, in a simpler lyric form, appear as well; and we are on the road to the Arcadian shepherdesses of the seventeenth and eighteenth centuries by way of such incongruous episodes as the tournament given by René d'Anjou known as the *Pas d'Armes de la Bergière*, where the setting of the tournament included the king's beloved dressed in pastoral costume, and with a real flock of sheep to guard in the midst of the heat and fury of the lists. But such diversions were not the real rivals of troubadour songs and love: it was the preference of the northern knights for epics to while away the long evenings, rather than lyrics brief as the Provençal dawn, that determined the issue. Into these longer poems the fruits of troubadour poetry were assimilated; and the echoes of the songs die away.

We have already glanced at the traditions of love in romance and love-letters in Germany, and the first German lyric poets emerge at the same time as the troubadours: 'der von Kürenberc', Dietmar von Aist, and Meinloh von Sevelingen, show what native talent might have made of the love song in the absence of the Provençal influence. Kürenberc's metaphors are drawn from knightly surroundings and pastimes; but his

95

ladies are human, pleading and hoping that love will endure in the hearts of their fickle knights. If they are proud and unyielding, the knight says 'Then she shall remain without my love' and goes in search of a warmer welcome, instead of throwing himself at her feet. In his most famous song, a lady sees her lover as a falcon, unsure whether she really has his love:

> I trained myself a falcon through a year's long days.
> When he was safely tamed to follow my ways
> And his plumage shone golden, painted by my hand.
> With powerful wingbeats rising, he sought another land.

> Since then I've often seen him, soaring in fair flight,
> For on his feet my silken jesses still shine bright
> And his plumage gleams with scarlet and with gold.
> May God grace lovers and reunite them as of old.[40]

When Kürenberc speaks as a man, women are fit subjects for conquest rather than adoration: 'women and falcons are easily tamed'. The pathos and high feeling are always on the woman's side; it is unmanly to be sentimental or subservient.

With Dietmar von Aist an occasional echo of new ideas creeps in: he can discreetly hint that his long service of his lady had made him a better man, and therefore more deserving of a reward. And he tosses and turns at night, thinking of 'the lady whom I'd like to love me'. The old forms of conversation and of the lady speaking alone continue in both his verse and that of the yet more courtly Meinloh; but they lack the sharp clarity of Kürenberc, while the poems addressed to the lady are more fiery and sharply drawn. Meinloh brings in the idea of *dienst*, service, which was to become an inseparable compound of *minne*, high love or *fin' amors*: *minnedienst*. With him, we are at the true beginning of *minnesang*, 'the songs of high love'.

There is one particular event within Meinloh's lifetime which marks the new epoch, the knighting of Frederick Barbarossa's sons, including the future emperor Henry VI, at Mainz at Whitsun 1184.[41] An international gathering on this scale was unknown since Charlemagne's day. Thanks to Frederick Barbarossa's able rule Germany was at peace, a rare enough state of affairs throughout the Middle Ages, and preparations had gone on without interruption for several months. All the lands under Frederick's rule were represented: and these included Burgundy (which reached as far

40 Sayce, *Poets of the Minnesang* 8; author's translation.
41 See Josef Fleckenstein, 'Friedrich Barbarossa und das Rittertum: zur Bedeutung der grossen Mainzer Hoftage von 1184 und 1188', in Borst, *Das Rittertum im Mittelalter*, 392-418.

as Arles) and Italy. These fiefs of the Holy Roman Empire led a political existence with little direct connection with Germany, and their magnates rarely appeared at the imperial court except on business. Now for once they gathered for more social purposes, and there were knights from France as well. Knightly society appears for the first time as the equivalent of court society. For an occasion of this kind, with its tournaments and festivals, Mainz was full of noble ladies, and to complete the court, all kinds of squires, minstrels and other members of the lords' retinues. It was they above all who benefited from the generosity proper to such occasions, the casual expenditure of fortunes as the lords vied with each other to make the greatest impression: the chroniclers emphasise the splendour of the event.

We know for certain of three singers present: Guiot de Provins, and Doetes de Troyes from Champagne, and Heinrich von Veldeke from Limburg in Belgium. Guiot was a *trouvère* of some repute who later described the feast in his poems; of Doetes de Troyes' work nothing survives. Veldeke, who was likewise to include in his version of the *Aeneid* a brilliant portrait of these days, of whose marvels 'men could talk until Doomsday without lying', is on the other hand a key figure in the development of *minnesang*, literally 'songs of love'. Even the young Emperor in whose honour the gathering took place, Henry VI, is reputed to have tried his hand at the new form. The latter, conscious of his imperial status, sings of an equal passion where man and woman are partners, not adoring and adored. But he is a minor figure compared with the more radical Veldeke. His *Aeneid* is based on an old French poem, not directly on Virgil, and turns the Trojans into models of chivalry; Eneas and Lavinia might be lovers from the court of Champagne. His poems, too, derive from the trouvères. Whether the great festival at Mainz affected his writing greatly we cannot tell; all the poets of this generation who show knowledge of troubadour or *trouvère* poetry come from the west of Germany, in areas where contact with France and the south was common. On the other hand, the nobles who flocked to Mainz heard the new songs for the first time, and certainly acquired their taste for such poetry about this period.

By the end of the century, there was no doubt as to the success of the new style. Veldeke's assertion that 'from love all good things come' is taken up and affirmed by Friedrich von Hausen and most of the others. Von Hausen is the first to acknowledge the complete superiority of his lady, a shadowy angel mirrored dimly in the poet's thoughts of despair and devotion. At its height, *Frauendienst*, the service of women, becomes a more intense experience in the hands of the German poets, an intensity which makes it liable to become entirely fantastic, as with Ulrich von Lichtenstein the following century, to whose adventures in tournaments we will return: but he is a law unto himself, a baroque figure from the ends of the empire. The greater poets saw *Minne* as an overwhelming, all-consuming force, but did not follow their arguments to an absurd conclusion in real life.

The golden age of *Minnesang* was the last decade of the twelfth and first decade of the thirteenth centuries.[42] German writers had absorbed the Provençal ideas, and proceeded to go beyond them in their own ways. At the Thuringian court, Heinrich von Morungen stood 'bewitched by great love'; and his insubstantial beloved appears to him in dreams rather than in cold daylight. At times he followed a Provençal model very closely as in the poem where he sees himself first as a child grasping at a mirror that delights him and breaking it, and again as Narcissus, bound by what he sees in the mirror of the spring to love for ever. (The practice of *contrafacta*, writing a poem to an existing melody, accounts for the similarity of some German and Provençal poems, though the evidence is not always clear. There may have been imitation of metrical forms as well, which made it possible to sing a poem to an existing French tune. For instance, Jaufre Rudel's poem on p. 83 and Walther von der Vogelweide's '*Nu alrest lebe ich mir werde*' can be sung to the same melody.) Here even the rhyme scheme and the number of lines is the same as in the original; the difference in content is barely more than that of a free translation. Yet Morungen's version is undoubtedly the greater poem; his images are sharper, his handling of the theme surer.

The great rival to Thuringia as a poetic centre was Vienna, ruled at this period by the Babenberg dukes. Here both 'the nightingale of Hagenau' and 'the nightingale of Vogelweide' sang. Reinmar of Hagenau, whom Gottfried von Strassburg mourned as the possessor of 'the master-secret of all music' represented classical *Minnesang* at its purest. His range of subjects is narrow: the unconditional and hopeless service of love through the lady is his dominant theme, which he dissects out until each nerve lies exposed in a fine pattern:

> *These long days when I've sweetly sighed*
> *For my true love's love are still renewed and endless.*
> *And I still marvel how my pride*
> *Regrets so little years of service spent and fruitless;*
> *Her messengers never come*
> *With comforting words; sadness and sorrow is all they bring.*
> *How shall I endure this pain a moment more?*
> *Her heart is cold; that is my grief.*
> *Could I but fire her, I would swear her lifelong love.*[43]

---

42 Bert Nagel, *Staufische Klassik: Deutsche Dichtung um 1200* (Heidelberg 1977) is the most comprehensive survey.

43 Sayce, *Poets of the Minnesang*, 1-2.

Love's fulfilment is as distant as for the most austere troubadours; but he still persists in his task. But there is a subtle shift in his reasoning: he argues that the lady loves him secretly and is fearful only of her reputation – she says 'What he desires, is death!'. He does not find the consolation in *joy d'amour*, the ecstasy of unfulfilled love with which the troubadours sustained themselves, though he still consoles himself, and answers his many critics, with the honour to be won through a lady's love. Love is a hard game (*swaerez spil*), but within this framework Reinmar has a great variety of moods and expressions: he is far from being the chronicler of love's despair, even though 'love is suffering' is writ large throughout his work, which is formal, serious and relies on understatement and nuance for its powerful effect. Even if his opponents disagreed with his idealised picture of love, they acknowledge his artistic skill, and particularly his poems in praise of his lady. Walther von der Vogelweide, his greater rival, in a generous elegy on a man whom he admired but did not like, quotes with approval Reinmar's famous line – 'O woman, greeting: how pure a name!'

Reinmar was keeper of the 'master-secret' not only for Gottfried, but also for a whole school of later poets. Here the terms of love-service became rigid and codified. The same theme of almost hopeless love within the private universe of poet and lady takes on an exclusive and esoteric air, as his successors seek for the *Minne* which he so finely analysed. *Minne* becomes a religion in itself; yet it does not contradict Christianity for the lady's beauty is also God's creation, and *Minne* is the feeling inspired by contemplation of this handiwork. *Gotes hulde*, divine favour, and *êre*, honour, are the chief goals of the lover beside his lady's love; the striving for both worldly and spiritual reward leads to one end, the old troubadour ideal of worth through love. The German poets, despite their more vivid imagery, make of this a more abstruse ideal. The troubadours never exclude love's fulfilment so vigorously: the world is still peopled by the jealous watchers who may prevent it, but it remains a possible goal. The idea of love as suffering had already arisen in Provence, but it was the Minnesingers, and Reinmar first and foremost, who made the two inseparable: 'Love without suffering cannot be.' The hopeless, introspective nature of their emotion demands an impossible goal; and in later days, their goddesses are specifically married women. Ulrich von Lichtenstein, as he describes his extravagant pursuit of his beloved, can speak of his 'dearest wife' in the same breath. *Minnedienst* has become a courtly ritual, to be performed as a diversion from reality, however earnest it may at moments seem.

Reinmar and his successors were poets working in an artificial convention, as the troubadours were, and no one had questioned the carefully contrived mythology of Provence. In Vienna the fantasy had not struck such deep roots. Walther von der Vogelweide extends the range of *Minnesang* and turns his verses to other ends besides. To us the result is more appealing, but he breaks the charmed circle in the process. There *is* a natural world outside the castle, which is more than the setting for a maying expedition. In returning to the roots from which the native German poetry of the mid-twelfth century had sprung, he saved the courtly lyric from the eclipse which it suffered in the knightly world of France. Yet his poems are not so different from those of, say, Thibaut de Champagne, or Charles d'Orléans in a later age; the background of courtly society no longer permeates them in the same way; instead a new and timeless charm distinguishes them:

> Under the lime tree, amongst the heather,
>   Down in the hollow where we lay
> Ah, passer-by, ah tell me whether
> The grasses lie in disarray.
> At the wood's edge, in the vale,
>   Tandaradei,
> Sweetly sang the nightingale.
> The meadow path was soft and easy
> For there my love awaited me.
> Ah, Blessed Mary, he received me
> And my heart still sings its ecstasy
> All his kisses seemed one kiss,
> Tandaradei,
> See how red my mouth is.
>
> He made. as rich as I could wish for,
> A bed from meadow flowers and grass;
> And as you walk the path which I walked,
> You'll smile, perhaps, there, as you pass.
> From the roses you still may,
> Tandaradei,
> See the place where my head lay.
>
> If anyone knew we'd lain together–
> Which God forbid! I'd die of shame.
> And what he did, ah, no one ever,
> Except for us, shall know that game;
> Except for us and one small bird,
> Tandaradei,
> And he, surely he will keep his word.[44]

---

44   Sayce, *Poets of the Minnesang,* 103-4; author's translation.

As the barriers separating the knightly world from that of burgher or peasant gradually disappear, there arise new divisions. The troubadour Peire Vidal had depicted the Germans as rough and unmannerly, and praised the ways of his native land in contrast; so Walther can defend German men as the most courtly of all, the women as angelic. Walther is the first German poet to extend the range of his subject matter to politics. His greatest poems are those on the state of the Empire, torn between two claimants to the imperial crown, as far above the Provençal *sirventes* as Ciceronian eloquence above a demagogue's taunts. It is this broader, wider view that characterises his work; and he himself had tasted life outside the charmed circle of court and castle. He 'learnt his singing and rhyming in Austria', but left Vienna in 1198 on the death of Duke Frederick, his patron, from an accident in a tournament. He then led a wandering existence, begging his way as necessary, like the Irish scholars before him. In 1203 he was in the company of bishop Wolfger of Passau, who gave him a fur coat at the first great church festival after he entered his service, just as another pauper singer, who went by the name of the Archpoet, had put in a Latin plea for one from Frederick Barbarossa's chancellor half a century before. In the end he seems to have pleaded successfully for a fief, where he settled at some time after 1220.

Broadly speaking, Walther's poems are at their most courtly during his wanderings, though his later patrons may have demanded an occasional verse in a lighter vein. He starts by singing of one lady only, his own personal lodestar; but she soon disappears, and the heresy that *Minne* is a matter not confined to the elegance of court life creeps in. Then, briefly, he takes up Reinmar's universal theme of the divinity present in all women, finds it too artificial, and turns aside to an increasing concern with politics, a phase which corresponds with his years of wandering.

After Walter, *Minnesang* divides into two schools of thought in the second quarter of the thirteenth century, both claiming him as their genius. The traditionalist theoretical poets predominate, becoming more and more involved with the nuances of the central situation of *Minne* until rhetoric turns to cold hair-splitting as they search for the last shadow of refinement that can be wrung from the old themes. A little great poetry does emerge in the process, but only three poets had any hand in it: Neidhart von Reuenthal, Ulrich von Lichtenstein and Gottfried von Neifen. Neidhart makes rather pedantic play on his surname, 'of the Vale of Sorrows', in his more formal poems, quite in the old vein, but his really original work arises from the introduction of new subject matter, in that many of his poems are in peasant settings, descriptions of village dances and conversations, moving outside the framework of courtly convention.

All that could be done with *Minnesang* proper was to make of it a baroque fancy, in the manner of Ulrich von Lichtenstein's exploits. The poems embedded in the phantasmagoria of his book, entitled simply *Frauendienst*, are in the classic style and almost normal compared with the strange adventures he undertakes in his lady's service; his successors, however. transfer the eccentricities to their poetry. The complexities of metre are occasionally put to enchanting use, as with the dancing lilt in Burkhard von Hohenfels's poem:

> *Welcome, soft breezes!   Come now who pleases!*
> *Maidens entrancing,   join youths in dancing,*
> *follow my paces:*
> *In gayest attire, you beckon Love's fire   with smiles and sweet faces.*[45]

More often, they are part of an overwhelming rush of images, which make the established themes seem a cornucopia of poetic visions. But description without conviction soon palls, as the competition for richer echoes, more intricate modes, increases. Satire, which Neidhart had directed against the rough ways of the peasants, was turned against the gates of love itself: and the last shreds of reality fell away. Towards the end of the great interregnum in the Empire which began in 1254, the burghers adopted the chivalric fashions and made of them the closely regulated art of *Meistergesang* which emerged about 1300. In the turbulent days that followed until Rudolf of Habsburg began to restore order, there was little time for the ways of knighthood, and much for those of war. Germany's contribution to the lyric poetry of chivalry was brief, eloquent, without lasting inheritance.

The most obvious and yet the most striking feature of the theory of *Minne* is its almost complete dependence on the Provençal *fin' amors*. The same premise lies at the roots of both: the lover's moral improvement through the spiritual love he bears his lady. Given this, the code cannot really vary in any great degree: if the love becomes passion in the modern sense it leads to physical union as well as spiritual, while it cannot diverge into pure friendship in the other direction. *Minne* tends to become a more generalised emotion, as in Reinmar's eulogy of the fair sex as a whole, of which his own lady is merely the fairest and most virtuous representative. The emphasis tends to be on love itself, its genesis and nature, rather than on the ancillary virtues which the troubadours delighted in. The moral rewards and ecstasies are less prominent; *hôher muot*, the equivalent of *joy d'amour*, rapidly becomes a state of mind inspired by circumstances rather than the lady herself; spring or, for Lichtenstein, a good horse or a noble banquet, inspiring the feeling. The relationship of lover and lady is in the foreground instead.

---

45   Sayce, *Poets of the Minnesang*, 153; author's translation.

Service *(dienst)* and faithfulness *(triuwe)* are the cardinal points of this relationship. It is a service which for Friedrich von Hausen (following Bernart de Ventadorn), and later for Ulrich von Lichtenstein, begins in childhood: Ulrich declares that he has loved his lady since he was twelve. The terms of the relationship are set out more sharply in the German poets. The lady is guarded by jealous watchers who prevent the lover from gaining free access to her, but also exclude all rivals. The poet rarely accuses his beloved of unfaithfulness, or even admits that she might have other admirers. It is only the ice within her heart that keeps him at a distance, and he hopes that his lyrical ardour will be able to melt that. Occasionally, under the spell of the romances, he may resort to deeds as well. This, and the increasingly physical descriptions of the lady, mark the decline of *Minnesang* with poets such as Tannhäuser: where the troubadours become more obscure and abstract as time goes on, the German poets come down to earth, and demand to 'pluck the roses' in return for their efforts in the tournament. For Veldeke or Reinmar, however, the lady offers no more than a token of favour, a smile, a word in private, as her part of the contract.

The setting of the *Minnesang* poems is exactly parallel to that of the troubadour lyrics: a courtly society where life is governed by conventions. These conventions were a matter of fashion, so much so that they almost seem a poetic fiction, yet the rules were so respected by the poets that they must have had some ground in reality. A poetry which has no such ground 'would indeed be an unheard-of phenomenon'. How seriously was the game played? We have too few independent witnesses to be able to tell, and most of them have a moral axe to grind. The attitudes struck by Reinmar and others may appear to be elegant poses; nonetheless, they are poses which arise from an exaggeration of real emotions, a dissection of the soul under the microscope true enough to its own premises, but out of scale with the rest of the world.

As *Minnesang* disappears at the end of the thirteenth century into contests of technique on the one hand and social satire on the other, it closes the great arc described by the lyric poetry of chivalry and the social convention of love attached to it. Rising from obscure origins, it starts as a mixture of high spirits and low morals in Guilhem IX's first poems and in some of Marcabru and Cercamon's work, rapidly climbs into the ethereal world of Jaufre Rudel's *amor de lonh*, and remains in these high regions until the inspiration and impulse evaporated completely in the south. The *trouvères* make it a little more mundane, but the Minnesingers briefly restore it to its old pretensions, at about the same time that it rises to its most abstruse in Provence. From then on the mode and mood change; poetry is a decoration to the knight's existence, not the oracle from which all truth proceeds. The idea of love-service survives, as an old but active custom which good knights ought to observe, well into the fifteenth century, long after the original social and poetic impulses which gave it life have failed. The decline is slow, almost imperceptible: the accepted ideas of knightly society as to love in 1250 would have been perfectly understood in 1450, despite the fact that no lyric poetry actively advocating such ideas had been written in the interval. For this enduring preservation of the high ideals we must turn to the romances.

5

The Romances of Chivalry

EPIC AND LYRIC, tales of war and songs of love, are only the precursors of the literature of chivalry proper. In northern France, towards the middle of the twelfth century, a new genre came to dominate secular writing. It drew on the ideas of love propounded in the troubadour poems, as well as on the older and simpler tradition of story-telling. There were traces of the late Classical romances, and the epics of the Trojan war and the founding of Rome were recast as stories in verse about the time that the new works appear; but most of the substance of the latter was drawn from the Celtic tales of Wales and Brittany, and, more remotely, Ireland. The result was a complex, exciting mixture of the psychological insights provided by the southern poets' intensive study of love, the high drama of fictional historical triumphs, and the supernatural world of the Celtic myths. This powerful blend of the imaginative and the real was to be the staple entertainment and inspiration of the knightly world for almost four centuries. It was in this fictional world that chivalry took its final shape, and it was here that it appeared in its most alluring guise.

Yet the romances need not necessarily have taken this particular course. The earliest exemplars are retellings of Classical history, and the first 'Celtic' romance is the *Tristan*, is a tale of what we would now call passionate love. It exists in two early versions, both fragmentary, by Béroul and Thomas, poets writing in the middle years of the twelfth century, one Norman, one Anglo-Norman.[1] Later writers confused the story of Tristan and Iseult with the ideas of courtly love, but the original version is *not* courtly. Its idea of love as an overwhelming, dark, supernatural and tragic force is at loggerheads with the troubadours' concepts. Indeed, in the troubadours' terms, Tristan actually loses *pretz* by falling in love with Iseult; and there is little *cortesia* in his actions. We are in a new world, a world of myth rather than manners. The figures of Tristan, Iseult

---

[1]   Translations: Gottfried von Strassburg, *Tristan . . . with the surviving fragments of the* Tristran *of Thomas*, tr. A.T.Hatto (Harmondsworth & Baltimore 1960); Béroul, *The Romance of Tristan*, tr. Alan Fedrick, (Harmondsworth & Baltimore 1970).

and Mark are close to their Celtic kin of the Irish legends. The tension in Tristan arises from Tristan's dual allegiance: to Iseult through love, to Mark through duty, exactly the conflict which the troubadour poets so carefully avoid. Here the bonds of love and the bonds of the feudal world are in open opposition, and the scrupulous, not to say artificial, constructs of the poets' philosophy of love are swept away by its reality.

The fate of the story of Tristan and Iseult is instructive. It disappeared in the thirteenth century into a huge compilation of other romances, the *Prose Tristan*, on which Malory drew for his account of Tristram in the *Morte Darthur*. By the time the story reached him the tension between Mark and Tristram is caused not by Isode, but by the wife of one Sir Segwarides, whom they both love before Isode is wedded to Mark. Isode is no more than Tristram's lady; the passion that sings through earlier and later versions of the tale has vanished. It is not a suitable subject for chivalric romance, because chivalric love does not make passion its ideal; instead, devotion, fidelity, service are its lodestars, inherited from the troubadours' concern with those restraints which prevent love from becoming passionate.

Among the poets of the mid-twelfth century who wrote on the Tristan legend — though his version is now lost — was the first master of French romance, Chrétien de Troyes.[2] Working at the sophisticated court of Champagne, whose countess, Marie, Eleanor of Aquitaine's daughter, was an enthusiastic follower of the southern poets, he nonetheless represents a new development in the ideas of chivalry. The writers of the *chansons de geste* were expert storytellers, heirs of local, almost tribal, traditions who kept to a realistic, active world, whose only touches of fantasy were the giants and monsters fighting for the enemy, and whose heroes were moved by simple emotions of loyalty and hate. The troubadours were lyric poets, and hence preferred to move in an introspective world where feeling was paramount and the setting of their love merely ornamental. Chrétien offers a very different atmosphere. He is international where the jongleurs are national, analytical where the troubadours are subjective. Drawing on the love of action of the knights and the longing for love stories of the ladies, and blending both with the newly current 'Breton tales' of Celtic marvels and enchantments, he created a new world and cast a spell over chivalry from which it never quite awoke.

Chrétien's earliest 'story of adventure', as he himself calls it, was written about 1160. The story of *Erec et Enide* is known to English readers from Tennyson's *Enid*: the knight 'forgetful of the tilt and tournament' for love of the fair maiden he has married.

---

2   Chrétien's romances are available in a number of English versions, the best being Chrétien de Troyes, *Arthurian Romances*, tr. D.D.R.Owen (London 1987), and Chrétien de Troyes, *Perceval: The Story of the Grail*, tr. Nigel Bryant (Cambridge & Totowa, N.J., 1982). The latter contains excerpts from the writers who continued Chrétien's unfinished Grail romance to provide a complete version of the main theme of the story.

At once there is a difference in ethics between Chrétien and the Provençal poets, for the greater part of the action takes place after Erec's marriage, and the crux is how Enide can prove her faith to him in the series of adventures that befall them. Here for the first time we meet the unequal heroic combats, the magical adversaries, and enchanted castles that are the stock in trade of the romances; here too tournaments and knight-errantry come into their own. For it is essential to the style of the romances that the knight should wander forth in search of adventures; the duels and marvels that befall him are rarely hindrances to his journey, but are usually its very purpose. Erec sets out to retrieve his reputation and to test his wife's love for him (though Chrétien never says so explicitly) and in the course of his adventures does both; on these threads are strung the individual episodes which enliven the narrative.

The adventures of Erec conform to certain rules which condition all later chivalric romances. For instance, the hero is never defeated unless suffering from a handicap, such as wounds from a recent combat. This is common to all heroic folk-tales: the central figure of such tales may commit all kinds of pillage and rape, as in the Irish epics, but his prowess remains unquestioned. Erec is harsh to his wife, though only while he suspects her fidelity, yet he is generous and courteous to the rest of the world. Chrétien overlays the basic simplicity of his marvels with other touches which become commonplace later. Knights who have never met before and with no reason to be aggressive fight each other without a challenge. In the latter type of combat, the protagonists are often within an ace of death, but never actually expire. Thus Erec not only overcomes Guivret le Petit in such an encounter, and is greeted warmly by him when he learns Erec's identity, but meets him again on a dark night and is nearly killed by Guivret because he is already badly wounded. Such episodes do not represent any knightly custom of real life, being largely devices to heighten the tension of the story; but their spirit inspired the chivalric episodes of the Hundred Years' War and in the fifteenth century *pas d'armes* which copied the romances. In all this, love seems to have disappeared into the background. In a sense, it has become part of the adventures: Erec's meeting with Enide in her father's threadbare house and his winning of her by defeating Yder in the duel for the sparrow hawk tell us nothing about the subtleties of love, but spin more golden threads into the texture of the romance. It is in the picture Chrétien paints of Enide and Erec's adoration of each other, Erec's forgetfulness of knighthood in her arms, and her unswerving loyalty in face of his trials, that his skill is apparent. It is a new window on the ways of men's hearts. Chrétien is concerned with what actually happens, not with the artificial theories and stylised courtships of the troubadours. Yet the troubadour influence is there in the background. Erec, at a pause in the battle for the sparrow hawk, looks towards his lady 'as she utters heartfelt prayers for him. No sooner has he seen her than great strength has surged back into him. Her love and beauty have restored his great fighting spirit.'[3] The lover wins physical, not moral, prowess, from his lady's eyes; for his moral worth is taken for granted in this magic world, and the power of love is needed more urgently as a charm to give might to his sword.

Chrétien's second work, *Cligès*, takes us into a new realm again: he exchanges the wilds of Wales for the imperial courts of Constantinople, and instead of physical adventures gives us intellectual debates. Cligès is the history of two pairs of lovers: Alexander and Soredamors, Cligès' parents, and Cligès and Fenice. The setting is a mixture of classical and Arthurian, but the former predominates. However, the main interest of the romance is in its study of love, and here Chrétien strikes another new note. He portrays the effect of love on Alexander, Soredamors, Cligès and Fenice in turn, but he does so as a detached observer and analyst of their feelings. The result is a series of introspective but acute monologues based on Ovid's ideas on love as the twelfth century understood them, but illumined by Chrétien's gift of bringing them vividly to life. Here is Soredamors wrestling with her pride when she discovers that she loves Alexander:

> 'Why, then, do I think more about him, if he's no more pleasing to me than any other? I don't know; I'm completely confused: for never before have I thought so much about any man alive; and if I had my way, I'd see him all the time, and would never take my eyes off him, such is my delight when I see him. Is this love? Yes, I believe so.' [4]

But this love is still turned towards marriage; it is Alexander's wooing of Soredamors that is depicted in the smallest detail, dwelt on as the copyist might dwell on the jewelled colours of the illuminations to his manuscript. Love and marriage are one and indivisible; and Fenice, loving Cligès but betrothed to his uncle, bewails her fate as hopeless:

> 'I'd rather be torn limb from limb than have people in referring to us recall the love of Iseut and Tristan, about whom such nonsense is talked that I'm ashamed to speak of it. I couldn't reconcile myself to the life Iseut led. With her, love was too debased, for her body was made over to two men, whilst her heart belonged entirely to one.' [5]

No clearer indictment of the morality behind the story of Tristan could be found; and Chrétien is fond of comparing his characters favourably with Tristan: for instance, Cligès knows far more about hunting than Tristan ever did.

---

3   Tr. D. D. R. Owen, 12.
4   *Ibid.,* 105.
5   *Ibid.,* 135.

So *Cligès* is in some respects a deliberate 'anti-Tristan', even though Chrétien boasts in the introduction of having written about King Mark and the fair Iseult. But he does not draw a high moral, and is more concerned to show that love admits of no division of affection. Fenice living with Cligès as his mistress he can approve, so long as Fenice does not also give herself to Alis, his uncle. As she is the latter's wife, Chrétien has recourse to a *dea ex machina*, in fact a witch, to keep his heroine pure. Cligès marries Fenice in the end, and this is the only fitting end to the story.

However, Chrétien's moral attitude is to some extent conditioned by his story. The tension arises not from the subtleties of divided loyalties but from the obstacles to the union of Cligès and Fenice. That Chrétien held no absolute brief for even the fairly broad morality of *Cligès* is shown by his next work *Le Chevalier de la Charrette*, or *Knight of the Cart*, admittedly written 'since my Lady of Champagne wishes me to undertake a romance'. There is a slightly defensive note about his insistence that 'the material and the treatment of it are given and furnished to him by the countess, and he is simply trying to carry out her concern and intention'. For this is the story of Lancelot and Guinevere, morally a Tristan and an Iseult without even the love potion to excuse them. Chrétien, the poet of the married heroes, Erec and Yvain, here writes of a love that exists entirely outside marriage: but he is more interested in the relationship between the two than in the ethics of the affair. Lancelot's complete subservience to Guinevere as his lady is the most remarkable feature of the story. He rides in shame in the hangman's cart (from which he earns the nickname of the title) purely to reach Guinevere more quickly when his horse has been killed. Even after Guinevere has surrendered herself to him, she still commands his every movement; whether her whim is for her lover to play the coward or the hero in a tournament, Lancelot obeys with equal alacrity.

Chrétien's famed skill in characterisation and psychology fail him here: Lancelot and Guinevere have become little more than archetypes of the courtly lover and his lady. Though they are made of flesh and blood – Lancelot hesitates an instant before getting into the cart – they are not human beings in the same way as his previous characters. Chrétien loves to keep his protagonists anonymous (we only learn Enide's name after Erec has won her) and Lancelot spends half the story described only as 'the best knight living wherever the four winds blow', but whereas Chrétien had previously depicted his heroes and heroines in glowing colours, here he is concerned to get on with the story, and scarcely pauses to dwell on his main characters. His skill in storytelling does not fail him, but there is a sense of unease about his handling of the subject; this is confirmed by the fact that the last thousand lines of the poem were written by Godefroy de Lagny under Chrétien's direction.

With *Yvain*, Chrétien's masterpiece, we return to the old ground of the wooing and winning of a bride within the knightly conventions, and of the history of the marriage. The parallel with *Erec et Enide* is close; the construction, and even the length of the sections, are very similar. A lengthy introduction brings us to the hero's marriage; no particular question is posed, and the story is a simple adventure. Then the crisis is reached with the danger of Yvain falling into slothful ways, described in a short passage of some three hundred lines. His adventures and their resolution, the core of the story, form the concluding and longest section. The pattern may be the same, but Chrétien profits from his familiarity with the scheme to weave a more subtle web of adventures and a more involved plot. The world of Yvain is that of Lancelot's journey to the land of Gorre in *Le Chevalier de la Charrette*, enchanted, magical and spellbinding for the reader, who is carried breathless from one marvel to the next as soon as Calogrenant starts his tale of the spring in the forest of Broceliande at which, if water is poured from it on to a stone, a tempest arises and a knight appears to overthrow the challenger. Chrétien plunders every mythology to hand, pagan, Christian, Celtic, to embellish his story; the easily consoled widow may be Jocasta, the tame and devoted lion belongs to Androcles, and the fountain comes from Breton lore. And beyond this, he draws his characters in bold strokes: Yvain, generous, noble, impulsive; Laudine, haughty, clever, yet truly loving; and Lunete (her confidante) shrewd and devoted. Only once does he fail to convince us that he knows exactly how their minds work, and that is in Yvain's desertion of Laudine after a mere fortnight of marriage, and his forgetfulness. Chrétien merely says 'as the year passed by my lord Yvain had such success that my lord Gawain strove to honour him and caused him to delay so long that the whole year slipped by'. Though this is the hinge on which his plot turns, it perhaps demands no greater suspension of disbelief than the marvels which precede and follow it.

Yvain remains a highly moral work. Punishment is meted out for Yvain's forgetfulness, and Laudine's determination not to forgive him is only softened by Yvain's great deeds in his disguise as the Knight of the Lion; he has to earn forgiveness through the quality of his knighthood. Chrétien's message is that knighthood practised aright brings its own salvation with it. The cycle of sin and redemption is closed within an earthly limit.

Perceval or *Le conte del Graal* takes us beyond the secular boundaries of chivalry to which Chrétien has so far kept, where the supernatural is mysterious but amoral. The old scenery remains, and with it the magical adventures, still separate from divine retribution; but the ultimate goal has changed. Chrétien did not complete the story, his longest and most ambitious undertaking; and the riddles he left unanswered, notably that of his concept of the Grail itself, have perplexed scholars for several generations. We can only assume that Perceval was to achieve the Grail quest and his spiritual journey in the finished version, but we cannot be certain.

Beneath the perhaps deliberate obscurities of the adventures, Chrétien found a new direction. *Perceval* is the moral tale of a knight's education, both worldly and spiritual. The hero does not begin as an accomplished warrior but as a raw simpleton, who has to be taught everything about the world of chivalry. In the process Chrétien's view of the real functions of knighthood emerge, as Perceval comes first to maturity in physical skills, and then grows to his full moral and spiritual stature. Yvain and Erec never progressed beyond secular experience, but here Chrétien treats both the physical and moral qualities of knighthood as though they could only find fulfilment in the spiritual end. Charity and faith supersede the thirst for glory, prowess and love as the ultimate goal.

Religious and secular chivalry are not exclusive in *Perceval*. Prowess and loyalty are cardinal virtues: maidens still insist on their lovers proving themselves, and oaths once pledged, however fantastic or impossible, are still kept at all costs. Indeed Chrétien's attention is divided between Perceval and his secular foil, Gawain, who plays the same part as in *Yvain*, the most peerless of knights in all things earthly, polished, courteous, fearless of danger. Perceval has these virtues too; and there is no insistence on his chastity, such as we shall meet in later poets. From the very first, however, he has a religious aura, which is totally foreign to Gawain: Gornemans knights him thus: 'Next the worthy man took the sword, girt it on him and kissed him, saying him that he had conferred on him with this sword the highest order created and ordained by God, namely the order of chivalry, which must be free of all baseness.'[6]

His mother's advice is largely religious in tone: succour the weak and helpless, and always turn aside to pray and hear mass. Such advice as she does give him on courtly ways he later misinterprets completely. Gornemans likewise tells him to avoid killing other knights, and to succour the helpless. Again, Perceval misinterprets Gornemans' worldly advice, which is simply not to talk too much. His uncle the hermit, much later in the story, repeats their religious advice, and adds the virtue of humility. This is a far cry from the hectic search for fame and hatred of idleness because it damages a knight's reputation which provides the crux of the matter in *Yvain* and *Erec*, and further still from Lancelot's adoration of Guinevere.

Chrétien is the poet of the moment when knighthood becomes chivalry: his work prefigures much of the later world of chivalry. Knight-errantry first appears in his work; heraldry and tournaments also make their literary début here. He is writing for a new audience of enthusiasts, the 'young king' (Henry II's eldest son), Richard Coeur de Lion, William Marshal, Philip of Flanders and the landless younger sons who formed their entourage, the so-called '*iuvenes*' or young men. The world he creates for them is the backbone of all the later mediaeval versions of the Arthurian romances, and for many stories in which Arthur is a mere figurehead or absent altogether. The court of

6   Tr. D. D. R. Owen, 396.

these tales became the paradise of which all secular knights dreamed, and the themes the birthright of every storyteller. So his influence on the ideal of knighthood was immense, both directly and indirectly. The very concept of knight-errantry is almost Chrétien's own; the events that in the Celtic romances merely happened to the heroes are now something to be sought after. Knighthood implies activity, activity to win one's beloved, activity to make a reputation and maintain it. For Chrétien, the greatest sin is idleness. His heroes are all too ready to fight the first comer, without inquiring who it may be, but on a higher level, we have seen how idleness and the fear of loss of fame is the hinge on which both *Erec* and *Yvain* turn.

In the unreal world of these romances, this diligent search for glory seems the only obligation a knight has to recognise beyond his lady's commandments. The attempts in *Perceval* to make a moral code out of knightly ideals are prophetic, but at odds with the rest of the story; the knights and the adventures still predominate, not the hermits and the sermons as in some later versions. (Knowing what the story of Parzival became in other hands, it is almost impossible not to read into Chrétien's story religious details which were never intended: one feels that Chrétien may only have realised the religious possibilities as he worked on the story.) Otherwise, knights have little duty to the everyday world; damsels in distress may profit from their assistance, but none of the duller chores of real life intrude. Chrétien's knights have forgotten their feudal duties, and have no truck with the holding of land. Before we dismiss them as pure escapist fantasy, however, there is one point to be considered. His heroes are always young, by implication not yet required for responsible duties. Knighthood may become the burden of lordship in later years, but for Chrétien's heroes its essence is this very youth and freedom. It does not reject responsibility, but is rather something to be enjoyed before responsibility becomes unavoidable.

Thus knighthood begins, by the end of the twelfth century, to become something apart from the social and feudal status we have already studied. It is this distinction that defines chivalry: the ideals of the knightly class pursued for their own sake. We shall hear little more of the feudal duties of a knight; henceforth chivalry is a prelude to or distraction from those burdens. So the escapism of the romances is paralleled in real life, and fantasy is increasingly chivalry's keynote. The romances themselves become more and more elaborate with Chrétien's successors, even though the flights of fancy which Chrétien took over from his Celtic predecessors die away into more prosaic sequences of jousts and tournaments.

The closest heirs of Chrétien were the German poets of the late twelfth and early thirteenth century. Chrétien's work was not the first to find its way across the Rhine from France: there were already versions of the Tristan story and of the Trojan legends taken from the French, and we have seen how troubadour and *trouvère* poetry won followers among German poets. Hartmann von Aue's adaptation of Chrétien's *Erec* is the first German romance of chivalry to survive. Hartmann came from the borders of southern Germany and Switzerland, and probably wrote his *Erek* in the last decade of the twelfth century, some thirty years after Chrétien. He prefers the splendours of knighthood's estate to Chrétien's poetic economy, and expands the text with long descriptions of the marvels of his hero's equipment or the luxuries of a great feast. The result is in a curious way simpler; the subtleties of Chrétien's psychology disappear under the elaborate trappings, and are replaced by an insistence on the high nature of knighthood itself. He is more interested in the knight's place in society, and the ethical values this implies, than in the analysis of character and emotion. He followed this some years later with a version of *Yvain* (*Iwein*) in which the same traits appear, though the details are less lavish and more acutely observed. The technical skill at his command was of a very high order; and this was to prove fatal to later imitators, who, dazzled by the outer brilliance, failed to perceive the central unity of his tales.[7]

Between the two translations, Hartmann produced works of his own, including the *Klage*, a lesson in love addressed to a young man who has just fallen in love for the first time, and a group of crusading songs. Hartmann spans a wider range of chivalric topics than his French counterparts, and indeed it is *Der arme Heinrich*, the story of which comes from a Latin moral tale for use in sermons, which is perhaps his masterpiece. It tells of a knight who has all the chivalric and Christian qualities save that of spiritual humility. His forgetfulness of God is punished by a terrible leprosy, which, he is told, can only be cured by the blood of a pure maiden willingly sacrificed for him. When he at last finds his paragon, the miracle is accomplished without her death; he marries her, although she is a poor man's daughter, and is restored to his former estate. He has learnt his lesson, and Hartmann allows his hero to return to his old ways and to a life of chivalry, although he remains conscious of the favour God has shown him. This is one of the rare examples where a moral tale is told, not against the knight's scale of values as a whole, but as an example of one particular sin. The clergy were apt to condemn the whole panoply of secular knighthood as vainglorious, and to see it as an entirely unrewarding occupation, preaching a powerful contempt of the world instead. Hartmann counters this with the idea of *mâze*, moderation, familiar to us as the *mezura* of the troubadours, and shows that it is only the abuse of knighthood, or its pursuit at the expense of one's devotions that really contravenes the Church laws, a point not often enough made by its champions, who preferred to regard their world as beyond the sphere of the Church.

The reconciliation of divine and knightly ideals was an exercise at which the German writers were adept. The greatest of the German romancers, Wolfram von Eschenbach,

---

7   On Hartmann, see W.H.Jackson, *Chivalry in Twelfth-Century Germany: the Works of Hartmann von Aue* (Woodbridge & Rochester, N. Y., 1994).

combines the highest philosophical themes and adventures in the manner of Chrétien with consummate skill in his *Parzival*,[8] written in the first decade of the thirteenth century. Chivalry becomes an ideal within which all man's highest aspirations are fulfilled, crowned by its own religious order, the knights of the Grail, and yet remains a real and actual experience.

Wolfram was a Bavarian knight, who came from the village now known as Wolframseschenbach. His family were *ministeriales,* knights in imperial service who remained officially of unfree status. Of his life we know only what he himself tells us: that he was poor – 'at home the mice rarely have enough to eat' – that he had various misfortunes in love (though he implies that he was happily married), that he was widely travelled in Germany. He came at some point in his journeyings to the court of Hermann of Thuringia, where Veldeke and Walther von der Vogelweide had also been honoured guests. His view of courtly life is not entirely approving; he has some sharp words for the disorderliness of Hermann's halls, where every insolent fellow who pretended to sing or make verses gained easy entrance. Addressing the Landgrave, he says 'you could have done with a Keie [King Arthur's uncompromising seneschal] seeing that your true generosity has brought you so mixed a following, here a vile rabble, there a noble throng.'[9] And in another passage he attacks the morals that all too often lay behind the outward show of courtly love, saying that he would not care to take his wife to King Arthur's court, where everyone's thoughts were always occupied with love. 'Someone or other would have whispered to her that her charms were stabbing him and blotting out his joy, and that if she would end his pangs, he would serve her before and after. Rather than that I would hurry away with her.'[10] Wolfram's wry humour marks him as a man with a down-to-earth view of life, at first blush an unlikely guide to exotic adventures and spiritual quests.

Chrétien's *Perceval* was left incomplete; what he did complete shows him exploring new dimensions; what begins as the moral education of the hero moves into uncharted territory. Wolfram claims to have used Chrétien's source, the work of a mysterious poet called Kyot, but this is almost certainly a disguise for his own inventions. He adds a prelude, giving the history of Parzival's father Gahmuret and and tells of Parzival's son Loherangrin at the story's end: crucially, he provides the conclusion of Parzival's quest for the Grail, just as Chrétien's French continuators had done, but in a wholly individual way.

The theme which Wolfram makes central to the story, Parzival's courtly and spiritual progress, is implicit but only partly explored in Chrétien. The old folk-tale

8   Wolfram von Eschenbach, *Parzival,* tr. A.T.Hatto (Harmondsworth 1980).

9   *Ibid.,* 155.

10   *Ibid.,* 116.

of the prince brought up in ignorance, the 'pure fool' of noble birth, began as merely another inherited *motif* from the Celtic past with which to embellish a new romance. Wolfram turns this into a deeply felt heroic example, yet does not preach or point a moral. Indeed, his portrait of Parzival's innocence is delightful and natural. The boy, kept from the ways of knighthood that have caused his father's death, is brought up by his mother in the depths of the forest, ignorant of the glittering world that is his birthright, ignorant even of the simplest ideas about life: he has learnt who God is, and that 'His love helps all who live on earth'. When he meets a knight who has fled into the deep forest to escape his pursuers, he can only imagine that this superior being is God: and although he is naturally disillusioned, his natural instinct for knighthood has been aroused.

Wolfram makes great play with the idea of an inherited nobility: Parzival's nature predisposes him to knighthood. From his father's family he inherits love as his destiny: from his mother's, the service of the Grail. This idea of a place in life at once fore-ordained and inherited is at the root of Wolfram's idea of society, which he conceives as a series of orders, of which knighthood is the chief. Man should not question his appointed lot, even if it be a less honourable one than knighthood.

So Parzival sets out: dressed in fool's clothing, and with the briefest of advice from his mother. She hopes that his attire will draw mockery and send him back to her; and he has misunderstood her advice. This provides the matter of his first adventures, and the wrongs he unwittingly inflicts will have to be atoned for later, including the killing of Ither, a knight who had done him little harm, but whose splendid armour he covets. It is not until he reaches the castle of Gurnemanz that he finds a mentor who is prepared to educate him in matters of chivalry. His fool's attire, which he still wears beneath the real armour, is taken from him, and with it his foolish ways. Gurnemanz instructs him in courtesy and, more important, in the ethics behind courtesy. 'Never lose your sense of shame', is his first precept, and the second to show compassion to those who suffer. Parzival remembers, but does not understand: he has learnt the outward forms but not the inner meaning.

His second series of exploits starts auspiciously. He wins the heart of Condwiramurs, and marries her. The contrast with Chrétien is sharp. Perceval and Blancheflor are deeply in love but their ties are only casual. Here Parzival and Condwiramurs are bound by the ideal love to which – in Wolfram's view – *Minne* aspires, the conjugal love of marriage and passionate physical love. When Condwiramurs comes to Parzival's room at dead of night to pour out her troubles to him, they do not even kiss; and when they marry, their love is so ethereal, 'they so shared togetherness', that Parzival does not think of making love to her for three nights after the wedding. The strength and joy of their earthly love shines clearly through the lovely scene when Parzival, now at the end of his adventures, comes to meet his wife at the edge of the lands of Munsalvaesche, the Grail castle, in the grey light of dawn, and finds her asleep with their twin sons. The seneschal wakes the queen; clad in only her shift and a sheet hastily flung round her, with one impetuous movement she is in Parzival's arms. Parzival embraces her; the children wake, and he stoops to kiss them too. The old seneschal and the attendant ladies discreetly retire with the children, and leave the pair alone to prolong the night until the sun stands high in the heavens.[11]

In this ideal marriage Parzival fulfils one half of his nature, the steadfastness in love inherited from his father. Most heroines of the romances are only truly won at the end of the tale: even Erec and Enide, Yvain and Laudine do not find the fullness of joy until their adventures are over. To Parzival, Condwiramurs is both the lady of his love-service and his sustaining hope in his adventures. At one moment. like Chrétien's hero, we find him sunk in ecstasy over three drops of blood on the snow, which remind him of his beloved. If we remember that she is also his wife, the difference between Chrétien and Wolfram is evident. The idea for this relationship may well be evolved from Chrétien's married heroes; yet what distinguishes it is Wolfram's complete acceptance of the situation. Chrétien cannot quite believe that knighthood and marriage are compatible; for Wolfram they are the most natural companions in the world. Even Gawain, whose adventures occupy about half the romance, and whose deeds and character are much closer to his French counterpart, ends by marrying the proud Orgeluse. Orgeluse is in the French romance an irrational, scornful figure; and it would seem difficult even for Wolfram to make her a convincing character. Yet she becomes entirely human in his hands; her pride and scorn are partly the result of the loss of her lover, partly a test by which she will find the hero who can revenge her on her lover's killer.

Parzival's other inheritance takes us into the moral and religious spheres only implicit (and that perhaps with hindsight, knowing what other writers made of it) in Chrétien's unfinished poem. A little time after their marriage, Parzival asks Condwiramurs to let him go in search of his mother; 'loving him truly, she could not disagree', and he sets out on a quest which, though he does not know it, is to lead not to his mother, but to his fulfilment of his part as guardian of the Grail. (Wolfram's idea of the Grail is a curious one: a stone of strange powers that fell from heaven during the struggle between Lucifer and the Angels. It has no particular associations as a relic, but its quality is such that it attracts all that is highest and best in men.[12]) It is a task

---

11   Tr. Hatto, 397.

12   Wolfram's ideas were religiously daring, not to say heretical; in another passage the hermit Trevrizent implies that the Grail can be won by strength of purpose alone, but later retracts this. He also talks of the 'neutral angels', who sided neither with Lucifer nor God, a highly unorthodox belief.

116

for which he is not yet ready: for though he comes to Munsalvaesche, the Grail castle, he heeds only Gurnemanz's warning that curiosity is rude, and does not ask the crucial question on seeing the Grail borne in procession, and the agony of the Grail-king, Anfortas. Anfortas has broken the laws of the Grail community in pursuing earthly love without permission, and lies wounded between the thighs in punishment, until an unknown knight shall come and ask him: 'Lord, what ails thee?' Parzival may observe the outward forms of courtesy, suppressing his curiosity; but he forgets its inward essence, humility and compassion. He leaves the desolate castle, which had shone with all the show of a splendid feast on the previous night, in a dark and lonely dawn, with only the curses of the gatekeeper to speed him on his way. As if to show that men cannot judge between inward and outward courtesy, Parzival rides on to his greatest triumph yet at Arthur's court, only to have it shattered by the arrival of Cundrie, the hideous messenger from the Grail castle who roundly curses him for his 'falseness', 'falseness' both to his nature and to his destiny.

However, Parzival can only ask the question when he is ready to do so: and his reactions to Cundrie's message show that he is far from such a state of mind or spirit. In the grip of black despair, he curses God for not rewarding his faithful service, and departs in search of the Grail again. He is now even more remote from it, seeking it despite God; the lesson he has to learn is not only compassion and humility, but penitence and the real nature of man's relationship to God. He sees it only in feudal terms as a contract by which man's service earns God's favour. It is not until he comes, after long wanderings, to his uncle, Anfortas' brother, the hermit Trevrizent, that the way begins to clear. In Chrétien's version, Perceval is quickly brought to penitence, and goes on his way with no more than a brief lesson and prescribed penance.

Wolfram makes this scene the crux of his hero's development. The pilgrims who reproach him for bearing arms on Good Friday bring him out of the heedless, timeless mood in which he declares that 'he once served a lord called God, until He chose to scorn and disgrace me'. Though he gives his horse its head that God may lead him to Trevrizent, he still defies and challenges: 'if this is His day for giving help, let Him help, if He is so inclined', and he only admits to his state of mind gradually under Trevrizent's patient questioning. As his story unfolds, so does the seriousness of his offences appear: the killing of Ither, which he had dismissed as something done when 'I was still a fool' proves to be the murder of a kinsman; and his equally thoughtless abandoning of his mother has caused her death from sorrow. Finally, his failure to ask the redeeming question when he was the knight chosen by God to do this has condemned his uncle – for Anfortas proves to be such – to continued years of pain. Parzival now sees that though he has indeed been a valiant and skilful knight, his own sins are so great that he his no claim on God; the way lies not through deeds alone, but also through belief. 'God Himself is loyalty', and cannot be disloyal, which had

117

been the burden of Parzival's complaint against him. The spiritual world cannot be conquered by earthly virtues and services. He departs, chastened; the seeds of penitence and redemption are sown.

When 'the story comes to its rightful theme' again, Parzival and Gawan fight a duel as strangers, in which Parzival is victor, though he recognises Gawan before they have done each other serious injury, a commonplace of the romances. A similar combat ensues with Parzival's half-brother Feirefiz, in which the combatants are equally matched; again, they recognise each other in time. In the meanwhile, he has also fought a mutual enemy of his and Gawan's, Gramoflanz. Each of these battles, at this stage in Parzival's spiritual progress, must represent more than another episode in the romance; at first sight they seem to reduce Parzival to Gawan's level, a mere knight-errant again. But in the wider symbolism of the poem, Gawan represents earthly chivalry, and Gramoflanz pride. Earthly chivalry and pride have to be overcome. And Feirefiz, Parzival's pagan half-brother from his father's marriage to the heathen Belakane, is the archetype of natural goodness; despite his strange black-and-white striped skin, he is as courteous as any of the knights of the Round Table, and as virtuous as any Christian. It is Feirefiz who is the one knight chosen by Parzival to go with him on his journey to claim the kingship of the Grail.

For Parzival's trials are now at an end; and on the day of Feirefiz's admission to the Round Table, a day of 'sweet pure clarity', the messenger from the Grail castle returns, to announce that he has been named as King of the Grail, in letters which have appeared on the magical stone itself. He rides to Munsalvaesche; the compassionate question is asked, Anfortas healed. The story moves swiftly to its end, telling how Condwiramurs rejoins Parzival, how Feirefiz is converted and married to the bearer of the Grail, Repanse de Schoye, and how Loherangrin succeeds his father. The two ways are reconciled: earthly and spiritual chivalry move in harmony.

Parzival is at once the greatest and most human figure in the mediaeval romances; in him chivalry is shot through with a warmth and natural ease which owes little to convention. By contrast, Gawan, the secondary hero of the story, is a formal figure, moving within a limited world but perfect within his own established limits. The idea of *orden* , levels of achievement according to each man's power, enables Wolfram to transcend the old ideals of knighthood, and set a higher goal without contradicting these cherished images. For this is his real insight: that chivalry is not merely a matter of rules of good behaviour, of *Minnedienst* or even of religious service. Its strength lies in its appeal to man's better nature while remaining in close contact with the realities of life. The marvellous is only an outward trapping, corresponding to the splendours of court festivals: what matters is the effect of these great ideals on the mind and soul. Chrétien had started to explore the effect of idealism in love on men's minds; in *Parzival*,

Wolfram extends and completes the search, until the way of chivalry becomes the way of Everyman to Salvation.

Wolfram's disrespect for courtly conventions, his inventiveness, sly humour (which recurs even at the most solemn moments) and his obscure and uneven style, won him harsh words from his great contemporary, Gottfried von Strassburg. In the middle of his *Tristan*, he breaks off to discuss his fellow poets, and the only one whom he cannot praise is 'the friend of the hare', as he calls Wolfram: the breadth of Wolfram's ideas, as well as his weakness for strange pieces of secondhand alchemists' lore, earned him that title. Gottfried is singleminded compared with him, and his purpose is quite different: so different as to be almost diametrically opposite.

The story of Tristan and Isolde has come briefly within our purview in its old French version, retaining traces of its original, an unpolished tale of elemental power. From this rough stone, Gottfried carves one of the masterpieces of erotic literature. Wolfram raises chivalry's idealism to its highest peak. Gottfried takes the world of courtly behaviour and infuses it with pure passion. The result is a highly individual and unconventional work, even though it is cast in the form of a romance.

Like *Parzival*, *Tristan* begins with an account of the hero's father and his exploits. But as soon as Tristan himself appears, there is a great gulf fixed between the two tales. Parzival begins as a simpleton, and his story is that of his development towards perfection; Tristan can do no wrong from the moment he is born. Image beyond all words of the perfect courtier and knight, every skill is at his command, no virtue is too taxing. Strong, handsome, gay, he turns his hand to chess, harping, the arts of venery, or war, speaks several languages, is at ease from the moment he sets foot in a strange court.

With such a beginning, we might well expect to find ourselves back in the world of Chrétien, amidst more extravagant fantasies than ever. Instead, the fantasies are kept to a minimum; the descriptions are extraordinarily real, yet nonetheless beautiful for it. The courtly world needs no apology, no excusing ethos: for Gottfried it is normal and natural. Tristan's loyalty to Mark, his duty to his subjects as ruler of Parmenie are part of this world; his adventures until he meets Isolde are purely chivalrous, and of a very simple type. The slaying of Morold, the Irish champion who comes to claim the annual tribute from Cornwall, belongs to the old heroic manner, as does the theme of the poisoned sword whose wounds only the dead man's relatives can heal.

Gottfried uses this perfect, self-contained world only as a starting point. As with Wolfram, there are higher ends in view. Wolfram looks to a perfection to be gained by striving and effort, and spiritual pilgrimage; Gottfried's higher world is very different. Tristan and Isolde are already perfect. It is this that qualifies them for the transcending experience. The mysticism of love is his theme, and he speaks only to those 'noble hearts' who can understand his message.

The crux of the story, the famous scene where Tristan and Isolde drink the love-potion, thinking it is common wine, has been given many different meanings. Gottfried uses the idea skilfully. He leaves us uncertain whether the drink merely confirms a love already begun, or is in itself the *coup de foudre* . For his own purposes he is well enough content to let it be regarded as a supernatural force; by this excuse he can tell his story of open adultery, treachery and broken oaths as a special case, and invoke magic as the cause of each transgression. On the other hand, the 'noble hearts' who understood his true meaning could see the potion merely as surrogate of love's power, a symbol of its workings.

Tristan and Isolde's love puts their relationship above the everyday ways of the world. They are no longer subject to the ordinary laws of men, and can only be judged in terms of their fidelity to each other and to love's ideals. The conflict and tension that arises between the two worlds, their unresolved discontent, shows that this is not an intensified version of the love described by the troubadours, but a more disturbing force. Passion is the word we have now come to use for this force, and it is a commonplace of our view of love. But to Gottfried's contemporaries, despite Chrétien's tentative descriptions of the symptoms, this was novelty indeed.

Tristan and Isolde are equal in love. There is no question of knight serving lady; instead, they are both servants of *Frau Minne*, Lady Love. Caution becomes impossible, compromise unthinkable once her mystic joys have been tasted. Love becomes the fountain of all goodness, and even provides them with physical sustenance. The climax of the poem is the episode in which the lovers, banished by Mark, take refuge in the 'fossiure à la gent amant', the Cave of Lovers. In this symbolically perfect retreat, whose every feature corresponds to one of Love's qualities:

> Their high feast was Love, who gilded all their joys; she brought them King Arthur's Round Table as homage and all its company a thousand times a day! What better food could they have for body or soul? Man was there with woman, Woman there with Man. What else should they be needing? They had what they were meant to have, they had reached the goal of their desire.[13]

But if love is a higher ideal than those of the courtly world in which the lovers move it affords them no protection. Its joys are balanced by its sorrows; and its sorrows stem from the lovers, concern for their reputation. When Mark discovers them lying with a naked sword between them and is persuaded of their innocence, they return to court 'for the sake of God and their place in society'. Mark represents the opposite side of love: lust and appetite aroused by Isolde's beauty. As such he cannot find peace either;

13   Tr. Hatto, 263.

a pitiful figure, he wavers between the unpalatable truth and the comfort of illusion. Despite its outward gaiety, the court of Cornwall which he rules is similarly tainted; suspicion is everywhere, misunderstanding and distrust abound. Only Brangane and Kurvenal remain loyal; and even their steadfastness is tested. Isolde, fearing lest Brangane should reveal their secrets, tries to have her killed, but repents as soon as she fears that the deed is really done. For loyalty exists only between the lovers themselves; all external claims are brushed aside, and there is left

> *A man, a woman; a woman, a man:*
> *Tristan, Isolde; Isolde, Tristan.* [14]

Their true world is an enclosed, charmed garden, the garden of the Cave of Lovers; in the everyday world, however splendid and gay, they move guiltily, forced to deny their desires, and the air grows thick with sorrow and evil.

Gottfried did not complete his poem; whether by design or accident, we cannot tell for certain. It ends with Tristan's thoughts as he is torn between the idea of marrying Isolde of the White Hands, whose love he has won during his self-imposed exile from Cornwall; and it seems likely that Gottfried was similarly torn between faithfully following the story as given in his original and the loyalty in love which had become both his main theme and the excuse for his hero and heroine's misdeeds. That this ideal meant a great deal to him is plain enough, and there are veiled references to personal experiences of such a love throughout the poem. Yet, even as a guiding light for those 'noble hearts' to whom he addresses himself, it is an uncertain star. Gottfried makes sensual love sublime by his artistry; it is the one way in which the great tale he tells comes to life, but the philosophy is incomplete and less subtle than that of the troubadours and Minnesingers. Indeed, it is scarcely a philosophy at all, though Gottfried would like us to think it was; it is a mysticism without a goal, the exaltation of emotion to the level of the divine through the element of suffering that emotion arouses. What he does tell us a great deal about is the psychology of love, how lovers behave and how their minds work; and his audience of 'noble hearts' are lovers who seek to find distraction for their own sorrows and perhaps a reflection of their own dilemmas.

In this lies the sharp distinction between Gottfried and Wolfram. Gottfried is a superb poet, a master of style whose cadences ring true, describing the deepest secrets of the emotions in a story well suited to his ends; Wolfram is less technically accomplished, but has a far broader view of life, which he expresses amidst the unlikely paraphernalia of a knightly romance. Both, however, have risen too far beyond the conventions of the world about which they were writing for their successors to do

---

14   Tr. Hatto 43.

more than admire their lofty concepts and to produce imitations of the outward forms from which the inner spirit is lacking. Wolfram and Gottfried represent, together with the greatest of the Minnesingers, a *ne plus ultra*. All that was left for later writers in the genre to do was to compile immense fantasies, drawing on the inherited stock-in-trade of endless combats, strange adventures, mysterious beautiful damsels, prolonged quests that never seem to reach an end. The romances reverted to type, and as Caxton says 'for to passe the tyme, thys book shal be pleasaunte to rede in, but for to gyve fayth and byleve that al is trewe that is conteyned herin, ye be at your lyberté'.

The main stream of chivalric romance in the thirteenth century is the vast assemblage of Arthurian stories in French called by modern scholars the Vulgate Cycle.[15] Drawing on all the main themes of Arthurian literature, it presents a vast panorama of every element in the romance literature of the period. The huge scheme of the work, from the bringing of the Grail to Britain to the death of Arthur, is an extended set of variations on the themes provided by Geoffrey of Monmouth in his *History of the Kings of Britain* and Chrétien, with borrowings from Celtic and Christian legend, and numerous inventions by the many lands who contributed to it. With the *Prose Tristan*, it contains almost all the memorable Arthurian stories. The Vulgate Cycle itself was complete by about 1230, and the major variations on it do not continue much beyond the middle of the thirteenth century. So the main body of the romantic tradition of chivalry remained fixed for the next 250 years. Only the details changed in the numerous translations into practically every European language; the stories of Arthur and his court were common ground for Spanish, Italian, Portuguese, French, German and English knights, and there are even pieces in Hebrew, Greek, Latin and Norse.

The great Arthurian heroes are the literary archetypes of the mediaeval knight. Again and again, whether in songs and tournaments, their names recur; and their parts in the history of Logres, Arthur's realm, reflect the development of the ideals to which all knights looked. Arthur himself, originally a warrior hero, never becomes a real knight-errant (except in the fantastic fourteenth-century romance of the *Chevalier du Papegau*, where a talking parrot leads him on his adventures). He is the fount of all honour, his court the magnet to which all knights are drawn. He is in many ways the knight's ideal monarch: generous, eager for the renown of his knights, concerned that there shall be adventures for them to undertake. Only in the opening and closing sections, where deep emotions and high affairs of state predominate, does he become a clear cut figure: and Arthur himself belongs to the great tragic heroes rather than to the world of chivalry. When we reach *La mort le Roi Artu*,[16] the last of the five sections

---

15 *Lancelot-Graal: The Old French Arthurian Vulgate and Post-Vulgate in Translation*, ed. Norris J. Lacy (New York & London 1993 –) will provide a complete modern English version.

of the Vulgate Cycle, chivalry is only the backdrop; even if Lancelot and Guinevere are lovers in the courtly tradition, the drama derives from the division of loyalties and the inexorable workings of fate.

Gawain, one of Arthur's earliest companions, likewise fails to shake off his pre-chivalric characteristics. In the first romances he figures not unflatteringly, and indeed is almost the co-hero of Chrétien's *Perceval.* But as the moral tone of the romances becomes more and more high-minded, Gawain's unremorseful wenching and killing comes in for increasing disapproval. In the Vulgate Cycle *Queste del Saint Graal* he is the exemplar of the folly of worldly glory without God; and in *La mort le Roi Artu* it is his stubborn pride that drives the tragedy on to its last agonies, through his refusal to forgive Lancelot for his accidental killing of Agravain and Gaheriet in rescuing Guinevere from the stake. The simple warrior seemed uncouth in the light of the newer, more polished ideals: and his casual amours were equally censured. Under pressure from those who saw chivalry as a potential religious ideal, secular knighthood had to clear itself of its worst faults, or stand condemned like Gawain.

Lancelot, on the other hand, who had never been anything other than a courtly lover and knight-errant, survived the contest with the religious standards in a better light. He was no longer the unvanquished hero, the model of perfection; but his standing was such that the main body of the Vulgate Cycle is still known as the *Prose Lancelot,* and many versions of the whole story bear his name. His romance with Guinevere is transmuted into a more passionate than courtly love. Where once his love for her had merely been a duty appropriate to his standing – the best knight of the court could only have the queen as his lady – here he loves her 'from the first day he was made knight' and receives his sword from her at his knighting. Though the element of service remains, Guinevere is no cool remote commander of his affections, but a warm and human partner, jealous to the point of despair when she seems to sense a rival in the maid of Escalot.

So long as the story moves on a secular plane, he remains the perfect knight, faithful to his lady and all-conquering in joust and tournament. Before he departs for Arthur's court, the Lady of the Lake outlines the qualities of the perfect knight to him, one of the few moments when theory replaces example. She begins by explaining why knighthood was instituted: how all men had been equal, but as envy and greed increased, knights were appointed to defend the weak against the strong, and how 'the tallest, strongest, fairest and most nimble, the most loyal and the bravest, those full of goodness of heart and body', were chosen for this office. A knight should be 'merciful without being uncouth, affable without being treacherous, kind towards the suffering, and

16   *The Death of Arthur,* tr. James Cable (Harmondsworth 1971).

generous. He must be ready to succour the needy and to confound robbers and murderers, a just judge without favour or hate.' He must prefer death to shame. Chivalry was also instituted to defend the Church, the Lady of the Lake goes on, and she explains the allegory, familiar from religious writers, of how the knight's armour symbolises his duties and position.[17]

Unfortunately the high moral tone and complete absence of any mention of the service of fair ladies make the religious origin of this passage all too clear; the knightly virtues of secular romance remain undefined. Lancelot, though he possesses most of the virtues listed above, plays a very different part. Once the religious marvels of the Grail appear he becomes a sinner who loves his lady and his reputation too well, and God too little. Whereas Gawain is almost past redemption, a great deal of time and many sermons are devoted to Lancelot's salvation. He is the only knight, apart from the three elect, to approach the Grail, though the consequences are dire; and he does achieve repentance at the end of the quest. It only lasts so long as he and Guinevere are separated. They fall into their old sin as soon as they meet again, with Bors, one of the three knights of the Grail, condoning them. He fails to see that he cannot reconcile the worldly ideal natural to him with the alien mystical ideal he has learnt in the Grail quest. However, he remains great-hearted, forgiving and generous to the end, and his fate in the closing scenes sums up the temptations and virtues of secular knighthood, his good qualities being balanced by his sensuality and pride.

The new ideal of spiritual knighthood is represented by Bors, Perceval and Galahad, who achieve the quest of the Grail. Bors and Galahad are unknown in early versions of the Grail story: Perceval's character and traditional adventures were too worldly for the author of the *Queste del Saint Graal,* and he is replaced as the protagonist by Galahad, the pure knight who also has something of the Messiah about him. He is a superhuman figure moving in an aura of mystical certainty towards his appointed goal, almost an incarnation of our Lord as knight-errant. And it says much for the author of the romance that he is nonetheless a clearly defined character. Perceval, in his traditional role as a naive innocent, represents redemption by faith: his purity shines through his foolish incomprehension. Bors, likewise, represents a type of the Christian knight: he earns his redemption by good works in expiation of his one casual sin. But because none of them play an important part in the stories outside the *Queste del Saint Graal,* being solitaries rather than brothers-in-arms and preferring dialogues with hermits to the glittering companies that belong to knighthood's very essence, they remain in the last analysis lay figures, symbolic characters from another world.

---

17   H. Oskar Sommer, *The Vulgate Version of the Arthurian Romances, edited from manuscripts in the British Museum* (Washington 1908-16) III, 133-6.

The *Queste del Saint Graal* stands alone in the romances as a deliberate attempt to bend the power of chivalry to new ends, the Church's ends. It is probably the work of a Cistercian monk, but a monk well acquainted with the matter of romance. Robert de Boron, whose less coherent version of the story was probably used by the writer of the *Queste*, had made of Chrétien de Troyes' mysterious Grail a Christian symbol; but the adventures attached to it remained pure adventures in the other world of romance. The atmosphere of Arthur's court within this other world, a centre of light continually threatened by the surrounding darkness and its marvels, corresponds to the knight's own conception of his place in life; but it also corresponds to the Christian life in this world as mediaeval churchmen saw it. In the *Queste* the two ideals are brought together. Knowing the connection between the Cistercians and the military order of Calatrava, it seems surprising that the result is not some new military order of the Grail, a spiritual counterweight to the order of the Round Table. But the romances themselves as already established could not be easily reshaped to such an end. So a new vision of chivalry, where secular knighthood became the highest inspiration of the lay world, emerged.

At much the same time as the *Queste del Saint Graal* was written, perhaps a decade or so earlier, another writer had realised the power and spiritual wealth of meaning in the story of Perceval, and had written the romance called *Perlesvaus* .[18] It is a strange work, at odds with much of the 'accepted' story of Arthur in its plot, and showing a markedly individual idea of the role of Christianity in a knight's life. The Old Law of the Old Testament is set against the New Law of the New Testament, as sharply as heathen and Christian are distinguished. The romance opens at Arthur's deserted court: Arthur, forgetful of the New Law, has lost all desire to honour knighthood and encourage great deeds. Only the renewal of his faith and the achievement of the Grail can remedy matters. Perlesvaus' (Perceval's) failure to ask the vital question at the castle of the Fisher King has already taken place, and it is this that has caused the decline of Arthur's court and kingdom. The New Law, which Arthur is to reintroduce and spread,is far from being the gentle teaching of Christ as opposed to Jehovah's tribal anger; it is to be imposed by force of arms. As in *Parzival*, the climax of the romance is Perlesvaus' reception at a castle with rich hangings worked with images of Christ, and occupied by two Masters and a company of thirty clad in white robes with a red cross on their breasts, which might well be an idealised version of a castle of one of the military orders. Perceval is destined to be king, not of that castle, but of one nearby, as though the Masters were sovereign rulers themselves. Both the militarism and earthly splendours of the leaders of the New Law echo the ideals of the crusaders and of the military orders; there is also a strong element of Mariolatry which coincides with

---

18   *The High Book of the Grail* tr. Nigel Bryant (Cambridge & Totowa, N. J. , 1978).

knightly attitudes. *Perlesvaus* is an unjustly neglected work, and possibly a very important one in the history of chivalry, but needs more attention from scholars before it can be really understood.

Later works on the Grail shrink back from the positive religious attitude of both the *Queste* and the *Perlesvaus*. The *Queste del Saint Graal* would not have achieved its standing as the accepted history of the Grail if it had not formed a part, though at odds in spirit, of the Vulgate Cycle as a whole. In the first of the many variations and compilations that followed, the *Roman du Graal*, the conflict of mood within the cycle as a whole is partially resolved by making Arthur a more central figure and linking the Grail with the fate of Arthur's kingdom by means of the story of the Dolorous Blow. The Grail and the Holy Lance, with which Balain strikes King Pellean and thus lays waste his kingdom, have returned to the world of marvels – or rather miracles, for they are still firmly Christian. The deeper allegory and argument are fading, however; the new knighthood has found no answering chord in reality. The process of attrition continues down to Malory; both the Grail knights and the Grail itself diminish in importance.

Another of the great Arthurian tales, that of Tristan and Iseult, suffered similar changes at the hands of thirteenth-century writers. The *courtois* ideal may never have been positively proclaimed in the romances as the one true mirror of life, but courtesy is nonetheless the accepted cornerstone of chivalric behaviour. It was Lancelot and Guinevere's romance that was the stumbling-block for the Grail ideal, and it was their courtly prowess which later writers re-emphasised. The same originally *courtois* ideas became grafted on to the legends of Cornwall, which, as we have already shown, were alien to the idea of courtesy in their passionate intensity; these stories lacked the *mezura* of the troubadours, and burned all the brighter for it.

The *Prose Tristan* [19] has as its central thread the original story, but the characters and relationships are almost unrecognisable. Tristan is now the central figure, Iseult becoming his lady rather than his soul-mate and partner in hardship. The old tension between feudal and amorous loyalties disappears. Mark is an evil and treacherous king, with scarcely a spark of humanity to redeem him; it is he who kills Tristan as he sits harping at Iseult's feet with a cowardly blow from behind. The story of the lovers is related entirely in the manner of knight-errantry. Tristan's growing fame and eventual place among the greatest knights of the Round Table become as important to the plot as his love for Iseult. Once again, the active ideal predominates over the passive and passionate basis of the story.

19   *The Prose Tristan*, tr.Renée Curtis (Oxford 1995).

One figure in the *Prose Tristan* stands out as something new. Dinadan is Tristan's companion-in-arms; and as such we might expect him to be a minor hero in his own right. Far from it; he is a cheerful but keen critic of the whole business of knight-errantry. On meeting an armed knight who greets him in the conventional way of the romances: 'Sir Knight, you must joust with me,' Dinadan replies, 'Sir Knight, as you hope that God will send you good adventures, don't you know any other way of greeting a knight-errant than "you must joust with me"? It is not very polite, and besides, how do you know I want to joust with you?' 'I don't know,' says the other, 'but I still say you must joust with me.' 'Out of friendship or out of hatred, then?' 'I don't hate you, of course; all I want is a friendly joust to pass the time.' 'Then I don't think much of your friendship or your pastimes; take your friendship elsewhere, for I'd rather be your enemy.'[20] Eventually the baffled knight agrees to leave Dinadan in peace; and the latter congratulates himself on having talked his way out of trouble yet again. The contrast between the singleminded, lumbering anonymous knight and Dinadan's quick-witted practical view of the matter is nicely done. On another occasion, he remarks to Agravain, just defeated and deprived of his horse by a mutual enemy whom Dinadan has avoided, 'My cowardice keeps me alive, and your boldness is the reason why you're on foot now', and to Agravain's angry exclamation he answers: 'I am a knight-errant who sets out each day in search of adventures and the sense of this world; but I can find neither.' 'Let cowards be cowards and leave prowess to the bold' is his motto; and in love he is careful to take his pleasure where he can and never lose his heart to a girl.

Despite all this, his sallies are greeted with enthusiasm by his knightly audiences; Guinevere laughs at his wry attacks on love, Tristan at his barbed remarks about knight-errants. He is still part of the chivalric world, not a new breath of critical realism from elsewhere. His part is that of a jester; when the unpalatable truth must be faced he disarms it by laughter. The attacks he makes are not meant as attacks on the ideals of knighthood; he accepts that prowess is for the bold, and never suggests that the expert knight-errants would be better employed in other fields. His humour is at his own expense; he is making fun of his own shortcomings as knight and lover.

The relationship between knight and lady is the most apparently important of the knightly ideals presented in the romances. The adventures undertaken by the members of the Round Table arise entirely from their desire for renown; and this renown is only valued when it increases their standing in their ladies' eyes. Guinevere may reproach herself for having robbed Lancelot of his honour since his passionate love for her prevents him from achieving the adventure of the Grail, but his answer

---

20   Eugène Vinaver, *Etudes sur le 'Tristan' en prose* (Paris 1925) 98 ff.

reassures her: 'I would never have risen to such heights without you, because my knighthood alone would never have led me to begin or undertake affairs which others had abandoned as beyond their power; but my devotion to you, and the thought of your great beauty has made my heart proud, and I cannot find any adventure I cannot accomplish.'

The lady remains at the centre of the chivalric world, but it is interesting that most of the lesser heroes have no specific lady to whom they are attached. They are very ready to succour damsels in distress, but just as prepared to sleep with their host's daughter if she is willing. Lancelot's fidelity to Guinevere is the exception, not the rule. It is a high ideal, and fully worthy of its place, at the summit of chivalric love stories. Lancelot's words towards the end of his career are an echo of his first admission of love to Guinevere: he tells her how he has loved her from the day he first saw her, and that all his deeds so far have been for her sake. 'When I took leave of my lord the King, fully armed save for my helmet, I commended you to God and said that I would be your knight and friend wherever I was; and you answered that you wished me to be your knight and your friend. And I bade you adieu, my lady; and you said "Adieu, fair sweet friend".'[21] These four words had been his comfort and safeguard in all his adventures. Other knights may serve their chosen ladies well, but without the qualms that beset Lancelot when the maid of Escalot offers her love; and although service is much spoken of, the examples are few and far between; indeed, only Galehaut's love for the lady of Malehaut offers a parallel.

Thus secular chivalry devolves into a code of conduct and a purely self-engendered search for 'adventure'. (One curiosity is the sanctity of a knight's oath, however fantastic or unreasonable. But this 'ideal' of a perfect faith is often only a device to further the plot, as the numerous episodes which arise from such undertakings show.) In the world of marvels which lies outside the gates of Arthur's court, the knights are the dispensers of justice in an evil and hostile world; and they themselves are a compact group, 150 in all, of whom the chief heroes come from two families, of Ban (Lancelot, Hector, Bors and Galahad) and Utherpendragon (Arthur, Gawain and his brothers, Mordred). It is a narrow circle, self-consciously aristocratic; and it reflects the vision of the knightly class of themselves as self-appointed leaders. Arthur, inactive himself but attracting a brilliant circle to his court by his generosity and care for his knights, when necessary a brilliant leader in war, is again the real knight's ideal king. 'Adventure' is another strand in the tissue of wish-fulfilment; but it must bear some resemblance to everyday life, which perhaps explains the increasing number of tournaments in later romances, and the tendency to play down the purely miraculous elements. Furthermore,

---

21   Sommer, *Vulgate Version*, III, 261.

'adventure' is a justification of the knight-errant's existence; for almost all the episodes end with some good deed being achieved – an evil custom abolished, a knight or damsel rescued, a giant slain.

But these ideals belong only to the *Lancelot* proper. *La mort le Roi Artu* and the *Queste del Saint Graal* have other themes. *La mort le Roi Artu* is furthest from the idea of 'adventure'; it is a return to the tale which originally engendered the whole cycle. It is concerned with blood feuds and the idea of Fate, both of which were part of the knight's world, however chivalrous he might be; chivalry only appears at intervals. Though the writer is more concerned with the action and characters of his drama, in Lancelot's fate we find the weaknesses and virtues of knighthood reflected. Adultery and pride are balanced by a simpler greatheartedness: forgiveness of enemies, generosity, justice. These are the real, observed, qualities that any knight should attain, not a complex code of prowess and honour. It was not for this that the audiences of the Middle Ages prized the tale, but for its play with the idea of Fate, and the eloquent laments for Gawain, Arthur and Lancelot as each in turn goes to his long home.

On a less exalted level, the knight's chief asset is his skill in arms. Lancelot, 'the best knight in the world', derives his position from his expert handling of lance and sword. His victories in jousts and tournaments earn him honour; honour earns him Guinevere's love; and that love spurs him on, for honour's sake, to seek fresh victories. His magical qualities as 'best knight in the world', enable him to achieve many adventures, such as the ending of the enchantments of the carol, which condemned its hearers to dance until the spell was broken, and of the self-moving chess set which no one could beat. Yet he has only to appear for the spell to be dissolved; his reputation alone is sufficient. Against this, the idea of victory as being in God's gift must be set: Lancelot's skill is a reflection of his other virtues. When his virtues are insufficient, as in the *Queste del Saint Graal* , he is overthrown by divine judgment: and there is a faint echo of the ideas behind the trial by battle in the outcome of each joust and tournament. Guinevere exerts a much more direct influence on his fortunes in the field: for example, at the last tournament at Winchester, she commands him to do badly, until the third day, when she relents, and allows him to display his usual prowess. Lancelot may attain to some spiritual standing in the Grail quest, but his real place is where we first met him, as ardent suitor to the queen of chivalry.

Outside the Arthurian cycle, *Perceforest* [22] is the most interesting of the French romances from a chivalric point of view. Its author had distinct ideas on the nature of chivalry, and saw it as a noble institution which had fallen on evil days. In olden times,

22   The relationship of this romance to Edward III's foundation of the Order of the Garter is still unresolved; it has generally been regarded as foreshadowing the Order, but I would see it as nearly contemporary, a reflection rather than a premonition of the newly-instituted Order.

he tells us, 'all those who were endowed with sense and good morals and bold at heart and strong and personable were regarded as gentle, wherever they came from, and became knights if they wished to.' He places great emphasis on the ceremony of knighting, which he describes in detail in its various styles, from the simple *colée* on the battlefield to the elaborate church ceremony. A knight's prime function is the search for honour, in his view: and he gives four rules for the knight errant. Never refuse a challenge: if you unhorse your opponent, offer to fight him with swords. Support the better cause in a war, to the death. Always support the weaker side in a tournament. Always help and assist those in need of aid. And as in the Arthurian romances there is a great order of knighthood, that of the Franc-Palais , which, like the Round Table, attracts the best among knights. If all this varies only slightly from the Arthurian romances, the similarities show how consistent the romantic theory of chivalry was.

English literature is little concerned with chivalry. French was the *lingua franca* of the knights, and the humbler origins of English writers before Chaucer meant that the world of chivalry lay outside their ken. With Chaucer and his successors we are already into the first stirrings of the new humanist world which was to replace the knightly ways of thought, and beyond the point at which original romances were being written. The one major exception to this rule is the famous *Sir Gawain and the Green Knight* . The anonymous poet took two stock themes of romances, no more, and interlinked them into a plot of great subtlety yet simplicity, in which the outcome of the magical challenge which Gawain has accepted depends on his success in resisting the seductions offered by the challenger's wife. The richness of the poetry almost obscures the poem's other great merit: a clearcut and uncompromising view of knighthood as the highest attainment of mankind. Gawain fights, not under the auspices of an earthly lady, but bearing the pentangle of virtue on his shield and vowing himself as 'Mary's knight'. But it is an attainment inescapably tainted by human weakness. Gawain acquits himself with great honour, except when he is offered a magic belt which will guarantee his safety, which he accepts and keeps, thus breaking faith with his host. Like Wolfram's *Parzival*, the theme of the poem is a search for earthly perfection. Wolfram, the optimist, believes that it can be attained in the end: the Gawain poet denies this, but paints just as moving and human a picture of the attempt.

By the end of the fourteenth century, vernacular literature had come of age, and the relatively unsophisticated allure of the romances was no longer as powerful for audience and authors alike. An increasingly literate secular society expected intellectual challenge as well as entertainment, and found it in the works of the Italian masters, Boccaccio, Petrarch and Dante, who were to be the models for Chaucer and his French contemporaries, leading towards new poetic forms which could embrace both traditional matter and much more subtle literary creations. At one end, the *nouvelle, novella* or tale – as in *The Decameron, The Canterbury Tales* or *Les Cent Nouvelles Nouvelles* –

may be no more than a folktale recast in literary form; at the other extreme, the complex images and structures of *Troilus and Criseyde, The Divine Comedy* or the French allegorical tradition which stems from the *Roman de la Rose* is learned, sometimes abstruse, and distinctly intellectual in tone and content. Chivalry already had its established literary canon, and authors saw no profit in trying to compete with it. The romances remained popular, as numerous late medieval copies attest, not only with their original knightly audience, but also with those who aspired to the social status of knighthood. It was by no means a dead tradition, but the weight of authority of the great romances meant that additions were few and far between.

6

Chivalric Biographies and Handbooks

F OR MANY KNIGHTS, the ideals of chivalry were passed down through
romances and poems; but there were also more formal exemplars, in the shape of
manuals about chivalry, love and courtly behaviour, and biographies of its great
exponents. Some of these were very influential, but there was never anything
approaching a set, formal code of chivalry, nor any systematic teaching of its concepts.
Some writers did indeed set out to instruct their audience by precept, and because their
works were in a learned and scholarly style, they have survived in libraries; but it is easy
to overestimate their influence and their place in history. There may well have been
simpler treatises which were passed from hand to hand and which have largely
disappeared, on the lines of the little twelfth century poem on knighthood from the
Rhineland quoted in chapter 2. There are other early manuals in this vein, but their
real subject is courtly conduct rather than chivalry. In the late twelfth century, however,
we find manuals which discuss the nature of love in terms of the concepts to be found
in Chrétien's romances and those of his German successors, with some elements from
troubadour poetry.

The most famous of these manuals often finds its way into the histories of chivalry,
but really has very little to do with it. Because it is so well-known, we need to look at
it briefly, to see why it acquired such a reputation, and what it really tells us. This is
the *De Amore*[1] of Andreas Capellanus ('the chaplain') who was believed to have been at
the court of Champagne in the 1180s; in fact the most likely candidate is a member
of the royal court at Paris, and the real context of the book is the intellectual world of
the capital, with its schools and reputation for learning.[2] It is indeed a scholarly treatise,
following the prescribed forms of such works, with its threefold division and discussion
in dialogue form. The first part explores the nature of love, the character of lovers, and

1   *The Art of Courtly Love*, tr. J.J.Parry (New York 1941; rptd 1959).
2   Alfred Karnein, 'Auf der Suche nach einem Autor: Andreas, Verfasser von "De Amore"',
     Germanisch-Romanische Monatsschrift 28, 1978, 1-20.

the various types of love. This is followed by an analysis of how love-affairs may develop, and various laws of love are given, supported, as laws should be, by a chapter containing the decisions reached in 'court': Andreas invents a system of love-courts, and attributes the verdicts to famous ladies of his day - Eleanor of Aquitaine, Ermengarde of Narbonne, Marie of Champagne: but the device is fictional, and the names are simply borrowed. A relatively brief third section is a formal retraction of much that has gone before, taking the strict religious view that carnal love is a sin, and explaining that the author's real purpose in writing the *De Amore* is to warn the young friend to whom it is addressed of the pleasures of the flesh, so that he will be able to reject such temptations and keep to the paths of spiritual safety.

Andreas carries out his scholarly exercise with grace and wit, and the result has been taken for a genuine handbook on the subject which was thought to have had considerable influence on succeeding generations. Because it attempts to present a code of love, complete with courts of ladies who sit in judgement on those who transgress, it seems to offer a systematic view of a complex and difficult subject, and it was eagerly studies by the nineteenth century scholars who first rediscovered it.[3] The courts of love have long since been shown to be a fiction, but the treatise itself is no more that a learned exercise, in the manner of Ovid's *Art of Love*, but with Ovid's poetic genius replaced by the pedestrian methods of the Paris schools. Its influence was on fellow-scholars rather than the world of the court, and although Andreas' name can be found in discussions of love in Spanish, German, Italian and French, only a handful of copies of the original survive. Indeed, mention of his name becomes more frequent after the work was condemned by the archbishop of Paris in 1277, and there is very little evidence of its use in vernacular literature before Jean de Meun invokes it in *Le Roman de la Rose*, a work which is in itself a product of a learned theological world rather than the secular chivalric or courtly tradition. The theologians and moralists who read the *De Amore* in order to write their own Latin treatises saw it as a satire, which exaggerated the claims of the secular writers to have invented an alternative morality based on love in order to demolish them; and they almost always worked, not from the text itself, but from an anthology of maxims (*auctoritates*) in which the *De Amore* was quoted. The quotations were chosen in such a way that the book appeared to be a treatise concerning sexual desire or *cupiditas*. In vernacular literature, authors like Richard de Fournival who were assumed to have derived their ideas from the *De Amore* are simply expressing in their own terms the ideas about love given currency by the poets, whether the troubadours or the writers of romances. Instead of the fixed code of 'courtly love' which Andreas so neatly offers, we must acknowledge instead the

---

3   What follows is based on Alfred Karnein's important article, 'La reception du *De Amore* d'André le Chapelain au xiiie siècle', *Romania* 102, 1981, 324-351, 501-542.

diversity and individuality of concepts of love in chivalric literature. There are themes and variations, but no rigid set of rules.

Indeed, chivalric manuals devote remarkably little time to the subject. Generally, love is not treated in the works which centre specifically on chivalry. It belongs more to the genre best described as 'courtesy books', which give advice on behaviour, with some ethical content, for the instruction of aspiring courtiers. Even *Die Klage*, a work by a poet as familiar with literary and knightly fashions as Hartmann von Aue is 'an optimistic plan of broad ethical and social instruction',[4] which draws on 'courtly' love and the chivalric ethos, but only insofar as they are relevant to his purpose. Other poems of this kind are addressed to a wider audience, including women and young townsmen. Love service becomes a means of social advancement, rather than a specific chivalric attribute: just as the romances found a broader audience as time passed, so the ideals behind them became part of the general cultural background, and were to be found in manuals of good conduct.

We have already looked at the earliest manual to concern itself exclusively with knighthood, *L'Ordene de chevalerie*. This focusses on the knighting ceremony and its symbolic meaning, but a contemporary (possibly slightly earlier) allegorical poem, the *Roman des Eles*, takes a wider view and aims to instruct its readers in chivalry proper, the 'fount of courtesy' which 'comes from God; knights possess it'. Or rather, should possess it, for in the author's view most knights know little of chivalry and can only say 'I am a knight'. He sets out to remedy this state of affairs, by way of an allegory depicting the two wings of prowess, largesse and courtesy. Largesse is treated first: knights should not be too proud to give, nor should they say: 'Why do I fear these gluttons? Shall I give them something? Why? What can they say about me? Am I not the man with the great shield? I have beaten everyone, and am the best of all; I even surpass Gawain in feats of arms.'[5] The victor should be all the more generous; the poet praises boldness, freedom and even carelessness in giving. Courtesy proves an all-embracing virtue, even though it is largely defined in negatives – avoid envy, slander, pride, boastfulness and gluttony. A knight should honour the church, and should be joyful and appreciate songs and music. The final feather in the wing of courtesy is of course love (which the poet compares in rapid succession to the sea, wine and roses!). The *Roman des Eles* is a conventional enough work, but interesting in showing how the ideals of chivalry were beginning to be defined in the early thirteenth century.

The most famous and popular of the manuals of chivalry concentrates on the spiritual and social function of the knight to the exclusion of love and the courtly aspects of his life. This is Raimon Llull's *Libre del Orde de Cavalleria*. Llull is one of the

4   Jackson, *Chivalry in Twelfth Century Germany*, 177.
5   Houdenc, *Roman des Eles*, 75.

most important philosophers of the late thirteenth century, but he was brought up as a knight and courtier, and led a conventional, even dissipated life, until he underwent a mystical experience at about the age of thirty, in 1265; as he wrote a cantilena to a lady whom he loved, he had five visions of the crucified Christ. He went on pilgrimage to Santiago de Compostela, and then devoted himself to plans for a crusade in North Africa and to writing religious and philosophical treatises. His ideas included the foundation of schools where missionaries could learn Arabic and other heathen languages, so that they could preach more effectively. He taught at Paris and Montpellier, and led an extraordinarily active life, as well as writing over 250 works, most of which survive, and which include notable romances as well as highly abstruse scholarly texts. From 1291 onwards he made a series of expeditions to North Africa to preach Christianity to the Muslims, in the course of one of which he was nearly stoned to death by his infuriated hearers. So we have here a major philosopher writing about knighthood, from a theoretical and religious standpoint, while retaining a firsthand understanding of knightly ways. He is interested in chivalry, not as a spiritual weapon, like St Bernard in his letter on the Order of the Temple, *De laude novae militiae*, but as part of the established pattern of Christian society. Llull's ideas on the subject are traditional, and derive substantially, if at second hand, from John of Salisbury's *Policraticus*; he is characteristic of the writers whose mission was to propagate chivalric ideas in order to 'improve, or at least change, the knights of the time',[6] and one aspect of his thinking is the need for a disciplined, well-trained army to carry out his crusading ideas.

But his treatise is also a lively piece of writing, well calculated to appeal to the knights themselves just as much as to Llull's fellow-scholars discussing theories of education. The book opens with a picture of the 'good hermit knight' who is to be Llull's spokesman:

> It once happened in a country that there was a wise knight, who had long sustained the order of knighthood and who by his nobility and strength and high courage and wisdom, and by risking his life, had been through wars, jousts and tournaments, and had had many noble and glorious victories in battle. Because, brave through he was, he realised that he could no longer live as he had done in the past and was approaching his end, he chose to live as a hermit . . .

He is visited by a young squire, who has fallen asleep on his journey to the royal court, and whose horse has strayed to the hermit's door as a result. The hermit knight, learning of his intention to seek knighthood, offers to instruct him in the ways of chivalry, and

---

6   Sidney Painter, *Feudalism and Liberty*, ed. Fred A.Cazel Jr (Baltimore 1961) 96..

gives him a little book on the subject, which is of course the book which Llull proceeds to write.

His object is stated in the prologue: 'May the knight through this book return to the devotion, loyalty and obedience which he owes to his order.' This order is an essential part of the hierarchy, coming below the prince and above the people. In serving the prince, the knight also serves God, and he must defend both the prince's honour and the Catholic faith. His greatest mission, however, is his duty to the people, to uphold justice. Llull sees the knight as someone who will inspire terror in ordinary people, so that they will be afraid to do wrong. But he also says that knights should 'ride warhorses, joust, go to tournaments, hold Round Tables, hunt stags and rabbits, bears, lions, and similar creatures' because these exercise him in the practice of arms. 'To despise and neglect things by which a knight is made more fit for his duties is to despise and neglect knighthood itself.'

But Llull goes on to warn that mere bodily strength and boldness are not enough to make a good knight: sense and spirit are needed as well. He then sets out a form of catechism for the squire, and emphasises true courage as the knight's first virtue:

> Seek not noble courage in speech, for speech is not always truth; seek it not in rich clothes, for many a fine habit conceals cowardice, treachery and evil; seek it not in your horse, for he cannot speak to you; seek it not in fine harness and equipment, for they too often conceal an evil and cowardly heart. Seek noble courage in faith, hope, charity, justice, strength, moderation and loyalty . . .

Llull requires of the knight nobility of spirit, which must at very least mean that knights 'are less inclined to do evil', and at its highest means that nobility is open to those whose way of life and deeds are noble. The knight must be an example to others, and should lead a virtuous and religious life. When he places these qualities at the service of the commonwealth, as he should, he is not expected to serve only in war, but also as a royal official. 'To a knyght apperteyneth that he be lover of the comyn wele. For by the comynalte of the people was the chyvalrye founden and establysshed. And the comyn wele is gretter and more necessary than propre good and specyall.'[7]

After the mission of the knight, he describes the knighting ceremony and the symbolism of the arms, in a passage which seems to be borrowed from the Lady of the Lake's speech. The remainder of the book deals with the virtues appropriate to knighthood, with suitable examples, and the privileges which he should enjoy: 'any noble baron or lord who does honour to a knight in his court and in his council and

---

7   Raimon Llull, tr. William Caxton, *The Book of the Order of Chyvalry*, ed. A.T.P.Byles, EETS OS 168 (London 1926) 113.

at his table, does honour to himself'. The relative brevity and clarity of the book won it a wide following: there are translations in French, English and Scots, and a Latin version seems to have been made. Caxton printed it in 1484 as *The Book of the Ordre of Chyvalry or Knyghthode*, adding his own epilogue.

Llull wrote as philosopher rather than as man of the world. For the views of a knight who was among the foremost of his generation, 'the most valiant and worthy of them all', according to Froissart, we must turn to the works of Geoffroi de Charny. He wrote two versions of his book on chivalry, one in verse[8] and one in prose, texts which reflect a lifetime's experience as a warrior. He served in Gascony in 1337 at the outset of the Hundred Years' War, and went on to campaign at the siege of Tournai in 1340; he next appeared in Brittany, where he was captured at Morlaix in 1342. He was ransomed soon afterwards, and set out on crusade with Humbert of Vienne in 1345, to Smyrna; the expedition was a failure, and he returned to France in time to serve under the duke of Normandy (later king John) in Gascony. He was appointed bearer of the royal standard or *oriflamme* in 1347. In 1350, he was captured after an abortive attempt to retake Calais, and taken to England; his ransom was set at 12,000 florins, but he was back in France the following year. In 1352, he was a founder-member of the royal 'Order of the Star', and it was probably for members of the Order that the prose version of the *Livre de Chevalerie* was written, at a moment when the question of the concept of chivalry was very much in the air: the Star was one of the first group of secular orders of knighthood to be founded in the mid-fourteenth century. When hostilities with England were renewed in 1355, Charny was again standard-bearer, and met his death defending the *oriflamme* at Poitiers in 1356.

Charny is not a great stylist, and his arguments are often long-winded and repetitious to modern ears. His views are largely traditional: his account of the ceremony of knighthood is close to that of the *Ordene de Chevalerie* a century and a half earlier, and much of his theoretical basis for knighthood can be found in Raimon Llull or the *Prose Lancelot*. But he has a much more practical grasp on the realities of chivalry than his predecessors, while exalting it to a key place in the structure of society: without chivalry, he believes, the ruler would have no effective authority, and order and justice would break down. The threat of knightly power is the ultimate sanction against wrongdoers, and he emphasises chivalry's place as a sacred order alongside that of priesthood. For this reason, knights should be pure in heart and fear God; but he reinforces his arguments by reminding his listeners that chivalry is the most dangerous of all callings, and puts the knight in daily peril of both body and soul. As for the view that those engaged in the calling of arms are beyond salvation, Charny points to the

---

8   Geoffroi de Charny, 'Le livre Messire Geoffroi de Charny', ed. Arthur Piaget, *Romania*, 26, 1897, 394-411.

necessity of war as a deterrent against malefactors, who could otherwise do as they pleased with impunity. It is chivalry which upholds peace and good government.

As to the knight's personal conduct, this should be an endless quest, not for perfection – which is beyond human reach – but for the achievement of greater deeds and more honour: 'he who does more, is more worthy'.[9] If on the one hand fame is the spur, on the other hand the knight's lady has a crucial role to play. Here Charny departs from the religious theorists like Llull, and proposes a secular ideal closer to that of the Arthurian romances. To 'love for love's sake' ('amer par amours') is a vital part of a knight's life, and is the reason why he aspires to great deeds. It is an entirely practical application of the theme which we have already traced from the troubadours through to the romances, and Charny makes the ladies into active mentors of the untutored novices:

> There is another category of men-at-arms who when they begin are so naive that they are unaware of the great honour that they could win through deeds of arms; nevertheless they succeed so well because they put their heart into winning the love of a lady. And they are so fortunate that their ladies themselves, from the great honour and superb qualities that reside in them, do not want to let them tarry nor delay in any way the winning of that honour to be achieved by deeds of arms, and advise them on this and then command them to set out and put all their efforts into winning renown and great honour where it is to be sought by valiant men .. [10].

Nor is this motivation confined to novices; experienced knights should 'love loyally' (in another phrase borrowed from the romances), and they and their ladies should be honoured. 'Love is the right state for those who want to acquire honour.'[11] Charny is emphatic that love-affairs should not be conducted in public: 'the most secret love is the most joyful, lasting and loyal'.[12] Even so, the lady whose lover is renowned for his prowess will derive her reward from his public appearances, when he is honoured and feted by his companions. But the knight should not be excessively involved in love - shades of Chrétien's Erec! - because love of honour and love of God are more desirable.

Charny also has much practical advice to offer, drawing on his own personal experience. Young knights should be gay and handsome, and versed in the social graces; but they should treat such matters lightly and should not draw attention to themselves

---

9   Charny, 'Le livre de chevalerie', 464

10   Tr. Elspeth Kennedy, 'Geoffroi de Charny's *Livre de chevalerie* and the Knights of the Round Table' in *Medieval Knighthood V*, ed. Ruth Harvey and Stephen Church (Woodbridge and Rochester N. Y., 1995, forthcoming).

11   Charny, 'Le livre de chevalerie', 483

12   *Ibid.*, 484

by excessive enthusiasm for dress or for good food and wine. They should avoid gambling, particularly betting on tennis matches, and they should not be idle; equally they should not be preoccupied with their own financial affairs or the management of their estates, which should be left to others. Generosity in word and deed is the hallmark of the knight when he is in society; in battle he must not think about injury, capture or flight. He should be wise and determined, and should not trust to fortune: as the proverb says, he who climbs highest, falls furthest, echoing the medieval image of the wheel of fortune.

Charny lays considerable stress on the merits of jousting as a pastime, as befits the author of a work on the subject of tournaments. He does, however, warn against over-enthusiasm and decries the knights who get so carried away by the sport that they forget that this is not the only way of bearing arms. It is in the harsh reality of campaigning that honour is won by true men of valour 'through great hardships, labours, fear and bodily danger, and loss of their dear friends whom they have seen die in various fortresses where they have been, which has made them uneasy and often angry at heart . . .'

In the poetic version of the *Livre*, Charny adds details from his own experience, and generally offers a more immediate picture of chivalry in action. He advises that a knight should be a good horseman before he tries his hand in the lists, and he gives us a sad little vignette of a knight who goes up to his lady, and is asked to joust for her. He cannot make his horse obey him and is unseated in the mêlée; muddy and dishevelled, he tries to keep out of her sight: there is no question of a prize for him! Again, Geoffroi emphasises the hardships of life in the field: 'to fast often, drink little, be badly paid and often in debt, get up early, often have bad horses and a hard end to the campaign'.[13] Poverty leads to the need to borrow to buy arms and horses; there is the danger of imprisonment, from which release may be difficult to obtain; and if the campaign is overseas, the hardships may be ever greater, as Geoffroi illustrates by examples from his own campaigns in the Levant.[14]

Charny's realism is overshadowed by the idealistic tradition in most poems which deal incidentally with knighthood: Langland's *Piers Plowman* repeats the concept of knights as agents of justice, summing up:

> *Trewely to take   and treweliche to fyghte*
> *Ys the profession and the pure ordre   that apendeth to knyghtes;*
> *Who-so passeth that poynt   ys apostata of knyght-hod.*
> *For thei shoulde not faste   ne for-bere sherte;*

13   Charny, 'Le livre messire Geoffroi de Charny', 409.
14   *Ibid.*, 409.

> *Bute feithfullich defende   and fyghte for truth,*
> *And never leve for love   in hope to lacche seluer.*[15]

And the tradition persists well into the fifteenth century with very little change: Alain Chartier in *Le breviaire des nobles*[16] produces a list of twelve virtues of knighthood based on those of Llull: nobility, loyalty, honour, righteousness, prowess, love, courtesy, diligence, cleanliness, generosity, sobriety and perseverance. Chartier's additions are interesting: by love he means not only the love of one's lady, which hardly appears in Llull, but the love of king and country. In courtesy, sobriety and generosity, the old virtues preached by the troubadours reappear – *cortesia, mezura* and *largesse.* Here a more strictly chivalrous ideal has been merged with that of knighthood Chartier's poem, in its pedestrian way, attempts to present an all-embracing definition of chivalry, but the 'knightly system of virtues',[17] whose ideas are the common stock of many writers, deriving from philosophical ideas then current, is really an illusion, just as much as the imaginary 'laws' governing courtly love. In German writers 'God's favour' and honour had predominated; in French writers, *courtoisie* prevailed. As the German influence lessened towards the middle of the fourteenth century, and chivalric fashions were set almost entirely by the French, so *courtoisie*, the attainment of all worldly virtues, becomes the keynote of chivalry. Much of *courtoisie* was concerned with questions of manners: hospitality and a warm welcome, 'debonnaireté' or gaiety and openheartedness, seemed to be as essential as loyalty, and generosity is as vital as compassion.

In the mid-fifteenth century, we find aspiring knights making their own collections of writings about chivalry, drawing on romances, heraldry, treatises, and accounts of contemporary deeds of arms. The 'Grete Boke' assembled by or for Sir John Paston in the 1470s is one of the best examples of this genre, containing descriptions of the major feats of arms of his time alongside a copy of the thirteenth century Statute of Arms and ordinances of war issued by Henry V in 1419; there are details of the ceremony for creating Knights of the Bath, and instructions for organising 'jousts of peace', together with the fictional preamble in romantic style for a passage of arms, as well as an English version of Vegetius on the art of war.[18] But in the last analysis chivalry was not something which lent itself to teaching by handbook or learning by rote; it

---

15   William Langland, *The Vision of William concerning Piers Plowman*, ed. W.W.Skeat, Oxford 1896, Text II 190 ff.

16   See W.H.Rice, 'Deux poèmes sur la chevalerie: *Le breviaire des nobles* d' Alain Chartier et *Le Psaultier des Vilains* de Michault Taillevent', *Romania*, 75, 1954, 54-97.

17   Gustav Ehrismann, 'Die Grundlagen des ritterlichen Tugendsystems', *Zeitschrift für deutsches Altertum*, 56, 1919, 137-216.

18   For contents, see G.A.Lester, *Sir John Paston's 'Grete Boke'* (Woodbridge and Totowa, N. J., 1984) 9-12.

was the example of heroic figures, whether from the romances or from real life, which was a far more potent inspiration. Sir Ector's lament for his brother Lancelot at the end of Malory's *Morte d'Arthur* overshadows all the host of other expressions of these virtues which are to be found in mediaeval writers:

> 'A, Launcelot!' he sayd, 'thou were hede of al Crysten knyghtes! And now I dare say,' sayd syr Ector, 'thou Sir Launcelot, there thou lyest, that thou were never matched of erthely knyghtes hande. And thou were the curtest knyght that ever bare shelde! And thou were the truest frende to thy lovar that ever bestrade hors, and thou were the trewest lover, of a synful man, that ever loved woman, and thou were the kyndest man that ever strake wyth swerde. And thou were the godelyest persone that ever came emonge prees of knyghtes, and thou was the mekest man and the jentyllest that ever ete in halle emonge ladyes, and thou were the sternest knyght to the mortal foo that ever put spere in the reste.'[19]

Chivalry draws its inspiration not only from the heroes of the romances, from the practical Gawain to the ethereal Galahad, but also from the heroes of real wars and tournaments. The *chansons de geste*, with their ideals rooted firmly in the world around them, are the most primitive form of these heroic examples whose deeds are used to inspire succeeding generations of knights; and as the concept of chivalry grows more complex, so Charlemagne and his paladins are replaced on the one hand by the heroes of the imagination and on the other by men inspired by the new ideas. The heroic biography plays an important part in the cult of chivalry: if Lancelot and Parzival are its gods, William Marshal and Boucicaut might fairly be called its saints, offering a more human and practical example to the aspiring knight.

The biography of William Marshal, written with the help of his squire by a jongleur at the end of the Marshal's long and brilliant career, is the only survivor of a possibly extensive number of poems on current events, most of which were composed as news items to be recited by travelling minstrels on their rounds. We know that the heralds used to proclaim the praises of their patrons at tournaments, and thus became deadly rivals of the minstrels whose task this had once been, and who had reaped generous rewards for it. The currency of such work would be brief, and only a figure such as the Marshal could expect (or afford) a more permanent record.

It is the only portrait from the life of a knight-errant in the twelfth century that has come down to us. William Marshal certainly deserved his posthumous fame; the account of his life is no artificial eulogy, for it was written largely at the dictation of

---

19   Sir Thomas Malory, *Works*, ed. E.Vinaver, rev. P.J.C.Field (Oxford 1990) III, 1259.

his squire and rings true in most of its details; yet he stands out as a shining example of what a knight could be and do.[20]

William was born in about 1144, the younger son of John FitzGilbert, marshal to Henry I. His father supported the empress Matilda in the civil wars that followed Henry's death, and in 1152 found himself defending Newbury against king Stephen. A truce was arranged, and William was one of the hostages, his father having promised to surrender if help did not arrive within a specified time. When the day came, FitzGilbert refused to hand over the castle, and when Stephen's followers threatened to hurl William from a siege-engine into the castle, FitzGilbert merely replied 'Do what you like; I still have the hammer and anvil on which to forge a better one than him'. William was spared, however, and three years later, when peace had been reestablished under Henry II, went to the count of Tancarville to become a squire in his household. Here he spent eight years, earning a reputation for 'doing nothing except drinking, eating and sleeping'; but when his opportunity came, in 1168, after he had left the Tancarville household, he was quick to seize it. He was in the service of his uncle, the earl of Salisbury, as he escorted queen Eleanor through Poitou. The party were ambushed by Geoffrey de Lusignan; the queen escaped, but the earl was killed and William was wounded and captured. Eleanor paid his ransom, and rewarded his courage with horses, armour, money and fine clothing; she evidently commended him to Henry II, for soon afterwards he became tutor in arms to Henry's eldest son, the 'young king' Henry, who was crowned in 1170. It was William, not Henry, who knighted him in 1174, during a quarrel with his father; and after 1174 the young king and William spent much time abroad at tournaments. William remembered it as a golden age of chivalry:

> It was the young king who revived chivalry, which at this time was almost dead. He was the gateway through which she returned, and he was her standardbearer. For then great men did nothing for knights, but he set them an example by retaining good men. And the other lords, seeing such men gather round him, regarded him as very wise, because they knew that no king or count is worth anything without good men at his side. They too started to do the same, retaining good knights and putting chivalry into good shape again. The count of Flanders did likewise, envying the young king and wishing to demonstrate his own prowess. King, count and lords all sought out good knights and gave them horses and arms and money, land or good maintenance. But now the great men have put chivalry in prison again by their idleness, and their miserly ways have locked up generosity: tournaments have been abandoned in favour of lawsuits.[21]

20 *L'histoire de Guillaume le Maréchal*, ed. Paul Meyer, SHF (Paris 1891-1901); see also Georges Duby, *William Marshal: The Flower of Chivalry* (London and New York 1986) and David Crouch, *William Marshal: Court, Career and Chivalry in the Angevin Empire 1147-1219* (London and New York 1990).

We shall explore William's career in the lists in our discussion of tournaments; this was the high point of his chivalric career, and his reputation and booty were very high. From tournaments, however, his career turned to politics; after the young king's death in 1183, William undertook his master's vow to go on crusade, returning in time to support Henry II in his final quarrel with Richard. Having unhorsed Richard in a skirmish a few days before Henry's death, he found himself facing his new master, charged with attempting to kill him; but his bold reply - that if he had wanted to do so, he would certainly have succeeded - won him a pardon. From then on his career was in the world of government, culminating in his appointment as regent during the minority of Henry III, from 1216 until shortly before his death in 1219.

This pattern of a career in which chivalric prowess enables the hero to rise from relatively humble origins to the greatest position in the land is repeated in the biographies of two fourteenth century knights, Du Guesclin and Boucicaut. The biographer of du Guesclin is a realist through and through. If he has a moral to convey to the rest of the chivalric world, it is that even the most unpromising squire can make good. There is something of the childhood uncouthness of Parzival in the description of du Guesclin's youth: how his strange, swarthy appearance made his parents reject him - although he was the eldest son, they treated him as a menial. Only the prediction of a visitor that he would have a great future persuaded them to relent; and even then his escapades, including running away from home and leading a gang of the village youths, were anything but knightly. In later years, this rough upbringing was reflected in his impetuousness, generosity and lack of the subtler points of courtesy. It was his feats of arms alone that made him a chivalric figure, though at moments, as when he scaled the walls of Melun alone, he seemed to belong to the *chansons de geste*. On the other hand, it was his military genius that earned him the post of Constable; and it is a reminder of the close connection of chivalry and war that this seasoned soldier could ever become one of its heroes.

His successors were portrayed in very different light, acquiring a veneer of romance even during their lifetime. By this time, it was recognised that the deeds of the great figures of chivalry could be an inspiration to their successors. In the thirteenth century, the author of the Vulgate Cycle shows such doings as being recorded for posterity: as Malory translates it at the end of his account of the quest for the Holy Grail: 'The Kynge made grete clerkes to com before hym, for cause they sulde cronycle of the hyghe adventures of the good knyghtes. . . . And all thys was made in grete bookes and put up in almeryes at Salysbury.'[22] In mid-thirteenth Spain, Alfonso X prescribed in his law code *Las Siete Partidas* that 'accounts of great deeds of arms should be read to

21   *L' histoire de Guillaume de Maréchal*, ll.2637-95, tr. F.M.Powicke, *EHR* 22, 1906, 40.
22   Malory, *Works*, II, 1036.

knights while they eat',[23] rather as religious texts were read to monks in their refectory. Alfonso explains that 'this was done in order that, hearing them, their minds and hearts might be enlarged and strengthened by the performance of good actions, and to awaken a desire to attain to what others had accomplished, or to surpass their efforts'. And in the statutes of the secular orders of knighthood from the mid-fourteenth century onwards, it is provided that the deeds of members should be recorded by an officer of the order. [24] The resulting volumes do not survive, but the concept is nonetheless important.

It is against this background that we need to read the lives of Boucicaut, Pero Niño and Lalaing. In these works, real episodes are woven into the conventional progress of a hero so that we find Boucicaut excelling in chivalrous games in his youth, 'and his manner was from then on lordly and haughty; and his bearing was upright, hand on hip, which suited him well. Thus he watched the other children at play, and never spoke much nor laughed too long.'[25] And at a suitable point that love which was the making of all good knights appears:

> When the winter was ended and the renewal of sweet spring came round in the season when all things rejoice and woods and meadows clothe themselves in flowers again, and the earth grows green, when the little birds in the branches sing loud and the nightingales give tongue, at the time when love is strongest in gentle lovers' hearts, and sets them on fire with pleasant memories which give birth to desire, desire which gives them pleasant torment and sweet languishing in fragrant sickness.[26]

Boucicaut is duly initiated into the ways of love, but his valiant nature cannot dwell for long in such soft arbours, and love becomes the motive for his first series of adventures and single combats. His travels in the East and in Prussia, and his appointment as marshal at the age of twenty-five, point the way to a more serious career; but before that come the jousts of St Inglevert in 1390, in which Boucicaut played a major part, and the foundation in 1399 of his Order, 'The White Lady on a Green Shield', whose avowed object was to protect defenceless and disinherited ladies against oppressive lords. The thirty knights were to wear a badge with the device from which the order took its name. It was the last of Boucicaut's purely chivalrous exploits, and was defunct within five years, while its founder went on to a political career as

23   Alfonso IX, *Las siete partidas*, tr. Samuel Parsons Scott, Chicago 1931, 428 (Book II title XX)

24   D'A.J.D.Boulton, *The Knights of the Crown: The Monarchical Orders of Knighthood in later Medieval Europe 1325-1520*, Woodbridge and New York 1987, 239-240.

25   *Le livre des faicts du bon messire Jean Le Maingre, dit Boucicaut* in Michaud et Poujoulat, *Nouvelle collection des mémoires pour servir à l'histoire de France* (Paris 1854) ii, 205-332.

26   *Ibid.*, i.xiii-xiv

career as governor of Genoa, and as representative of French interests in northern Italy, a career which did not prove entirely successful. (He did not abandon his courteous ways. Once, in the streets of Genoa, he bade good day to two prostitutes, and when his companion pointed out his mistake, he said that he preferred to greet two prostitutes by mistake, rather than fail in politeness to one noblewoman.) He returned to France and was captured at Agincourt, dying in prison in 1421. His biography ends, however, on a less dark note, as it was written in about 1408: and the last part is an encomium of the marshal's personality and qualities in which his religious devotion and wisdom figure as largely as his boldness and generosity.

A better known example was offered by Jacques de Lalaing, of whom two chroniclers wrote memorials.[27] Born in 1421, he was brought up in the entourage of the duke of Cleves at the Burgundian court, and distinguished himself at an early age in tournaments. From the age of twenty-four onwards he held a series of single combats and challenges, culminating in the *pas d'armes de la Fontaine des Pleurs* which lasted from November 1449 for one year. His death at the siege of Poucques in 1453 meant that these feats were still fresh in men's minds when the time for eulogies came. If the results are less overlaid with romance than the life of Boucicaut, it is because Lalaing's record needed few embellishments. Indeed, Jean le Fèvre de St Remy, who was herald to the order of the Golden Fleece (of which Lalaing was a member) does not gloss over the occasions when an opponent breaks more lances than his hero.

Lalaing is the exception among these exemplary knights. If we turn to a Spanish history in similar vein, *The Victorious Knight*, a biography of Don Pero Niño of Castile finished in 1449, the romantic prelude to a prosaic career reappears.[28] Pero Niño began his knightly deeds at the age of fifteen in 1394, jousting with cane lances and bullfighting, 'and there was there no one who did such good service, as well afoot as mounted'. He soon took up a military career, and at the siege of Pontevedra we find him jousting again: 'Battle was given on a ground well chosen for those who would distinguish themselves in arms for the love of their ladies; for all the ladies and damsels of Pontevedra were there to look on from he height of the ramparts'.[29] Shunning a political career for the moment, 'since among ministers there are of necessity found certain deceiving ways, and matters which spring not from the same root as chivalry', he entered the service of love, and sought feats of arms.

27   *Chronique de J. de Lalain*, in J.A.Buchon, *Collection des chroniques nationales françaises du treizième au seizième siècle*, Paris 1825; Georges Chastellain, *Le livre des faits de Jacques de Lalaing* , in *Oeuvres*, ed. Kervyn de Lettenhove (Brussels 1866) VIII.

28   Gutierrez Diaz de Gamez, *The Unconquered Knight: a chronicle of the deeds of Don Pero Niño*, tr. Joan Evans (London 1928).

29   *Ibid.*, 35.

Yet he saw nothing incompatible with chivalry in becoming captain of a galley in the Spanish fleet which was little more than a licensed corsair, raiding in reprisal the Barbary coast and the Mediterranean, as well as an expedition to Cornwall. He cheerfully returned to chivalry after this interlude, jousting in France and defeating two champions, and finally being knighted in 1407, at the end of his chivalric career. He continued in the royal service as sea-captain and minister, and these events take up most of the latter part of his story. *The Victorious Knight is* less an example to others than an ordinary biography written in an idiom which no longer has much to do with the subject, a formal decoration suitable to a successful career.

A more worthy close to the roll of heroes is the Chevalier Bayart, *'sans peur et sans reproche'*. His life, as described by the 'loyal servitor' Jacques de Mailles,[30] begins as an idyllic story of chivalry, from the moment when he challenges Claude de Vauldray at a *pas d'armes*, and is told by the herald: 'Your beard is not of three years growth, and do you undertake to fight with Messire Claude de Vauldrè, who is one of the fiercest knights that you may hear of?' Bayart answers that he wants to learn, 'and God, if He please, may give me grace to do something which shall please the ladies'.[31] Which indeed he does, at the cost of his reluctant uncle, the abbot of Esnay, who has to provide him with arms. More serious considerations prevail, with his service in the Italian war, though even here he contrives intervals in the lists. His virtues are in the traditional mould: courtesy, generosity even when he 'knew not how to come by ten crowns', and above all courage: at Milan he was so intent on the pursuit of his enemies that he was captured right inside the town, though the skirmish had begun some miles outside.

Yet the new ways are upon us: Bayart's duel with Alonso de Sotomayor was fought in the Italian fashion with rapiers, a fencing match and not an old-fashioned exercise with axe or sword. Bayart had also to resist suggestions by the duke of Ferrara that the best means of overcoming the pope was by poison; and little quarter was shown in the ferocious battle between Italians, French, Spaniards and Germans. The latter with their fearsome pikes now dominated the field. Only Francis I maintained the old estate of chivalry, and the scene in which Bayart, a penniless knight, confers knighthood on the king is the epitaph for all those who had made their name by their knightly prowess:

> On the evening of the Friday, when the battle terminated to the glory of France, rejoicings were made in the camp, and the affair was spoken of in divers fashions. And some were found to have behaved better than others; but above all it was determined that the good Knight had approved himself such as he had even done on all former

30 Jacques de Mailles, *The right joyous and pleasant history of the feats, gests and prowesses of the chevalier Bayart*, tr. Sara Coleridge (London 1906).
31 *Ibid.*, 20

occasions, when he had been in similar circumstances. The King, desirous of doing him signal honour, received the order of knighthood from his hands. Wherein he did wisely; for by one more worthy it could not have been conferred on him.[32]

Beside chivalric biographies, concerned with individual knights, we need to set the chivalric chronicle, painting a wider canvas, but still with the figures of the heroes of the day very much in the foreground. The most famous of these are of course the chronicles of Jean Froissart, canon of Chimay and self-appointed 'Secretary of Chivalry'.[33] He modelled his work on that of Jean le Bel, canon of Liège, who had recorded the early years of the Hundred Years' War, and like Le Bel, his main interest was not in the broader political view, but in the individual protagonists. His prologue is the key to his attitude; he roundly declare that the object of his work is

> that the honourable enterprises, noble adventures, and deeds of arms, performed in the wars between England and France, may be properly related, and held in perpetual remembrance – to the end that brave men, taking example from them, may be encouraged in their well-doing. I sit down to record a history deserving great praise...

Froissart had written poetry and romances before he came to write chronicles, and his pages are strongly coloured by the concepts and values of the romances. Even when he conveys a large amount of factual information, the focus is always on the protagonists, and the military manoeuvres and larger strategic issues take second place to the feats of arms of his heroes. As an eye-witness and indefatigable collector of the reminiscences of eye-witnesses, he is invaluable as a historian, but it is personality rather than politics which fascinates him. His eulogies of individual knights amount to heroic lives in miniature. Sir Walter Manny was a compatriot of Froissart's in Hainault and like him enjoyed Queen Philippa's patronage after her marriage to Edward III in 1328. He is one of the six knights mentioned by both writers in their prologues. Knighted for his exploits on the Scottish campaign of 1333, it was he who led the English troops into France in 1338 as a result of a vow to be the first to strike a blow. During 1342 he was active in Brittany, helping the countess of Montfort to defend her husband's territories. At one point, he and his men were besieged with her at Guingamp; after dinner one evening, Manny looked out of the window at the great siege engine which the French had built, and turning to his companions suggested that they go out and destroy it as a fitting conclusion to the entertainment, which they proceeded to do. As they retired, the enemy set out in pursuit: 'Sir Walter Manny, seeing this, exclaimed,

---

32   *Ibid.*, 301.

33   The phrase is from Peter J.Ainsworth, *Jean Froissart and the Fabric of History* (Oxford 1990) 8.

"May I never be embraced by my mistress and dear friend, if I enter castle or fortress before I have unhorsed one of these gallopers."[34] At which a skirmish ensues in which 'many brilliant actions, captures and rescues might have been seen'. Later in the same expedition, when two of his compatriots were about to be beheaded to satisfy Louis d'Espagne's wrath, Manny rescued them by a daring sally from the castle of Hennebont into the besieging army. Froissart also has his examples of the power of love for a knight: Eustace d'Aubrecicourt, one of the English allies, was 'much in love with the lady Isabella de Juliers.... This lady was greatly attached to Sir Eustace, for his gallant deeds of arms, which had been related to her; and she sent him coursers, hackneys, and letters full of love which so much emboldened Sir Eustace, and spurred him to perform such feats of chivalry and arms, that all those under him made fortunes.'[35] But the dénouement — he married her — is not within the chivalric conventions.

Nor is it only deeds of arms that Froissart relates: his story of how the Black Prince honoured king John of France after defeating and capturing him at Poitiers is the ideal example of the knightly virtue of courtesy:

> The prince himself served the king's table, as well as the others, with every mark of humility. and would not sit down at it, in spite of all his entreaties for him so to do, saying, that 'he was not worthy of such an honour, nor did it appertain to him to seat himself at the table of so great a king, or of so valiant a man as he had shown himself by his actions that day'. He added also with a noble air: 'Dear sir, do not make a poor meal because the Almighty God has not gratified your wishes in the event of this day... In my opinion, you have cause to be glad that the success of this battle did not turn out as you desired; for you have this day acquired such high renown for prowess, that you have surpassed all the best knights on your side. I do not, dear sir, say this to flatter you, for all those of our side who have seen and observed the actions of each party, have unanimously allowed this to be your due, and decree you the prize and garland for it.'[36]

In Froissart's eyes, the loss of a kingdom is as nothing against the winning of personal renown.

Again, Froissart explains how in 1388 he considered 'that great deeds of arms would not happen for a long while in the borders of Picardy and in Flanders, because there was peace there,' so for fear of idleness he set off to visit the count of Foix at Orthez in the foothills of the Pyrenees, gathering news as he went. The count, Gaston Phoebus, made him welcome and readily answered his questions, 'saying that the history I was employed on would in times to come be more sought after thatn any

---

34   Froissart, *Chronicles*, ed. Lettenhove, IV, 46; tr. Johnes, I, 108.

35   *Ibid*, VI, 254; I, 258

36   *Ibid.*, V, 460-1; I, 226-7.

other, "because", he added, "more gallant deeds of arms have been performed within these last fifty years, and more wonderful things have happened, than for three hundred years before." ' With this encouragement, Froissart set to work and gathered much information, which, he says, he will set down 'to give examples to these worthies who wish to advance themselves in renown. If I have heretofore dwelt on gallant deeds, attacks and captures, of castles, towns and forts, on hard-fought battles and skirmishes, many more will now ensue; all of which, by God's grace, I will truly narrate.'[37] Among these deeds, to take just one example, are the jousts held at St Inglevert near Paris in 1390, which, being an eminently chivalric occasion, are accorded a very much lengthier description than the whole of the battle of Poitiers.

Other secular chroniclers adopted the same chivalric stance, though to a lesser degree. The poem on the Black Prince by Chandos Herald (who decries *jongleurs* and proclaims his historical intent) written *c.* 1385, was one of Froissart's sources, and is an excellent illustration of the contrast between Froissart's achievement and the usual tradition of secular historical writing for the same audience. Chandos Herald is very brief — he recounts the whole of the prince's career in 4,000 short lines — and chivalry provides no more than the occasional flourish: of a skirmish which no other historian felt worthy of mention, Chandos Herald can say, 'such deeds of arms were done there that Roland and Oliver and Ogier le Danois, who was so courteous, might have met their match',[38] but it probably disguises the fact that he has no information on the details.

This genre was clearly in demand, as the work of other heralds, Gelre Herald from Flanders and Peter Suchenwirt from Austria, is in the same vein: brief poetic sketches of the careers of contemporary chivalric heroes, executed with a greater or lesser degree of literary sophistication. They were primarily, like so much of the heralds' work, matters of record; only in Froissart's hands do the same topics become matters of inspiration and example.

A similar desire to record lies behind another chivalric biography which is an artistic rather than poetic record, the so-called *Beauchamp Pageant*, written in the 1470s and illustrated with miniatures on alternate pages. It describes the career of Sir Richard Beauchamp, earl of Warwick, who died in 1439, and was probably written for one of his descendants. The emphasis of the book is very much on his career as a jouster, and it was composed at a time when the English court, under Edward IV, was once again enthusiastic about tournaments and chivalry. It describes Beauchamp's pilgrimage to Jerusalem and his travels in eastern Europe, 'by such Coostes as his Auncestry hadde

---

37   Froissart, *Chroniques*, ed Lettenhove, XI, 4; tr. Johnes, II, 68-9.

38   Chandos Herald, *Life of the Black Prince*, in *The Life and Campaigns of the Black Prince*, tr. and ed. Richard Barber (Woodbridge and New York 1986) 87

labored in and specially Erle Thomas his grauntfadre';[39] but he was unable to join the Teutonic Knights in fighting the heathen, as they were recovering from their disastrous defeat at Grünwald in 1410, and diverted himself instead with 'many turnamentes and other faites of werre'.[40] Even when he was appointed governor of Calais, his biographer records how, since the French refused to attack, 'he cast in his mynde to do some newe poynt of chevalry' and challenged them to joust instead. This is very much in the tradition of Froissart, but on a smaller, almost domestic canvas – a personal reminder and example to Beauchamp's descendants.

We also catch glimpses of individual chivalric exploits in other chronicles which lack the overall chivalric bias of Froissart's work. The story of Louis Robessart's death is found in two contemporary chronicles and in a book of instruction for his sons written by the Burgundian knight Ghillebert de Lannoy. The story, which is substantially the same in all three versions, tells how in the Anglo-French war in 1430, Louis Robessart, a knight of the Garter, was attacked in a skirmish in northern France, and drove off the enemy despite their superior numbers. However, they returned with reinforcements, and although Robessart had ample warning of their arrival, he refused even to take refuge in the nearby castle, but held his ground, sending his men to safety when he saw that they could not hold out: 'and there he died gloriously, honourably, and with very few of his company'. And it is as an example of chivalrous courage that he earns his place in de Lannoy's moral precepts.[41]

Perhaps the strangest, and certainly the most elusive, of the literary heroes of chivalry is Ulrich von Lichtenstein. He was a poet and knight from Styria in southern Austria, and wrote his chivalric autobiography in the mid-thirteenth century.[42] His 'device' for the series of tournaments which he fought in honour of his lady was Frau Venus, deriving from the poems of the Minnesingers, and he claimed to have carried out the 'quest', a journey which took him from the Tirol as far afield as Venice, dressed in woman's clothing. Within the imaginative framework of his adventures in love, Ulrich describes with some degree of truth and at least as much fiction his jousting exploits, of which he seems to have kept some kind of record. The 'Venus journey' took place in 1226, and lasted for a month; he attempted to repeat it in 1240, with an 'Arthur journey', but politics intervened. *The Service of Ladies*, as Ulrich called his work,

---

39 *Pageant of the Birth Life and Death of Richard Beauchamp Earl of Warwick K.G.* ed. Viscount Dillon and W.H.St John Hope (London 1914) 44

40 *Ibid..,52*

41 See David Morgan, 'From a Death to a View: Louis Robessart, Johan Huizinga, and the Political Significance of Chivalry' in *Chivalry in the Renaissance,* ed. Sydney Anglo, (Woodbridge & Rochester N. Y., 1990) 93-106.

42 *Ulrich von Liechtenstein's* Service of Ladies, tr. J.W.Thomas (Chapel Hill, N.C. 1969)

is a remarkable book; but whenever we look at the detail closely, he has quietly exaggerated the number of contenders or the number of spears broken until the total reaches fictional proportions – 307 broken in a month, or a hundred in one day. It is the work of a successful man of the world – when Ulrich wrote it he was a highly placed court official – who is writing for his friends' entertainment, with a sly dig at the more extravagant ideas of courtly love, but who completely accepts the basic convention. Some of his adventures are Falstaffian, as when Ulrich/Venus finds himself trapped in his bath by his lady's page, who pelts him with rose-petals, or when he attempts to climb a rope of sheets to his lady's chamber and is left suspended a few feet off the ground. Yet he is proud of his thirty-three years as a chivalrous knight, and writes for instruction as well as entertainment. However, his parting advice is disarmingly simple and far from the artificial emotion of his adventures. As usual, he sees the days of his youth as ideal: men nowadays are out to deceive women. His advice is to return to a simpler way of life than that which he attempted: a knight should not seek God's grace, honour, ease and wealth all at once, as he did, but take each in turn. There is a little of everything in Ulrich's book – romance, autobiography, poetry, moral instruction – and it is a fitting note on which to end our survey of chivalric biographies, as his story merges back into the literature which was chivalry's original inspiration.

PART THREE

Chivalry in the Field

7

The development of the tournament

THE TOURNAMENT may be fairly described as the central ritual of chivalry.[1] It draws on both military tradition and the ideals of chivalry; it first appears when chivalry is in its infancy, and only vanishes when chivalry itself is no longer an active inspiration. Its origins lie in military games and exercises as old as the history of war itself. At what point the tournament emerged as a distinct form of martial sport is not clear, and the question has been further obfuscated by chroniclers anxious to claim the longest possible record of participation in tournaments for the ancestors of their patrons. The games of horsemanship held in 842 to celebrate the alliance of Louis the German and Charles the Bald have been claimed as the first tournament on record, though it is clear that these simple manoeuvres, where the two teams charged each other, wheeled about and took turns to simulate flight, involved none of the actual combat which was an essential part of the tournament.[2]

The tournament seems to have emerged as a distinct form of martial game at the end of the eleventh century, somewhere in the environs of northern France, and this coincides with the first appearance of the couched lance in warfare. The significance of the new technique was that it required training and practice in order to use it effectively. Moreover, as its maximum effect could only be obtained by a number of knights acting in unison, team training and team practice were necessary. The tournament fulfilled all these needs admirably, and indeed may have developed precisely as a result of those needs. There are a smattering of references to tournaments which fall in the late eleventh century. The earliest of these occurs in Geoffrey of Malaterra's account of the wars of the Norman adventurers, Robert Guiscard, duke of Calabria and Roger, Count of Sicily. At a siege in 1062 the young men from both armies who were 'ambitious for praise' tourneyed together under the city walls and one Arnold, the count's brother-in-law was killed.[3] Geoffrey was writing in 1110, so that even if

1   The following three chapters are based on Richard Barber and Juliet Barker, *Tournaments: Jousts, Chivalry and Pageants in the Middle Ages* , (Woodbridge and New York 1989); the detailed references to archive material have not been repeated here. I am most grateful to Juliet Barker for allowing me to rework this material.
2   Nithard, *Carolingian Chronicles* ed. J. W. Scholz (Michigan 1970) 164.

his account may be anachronistic for the year 1062, jousting of this kind must have been familiar by the turn of the twelfth century.

The second, more famous reference occurs in two local chronicles of the town of Tours in northern France. Under the year 1066 the *Chronicle of St Martin of Tours* records:

> In the seventh year of the emperor Henry and the third year of king Philip, there was a treacherous plot at Angers, where Geoffrey de Preuilly and other barons were killed. This Geoffrey de Preuilly invented tournaments.[4]

Unfortunately for the early history of tournaments, this chronicle was written in the first two decades of the thirteenth century when the sport was already very popular. The contemporary sources on which it is based, while relating Geoffrey de Preuilly's treachery and subsequent murder, make no mention of tournaments in any form. The suggestion, therefore, that Geoffrey invented tournaments, unless it relies on some oral tradition, is without solid foundation.

By the beginning of the twelfth century, references to tournaments are on the increase and the sources are more reliable. The Byzantine princess, Anna Comnena, who had no interest in claiming early origins for the sport, relates a most fascinating anecdote in her *Alexiad*. One of the French knights who went on the First Crusade sat on the Imperial throne in the presence of the Emperor. When this insolent gesture was reproved he made a defiant speech challenging the Emperor:

> I am a pure Frank and of noble birth. One thing I know: at a crossroads in the country where I was born is an ancient shrine; to this anyone who wishes to engage in single combat goes, prepared to fight; there he prays to God for help and there he stays awaiting the man who will dare to answer his challenge. At that crossroads I myself have spent time, waiting and longing for the man who would fight – there was never one who dared.[5]

Although a tournament is not specifically mentioned by name in this account, all the elements of the game are here including the crossroads, the challenge and the chance encounter which became such features of knight errantry in the chivalric romances and the historic *pas d'armes*. Indeed, this appears to be a very early reference to the specific form of the sport known as 'seeking adventures'.

3   Geoffrey of Malaterra, 'De rebus gestis Roberti Guiscardi, Ducis Calabriae, et Rogerii, Comitis Siciliae' in *Thesaurus Antiquitatem et Historiarum Siciliae* ed. J.G.Graevius (Amsterdam 1723) iv, bk.ii, ch.xxiii, col.26.

4   *Recueil des chroniques de Touraine* ed André Salon, Société archéologique de Touraine, *Collection des documents sur l'histoire de Touraine* I (Tours 1854) xvi,125; xxxviii,189.

5   Anna Comnena, *The Alexiad* ed. & tr. E. R. A. Sewter (Harmondsworth 1979) 326.

The usual context of the first 'tournaments' was warfare itself. William of Malmesbury, for instance, describes how King Stephen's men, confronted at the siege of Lincoln in 1141 by the knights of Robert, earl of Gloucester, began the battle by performing 'the prelude to battle, which they call a joust, because they were skilled in the art'.[6] On this occasion, however, they had chosen the wrong moment and their less chivalrous opponents promptly rode them down and began the battle in earnest. This did not mean that the king's men had a monopoly on the sport: shortly afterwards, at the siege of Winchester, it was the earl's knights who daily rode out of the city 'to perform chivalrous deeds'.

The tournament was being used as a cover for rebellion as early as the 1140s. When Frederick Barbarossa, himself a knight 'trained, as is customary, in military sports', invaded Bavaria to attack his enemy Henry of Wolfratshausen, the Bavarians, and particularly the counts and other nobles, according to the chronicler Otto of Freising, 'betook themselves to the stronghold of the aforesaid count, as though to celebrate a passage of arms (which we are now accustomed to call a tournament). And so that most redoubtable youth (Frederick Barbarossa), coming upon the Bavarians as they stood outside the wall awaiting him under arms, assaulted them not as in play, but manfully making a serious assault.'[7]

In both cases what actually followed was a military action: Lincoln is a skirmish, Wolfratshausen the prelude to an actual battle. In Spain this usage continues much later than elsewhere in Europe. In a set of statutes of Aragon about 1300, the paragraph in which 'torneo' occurs is entirely concerned with warfare. This meaning also appears in the law code of Alfonso X of Castile in the mid-thirteenth century, the *Siete Partidas*: Alfonso explains that the *torneo*, a sally by the defenders or besiegers of a castle, after which both sides return (*tornanse*) to their respective camps, is a warlike manoeuvre not to be confused 'with these tournaments (*torneamientos*) practised by men in some countries, not in order to kill each other, but in order not to forget the use of arms.'[8] The statutes of Navarre use *torneamiento* in the sense of *torneo* in a similar passage. We have to remember also that 'torneo' in Spanish was for a long time an exclusively warlike manoeuvre, before it came to mean 'tournament' in our sense in the thirteenth century. Yet these episodes are not simply to be dismissed as evidence that tournaments at this time were hostile engagements only. Otto of Freising is sure of the difference: 'not as in play', he says, implying that the element of play is the distinguishing mark of the tournament.

When twelfth century knights fought a tournament in peacetime for sport, it was a *mêlée* or free for all involving a number of knights, fought out over several miles of

---

6   William of Malmesbury, *Historia Novella*, ed. K.R.Potter (Oxford 1955) 48-9.

7   Otto of Freising, *Gesta Friderici seu rectius Chronica* ed. F.-J. Schmale (Berlin 1965) 180.

8   Alfonso X, *Las siete Partidas*, II, bk. XXIII, ch. xxvii (author's translation).

open countryside encompassing rivers, woods, vineyards and farm buildings – all of which provided useful opportunities for ambush and sortie. The boundaries were unmarked in the early days, though the field was vaguely designated by reference to two towns: tournaments were thus proclaimed 'between Gournai and Ressons', for example, or 'between Anet and Sorel'. The only formal limits were certain specially designated areas which were fenced off as refuges where knights could rest or rearm in safety during the combat.

Several companies of knights took part, under the leadership of the same lords whom they followed and served in warfare, and often as many as two hundred knights participated on each side. At this early period there were no rules to distinguish the tournament from real battle: there were no foul strokes or prohibited tactics and, even if there had been, there was no-one to supervise or enforce them. It was thus quite common for several knights to band together to attack a single tourneyer: there were instances of tourneyers being attacked despite the fact that they had lost vital parts of their armour in the skirmishes and occasions on which any weapon to hand was used – including bows and arrows and crossbows. The only concessions to the sporting nature of the combat were the provision of refuges and the *sine qua non* that the object of the game was to capture and ransom the opposing knights, not to kill them. Here was a rough and tumble game which was so strongly imitative of battle that it often became indistinguishable from it.

By 1130 the sport had proliferated to such a degree that it attracted the attention of the Church. Significantly, the first official pronouncement on the subject was a condemnation. This was hardly surprising as the Church had played a leading role in Europe in its efforts to control the violence of medieval society. The Peace of God movement had for over a century formally attempted to limit martial activity and protect non-combatants. Local church councils had prohibited fighting from Friday to Monday and on feast days. Enforcers of these rules were sought among the local knights who acted as champions of the church and their efforts were backed up by ecclesiastical sanctions against offenders. It was therefore inevitable that the Church would set its face against the imitation warfare of tournaments. At the Council of Clermont in 1130 the ninth canon issued stated that

> we firmly prohibit those detestable markets or fairs (*nundinas vel ferias*) at which knights are accustomed to meet to show off their strength and their boldness and at which the deaths of men and dangers to the soul often occur. But if anyone is killed there, even if he demands and is not denied penance and the *viaticum*, ecclesiastical burial shall be withheld from him.[9]

9   C.-J. Hefele & H. Leclercq, *Histoire des Conciles* (Paris 1912) V.i, 729.

Apart from its spiritual dangers, the tournament was soon associated with political unrest. In England, Stephen's troubled reign seems to have seen a particularly enthusiastic outbreak of tourneying. In addition to the instance already cited, in 1140 Ranulph, earl of Chester was able to recapture Lincoln castle from the royalists with only three men-at-arms because the military garrison had deserted their posts in order to take part in martial sports elsewhere. Contemporary chroniclers pointed out the connection between anarchy and the new sport. According to William of Newburgh, in the days of Henry I and Henry II, tourneying was placed under firm royal prohibition and anyone wishing to indulge in the sport had to travel overseas to do so. However, due to the shameful weakness of Stephen's rule, there was no proper government and therefore tournaments flourished.[10] He is pointing out for the first time what was later to become almost a truism: that there was a distinct correlation between the amount of (particularly illicit) tourneying activity and the amount of government control. During periods of weak kingship, such as the reigns of Stephen, John and Henry III in England, tournaments became increasingly frequent and often had distinctly subversive overtones.

It is only towards the end of the twelfth century that the tournament acquires a degree of respectability, through the new chivalric romances. In this new set of values, stressing the importance of courtly love and service to the mistress who inspired that love, played out against a background of court ceremonial, the tournament took a central role. It was here that the heroes of romance won their ladies, proved their prowess and displayed their legendary strength and courage.

It is no accident that the patrons of the arch-romancer and great innovator of the genre, Chrétien de Troyes, were Henry, count of Champagne and Philip, count of Flanders, both devotees and patrons of the tournament. The importance of this connection cannot be over-emphasised, for Henry of Champagne was married to the daughter of Eleanor of Aquitaine, and his brothers-in-law were Henry the Young King, Geoffrey of Brittany and Richard I. Eleanor's family were equally lavish in their patronage of courtly literature and chivalric sport. A small circle of inter-related, powerful, rich and cultured young men met regularly on the tournament fields of northern France and the Low Countries. During the day they exercised themselves in arms and in the evenings they would gather round the fires and tell stories. Arnold count of Ardres, who was also part of this charmed chivalric circle, employed several *jongleurs* and ancient knights, each with a different speciality – tales of the Holy Land, Arthurian romances or Carolingian *chansons de geste*.[11]

---

10 William of Newburgh, II, 422-3.

11 Lambert of Ardres, *Chronicon Ghisnense et Ardense* ed. D. Godefroy (Paris 1855) 215-7.

Patronage of chivalrous sport and courtly literature went hand in hand. Naturally, because they were catering for the interests of tourneyers, the romance writers dwelt at great length on the sport and painted it in glowing colours. This, in turn, helped to give tournaments greater prestige because they played such a decisive role in the lives of romance heroes. Thus a kind of symbiosis developed between tournaments and courtly literature, each feeding the other and thereby encouraging their mutual development. It was largely due to this meeting of like minds – the Young King, Henry of Champagne and Philip of Flanders – that in the 1170s and the 1180s there was such a proliferation of tournaments. If the texts about Arnold of Ardres and William Marshal are to be believed, tournaments were held almost fortnightly in the region at this time. Many of the protagonists were young men, recently knighted, the eldest sons of nobles sent out with a band of similarly placed peers to learn the skills of knighthood. Thus began what became a great tradition: a period – perhaps months, perhaps years – of chivalrous apprenticeship spent on the tourneying circuits of northern France. Nearly a hundred years later, despite the fact that tournaments were no longer prohibited by the secular authorities elsewhere in Europe, the tradition was still in force and young knights like Edward I of England, for example, still travelled to this area for two years of tourneying.

There were a number of outstanding personalities tourneying at the time and their patronage of literature ensured that their feats were recorded for posterity. The most informative and important of these chronicles was the biography of William Marshal, already discussed in the last chapter. His skill at tournaments was renowned. At his first outing, at Le Mans in 1167, riding a borrowed mount in the company of his lord, William of Tancarville, he won four and a half horses for himself together with a similar number of horses for his esquires, as well as baggage horses and equipment.[12] This success encouraged him to adopt a business-like approach, completely at odds with the idealism of romance tourneyers. William's object was to win as much booty, in the form of ransoms, horses and equipment, as possible. He even went so far as to enter into a partnership with another knight of the Young King's household. For two years they followed the tourneying circuit, fighting as a team and dividing their winnings. A royal clerk kept a record of their successes and he noted that in the ten months between Pentecost and Lent, they captured one hundred and three knights, together with their horses, harness and baggage.[13] For a knight without a patrimony, success at the tournament could be a means of gaining wealth without the social stigma attached to trade and at the same time enhancing his reputation for knightly skills.

12   *L'histoire de Guillaume le Maréchal* ll.1374–80.
13   *Ibid,* ll.3381–425.

The descriptions of tournaments in the history of William Marshal, which are some of the fullest in medieval sources, are nonetheless perfunctory. The companies line up to face one another; one company usually conducts itself in a disciplined and orderly fashion, the other in a disorganized muddle, as the leaders vie for the privilege of striking the first blow. Inevitably, the company proceeding in serried ranks is victorious – it is the company manoeuvre, not the skill of the individual, which wins the day. There are no love tokens or devices and (except on one occasion) no watching ladies. Though outstanding feats of arms and public acclamation of success are valued, it is victory and booty which are the prime concerns. Instances of the pragmatism of participants in tournaments in northern France at the end of the twelfth century abound. The flower of chivalry, Philip of Flanders, was not above holding his men back from the fighting until the other tourneyers were exhausted and therefore made easy pickings. He was only out-manoeuvred when William Marshal persuaded the Young King to adopt the same tactic and thereby turned the tables on the Flemish.[14] William himself, when dining at an inn while a tournament was taking place round him, could not resist capturing a tourneyer who fell off his horse and broke his leg in front of him, even though he was not actually participating on this occasion.[15] There are other good stories about William: he once lost a prisoner as he was leading him back to his tent when the latter was knocked off his horse by a drainpipe unnoticed by his captor; on another occasion, he won the prize at a tournament, but could not be found for the presentation, and was eventually traced to the local forge, where he had his head on an anvil for a blacksmith to beat his helm back into shape so that it could be removed.[16]

There was a much more serious side to the sport, nevertheless, which was minimized or ignored even by the author of the *History of William Marshal*. Although rules and regulations were rudimentary, customs quickly developed and became universally accepted. For instance, the division into tournament teams was usually decided by the area from which the participants came but an alignment of teams contrary to custom could cause real offence. When Baldwin of Hainault joined the French (who would otherwise have been outnumbered) instead of his natural allies, the Flemish, at a tournament between Gournay and Resson in 1169, Philip of Flanders was so infuriated that he immediately attacked with all his horse and foot drawn up 'as if for war'.[17]

---

14   *Ibid.*, ll.2723 ff.
15   *Ibid.*, ll.7209-32.
16   *Ibid.*, ll.2840ff, 3102ff.
17   Gislebert of Mons, *La Chronique* ed. L.Vanderkindere (Brussels 1904) 97-8.

Another problem, also minimized in the *History of William Marshal*, was the number of deaths caused by tourneying. In the rough and tumble of the *mêlée*, particularly when real hostilities had prompted the tournament in the first place, the dangers were considerable. The twelfth century had already seen a large list of prominent tournament casualties including Geoffrey of Brittany, son of Henry II, who was killed in a tournament near Paris in 1186 and Leopold of Austria, who died in 1194 after his horse had fallen on him 'while he passed the time in a warlike exercise and game'. Attempts were made to avoid such loss of life: the church's prohibition on the sport was generally ineffectual but in 1175, however, archbishop Wichmann of Magdeburg ordered that the church's decree of excommunication and refusal of ecclesiastical burial to those killed in tournaments should be strictly observed, after he had heard of the death of Conrad, son of the margrave Dietrich von der Lausitz, who had received a fatal wound in an Austrian tournament. It was not simply Conrad's status which prompted this action but the fact that this 'plague of a sport', as the chronicler calls tournaments, had already claimed the lives of sixteen knights in Saxony that year. The archbishop sent messengers to Austria to ensure that Conrad was not given ecclesiastical burial. He refused to relent until evidence was provided that Conrad had repented and taken the Cross before his death; his relatives also had to swear on holy relics 'to abstain from tournaments forever, not to permit any such occasion on their domains, and to prevent their men and knights by all possible means from taking part in them'.[18]

Despite such occasional action by the church, it fell very largely to the secular authorities to attempt to control the sport. In England this was achieved quite brilliantly by Richard I who, well aware of all the problems caused by tournaments, drew up his innovative and unique decree of 1194 by which, in blatant contravention of the church's ban on tournaments, he laid down a licensing system which would enable them to be held legitimately on English soil – it is interesting that the decree did not cover his foreign dominions where tournaments were already rife. Richard, as we have already noted, was one of the charmed inner circle of chivalrous patrons in northern France, although before he came to the throne, he himself had preferred the minor warfare that went on almost continually in the duchy of Aquitaine to tournaments, and rarely, if ever, took part in them. Yet Richard appreciated not only the overpowering attraction which it held for his knightly subjects, who would tourney whether or not he permitted it, but also the advantages of an apprenticeship in arms served in the lists.

To this end, Richard introduced a decree which recognized five places in England as official tournament sites: between Salisbury and Wilton (Wiltshire), Warwick and

18   *MGH SS* XXIII 155-6.

Kenilworth (Warwickshire), Stamford and Warinford (probably Suffolk), Brackley and Mixbury (Northamptonshire) and Blyth and Tickhill (Nottinghamshire). Any knights who wished to tourney could go to any of these sites having first obtained a licence for the tournament to take place for which he had to pay ten marks. In addition to this, he had also to obtain a personal licence in the form of a fee graduated according to rank, from twenty marks for an earl to two marks for a landless knight. It is significant that no tourneyer of lower status than a landless knight was envisaged and that foreign knights were specifically prohibited from tourneying in England.[19]

This tournament decree set up a system whereby English knights could tourney legitimately (as far as the state was concerned) and peacefully against their fellow countrymen. Perhaps it was his own or his brothers' personal experiences of tourneying which made Richard exclude foreign knights, for this effectively prevented the setting up of a tourneying circuit in England like the one in northern France and the Low Countries which they had frequented. It was certainly one way of trying to limit the potential for disaster by excluding the sort of political rivalry consequent upon a mix of knights of different origins. The choice of five sites was also a deliberate attempt to limit destruction. As the tournament ranged over a wide area of countryside it was definitely an advantage to have a location designated in advance, well away from the most vulnerable places such as towns, monastic houses and royal forests. Richard certainly seems to have had an eye for the preservation of his forests as the preamble to his decree specifically stated that its purpose was:

> so that our peace shall not be broken, the power of our justiciar shall not be threatened and loss shall not fall on our royal forests.

The five designated sites were fairly well spread over the country to serve the needs of the knightly classes but there was noticeably no provision of sites in either the west or the north of England – both areas where royal control was comparatively weak and therefore most vulnerable.

Richard's decree of 1194 was unparalleled elsewhere, and allowed the pattern of English tournaments to develop in a separate and distinct way from those on the Continent. Though the counts of Flanders, Hainault, Champagne and the rest patronized and personally participated in the sport, just as Richard did, they made no effort to legitimise it or monopolise its control. The kings of France similarly ignored the possibilities presented by licensing the sport and, with singular ineffectiveness, continued to issue prohibitions of tournaments alongside prohibitions on private war.

19   *Foedera* I. i, 65. For a full discussion of the decree, see Juliet Barker, *The Tournament in England* (Woodbridge 1986) 53-6.

In England, the fact that a tournament was either legitimate or illegitimate, licensed or unlicensed, gave it a special relationship with politics and therefore nuances which were simply non-existent elsewhere. Similarly, the fact that the sport was under royal control in due course enabled the kings of England to use their patronage to considerable propagandist effect.

Records of tournaments in the first half of the thirteenth century are much more variable than in the late twelfth century. In England, they were frequently banned in periods of political uncertainty, for example during Henry III's minority, during the power struggle between the English barons and the French court party, and during the events leading up to Simon de Montfort's rebellion. Such tournaments as did take place were marred by excessive violence and ill-feeling. And other necessities of state might put a damper on tourneying activity. Even Edward I, whose enthusiasm for tournaments we shall examine, was obliged by war on three fronts and the necessity of sending armies to Gascony, Wales and Scotland at the end of the 1290s to seriously attempt the suppression of tourneying activity. On at least two occasions, large numbers of knights were committed to prison and had their lands seized for leaving the king's army without permission during lulls in the fighting to attend jousts in England.

In times of peace, however, they were positively encouraged. In 1228 Henry III undertook to secure an ecclesiastical licence from the Pope for a tournament at Northampton so that the participants would not be excommunicated; when it actually took place, he sent letters to all his household knights positively ordering them to attend,[20] and four years later, he allowed tournaments at Dunstable, Brackley, Stamford and Blyth.

We can detect some developments in the sport during this period, despite its varying political fortunes. In 1216 the English barons tourneying with the French knights who, under Prince Louis, had invaded England in support of the baronial cause. A particularly interesting feature of this hastilude was that the participants were all clad in padded garments instead of armour and using lightweight lances instead of the usual heavy war ones. These are the classic hallmarks of a *béhourd*, an informal or practice tournament, and reinforce the idea that this was a friendly meeting in arms, even though, despite these precautions, a prominent English baron, Geoffrey de Mandeville, was killed.[21]

Evidence from Germany shows that individual jousts, as depicted by Matthew Paris in the margins of the English chronicles he wrote at this time, had begun to predominate, and that literary accounts of knightly exploits were being deliberately imitated. In 1227 a knight from Thuringia named Waltmann von Setenstete

20   *Calendar of Close Rolls 1227-1231* , 113.
21   Matthew Paris, *Chronica Majora* ed. H. R. Luard, RS 57 (London 1872-83) II, 614-5.

announced that he was setting up a 'forest' (a German name for a type of 'round table' joust) near the town of Merseburg, to which he would bring a beautiful girl.[22] Imitating a familiar pattern in the romances of chivalry, he would fight three courses with anyone who challenged him on the way, and if he was defeated, the victor could lead away the girl and take his arms and equipment as well. However, he reached the place named as the 'forest' unscathed, despite numerous challenges from knights who had come from far and wide. At the 'forest', some kind of festival was held, and he returned home in triumph with his companion. The literary overtones of this event are paralleled by Ulrich von Lichtenstein's journey the previous year, which we have already discussed.

Another new aspect of tourneying, royal patronage based on personal enthusiasm on the part of the king, emerged with the accession of Edward I in England; he and his successors did not lose their royal dignity by participating in a sport which was no respecter of persons; indeed, by so doing they enhanced their chivalric reputations and won an international renown. Edward's tourneying career began when he was still heir to the throne with a *béhourd* at Blyth in 1258, in padded clothing and with light weapons. Despite these precautions, William Longsword and Robert de Quincy were killed and Roger Bigod's faculties were permanently impaired as a result of injuries received in the combat: Edward himself escaped unscathed.[23] Tournaments occurred frequently in his reign: in 1278, Edward himself sponsored what was clearly a classic example of a *béhourd* at Windsor; thirty-eight knights, including the king, took part wearing specially-commissioned armour made of *cuir bouilli*, leather boiled until it was almost as hard as metal though much lighter. Whalebone swords and wooden shields were also used. Although the accounts for preparing the armour are extant, there is no record of what actually occurred in the field.[24] Edward's victories over the Welsh were celebrated with a great show of chivalric strength; and in 1284 a splendid tournament was held at Caernarvon to celebrate the birth of the prince of Wales. The frequency of tournaments in his reign is shown by the royal household accounts; among other entries, these record six tournaments attended by John of Brittany in 1285–6 and seven attended by John of Brabant in 1292–3, none of which are mentioned in other sources. Both young men were affianced to Edward's daughters, and their expenses were met by him.

By contrast, the kings of France evinced an extreme reluctance to take part in any kind of military sports in their own person and patronage therefore passed into the hands of the great barons. Although in the thirteenth century there was no single focal

---

22   *MGH SS XXX*, 608 (*Cronica Reinhardsbrunnensis*).

23   Matthew Paris, *Chronica Majora*, V, 557.

24   'Copy of a Roll of Purchases for a Tournament at Windsor Park in the Sixth Year of Edward I', ed. S. Lyons, *Archaeologia* First Series, XVII, 1814, 297-310.

point for the sport, and references to hastiludes in France are few and far between, we do have two poems which document in detail specific tournaments. The first of these is the earliest detailed record of a festival which included play-acting as a framework for jousting. In 1278, a hastilude was held at Le Hem in Picardy; it was a spectacular Arthurian festival arranged by the lords of Longueval and Bazentin.[25] The proceedings were initiated by 'Dame Courtoisie' and presided over by a 'Queen Guinevere'; all the attendant knights had to bring a damsel with them, in imitation of the knights-errant of the romances, and an elaborate scenario was created for them. Seven knights came to surrender themselves to the 'queen' because they had been defeated in combat elsewhere by the 'Chevalier au Lyon' or 'Knight with the Lion'. They were followed by the Chevalier au Lyon himself, entering in triumph with the queen's damsels, whom he had supposedly rescued, and even a real lion in his retinue.

The occasion for the jousts in question, which lasted for two days, was the public beating of a damsel who was being punished on her lover's orders for declaring that Guinevere's knights were the best in the world. This provided the opportunity for various knights to vindicate her claim against her lover. The complex arrangements involved not only the knights, but also the ladies and spectators, so that each had an integral role to play. The festival at Le Hem was held in contravention of Louis IX's prohibition on tournaments and this may explain the absence of a *mêlée* tournament on the third day of the proceedings which was the usual format for this type of event.

The other tournament of which we have a full account was held at Chauvency, just outside the French king's jurisdiction, and included a *mêlée* tournament, but had no 'festival' or theatrical elements.[26] In 1285, Louis de Looz, count of Chiny, held a week-long festival; there were jousts on the Monday and Tuesday, but those on the Wednesday were cancelled when a knight was injured and it was feared that the tournament might be at risk. The event culminated in a *mêlée* tournament on the Thursday. The French visitors lodged at Chauvency with the count's younger brother, while the count of Luxembourg and his men and the knights of Flanders, Hainault and Ruy lodged at the count's own castle of Montmedy. The lodging arrangements provided a natural division into two sides for the actual combat.

A similar convergence of tournaments and festivals was meanwhile taking place in the Low Countries — Flanders, Hainault and Brabant.[27] In this comparatively urban area, hastiludes were not solely the province of the knightly ranks of society, but were

25   Sarrazin, 'Le Roman du Hem' ed. F. Michel in *Histoire des Ducs de Normandie et des Rois d'Angleterre*, SHF (Paris 1840).
26   Jacques Bretel, *Le Tournoi de Chauvency* ed M. Delbouille (Liège 1932).
27   For the civic festivals in the Low Countries see Juliet Vale, *Edward III and Chivalry* (Woodbridge 1982)

also patronised and fought by burghers of the towns and cities. This is not to say that the nobility had no role to play: far from it, for the counts of Flanders were amongst the greatest patrons of chivalry from the twelfth to the fourteenth centuries. But they, like their nobility, were town based and therefore the jousts began to take place in the market squares from the mid-thirteenth century onwards, and became civic festivals. They always involved elaborate pageantry and role-playing, with an emphasis on chivalric romance. At Tournai in 1330–1, thirty-one burghers held an immensely elaborate round table; each of the defenders dressed as and bore the arms of one of the thirty-one kings contemporary with king Arthur. The year previously they had formed a Society of the Round Table, and had sent out invitations to the festival which were accepted by fourteen cities, including Valenciennes, Paris, Bruges, Amiens and Sluys. The jousts themselves took place in the market square, and there was an impressive procession of the participants to the lists. Jean de Sottenghien won the prize, a golden vulture, and the affair was concluded by a banquet at the *hotel de ville* organised by one of the citizens, Jacques de Corbry.

Perhaps the most important of all the festivals of this type was that of the 'Roys de l'Espinette' (King of the Thorn) or 'L'Epervier d'Or' (The Golden Sparrowhawk) held each year at Lille since at least 1278. In 1335, for example, knights from Valenciennes attended dressed in scarlet and carrying three live swans as a rebus on the town's name – 'val aux cygnes' or valley of the swans; they presented a model of the town flanked by towers and bearing standards of the city's arms to the 'roi d'espinette' himself, who appears to have been the victor of the previous year. A Valenciennes citizen, Jacques Grebert, won the prize in the jousts, and was carried off in triumph by four damsels.

The importance of the annual Lille festival was acknowledged by Philip VI of France when he exempted it from a general prohibition on jousts in 1338. Winning the jousts carried immense prestige, and the triumphant knight was often honoured by his own city; in 1352, for example, Michiel Anguille of Ypres was rewarded by his fellow citizens with a gift of Rhenish wine. The main prize of the festival was a golden thorn, which seems to have been a symbol of Christ's crown of thorns. On the other hand, the festivals were firmly rooted in the literary tradition of the romances, and were even called the 'festival of the lord of Joy', a direct reference to the twelfth century romance *Erec et Enide* by Chrétien de Troyes. As at the other urban festivals, great emphasis was placed on the procession of jousters through the streets to the lists, with the important corollary that the civic pride of the participating towns led to great ingenuity in creating mechanical effects rather than simply the wearing of liveries, which seems to have been the custom in England and France. The presiding 'roys de l'espinette' was assured of great honour throughout the year of his office and rode in triumph to a formal coronation which preceded the jousts; the festivities as a whole lasted up to two weeks. At some time in the fourteenth century, the appointment of the new 'roys de l'espinette' came to be made by a college of former 'roys', and thus took on something of the format of an order of chivalry.

The German city records reveal whole series of regular jousts within the towns. At Frankfurt the records start in 1351; there were six up to 1358, followed by annual jousts from 1361–9, and then a less regular series, roughly once every three years to 1400.[28] At Cologne, the town accounts from 1371 to 1381 show a fee paid on twelve occasions to a family whose house was taken over by the city council so that they could watch the jousting from it. At Munich, there were tournaments almost every other year from 1370 to 1440; the city paid for the construction work at the place of the tournament, and for the extra archers and watchmen on the towers and gates.

In Italy, we have a delightful picture of civic jousts in about 1310 from the pen of Folgore di San Gimignano, so called because of the dazzling (*folgorante*) life-style he maintained in the little Italian city of San Gimignano in Tuscany. He wrote two sequences of sonnets in which he mentioned tournaments: in the days of the week, Thursday is the day for combat, 'every Thursday a tournament, knights jousting one against one; let the battle be in a public place, fifty against fifty, a hundred against a hundred.' And for May, in the sequence for the months, he wrote:

> *I give you horses for your games in May*
> *And all of them well trained unto the course,*
> *Each docile, swift, erect, a goodly horse;*
> *With armour on their chests, and bells at play*
> *Between their brows, and pennons fair and gay*
> *Fine nets, and housings meet for warriors*
> *Emblazoned with the shields ye claim for yours,*
> *Gules, argent, or, all dizzy at noon day:*
> *And spears shall split, and fruit go flying up*
> *In merry interchange for wreaths that drop*
> *From balconies and casements far above;*
> *And tender damsels with young men and youths*
> *Shall kiss together on the cheeks and mouths;*
> *And every day be glad with joyful love.*[29]

28   G.L. Kriegk, *Deutsches Burgerthum in Mittelalter* (Frankfurt 1868) 586.

29   *Le rime di Folgore di San Gemignano* ed. Giulio Navone (rptd Bologna 1968) 13; translated by William Heywood, *Palio and Ponte* (London 1904) 191-2.

The different social structure in Italy, where there was none of the tension between landed gentry and city-dwellers, but where the richest and most powerful men were proud of their citizenship, meant that jousts were exclusively a city phenomenon, even when the cities moved from republics and oligarchies towards princely rule. Enthusiasm for jousting in a particular ruling family came to be an important factor from the mid-fourteenth century onwards, as in the jousts held at the Mantuan court of the Gonzagas in 1340, 1366, and 1380.

In Italy, Florence was alone among the merchant cities of Tuscany in having a substantial tradition of jousting. Between 1387 and the seizure of power by Lorenzo de' Medici in 1434, there were at least a dozen jousts. We know of those in 1392 and 1396 from accounts: £100 was paid to three leading citizens in 1392 for expenses for the tournament to be celebrated in Florence 'for the honour and dignity of the commune of Florence', while in 1396 146 florins was spent on two ornate helmets for those who 'ran the best course in the jousts held this month for the honour and magnificence of the commune of Florence.' The diarist who recorded the three jousts held in October and November 1406 also lays great emphasis on prizes: on 24 October the eighteen jousters in the piazza Santa Croce competed for a silver-gilt lion and a velvet cap, while on 31 October, following the knighting of 60 squires from the Guelf faction, eight jousters braved the rain in the piazza Santa Maria Novella to compete for a helmet. The writer notes that the lists 'were not covered', implying that this was sometimes done. The jousts four weeks later were again in the piazza Santa Croce, apparently the traditional site for such events, but the lists were exceptionally large, occupying almost the whole square, 125 paces by 60 paces. There were fourteen to sixteen jousters, the prizes being a helmet with a silver dragon's head, and a 'jousting helm with two golden wings with many green, white and red feathers.' In 1415, it was minuted that 'Saracens' or quintains should be erected on the piazza della Signoria 'as usual', and jousts held, for St Barnabas' day (11 June).

What is remarkable about the civic festivals is that they continued to be held, year in, year out, every year, particularly in the Low Countries, where the longest series runs from the end of the thirteenth century to the last part of the fifteenth century. The expenses were borne by the city, sometimes in conjunction with prominent citizens, and there was no distinction between the social rank of the participants. Burghers assumed the right to carry arms and to armorial bearings without hesitation, even if these were normally regarded as the jealously-guarded privileges of the knightly classes, and they jousted indiscriminately against the hereditary nobles in the lists. It is true that these festivals tended to be purely local in character – it was exceptional for foreign knights to attend – but they provided a continuity of practice and a standard of spectacle unique in Europe.

Such festivals soon began to appear under princely patronage, as for example Edward I's round tables held under his auspices at Kenilworth and Warwick in 1279, Warwick in 1281, Nefyn in 1284 and Falkirk in 1302. We have few details of Edward's feasts, and to learn more about round tables we have to turn to Aragon, where the chronicler Ramon Muntaner (himself a knight) gives us a detailed account of a round table held in the same year by the admiral of Aragon, Roger de Luria, whose triumphant career had included the defeat of the Sicilian fleet, which led to the capture of Sicily by the Aragonese. This was a festival comparable to anything mounted elsewhere in Europe in the thirteenth century. Roger de Luria had lists built with scaffolds for spectators and a wooden castle at one end, 'from which he would issue at the approach of a knight. And on the first day of the round table he, all alone, wished to hold the castle against any man who wished to break a lance.'[30] Jaime I and Sancho IV of Castile were among the spectators, as well as lords from all over Christian Spain and as far afield as Gascony. The first challenger was a knight of the king of Castile's court, Berenguer de Anguera, and the encounter was so fierce that the admiral's lance was shattered and Berenguer de Anguera's helmet was forced off, injuring his face; at which the kings were very concerned, and, although the injuries were not serious, the round table was stopped 'for fear a quarrel should ensue'.

From Germany, we have a description of a spectacular tournament in the form of a 'forest' held by Heinrich, margrave of Meissen and landgrave of Thuringia, at Nordhausen in either 1263 or 1267. Heinrich had a 'marvellously beautiful wood of green trees' built outside the town, among which was a tree with gold and silver leaves.[31] A large number of eminent lords gathered for the tournament, 'some spurred on by courage, others spurred on by love' and if any of them broke a spear on his opponent, he was awarded a silver leaf from the tree. If he succeeded in unhorsing his opponent, he was given a golden leaf. The chronicler notes that it was a spectacle 'worthy of an emperor', and even allowing for the fact that he was writing a century after the events he describes, the way in which the margrave is the undoubted driving force behind the tournament, and uses it to display his own wealth to best effect, points forward to the elaborate royal festivals of the later middle ages. The carefully contrived scenery and the hint of some kind of 'programme' belong to the new style of jousts, highly organised and much more formal.

One of the oddest tournament stories comes to us from Saxony a couple of years later, in 1281–2. According to the town chronicler of Magdeburg, Brun von

---

30   Ramon Muntaner, *The Chronicle of Muntaner* tr. Lady Goodenough, Hakluyt Society Series II, XLVII, L (London 1920-1) II, 433-4.

31   *Annales Vetero-Cellenses*, ed. J.O.Opel, *Mittheilungen der deutschen Gesellschaft zur Erforschung vaterländischer Sprache* I.ii (Leipzig 1874) 206; MGH *Chroniken* II, 563 *Braunschweigische Reimchronik*.

Schonebeck, one of the constables of the town – 'he was a learned man' – presented a joyous entertainment.[32] He 'made a grail', and wrote courtly letters to Goslar, Hildesheim, Brunswick and other places, inviting all those who wished to practice knightly skills to come to Magdeburg. He and his fellow-constables found a beautiful woman, of doubtful morals, whom they called 'Frau Feie' and who was to be given to the victor in the jousts. This aroused great enthusiasm in the surrounding towns. The 'grail' was set up outside the town, with a tree on which the shields of the defenders (two of the town constables) hung. Any would-be challenger rode up and touched one of the shields, and its owner came out to joust with him. But the end was pure anti-climax: 'an old merchant from Goslar' won the hand of 'Frau Feie', married her off with a good dowry and persuaded her to abandon her wild ways. The chronicler notes that 'a whole book in German was made about this', and that Brun von Schonebeck wrote a number of works in German. So was the whole episode perhaps a satire on the knightly aspirations of the young bloods of the city? The downbeat ending might well be taken for satire: but the chronicler draws attention to the regularity of the Whitsuntide games at Magdeburg of 'Roland, Schildekenboom (a tree of shields), round tables and other sports', and this seems to have been a more elaborate version of the regular event. The enthusiasm of the Magdeburg citizens for tournaments is confirmed by a strip of tin figures found in the old marketplace, contemporary with this festival, which shows knights tourneying and what may be allegorical figures referring to such an occasion. So we can award the old merchant riding off home with his unlikely companion his improbable place in the list of tournament champions.

We get a more direct glimpse of the knight's involvement in tournaments from Austria at about the same time, in a collection of letters from Lâa, near Vienna.[33] The letters are rather formal, and may have been kept as models for letter-writing: but the people and events seem real enough. They concern Kadolt von Wehing, captain of the garrison at Lâa; we find him invited to a tournament in nearby St Polten, to which he replies that it is such short notice that he cannot make the necessary preparations; unwilling to let his friend down, he will nonetheless come rather than let their challengers win the day because of his absence.

And when he is invited to a tournament at Eggenburg against newly-made knights from Vienna, he replies that although he is suffering from severe pains from an injury to his armpit, he will come to the tournament for the chance of showing off his skill in arms. Again, Kadolt writes to a knight coming from Znaím in Czechoslovakia, some

32   *Die Chroniken der niedersächsischen Städte: Magdeburg I*, CDS VII (Leipzig 1869) 168-9.
33   *Die 'Laaer Briefsammlung'* ed. Marx Weltlin, Veröffentlichungen des Instituts für Osterreichische Geschichtsforschung XXI (Wien 1975) 104.

sixty miles away, for a tournament in Vienna, suggesting that he should come and rest his horses for a few days, so that they can proceed to the tournament together in good shape.

Under Edward I, knights habitually looked to the royal court for leadership and patronage of chivalric sports, a situation unique to England. The joust, which had been rare before his accession, was already overtaking the tournament in popularity. Most important of all, however, Edward I had established himself as the great patron of all forms of the sport, and had also made the crucial discovery that it had a valuable potential for enhancing his political prestige, a discovery which was to have a major influence on the later history of the tournament. At the end of the thirteenth century, the tournament was a regular feature of the gatherings of princely courts. In December 1290, Rudolf of Habsburg was at Nuremberg, negotiating with the princes of the empire. 'Among the other things they did there, as is the custom at royal courts, the nobles of the court took part in fierce jousts, while the populace watched them.'[34] Ludwig, son of the duke of Bavaria, 'contrary to the practice of princes' insisted on taking part. Unable to find an opponent of equal rank, he challenged a nobleman from Hohenlohe, who at first declined out of respect for the duke; but Ludwig insisted, and they charged at each other. Two or three courses were run, in which the lord of Hohenlohe let his lance drop away, in order to spare Ludwig. In the end, however, he held his lance firm and struck the duke on the neck-armour, penetrating it and causing a fatal wound. When the lance was drawn out, it was found to have a sharpened point, 'for which nothing is impenetrable, but which goes through anything'. Amid suspicions of treachery, the lord of Hohenlohe fled, and Ludwig died some days later.

Other princes were more fortunate. The career of one of the most enthusiastic of all royal tourneyers began when the emperor Henry VII celebrated the wedding of his son John to Elisabeth of Bohemia at Speyer in 1310 with a tournament in which the Bohemian knights aroused the admiration of the spectators by jousting with spears longer and thicker than those to which the knights of the Rhineland were accustomed.[35] Whenever a Bohemian appeared in the lists, the onlookers shouted 'Here's a Bohemian! Here's a Bohemian!' and anyone incautious enough to challenge him found that the force of a Bohemian charge was enough to splinter one of their formidable spears. But it was not always easy to stage such events, as John of Bohemia discovered in 1319, when he and other Bohemian knights announced a 'court of king Arthur', for which scaffolds were erected in one of Prague's marketplaces: but no outsiders responded to the invitation, and the would-be 'defenders' had to joust among themselves. Two years

---

34   *Chronica de gestis principum* in *Fontes rerum germanicarum* ed. J.F.Boehmer (Stuttgart 1843) 14-15.

35   *Die Königssaaler Geschichtsquellen* ed. Johann Loserth, in *Fontes rerum Austriacarum, Scriptores* (Wien 1875) VIII, 275. For subsequent episodes of John's career see *ibid.*, 404-5, 413-4, 450, 520.

later, another great tournament was held in Prague, at Shrovetide; when king John entered the lists he was knocked from his horse by a lance-thrust, and trampled on by the horses. In the end, unconscious and covered in mud, he was dragged to safety by his servants, while some of the onlookers, hostile to the king, applauded the disaster which had befallen him.

His enthusiasm for tournaments was undiminished, however; even if he does not seem to have held them in Prague again, he was to be found at other European courts in pursuit of his favourite sport. In 1324, having raised a huge ransom from Frederick, duke of Austria, he held a tournament at Cambrai in honour of the marriage of Charles IV and Jeanne d'Evreux at which substantial gifts were distributed to knights, lords and squires. Reports of his deeds were rife, and wild rumours were current: in one year, he was said to have travelled from the Atlantic to the border of eastern Poland, taking part in jousts all along his journey, while on another occasion he was said to have killed a knight in a Burgundian tournament. Another chronicler records that his choice of a second wife, Beatrice, daughter of the duke of Bourbon, was influenced by her love of tournaments; she gave him magnificent presents when he was the victor. In the jousts which followed their wedding in 1335, he was seriously wounded, and, because tournaments were forbidden in France, the other participants were imprisoned. Only John's personal intervention with the French king, Philip VI, secured their release.

In Castile, we find the tournament as an integral part of one of the earliest secular orders of knighthood,[36] in the statutes of the Order of the Banda, founded by Alfonso in 1330 at Vitoria. We know of two occasions when the knights held tournaments: the first was in 1332, when the king was at Santiago de Compostela before his coronation:

> Moreover they maintained two tablas[37] for jousting, and the knights of the Banda, whom the king had made and ordained a short time before, remained all day, four of them arrived in each tabla, and would joust with all who sought to joust with them.

The second occasion was at Valladolid at Eastertide in 1334. The chronicler describes how Alfonso was always involved in 'tournaments and round tables and jousting' (if he was not out hunting), and how he regarded such occasions as a valuable means of ensuring that 'the knights would not lose the use of arms, and would be prepared for war when the need arose'. The knights of the Banda fought together as a team against an equal number chosen from all comers, the king being incognito as a member of the Banda. Two tents were pitched at either end of the lists, and the tournament began

---

36   See ch. 16 below

37   A *tabla* is an open flat space; in this context, it is probably a technical word for a type of tournament enclosure.

under the supervision of four judges. It was fiercely fought, and the king, because he was incognito, received heavy blows in the thick of the press. The judges, seeing that the contest was becoming too heated, entered the lists and forced them to part. The two sides charged each other twice more and the fighting moved to a little bridge over a river outside the town gate, where the combat continued until after noon. The judges parted the two sides, and they went to eat in their respective tents. After dinner, the knights who formed the all comers' team went to visit the knights of the Banda and the king, to hear the judges' verdict as to who had performed best; and they talked at length of the day's doings.

In England, under Edward III, the royal jousts take on aspects of the civic jousts of the Low Countries, in the golden age of English tournaments. Edward may have been influenced by knights familiar with the festivals of the Low Countries in the retinue of Philippa of Hainault, whom he married in January 1328; he held a three week long festival of jousts and *béhourds* to celebrate his marriage, and she seems to have encouraged his taste for chivalric pursuits. After their marriage she was to be found in regular attendance at the innumerable jousts he patronised, and her presence in the stands gave increased respectability to the sport and encouraged other women to attend. Undoubtedly, the presence of women lent lustre to the proceedings and promoted those aspects of the sport most calculated to appeal to spectators. There was indeed a remarkable growth in pageantry in Edward's reign; colourful costumes, processions of participants, fantastic themes, role-playing and play-acting became part and parcel of the fourteenth century joust and tournament.

The overthrow of Mortimer and Edward's return from France after doing homage for Gascony were marked by a series of small-scale jousts, in one of which the king rode under the banner of William de Clinton. Comparatively detailed accounts exist for two other occasions in 1331 which reveal how far the organisation of these jousts had developed. At Stepney on 16 June Robert Morley held three days of jousts: the festivities were opened by a procession of the twenty-six defenders and their challengers, all clad in similar costumes bearing a golden arrow motif, through the streets to St Paul's, where they offered oblations before processing to the market place, which had been enclosed and sanded for the occasion.[38]

Three months later, on 22 September, another of Edward's closest companions, William Montacute, held a three day jousting festival at Cheapside. Once again the market place was enclosed and a stand built for the ladies; it collapsed while the jousts were in progress, causing a number of injuries. Again, the whole affair was opened by a splendid procession in which the defenders, all dressed as Tartars, were each led

---

38   *Chronicles of the Reigns of Edward I and Edward II* ed. W.Stubbs, RS 76 (London 1882) I, 352-3.

through the streets by a damsel in matching costume. Edward III ordered all the able-bodied knights of the realm to attend, presumably to ensure the success of the occasion; this was unusual enough to draw comments from the chroniclers.[39]

The successful conclusion of the Scottish campaign in 1342 provided the excuse for a series of elaborate jousting festivals held under the king's aegis, culminating in a fifteen day long festival in London which was proclaimed throughout Europe and attracted many foreign knights, including those from Hainault who had fought on his campaign. Five years later, Edward's triumphant homecoming from the Calais campaign was marked by celebrations in which the king and the Black Prince played a prominent role; the royal wardrobe provided fabulous costumes for jousts at Reading, Eltham, Windsor, Lichfield, Bury St Edmunds and Canterbury, which were issued to the king, his household, his minstrels, the queen and her ladies, and, perhaps most significantly of all, to the captive nobility of France and Scotland, among them the king of Scotland himself.[40]

Events such as these not only commemorated Edward III's success in war by the obvious parading of his prisoners, but also contributed greatly to his international reputation as a chivalric figure. Ten years later, after the victory at Poitiers, he was able to repeat the exercise with even greater glory and acclaim, because among the captives present were not only the king of Scotland but also the king of France. Edward's latest victories were marked by jousts at Smithfield in June, an unusual torch-lit jousting festival at night in Bristol, and a magnificent round table at Windsor in 1358, which Edward had proclaimed by heralds throughout France, Germany, Brabant, Flanders and Scotland at a cost of £32. By personal example and lavish patronage, Edward III made the joust à plaisance a court monopoly.

After the glorious pageantry in the wake of the English victories in France there were comparatively few hastiludes in Edward's later years. A few notable ones did occur, but at irregular intervals: for the marriage of John of Gaunt and Blanche of Lancaster, the king with his sons and nineteen other nobles held the field against all comers, dressed as the mayor and aldermen of London. At Cheapside in 1362 seven knights jousted as the Seven Deadly Sins against all comers – uch to the pious horror of the chroniclers. In April of the same year, a five day festival of jousts was held by the king at Smithfield; a great number of foreign knights attended, including Spanish, Cypriot and Armenian knights. Ironically, the last recorded jousts of Edward's reign were in London in 1375, where the proceedings were dominated by his mistress, Alice Perrers, who flaunted her relationship with the now enfeebled king by appearing as the

39   *Ibid.*, I, 353-5.

40   N.H.Nicolas, 'Observations on the Institution of the Most Noble Order of the Garter', *Archaeologia* First Series XXXI, 1846, 37ff.

'Lady of the Sun' (the sun being Edward's personal badge) and leading the tourneyers in procession to the lists for a festival which lasted seven days.

In Savoy, the enthusiasm of the 'Green Count', Amadeus VI of Savoy, for tournaments was similar to that of his slightly older contemporary, the Black Prince. The most magnificent of these occasions, the moment at which 'the count, "beau et gracieux adolescent" ', created the sensation that subsequently earned him a place among the chivalrous figures of his century' was held at Bourg-en-Bresse at Christmas 1352.[41] When the trumpets announced the entry of the combatants into the lists, the count appeared at their head resplendent in green silk and velvet vestments under his armor, an emerald plume on the crest of his silver helmet, and astride a magnificent charger richly caparisoned in silver and green. Behind him rode eleven of his noblest knights, also in green, and all were led into the arena by lovely ladies, each holding her champion captive by means of a long green cord attached to the bridle of his charger. Then the damsels, also in green robes, released their knights, and the tournament began. When the jousting had ended for the day, the ladies descended once more into the arena to 'recapture' their champions and lead them back into the castle. Then the banqueting began in the great hall, in the course of which gold rings or batons were awarded to those adjudged the most valorous in the day's contests of skill and strength.

Although other knights were declared the individual winners on each day Amadeus was acclaimed as the overall winner; according to the romantic chroniclers of the next century, he was offered all three gold rings and the traditional kisses by the ladies who awarded the prizes. He accepted the kisses and asked for the gold rings to be given to the victors of the different days; at which the latter gallantly protested that they would have much preferred the kisses. The household accounts give the more prosaic detail that there were 1460 horses at Bourg over Christmas, and generous gifts — forty florins in one case — were given to minstrels and heralds. The green silk and cloth bought on this occasion was to become the count's livery in future years. This was the high point of a long tradition of tournaments at the court of Savoy, beginning at Chambéry in 1344 and which continued through the reign of Amadeus VII, 'the Red Count' into the early fifteenth century. The Red Count earned as high a reputation as his father in the lists: in 1383, in a single combat with the earl of Pembroke and another English nobleman, he broke 47 lances. Under Amadeus VIII, his son, there were tournaments almost every year between 1400 and 1412.

The international nature of the tournament is best illustrated by the joustings of Peter I of Cyprus throughout western Europe in the years 1361 to 1365.[42] Peter was

41   Eugene L.Cox, *The Green Count of Savoy* (Princeton 1967) 98-9.
42   Nicolas Jorga, *Philippe de Mezières 1327-1405 et la croisade au xive siècle* , Bibliothèque de l'école des hautes études 110, (Paris 1896; rptd London 1973) 144-201.

I   Count Wernier von Honberg in a mêlée outside a castle with his banner
displayed, early fourteenth century, from the *Manessische Liederhandschrift*
(Universitätsbibliothek, Heidelberg, MS pal. germ. 848 f. 237)

II   Jongleur, tenth century
(BL MS Add. 11695 f. 86)

III   Making a knight: girding on the
sword (BL MS Royal 20 D XI f. 134v)

IV   Ulrich von Lichtenstein

(Universitätsbibliothek, Heidelberg, MS pal. germ. 848 f. 237)

V The magic fountain at dawn: scene from *Le Livre de cuer d'amour espris*
by René d'Anjou

(Vienna, Staatsbibliothek, MS 2597 f. 15; fifteenth century)

VI   The knight takes leave of his lady
(BL MS Harley 4431 f. 135; early fifteenth century)

VII   The English fight the French on a bridge over the Seine, 1346
(BL MS Royal 20 C VII f. 137; late fourteenth century)

VIII   Battle scene, fourteenth century
(BL MS Harley 6631 f. 110)

IX   Prisoners being taken
(BL MS Royal 20 C VII f. 28v;
fourteenth century)

X   Jousts at St Inglevert, 1389

(BL MS Harley 4379 f. 43; early fifteenth century)

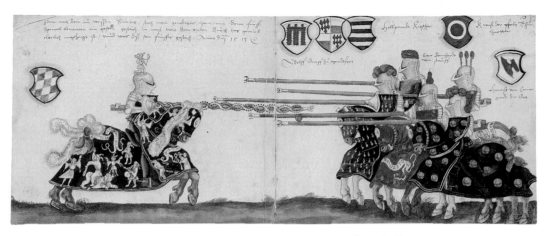

XI   Wilhelm IV of Bavaria jousting against five challengers, 1513

(Munich, Bayerische Staatsbibliothek, MS CGM 1929 f. 12v-13)

XII   Burning of the Templars at Paris. 1312

(BL MS Royal C VIII f. 48; fourteenth century)

seeking support for his plans for a new crusade to be launched from Cyprus to regain the Holy Land. He arrived in the west in December 1361, and in April 1363, he set out on his recruiting drive in earnest, travelling by slow stages through France and reaching Strassburg about July 4 where a joust was held in the Rossmarkt in the presence of a large number of ladies. He continued through northern France on his way to England, where Edward III held a joust in his honour at Smithfield in November. Peter returned once more to France, where he stayed from December 1363 until June 1364; at the end of May, he took part in the jousts after the coronation of Charles VI. A few weeks later he was in Brussels, if we are to believe Froissart, being entertained by another tournament; other sources claim that he took part in the great tournament at Venice witnessed by Petrarch in June that year, his opponent being named as the 'son of Luchino del Verme'.

At all events, he set out for eastern Germany soon afterwards, and jousts were held in his honour in Saxony. He met the emperor Charles IV in Prague in August, and here he won the prize at the tournament held in his honour. In October he was in Cracow in the emperor's company, and when Charles IV took part in jousts there, a courtier remarked that no-one had ever seen an emperor joust before; to which the emperor replied that a king of Cyprus had never been seen in that part of the world before. Peter's journey continued to Vienna, where duke Rudolf arranged yet another tournament in his honour, and yet another prize fell to his lance. He then ended his journey in Venice; but his fame as a jouster was such that he was reputed to have been at the jousts for the christening of Edward the Black Prince's eldest son at Angoulême in April 1365, but this would have required a journey both from Venice to Bordeaux and back at considerable speed.

The events which Peter of Cyprus attended ranged across the whole variety of occasions when jousts were deemed appropriate: the arrival of an important visitor, a coronation, the birth of a prince. Diplomacy, state affairs and dynastic celebrations alike were an excuse for chivalric display of this kind, and gradually the tournament itself became a social ritual. The etiquette surrounding the event and the dramatic framework created for it overshadowed the actual fighting.

The jousts at St Denis in 1389, according to the chronicler of St Denis itself, were held after the coronation of Charles VI's queen Isabella in order to 'ensure powerful friendships and gain the favour of strangers'.[44] This did not impress the populace, who muttered – no doubt thinking of their taxes – that such amusements were unbecoming to the king's majesty. Charles himself was one of the thirty knights who challenged an equal number of defenders, the latter wearing the royal device of the blazing sun. Three

44   *Chronique de Réligieux de St Denys* I, 568-98.

days of jousting followed: on the first day, Froissart records that 'the number of knights made it difficult to give a full stroke, and the dust was so troublesome that it increased their difficulties'.[45] The next day, when the esquires fought, two hundred water-carriers were employed to water the square, but 'notwithstanding their efforts, there was still a sufficiency of dust'. The ladies, who watched from scaffolds around the square, joined with the heralds in adjudging the prizes each evening, and on the Friday, after the main jousts had ended, knights appeared in the wooden hall which had been specially built for the occasion and tilted for two hours indoors. Something of the splendour of the occasion can be gleaned from the accounts of the duke of Burgundy: his son, the count of Nevers, had only just begun to joust, appearing in the lists for the first time in the previous year; and he gave Mlle de la Riviere, daughter of one of Charles VI's counsellors, a diamond ring for leading him into the lists. The gold which was taken off the duke's doublets after the festival fetched over 1000 francs, and more than 500 ostrich feathers were used, including one on the beaver hat, lined with sendal silk and adorned with a silver fringe and three pheasant feathers as well, which the duke wore as he entered the lists.

Although Froissart's account might imply that there was a general *mêlée* on the first day, it seems more likely that these were multiple jousts going on at the same time. When the Spanish knight Pero Niño came to Paris twenty years later, he found that:

> There is neither one that holds the lists, nor joust of one man against another by champions assigned; but each attacks whomsoever he will. All are assailants; ten, or twenty, or thirty, or more, take their place on one side, and as many on the other. As soon as one takes his lance, the other at once grasps his; and not only one goes out against him, but in their great ardour it happens that two or three come forward together against him who has stood forth, notwithstanding their courtesy.[46]

The most famous French jousts of the fourteenth century were held at St Inglevert near Calais in 1390.[47] In the letter outlining the details of the jousts, the defenders offered to hold the lists for thirty days from May 20 next, and to 'deliver from their vows all knights, squires and gentlemen, from whatever countries they may come, with five courses with a sharp or blunt lance. . . . or with both lances'. The challengers were to touch a shield of war or of peace belonging to one of the defenders on the previous day, to give notice of their intention to fight, and to indicate which lance was to be used. The letters were widely circulated, and aroused particular enthusiasm in England,

45   Froissart, *Chroniques*, ed. Lettenhove, XIV, 151; tr. Johnes, II, 404.
46   de Gamez, *The Unconquered Knight*, 142-3.
47   *Le livre des faits du Jean le Maingre, dit Boucicaut*, II, 230-233.

as a year's truce with France was in force, and the younger knights were eager for action. About a hundred English knights and squires crossed the Channel to take up the challenge, and many more came to watch; about forty knights came from other countries. In the event, the total number of jousters was in fact only thirty-nine, and the whole of the proceedings lasted four days, from 21 May to 24 May. There were no serious injuries, even though most of the English knights chose to joust *à outrance*, and the jousting was generally reckoned to have been of a high standard, with several knights unhorsed and many unhelmed, and a good number of spears broken. When the English party left on the evening of 24 May, no other challengers appeared, although the three knights held their places until the end of the thirty days, when they returned to France covered with glory, and donated their arms in triumph to the church at Boulogne.

The popularity of the joust *à plaisance* with its sophisticated settings and its appeal to spectators sounded the death-knell of the old *mêlée* style tournament. These had been kept alive by the need to approximate the conditions of real battle so that knights could train and practise handling their weapons. Jousting also fulfilled these requirements, but had the added attraction of being safer because fewer knights were involved. It also appealed to knightly vanity because the combatant's prowess was so much more evident to the spectators. As it faded into obscurity, those knights who enjoyed the dangers of mixed combat sought their excitement in other spheres.

8

Pas d'armes and fifteenth century tournaments

PRINCELY PATRONAGE of the tournament, by the early fifteenth century, led to an increasing emphasis on splendour, display and a literary framework. The magnificent costume jousts of Edward III's tournaments were outshone by the theatrical tournaments which appear fifty years later, combining the tradition of Le Hem with that of Edward's Smithfield jousts. The first of these elaborate occasions on record comes from Spain; there is reason to believe that the tilt, a cloth or wooden barrier down the centre of the lists which separated the jousters and prevented collisions, was a Spanish or Portuguese innovation, and the extra safety that it offered may have encouraged royal participation in such occasions. The series of great Spanish tournaments belong to the reign of Juan II of Castile who patronised tournaments as a young man, from 1414 onwards, when jousts were held at his coronation at Saragossa: these were marked by 'many outstanding encounters', culminating in 'a tournament of a hundred versus a hundred, white against colours'. At his betrothal to Maria of Aragon in 1418 and at his marriage to her in 1420, there were jousts and tournaments and bullfights. We have a detailed account of another tournament in Madrid in 1419, at which Alvaro de Luna, later constable and the most powerful figure in the realm, was wounded. He appeared in splendid array at the jousts, wearing a favour from his mistress, and broke many lances, until the king sent orders that he should leave the lists, because he had done enough, and won great honour. But Alvaro de Luna begged permission for one more joust. His opponent on the other side of the tilt was one of the best jousters at court, Gonzalez de Quadros; Alvaro de Luna struck him on the shield, while Gonzalez' lance struck Alvaro on the visor, lifting it, and striking him on the forehead with the coronal, stunning him and causing a deep wound. The joust was abandoned, and the constable only narrowly escaped death from his injuries.[1]

1   *Crónica de don Alvaro de Luna* ed. Juan de Mata Carriazo (Madrid 1940) 28-31.

In 1423, at the age of eighteen, we find Juan himself taking part in jousts, and the remainder of his long reign, which ended in 1454, was the golden age of jousting in Spain. Juan was a skilled jouster, and even at the age of twenty in what seems to have been his first proper joust he could hold his own against more experienced knights: at a joust near Tordesillas, he impressed onlookers by his accurate aim and firm seat, scoring several hits on his opponents' shields. Jousts were held on most formal occasions, such as the ceremony at Toledo when Doña Catalina, Juan's eldest daughter, was recognised as heiress of Castile, at Tordesillas when Alvaro de Luna was appointed constable, for the king's ceremonial first entry into Burgos, for the recognition of his son Juan as his heir at Valladolid. But both the king and the constable also held jousts purely for the pleasure of it; the king's 'natural condition was to hold jousts and to do things which he enjoyed', while Alvaro de Luna, during a period of banishment from court, entertained his followers with jousts.

The most spectacular festival of the period was that given by Juan's son, Prince Enrique, at Valladolid in 1428 which lasted from 28 May to 8 June, with a very complicated setting and scenario.[2] In the main square a fortress was built, with a high central tower and four surrounding towers. At its foot was a belfry and a pillar painted to look like stone, on which a gilded gryphon stood, holding a great standard. A high fence with four towers surrounded it, and an outer fence with twelve towers completed the fortifications. In each of these towers stood a lady dressed in finery. Inside the fortress were rooms for the prince and mangers for the horses. A tilt made of cane ran from the fortress across the square to two more towers and an arch inscribed 'This is the arch of the perilous passage of great adventure'; on one of the towers was fixed a great golden wheel, called the 'wheel of fortune'. Before the defenders went to arm themselves, there was dancing, feasting and a musical interlude. When the challengers arrived, they were greeted by fanfares and a lady who warned them that they could go no further without jousting; they replied that they were ready. The king, on a horse caparisoned in silver and gold, took up the challenge, and broke two spears; he was followed by the king of Navarre, with twelve knights 'all like windmills', who also broke a spear. But despite all the ceremonial, the jousting was fierce: Enrique was stunned by his opponent, and one of his squires was so badly wounded that he died two hours later.

Six days later, the king of Navarre gave another festival; he and five other knights were the defenders. He broke a number of spears on the first challengers; then Juan

2   Pedro Carrillo de Huete, *Crónica del halconero de Juan II* ed. Juan de Mata Carriazo (Madrid 1946) 24-6; Lope Barrientos, *Refundicion de la crónica del halconero* ed. Juan de Mata Carriazo (Madrid 1946) 59-66; Diez de Games, *The Unconquered Knight* 328-9; *Crónicas de los reyes de Castilla*, in *Biblioteca del autores españoles* ed. Cayetano Rosell, 66, 68 (rptd. Madrid 1953) II, 446-7.

appeared, his lance on his shoulder, with twelve knights riding in similar fashion. In two courses, he carried off his opponent's crest, a highly skilled feat, and broke a lance; many other lances were broken before the proceedings ended with a magnificent dinner, during which many knights jousted in war armour by torchlight.

A fortnight later, on Sunday 6 June, the king gave his own festival, in honour of his daughter's forthcoming marriage to Duarte, the heir of Portugal. A tent was pitched at the top of a flight of steps covered in cloth of gold, and the king appeared in the lists dressed as God the Father, each of his accompanying knights as an apostle with a scroll bearing his name and carrying one of the instruments of the Passion. Six of the prince's men appeared in surcoats decorated with smoke and flame, and six with mulberry leaves on theirs. They fought a number of courses, in which the king broke three spears and the prince five; and then the prince and his men retired to disarm. The prince returned alone, to fight three more courses, and the king of Navarre followed him into the lists; then other challengers fought, 'and the jousts lasted until there were stars in the sky'.

This was followed two days later by a duel between Gonzalez de Guzman of Castile and Luis de Fazes of Aragon, consisting of eight courses on horseback and fifty blows with a dagger on foot: in each of the eight courses, they both broke their lances, and the fifty blows were accomplished without injury. Finally Alvaro de Luna held a tournament of fifty against fifty, in which he was acclaimed as the best jouster of the day, but this was overshadowed by the magnificence of the earlier celebrations.

Two years later, in 1430, the marriage of a Portuguese princess, Isabella, to Philip the Good, duke of Burgundy, was the occasion for a great tournament at Bruges, the scene of notable civic jousts in earlier years.[3] The day after the marriage, which took place at the nearby town of Sluys, the new duchess made her formal entry into Bruges, where a range of elaborate temporary buildings had been added to the ducal palace to provide a huge banqueting hall and the necessary kitchens and larders. Outside the palace, a great wooden lion crouched, a gun beneath one paw and a stone under the other, from which red and white wine flowed into a basin day and night. Within the courtyard, a stag and a unicorn held flasks from which hippocras and rosewater poured. And inside the hall itself a gallery was provided with space for sixty men - heralds to announce the different stages of the feast and musicians to play for the dances. On a gilded tree, standing on a lawn within the hall, hung the arms of the duke's various lordships, with his own arms in the midst.

When the duchess made her entry into the town, in a gilded litter carried by two horses, the crowds were such that it took her two hours to make her way, through

3   Jean le Fèvre, sieur de St Rémy, *Chronique*, ed. F.Morand, SHF (Paris 1876-81) II, 172-4

streets entirely hung in vermilion cloth, to the ducal palace, where a fanfare of 76 trumpets welcomed her. After attending church, a great banquet took place; we have a minute description of it from the duke's herald, Jean le Fèvre, lord of St Rémy. He tells us exactly who sat where and what was served, particularly the elaborate confectioneries displayed on the sideboard of ladies holding unicorns mantled with the duke's arms, or a wild man on the ramparts of a castle, with the same arms displayed on his banner. The culmination was a vast pie, containing a man dressed as a wild beast and a live sheep which had been dyed blue, with gilded horns. The feast was followed by dancing, at which both ladies and knights changed their dress two or three times, and which continued until after midnight, when a tournament was proclaimed for the following day.

The tournament lasted from Monday to the following Sunday, with Friday as a rest day: the first three days were taken up with individual jousts, for which the market place was divided into three sets of lists, each with barriers along the sides, and a low tilt down the centre. The contestants were divided into two teams, defenders and attackers; each day a prize in the form of a jewel or a golden chain was given to the best knight and squire from each team. There was great display among both spectators and participants; Jean le Fèvre comments that even the duke's officers and pages appeared in several different costumes, and the silken dresses of the ladies were weighed down with jewellery and furs. Each evening there was dancing. To crown these festivities, Philip the Good announced the foundation of a new order of knighthood, that of the Golden Fleece, which like the legendary Round Table of King Arthur and the English order of the Garter, was to consist of 24 knights only. Among the members of the new order were several knights who had taken part in the tournament.

Jousting was now a matter of princely, if not national, prestige, as we learn from an episode at a joust in Milan in 1435.[4] Filippo Visconti had just returned to Milan after his victory at Pavia, bringing king Alfonso of Aragon, his brothers and four hundred Aragonese nobles as prisoners. Jousts were held to celebrate his triumph, and the duke was eager that one of his men should be the first to win the honours of the day. However, Carlo Gonzaga was the easy victor on the first two days, and when the duke bemoaned this among his intimates, one of them told him: 'You have in your prison one of the best lances in Italy, my nephew Venturino Benzone; if you deign to set him free, I am sure that the prize will not be carried out of your realm.' Venturino was summoned and agreed to take on all comers, provided he was allowed a little time to rest and was given a good horse. The next day Venturino jousted with Carlo Gonzaga, and on the last course succeeded in striking him on the helm with a heavy lance; Carlo and

4   Riccardo Truffi, *Giostre e cantori di giostre* (Rocca S.Casciano 1911) 153-4.

his horse came down, and Venturino was declared the victor, to the delight of the duke, who had regained his prestige, and of Venturino himself, who had regained his liberty.

A decade later, for the marriage by proxy of his daughter Margaret to Henry VI of England, René, duke of Anjou and Lorraine and titular king of Naples, mounted a suitably grand tournament at Nancy.[5] Of the heads of the junior branches of the royal house of France, Philip the Good as duke of Burgundy could boast a more distinguished following of knights, but René, with much more limited resources, made as great an impression on his contemporaries in the world of jousts. This was the first of a series of festivals of which his book on the organisation of tournaments was the literary and artistic summary. The *Treatise on the form and devising of tournaments* was the first of several chivalric works, culminating in his masterpiece, *Le Livre du Cuers d'Amours Espris (The Book of Heart seized by Love)* in which the allegorical adventures of Heart in search of his lady, Sweet Grace, are described. It survives in one of the most magical of all medieval manuscripts, whose exquisite miniatures are sometimes attributed to René's own hand. That René had a powerful visual imagination and a taste for opulent surroundings is undisputed, and he saw the tournament as part of the rich artistic possibilities of princely life. A miniature from *Le Livre de Cuers d'Amours Espris* gives us a marvellously realistic image of how the results of literary influence on the ceremonial surrounding a fifteenth century tournament might have looked: the superb design of the knight's crests and horse-trappings, the fairylike figures of the ladies in the pageants, the wonderful tents, the columns of precious marble bearing enigmatic descriptions. It is a glimpse direct into the world of romance; and this recreation of a golden, romantic world is a powerful current in the visual element of contemporary jousts.

At the jousts at Nancy, a tent of red, white and green silk stood at one end of the lists, at the other a massive green pillar, to which were affixed the articles of the jousts. René d'Anjou made his entry, followed by six horses, each with different trappings. René's own mount was in purple velvet and gold, and the others in crimson, black, blue, yellow and grey velvet, with one in white cloth of gold, each surcloth embroidered with different devices. But this magnificence was rivalled by the count of St Pol, messire de Brézé, the sieur de Lorraine, and the other defenders; and even when it came to the actual jousts, the contestants appeared in equally rich attire. Charles VII himself opened the jousting, even though he had the reputation of disliking such exercises; in the three courses he ran against René d'Anjou, he acquitted himself well, but his other opponent, Pierre de Brézé, one of his favourites, was blamed for jousting against the king with too solid a lance, the implication perhaps being that it was unnecessary; the king lost his shield when de Brézé struck it, but both riders broke their lances. The king was

---

5   Guillaume Leseur, *Histoire de Gaston IV, comte de Foix* ed. Henri Courteault, SHF (Paris 1893) I, 144-70.

followed as challenger by the count of Foix, Gaston IV, whose biographer has left us a vivid eye-witness account of the event. Gaston IV almost unseated the count of St Pol in the first encounter, and at his third course, against the lord of Lorraine, he shattered his spear with such force that the pieces flew high in the air, to the wild cheers of the crowd. The fourth course, against Pierre de Brézé, failed, because de Brézé's horse shied away: Gaston continued down the lists, turning his Spanish steed at the end with a caracole. In all, Gaston ran twelve courses, breaking eleven 'good stout lances', unhorsing one opponent and almost unseating another. Ten further challengers followed, each of whom succeeded in breaking between six and eleven lances; but at the end of the day the challengers' prize went to Gaston of Foix, and that for the defenders to the count of St Pol.

René d'Anjou's next two enterprises were held in his own duchy in 1446. The first, the *Emprise de la gueule de dragon*, was held near Chinon; a raging dragon was depicted on the pillar which marked the place of the jousts, with the shields of the four defenders on it.[6] Any lady who passed was to be accompanied by a knight who would break two lances for the love of her. The king jousted with a black shield sown with gold tears and a black lance, to mark the various misfortunes which had recently befallen him.

The *Pas de la joyeuse garde*, named after the famous castle of lovers in Arthurian romance to which both Tristan and Iseult and Lancelot and Guinevere retreated, was more elaborate: a wooden castle was built outside Saumur, and the jousting was opened with a procession consisting of two Turks, dressed in white and leading real lions, drummers and pipers on horseback, trumpeters, and kings-at-arms and judges on horseback; they were followed by a dwarf, bearing René's yellow shield painted with 'natural thoughts', and finally the king himself, led by a lady with her scarf tied through his bridle. The two lions were chained by strong silver chains to the pillar which bore the shields of the defenders. Among the judges was Antoine de la Sale, and the defenders included Ferry de Lorraine, a notable jouster who was the winner of the gold clasp decorated with diamonds and rubies which went to the best performer among those 'holding' the *pas d'armes*.

René's last festival, held at Tarascon in 1449, was also the most intricate in both programme and setting.[7] The *Pas d'armes de la bergiere* was a mixture of pastoral and tournament. The centrepiece of the occasion was a cottage outside which a shepherdess, played by Isabella de Lénoncourt, tended a flock of sheep, and the two knights who defended the pas were dressed as shepherds. The whole event was on a modest scale, and was designed as a private entertainment for the king and his court rather than a

---

6   See M.Vulson de la Colombière, *Le vray theatre d'honneur et de chevalerie* (Paris 1648) 81-84, which uses a lost contemporary account.

7   G.A.Crapelet, *Le pas d'armes de la bergère* , 2nd. edn. (Paris 1835).

great public spectacle, drawing knights from far afield. It was proclaimed by just one herald, who travelled no more than sixty miles from Tarascon in search of would-be challengers, and there were only three days of actual sport. Louis de Beauvau's poem describing the events has preserved for us a detailed picture of an occasion which must have been commonplace among princely courts in the fourteenth and fifteenth centuries, a private celebration of chivalry. Everyone, from the king's councillors to relatively inexperienced knights, took part, and no-one was too critical of their performance; the king at one point went into the lists to encourage a young knight who had been stunned by a blow from the defender, and gave him a new lance when he succeeded in breaking his own.

Burgundy certainly had the advantage in terms of propaganda, in that jousts were assiduously recorded there: in the statutes of the Order of the Golden Fleece, one of the duties of the king of arms of the order was to record the notable deeds of the knights. The marriage of Charles the Bold to Margaret of York at Damme, near Bruges, on 3 July 1468, was a major dynastic and political event, cementing the alliance of England and Burgundy against France, and the celebrations represented the real coming-together of the Burgundian state feasts and Burgundian chivalry: splendour represented power, and power was the underlying theme of the day.[8] Among the English embassy was Sir John Paston, and his letter home to his mother five days later gives the most immediate impression:

> And the same Sunday my lord the Bastard took upon him to answer twenty-four knights and gentlemen within eight days at jousts of peace; and when that they were answered those twenty-four and himself should tourney with another twenty-five the next day after, which is on Monday next coming. And they that have jousted with him up to today have been as richly equipped (and he himself as well) as cloth of gold and silk and silver and goldsmiths' work might make them; for those of the duke's court, whether gentlemen or gentlewomen, lack nothing for such gear, and gold and pearls and jewels; unless they get it by wishing for it, I never heard of such plenty as is here..... And as for the duke's court, for lords, ladies and gentlewomen, knights, squires and gentlemen, I never heard of one like it except king Arthur's court.[9]

We can fill in the omissions from other sources, including Sir John Paston's own 'great book' of treatises, which includes a copy of the challenge issued by Anthony, bastard of Burgundy. It is based on a contemporary romance, the story of Florimont; the knight of the Golden Tree (Arbre d'Or), who serves the Lady of the Secret Isle,

8   Olivier de la Marche, *Mémoires* ed. H.Beaune and J.d'Arbaumont , SHF (Paris 1883) II, 123-201.
9   Version from Richard Barber, *The Pastons* (London 1984, rptd Woodbridge 1993) 140-1.

has travelled from afar to set up his tree in the market place at Bruges, where he will defend it for eight days against four opponents each day, concluding with a tournament: the tournament is to open with one charge with the lance and continue as a *mêlée* 'for as long as the ladies wish'. A very carefully defined ritual is to be followed by all the challengers. A giant and a dwarf guard the tree: the latter is seated on a *perron* or pillar, and has a horn and an hour-glass. The knight must knock three times on the barrier with a wooden hammer, and a herald will emerge to question him. He is to ride once round the lists, and then choose one of two lances, at which the dwarf sounds his horn. When they start to joust, the hourglass is set, and the knight who breaks most lances in half an hour is to be the winner. This timed joust is without parallel in earlier tournaments, in which the number of courses is prescribed in advance. In addition, each knight was formally introduced to the ladies present.

Olivier de la Marche, who was on the judges' stand for part of the proceedings, has left us the fullest account of the jousting itself. On the first day, after the wedding itself, there was only time for one challenger, Adolf of Cleves, because the earlier ceremonies had taken so long. Each day of jousting ended with a magnificent feast, with theatrical *entremets* of suitably allegorical and heraldic significance, such as the unicorn and leopard bearing the English arms which opened the first feast, a singing lion ridden by a dwarf, and a dromedary whose rider released richly painted birds. The second day's jousting was opened by a novice, the lord of Châteauguyon, who nonetheless broke nine lances in eighteen courses; but the knight of the Golden Tree was the winner in all three of the day's encounters. The banquet that evening was on the theme of Hercules, almost in the form of a play, with a series of tableaux. On the third day, Jean de Luxembourg, count of St Pol, was the first jouster, but unfortunately, a piece of his armour broke and he was unable to continue. The nephew of the duke of Brittany followed, and matched the defender's total of thirteen lances broken; the next knight, Anthoine de Hallewin, succeeded in defeating the knight of the Golden Tree. The evening's banquet centred round a model of Charles the Bold's new castle at Gorcum, which rose to the roof of the hall and was occupied by singers disguised as animals. The fourth day's proceedings began promisingly, with the appearance of the Enslaved Knight, servant of a Slavonian lady, who told a long story of his love in the challenge; but his armour was deemed inadequate, and he was told that he was unlikely to joust successfully. To avoid wasting time, he was allowed to go without attempting a course. Jacques de Luxembourg, the count of St Pol's brother, followed and broke seven lances to the defender's six. The next day, the fifth of the pas, went off without problems: the knight of the Golden Tree defeated his brother, was beaten by another knight and drew with the third. The banquet in the evening was the most splendid of all with a joust between Hercules, Theseus and two Amazons as the centrepiece, continuing the earlier theme of the labours of Hercules.

On the sixth day, the challenger was Lord Scales, with whom the bastard of Burgundy had fought a duel in London in the previous year; because of this, they were sworn brothers-in-arms and the bastard delegated his role as defender to Adolf of Cleves. The joust was one of the best of the series, Cleves breaking seventeen lances against Scales' eleven: but the bastard of Burgundy, who was watching, was badly injured when a horse kicked him above the knee. The wound was so serious that he was in danger of his life, but he insisted that the *pas* must continue, at his expense, and he provided trappings for all those who deputised for him. The next challenger, Jean de Luxembourg's son, the count of Roussy, arrived in a castle with four towers, which opened to reveal him fully armed and on horseback. His character was that of a knight held prisoner by Danger and Little Hope, who had to fight at the *pas* in order to win his freedom. Charles de Visan was the defender for the rest of the day, but lost against both the count and Jean de Rochefay. Being a Friday and therefore a fast-day, there was no feast: on the Saturday, Philippe de Poitiers took over as defendant and fought five opponents, of whom he defeated three. Again, there was no feast, and Philippe de Poitiers also defended the lists on the Sunday, the last full day of jousting. However, he was wounded by the lord of Contay, the second challenger, at the first course, and had to be disarmed. So the next challenger, the marquis of Ferrara, was appointed defender, as it would have taken too long to arm anyone else. But his horse flatly refused to come up to the barrier, and to run the course, so he had to retire without having encountered his opponent. Contay took over as defender, but at his first joust with the English knight who was the next challenger he disarmed the latter, and the jousting came to an end. The feast that night continued the theme of the labours of Hercules, completing the portrayal of the remaining tasks.

The final day was devoted to a tournament. Despite his injury, the bastard of Burgundy arrived in a superb horse-litter, wearing a jewelled cloak and accompanied by his archers, knights and gentlemen, in such style that he 'did not seem just a bastard of the Burgundian house, but heir to one of the greatest lordships in the world'. His litter was placed on a special scaffold, separated by a palisade from the action of the tournament. The duke followed him, as leader of the challengers, and Adolf of Cleves headed the defenders. They jousted, and Cleves broke eleven lances to the duke's eight. Then the judges' stand and the barrier were quickly removed, and the two teams of twenty-five knights each ranged themselves in the square. The lance charge was followed by swordplay, which became so heated that the two teams could not be parted, and the duke had to take off his helmet, so that he could be recognised, and ride through the lists separating the duelling knights. When the tournament was finally broken off, the knights fought in small groups by their own request. The final feast repeated the theme of the Golden Tree, with thirty centrepieces of gardens, each with a golden hedge and a golden tree laden with fruit in the centre. The chief diversion was the arrival of a whale, accompanied by giants; sirens appeared from within the whale and sang, and the episode ended with a battle between twelve sea-knights and the giants. At the end of the feast, the prizes were presented. The lord of Arguel won the prize for the joust, and that for the tournament was unanimously awarded to the duke; but he refused it, and it was given to John Woodville, brother of the queen of England. The knights' enthusiasm for jousting was still not satisfied: Arguel proclaimed a further joust for the next day, but as 'it is a common thing for a crowd to joust together', La Marche gives us no account of the proceedings. On the following day, the proceedings closed with a dinner, followed by the payment of the heralds and promotion of various heralds to new offices.

The other great centre for magnificent festivals which included jousting was Florence under the Medici rule. Here, even the fantasies of gilded youth could be spectacular. A certain Bartolomeo Benci, anxious to improve his standing with his lady, decided to serenade her on the night of carnival (Shrove Tuesday) 1473 in high style.[10] He and eight companions, 'splendidly dressed and with newly caparisoned horses, set out from his house at one in the morning, each attended by thirty youths bearing torches in their lord's livery, and by eight youths on horseback. They took with them a "triumph of love", consisting of cupids armed with bows set in greenery, surmounted by a bleeding heart surrounded by flames.' Machinery within made the cupids fly up and down 'as if they were alive'. At the lady's house, the leaders took up their lances and jousted under her balcony; and they proceeded to do likewise at the houses of the ladies of the other eight participants, 'so that the feast lasted all night.' Benci had been prudent enough to get official permission for his serenades and jousts, for the town council decreed that if anyone was accidentally killed, no penalties would be levied.

A whole series of tournaments was held in the 1460s and 1470s at Florence[11]; the enthusiasm of the Medici court for jousts outstripped that of any other Italian principality. Giuliano di Piero di Medici's jousts in 1475 were celebrated in the high classical style of the Renaissance in a poem by Angelo Poliziano, and we have a very careful description of his appearance at what may have been the same joust. He rode a grey horse called The Bear, and his shield bore a Medusa's head at the top decorated with large pearls, all of which were lost in the joust. The shield was lavishly trimmed, fringed with gold and jewels, and in the centre a great flame was shown, with balas rubies for the glowing coals. His cloak was decorated with brooches and pendants and his elaborate silk head-covering had two white feathers, a balas ruby, a diamond and three pearls.[12] Other jousters appeared with as much as twenty pounds of pearls on

---

10   Truffi, *Giostre e cantari di giostre*, 68-9.

11   See Lucia Ricciardi, *Col senno, col tesoro e colla lancia: Riti e giochi cavallereschi nella Firenze del Magnifico Lorenzo* (Firenze 1992) esp. chs. VII & VIII.

their costumes. Interestingly, none of the costumed jousters are mentioned as breaking spears, and their entry into the lists may have been largely for show.

The emphasis in other descriptions of Italian jousts is on the appearance of the jousters and the lavish costumes, armour and sometimes scenery, as much as on the results. At the double marriage of Beatrice d'Este and Anna Sforza in Milan in 1491, the costumes were minutely recorded: Galeazzo Sanseverino, for instance, had ten attendants dressed as wild men, while others rode 'wild horses', as did Galeazzo himself. Wild men were a common enough theme in medieval festivals, but in this case Leonardo da Vinci had had a hand in their design, and they may well have been a sight out of the ordinary. All the costumes were either luxurious or elaborate, or both; Turkish costume was popular, and the crests included such flights of fancy as 'a mountain in front of which is a naked man with a letter in his hand and a book, and a star above his head'. In the jousting Galeazzo Sforza distinguished himself by breaking nine spears in twelve courses; in the other three he hit his opponent's shield, but the spear did not break. The duke of Milan, Giangaleazzo Sforza, was justly proud of his festival, claiming that 'as many lances were broken in the lists as in any joust in Italy for very many years, and these were lances of a size not merely above the normal, but beyond all belief to anyone who did not witness it'.[13]

In Germany, where princely magnificence was far less in evidence, enthusiasm for straightforward jousting continued. We can glimpse a little of the world of the individual enthusiasts, notably through letters in the archives of the princely families of Saxony and Brandenburg. Perhaps the most intimate glimpse is in the papers of the Cronberg family, where a proud father has made a note at the end of the family deeds:

> My eldest son Philip's first tournament was at Wiesbaden on October 5, 1410. After that, at Mainz on 18 November, and a week afterwards at Frankfurt, then one at Boppard at Christmas and one at Mainz the following Easter (1411), and one at Worms a fortnight after Easter. Then one at Würzburg three weeks after Whitsun and one about November 11 at Frankfurt, and one at Landau a fortnight after Easter (1412) and one at Heilbronn and one at Wiesbaden on Shrove Tuesday (1413) and one in November at Boppard and one in November at Worms.[14]

Philip was born in April 1393, and was therefore seventeen when he entered the lists at Wiesbaden. His father had reason to be proud not only of his son, but also of

12   *Ibid.*, 179
13   Giulio Porro, 'Nozze di Beatrice d'Este e di Anna Sforza', *Archivio storico lombardo* IX 1882, 529-34.
14   'Cronbergsches Diplomatarium', ed. O.Freiherr von Stotzingen, *Annalen des Vereins für Nassauische Altertumskunde und Geschichtsforschung* 37, 1907, 217. Conjectural years have been added, and dates modernised.

his own achievement in providing Philip with the means to fight so regularly. We find members of the house of Jülich and Berg writing to each other about the problems of equipping themselves and their followers for tournaments in the 1420s. Adolf von Berg had to borrow horses from his sister-in-law for a tournament at Cologne in 1417, and was in turn asked for the loan of horses by Rupert, the count palatine, for an event at Creuznach in 1423. In the following years, he was frequently asked for the loan of horses, and most of the other surviving letters about tournaments from this period are concerned with the same problem. Requests for the loan of armour are much less common, simply because so much of it was close-fitting and hence made to measure for an individual.[15]

The German tournament in the late fifteenth century had in theory become the exclusive preserve of the highest aristocracy, particularly with regard to admission to such events. Only those who could produce evidence of noble birth on both sides of the family for four generations – 'four ancestors' is the phrase used – were technically allowed to take part. The huge costs of such occasions led, in the absence of wealthy patrons, to the formation of tourneying societies. Knightly societies of various kinds had existed for centuries; the idea of a confraternity of knights was a familiar one, and it was a natural step to create such confraternities for the purpose of holding tournaments. The distinguishing mark of the societies was that they were outside the patronage of lords and princes, and were democratic in structure, with leaders elected from the membership: their rules were created by common consent of those concerned. Regulations of this kind appear as early as the 1430s, when a Spanish diplomat named Pero Tafur watched a tournament held at Schaffhausen, not far from Basle:

> . . . . the nobles and ladies assembled at their own cost, and when all were gathered together the elders went apart with certain matrons and took counsel, and enquired whether any nobleman had done ought amiss, whether any had forced or dishonoured matron or maid, or had seized the goods of a minor who had no protector, or had debased himself for greed of money by marrying a woman of low birth, or had otherwise degraded his rank. Thus the misdeeds of each were brought to light, and when any culprit was found they provided as follows. Certain knights were summoned, and when such an one appeared in the lists, they were ordered to fall upon him and beat him with rods and drive him thence. This was done, and afterwards the older knights and ladies drew near to the culprit and told him why he had been beaten. Then they escorted him back and allowed him to take his place with the other noblemen in the tourney, as if he had purged his offence and done his penance. But if he refused to attend he was sentenced to a double punishment, and if, after a third summons, he still remained obdurate, he was no longer regarded as a noble since he had refused to joust with his peers. In these

---

15 *Deutsche Privatbriefe des Mittelalters* ed. Georg Steinhausen (Berlin 1899) I, 23-24, 173, 69.

parts all can joust and join in any knightly sports, but only nobles of known escutcheon can take part in the tourney.[16]

Tafur remarks on the sharp distinction between jousting – 'all can joust and join in any knightly sports' – and the tournament proper, to which entry is strictly limited. This exclusiveness seems to have been a purely German phenomenon; the display of helms and shields which preceded the tournament was a rigorous test of aristocratic descent and chivalrous behaviour. By 1485, there were no less than fourteen tournament societies in existence, and their representatives met at Heilbronn to discuss the formation of a kind of union. Individual societies had merged over the years, and this attempt at unification was a symptom of the problem that faced all the societies. Tournaments were immensely expensive to stage, and because the societies valued their independence from the great princes, they relied on their members' own more modest resources. The ordinances agreed at Heilbronn make a point of banning excessive display, and only one general tournament was to be held each year in order to keep costs down. But precisely this need for moderation was the downfall of the grandiose scheme: the demand was for more tournaments, and if the societies could not provide them, their members would turn elsewhere, to the courts which could afford such occasions. Two years after the agreement at Heilbronn, the last tournament of the united societies was held.

The aristocratic element in German tournaments is reflected in a whole series of books, both manuscript and printed, from the early sixteenth century, the most spectacular visual record of the sport to survive. Beginning with the tournament books of the electors of Saxony, one of which may have been executed by Lucas Cranach the elder, there is a similar compilation for Wilhelm IV of Bavaria by Hans Ostendorfer (1529) and the genre culminates in Hans Burgkmair's triumphal images of the imperial tournaments held by the emperor Maximilian, and the romances written around him, *Freydal* and *Weisskuenig*. Hans Burgkmair produced a record of the jousts held at the wedding of Caterina Fugger, a member of the great Augsburg banking family, in 1553; it was a fairly modest affair of seven encounters of three courses each. By comparison, the tournament book of Marx Walther of Augsburg is much more lively; his crest appears to have been three sausages on a spike, and he seems to have been a skilled and respected jouster who enjoyed thumbing his nose at the pretensions of the nobles. Marx Walther and his fellow-patricians were considered worthy competitors by dukes Christoph and Wolfgang of Bavaria; in 1452, they challenged them to a joust, with four participants on each side, in which Marx Walther and his companions came off victors. Marx Walther's book also records what seems to be a Shrovetide joust, with men in

16   Pero Tafur, *Travels and Adventures* tr. Malcolm Letts (London 1926) 209.

fool's clothing surrounding the jousters and, most impressive of all, the day when Marx rode into the Fronhof at Augsburg with a small boy sitting on the end of his massive lance.

In the late fifteenth century, jousting became chiefly the preserve of imperial and princely courts, where participation was by invitation only, though the city tournaments continued at Augsburg and elsewhere into the sixteenth century. At the emperor Maximilian's court, chivalric sports attained an unprecedented variety, particularly in terms of fighting on foot, which was a relatively minor part of earlier tournaments and jousts. These were single combats, well adapted to display the prowess of a would-be hero-king, but also closely related to the changing style of real warfare; for example there are duels with pikes following the dramatic victories of the Swiss pikemen in the 1470s. Maximilian's activities in this sphere take us beyond the world of the tournament proper into the foot-tournaments of the sixteenth century and into the history of the duel. His tournaments are more orthodox, though they do contain increasingly artificial apparatus, such as spring-loaded shields which fly apart when struck on the right spot, and highly specialised armour. The emperor's own enthusiasm for the joust is paralleled by that of Henry VIII in England and Francis II in France, and it is still a genuine interest in warlike pursuits; a revealing picture in *Weisskuenig* shows the emperor as a child playing with toy tournament figures, emphasising the way in which his whole upbringing had centred round chivalry.[17]

But the role of the tournament in the political and social world, whatever Maximilian's personal feelings about it, had moved on; we are deep in the Renaissance world of princely magnificence, and despite the emphasis on foot combat, the realities of warfare have moved elsewhere. It is only Maximilian's own prowess, 'so skilled with the lance that no opponent of equal birth was to be found in Germany or elsewhere', that sets him firmly in the medieval tradition: he was known to joust with men-at-arms of humble origin in order to find a match for his dexterity.

The *pas d'armes*

For the real enthusiast, there was another way of holding jousts which was less demanding on the purse than mounting a full-scale tournament with its attendant pageantry. Through the influence of the romances, the quest for individual prowess

---

17   W.H.Jackson, 'The Tournament and Chivalry in the German Tournament Books of the Sixteenth Century and the Literary Works of Emperor Maximilian I' in *The Ideals and Practice of Medieval Knighthood* ed. Christopher Harper-Bill and Ruth Harvey (Woodbridge and Dover, N.H., 1986) 58-68.

had become the overriding theme of chivalric ambitions by the fifteenth century, and the most successful of the secular orders of chivalry reflected this: it was those with an exclusive membership, such as the Garter and the Golden Fleece, which outlasted the more amorphous larger orders such as the French Order of the Star. At the outset, the Order of the Garter had successfully capitalised on the camaraderie of the tournament team to produce a body of knights with a strong corporate identity: a hundred years later, its exclusiveness appealed to a different sense of chivalric values which placed individual achievement above all else.

If the skilled jouster imagined himself as a Lancelot or a Tristan, winning his lady's heart by his exploits in the lists, he also imitated the heroes of romance by the use of extravagant vows. At St Inglevert in 1390, the defenders did not actually take any vows themselves, but they offered 'to deliver from their vows' anyone who challenged them. In the 'emprise' or enterprise of the 'Prisoner's Iron' which the duke of Bourbon instituted on I January 1415, the knights professed, not individual devotion, but a generalised devotion to women. They were to wear a badge of a golden chain and collar every Sunday for two years until they had found sixteen opponents who would fight them on foot, with weapons of war; the losers were to yield themselves as prisoners. Boucicaut's order of 'the White Lady on a Green Shield' is in one respect a continuation of the jousts at St Inglevert, in that its members, in addition to a general commitment to the defence of the honour of women, were pledged to provide opponents for anyone unable to gain release from a vow to perform a specific deed of arms in the lists because of a lack of challengers. Vows were after all a commonplace of medieval life: in the religious world, vows to go on pilgrimage or on crusade were usual, and as so often, the chivalric world mirrored that of religion in its outward forms.

The idea of a vow led on to the imitation of romance episodes where a knight defends a particular place against all comers, the prototype for which is Anna Comnena's Frankish knight waiting at the crossroads for someone to fight with him. In Arthurian romance, the concept of such challenges had been commonplace since the twelfth century. In Chrétien de Troyes' *Yvain*, Yvain defeats a knight who is committed to defending the magic fountain in the forest of Broceliande against anyone who challenges him by pouring water on a nearby stone and thus raising a violent storm. This kind of story forms the literary framework of the *pas d'armes*, or passage of arms, of which the most famous is the *Passo Honroso*, held at the bridge at Orbigo by Suero de Quiñones and his companions in July 1434, described in detail for us by Pero Rodriguez de Lena.[18] These festivals predate and foreshadow the great Burgundian festivals. While both Spanish and Burgundian knights were probably imitating earlier and less

18   Pero Rodriguez de Lena, *El passo honroso de Suero de Quiñones*, ed. Amancio Labandeira Fernandez, (Madrid 1977).

well-recorded French and Flemish festivals, the pre-eminence of Burgundy in terms of chivalric activity is almost certainly exaggerated, and the Spanish achievement needs to be recognised.

The *Passo Honroso* unfolds against a background of political intrigue. The jousts at Valladolid had aroused much rancour; it seems that Alvaro de Luna, anxious to maintain his chivalric reputation, was behind the venture, though it was Suero's father who supplied the necessary funds by giving Suero part of his inheritance. This demonstration of the power and wealth of the Castilian nobility was merely another stage in the long struggle between the princes and Alvaro de Luna, but it shows how highly regarded such chivalric displays had become in Spain.

The terms of the *Passo Honroso* were published as soon as the king gave his formal permission, seven months before the appointed day for the opening of the passo, which was to last for thirty days or until 300 lances were broken. One of the royal heralds, León king-at-arms, was given the mission of publicising the event. The rules stated that if any knight lost a piece of armour in the lists, his opponent was to keep it; two knights succeeded in winning helms in this way. Pero Niño, 'the unconquered knight', was one of the judges, and the teams were made up of Alvaro de Luna's close associates. An encampment of twenty-two tents had been erected at Orbigo, to house the knights, judges, heralds, musicians, scriveners, armourers, surgeons, physicians, lance-makers, and others. A wooden dining hall was built, where Suero and his companions and the challengers dined at one table, and visiting gentlemen 'who had come in honour of the passo, at the other.

The first arrivals, on 10 July, were two knights from Aragon and a German knight from Brandenburg: the latter was accorded the honour of the first joust. On the Sunday, Suero de Quiñones took formal possession of the field, with suitable ceremonies. On Monday the jousts began with the herald's cry of 'Laissiez-les aller, laissiez-les aller, pour faire leur devoir' (Let them go, let them go, to do their duty). The first jousts were successful, with 3 lances broken in 6 courses; but when Lope de Stuñiga came on as defender to meet the Aragonese Johan Fabra, the score dropped to 2 lances in 19 courses. A large number of knights arrived on this day, and the defenders were kept busy for the next four days: on the Friday 54 courses were run by three pairs of opponents, with nine spears broken, and on the Thursday Pedro de Nava and Francisco de Faces ran 27 courses against each other, the highest number during the jousts. Injuries were rare, though Suero de Quiñones himself dislocated his right hand. Two squires were knighted by him during the week, this being regarded as a highly auspicious moment for chivalric ceremonies.

The second week was less successful: on the Wednesday and Thursday, 21 and 22 July, there was no challengers, but many more knights arrived at the end of the week. The number of lances broken was nowhere near the target of three hundred: two weeks in the lists had brought a total of ninety. Furthermore, two Catalan knights, apparently hostile to the enterprise because it supposedly hindered pilgrims on the road to Santiago, had issued letters of challenge attempting to bring the enterprise to a rapid end by undertaking to break all three hundred lances in combats between themselves and the defenders: and when Suero pointed out that the articles of the *passo* limited each challenger to three lances, they defied him to fight a joust *à outrance*.

The week following St James's day saw much more activity. At least 30 courses were run each day, reaching a peak of 60 on Friday, with nine spears broken. The greatest number of spears (13) were broken on the Wednesday, but Suero himself was wounded again, in the right arm: this was the fourth and last time he was to enter the lists. By the last week of the *passo* there was no hope of reaching the target of three hundred lances, largely from lack of challengers: on Wednesday 4 August, only one pair of jousters fought, breaking 3 lances in 15 courses. On the Friday, the Aragonese knight Asbert de Claramunt, riding against Suero, the son of Alvaro Gomez, who was one of the most active of the defenders, was struck in the left eye by a spear which broke his visor: he died instantly. There were friars at the *passo* who said their devotions each day, and Suero de Quiñones sent for them, asking them to take charge of the body and for one of them to obtain permission from the local bishop for burial in sacred ground: death in a tournament was still regarded as a reason for refusing Christian burial. Meanwhile, the corpse was taken to the hermitage at the head of the bridge at Orbigo, where Suero waited until nightfall, hoping to hear that the licence had been granted. But the friar returned to say that the bishop had refused permission. A makeshift grave was dug outside the hermitage, and at nightfall the body of Asbert de Claramunt was lowered into its last resting place by the flickering light of torches, in the presence of the assembled knights, but without the church's blessing. Pero Rodriguez de Lena, much troubled by this disaster, carefully explains in his account of the proceedings that Claramunt was a very tall and strong man, and although he had been wearing a helmet which was not his, but had been borrowed from one of the defenders, he had declared that it was the best he had ever put on: the whole episode was, in Lena's view, deplorable, but a complete accident.

Despite the dramatic circumstances of Claramunt's death and burial the jousting continued the following day, when another mishap occured, Lope de Stuñiga breaking his lance on his opponent's horse. On Sunday, 8 August, normally a rest day, the jousts continued in an attempt to raise the total of spears broken, but although eighteen courses were run, only one was added to the total, and the final figure was 180 when the jousting ended the next day.

The *Passo Honroso* was, at least nominally, held in order to redeem a vow; but vows were not the exclusive reason for a *pas d'armes*, however. The jousts at Dijon in 1443, according to Monstrelet, were held with the permission of the duke of Burgundy 'and for his amusement'; the letters of challenge state simply that the jousts are 'for the augmentation and extension of the most noble profession and exercise of arms', and Olivier de la Marche opens his account of them by saying 'As the times happened to be idle ...'[19] This was the first major pas d'armes to be held in Burgundy on record, and was to last six weeks, defended by thirteen knights and squires, an arrangement similar to that of the *Passo Honroso*. The venue was the hornbeam wood at Marsannay-la-Côte near Dijon, in which was to be found 'Charlemagne's tree'; here the challengers would find two shields displayed, black with gold tears and violet with black tears.

Anyone striking the first would run eleven courses in war harness; the second entailed a duel with axes or swords. The leader of the defenders was the lord of Charny, Pierre de Bauffremont, chamberlain of Philip the Good. He arranged for the necessary lists to be built near Charlemagne's tree, and raised a stone pillar, on which were images of God, our Lady and St Anne and the thirteen shields of the defendants. A crucifix, with the figure of Bauffremont in his jousting armour as donor, was erected on the road to Dijon, as a kind of signpost. Three neighbouring castles were commandeered for the lodging of defendants and challengers.

The first challenger was a Spaniard, Pedro Vasquez de Saavedra, who had a considerable reputation, having fought in Germany and England. Bauffremont undertook the first encounter. Olivier de la Marche describes the proceedings in detail because they were the first jousts he had ever seen. The duel with axes was fought with visors raised, because the Spaniard came into the lists in this fashion, and his opponent chivalrously matched his gesture; both this and the combat on horseback passed off without injury. A succession of challengers followed, though not all the challengers proved to be as expert as they claimed; a Piedmontese named Martin Ballart boasted that he would fight three or four of the best defenders on foot, having touched the shield for combat on horseback. When he missed in all eleven courses, his opponent reminded him of his words, and offered to take him up, but Ballart made excuses about lack of armour and left hurriedly. With this exception, the *pas d'armes* was fought courageously and with few injuries. The shields were displayed for six weeks, and at the end of the event they were taken to the church of Our Lady at Dijon and offered to her; they survived for many years in one of the chapels.

In 1449, Jean de Luxembourg held a *pas d'armes* near Calais, the letters for which were prefaced with a long tale of how he had rescued a beautiful lady, on her way to Rome as a pilgrim, from the hands of robbers.[20] She begged him to accompany her

---

19   Olivier de la Marche, *Mémoires*, I, 282-335.

20   Ibid., II, 118-23; M.Eudes, 'Relation du pas d'armes près de la croix pèlerine', *Mémoires de la société des antiquaires de la Morinie* I, 1833, 302-337.

for the rest of her journey but her rescuer pleaded that, although he would be happy to help her, he could not honourably abandon his announced intention to hold a *pas* near Calais from 15 July following 'until the feast of our Lady in mid August'. Thereafter he would be free to accompany her. In the letters announcing the event, the lady begged knights to come forward so that her protector could accomplish his vow. His shield was duly hung on the 'cross of the pilgrim' on the date announced. The regulations were particularly detailed: lances were to be supplied by the lady, as the patron of the jousts, but knights were to provide their own iron tips; and in the combats no wrestling was allowed. The *pas* was widely proclaimed: heralds went to England, Scotland, Germany and Spain at the duke of Burgundy's expense to publicise it.

Jean de Luxembourg was an experienced jouster who had fought in tournaments for at least a decade: we first hear of him at the jousts for the betrothal of Charles the Bold and Catherine of France in 1439. However, relatively few knights took up the challenge, largely because they felt that if there was only one defendant, he might be wounded before they reached Calais, and hence be unable to complete his intended time. Those who did arrive included a knight from Swabia, aged 65, who fought skilfully with an axe, and Bernard de Béarn, who was delayed by illness and was therefore allowed to fight after the time limit had expired: his challenge ended after the first joust, when an unlucky blow removed his helmet, which injured him as it came away.

The expenses of the occasion, as far as the neighbouring town of St Omer was concerned, were considerable: they paid 1600 écus for the privilege of having the jousts nearby; Lille and Bruges had also tried to come to terms with Jean de Luxembourg for this privilege. The cost of building the houses and lists for the jousts amounted to £333, and the general works, such as levelling the ground and providing transport and guards, £687; without the town's support, the occasion would have been difficult to mount, but the sponsorship was evidently undertaken in the hope of a good profit from crowds of visitors, and the townspeople must have been disappointed by the poor attendance.

A much more successful event was the *pas d'armes* of the Fountain of Tears, in which there was once again just one defender, Jacques de Lalaing, councillor and chamberlain of Philip the Good of Burgundy, and already one of the most famous jousters of the age.[21] He vowed to set up a pavilion in a meadow near Chalon sur Saône, where the 'Fountain of Tears' ran on the first day of each month for a whole year. The site was a strategic one, lying on the boundary of France and the Holy Roman Empire, but in the middle of Burgundian territory. Outside the pavilion, a herald was to accompany a damsel with a unicorn; the damsel's attitude of grief gave the event its name. The

---

21   Georges Chastellain, 'Le Livre des Faits', 188-246.

first arrival on each day was to fight within the first week of the month, and so on up to a maximum of four challengers for each new month. Weapons were to be provided, and even horses for knights who happened to be passing without suitable steeds: we have already seen from German sources how rare good jousting horses could be.

The pavilion was pitched for the first time on I November 1449. At the pinnacle was an image of the Virgin, and below, the lady of the fountain, with her unicorn and three shields; a cunningly arranged jet of water made her weep copiously, her tears running down over the shields. The three shields, each strewn with tears, were of different colours to indicate the type of combat offered. Anyone striking the white shield fought with an axe; if defeated, he had to wear a golden bracelet for a year unless he could find the damsel who held the key; once released, he had to present her with the bracelet. The violet shield indicated a sword combat on foot; if one of the combatants was forced to the ground he had to present a ruby to the most beautiful lady in the realm. The black shield indicated a wish to fight twenty-five courses with lances in war saddles; a knight who was unhorsed had to send a lance to the sovereign lord of the victor. In each case, the prize for the best performance was a golden replica of the weapon with which the challenger had fought. In all, forty-eight combats would have been possible, and Lalaing actually fought eleven opponents: but he had a long wait before the first of his challengers appeared, since no-one touched the shields until I February, when Pierre de Chandio, a squire aged 25, became the first to take up the challenge, selecting the axe as his weapon. The following month, a more formidable figure appeared, the Sicilian knight Jean de Boniface; he came across the pavilion without knowing of the enterprise and claimed 25 courses with lances and 25 blows with axes: this was in excess of the rules, as only one shield could be touched. But Boniface had already fought Lalaing in single combat at Ghent in 1445, and Lalaing allowed him this exception. In the lance-combat, Lalaing split his lance from iron to guard, without breaking it and there was some argument as to whether he was entitled to another one, but Boniface also lost an irreplaceable piece of his armour, and the joust ended after eight courses. In the duel with axes, Boniface was knocked down, and had to wear the locked gold bracelet as the rules provided.

A further three months elapsed before the next challenge, but in October, the last month of the *pas*, no less than seven knights appeared. Anxious to bring the event to a triumphant conclusion, Lalaing waived the articles in order to allow them all their turn. One of them, the lord of St Bonnet, was brought down in a duel with axes, but refused to wear the gold bracelet, claiming that Lalaing had fallen with him, and the penalty did not apply. The next knight presented himself anonymously, in best romance tradition, but there was a reason for this; he had already watched the jousts, and no spectator was supposed to become a challenger. However, the rules were waived, and he was allowed to fight. All these challengers except one chose to fight with axes.

The concluding ceremonies took place on 15 October, with a great banquet and a little theatrical scene, in which the figures of the Virgin and the lady of the fountain – doubtless played by actors – addressed each other; Lalaing approached the lady of the fountain, and asked if she had further need of his services. With her gracious dismissal, and the distribution of prizes, the *pas* was at an end.

The Burgundian court, even in its heyday, was far from having a monopoly of the *pas d'armes*; and a lavish, if brief occasion of this kind was held by Gaston IV, count of Foix, whom we have already met in the lists at Nancy in 1445. On a diplomatic visit to John II of Navarre at Barcelona in 1455, he declared a pas d'armes, calling himself the knight of the pine with golden fir-cones, servant of the lady of the Secret Forest.[22]

Challengers were to break three lances in jousting armour, and if the defender won, his opponent was to present a jewel to the lady of the Secret Forest; if he was defeated, he would present a similar jewel to the victor's lady. The lists were erected on one of the town squares, with a pine tree with golden cones at one end. The count of Foix made his entry on a particularly fine charger, amidst the usual procession of heralds, knights and squires, as well as two Moors as footsoldiers. The event was very well attended: in two days Gaston fought 42 opponents, broke 82 lances and had 75 lances broken on him, all apparently without mishap. Admittedly the challengers were restricted to three courses, but it was one of the finest feats of arms of the period, and one which has not been given its due place in the history of jousting. The nobles of Aragon and Navarre were evidently ready and skilful jousters, yet we know so little of jousting in these countries in the fifteenth century.

With the end of the Burgundian dynasty in 1477 and the French wars in Italy, the peace and prosperity needed for the great festivals vanished. Two last *pas d'armes* claim our attention, those of the *Dame Sauvage* held by Claude de Vauldray and the Arthurian jousting at Sandricourt in 1493.

The proceedings at Claude de Vauldray's challenge, held at Ghent in January 1470 in the presence of the duke and duchess of Burgundy, were marked by a romantic letter of introduction, describing how he had been rescued by a wild lady when he had been wounded on his first adventure, described in highly allegorical terms reminiscent of René d'Anjou's *Livre du Cuers d'Amours Espris*.[23] The appearance of the jousters in the lists was similarly inspired by romances. The count of Roussy, the first challenger, arrived under the device of 'The Innocent', preceded by his fool, riding a donkey and designated his 'Chancellor', while he also rode in on a mule accompanied by his two smallest pages as his 'Chief Councillors'; the allusion was either satire or, more probably, a play on the idea of innocence related to characters such as Perceval in

22   Leseur, *Histoire de Gaston IV*, II 39-59.
23   Felix Brassart, *Le pas du perron fée* (Douai 1874).

Arthurian stories, the 'pure fool' who is really a peerless knight. De Vauldray appeared with an escort of wild men and women, dressed only in long blond hair and, for the women, strangely-cut mantles. The jousts were fiercely fought; on the last of the five days of jousting, de Vauldray could not be separated from his opponent, and they exchanged more than thirty blows instead of the prescribed seventeen. De Vauldray had an impressive variety of costumes, and one wonders where he managed to finance this highly expensive display; even as chamberlain to Charles the Bold, he must have needed ducal help.

We know that Louis de Hédouville, who organised the pas d'armes at Sandricourt in 1493, was subsidised by the duke of Orleans to the tune of 100 gold crowns.[24] De Hédouville was evidently one of the rising stars of the French royal court, and he produced a scenario in which each stage of the proceedings took place in a suitable location: the 'perilous barrier' was outside the castle, with lists for the tournament at the 'dark crossroads' and the jousts at the 'field of thorns', while the closing day of the tournament took place in the 'forest without tracks'; here the ten defenders of the pas d'armes stationed themselves to await the challengers, 'like knights errant seeking adventures, just as the knights of the Round Table used to do in former days'.

And with this echo of round tables, 'forests' and other tournaments in dramatic form we take our leave of the last of the golden age of the *pas d'armes*.

The individual challenge and combats *à outrance*

In complete contrast to the development of the courtly spectacle of the *pas d'armes*, and perhaps as a kind of reaction to it, we find an increasing number of combats *á outrance*. These continued to attract knights and esquires anxious for real fighting throughout the fourteenth and fifteenth centuries. Although they were essentially in the tradition of the border encounters during war, they nonetheless began to acquire a courtly veneer, and we find formal letters of challenge just as with the *pas d'armes*. Most of these are preserved as examples for future generations; some relate to individuals who sought self-glorification in feats of arms; others concern groups of knights who had formed themselves into a sort of order of knighthood whose sole object was to perform feats of arms. In both cases the readiness of the challengers to fight was often shown by the adoption of a motif, badge or device, which might also be the prize for success.

The earliest extant challenge to hastiludes *à outrance* dates from 1398, when seven French knights challenged seven English knights to a series of combats.[25] The French

24   A.Vayssière, *Le pas d'armes de Sandricourt* (Paris 1874).
25   F.H.Cripps-Day, *The History of the Tournament in England* (London 1918) 126-8.

had undertaken to wear a diamond for three years as a sign of their membership of the group and of their willingness to undertake feats of arms. Any knight who wished to challenge either an individual or the group could win the diamond by a successful combat in courses with lance, sword, axe and dagger. If he failed, he was to give each of the group a golden rod for their ladies. The English knights who took up the challenge did so on condition that the combats were fought *à outrance* and suggested that the English king should preside over the undertaking, either in person or through his lieutenant in command of Calais.

Such combats could also be fought as one-to-one combats. Michel d'Oris, an Aragonese esquire in French service, issued letters of challenge from Paris in 1400, declaring that he had undertaken to wear a piece of armour continually until delivered of it by an English knight. They were to fight a series of courses in different types of combat, which were specified in some detail. An English knight, Sir John Prendergast, took up the challenge; he explained that he did so partly to relieve the misery of the esquire and partly to fulfil a long-held wish to fight against a French opponent. Letters, almost certainly written for the protagonists by heralds, were exchanged in a rather desultory fashion, and the project came to nothing, probably because Oris had to return to Aragon. A similar set of challenges which passed between the seneschal of Hainault and John Cornwall in 1408–9 resulted in a protracted correspondence in which Chester Herald acted as go-between for the two parties. The delays meant that the seneschal eventually found himself facing the prospect of two sets of jousts *à outrance* within six weeks of each other. In the end, after much discussion, the seneschal's combat against John Cornwall was organised to take place at St Omer, before the duke of Burgundy; there is no record of the combat having actually taken place, but it seems likely that the challenges were fulfilled.

One of the hallmarks of the fifteenth century challenges of which we have records seems to have been the great distance travelled by the knights. In 1435, Philip the Good presided over a duel between Juan de Merlo, a Spanish or Portuguese knight, and Pierre de Bauffremont: Monstrelet specifically points out that the contest was fought 'without any defamatory quarrel, but solely to acquire honour'.[26] There was some difficulty over the lances to be used, as Bauffremont's were longer than those brought by Merlo; so they agreed to use pairs of lances from each set in alternate courses; this, together with the Spaniard's problem with his horse, which shied at the lances, perhaps explains why only one was broken. The next day, they fought with axes, and Merlo disconcerted his opponent by fighting with his visor raised; when the combat was halted by the duke 'the Spaniard . . . twice declared aloud that he was far from

---

26   *La chronique d'Enguerran de Monstrelet* ed. L.Douët d'Arcq, SHF (Paris 1857-62) V 138-43.

being pleased that so little had been done; for that he had come at a great expense, and with much fatigue by sea and land, from a far country, to acquire honour and renown'. The duke managed to reassure him that he had indeed acquired much honour.

The danger of such combats is underlined by the challenge fought at Paris by John Astley and Piers de Massy on August 29 1438, in the presence of Charles VII; Astley ran Massy through the head with a lance, killing him. This did not deter Philip Boyle, a knight from Aragon, from challenging Astley at Smithfield in January 1442: Astley was again the victor, but his opponent was only slightly wounded. Henry VI, who halted the fight when Astley had Boyle at his mercy and was about to strike him in the face with his dagger, knighted Astley on the spot, and granted him a hundred marks a year for life.[27]

Four years later, at Arras, Galeotto Balthazar, a Spanish squire in the service of Filippo Maria, duke of Milan, who had left Milan about Michaelmas 1445 in order to travel, see the world, and perform deeds of arms to advance his reputation, fought Philippe de Ternant, his opposite number as chamberlain at the Burgundian court.[28] The dukes of Milan and Burgundy were brothers-in-arms, and Galeotto had been specifically forbidden by his master to fight in Burgundy unless he obtained permission from the duke. If he failed to find an opponent in Burgundy, or was refused permission, he intended to go on to England to fulfil his emprise. Philippe de Ternant met him and, having wanted for a long time to take up a challenge of this sort, negotiated the necessary approval. On 27 or 28 April, the combat duly took place, in the great market at Arras, within double-fenced lists 'of very large and spacious size'. La Marche, who has left the best account of the occasion, was the duke's only page that day. After the usual ceremonial, the fighting began with seven lance thrusts on foot. The Milanese squire, 'as soon as he held his lance, started to handle it and run as if he held no more than an arrow; and he jumped in the air once or twice so lightly and quickly that you could see that his armour and equipment did not hinder him in the least'. Philippe de Ternant adopted the opposite approach, thrusting himself solidly into the ground at each step; when the two encountered each other, he drove his leg almost a foot into the sand. The run-up was carefully marked out with cords as seven paces of two and a half feet each. The lance thrusts were followed by eleven sword blows, all of which passed off without incident, except some damage to the armour, even though the blows were heavy and skilful on both sides. In the combat with axes, Ternant managed to sidestep as the Milanese squire came towards him on the first encounter, and nearly felled him with a massive blow on the neck. However, the fifty blows with axes were accomplished, and the proceedings continued the following Monday on horseback.

27   G.A.Lester, *Sir John Paston's 'Grete Boke'* (Cambridge and Totowa, N.J., 1984) 96-7, 92-5.
28   Olivier de la Marche, *Mémoires*, II, 64-79.

Galeotto appeared on a horse equipped with armour studded with 'great steel spikes', and the marshal in charge of the lists ordered these to be removed, since they were not allowed in the lists. Galeotto's tactics were evidently designed to make use of this armament, as he charged at his opponent and nearly knocked him off his horse with the force of the collision. Ternant's sword-strap broke, and he was unable to reach it as it hung from his horse's neck; it finally fell from its scabbard as Galeotto rained blows on him, and the combat was stopped while it was restored to him, in accordance with the rules. The swordplay was fiercely fought, and the duke stopped it after Ternant had probed the chinks of his opponent's armour with the point of his sword; he was unable to injure him, because his armour was so good. The prescribed thirty-one blows were not accomplished, but the duke declared himself satisfied, and the Milanese squire was feasted in the traditional way before his return home: it was judged one of the finest feats of arms for many years.

In 1465, Edward IV's brother-in-law, Anthony Woodville, Lord Scales, issued a challenge to Anthony, bastard of Burgundy.[29] Such events were rare in England, and this seems to have been part of the imitation of Burgundian courtly life by the courtiers of Edward IV. The challenge was said to have been imposed on Lord Scales by the ladies of the English court, who on 13 April 1465 surrounded him and tied a gold band to his thigh, containing a 'flower of remembrance' and articles for a joust. It was two years before the challenge was taken up; when the Bastard finally reached London, he did so in high style, and there were conferences over the precise terms of the combat, and the king took a close interest in the arrangements. Spiked horse armour was specifically forbidden, but despite this, the Bastard's horse was severely wounded in a collision with Lord Scales, and died either on the spot or the next day. There was immediate suspicion that Scales had used spiked armour, but he was able to clear himself, though a piece of metal, apparently from his sword, was said to have been found in the unfortunate beast. The combat on horseback had been brief, and that on foot was not much longer; when Lord Scales had the advantage after a few strokes of the axe, the king stopped the fight. The proceedings continued with other challenges by Burgundian knights against Englishmen, but it was Scales' fight which was remembered.

Perhaps the most remarkable of all chivalric duels were those fought by the emperor Maximilian. He fought a large number of such combats, with a great variety of weapons. A good example is the fight between him and Claude de Vauldray, the defender of the *pas d'armes de la Dame Sauvage* twenty-five years earlier, at the imperial parliament at Worms in 1495. Although the fighting was not spectacular, the eagerness of

---

29   Lester, *Sir John Paston's 'Grete Boke'*, 103-117, 123-33.

Maximilian for chivalric as opposed to inherited fame is extraordinary. Claude de Vauldray was probably careful not to press his opponent too hard, but there is no suggestion that the match was anything other than a normal challenge. Maximilian succeeding in taking de Vauldray's sword from him, and at this point the fight was stopped.

The individual challenge, which had always had an element of trial by battle in it, gives way in the seventeenth century to the duel, with its heightened emphasis on honour, and hence a greater insistence on a decisive outcome: for a knight to have fought a challenge was deemed honourable enough, and there was less emphasis on victory or defeat. But if the individual challenge became more deadly, the tournament became more ritualised. The private tournament, already becoming rare in the fifteenth century, disappears entirely with the emergence of the new autocratic monarchies, where the royal court was the only place for such events. It is in the context of the prince's attitude towards chivalry that we shall return to the last days of the tournament.

9

The Tournament as Chivalric Occasion

THE TOURNAMENT brought together the practical and social aspects of chivalry in a way that no other occasion could rival. Its basic function, as a means of providing practice in the use of arms, remained valid to the last; even if the mounted charge was no longer one of the key manoeuvres in warfare, the tournament encouraged good horsemanship and dexterity in handling a variety of weapons.

In the absence of manuals on training in arms, we have to rely on incidental, often literary, descriptions of how a knight learnt his skills. For jousting, practice in its simplest form was provided by the quintain, a wooden device mounted on a pole at which the knight aimed with his lance; it usually represented a Saracen with a shield, and if the shield was struck fairly, it swung aside to give the knight a clear path. Another form was a ring suspended on a cord, which was to be carried off on the tip of the lance. These exercises involved only one knight; of more interest to us is the *béhourd* or *bohort*, which has been something of a mystery until now. The earliest use of the word *buhurt*, a term which seems to describe informal jousts, is to be found in a chronicle from south Germany about 1150; it is possible that it was the original German term for tournaments, and the French-derived word *turnier* only later supplanted it. The verb *béhourder*, to hold a *béhourd*, is found in French from about the same period; the earliest French translation of Geoffrey of Monmouth's *History of the Kings of Britain* uses the word as the equivalent of 'imitation battle'. An early thirteenth century German romance describes a fierce *béhourd* which 'would have been a tournament if they had been wearing armour'.[1] It is mentioned in the rules of the Order of Knights Templars in the mid twelfth century: whereas tournaments were strictly forbidden as a breach of canon law, the brothers were allowed to *bohort* provided that no spears were thrown.[2] An Italian writer in the fifteenth century claims that it is so called from the light spears used, named 'bigordi'.[3]

1   Wirnt von Gravenberg, *Wigalois*, quoted by W.H.Jackson in *Das ritterliche Turnier im Mittelalter*, ed. Josef Fleckenstein (Göttingen 1985) 264n; see also *ibid.*, 63-6, 354-5.
2   *La règle du Temple* ed. H.Curzon, SHF (Paris 1886) 184.
3   Francesco da Barberino, *I Documenti d'Amore*, Società Filologica Romana, Documenti di storia letteraria (Rome 1905) I, 329-336.

And in the literary tradition of the period the *béhourd* is an essential part of court festivities: knightings and weddings end with a *béhourd* and a dance. We have no specific historical evidence for the *béhourd* in this period, probably because it was an informal and impromptu occasion, by contrast with the more highly organised tournament. It may also have been less dangerous and less controversial, in that it fell outside the church's condemnation of tournaments. In Italy in 1208, we find a nobleman near Rome who was a vassal of the Pope 'playing at buhurts from afternoon until suppertime' when Innocent III came to visit him.[4]

The *béhourd* continued to be practiced alongside the tournament in both Germany and Italy; it appears most frequently in thirteenth century sources, and then gradually vanishes. It is almost always associated with festivities: at a great court in Verona in 1242, 'the knights held a *béhourd* in the marketplace and the ladies danced on a kind of stage built outside the town hall.' But the sheer informality of the *béhourd* entailed other dangers: in Venice in 1288, an ordinance was issued, in connection with highway regulations, that anyone who was taking part in a *béhourd* should have bells on his harness, so that he could be heard as he approached, implying that the sport was practised at large in the streets; and in Bologna in 1259 a statute was enacted against those taking part in a *béhourd* attacking bystanders with a spear, if the latter were on foot.

They were always a popular recreation with squires and others who were not knights, particularly in England, and this may have added to the risk of disorder. They were banned in England in 1234 because of the ill-will they caused, and the 'fair of Boston' in 1288 which ended in a riot was technically a *béhourd*. In Germany, as the full-scale tournaments became better-regulated and more peaceful, so the *béhourd* slowly disappeared and the distinction between the two forms was largely forgotten. The word itself was gradually supplanted by the French-derived *turnier* and only appeared as an old-fashioned name for the sport in chivalric romances which harked back to the golden days of knighthood. In Italy, on the other hand, the *béhourd*, or, to give it its Italian name, *bagordo*, flourished to the end of the fifteenth century, and contributed to the emergence of the *carrousel* or non-combatant display of horsemanship, in the sixteenth and seventeenth century. Because the equipment required was minimal – a shield and a spear, without the expense of full armour – it became a pastime for the citizens as well as the nobles. It was not regarded purely as training for the joust or tournament, but as a sport in its own right, and hence was not dependent on enthusiasm for the tournament proper. Its rough and tumble informality was little use as practice for the highly formal joust.

---

4   *Annales Ceccanenses*, quoted by Szábo in Fleckenstein, *Das ritterliche Turnier*, 354n.

There is little doubt that tournaments were held because the participants enjoyed them, rather than as a form of compulsory training. However, they were also held because the participants enjoyed real warfare, and it is not surprising that truce or peace was generally a pre-condition for tourneying—real war brought other preoccupations with it. During times when warfare proper was in abeyance, tournaments were a means of keeping one's hand in. Truces in particular, a time when hostilities were merely suspended and rivalry had deeper undertones than usual, were a fertile time for tournaments, especially those fought with weapons of war. Examples can be found as early as 1197, when Richard I's army is said to have fought tournaments at Tours during a truce,[5] and as late as 1495, when Bayart was fighting the Spanish in Naples and arranged a combat of thirteen against thirteen during a two months' truce.[6]

During the Hundred Years' War, tournaments were a regular feature of periods of truce or peace, the jousts at St Inglevert in 1390 being the most notable example. In such circumstances, the argument that tournaments were the best form of practice for real warfare was entirely convincing. Sieges were also a period when jousts of a more or less serious nature were frequently held. Three of our earliest examples of jousting are found in connection with sieges, at Würzburg in 1127 and at Winchester and Lincoln in 1141, and the borderline between jousting in play and a lance-combat in deadly earnest is very slender.

The end of a campaign could also be marked by jousts or tournaments. In 1225, in eastern Germany, the knights of Ludwig of Thuringia marked the capture of the castle at Lebus by holding jousts. In fourteenth century Italy there are half a dozen examples: at Florence in 1329 to mark the end of war with the neighbouring town of Pistoia, at Padua to mark a victory over the Venetians in 1379, at Venice for the capture of Treviso in 1338 and for the surrender of Candia in 1364, at Bologna in 1392 for the end of a campaign against Genoa. These occasions, as we know from Petrarch's description of that at Venice in 1364, had something of the old classical triumph about them, with processions and organised manoeuvres on horseback as well as jousting, but the fashion does not seem to have spread much beyond the Italian city-states.

For knights who had acquired a basic skill in arms, tournaments also provided a means of gaining experience. Warfare was by no means continuous, however much it might seem to dominate medieval history. Tournaments were therefore sought out by knights anxious to make a reputation for themselves. In the twelfth century, given that tournaments were banned by the Church and also by secular rulers, the arrangements were evidently made among a small circle of enthusiasts, augmented

5   *Chronica Monasterii de Melsa* ed. E.A.Bond, RS 43 (London 1868) I.279.
6   de Mailles, *Chevalier Bayart, 84-86.*

by knights who 'rode in search of tournaments' like St Bernard's visitors in 1149. The enthusiasm for tournaments in Picardy and the Low Countries in the 1170s and 1180s was relatively local, and developed from the eagerness of a small group of great lords to take part in the new sport. Each of these maintained a retinue for tourneying purposes, and it was therefore a relatively simple matter to arrange a tournament: indeed, they were so frequent that in many cases the date and place for the next encounter must have been fixed at the end of the preceding tournament. A book of formula letters prepared by a Florentine lawyer with connections in the German imperial court in the early thirteenth century contains a specimen letter inviting a knight to a tournament:

> Word has gone out in various parts of France that various princes and an infinite number of knights are to gather for a tournament in Flanders next Whitsun. So that you may increase your fame, we exhort you not to delay in coming to such a joyful and exciting gathering.

This is followed by another specimen letter, dissuading a knight from tourneying on the grounds of danger and expense![7]

Expeditions by a lord in search of tournaments could produce a series of encounters. Edward I set out on such a tour with a large company of knights in 1260, and fought in tournaments in France: he met with little success, losing horses and armour and finally being wounded himself in June 1262. Bursts of local enthusiasm for the sport leading to a series of tournaments can be found throughout the middle ages, usually inspired by the interest of an influential nobleman or prince, though occasionally they seem to have been spontaneous, as in Germany in 1377, when the Augsburg chronicler notes that 'the lords, knights and squires held numerous tournaments throughout the country'.[8]

If the tournament had been no more than a question of practice and experience of mock warfare, it would belong to military history pure and simple rather than the history of chivalry. But the concept of the tournament as a sport with set rules takes us into a different world. The rules to be observed during a tournament grew in complexity as the sport matured. Originally, in the twelfth century, there were only a handful of limitations. The critical distinction between tournaments and war was of course that the object was to unhorse and capture opponents, never to kill them and preferably not to injure them. From a very early date, areas of retreat were provided,

---

7   Ludwig Rockinger, *Briefsteller und formelbücher des eilften bis vierzehnten jahrhunderts* , Quellen zur bayerischen und deutschen Geschichte 9.i (Munich 1863) 162.

8   *Annales Monastici* ed. H.R.Luard, RS 36 (London 1866) III 216-8 (*Annals of Dunstable*).

where knights could retire to rest themselves and their horses, and repair their armour. There were also boundaries of a kind by the end of the twelfth century. It was agreed that knights who were captured forfeited their horses and had to find a ransom, but could not be held prisoner once they had promised to pay. This had not always been the case, as a letter from Henry, son of count Theobald of Blois, to abbot Suger in 1149 shows: he asks Suger to intervene to get his vassal Reginald to release Anseric of Royaumont, whom he had captured in a tournament.[9]

There were also quite complicated arrangements about the intervention of footsoldiers in support of a knight, either to help him to capture another knight or to prevent him from being taken himself. By the early thirteenth century, there were evidently agreements that certain types of blunted weapons would be used on a particular occasion, and it seems that the 'round tables' were a kind of temporary association in which each member swore to obey set rules covering the combat. In effect, the ethos behind the regulations has become a desire to see 'fair play', that fundamental criterion for all true sporting events. These rules developed into the pre-conditions attached to all the great passages of arms in the fifteenth century, and into the ordinances of the German tourneying societies: we know little about the actual rules for fourteenth century tournaments, though there is evidence for tournament judges and even scoring in Bologna in 1339. The three 'superestantes zostrae', 'overseeing the joust' are named, their duty being to see who won; a notary was present to write down the blows at their dictation.

The most interesting evidence for the ideas behind the regulation of tournaments in the fourteenth century regulations is also the most tantalising, Geoffroi de Charny's 'Questions on jousting and tournaments' written in the 1350s for the members of the shortlived French Order of the Star.[10] Alas, we have only the questions, none of the answers. But the questions do shed some light on the problems that arose. The 'Questions on jousting' are concerned almost entirely with the winning and losing of horses. When should a knight be awarded the horse of the opponent he has just vanquished: for instance, does this apply if no terms have been proclaimed before the joust, and is it also valid for squires? And when should a knight who had killed or injured his opponent's horse make reparation? If both knights fall, should they exchange horses? If a knight acts as a substitute for another who is wounded, and wins a prize, should the prize go to the wounded knight or to his stand-in? Evidently the capture of horses was of just as much concern in Geoffroi de Charny's day as it had been when William Marshal made his fortune in the tournaments of the 1180s.

9   *RHGF*, XV 511 (letter of Abbot Suger).

10 Geoffroi de Charny, 'Demandes pour la jouste...' Brussels, Bibliothèque Royale Albert Ier, MS 11125, fos. 41-50v.

The questions on tournaments open with a different set of problems, chiefly those of service in a retinue, and the occasions on which a knight retained by one lord can fight under another's banner. We learn that it was the custom for all knights to swear an oath at the beginning of a tournament; if a knight failed to swear such an oath, should he be excluded? What exactly constitutes a tournament, and what happens if knights continue to fight after it has officially been declared at an end? Here we learn of the presence of *diseurs*, arbitrators or judges: the word occurs as early as the 1270s in the romance of *Fulk Fitz-Warin*, where 'judges, heralds and *diseurs*' are grouped together; by the fifteenth century, René d'Anjou talks of '*juges-diseurs*', and the two functions have evidently merged, if indeed they were ever separate. The problem of whether a horse should be forfeited or not reappears in later questions; other points of debate concern late entries, and what should happen if knights continue to fight of their own accord after the tournament is formally declared at an end.

All this paints a more mercenary picture of the sport than we get from other sources. The capture of horses was highly important, as the overall prizes were often of less value than a single horse, though the honour of winning the prize was more important than the financial gain: William Marshal was once awarded a 'fine pike' as a prize, and one source even claims that talking parrots were offered to the winner.[11] The Italian civic tournaments give a fairly consistent pattern, such as the splendid helmets created by the jewellers of Florence as prizes for jousts there; French and Burgundian tournaments usually had a jewel as a prize, and the 'dank' at a fifteenth century German tournament was similar. Lengths of cloth were also occasionally given, but the prizes at Bruges in 1429 are typical: rubies, gold chains and diamonds. A skilled knight could do very well financially out of tournaments.

The final touch which ensured fair play and fair judgements of the results was the introduction of scoring. It is only in the late fifteenth century that real evidence of scoring has come down to us: until then, it appears that breaking lances or unseating opponents were the only incidents which had a definite 'scoring' value. Sir John Tiptoft's ordinances of 1466 set out a scoring system, 'reserving always to the queen and to the ladies present the attribution and gift of the prize, after the manner and form accustomed'.[12] The provisions are complex, and must have required close attention on the part of the judges: it must have been difficult to see whether spears were broken tip to tip, or whether they had broken within a foot of the tip. The first was very high-scoring, while the second instance scarcely counted. We have a few surviving scorecards or jousting cheques from Tudor times: these indicate, however,

11   Werner Meyer-Hofmann, 'Psitticher und Sterner', *Basler Zeitschrift für Geschichte und Altertumskunde* 67, 1967, 9.
12   Sir John Tiptoft, 'Ordinances, Statues and Rules', in Cripps-Day, *History of the Tournament*, xxvii ff.

that scoring had become less complicated since Tiptoft's day, and only broken spears were usually being counted.[13] Rules which entail disqualification are found from the fourteenth century onwards: a blow beneath the waist or under the barrier with a pike, use of any device to fasten the sword to the hand, dropping a sword, resting on the barrier during the fight, and failing to show a sword to the judges beforehand.

When it comes to the actual techniques involved in jousting, by far the most detailed information on jousting technique is to be found in *The Art of Good Horsemanship*, written in about 1434 by no less a personage than Duarte, king of Portugal. It gives a vivid picture of what it was like to enter the lists; it is very rare to find a medieval text that speaks so directly of practical matters, the nearest parallels being the aristocratic manuals on hunting and falconry. Duarte's prime concern is of course with horsemanship pure and simple, but several chapters deal specifically with jousting, and remind us once again that behind the elaborate rituals and accomplishments of chivalry lay a hard basic training in warfare and horsemanship:

> For, in my opinion, I do not regard as good jousters those whose horse is brought to them by the rein; then somebody else goads the horse for them with a stick. A good jouster must bring in his own horse, controlling it with the reins or the spurs, holding it back or spurring it on, and bringing it up to the tilt or heading it away as appropriate. For if the horse is handled in any other fashion, few can control their lances and perform well as jousters, even though a horse that charges very fast and wears head armour allows the lances to be held more steadily once these have been fitted into the lance rest.[14]

Much of the advice on handling a horse in the lists applies to riding in general; riders who are unable to control their horses because they have unsuitable bits, or who are unable to get their horses to charge in the desired direction lack basic skills. But it is fascinating to find the theme of the rider who does not attempt to control his horse, already mentioned in the previous chapter, brought up again; evidently there was a class of jouster, whether from inexperience or choice, who launched himself like a missile down the lists and hoped that he would make contact.

Duarte also deals with the psychology needed to become a successful jouster. No chronicler (and indeed, although we have not included them in our witnesses, no poet) gives us anything approaching the feel of entering the lists in the way that Duarte's down-to-earth description does:

13   Sidney Anglo, 'Archives of the English Tournament: Score Cheques and List', *Journal of the Society of Archivists* II, 153-62.

14   Duarte, king of Portugal, *Livro da ensinança de bem cavalgar toda sela* ed. Joseph M. Piel (Lisboa 1944) 86, translated by Amélia Hutchinson.

Owing to a lack of confidence, those who joust can fail in four different ways:

Firstly, because they want to avoid the encounter.

Secondly, because they veer away, fearing the moment of encounter.

Thirdly, by failing to keep their body and lance steady because of the effort required.

Fourthly, they are so anxious to gain an advantage over their adversary that they end up by failing.

As to the first point, some fail because they are led by their own instinct to avoid the encounter, wanting to protect themselves from a certain opponent or because their horse is so weak or their lance is so thick that they know that they cannot enter the encounter without receiving some injury . . . . Some fail because of this first attitude, however, when people seek their own safety and avoid danger and trouble. It happens like this. When someone enters a joust, he is determined to fight, and this determination is still present when he takes hold of his lance. But as he approaches his adversary, his instinct advises him to avoid the encounter; his determination immediately contradicts this, and this inner struggle is conducted all the time he is charging down the lists. Sometimes his instinct pulls his body away from the line of charge and aims his lance away in order not to encounter his opponent. And as soon as he has missed his adversary, the jouster is very disappointed with himself and determined to be firmer next time. But when he takes part in other jousts, his free will decides to follow this weak and evil instinct rather than his strong and virtuous determination.

The second way in which you can fail—namely because fear leads you into straying away from the line of the charge—is also caused by the weakness of the flesh; but there is this difference. The first group I referred to simply decide to avoid the encounter and pull their lances away, but the latter are determined to be firm, and in bracing themselves and their whole bodies, they close their eyes, thus failing to encounter their opponent; or else in bracing their bodies, they brace their arm too tightly and cause the lance to deviate from its target.

The last error comes from wanting to be in a position of advantage over your opponent; here the instinct is to avoid danger but nonetheless to strike and injure the adversary. If such a position of advantage does not present itself, this kind of jouster prefers to miss the encounter altogether. . . . This is done without taking any account of who or what they are competing against, or of what sort of horse they are riding . . . . In order to avoid the attitudes described above, you must follow your reason and understanding. Consider what is the right course of action to take, and force yourself along that path, supported by your effort, reason and practice . . . . Think of your initial determination to strike home in the encounter as you first started riding the tilt; remember it throughout and do not allow yourself to be distracted from it. Remember how few accidents result from taking part in an encounter of this kind compared with the accidents which result from taking part in the 'juego de cañas' (game with canes) or from hunting or fighting in battle, in which people engage without any great fear. You should feel the same about jousting, and you will then be prepared beforehand for any shortcomings or fall, rather than wanting to avoid meeting your adversary. And if you hold firmly to this decision and are quite determined to follow it, you will perforce meet your adversary in the end. To guard against the tendency to brace yourself too firmly in preparation for the encounter, you can chose one of three alternatives: either to hold yourself and the lance in a relaxed fashion, or to hold yourself so tight that it is difficult to hold that position for long and by the time you come to the encounter you will already be more relaxed. And the third alternative is to carry the lance a little loosely so that by the time you tense yourself to get courage, it naturally comes into the right position to strike the adversary.

As to wanting to be protected by unfair advantage, this should be avoided by any reasonable jouster. He should take into account himself, his adversary, his horse, the lances being used, and then encounter his opponent. And if you think that you have an advantage, lower your shield, for I always feel that you cannot be a good jouster if you are unable to take some risk. And besides this, you can also take the following two pieces of advice. First, when you lower your lance under your arm, if your adversary is not too near, let the lance point a little lower than where you intend to hit. This is done for two reasons: first, in order to see more clearly the place where you intend to hit; second, in order to stop yourself from lowering the lance too far when you are bringing it down. The second piece of advice, and this is the main method of striking on target, is to have your eyes set firmly on your target and force your body and intention to remain set until you think you can see the iron tip of the lance arrive at its intended target.[15]

Duarte's point that jousters should not seek an advantage over their opponents is echoed in other sources in a slightly different context. Diego Gutierre de Gamez notes that the French fought with lances of equal size, and that only three master craftsmen were allowed to make them. The articles of many of the challenges of the fifteenth century stipulate that only lances and swords provided by the defender are to be used, and that the challenger is to have first choice. In 1481, Albrecht Achilles of Brandenburg wrote to Wilhelm of Jülich about arrangements for wedding jousts to establish the standard for armour and to set the measurement for the lances – 11 feet long from the coronal to the vambrace.[16] Again, the concern to see fair play is an essential part of the concept of the tournament.

Throughout Europe, the tournament was accepted as part of the social aspect of great ceremonial occasions in peacetime by the fifteenth century. We find examples in connection with formal royal entries into cities, diplomatic meetings, coronations, knightings, and on a more personal level, christenings and – above all – weddings. The idea of knightly sports as part of solemn occasions such as the assembly of a royal court is to be found as early as 1135 in Geoffrey of Monmouth's *History of the Kings of*

15   Duarte, *Livro da ensinança*, 96-101.
16   *Deutsche Privatbriefe des Mittelalters* I 23-24.

Britain,[17] and there were plans for a tournament at Frederick Barbarossa's great court at Mainz in 1184. About the same time, John of Marmoutier, in his biography of Geoffrey duke of Anjou, describes how a tournament was fought immediately after his knighting, and two of the round tables recorded in the thirteenth century were associated with knighting ceremonies. As Raimon Llull put it in the *Book of the Order of Chivalry,* when describing the making of a knight, 'that same day him behoveth to make a great feast and to give fair gifts and great dinners, to joust and sport and do other things that appertaineth to the order of chivalry . . . .'[18]

Because other state ceremonies involved the holding of great courts, at which large numbers of knights assembled, the tournament became associated with these as well. Three particular occasions, however, regularly provide mentions of tournaments or jousts: coronations, royal entries into cities and diplomatic occasions. The earliest mention of jousting at a coronation or its equivalent comes from the election of Rainieri Zeno as doge at Venice in 1253,[19] and at Acre in 1286 there was a round table at the coronation of Henry of Cyprus as king of Jerusalem. Early in the fourteenth century we find jousting at the coronations of Edward II of England in 1308, Philip VI of France in 1326, Alfonso IV of Aragon in 1328, and as far afield as Sweden, for the coronation of Magnus in 1336. Similarly, the ritual of royal entry into a town was largely a French and Spanish custom in the fourteenth and fifteenth centuries; the earliest example of a tournament in this context is that at the entry of Philip VI into Paris in 1328, when thirty knights took part. The arrival of the king at a major city was in a sense a diplomatic occasion: both the ruler and the citizens were mindful of their respective privileges and authority, and hence a formal welcome was needed, to display the goodwill of both sides. We find tournaments at international diplomatic occasions as well, such as the tournament at Friesach on 12 May 1224, when Leopold of Austria and two local magnates met for a conference. [20]

We have already noted the series of jousts held for the king of Cyprus in 1363–5, and in the fifteenth century we find a number of jousts held specifically in honour of an embassy, such as the English ambassadors at Paris in 1415, or the ambassadors sent to Lisbon in 1428 to fetch Isabella of Portugal for her wedding to Philip the Good: there were two days of jousting, described in some detail by the official who reported to Philip on the proceedings. Interestingly, he appears to have been unfamiliar with both jousting challenges and the use of a barrier in the lists; it is not impossible that this diplomatic contact had a considerable influence on the shape of later Burgundian

17   *The Historia Regum Britannie of Geoffrey of Monmouth* ed. Neil Wright (Woodbridge 1985) 112.
18   Ramon Llull, *The Book of the Ordre of Chyvalry* , 75.
19   Pompeo G.Molmenti, *La storia di Venezia nella vita privata* (rptd Trieste 1976) I, 189.
20   Thomas, *Ulrich von Liechtenstein, Service of Ladies,* 15-16.

festivals. The culmination of diplomatic encounters in the lists was of course the Field of Cloth of Gold in 1520, when the tournament scores were on the verge of becoming a major factor in the outcome of the negotiations themselves.

Such diplomatic tournaments often involved princely prestige, and were akin to a display of military strength, but the individual participants may have viewed the matter differently. The enthusiasm aroused by tournaments was not confined to the knights who took part. The tournament was a major social occasion from the early thirteenth century onwards, and the presence of ladies at such gatherings was taken for granted, though there is little direct mention of them. Pedro II of Aragon's tournament at Montpellier in 1207 in honour of his mistress is the earliest specific record of the patronage of ladies. About 1270, we hear of the marquis of Este holding a tournament in honour of a lady who was present, and ladies were present at Roger Mortimer's festival at Kenilworth in 1279, and at Chauvency in 1285. At Basle in 1315 many ladies were injured, and many jewels stolen, when a stand collapsed. By the 1330s, ladies were regular spectators at English jousts, and in 1331 the stands at Cheapside collapsed, again injuring many ladies. The implication is that the practice of building stands was a result of the presence of ladies, who could not be expected to mix with the excited rabble of citizens who were also watching. We catch glimpses of individual enthusiasts such as the countess of Luxembourg at Chauvency, and John of Bohemia's second wife Beatrice; he is said to have married her precisely because of her love of tournaments.

In the 1480s Friedrich of Brandenburg held a tournament to entertain his mother, who was recovering from an illness. It is most unusual to find a lady who positively refused to watch, as was the case with Isabella of Burgundy: Olivier de la Marche describes how she would not watch a passage of arms in 1449, 'and I had never seen her come to watch a combat on foot'. Other ladies probably came simply for social reasons: Dorothea of Mecklenburg's request for a gilded coach to go to tournaments in 1467 reflects this side of the occasion.

Tournaments were from the beginning associated with dances; we catch a glimpse of this even in William Marshal's day, and there were dances at Kenilworth and at the tournaments of Edward III. At Chauvency, there was dancing every evening, and the ladies danced among themselves while waiting for the tournament to begin on the last day. Dancing was an essential part of Spanish and Burgundian tournaments, and it became formalised in the German tournament society regulations: those who committed a foul in the tournament were to be excluded from the dance, as were those who took part in the tournament without licence or without being properly qualified.

The prizes were traditionally given by ladies: William Marshal's prize of a fine pike was sent by the lady of a local castle, and a lady presented the bear which was a prize at the tournament near London in 1216. Sir John Tiptoft says that the award of the prizes was traditionally at the discretion of the ladies: again, we find this formalised in Germany in the shape of a *frauendank* or ladies' prize. However, the occasion at Ferrara when the ladies themselves competed for prizes in 1438 seems to have been an exception: after the jousts ended, 'all the ladies ran on foot in the lists. They had to run as far as a man could throw a stone.'[21] The prizes were laid out at the other end, and were three fine pieces of cloth. Here at least there would have been an easily distinguished winner: in the complicated scoring for jousts or the confusion of a tournament, the ladies' role in judging the results must have been a ceremonial one, the real work being done by the officers responsible for organising the tournament or by the judges themselves, as in René d'Anjou's description.

The other social aspect of tournaments was their function as spectacle, often involving ladies. The theme of the lady as inspiration goes back in literature to Geoffrey of Monmouth's *History of the Kings of Britain,* and reaches its height in Chrétien de Troyes' romance of Lancelot and Guinevere, in which Guinevere, unsure of the identity of a knight who has entered the lists incognito, sends word by a messenger ordering him to fight badly: when he at once turns from victor into vanquished, she knows that it is Lancelot. Perhaps because of the intimate involvement of Guinevere with tournaments in the romances, the proceedings at Le Hem in 1278 were under the direction of a lady playing 'Queen Guinevere'. We have already noted the 'round tables' which were a frequent form of tournament, and Sarrasin's poem about Le Hem provides us with a picture of a festival conceived in almost theatrical terms which may well have been typical of such occasions. In the Cyprus festivities of 1223, the courtiers are said to have 'imitated' the adventures of Arthur and his knights, and at Le Hem we find knights playing specific parts: Robert count of Artois acted Yvain, the knight with the lion; seven identically dressed knights appeared as knights who he had earlier rescued and sent to Guinevere, in the best tradition of the romances, and another took the unrewarding part of Kay, Arthur's bad-tempered seneschal. There was an ugly damsel as messenger, and all challengers had to be accompanied by a lady, and had to joust before they were admitted to the court.

So the literary framework of the round table tournaments had led into the theatrical world; and the jousters appear in many different guises. Ulrich von Lichtenstein is the earliest example of this, and his Lady Venus is countered by a knight dressed as a monk. His apparently shocked response to the appearance of this challenger would imply that such impious disguises were still a novelty: in 1286 the courtiers at Acre appeared as nuns and monks at the festivities for king Henry's coronation, and we have already noted a series of jousts in religious disguises from the fourteenth and fifteenth century.

21   Pero Tafur, *Travels* 178.

The costumes would obviously have been simple enough to wear over armour, and must have been little more than a surcoat, a special crest and arms and perhaps devices on the horsecloths and trappings to indicate the character in question. The complicated tournament crests in standard use already represented a kind of costume; the jousters were already dressed for the part, and from there it was only a short step to playing with different costumes and identities.

The tournament's function as a social occasion is shown most clearly by its association with weddings. This apparently surprising conjunction is very frequent from the end of the thirteenth century to the middle of the sixteenth century, and in German princely families the tournament became almost de rigueur. The first notice of a tournament at a wedding is in Lambert of Ardres' history of the counts of Ardres in the 1180s, when Arnold of Ardres married Gertrude of Flanders.[22] In the thirteenth century we only hear of tournaments at weddings when some disaster or drama is involved: at Merseburg in 1268, the bride, Cunegunde of Saxony, saw her brother mortally wounded, while at the wedding of Edward I's daughter Eleanor in 1293 to the count of Bar, John duke of Brabant was run through by the spear of his opponent and killed. At the wedding of Philip VI of France and Jeanne of Burgundy at Paris in 1328, the jousting was of a high standard, and the lord of St Venant distinguished himself by unseating the duke of Normandy at the first encounter: but the chronicler ends more sombrely by relating the death of the count of Eu, constable of France, from an accidental lance-thrust in the stomach.[23]

By this time, tournaments were an accepted feature of noblemen's weddings, from the Holy Roman Emperor down to relatively minor figures. The great Burgundian festivals of the fifteenth century were closely linked to weddings: Philip the Good and Isabella of Portugal at Bruges in 1429, Charles the Bold and Margaret of York in the same town forty years later. Likewise, when Wilwolt von Schaumburg married the daughter of a court official at Würzburg towards the end of the fifteenth century, there were about a thousand guests, and jousts of three types were held, the festivities lasting for three days.[24] Wilwolt had something of a reputation as a warrior, and this display is in keeping with his character, but in 1553, a tournament also figured in the wedding ceremonies of Caterina Fugger, who belonged to the great Augsburg banking family, an event carefully recorded by Hans Burgkmair in a specially commissioned tournament book. However, only the very wealthy or the very enthusiastic could afford to mount

---

22   *MGH SS XXV*, 480 (*Chronicae principum Saxoniae*), 546 (*Balduini Ninovensis Chronicon*).

23   *Petite chronique française de l'an 1270 à l'an 1356* ed. M.Douët d'Arcq, *Mélanges publiés par la société des bibliophiles françois* , III, Paris 1867, 18-20.

24   *Die Geschichte und Taten Wilwolts von Schaumburg* ed. Adalbert von Keller, Bibliothek des Litterarischen Vereins in Stuttgart 50 (Stuttgart 1859) 36.

such an event: cost as much as snobbery restricted the holding of wedding tournaments to a very small elite.

A knight's first joust could in itself be something of an occasion. At a relatively modest level, we have already noted the lord of Cronberg proudly recording in the family deeds that 'Philip my eldest son took part in a tournament for the first time at Wiesbaden' in October 1410. A much grander entry into the lists for the first time was that of John count of Nevers, later duke of Burgundy, in 1388: the ducal accounts record payments not only to the heralds who attended the jousts and the squire against whom he fought, but also furs given to the wife of Josset the armourer when the latter armed the count for jousting for the first time.[25]

The social aspect of the tournament is further underlined by its links to Shrovetide. The association may go back as far as the very beginnings of the tournament: when a group of young nobles came to visit St Bernard at Clairvaux just before Lent, in the course of a tour in search of tournaments, St Bernard tried to persuade them not to bear arms in the few days before the fast, and, not without difficulty, succeeded.[26] In this case, the association with Lent may have been pure coincidence, but there is at least a hint that this was a likely time for 'those detestable fairs called tourneys'. The first certain evidence is appropriately from Venice, home of the carnival in succeeding centuries: six gentlemen from Friuli on the mainland challenged the men of Venice at Shrovetide 1272. Sixty years later, we find Edward III jousting at Guildford in March 1329 just before Lent, and a specifically Shrovetide joust at Pegau in central Germany in 1331 in which a local nobleman was killed.

Shrovetide carnivals — from the Latin 'carni vale', or 'farewell to the flesh' — were by no means general at this period, and it is only from the late fourteenth century that we find continuous series of Shrovetide tournaments, as at Cologne from 1371 onwards, where the city council regularly rented a house overlooking the hay market so that they could watch the jousting. But there seems to have been such a tradition in Italy, despite the absence of specific records, because we know that the month of February was connected with tournaments. We find this link in a series of poems on the months by Folgore di San Gimignano, and in a similar series of frescoes depicting the months at the castle of Buonconsiglio in the north-east of Italy, where the month of February is represented by a tournament. In France, Charles VI held a Shrovetide joust at Troyes in 1420, and the first Sunday in Lent is called 'béhourd Sunday' in documents of that period; but it is in Germany that the tradition was strongest, with examples from Nuremberg in 1401, 1446, and 1454: in the latter year Albrecht of Bavaria and Ladislaus of Bohemia took part, and the nobles jousted against the

---

25   *Inventaires mobiliers de ducs de Bourgogne*, ed. Bernard Prost (Paris 1902-8) II, 409, 415, 483.
26   *PL* CLXXXV, 157 (*Life of St Bernard of Clairvaux*, c.1140-5).

Nuremberg patricians. Jousting made one of its very rare appearances in Rome itself during the carnival of 1473, when cardinal Riario, nephew of Sixtus IV, gave two prizes for jousting, to be awarded by a panel of judges.

Tournaments were also associated with Christmas and Easter, but to a much lesser degree, and Martinmas, at the beginning of November before winter set in, is another date that recurs in the records. Christmas jousts were very much a question of the enthusiasm of a given household for jousting: the three best examples are the court of Savoy in the 1340s, the English court in the second half of the fourteenth century and the court of Saxony at Ansbach in the 1480s, all groups renowned for their interest in the sport who evidently held fairly informal jousts during the Christmas period. Easter and Whitsun, which were equally times when royal courts assembled, also saw jousting: the most memorable example is the Castilian joust on Whitsunday with the king and his team dressed as God and the Twelve Apostles.

Essentially, the tournament was the natural corollary of any major gathering where a number of knights were present. Despite its dangers, it provided a popular spectator sport, an opportunity for conversation and display on the part of the onlookers, and it fitted well with the other events, filling the 'tedious brief interval' between ceremony and feast.

In the early days of tournaments, there seems to have been little restriction on those who could take part: anyone who could acquire a suit of armour was welcome. In practice, this usually meant that the participants were knights and squires, but this was only gradually formalised. The concept of a separate event for younger knights and squires was an early development, and this gradually grew into the idea that only knights could take part in tournaments. But this was far from universally accepted: we have already discussed the long tradition of bourgeois tournaments in the Low Countries, where the citizens would assemble for an annual joust. In the Baltic towns we find the 'courts of king Arthur' or *Artushofe*, a kind of bourgeois order of the Round Table; these often included annual jousts as part of their ceremonial. And in the great south German cities, we find the leading citizens, such as Marx Walther, jousting as a team against the nobles. In Italy, where knighthood and feudalism were less sharply defined, jousting was an almost entirely civic sport.

The tournament is arguably one of the areas in which early heraldry emerged, as a means of identifying combatants, and heralds were prominent from the first. Their involvement was to lead to an insistence that only those who could prove their nobility should take part in tournaments. This process is part of the retreat into knighthood as an exclusive inherited status, rather than an order open to merit and ambition, and begins to appear in the fourteenth century. It appears clearly in the best account of the organisation of a tournament that we have, in René d'Anjou's treatise on the form and devising of a tournament, written about 1455–60, after his series of splendid festivals. All those wishing to take part are to assemble four days before the tournament itself, when the princes and other lords who wish to display their banners at the tournament – a sign of status which also implies that they are producing a team of jousters for the occasion – enter the town where the event is to be held in solemn procession. All those taking part have to display their shields at the window of their inn. The judges are to take up lodgings in a house of religion or somewhere where there is a cloister or courtyard in which the shields of the tourneyers can be displayed on the evening of the tournament. On the evening of the day of arrival, a dance is held, during which the shields are inspected: four instances are given for which a knight may be excluded from the tournament, a question to which we shall return later.

It was only in England, France and Spain that knighthood and tournaments were closely associated, and the patronage of tournaments was the exclusive preserve of the magnates. However, perhaps the most exclusive tournaments of all were to be found in Germany, as a kind of reaction to the general openness of entry into the lists in the towns. From the late fourteenth century onwards there was a determined attempt to restrict admission to tournaments to those of knightly descent, a movement closely linked with efforts to rally the knightly class as a political force. Only those whose great-grandfathers had taken part in tournaments were to be allowed to participate, and stringent rules against unknightly behaviour were introduced. These regulations reached their height in the 1480s, but their origins go back at least a century, and owe something to French customs: Antoine de la Sale notes wryly that some would-be jousters in a tournament in Lorraine in 1445 had difficulty in remembering how to describe (or blazon) their arms, and were afraid that they might be refused entrance, so he did his best to help them. The exclusions are found at their most elaborate in the regulations for a tournament at Würzburg in 1479 which deliberately set out to revive the then neglected sport. Fourteen clauses list those who are not to be admitted, ranging through perjurers, slanderers, cheats, cowards, adulterers, destroyers of churches, and bandits to those who cannot show that their ancestors tourneyed in the last fifty years and anyone tainted by trade.

Two years later, at Heilbronn, ordinances consist of 43 articles, and the offences are divided into two classes: minor offences for which a beating only is decreed before the knight is expelled, and those for which the knight is to be placed 'on the barrier' as well.[27] 'Anyone who lives in a town of his own free will. . . . or engages in trade' cannot take part in a tournament. The ordinances are much more concerned with the status and morals of the participants than with the regulation of the fighting. A long

---

27   L.A. von Gumppenberg, *Die Gumppenberger auf Turnieren* (Würzburg 1882) 125-131.

list of offences merit the drastic punishment of being 'put on the barrier'; the offender was beaten, unhorsed, and put on his saddle on the wooden fence which enclosed the lists, rather as though he was in the stocks. Many of the offences for which this punishment was prescribed were criminal – murder, highway robbery, rape and arson – but others, such as pursuit of a feud without due and proper notice, are questions of knightly ethics. Such a punishment could only be carried out if the offender was notified beforehand at the inspection of coats of arms and helms, and false accusations were severely dealt with. Lesser misdeeds, such as marrying outside the nobility or engaging in trade, were punished simply by confiscating the offender's horse. The social regulations extended to the dance after the tournament as well; only participants in the tournament were to be allowed to dance, and elaborate prohibitions against excessively costly dresses were laid down: women were only to bring three or four embroidered dresses, and noblemen were not to wear gold and silver ornaments on their doublets. It is only at the end that the regulations touch on the actual organisation of the tournament, and even then it is principally to ensure correct announcement of the event, to limit the number of retainers, and to provide for safe-conducts for participants. The actual fighting is scarcely mentioned; one of the last clauses decrees that only one tournament each year is to be held in the boundaries of the 'four lands' (Bavaria, Swabia, Rhineland and Franconia) so that such events may be properly regulated and suitably impressive. There is a distinct feeling that the occasion has become more important than the sport, because frequent tournaments would have undoubtedly enhanced knightly skills.

The tournament thus became briefly a kind of social court of honour. We first hear of this association of matters of honour with the tournament in 1286. The duke of Bavaria was widely believed to have executed his wife on a trumped-up charge of adultery; at a tournament at the imperial court held at Cologne, a hundred knights appeared bearing shields showing a headless lady, 'to shame the duke', at which the court was disbanded. We have already quoted Pero Tafur's eyewitness account of a tournament at Schaffhausen in 1434, where social regulations similar to those at Würzburg were in force.[28]

The real aim of these rules is to preserve the unity and character of the old nobility of birth against the threat posed by the increasing wealth of the townsmen and merchants, and the stress laid on the exclusion of children of misalliances between men of noble birth and the daughters of merchants – a traditional way of restoring aristocratic family fortunes – is particularly interesting. The most tangible form of this deliberate revival of knighthood as a class is to be found in the tourneying societies,

---

28   Pero Tafur, *Travels*, 208-9.

which aimed to become a kind of guild of knights centred round their favourite sport, but also with distinct political overtones. Confraternities of knights were not uncommon throughout the middle ages, and we have seen how secular royal orders like the Banda and the Garter had strong links with the world of tournaments.

The earliest German records which give us details of a tourneying society date from 1361, when a group of nobles from upper Bavaria formed a confederation with the political objective of bringing the young duke Meinhard of Bavaria under their control. The tournament was to act as a kind of annual assembly for the association, whose members were to wear the same livery at social occasions: 'and the society shall hold a court once a year, namely that is a tournament'. All members are to attend, or to pay a fine equal to the cost of actual attendance. A council of four is to be appointed to oversee the members, and members are to help each other in war. A chapel is to be founded in Freising, where masses are to be said for the members. All members are to own a warhorse if they can. At the annual meeting, all members must bring their wife, sister or adult daughter 'to honour the society'. Other rules provide for the recruiting and expulsion of members.[29]

Again, we know little of what became of the society after its foundation: but with the *Gesellschaft mit dem Esel* (Society of the Donkey) we are able to trace its existence from 1387 to 1435.[30] Its rules, which do not survive in their original form, seem to have been similar to those for the Bavarian society, but the leader was a 'king' who was elected annually. The primary object was to form an association of knights who would offer each other mutual support in adversity; beyond that, the society was intended to offer a suitable atmosphere in which chivalric culture could flourish. This was done through the society's feasts, of which the tournament was an essential part. The meetings were usually at Frankfurt, where the society rented its own quarters, including a dance-hall, from the town, and held jousts on the Romerberg. Unfortunately, we have only a very late version of the tournament regulations, dating from 1481, which seems to be copied from other sources.

By the 1470s and 1480s, after a period of relative decline, we find a dozen or more societies, who eventually grouped themselves into four 'lands', Rhineland, Swabia, Franconia and Bavaria, to give the sport a kind of overall controlling organisation. The members were rarely the great princes, though we find Albrecht of Brandenburg writing to his son about his family's connection with the 'Perner' tourneying society. He describes how his ancestors and his father had belonged to the society, and he has

29   Karl-Ludwig Ay, *Altbayern von 1180 bis 1550*, Dokumente zur Geschichte von Staat und Gesellschaft im Bayern I.ii (Munich 1977) 230-1.

30   Alfred Fries, 'Die Ritter- und Turniergesellschaft mit dem Esel', *Archiv für hessische Geschichte und Altertümskunde* XXIV, 154ff.

joined the revived society in his own name and for his sons: 'we were always, with God's help, foremost in tournaments, and intend with God's help to stay there'. The officers were usually elected from the lesser nobles: a letter from Konrad von Schellenberg, deputy of the king of the society of the Falcon and Fish, summoning a member to a tournament at Constance on June 19 1486 survives: he calls himself simply 'knight', with no higher title.[31]

The tournament began as an informal affair, martial exercises or mock warfare for knights and squires; by the beginning of the sixteenth century, form and formality have taken over, and the tournament is essentially an occasion, carefully planned in advance, held at specific times or for specific reasons, with its own literary and dramatic conventions. The apogee of the tournament is in the fifteenth century, when the reality of the fighting still balances the structure of ritual and theatrical invention superimposed on the martial exercise.

31   *Deutsche Privatbriefe*, I, 240.

10

The Knight on the Battlefield

1. The knight's role in warfare

REAL WAR AND TOURNAMENTS are never very far apart throughout the history of chivalry. Tournaments begin as mimic wars in the twelfth century; wars take on the appearance of mimic tournaments in the pages of Froissart in the fourteenth century. In both, the knight seems to be the sole protagonist, deciding the outcome of the day in a series of charges, against which infantry are powerless, and in hand to hand combats. Deaths are rare, the same rules seem to apply; and the knights, living for warfare, have made even this real warfare a kind of exciting, unreal game.

Mediaeval warfare was in fact a very much rougher and bloodier business than Froissart would have us believe, and much more complex than the pages of the chroniclers, themselves unskilled in its arts, would lead us to think. There is nothing quite so difficult to portray accurately as a mediaeval battle. First of all, the numbers are almost impossible to gauge, but are certainly exaggerated by contemporary writers. The greatest armies of classical times are estimated at about 35,000 men; Caesar at the height of his career may have had this number at Pharsalia in 48BC. With the fragmentation of the Empire, the numbers involved grow less and less, though reliable estimates are impossible until the twelfth century. When numbers can once again be reckoned, the mediaeval army appears as a force of between 7,000 and 10,000 men though there is no definite instance of the latter number being engaged in a single battle. If we set these figures, based on the study of royal accounts, and occasionally of the terrain of the battlefield itself, against the reports of the chroniclers, the unreliability of their figures, and indeed of their whole reports, becomes evident. To take a single instance: at Bouvines in 1214, when Philip Augustus of France defeated the combined Angevin and Imperial army, the chroniclers record up to 9,000 knights and 50,000 infantry on the French side, the real figure being a little over one-tenth of these; and a Scottish chronicle succeeds in attributing nearly quarter of a million men to the opposing army, which may have numbered 10,000.

The accounts of the course of the battles themselves are equally suspect in some respects. While the broad details may be accurate, the writers are rarely interested in the minutiae, or well-informed enough to know what happened. So every battle becomes a cavalry action in which the infantry are mere bystanders, unless some exceptional reversal of fortune occurs. The idea of mediaeval tactics as consisting of massive charges by heavily armed knights, invariably on horseback, captures the imagination all too easily: and the shadow of this attractive oversimplification still hangs over the history of mediaeval warfare.

The apparent improvisation and lack of theoretical manuals which are the chief features of mediaeval tactics belie the true nature of the warfare of the period. Selection of terrain, disposition of forces, and discipline were as important as the strength of the cavalry force and their fighting skill; the slow evolution of new ideas meant that the individual skill of the commander was at a premium, and that it was the quality of the troops rather than possession of the latest weapons that decided the outcome of the campaign.

The approach of a skilled general such as Richard I of England 'was methodical and carefully prepared. His strategy was based on the systematic use of magazines, supply lines and ravaging, 'the strategy of manoeuvre' which is usually associated with a later period, but the strategy which was in fact adopted by all good medieval generals.'[1] This was *guerre guerroyante*, as practiced in the campaigns of Edward III and the Black Prince in France. Full-scale battles were very unusual during the period of the knight's ascendancy as a warrior, and strategy on the battlefield was the supreme challenge for a commander, who was unlikely to have any experience of such a situation, and was equally unlikely to encounter it again. The endemic warfare of the middle ages, the kind of war most knights would be familiar with, depended far more on practicalities of administration and supply, recruitment and support, than on the spectacular occasions which found their way into the chronicles.

A great deal of medieval campaigning was economic warfare, designed to destroy the source of the enemy's revenue rather than to defeat his army. By removing his source of supplies, both immediately and in the long term, far more damage might be inflicted than by a victory in the field. William I's ruthless 'harrying of the North' in 1068-9 is an early example of this, and parallels can be found in Crusader warfare in the east and in the actions of the papal forces in the Albigensian crusade. Most of the campaigns of the Hundred Years' War consist of devastations rather than sieges and skirmishes:

1   John Gillingham, 'Richard I and the Science of War in the Middle Ages' in *War and Government in the Middle Ages* ed. John Gillingham and J.C.Holt (Woodbridge 1984) 90.

the Black Prince's expedition of 1355-7, for example, was intended to be no more than an armed raid for the purpose of economic warfare, and the battle at Poitiers only came about because the prince had made such an effective nuisance of himself that a drastic response became necessary.[2] The pillaging and burning may have seemed wanton and merely designed to demoralise the population and persuade them that their French masters were broken reeds as protectors; but the prince's steward, Sir John Wengfeld, gave a classic exposition of the reasoning behind this kind of war in his report home:

> And my lord rode against his enemies eight whole weeks, and sojourned not in all these places save eleven days. And know for certain that, since this war began against the king of France, there was never such loss nor such destruction as hath been in this raid. For the lands and the good towns which are destroyed in this raid found for the king of France each year more to maintain his war than did the half of his kingdom, not reckoning the exchange which he hath made each year of his money and of the profit and custom which he taketh of them of Poitou, as I could show you by good records which were found in divers towns in the houses of receivers.[3]

When a battle did occur, the basic dispositions remained the same from the twelfth to the fifteenth century. Cavalry formed the attacking force, with infantry as supporting and defensive troops. Even the introduction of the longbow and the successes of the Hussite infantry, using fortified wagons in a ring, the *Wagenburg* did nothing to alter this. In the twelfth century, the infantry role was necessarily smaller, since the crossbow was a slow and difficult weapon to handle. If there were no crossbowmen, the battle would open without a preliminary volley, in skirmishes between outriders, as the two armies manoeuvred and each tried to persuade the other side to charge. A first charge rarely succeeded, and if the enemy could be persuaded to commit himself too heavily to his initial effort, the chances of an effective counter-charge before he could recover were increased. There are innumerable examples of battles being lost by an impulsive opening attack by over-eager knights, a problem to which we shall return.

Equally, the two armies might confront each other for a long time before battle was joined, as at Las Navas de Tolosa in 1212, where the Christians refused to be drawn by the Muslim armies for two days, while they encamped and rested, despite exchanges between archers and light horsemen. Again, in Henry II's wars against his French overlord, a pitched battle never occurred, though the armies came face to face in 1173 near Conches and in 1174 after the siege of Rouen. The number of actual

---

2   Clifford J.Rogers, 'Edward III and the Dialects of Strategy', *Transactions of the Royal Historical Society*, Sixth Series, IV, 1994, 83-103.

3   Robert of Avesbury, *De gestis mirabilibus regis Edwardi tertii*, ed. Edward Maunde Thompson, RS 93 (London 1889) 445.

battles in the twelfth century is also very small: Tinchebray in 1106, Northallerton in 1138, Lincoln in 1141, Fornham in 1173, Alarcos in 1195. Of these, Lincoln and Fornham were on a very small scale, scarcely bigger than the skirmish at Courcelles in 1198 in which Richard defeated Philip Augustus and proudly announced in his letter reporting the victory that ninety French knights were captured, two hundred had been drowned, and that he had taken two hundred horses. The basic unit was a group of about thirty to forty knights around their leader's banner. In the twelfth and thirteenth centuries, these groups or *conrois* probably fought in tournaments in similar formation; the Brabançon mercenaries of the twelfth century came from an area where the tournament was almost a national sport. The 'battle' was composed of a number of these units, in close formation, and two or three such battles would probably be deployed, one sometimes being left in reserve or in ambush if a feigned retreat (as at Hastings) was to be used.

Sieges were a much more important ingredient of any twelfth-century campaign, given that the real object of military manoeuvres was to deprive the enemy of control of the countryside; this could either be done by ravaging, or by systematically ejecting the enemy from his fortresses. Henry II's successes were largely due to his skill in siegecraft and use of mercenaries who were prepared to sit out a long siege, unlike the feudal levies who were liable to go home at the end of their allotted time, regardless of the state of the campaign. If one could take a stronghold like Castillon in Gascony as swiftly as Henry did in 1161, reducing the local lords to a state of terror and amazement, none of the latter were likely to risk a pitched battle. Siege warfare and machinery lay outside the knight's province; experts were employed from a very early date, mercenaries recruited for the purpose on a similar footing to the Genoese crossbowmen. Only a commander of some standing was likely to have to direct a siege. On the other hand, knights were often to be found as defenders, either because castle-guard was one of their feudal duties, or as a professional garrison. By the early thirteenth century, castle-guard was almost always commuted by payments, and the professional garrison took over. Nonetheless, the ordinary knight was likely to see more of sieges than of battles in his military service, and after the arts of the engineers had effected a breach with mangonels, battering rams or mines, it was the knights who formed the assault troops who actually stormed the citadel. They were the ones who would scale the walls on ladders, or would be wheeled forward on wooden towers to leap onto the ramparts. At the siege of Ascalon in 1153 the Templars were so eager to gain the glory of capturing the town that when a breach was accidentally made in the part of the wall opposite their encampment, a small body of forty knights went through it to come to grips with the defenders, while their fellows prevented other Christian troops from entering. They paid dearly for their pride, however, and were overwhelmed.

We also have to remember that there were long periods of peace, particularly in the twelfth and thirteenth centuries. Under St Louis and Henry III, England and France had many periods when warfare was very much the exception,[4] and knights could only practice their skill in arms by going on crusade in the East or in the Baltic. Only in Italy and Germany was warfare frequent in this period. By contrast, the fourteenth and fifteenth centuries saw much longer periods of warfare; but even the Hundred Years' War was punctuated by decades of peace.

The pattern of warfare changed very little in the thirteenth century. Edward I's Scottish wars were fought on entirely orthodox lines, and there was very little difference in the tactics or proportion of foot to horse between Bouvines in 1214 and Falkirk in 1298, though the Welsh archers' part in the latter battle was an omen for the future. From a tactical point of view, there seems to have been very little coordination on either side at Bouvines; and only the action of a Templar, Guérin, ensured that the French drew up in such a way that they could not be outflanked. His evidently greater experience underlines the amateur nature of the feudal levies when compared with the more permanent armies in the East.

The more we look at medieval warfare, the more discipline emerges as the key factor. The idea of discipline and its importance, which ran directly counter to the quest for individual glory so often emphasised in chivalry, could only be instilled on the battlefield. To be effective knights needed experience of campaigning under disciplined conditions; a knight who did not go on crusade had little hope of seeing more than intermittent warfare. Its value was clearly realised: in an apocryphal speech of Henry the Fowler to his troops before a battle against the Hungarians (written in the twelfth century) he is made to say: 'Let no one try to pass his companions because his horse is swifter. But, using your shields as cover, take their first arrows on them; then charge them quickly and violently so that they cannot fire again before you have wounded them.'[5] Yet discipline was the weakest point of the mediaeval army, and especially of the knights.

The emphasis on individual glory (or in the case of the military orders, the glory of the order) was so strong that even experienced knights were unable to argue reasonably against it. In the East it was all too often the downfall of the Frankish troops. At Mansourah in 1250 Robert d'Artois nearly brought disaster on the entire army by disobeying specific instructions not to attack. True, he succeeded in surprising the Egyptians with the vanguard he commanded, but his initial success was too much for him, and he swept on into the town, and into an improvised ambush. The counter-attack almost swept the rest of the crusading army back into the canal they

---

4   Philippe Contamine, *War in the Middle Ages* , tr. Michael Jones (Oxford 1984) 65
5   J.F.Verbruggen, 'La tactique militaire des armées des chevaliers', *Revue du Nord*, xxix, 1947, 175.

had just so laboriously crossed. Repeatedly in the Frankish councils of war the barons urged attacks against unfavourable odds, or against strong positions, because they were so eager for battle and glory. The Templar Gerard of Ridfort was one of the most impetuous: at Cresson in 1187 he attacked a large Muslim force with a hundred or so knights and was one of only three survivors. When the entire resources of the kingdom were perhaps 1,500 knights, this was a disaster of the first order: and that the attack should have been made against saner counsels simply because Gerard had taunted the knights with cowardice was sheer folly. Tactics which involved use of a strong defensive position were often impossible to carry out, or were overruled by the opinions of such knights: at Gaza in 1244, the wiser heads among the Christian army, and particularly their Muslim allies, urged that their strong position should be held; if they had, the Egyptian armies would either have been defeated or would have withdrawn, but the temptation to try and overwhelm their opponents was too much for the count of Jaffa. In the event it was the Christians who, moving out into the plain, were massacred. The lesson of order was only learnt in the bitter days of defeat.

Part of the problem was undoubtedly that it was very difficult to deliver an effective cavalry charge which enabled the cavalry to regroup; in most instances, two or three successive charges would be launched by separate groups in turn, and it is very unusual to find a case where a group reformed successfully and attacked again.[6] The rule of the Order of the Temple show that this problem was a difficult one. Banners were used to form a rallying-point, and were crucial to the success of such a manoeuvre: 'Should [a brother] be unable to return to his banner, he was to rally to one of the Hospital, or failing that, any Christian banner... '.[7] The importance of banners on the battlefield cannot be overstated. In the *geste* of Girart de Roussillon a divine thunderbolt destroys the gonfanons of both the rebel and Charlemagne; the battle is immediately brought to an end in confusion. Given that the horseman might have to fight his way back to the banner to which he was rallying, the chances of actually coming together in good order were small. Yet again, the skill required by a heavily armed rider in combat needs to be emphasised:

> There is a vast difference between riding a linear route and being able to fight on horseback; the latter requires a degree of confidence in one's own riding ability so well founded that violent movement, either of aggression or defence, causes no loss of equilibrium.[8]

6   R.C. Smail, *Crusading Warfare 1097-1193* (Cambridge 1956) 114-5

7   Matthew Bennett, 'La Règle du Temple as a Military Manual, or How to deliver a cavalry charge', in *Studies in Medieval History presented to R. Allen Brown*, edited by Christopher Harper-Bill, Christopher Holdsworth, and Janet L.Nelson, (Woodbridge and Wolfeboro, N.H., 1989) 17-18

8   Ann Hyland, *The Medieval Warhorse: from Byzantium to the Crusades* (Far Thrupp & Dover 1994) 95

The medieval cavalry of the west were not normally capable of swift manoeuvres, as Monstrelet's surprise at the flexibility of the light cavalry raised by the duke of Orléans in 1410 shows:

> A number of Lombards and Gascons ... were mounted on terrible horses, that were taught to wheel round when on full gallop, which seemed very astonishing to the French, Flemings, Picards and Brabanters.[9]

Furthermore, it was easy for a charging horseman to pass straight through the enemy lines, or indeed to take flight on the slightest provocation. The footsoldiers were the fixed point around which the battle revolved. If they scattered, the cavalry at once had the upper hand; if they stood firm, they were proof against anything the cavalry could do. It is not easy to force a horse to actually ride down a man who stands firm, and the impetus of the charge would fade as the horses came to close quarters with the enemy. We occasionally hear of horses being trained to fight with hooves and teeth, but they became dangerous to their owners; the Templars used stallions, as being more aggressive.[10] The Anglo-Saxons at Hastings, the Flemish pikemen at Courtrai, the English dismounted knights and archers at Poitiers, all demonstrate the effectiveness of a disciplined infantry in defence.[11]

The knight's role in the actual fighting was strongly influenced by the development of armour.[12] To some extent, armour evolved to meet the knight's needs, but the lure of greater protection at the expense of mobility proved too strong. The chain mail of the eleventh to thirteenth centuries allowed great freedom of movement, and was comparatively light. On the other hand, it might not stop the sword's edge or the lance's point. A quilted undergarment came to be used as a shock absorber in the twelfth century, but the force of the blow might still produce a fairly serious wound. Made from a series of forged or riveted rings, chain mail (or mail) could easily break, and it was very difficult to keep clean and free from rust. Attempts at making a more effective yet reasonably light defence began with hardened leather garments to shield the chest and back; and at about the same time in the early thirteenth century plate-armour proper appeared. At first the mail coat was reinforced with small patches of solid metal plate at vital places, on the knees and elbows especially; then a construction of jointed plates on a leather base was used to cover the trunk. The progress of the new ideas was

---

9   Enguerrand de Monstrelet, *The Chronicles*, tr. Thomas Johnes (London 1840) II 205

10   Hyland, *Medieval Warhorse*, 114, 165; R.H.C.Davis, *The Medieval Warhorse: origin, development and redevelopment* (London 1989) 18 claims that mares and geldings were never used.

11   Stephen Morillo, *Warfare under the Anglo-Norman Kings 1066-1135* (Woodbridge and Rochester, N.Y. 1994) 158-61

12   See Claude Blair, *European Armour circa 1066 to circa 1700* (London 1958).

largely limited by the armourer's technical skill: it was not until the end of the century that gauntlets made on the same principle, which needed much closer fitting and accurate work, appeared. It was at this point that the armourer's craft moves from the local workers, who were little more than skilled blacksmiths, to the great international centres: the north Italian armourers established themselves at this time, and dominated the trade until its decline.

Armour reached its most complex point in the days of early plate-armour, about 1330, in that it was made up of a large number of individual pieces, often forming several layers, with complex lacing to hold each in its proper place. The length of time needed to don this equipment was underlined by the occasions when an army was taken by surprise. Later armour, being closely tailored to the body, was probably no easier to put on, but its construction was simpler and stronger as techniques of working metal improved after 1400, and steel was introduced. The breastplate, which seems such an essential part of the knight's equipment, did not in fact appear until the late fourteenth century, and the complete body armour of polished steel (alwhite armour) in which the Pre-Raphaelite painters clad Tennyson's heroes is of the mid-fifteenth century.

Nonetheless, the knight of the fourteenth century was sufficiently impregnable on his armoured horse to resist almost anything a footsoldier could do; only the Flemish pikemen at Courtrai in 1302, forebears of the Swiss companies of the fifteenth century, and the Turkish horse at Nicopolis in 1396 — the latter vastly superior in numbers — were able to inflict serious defeats on them. However, the dismounted knight, who had played an effective part in battles such as Northallerton in 1138, was now at a disadvantage on the attack; unable to move swiftly, less because of the weight of the armour than because armour was not designed for movement on foot, he was an easy prey to the dagger of a lightly armed soldier thrust between the joints of his carapace. The classic example of this was the experience of the French at Poitiers in 1356, when their first charge failed to break through the English archers who lined both sides of the road leading to the main body of the enemy, because their horses were shot beneath them, and both they and the dismounted second wave were cut down or killed by the English arrows used at short range.

The development of this elaborate defensive armour was not paralleled by a similar degree of development in the knight's aggressive weapons. Up to the end of the fourteenth century, the lance was held under the arm; before a charge it had to be brought from the riding position, sloped back on the shoulder, and aimed horizontally, a difficult movement while riding in formation, probably under archery fire. The introduction of the lance rest made this much easier, since the lance was now attached to armour by a swivelled mount, and could be controlled with one hand. The result was the use of heavier lances; the impact was more massive, because the whole weight of rider and horse could be brought to bear, and the strength of the blow no longer depended on the power of his grip on the lance. There were, however, far greater advances in the field of ballistics. For the knight was essentially conservative in his attitude to new modes of warfare, which he was apt to declare unknightly. No knight would have dreamt of using a bow; with some reason, for a horseman would have great difficulty in handling six feet of yew, and the short eastern bow was no match for the longbow. Both longbow and crossbow were introduced after cavalry warfare had become the universal pattern of warfare. The crossbow evolved from a late Roman weapon in north Italy in the tenth century, and became a speciality of the Genoese. It is a powerful but slow-firing weapon: on the later types, the tension is produced by a ratchet and screw, and experiments in 1894 showed that in order to load it, the archer's hand had to travel thirty feet in a circular motion as he wound back the cord.[13] Two shots a minute would be a good rate of fire, though this could be overcome by using one archer as a loader while the other aimed and fired, as at Jaffa in 1192. The squat bolt, known as a quarrel, made up for this slow delivery by its power when launched; it was still effective at 300 yards to the extent of piercing armour easily. Its devastating impact on warfare when it first appeared is reflected in Innocent II's condemnation of it at the Lateran Council in 1139: 'The deadly art, hated of God, of crossbowmen and archers should not be used against Christians and Catholics on pain of anathema.'[14]

The Genoese had a virtual monopoly both of manufacture and use of the crossbow, probably because it required a very high degree of training; and this meant that relatively few crossbowmen were available at any one time. The cost of employing them was accordingly high, and like all mercenaries their loyalties were at best uncertain; as a result it never became a general weapon.

The longbow, on the other hand, was a weapon which required much less training for efficient use, and was relatively easy to manufacture. It first appears in South Wales in the twelfth century (in North Wales the lance was the prevalent weapon: thus Giraldus, at least) though similar, shorter bows had been used since Roman days, and appear on the Bayeux Tapestry. Giraldus Cambrensis has this to say of the men of Gwent in South Wales about this time 'This people ... very accustomed to warlike ways, and most renowned for their powers, are also the most skilled archers among the Welsh.'[15] He claims that their arrows can penetrate an oak door for a hand's breadth, and that they have been known to transfix both knight and horse with a single arrow. Modern writers estimate the arrow's penetrating power as equal to that of a rifle bullet, as elephant hunters have shown; but its penetration is cleaner, and it kills only if used accurately, since it lacks the effect of the bullet, which produces shock and bruising as

13   C.J.Longman and H.Walrond, *Archery* (London 1894) 115.

14   Hefele, *Conciliengeschichte*, V, 441.

15   Giraldus Cambrensis, *Itinerarium Kambriae* ed. J.F.Dimock, RS 21 (London 1868) VI, 54.

well. With a rate of fire over six times that of the crossbow, it rapidly achieved a predominant role in warfare after Edward I's conquest of Wales. The companies of archers from Wales and the border counties first began to play an important part in Edward's Scottish campaigns at the end of the thirteenth century; the battle of Falkirk in 1298 is a good example. Their full tactical potential was only realised under Edward III, at Dupplin Moor (1332) and Halidon Hill (1333); and from then until the end of the next century, they were the key to the defensive tactics which brought the English armies such success.

There was no question of the knights adopting either crossbow or longbow for their own use. Apart from the impossibility of handling them on horseback, they were both supporting weapons, which required an offensive squadron to press home the advantage. It was not merely the knightly disdain for such servile weapons — the longbowmen were English peasants, the crossbowmen Italian mercenaries — which the *chanson de geste* of Girart de Roussillon forcefully expresses: 'Cursed be the first man who became an archer: he was afraid and did not dare approach.'[16] There were also sound tactical requirements which ensured that neither innovation dislodged the knight from his position as the mainstay of the army. Nor did either weapon appreciably increase the number of deaths on the battlefield; only a very small percentage of the missiles fired inflicted mortal wounds.

For similar reasons the knight was not interested in learning the skills of firearms, especially since gunpowder and artillery were until 1400 little more than a curiosity, like Greek fire, with very specialised uses. It was only well after the knight had ceased to be master of the battlefield for quite other reasons that the musket and arquebus appeared as practical infantry weapons, and examples of knights being killed by cannon are rare: the most famous to perish in this way was Jacques de Lalaing in 1453, at the siege of Poucques, though Talbot at Castillon in 1435 had been thrown from his horse by a shot from the strong position he was trying to storm, which had been entrenched and provided with artillery; and the earl of Salisbury was killed by a stone from a veuglaire at the siege of Orléans in 1428. It was only in the closing stages of the Hundred Years' War that artillery played any serious part, and the difficulty of transporting it meant that it was confined to sieges. The giant cannon known as bombards which appeared in the 1380s were so inefficient that they were superseded by smaller weapons by 1450. In that year a chronicler records of Charles VII setting out for Normandy that 'he had the greatest number and variety of battering cannon and bombards, veuglaires, serpentines, crapaudines, culverines and ribaudequins that had ever been collected in the memory of man'.[17]

16   A.T.Hatto, 'Archery and Chivalry: a noble prejudice', *Modern Language Review* xxxv, 1940, 50.
17   Monstrelet, *Chronicles*, tr. Johnes, II,158.

It is the variety, not the size of the pieces, that matters: veuglaires and serpentines are smaller pieces which we should call cannon pure and simple; crapaudines are a kind of mortar; and the culverines and ribaudequins are hand-firearms. Even so, the technical development of firearms was still in its infancy. James I of Scotland was killed at a test-firing of a new cannon in 1437 when the barrel burst. Hand-firearms, which appear from 1369 onwards, also had their problems. Two men were needed to operate a culverine, one to aim and support it, the other to fire. Despite the appearance of the shoulder-butt in the 1420s, the bow still retained its ancient pre-eminence; at Rupelmonde in 1452, 'the Ghent men made good use of their culverines; but they could not withstand the arrows of the Picards, and, turning about, fled'.[18] And in 1471, first of many such episodes, a band of 300 Flemish mercenaries armed with handguns were put out of action by a storm which extinguished their matches and damped their powder.

However, it was neither the longbow nor firearms by themselves which put an end to the knight's domination of the battlefield. The defensive tactics already mentioned, which had won the English their successes in the mid-fourteenth century, relied not merely on archers, but on archers and dismounted knights. We can see the changing status and deployment of the knight reflected in the careful accounts relating to horses kept by the English officials during this period. By the mid-fourteenth century, the knights no longer ride the very expensive *destriers*, capable of bearing them into battle in full armour, but take horses on campaign suitable for ordinary riding. The casualties which appear in the records are incurred on the march, not on the battlefield, and the payments made for loss or damage to horses, which first appear in the mid-thirteenth century, are replaced by a lump sum for campaign expenses. The point at which a knight's horse is valued and entered on the official list ceases to be the date at which his pay begins. And there is a tendency to buy horses abroad, rather than risk valuable mounts on a sea-crossing, which implies that the need to provide top-quality horses, which might not be readily available on arrival, was tending to diminish.[19]

Yet to some extent this was a temporary respite: the battles of the fifteenth century were still dominated by heavy cavalry and archers, even if both were challenged by a new kind of soldier, the fully professional infantryman, who was a soldier all year round, and who worked with his comrades at arms in a system of regiments, rather than being hired campaign by campaign, often in different retinues. State infantry regiments appear in France in the 1450s and again in Burgundy in the 1470s, but the Swiss troops, with their strict discipline typified by their use of uniforms and their marching in time to music were the model for these endeavours. At the same time, the

18   *Ibid.*, II, 162.
19   A.J.Ayton, *Knights and Warhorses* (Woodbridge & Rochester N.Y. 1994) 99-100, 122

royal and noble retinues were developing into small permanent military institutions, and the way was paved for the modern standing army. Once the professional soldier emerged, the knight's days were numbered: his social and financial standing depended precisely on the fact that he was not merely a soldier, but a member of a court, however modest, and a landowner as well.

Chivalry on campaign

Until the fifteenth century, war to the death, *guerre mortelle*, was a rarity: the French standard or *oriflamme* was unfurled at Crécy and Poitiers as a signal that no prisoners were to be taken, but it was the French who found themselves captive. This changed because of the tactics of the Swiss infantry, who regarded prisoners as a hindrance to their movements and their quest for booty. War between noble and commoner was much more vicious than war between social equals.[20] In earlier centuries, warfare could, despite the hardships of campaigning, be turned into an opportunity for chivalric encounters. This was particularly true of the long inactivity of sieges, where knights sought diversions to while away the time. Challenges between garrison and besiegers were quite common, usually for a skirmish at the barriers. Froissart describes one of these at Noya (in Galicia) in 1387. The French are already in position:

> [The besiegers] gave their horses to the pages and servants, and marched in a compact body, each knight and squire with his spear in hand, towards the barriers: every six paces they halted, to dress themselves without opening their ranks. To say the truth, it was a beautiful sight. When they were come as far as they wished, they halted for a short time, and then advanced their front to begin the action. They were gallantly received; and, I believe, had the two parties been in the plain, many more bold actions would have taken place than it was possible to find an opportunity for where they were; for the barriers being closely shut, prevented them from touching each other.... so every man had his match; and when they were fatigued or heated, they retired and other fresh knights and squires renewed the skirmish.[21]

The most famous of siege combats was that of the 'Combat of the Thirty' at Ploermel in 1351, when the commanders of two Breton castles arranged a joust to the death, with no restriction as to weapons, between thirty of their men on each side, in the open field. Initially, a contest of three knights on each side armed with daggers was offered and declined as too dangerous, but the final casualties, nine English and Germans and

20   Malcolm Vale, *War and Chivalry* (London 1981) 156-7.
21   Froissart, *Chroniques*, ed. Lettenhove, XII, 212-3; tr. Johnes, II, 257.

six Frenchmen killed, were very high. Jean Le Bel, who records the episode, is full of admiration: 'I never heard tell of such an enterprise taking place save this. And the survivors of this battle should be all the more honoured for it, wherever they go.'[22] According to Jean le Bel, the English had demanded jousts on behalf of their respective ladies, but this appears to be a romantic view of a challenge which really arose between two garrisons attached to the rival parties claiming the duchy of Brittany. Unusually for a chivalric combat, all the fighting took place on foot, and most of the participants were mercenaries. The widespread fame achieved by this 'Combat of Thirty' probably inspired a similar event on the marches of Gascony the following year: twenty French knights challenged twenty Gascons attached to the English cause to mortal combat, and casualties were again very high.

When a brief spell of peace intervened, these challenges became jousts. Miles Windsor, in the service of the king of Portugal, finding to his dismay on his arrival 'that as peace was concluded, there would not be any engagement, he determined not to quit Spain without doing something to be talked of', and arranged a joust against Sir Tristan de Roye, a Frenchman in Spanish service.

The almost continual warfare between England and France, and between England and Scotland, gave rise to a new variant, the border feat of arms, which contemporaries usually called a 'hostile combat' or 'jousts of war'. Jousts of war between English and Scottish knights were fought during the sieges of Cupar, Perth and Alnwick Castle; on the last occasion they were described as 'great jousts of war on agreed terms'.

In 1341 Henry earl of Derby, who was already a noted tourneyer in England, held two important border combats. The first was at Roxburgh, where the earl and three companions jousted à outrance against a party of equal numbers led by William Douglas; Douglas was mortally wounded. The second, more elaborate, affair was at Berwick, when twenty English knights challenged twenty Scots to three days of jousts à outrance. There were three deaths and many casualties, including one English knight, Richard Talbot, who would have been killed if he had not been wearing protective armour contrary to the agreed terms of the combat. In what seems a curiously inappropriate conclusion to the hostilities, the heralds present awarded prizes to the best performers on each side.[23]

More commonplace were the single combats which seem to have been an accepted part of any campaign or siege. In 1343, Thomas Colville, an English knight, forded a river to joust against (and kill) a French knight who had offered a challenge from the supposed safety of the opposite bank. At the siege of Rennes in Brittany, the young Bertrand du Guesclin fought three courses with lances, three with battle-axes and three

22   Jean Le Bel, *Chronique*, ed.Jules Viard and Eugène Déprez, SHF (Paris 1904) II,194-7.
23   Andrew of Wyntoun, *Original Chronicle* ed. F. J. Amours, Scottish Text Society (Edinburgh 1903-14) VI, 104-5.

with daggers against an English esquire, Nicholas Dagworth. Both parties fought valiantly, no harm was inflicted, and the whole affair was viewed with great pleasure by both armies.

The revival of hostilities with Scotland in the 1390s led to a number of applications to the king for licence to perform 'feats of arms' against various named and unnamed Scottish knights. The most famous of these encounters was held not in the Borders, however, but on London Bridge, where it was assured of maximum publicity. Four Scots, led by David Lindsay, fought single combats against four Englishmen, first with lances of war and then on foot with daggers. Despite the defeat of the English, Richard II rewarded the triumphant Scots with valuable gifts.[24] Three years later, in 1393, three Scottish lords returned to repeat their victory in London, but this time the English had their revenge and carried the day.

This persistence of hostilities in times of official peace leads us to the deeper question of the knight's attitude to war. The modern attitude is to regard peace as normal, war as the exception, and as immoral and evil. Late mediaeval attitudes were very different. The knight regarded war as the normal state of mankind, partly through dim memories of days when this had been true, and his services as defender of society had been essential, and partly because war was so strongly in his financial interest if he were a fighting man and not a merely titular knight. And at the most abstract level, that of the Roman lawyers and political theorists, war was part of the established order of things. In the fifteenth century, Honoré Bonet, in his *Tree of Battles*, drawn largely from earlier writers, declares:

> War is not an evil thing, but good and virtuous; for war, by its very nature, seeks nothing other than to set wrong right, and turn dissension to peace, in accordance with Scripture. And if in war many evil things are done, they never come from the nature of war, but from false usage.[25]

The right to make private war was another complication in knights' attitudes to warfare. Although this right was virtually non-existent in England after the thirteenth century, it was a generally recognised phenomenon in France, as *guerre couverte*: the legal right remained — 'A gentleman may make war according to custom', says a leading legal authority in the mid-fourteenth century.[26] However, the king could issue edicts forbidding it for a time; despite St Louis' attempts to suppress it entirely, we find royal edicts enforcing temporary bans until the end of the fourteenth century. Charles V

---

24 *Ibid.*, VI, 359-62.
25 Honoré Bonet, *The Tree of Battles*, tr. G.W.Copeland (Liverpool 1949) 125
26 Philippe de Beaumanoir, *Coutumes de Beauvaisis*, quoted in Richard W. Kaeuper, *War, Public Order: England and France In the Later Middle Ages* (Oxford, 1988) 228.

had to acknowledge the right of private war, if properly conducted, as late as 1378. [27]
Formal defiance had to be made, and due cause given, and burning and ravaging were
technically forbidden. In practice, the greater struggle between England and France
provided cover for any number of private feuds and raids. In Germany the right to
private war was jealously guarded by the nobility. Even in Charles IV's Golden Bull
of 1356 private war is acknowledged as legal provided due notice of three days is given,
and it is only unjust war, and other such disorders, that are prohibited. War was a
perfectly normal method of settling a dispute in the knight's view; the enthusiasm of
the Church for endless parleys and negotiated settlements only gained ground among
the lay nobles in the fifteenth century, and the idea that assemblies could make peace
as well as war was first tested at the Congress of Arras in 1435. Even then pacifism
remained the mark of the bourgeois whose trade was disturbed, or the peasant whose
crops were burnt.

If private war was gradually limited by the kings, the Church and the common
people had at one time managed to impose considerable restrictions on normal warfare.
War to the death was normally reserved for battles against the infidel. In 'open war',
where quarter and ransoms were allowed, the combatants escaped lightly, and it was
the non-combatants who suffered most, from the fire and sword of a ravaging army.

While knights were expected to uphold the standards of chivalry in such warfare,
it was an open question as to how far they should try to restrain their men, and even then
they were often powerless. Neither the Black Prince in 1355 nor his father in 1346 were
able to prevent the burning of Church property; at Carcassonne, explicit orders that it
was to be spared were ignored. The taking of a town by siege was likewise governed by
legal provisions. If a siege had been properly declared by a herald, the besieged could
make terms at any point until the actual storming of the walls. If they remained
adamant, the town lay at the besiegers' mercy. Churches and clergy were immune, in
theory, but the inhabitants were regarded as rebels and their goods as forfeit. Plunder and
slaughter might be carried out in cold blood, after formal possession had been taken and
the victorious general had made his entry. It is the idea that rapine is a legal remedy for
defiance that underlies the incredible cruelties of mediaeval sieges. A horrifying example
had been set by the knights of the First Crusade, when they avenged themselves not
only for the agonies of a month encamped in the desert, but for centuries of Muslim
'desecration' of the Holy Places, in the blood bath at Jerusalem in 1099:

> The crusaders, maddened by so great a victory after such suffering, rushed through the
> streets and into the houses and mosques killing all that they met, men, women and
> children alike. All that afternoon and all through the night the massacre continued.

---

27   *Ibid.*, 235.

Tancred's banner was no protection to the refugees in the mosque of al-Aqsa. Early next morning a band of Crusaders forced an entry into the mosque and slew everyone. When Raymond of Aguilers later that morning went to visit the Temple area, he had to pick his way through corpses and blood that reached up to his knees.[28]

If the crusaders can be excused in some measure as an army of fanatics, whipped into fervour by their preachers, their example was followed in all too many cases where there was no such excuse. Froissart tells how when the bishop of Limoges, a close ally of the Black Prince went over to the French in 1370, the latter, already a sick man, vowed to take vengeance for this treason: and when a breach was made, his men went in with instructions to spare no one.

> You would have then seen pillagers, active to do mischief, running through the town, slaying men, women and children, according to their orders. It was a most melancholy business: for all ranks, ages and sexes cast themselves on their knees before the prince, begging for mercy: but he was so inflamed with passion and revenge that he listened to none, but all were put to the sword, wherever they could be found, even those who were not guilty: for I know not why the poor were not spared, who could not have had any part in this treason; but they suffered for it.... Upwards of three thousand men, women and children were put to death that day.[29]

The irony is that the evidence of local chroniclers suggests that the sack never took place, and if it did was not particularly savage. What Froissart is depicting is the *expected* behaviour of a successful army after a siege; he does not deny the Black Prince's right to carry out such deeds when he suggests that mercy would have been well placed.

Real parallels for the supposed sack of Limoges are by no means rare: some are intentional warnings to other towns of the wrath that will fall upon them; in other cases, the commander has been unable to control his men. In the narrow streets of the mediaeval town, there was little a handful of knights could do, even when they did try, to stop a massacre. Only dire threats before the assault began were likely to have much effect, backed up by an occasional example after the event.

At the siege of Dinant in 1342, Louis d'Espagne was so angered by the burning of churches by pillagers that 'he immediately ordered twenty-four of the most active to be hanged and strangled upon the spot'.[30] The common soldier might not be sure to whom he owed obedience, and as devastation was part of the normal business of a raid into enemy territory, and loot the only pay he was likely to get, it was difficult to

---

28   Steven Runciman, *A History of the Crusades* (Cambridge 1951) I, 287.
29   Froissart, *Chroniques*, ed. Lettenhove, VIII, 39; tr. Johnes, I, 453.
30   Froissart, *Chroniques*, ed. Lettenhove, IV, 63; tr. Johnes, I, 109.

31   The youthful pastimes of 'Der Weisskunig' (Maximilian I)

32   Jousting and a tournament

3   Fighting in full armour with halberds

34   Fighting with shields in full armour

(31-34 from *Der Weisskunig* in *Jahrbuch der Kunsthistorischen Sammlung in Wien* 6, 1888)

35   German tournament armour (Germanisches Nationalmuseum, Nuremberg)

36   Drawing by Jacopo Bellini for a jousting costume
(Jacopo Bellini, *The Louvre Sketchbook*, Woodbridge 1986)

37   St George's Portico, design by Inigo Jones for Ben Jonson's
Barriers of 1610 (The Trustees of the Chatsworth Settlement)

Cy parle cõment charles le
bien aÿme regna en france apres
quil eut este sacre a rains. Lan mil
trois cens et quatre vingtz.

Premier chapitre.
Pource que en mõ
prologue aÿ au
cunement touche
que parleray au
commencement de
ce present liure de lestat et gouuer
nement du roÿ de france charles le

bien aÿme sixiesme de ce nom. Et
affin que plus plainement il soit
sceu les causes et raisons pour quoÿ
les seigneurs du sang roÿal furent
durant son regne et depuis en diui
sion en feray en ce present chapitre
aucune mention. Or est que le
dessusdit roÿ charles le bien aÿme filz
du roÿ charles le riche commenca a
regner et fut sacre a rains le dÿmen
che de deuant la feste de toussains lan
de grace mil trois cens et quatre vigtz

38   Enguerrand de Monstrelet writing his chronicle; battle scene; fifteenth
century (BN MS fr. 2678 f. I)

39   Defeat of Owen Glendower by Richard Beauchamp;
fifteenth century (BL MS Cotton Julius E IV art (6) f. 3v)

40   Early fourteenth century siege with crossbows,
trebuchets and scaling ladders
(BL MS Add 10294 f. 81v)

41   Fifteenth century siege with early artillery and siege tower
(BL MS Royal 14 E IV f. 281v)

42   Looting a house, fourteenth century (BL MS Royal 20 C VII f. 41v)

43   Christ leading the Crusaders, thirteenth century
(BL MS Royal 19 B XV f. 31)

44   Two Templars on one horse, by Matthew Paris,
early thirteenth century (BL MS Royal 14 C VIII f. 42v)

45   Kneeling crusader, by Matthew Paris, early thirteenth century
(BL MS Royal 2 A XXII f. 220)

46   The crusaders fight the Turks
before Ascolon; eighteenth century drawing
of a lost twelfth-century window from St Denis
(BN MS fr. 15634 f. 151)

47   Crac des Chevaliers (A. F. Kersting)

48   Gift of the castle of Uclés to the Order of Santiago (Madrid, Archivo Historico
Nacional. Tumbo Menor de Castilla, f. 15; twelfth century. Photo MAS, Barcelona)

49   Schloss Marienburg, Prussia, in 1938 (Paul Popper)

50   Chapel at Schloss Marienburg, showing the huge figure of the Virgin Mary

(From *Schloss Marienburg in Preussen .. Ansichten hergestellt von F. Frich*, Berlin 1799)

51   Preparations for the defence
of Rhodes, fifteenth century
(BN MS Lat. 6067 f. 33v)

52   The old hermit instructs a squire,
fifteenth century (BL MS Royal 14 E II f. 338)

53   Knight in the insignia of the Golden
          Fleece, fifteenth century
          (BL MS Harley 6199 f. 57v)

54   Knights of the Order of Santiago

(Burgos, Archivo Municipal, *Libro de la cofradía de Santiago*; Photo MAS, Barcelona)

55   *Forest with St George* by Albrecht Altdorfer (Munich, Alte Pinakothek)

restrain him. The problem was aggravated by the general pardons issued to criminals and outlaws if they would serve in France, which meant that the English armies had a certain element of troublemakers from the outset; and the free companies were largely self-formed bands of such men, though a strict captain like Perrot le Béarnois could protect the inhabitants of towns to some extent. Even knights on the opposing side might find themselves in danger, like the garrison at Caen in 1346, who shut themselves in a tower and made such defence as they could, until Thomas Holland arrived, whom they knew from crusades made with him to Prussia and Granada.

The horrors of the fate of the common people contrast sharply with the treatment of noble prisoners. From the mid-eleventh century onwards, it was extremely rare for captives of any standing to be killed, partly because of the very lucrative systems of ransoms. Ransoms were a question of business rather than chivalry, but they, in a sense, made chivalry on the battlefield possible by reducing the likelihood that a knight would be killed. On the other hand, when a battle became desperate, commanders might order prisoners to be killed, or might be unable to restrain their men. At Bouvines, knights were killed with special three edged daggers designed to penetrate chinks in their armour; and the slaughter of prisoners at Agincourt is perhaps the most famous example of a deliberate decision of this kind. There are other parallels, however, and when Froissart sorrowfully recorded that the English and Portuguese, fearing a reverse of fortune at the battle of Aljubarota, were forced to slay their prisoners, he lamented the financial loss: 'for whom they might otherwise have had ransoms of 400,000 francs'.[31]

The custom of ransoming goes back to classical times; Bede cites a case of a thane, Imma, captured in battle in 679, whose chains miraculously loosed themselves whenever they were put on, and who was allowed to go in search of ransom money on giving his word that he would return if he failed to find it.[32] But it was in some degree forgotten during the ninth and tenth centuries: and its revival was only gradual. Guibert de Nogent says of William the Conqueror that it was his custom never to hold his prisoners to ransom, but to condemn them to life-long captivity, but chroniclers more favourable to William emphasise the clemency which he practised on some occasions. It was certainly established by the end of the eleventh century, when Orderic Vitalis describes Norman magnates engaged in the border warfare of the period as making 'an honourable fortune out of ransoms',[33] but it was not until the latter part of the twelfth

---

31 *Ibid.*, XI, 180; II, 123..

32 Bede, *Ecclesiastical History of the English People*, ed & tr. B. Colgrave and R.A.B.Mynors (Oxford 1969) bk.IV ch.22, pp 400-4.

33 Quoted in Matthew Strickland, *War and Chivalry: the Conduct and Perception of War in England and Normandy, 1066-1217* (Cambridge 1996) (forthcoming), ch.8, 'Ransom and the treatment of prisoners'; I am most grateful to Dr Strickland for sending me a typescript of this important study.

century that it was clearly the norm; many of the nobles captured by Henry I remained in prison. As the practice grew, however, the agreement to ransom came to imply slightly more than merely buying one's way out of imprisonment. The prisoner had to be protected from other members of the opposing army, and he could not be severely treated while in prison; irons were permitted but very rarely used, but threats of death or blackmail to make him do something dishonourable voided the agreement and he was then at liberty to escape.

These conditions were by no means universal: the Spanish and the Germans had a bad name for their treatment of prisoners. When the earl of Pembroke and other knights were captured in Spain in 1372, 'they conducted their prisoners to a strong castle and fastened them with iron chains according to their usual custom; for the Spaniards know not how to show courtesy to their prisoners'. Froissart contrasts the French and German usage thus:

> They neither shut them up in prison, nor put on shackles and fetters, as the Germans do in order to obtain a heavier ransom. Curses on them for it! These people are without pity or honour, and they ought never to receive quarter. The French entertained their prisoners well, and ransomed them courteously without being too hard on them.[34]

Though there was a tacit understanding that a ransom should be related to a knight's estate, and should not ruin him financially to such an extent that he could no longer live as a knight should, ransoms occasionally reached huge proportions. At the head of the list stand the 'king's ransoms' demanded after Poitiers for John the Good, and that paid by Richard Coeur de Lion. Below this, princes of the blood royal such as Charles d'Orléans were held for very high sums; and Charles languished in the Tower, bewailing his lost youth in some of the loveliest of French poetry, for twenty-five years until Philip the Good of Burgundy ransomed him for his own political ends. Edward III received about £268,000 for three major ransoms in the period 1360-70. A great captain like du Guesclin was also highly valued; indeed, when he was captured in Spain, the Black Prince was reluctant to let him go at all, and finally asked du Guesclin what ransom he ought to pay. Du Guesclin named the impossible figure of 100,000 francs, at which the prince remitted half of it, and sent him to raise the remainder. The story that he distributed all the money he had been given by his friends in Brittany to ransom his old comrades-at-arms whom he met on the road is probably apocryphal; in any event, the sum was paid by the king of France, Louis of Anjou, and Henry of Trastamare (in whose service he had been when captured). At the very humblest end of the scale a sum of a few crowns might well suffice if the prisoner were a mere man-at-arms, or

34   Froissart, *Chroniques*, ed. Lettenhove, VIII, 144; tr. Johnes, I, 475.

the captor might settle for a suit of armour or a horse. So episodes such as the incident at Tournai in 1339 when Raymond, nephew to Pope Clement, 'was killed for the sake of his beautiful armour after he had surrendered, which made many good men angry'[35] were fortunately rare, as the armour could easily have been made part of his ransom. The custom was so generally accepted that it spread even to tournaments, and we have seen how the vanquished knight's horse and armour fell to the victor.

As Matthew Strickland points out, 'paradoxically, the convention of ransom at once both limited the execution of warfare itself by the prevention of wholesale killing among the warrior nobility, and yet ... acted as an incentive to the prosecution of ... hostilities.'[36] War, like tournaments, could make a knight's fortune as well as his reputation. When a simple squire like one Croquart in the count of Holland's household in 1347 could make 40,000 écus and thirty or forty good horses in a very short time in Brittany, the monetary side became very important. War had long been almost an economic necessity for the poorer knights, whose small fiefs could hardly support them. Bertran de Born's *sirventes* in praise of war brushes aside the idea that war is fought for anything but sheer love of fighting; but from the eleventh to the fifteenth century there were always knights who had to find employment for their swords. In the *Life of the Emperor Henry IV* the German knights of the early twelfth century are vigorously attacked for destroying the prosperity of the country, when the emperor's successful enforcement of peace led to a conspiracy in 1104:

> When the lords and their accomplices had been restrained by this law for some years, displeased that they could not practise their misdeeds, they began to murmur against the emperor. What wrong had the emperor done? Only this: he had prevented crimes, restored peace and justice, so that robbers no longer lorded it on the highways and bandits no longer lurked in the forests, so that merchants and sailors could go their various ways freely, so that robbers starved while robbery was forbidden. Why, I adjure you, can you only live by robbery? Give the men back to the fields, whom you took away for war: keep as many followers as your means allow, buy back your estates that you probably squandered in order to hire as many warriors as you could, and your boards and cellars will groan with plenty; and you will no longer need to take other people's goods, having more than enough of your own. Men, you will no longer need to mutter against the king, and the Empire will have peace. You will have what you need for your body, and, best of all, will save your souls. But my words are vain; I am asking the ass to play the lute; evil ways are rarely forsaken.[37]

35   *Ibid.*, I 64.
36   Strickland, *War and Chivalry*, ch 8.
37   *Vita Heinrici IV imperatoris*, in Franz-Joseph Schmale, *Quellen zur Geschichte Kaiser Heinrichs IV* (Berlin 1963) 438-41.

When these words were written, it was only half a century since the Normans had conquered Sicily and England by the sword, and in the process many individual fortunes had been made. The same impulse lay behind some of the crusaders' zeal: in the East it was possible both to win wide lands and save one's soul. As opportunities of this kind diminished, so the mercenary appeared on a humbler, non-knightly level, and ordinary war became a matter of business contracts as well as the clash of arms.

By the fourteenth century, fortunes could be made, not only from a lucky capture, but also from loot: the increasing prosperity of the towns of France provided both English and French troops with ample opportunities, for if a town failed to surrender or agree terms and was taken by assault, it was regarded as being 'at mercy', and only churches and clergy were immune. And such plundering could be done not only in the heat of the moment, but also systematically after the victorious commander had made his formal entry, because the town was technically forfeit for having rebelled against its lawful lord. This lies behind Froissart's picture of the sack of Limoges. The spoils so taken were usually divided in a fixed proportion, which was usually one-third to the soldiers, one-third to the commanders, and one-third to the crown. At the sack of Constantinople in 1204, churches were used to store the booty, which was then divided up: 'one mounted serjeant received as much as two serjeants on foot, one knight as much as two mounted serjeants'.[38]

In the indentures of war of the 1360s and 1370s which mark the final development of the system, and put the conduct of war on to an entirely commercial basis, the captain has to surrender the most important castles and lands to the king, and any prisoners whom the king regards as influential in return for a reasonable reward. Any other spoil is divided between the captain and the crown, the latter usually taking one-third. So far as the ordinary English soldier was concerned, the Ordinances of Durham of 1385 laid down that he was to surrender one-third to his commander, who then surrendered one-third of this to the crown. Hence it was the successful commander who stood to make the greatest amount; and quite apart from the mercenary captains who rarely surrendered any of their spoils, such eminent figures as du Guesclin, Sir John Chandos, and Sir Hugh Calverley founded their fortunes in this way.

On the other hand, sieges were not all that frequent, and many were unsuccessful; and in the lean periods there might be very little to live on, and no pay forthcoming. Spoils of war were probably deducted from pay, so a rich haul of booty might well prove to be nothing more than a year's wages in advance. The author of the *Boke of Noblesse*, addressed to Edward IV before his expedition to France in 1475, attributes the excesses of previous campaigns to lack of proper and regular pay. One means of

---

38   Villehardouin, *Conquest of Constantinople*, in Joinville, *Life of St Louis*, tr. M.R.B.Shaw (London and Baltimore 1963) 94.

dealing with the problem was by an agreement to share spoils with another knight, the 'brotherhood in arms' whose high-sounding title conceals a very practical arrangement. for instance, in the contract between Nicholas Molyneux and John Winter signed at Harfleur in 1421, all gains in war were to be sent to London to be banked, and each is responsible for raising the first £1,000 of the other's ransom in the event of capture, and we have already noticed William Marshal's partnership with Roger de Gaugi in the tournaments of 1177-9, the earliest appearance of such an arrangement. Brothers-in-arms would also inherit the other's military fortune on his death.

Yet, despite the financial basis of such agreements, brotherhood-in-arms acquired a veneer of idealism. Its deepest roots may go back to the primitive oath of blood brotherhood, in which blood was mingled in a cup. At its highest, it was a bond of alliance second only to those of family and liege homage, and acquired a special mystique of its own. Brothers-in-arms were supposedly 'bound to one another in such a way, that each will stand by the other to the death if need be, saving his honour,' in both counsel and action, and such a bond could sometimes be forged without a formal oath. The curious custom of fighting in mines – dug at a siege to bring down the wall of a fortress – was one such occasion. If a mine and countermine met, a skirmish would often ensue; and this often became a form of tournament. Knights who fought in such a combat became brothers-in-arms by the mere fact of having taken part, even though on opposing sides. At Melun Henry V himself is supposed to have taken part in such a combat, on horseback and with the mine lit by torches. At Limoges, John of Gaunt fought Jean de Villemur in a mine; and Jean was said to have been one of the few knights spared when the town was taken. More usually, the agreement was drawn up in proper legal form, and could be a form of alliance. Between princes, it became an important diplomatic weapon; but it was practised by the lowest kind of soldiers as well, including the mercenary captains. Froissart tells of one Louis Raimbaut, who left his mistress with his brother-in-arms, Limousin, only to find that he had taken too good care of her, and had obtained every favour from her. Raimbaut revenged himself by flogging his brother-in-arms out of the town; but Limousin betrayed him to a neighbouring lord, and he was ambushed and executed. At the other extreme is the remarkable tomb slab, now in the Archeological Museum at Istanbul, which records the burial of Sir William Neville and Sir John Clanvowe, who died near Constantinople in 1391. The arms of the two men are combined, so that they both bear the same shields, Neville's arms on the left, Clanvowe's on the right: technically, they impale each other. They had been constant companions since 1378, and were both knights of the Garter. Clanvowe is said to have died first, at which Neville refused all food and died three days later. Although there is no formal record of their brotherhood-in-arms, it seems almost certain that this was indeed the case.[39] Like homage and liege homage, which promised an exclusive bond when first introduced, brotherhood-in-arms became adulterated, and could be extended to more than one knight, but it remained the strongest of the various ties between man and man.[40]

A byproduct of the idea of brotherhood is the various small confraternities of knights which appear at the end of the fourteenth century. These are apparently small orders of knighthood, with insignia and chapters. Instead of being an honorific institution, however, they are practical, very much based on the practice of brotherhood-in-arms: the 'Pomme d'Or' in Auvergne, the 'St George' in Rougemont and the 'Tiercelet' in Poitou are a mixture between fighting companies, mutual protection associations and commercial organisations, but with an element of idealism as well. The statutes of the 'Tiercelet' provide for two special kinds of insignia, both for those who have been to Prussia to help the Teutonic knights; one is for those who have not been in action, and one for those who have actually fought the heathen. At the other extreme, the members are expected to help each other in lawsuits, and warn each other of any action likely to be taken against them.

The confraternities sum up the chivalrous attitude to war; beneath the high idealism of chivalric honour, war continues much as before, as cruel, atrocious and thoughtless as ever. Knighthood becomes a kind of guild of warriors, who may put the ordinary soldier and the civilian to the sword, but who rarely kill each other intentionally on the battlefield, and who see to it that military enterprises have a suitable financial reward. The occasional feat of arms is a diversion from the more serious business of pillage and destruction, and chivalry owes more to the pen than the sword. The glowing words of Froissart's preamble to his chronicles, 'that the honourable enterprises, noble adventures and deeds of arms, performed in the wars between England and France, may be properly related, and held in perpetual remembrance — to the end that brave men taking example from them may be encouraged in their well doing',[41] cast a golden spell of chivalry over the black harshness of war, an illusion in which the knights themselves believed, but which was nonetheless unreal.

39   Siegrid Düll, Anthony Luttrell & Maurice Keen, 'Faithful unto Death: the Tomb Slab of Sir William Neville and Sir John Clanvowe, Constantinople 1391', *Antiquaries Journal* 71, 1991, 174-190.

40   A parallel idea to that of brotherhood in arms is to be found in the 'godfather' relationship described in the *Siete Partidas*: the man who ungirds the sword of a newly-made knight becomes his godfather in arms, and the knight should never oppose him in war or do anything else which might harm him, and should always aid him in his quarrels unless the other party is his own liege lord or a member of his own family. Alfonso X, *Las Siete Partidas*, 426.

41   Froissart, *Chroniques*, ed. Lettenhove, II, I; tr. Johnes, I, I.

PART FOUR

Chivalry and Religion

II

The Church, Warfare and Crusades

THE TRADITIONS of the primitive Christian Church were wholly opposed to warfare of any kind, in sharp contrast to the *djihad* or holy war which played so great a part in the early history of Islam. Indeed, the early fathers questioned whether any part in warfare, however slight, was lawful for a Christian. It was not until Constantine's adoption of Christianity in 313 that practical considerations forced a change in this attitude, and thereafter the traditions of eastern and western Christendom divided. The east rapidly went over to a militaristic cult, complete with soldier-saints, of whom St George was one, and emphasised the image of St Paul, portraying the Christian life as that of a soldier in God's wars, as justification for this. The Roman church, less immediately involved in imperial politics, continued to regard war with suspicion, and when Augustine came to write on the subject, he could still insist that war was always evil, qualifying this very slightly by allowing that one side might have just cause for war; he also absolved the individual soldier who took part in an unjust war without being able to judge the rights and wrongs of the case.

Yet even as Augustine wrote, the eastern emperors were engaged in suppressing by force the Donatist heresy in his native North Africa. By the end of the sixth century, the idea that heretics and infidels could legitimately be converted by force appears in one of Gregory the Great's letters: 'Wars are to be sought for the sake of spreading the republic in which we perceive God to be revered ... inasmuch as the name of Christ may be spread throughout the peoples thus made subject by the preaching of the faith.'[1]

It was not until the eighth century that such wars became politically possible. The Carolingian wars against the Saxons had a definite political objective, but were presented as religious exercises. A mission to the soldiers first appeared in the west about this time. Mass was said before battle, and saints' relics accompanied the troops. This change was in some degree due to the Germanic element in Frankish civilisation: the old heroic ethos had been adapted rather than completely suppressed, and the

---

[1]   Carl Erdmann, *Die Entstehung des Kreuzzugsgedankens* (Stuttgart 1935) 8.

German cult of warfare was so fervent that it was impossible to expect a complete change in ways of thought and feeling. Hence the idea of the 'soldiers of Christ' led by St Michael is brought in to replace the old warrior paganism with Wotan as its deity, and the *militia Christi* of St Paul are no longer the meek and spiritual martyrs, but the all too earthly soldiers of Charlemagne's armies. Charlemagne's opponents were those German tribes who had remained unconverted, and hence the Church had few qualms of conscience about giving its blessing, and indeed its encouragement. If conversion had sometimes been part of a political settlement at the end of a war, it now became one of the avowed aims at the outset of the campaign.

The Church's growing material wealth and involvement in secular affairs helped to assist this change of attitude. Bishops and abbots invested with lay estates, born into and brought up in an aristocratic warrior world, were quite liable to decide to take up arms, both in their own defence or in the king's service, despite the edicts (enacted in the fourth century) against the clergy bearing weapons. The popes themselves accompanied armies raised to fight the Muslim pirates at the mouth of the Tiber; Leo IX in 849, and John X in 915 both did so. The defence of the Church against heathens and robbers in the troubled times of the ninth and tenth centuries became a sacred duty, and the reward for those who fell in such battles was eternal life. The liturgy included prayers not only for the destruction of enemies, but also that the Roman emperor might subject the heathen.

With the Cluniac reform of the monastic movement, and the insistence that the Church must take a greater part in everyday life, the warrior came to be regarded as one of the many professions of secular existence. We have seen how his activities were blessed by the Church so long as they conformed with the Christian ideal, though penance might still be exacted for actual killing in battle if a general absolution had not previously been issued. So along with prayers for the harvest and for the fishermen's catches, that seed and nets might produce a plentiful reward, prayers were said over the knight's sword, prayers which later became the service of knighthood. The army on campaign was provided with sacred banners bearing a saint's image, which quickly became the subject of miraculous tales. These were sometimes carried by the clergy: witness the deaths of a priest and deacon acting as standard-bearers in battles against the Slavs in 992.

Yet the Church's attitude was still guarded: it encouraged knighthood, but only in order to control and tame the warrior instinct. Even in the tenth century the life of St Edmund, martyred by the Danes in 870, portrays him as a passive martyr, not a soldier dying bravely against great odds. The general lawlessness of the tenth century provoked a strong reaction among people and clergy, as did the menace of unrestricted warfare. At the council of Charroux in 989 it was suggested that the Church should act as the protector of the poor, and laws from Carolingian capitularies were adopted as Church law to this end. At the council of Le Puy in 990 and at other synods of the Church in southern France the idea was taken up, and was put into a solemn declaration at Poitiers in 1000, to which not only Guilhem of Aquitaine but also the French king subscribed. Quarrels were no longer to be settled by force of arms, but in the courts of justice, and the threat of excommunication was levelled at those inclined to think otherwise. By the second decade of the eleventh century, this movement, which came to be known as the *pax Dei* or Peace of God, had spread to northern France, despite some opposition from those who, like the bishop of Cambrai in 1023, objected that this was a matter for the temporal powers.

The protection under this peace movement extended in the first place to churches and clerics, and secondly to those liable to oppression, the merchants and peasants. Lords were not to destroy the peasants' livelihood; mills, vines and cattle were to be immune, though certain exceptions to the last were made. More important, however, was the general peace or 'truce of God' to be observed on certain days. This began with the Carolingian ban on private warfare on Sundays, and was revived in 1027 in southern France. Eventually the great festivals and the period from sunset on Wednesday to dawn on Monday, regarded as the vigil for Sunday, were included, and there was less time for war than peace'.[2]

Perhaps the movement might have had greater success if less had been demanded. As it was, from the council of Narbonne in 1054 onwards, the Church regarded these days of peace as sacrosanct, until the end of the Middle Ages. Yet in practice the First Crusade attacked Constantinople on Thursday of Holy Week, and it is hard to find a single instance where a battle was postponed because of the day. However, the rules were apparently observed during sieges, where they were less of an obstacle to military success: for instance, at Rouen in 1174 a one-day truce was declared on St Lawrence's Day, 10 August, during a siege by Louis VII, though the latter broke it with a surprise attack which was only just repulsed.

Popular enthusiasm for the truce of God was such, and the breaches of the laws of protection and peace-days so flagrant, that the idea of a militia to enforce the idea was soon mooted. At Bourges in 1038 such a confederation was formed by administering an oath to maintain order to all men over fifteen, but it became such a potential menace to public order with its own burning of castles (which were the strongholds of lawlessness in popular eyes) that Odo de Déols massacred its members after it had burnt an entire village. The objection to such movements was that the peasants and clergy were usurping functions which did not belong to them, and setting themselves up as arbiters of justice. Properly directed, and armed with royal authority,

2   Bloch, *Feudal Society*, 414.

some degree of success might have been possible, but the peace armies resembled social revolution too closely to be tolerated.

There was, however, an increasing change of attitude on the part of the knights themselves. With the ecclesiastical revival of the late tenth and eleventh centuries, secular piety had become much more usual; knights founded churches on their estates, collected relics for the great churches, and were generally more devout as the church re-established its position in society. In the monastic histories of the period, we hear of knights who abandoned secular life in favour of the monastic habit, like the knights returning from a tournament at Worms in the 1150s who, resting in a meadow, had a dream-vision which persuaded them to 'join the wolf-coats of Kloster Himmerod', in other words to take up the grey habits of the local monks.[3]

On the borders of Christendom greater matters were afoot than the petty maraudings of feudal barons, matters which affected the whole Christian world. From the third century onwards, through all the vicissitudes of Roman, Byzantine and Muslim rule, pilgrims had gone to Jerusalem to worship at the holy places of Christendom. The custom had grown to considerable proportions in the tenth century as trade routes reopened and contacts with the east renewed, and had become a recognised form of penance for crimes. Pilgrimages were no longer purely matters of private enterprise, as the local monks had begun to organise the means of travel, and pilgrims came from all corners of Europe, from Iceland to Sicily.

The journey to Jerusalem had always been difficult and dangerous, but the problems were those of any long journey at the time: brigands and bad roads, disease and famine. Though the Muslims had held Jerusalem since 638, they tolerated Christian visitors and even encouraged them. It is true that there was a brief interlude of persecution under the caliph Hakim in the early eleventh century: the reasons for this change of policy are obscure, but as Hakim was a megalomaniac who finally declared himself divine, it seems to have been a purely personal action. His destruction of the Church of the Holy Sepulchre in 1009 had alarmed Christians everywhere, but they were reassured by his change of heart five years later. In 1020 he restored the damaged churches, and the numbers of pilgrims began to increase rapidly. In 1064-5, we hear of a party as large as 7,000 under the leadership of the bishop of Bamberg. Such a large body evidently contained some kind of armed guard, for when they were attacked by Muslims, they fought a defensive action lasting several days. Such attacks were by no means unknown, and in general there was no great change in conditions of pilgrimage. What was changing, however, was the attitude of the Papacy. The reformed

3   MGH SS XXV 220-1 (*Ex gestis Sanctorum Villarensium*).

Papacy of the eleventh century was now an aggressive temporal power as well, seeing itself as arbiter of Italy's affairs. It was thus by no means illogical for Leo IX to invoke war as a means of defence against his spiritual opponent, Benedict IX, and against the invading Normans in southern Italy in 1053. He led his troops in person on the latter expedition, and was defeated and captured at Civitá, a fate which more orthodox contemporaries saw as a divine retribution, less for taking part in war at all than for using war as a means to temporal ends, though Leo had been careful to portray his campaign as being designed 'to liberate Christendom'. Those who fell at Civitá were regarded by the pope as martyrs, and a cult was instituted to honour them.

This episode was followed by papal sponsorship of the expedition against the Muslims in Spain in 1063. Any hint of early Christian pacifism had long since been eradicated from the strategy of the Curia; and the international force that was led by William Montreuil, 'Captain of the Cavalry of Rome' as a Muslim historian calls him, probably had a papal banner, and its members certainly enjoyed papal absolution in advance – as well they might, for their massacre of prisoners at Barbastro and subsequent lascivious existence, 'utter abandonment. . . to the pleasures of the harem',[4] was hardly the behaviour expected of crusaders.

The papal blessing on military expeditions was likewise used to political ends. By placing the later stages of the Norman conquest of Italy under its protection, and encouraging the Norman invasion of England (a papal banner was carried at Hastings), the Papacy obtained a nominal overlordship and tribute from both countries. Gregory VII used the same methods to support the commune of Milan in its early days, and transferred the *militia Christi* completely from the spiritual to the material world, raising armies of papal troops among his vassals and among mercenaries, by means of both financial and spiritual rewards. This scheme did not meet with any great success: yet the idea of the Pope as a summoner of armies and as a leader in warfare was established. Gregory VII attempted to use 'the men of St Peter' (*fideles sancti Petri*) in 1074 to further his favourite project of a union between the Orthodox and Catholic Churches, and appealed to 'all those who wish to defend the Christian faith'.[5] The response was small: only Guilhem of Aquitaine, who had fought in Spain in 1064, answered favourably, and the problems of Italian politics intervened before any definite plans could be made.

The idea of a holy war in itself, despite the great attraction of the east for pilgrims, was not the only reason that led ordinary knights to undertake such lengthy and dangerous expeditions merely for the sake of adventure. If some set out from pious motives, there were more practical reasons for the eagerness of many knights to enlist for distant parts with only a slender chance of tangible reward. We have already come

4   Ramon Menéndez Pidal, *The Cid and his Spain*, tr. Harold Sutherland (London 1934) 85.
5   Erdmann, *Die Entstehung des Kreuzzugsgedankens*, 149.

across the wandering, landless younger sons of knights: and it was precisely they who were becoming more numerous during the eleventh century. Rather than eke out an uncertain existence at home, they were ready to gamble on such expeditions, since the possible prizes, if they were ever achieved, were mouthwatering. This would explain the behaviour of the French army at Barbastro: whatever the motives of their leaders, booty was what interested their followers. The same dichotomy of attitude is a recurrent theme in later crusades: we shall find it in the Frankish troops revelling in eastern pleasures on the Third Crusade, the diversion of the Fourth Crusade to Constantinople, and the sack of Alexandria by a crusade in 1365. The Papacy saw the crusades as a way of harnessing the concept of knighthood to spiritual ends: the knights saw them as a solution to earthly ills, with the promise of absolution and heavenly reward as well, a form of pilgrimage which allowed them to pursue their career as fighting men. Furthermore, by removing the discontented knights from their homes in the west, the popes believed that they would bring peace to Europe as well as helping their fellow-Christians in Palestine and Byzantium.

For help was needed urgently in the east. Hakim's whims had shown that the Christians in Jerusalem were at the mercy of their secular rulers. Though Muslim rule was comfortable enough, there was always a possibility of change, and with the advent of the Seljuk Turks the old ease of access disappeared, not because of religious hostility but from bad government, brigandage and extortionate taxation. The defeat of the armies of Byzantium at Manzikert in 1071 and the Seljuk capture of the great cities of Asia Minor along the pilgrim route meant that little help was likely to come from eastern Christendom: and indeed both the emperors Michael VII and Alexius had appealed to the west for help against the invaders. Urban II, who had in some measure re-established the papal position at home, had maintained friendly relations with Alexius; when the latter's envoys appealed for troops at the council of Piacenza in March 1095, his own ideas on the eastern problem had turned in the same direction. At the council of Clermont in November 1095, he appealed for a crusading force, a military expedition that would also be a pilgrimage to Jerusalem. His exact words are lost, though we know that his speech was eloquent and aroused immense enthusiasm:

> You have strapped on the belt of knighthood and strut around with pride in your eye. You butcher your brothers and create factions among yourselves. This, which scatters the sheepfold of the Redeemer, is not the knighthood of Christ. The Holy Church keeps for herself an army to come to the aid of her own people, but you pervert it with knavery. To speak the truth, the preachers of which it is our duty to be, you are not following the path that leads you to life. You oppressors of orphans, you robbers of widows, you homicides, you blasphemers, you plunderers of others' rights; you hope for the rewards of brigands for the shedding of Christian blood and just as vultures nose out corpses you watch and follow wars from afar. Certainly this is the worst course to follow because

it is utterly removed from God. And if you want to take counsel for your souls you must either cast off as quickly as possible the belt of this sort of knighthood or go forward boldly as knights of Christ, hurrying swiftly to defend the eastern Church. It is from her that all the delights of your salvation have come... We say these things, brethren, so that you may restrain your murdering hands from slaughtering your brothers, go to fight nations abroad for the household servants of the faith and, following Jesus Christ your leader, you the Christian force, a force most invincible, better than the ancient tribe of Jacobites themselves, wage war for your own rights over Jerusalem and throw out the Turks, more unholy than the Jebusites, who are there. It ought to be a beautiful ideal for you to die for Christ in that city where Christ died for you, but if it should happen that you should die here, you may be sure that it will be as if you had died on the way, provided that is, Christ finds you in his company of knights ... [6]

His hearers, crying 'Deus le volt' (God wills it), crowded round him at the end of his speech, begging to be allowed to take part in the great expedition. But much planning was still needed, and though a series of resolutions were passed concerned with the administration of the crusade it was now a question of obtaining lay support. To complicate matters further, Urban really wanted only able-bodied fighting men: it was a specific, not a general, summons. Those who wished to go were to vow – like pilgrims – not to turn back before Jerusalem, and in token of this to wear a red cross on their shoulders. They were to be ready to leave by August 1096. Constantinople was to be the place of assembly for the army so raised, and Byzantine support was expected. We know from the charters drawn up by departing crusaders and other laymen's comments that this was a new and distinctive spiritual exercise, a holy expedition: and in line with this Adhémar, bishop of Le Puy, was named as leader and papal legate.

The secular response was overwhelming. Members of many of the leading families of France, the Low Countries and Italy, took the crusading vows, including Raymond of Toulouse and Bohemond of Taranto, the dukes of Flanders and Normandy, and Godfrey of Bouillon. Sermons by bishops and itinerant preachers brought in not only knights and soldiers, but also immense crowds of the common people. The message which Urban had intended for the knights alone was distorted as popular enthusiasm grew, and one Peter the Hermit became the leader of what was a second, unofficial movement among the peasants, who may have understood him to promise to lead them out of their misery to a visionary Jerusalem of plenty. It was this expedition that departed first, in the spring of 1096, a purely religious movement with only a handful of experienced warriors; and it seriously hampered the real crusade, which followed

---

6   Baldric of Bourgueil, quoted in Louise and Jonathan Riley-Smith, *The Crusades: Idea and Reality, 1095-1274* (London 1986) 49-50.

some three months later, by its indiscipline at Constantinople. It finally came to a disastrous end on the coast just across from Constantinople, the peasants massacred in a Turkish ambush while Peter the Hermit was absent in the Byzantine capital. Three other armies came to grief in Hungary, having achieved little: their only memorable deeds had been horrific attacks on the Jews of the Rhineland, inspired partly by greed, partly by the feeling of vendetta which had already begun to insinuate itself into secular crusading thought. The crusade was seen as vengeance on the infidel for the Crucifixion itself as well as for subsequent persecutions of Christians.

The leaders of the main crusade, which followed in the summer of the same year, were more cautious: for them God was indeed on their side, but they did not expect him to cause the obstacles that beset their path to crumble away like the walls of Jericho. They reached Constantinople by April 1097, and won their first great victory at Dorylaeum in Asia Minor on July I, against the Seljuk Turks. The religious enthusiasm that had attended their original vows was nonetheless the mainstay of their morale, and remained so throughout. At the blackest moment of the whole expedition, when it seemed that, having taken Antioch in June 1098 after an eight month siege, they would be starved into surrender by a relief force which was in turn besieging them, it was the finding of the Holy Lance, said to have pierced Christ's side at the Crucifixion, that restored their wavering faith: they made a successful sortie and drove off their besiegers. Whether the find was genuine or not— and there is strong evidence to suggest that it was invented by a cleric—the belief was what mattered. Those who doubted (including the pope's deputy, Adhémar, bishop of Le Puy) held their tongues, seeing the value of miracles in a dispirited army. God favoured them once more, it seemed, and the discovery reassured them that they were indeed fighting for an invincible cause.

Again, the capture of Jerusalem a year later after a siege of a little under four weeks, with an army weary from its long journey, short of provisions, ill-equipped, and not large enough to encircle the city completely, was a remarkable feat. That it was accomplished at all was once more due to a revival of the enthusiasm which had originally launched the crusade. Though the garrison was small, the great danger was the arrival of a relieving force from Egypt. Hence it was realised from the beginning that action would have to be swift, and a general assault was attempted within five days of arrival, but failed for lack of siege-ladders. The arrival of the materials needed for siege-towers improved the situation, and two huge siege-castles were begun. As time ran out, the army grew exhausted and dispirited in the great heat; but once again a vision came to their aid. A three-day fast was enjoined, and a solemn procession round the walls ended with three sermons from the finest preachers in the army. The old fire was rekindled, and with victory so near, the great towers were completed in two days. The general assault, which began on the night of 13 July, ended on the afternoon of the 15th, and the triumphant crusaders poured into Jerusalem.

It was a triumph marred in the very hour of its achievement. Knowing that all Christians had been expelled from the city before the siege began, the Franks repeated horrors which they had already perpetrated earlier, at Antioch, on a grander scale: almost all the inhabitants were slaughtered by the Christian soldiers, whose enthusiasm turned to fanaticism. It was a moment of folly and bloodthirstiness which was to be repaid in full by an enemy whose instincts might otherwise have been far more civilised.

For as the crusade had made its weary way across Europe and Asia Minor, it had become clear that even the highest and holiest of wars was still much the same as other wars, and that an army dedicated to God's service was as sinful as any other. It is true that there had been no scenes of complete riot such as the massacres of Jews in Germany for which the wilder elements of the people's crusade had been responsible. There was, on the other hand, no lack of quarrels between leaders and indiscipline among the troops, perhaps because there were a number of minor princes but no one great figure in overall command. In Byzantine territory, towns had been plundered, and the Emperor, Alexius Comnenus, had had to send a heavy escort with the crusaders in order to prevent such excesses. His well-founded doubts as to the army's good behaviour had been confirmed by an attack on Constantinople itself on Maundy Thursday, which was partly a political move by the less responsible leaders, and partly a protest by the troops against what they considered to be the inhospitality of the Greeks.

The very nature of the crusading enterprise tended to attract those men who were least amenable to discipline: there were as many adventurers and the landless, lawless younger sons as the devout lords of settled estates who had come only at the dictates of their belief. Pope Urban had foreseen this when he limited any spiritual benefit from the crusade to those who went 'for devotion only, not to gain honour or money'.[7] Even Godfrey of Bouillon, whom later ages transformed into a golden hero, had some political reasons for setting out. Added to the temptations of adventure itself, was the possibility of winning great estates in the east, and men who might not have been interested in mere soldiering came because there were hopes of a fortune to be won. On the other hand, this provided the Frankish kingdom of Jerusalem with its original settlers, and meant that the moment of triumph could be turned into a material achievement: without these men, there would have been no permanent Christian state in the east.

Again, the crusade might have been inspired by religious ideals, and prayer and religious observances were very prominent in the army's daily life; but it also moved among political realities. The problems of the crusaders at Constantinople were greatly

---

7   Riley-Smith, *The Crusades*, 29.

complicated by the Byzantine claims to overlordship of the Holy Land, and the oaths of loyalty which Alexius demanded in order to safeguard that title. And it proved impossible to reconcile religion and politics either in the organisation of the crusade or in the structure of the new state. The leadership came from secular princes, with secular aims: Baldwin of Boulogne saw his opportunity at Edessa, and founded a principality there, while Bohemond claimed Antioch as his own. The commander-in-chief was elected by the 'common counsel of the whole army'; and it is remarkable that the military direction of the crusade was successful, given its unexpectedly democratic nature: it was pressure from the knights and ordinary soldiers that led to the successful final push to Jerusalem. And it was only at Jerusalem itself that idealism briefly prevailed. Godfrey of Bouillon ruled there not as king, but as 'advocate of the Holy Sepulchre', refusing to wear a royal crown in the city where Christ had been crowned with thorns. But there was no ecclesiastical figure of sufficient stature either to assume leadership of the crusade or to control the barons of the new state. Adhémar of Le Puy provided wise counsel, but was unable to assert his authority against the headstrong lords; and with his death at Antioch, the ecclesiastical element lost much of its influence. Baldwin of Edessa was crowned king of Jerusalem on Godfrey's death, despite the latter's wish that the Patriarch of the city should be ruler of the Franks in Palestine. Visions had yielded to the needs of the moment: the knights who had settled in the east understood only the familiar forms of government.

And so in times of peace the Frankish settlements of Outremer (Overseas), as it came to be called, were no different from their European counterparts; their institutions were closely modelled on those of their homelands, and normal relations began to be established with the surrounding, infidel, states. As Fulcher of Chartres wrote in 1127

> we who had been westerners have become part of the east; the man who was once a Roman or a Frank has become a Galilean or a Palestinian; and the man who used to live in Reims or Chartres now finds himself a citizen of Tyre or Acre . . . He who was poor in the west finds that God has made him rich here . . . . Why should anyone return to the west who has found an east like this? [8]

It was only in times of distress that the crusading cry was raised, when the forces of the new state were inadequate against the greater resources of their Muslim foes. For those who went on crusade, the ideal situation was a state of permanent war against the heathen which was far beyond the resources of the settlers, and which would have made the establishment of a settled Christian state well nigh impossible. In practice,

---

[8]   Fulcher of Chartres, *Historia Hierosolymitana (1095–1127)* ed. Heinrich Hagenmeyer (Heidelberg 1913) 748.

as the First Crusade had shown, it resulted in a mixture of petty jealousies, bad organisation and credulousness on the one hand, and immense resolve and real religious enthusiasm on the other. The discipline of the time was not strong enough to contain the zeal aroused by crusading; in the hour of triumph, religion was seen to have provided abundant fervour, but all too few moral qualities. The balance between ideal and reality remained unachieved.

The First Crusade had been conceived as an expedition which would settle once and for all the control of the Holy Places. Its triumph echoed through Europe, and in the confidence it engendered, the disasters which overtook those crusaders who had set out after the main expedition went unnoticed. Annihilated by the Turkish armies of Kilij Arslan in Asia Minor, very few escaped with their lives, let alone reached Palestine. Because these reverses were ignored, or used as a contrast to the spectacular achievement of the first crusade, the realisation that the victory of 1099 was not a permanent one did not penetrate men's minds until the third decade of the twelfth century. The newly formed Military Orders and the resources of Outremer seemed sufficient, until in 1146 Antioch was threatened by a Muslim army which had already overpowered Edessa. The weakness of the Frankish position now became evident, and an appeal went out to the west.

The Second Crusade set out when the memory of the First was still fresh in men's minds, and the response it aroused was great. Both Louis VII of France and the pope wished to take the credit for having set it in motion, a dispute which led to the papal bull known as 'Quantum predecessores'. This became the classic statement of the appeal to knights to go on crusade, setting out the papal claim to be the sole authority who could initiate a crusade. In it, the pope declared that the sins of Christendom at large had brought God's anger on the Christians in the east. All true Christian knights would wish to set this right, and he set out the privileges that they would obtain by so doing, both worldly and spiritual. The preaching of the crusade was entrusted to Bernard of Clairvaux, the greatest orator of his day. But these impressive preparations were not matched by the results. The failure of the crusaders to take Damascus (which was in any case an ally of the kingdom of Jerusalem) and their subsequent ignominious retreat seriously damaged the philosophy behind the crusade, because much of the morale of the crusader depended on his conviction that he was invincible, protected by the God for whom he was fighting. Even St Bernard found it difficult to accept the disappointment of the crusade's failure. The reverses might be attributed to sinfulness on the part of those involved, but such excuses wore thin as expedition after expedition failed to achieve its objectives. The problems facing crusades were persistently underestimated for the same reason; to an age which was convinced that God gave the victory to the righteous in secular battles, His help seemed certain in so holy a cause.

The Second Crusade had set out in response to a specific crisis. After the disaster at Hattin in 1187, when the army of the kingdom of Jerusalem was annihilated, King Guy was captured, and the Holy Cross fell into infidel hands, the state of crisis was to remain almost permanent, especially as Jerusalem was now under Muslim rule again. The crusader could once more hope to achieve the glory of reconquering the Holy Places. The pattern of 1145-7 was repeated: the pope issued a bull appealing for a new crusade, and sent out preachers to make his appeal known. The response was very impressive, exceeding even that for the First Crusade: the Emperor, Frederick Barbarossa, and the kings of England and France, Richard Coeur de Lion and Philip Augustus. It was well organised and equipped, lacking only an overall commander. The death of Frederick Barbarossa, drowned while bathing in a river in Asia Minor, and the departure of Philip owing to a quarrel with Richard which had developed en route, left the latter in sole command. Only the astuteness of the Muslim leader Saladin as a diplomat and his skill as a general prevented Richard from achieving the recapture of Jerusalem. The eventual failure of the Third Crusade was even more damaging, in a different way, than that of the Second: the greatest princes of the west had made common cause, and had still failed to attain their goal.

Worse was still to come, with the Fourth Crusade's attack on Byzantium. At the beginning of the First Crusade, the west was not politically involved in the Mediterranean beyond Sicily; but increasing attention was paid to the possibilities of diplomatic manoeuvres which would strengthen the position of the Frankish kingdom, and trading interests in the area had been built up by the Italians. Venetian hopes of commercial gain, the presence of a pretender to the Byzantine throne, and, more distantly, papal dreams of a reunion of the Roman and Orthodox Churches combined to divert the Fourth Crusade from its original objective, Egypt, to the destruction of the Greek empire. This was disastrous both in its tangible effects on the balance of power in the east and its impact on the crusading ideal. Europe was treated to the spectacle of an entire crusade being excommunicated, while Byzantium never recovered from the blow. The Latin empire which was established there was too concerned with maintaining its own precarious power to assist future crusades. It is only fair to say that the Venetians duped and blackmailed the crusaders at every turn, exploiting their shortage of money, and to this extent poor organisation was to blame. It was extremely difficult to raise a crusading tithe without the full royal support which the Third Crusade had enjoyed. Nor was there a leader of sufficient stature to resist the Venetian demands, though some crusaders, to their credit, left the expedition before its raids on Christian territory, and sailed straight for Palestine.

The outcome of the Fourth Crusade persuaded the pope, Innocent III, that any future crusade must be firmly under the church's control, and when a renewed call to arms was made in November 1215 at the Lateran Council in Rome, one of the most important gatherings of the medieval church, it was proclaimed as a papal crusade. It was not greeted with the enthusiastic reception accorded to the Third Crusade, and there was great difficulty in persuading magnates to take part. The main body of the resulting expedition gathered in the Holy Land in the spring of 1218, composed largely of Germans: John of Brienne, king of Jerusalem, and Leopold of Austria became its leaders, and launched an attack on Damietta, at the mouth of the Nile, in an attempt to break the power of Egypt, whose sultans controlled Jerusalem. In the early autumn, Pelagius, cardinal-bishop of Albano, arrived to take charge of the crusade. Despite the capture of Damietta on 5 November 1219, the crusade ended in failure when Pelagius insisted on marching to attack the Egyptian camp at Mansourah against the advice of John of Brienne. The crusading army was trapped on the bank opposite Mansourah when the Moslems flooded the dykes in the Nile valley, and was forced to surrender.

Jerusalem was to be briefly recovered some years later by the antithesis of the Fifth Crusade, an expedition which set out despite the pope's express commands to the contrary, headed by a ruler who was under sentence of excommunication. Frederick II's bitter struggle to assert the Emperor's authority in face of Gregory VII's attack on his position as ruler had led to his excommunication; yet it was he who succeeded where the popes had failed. Arriving in Palestine in 1228, he found the Egyptian sultan at odds with his brother the governor of Damascus, and by exploiting their differences, regained the Holy City on March 17, 1229, against the wishes of the Christian patriarch and the local Frankish knights, who disliked the terms of the treaty. It was a remarkable piece of statesmanship, but was not destined to last: Jerusalem was retaken with little difficulty by the Muslims fifteen years later.

It was only with the Sixth Crusade in 1249 that a capable leader again appeared at the head of an army in the east. St Louis was the most remarkable of all crusaders. His stern devotion to religion and justice had something of the puritan in it; he refused at first to entertain any approaches from the infidel, showed no mercy to those who broke his laws, and lived an austere life in an age when monarchy and ostentation were usually synonymous. That such a man should respond to the appeal for a crusade after the second fall of Jerusalem was only to be expected. The interval between his taking the crusading vows in December 1244 and his departure in August 1248 was occupied by elaborate preparations, and a large number of the French nobility joined the expedition. There were very few contingents from other countries, a symptom of the rising national feeling within Europe. But even Louis failed to overcome the vast problems that now beset any attempt at a large-scale campaign in the east. He took Damietta, and could have exchanged it for Jerusalem, only to be betrayed by the indiscipline of his brother at Mansourah when a great victory was almost within the crusaders' grasp. What had begun triumphantly ended in dark defeat: Louis and his whole army were captured, and the price in lives and ransom was enormous. Even the years of his wise government of Outremer after his release could not repair the damage.

And yet, despite popular murmurings in the west, the crusade was not discredited, nor the crusaders discouraged. The theory behind the crusades began to take a different shape. The crusading movement had to some extent originated in the Papacy's attempts to wield secular power against its enemies, and had always included a certain number of expeditions of this type, whether directly instigated by or merely approved by the Pope. A crusade could be used to suppress a dissident monarch: Innocent IV had appealed for a crusade against the heir of Frederick II in 1251; or it could be used against heretics, as in the blood-thirsty Albigensian crusade of 1209-12. The political and religious reasons which led to the destruction of the counts of Provence and the laying waste of the fertile lands of the south of France were complex, and to call a crusade against heretics whose preaching against early corruption had won much sympathy seemed to be making such campaigns a means of doing the Church's work rather than God's. The success of Frederick II's expedition in 1228-9, while he was still excommunicate, did little to strengthen men's faith.

The later crusades, with the exception of St Louis' attempt to convert the Emir of Tunis by a show of arms in 1270, begin to look like an extension of the search for *gloire*, renown. Knightly conduct was above all governed by tradition, and tradition decreed that crusading was one of the great knightly activities. Henceforward it was to be either younger men who became crusaders, men who had not yet come into their inheritance, as though an expedition to the east was part of their training for high estate; or men who had never lost their youthful vision of knightly fame. The secular knights who in all earnestness regarded the crusade as a holy war – and they had once been legion – dwindled to a mere handful, and those who had once gone on crusade in the hope of making their fortune realised that the east offered little prospect of riches. Both types of knight had a real cause for which to fight; they were replaced by men whose incentives were less powerful.

Nor were conditions in the east growing more favourable to the success of the crusades. Egypt and the lands to the east of Palestine had been weak and internally divided at the time of the First Crusade; there had been dissensions since then, but the passage of time had seen the rise of a formidable kingdom in Egypt which finally destroyed the Frankish kingdom of Jerusalem in 1291 by taking Acre, and without a foothold in the Holy Land, the last real impetus of the crusading movement faded into dreams and visions: reconquest was no longer an immediate and practical prospect.

But crusading was not merely a question of practicalities; even as Acre fell, Pope Nicholas IV had been actively campaigning for a crusade. He had collected advice from men with experience of the east, and one book written for him, Fidenzio of Padua's book *On the Recovery of the Holy Land*, contained much valuable advice.

Unfortunately, it was not to be the precursor of a crusade, but of a series of such projects, all ably argued and largely realistic. It is these books which show how real the idea of a crusade remained, even if the dream was never accomplished. They were not the work of isolated eccentrics, but of men with a sound knowledge of affairs, and who well understood the difficulties involved. However, the schemes were not always quite what they purported to be. Pierre Dubois' tract entitled *The Recovery of the Holy Land*,[9] like his other works, was propaganda aimed at enhancing the prestige of Philip the Fair, and its appearance in 1306 coincided with the campaign against the Templars. Their possessions were to be confiscated to pay for the expedition, and the Order abolished or merged with the Hospitallers. When we also find a memoir from de Nogaret, another of Philip's close advisers, written four years later, which advocates the diversion of the revenues of *both* Orders into a treasury to be controlled by the French king, the real purpose of the schemes becomes apparent. Like so many previous crusading taxes, little of this would have found its way to the east.

About the same time as Dubois' tract, Raimon Llull, whose theories on secular chivalry we have already noticed, produced a scheme for a crusade which was a thorough study of the theoretical aspects of the problem. It was typical of the change that was beginning to appear in European attitudes that he felt it necessary to start the work with a tract against the infidels. His remarks on the waging of the crusade are well thought out, and his proposed 'dominus bellator rex', a single commander of royal blood chosen by the Pope with jurisdiction over a united military order, shows that he had realised the dangers of divided leadership. As to the route of the crusade, he advocates an invasion of Moorish Spain and a gradual conquest of North Africa, to be supported by naval action in the Mediterranean and a trade blockade against the Muslims. But Llull's schemes ignored the realities of European politics just as those of Dubois and Nogaret had been all too down-to-earth; Llull died on his way back from Tunis in 1316 not as a conquering crusader but as a failed missionary.

It was not until the middle years of the century that any tangible results came from all these exhortations.[10] A raid on Smyrna in 1345 by a small papal and Hospitaller force had resulted in the town's capture and new enthusiasm for the crusading ideal, but there was now a distinct change of emphasis in the objectives involved. The recovery of the Holy Land remained the ultimate goal: meanwhile, any expedition against the Turks, even if only to relieve pressure on Smyrna, was dignified with the name of crusade, in sharp contrast to the grandiose expeditions envisaged by propagandists. Such was Humbert of Vienne's crusade in 1345-7; Amadeus VI of

9   Pierre Dubois, *The Recovery of the Holy Land*, tr. Walther I.Brandt (New York 1956).

10   On the crusading ethos after St Louis, see Norman Housley, *The Later Crusades: from Lyons to Alcazar 1274-1580* (Oxford & New York 1992).

Savoy went to the rescue of his cousin John V Palaeologos in 1366 wearing the cross; and following the example of St Louis in 1270, Louis de Bourbon crusaded against Tunis in 1390. And even the promising expedition of 1365, largely supported by the Cypriots under their king, Peter of Lusignan and the Hospitallers, with small Italian contingents, achieved no more than its initial success at Alexandria, where the booty was so great – greater even than the massacre of the inhabitants – that the majority of the crusaders refused to continue, and the fleet returned to Cyprus, having merely added another black page of bloodthirstiness to the history of the crusades, and having burnt the great library there, with its priceless collection of ancient manuscripts.

Yet among these failures, the vision persisted. Philippe de Mézières, chancellor of Cyprus from 1360, had been at Smyrna with Humbert of Vienne in 1346, and with the Carmelite friar Pierre Thomas had been deeply involved in Peter's crusade. At Alexandria, Philippe had seen that it was not the fervour that Pierre Thomas had so ardently preached that was lacking, but discipline. Peter did not launch another expedition before his death in 1369, and Philippe returned to France. Here he led a life of literary activity. His great ideal was to create a new military order, 'The Order of the Passion of Our Lord Jesus Christ'; and he worked out a detailed scheme for this; but he also saw that reforms were needed in the whole of Christian society before the west would be ready to launch a successful crusade. The evils of the world in which he lived were analysed in his polemic work, *The Dream of the Old Pilgrim*, an appeal for the launching of a new crusade, which he addressed to Charles VI of France. Philippe's experience, sincerity and power as a writer command respect, and of all the great schemes put forward, his is the most impressive.

His requirements were too great, however, to be put into effect; instead his preaching produced in 1396 exactly the kind of expedition he wished to avoid, under the youthful duke of Nevers, heir to the duchy of Burgundy, consisting of the chivalry of Burgundy and France.[11] It was bent on the pursuit of glory rather than the waging of scientific warfare, and above all lacked discipline, despite the presence of experienced leaders such as Marshal Boucicaut.

When the army went into action at Nicopolis on the Danube, the blockade of the town was scarcely taken seriously. Feasts and jousts were the order of the day, and rumours of the Muslim sultan Bajazet's approach to relieve the town were not seriously heeded. When battle became inevitable, divided counsels prevailed. The French refused to take Sigismund of Hungary's advice and place those of his local allies whose loyalty was dubious in the vanguard, so that they could not desert; the van, they said, was the place of honour, and theirs of right. Nor did they understand the Turkish tactics,

11   See Aziz Suryal Atiya, *The Crusade of Nicopolis* (London 1934).

which relied on light-armed horsemen who could wheel round and take up their formation again if their line was broken. Sigismund wanted to wait until the Turks had worn themselves out against the solid line of the Christian forces, but the French charged first, breaking the Turkish line, only to find a line of stakes. As they dismounted and made their way through, the archers kept up a constant fire, and the light horsemen regrouped; when they reached the crest of the hill, these and the reserve troops put them to flight, and the local Hungarian allies deserted. The arrival of more reinforcements under a Christian prince in Bajazet's service turned the rout into a massacre. Bajazet had all Christian prisoners except the most important killed, and a mere handful of the leaders were able to return to the west on payment of immense ransoms. Yet such was the magic of the crusading ideal and the aura attached to those who had been on crusade that John of Nevers was able to make a triumphal progress through Flanders on his return.

The crusade of Nicopolis was the last great expedition to set out for the east, not because the crusading spirit died with the disaster that overtook it, but because that spirit belonged to another age, that of a united Church and Christendom. The weakness of the Papacy during the period of the Great Schism and the conciliar movement meant that there was no strong appeal from that quarter for a renewal of the crusade. Nationalism had undermined the possibility of concerted, international action; chivalry might transcend national feeling at times, but practical politics offered too many obstacles. The balance of power was too delicate for such a major military undertaking to be agreed upon; national suspicions had become too strong. On the other hand, the rise of international trade militated strongly against the crusade. The Italian ports were prepared to engage in almost any kind of mercantile operation so long as it was profitable, selling Christians into slavery or even armaments to the Turks in return for the luxury goods of the east; and the immediate effect of the success of the crusade at Alexandria in 1365 was a vast increase in the price of spices because supplies were cut off. Finally, the great shield of Byzantium to the north and west of the Holy Land had been slowly disintegrating over the centuries, until only the Tartar victory at Angora in 1402 saved Byzantium itself from the Turks for another fifty years, while the Muslim states went from strength to strength. The crusade had been a difficult enough undertaking in the twelfth century, with a divided Muslim world and the Byzantine imperial power a real presence; now the odds had become impossible. Yet even after Byzantium fell in 1453, Pius II, an experienced diplomat and very much a man with a grasp of secular affairs, attempted to a launch a crusade, and died at Ancona in 1464, on his way to the east. The ideal that had begun with a pope died with a pope.

12

The Military Orders in Palestine

ONCE THE INITIAL IMPETUS which had carried the First Crusade into Jerusalem and established the Frankish kingdom in Palestine began to wane, the problems raised by a Christian state dependent on the West in such remote lands began to appear. The Holy War gave way to pilgrimages again; and instead of the crusading forces, lightly armed bands of pilgrims began to make their way through Asia Minor to Jerusalem. What the Frankish knights needed were either settlers or reinforcements, not this added liability; they existed uneasily with the indifferent support or downright hostility of the native population on whom they depended for the daily necessities of life. The crusade had been launched to recover the Holy Places for Christendom; but Western Christendom had never possessed them before, and was unwilling to face the problems of maintaining them, while the Eastern Empire regarded the Franks as intruders, and was not disposed to support them to any great extent.

The Kingdom of Jerusalem had arisen in the absence of any planned alternative; and in its first decades it was chiefly concerned with preserving its own existence, rather than with the function of guardian of the Holy Places with which it found itself endowed. Yet pilgrims could not be turned away; they had therefore to be protected. In the absence of official action, it was left to a small group of knights to act. Under one Hugh de Payens, they banded together to protect pilgrims on passage and to guard and keep open the public roads. The knights formed a small military confraternity: confraternities were a type of association familiar throughout the middle ages. There is some evidence that confraternities were behind the foundation of the Spanish military orders, and there were formal links between the monastic world and that of the knights in the shape of the 'advocates and defenders' whom we have already discussed as the putative subjects of the church ceremonies for the blessing of the sword. Such pacts between knights and monasteries, by which the knights exercised their secular power (whether as landowners, administrators of justice or soldiers) in the monastery's defence or favour in return for being remembered in the monks' prayers both during their lifetime, and, as benefactors, after their death, are well documented.

266

Even if formal associations sworn to defend monasteries may not have existed, the links between chivalry and religion which developed through the 'defensores et advocatos' are important. They showed in a practical way that the knight's skills could be enlisted for God's purposes; and in a sense Hugh de Payens was acting in just such a role for the pilgrims on the road to Jerusalem. The closest parallel, which has been claimed, though on dubious grounds, as a confraternity, concerns the abbey of La Sauve Majeure near Bordeaux, on the pilgrim road to Compostela.[1] It is interesting that Godfrey of Bouillon used the title 'advocatus' during his brief reign at Jerusalem after the First Crusade. We have also seen how ceremonies for the consecration of swords were part of a pact between local knights and monasteries for the defence of the latter. Soon after Hugh de Payens and his fellow-knights made their pact, in 1118, king Baldwin granted them a royal house near the Temple as their residence; the association became formal when they took a vow before the patriarch of Jerusalem, in the usual monastic form of poverty, obedience and chastity. The official foundation of the order, as a formally accepted institution, probably took place in 1120.[2] It seems most probable, in the absence of all records of these early years, that the idea of an association to protect pilgrims must have preceded that of a monastic vow. The latter was the means of giving the group a coherent form: and it was probably chosen to underline the devotional nature of the undertaking. For the idea of a full-scale Order at once military and religious would have been almost unthinkable anywhere except in Palestine. 'He that liveth by the sword shall perish by the sword', had been the Church's teaching since time immemorial; and the preaching of a Holy War was a revolutionary enough idea, invoked only in order to recover Jerusalem. To combine monasticism and war was to make a temporary departure from scriptural teaching into a permanent change of attitude. The unfamiliar nature of the concept behind the order was repeatedly emphasised by contemporaries: even the Templars themselves said that theirs was 'a new kind of religion'.[3] But in the context of the change in the church's view of knighthood in the early twelfth century, it was a novelty which was more than acceptable to society at large.

The 'poor knights of Christ', as they called themselves, were too urgently needed for anyone to raise objections; at the outset, they merely defended pilgrims, a role which was an echo of the church's current teaching about the knight's place in society. But

1   Marcus Bull, 'The confraternity of La Sauve-Majeure' in *The Military Orders: Fighting for the Faith and Caring for the Sick*, ed. Malcolm Barber (Aldershot 1994) 311-319.
2   Malcolm Barber, *The New Knighthood: a history of the Order of the Temple* (Cambridge and New York 1994), 9.
3   A. J. Forey, 'The emergence of the military orders in the twelfth century', *Journal of Ecclesiastical History* 36, 1985, 175-195; the quotation is on p.176.

they turned fairly quickly to a more general war to keep the infidel at bay and preserve the whole Frankish kingdom; at the same time, active support began to increase. Fulk of Anjou gave the knights £30 in silver in 1120; and their riches soon began to accumulate. Hugh, count of Champagne, renounced his rank to become a member in 1125; by 1126 the knights were too influential to remain a merely local arrangement between king, patriarch and members; and a rule on the lines of those granted to the normal monastic orders was sought from the Pope.

The rule of the Templars and their status in relation to the rest of the Church was determined by two documents: the rule granted at the council of Troyes in 1129, and the bull *Omne datum optimum* of Innocent II in 1139. The original precepts which the brothers followed had been simply those of the Augustinian canons, with the three vows of chastity, poverty and obedience. But something more specific was needed for a body whose importance and wealth were rapidly increasing, and Bernard of Clairvaux, one of the great figures of the Christian West was enlisted for the purpose. Bernard had been the chief instrument in the spread of the new Cistercian rule and the revival of monasticism; and in some ways the military orders were very much part of this movement. He had been a vigorous supporter of the Temple when its existence was still uncertain, and had written a pamphlet in support of their ideals, *De laude novae militiae* (In praise of the new soldiery).[4] It was specifically addressed to the Templars – *Liber ad milites Templi* – and as it preceded the drawing up of the Rule, it is a manifesto for the new ideal rather than a detailed organisational blueprint. It seems to have been written in response to a letter from 'Hugo the sinner' (who may or may not have been Hugh de Payens himself) setting out the hopes and fears of the knights, anxious to acquire the formal status of an order, but uncertain of their ground.[5] Bernard contrasts the new knighthood he has in mind, the *milites Christi*, with the secular knighthood. The latter fight in their own interest: therefore, if they kill, they commit a deadly sin, if they are killed, their souls perish. Their splendid equipment – silken saddles, painted lances and shields, harness decorated with gold, silver and precious stones – is mere 'feminine ornament' to Bernard's austere eye, like their long hair and fashionable clothing. True knights need none of this; but however brave and skilled they may be, they are condemned so long as they fight only for earthly possessions. They should be 'God's ministers to take revenge on evildoers, and should honour good men.' The new knights slay the heathen, but only if they refuse to end their oppression of Christians. Bernard goes on to outline the life of the knights: they should live in chastity and obedience,

4   Josef Fleckenstein, 'Die Rechtfertigung der geistlichen Ritterorden nach der Schrift >De laude novae militiae< Bernhards von Clairvaux' in *Die geistliche Ritterorden Europas* ed. Josef Fleckenstein and Manfred Hellman, Vorträge und Forschungen XXVI (Sigmaringen 1980).

5   J.Leclercq, 'Un document sur les débuts des Templiers'. *Revue d'histoire ecclesiastique* 52, 1957, 80.

holding all things in common, in other words, they should follow the three ideals of a monastic existence. They are to avoid the rich trappings and licentious existence of secular knights, the songs of minstrels and the mock war of tournaments.

The final version of the rule of the Templars, which served as model for that of the Hospitallers, was largely the work of Bernard and Hugh de Payens; and it in turn largely reflects the thinking behind the Cistercian rule.[6] The hierarchy of the Order was carefully defined. The Grand Master, or more simply, the Master, enjoyed wide powers, but there were severe restrictions nonetheless. He could dispose of minor matters as he wished, and was even allowed his own treasury. If, however, the question of a gift of the Order's land, alteration of a decree of the Chapter General, or admission of a candidate came up, he had to refer it to the Chapter General of the Order. Any diplomatic problem had to be decided by them, such as the signing of treaties or declaring of war; the military undertakings such as sieges required their approval. The Chapter General consisted of high officers and seems to have varied with the subject to be discussed; it was paralleled by lower chapters with jurisdiction over a single province, who could be summoned by the local master. Besides the Master, the central officers consisted of the Seneschal, the Master's deputy; and the Marshal, who was responsible for the direction of military affairs. The commanders of provinces made up the remainder of the senior hierarchy. The commander of the land and Kingdom of Jerusalem acted as treasurer, the commander of the city of Jerusalem as hospitaller was responsible for the welfare of pilgrims; while the nine remaining commanders, of Tripoli, Antioch, France, England, Poitou, Aragon, Portugal, Apulia and Hungary, had no special tasks beyond those entailed by the care of their respective provinces. The provinces were divided into houses, each again with its commander, and the houses were controlled by the knights-commander acting as the latter's lieutenant. The organisation was thus equally well adapted for monastic and military discipline: in war, the divisions of command in the field corresponded to the administrative ranks.

The everyday administration and discipline of the Order was in the hands of the ordinary Chapters, at which all Knights were bound to attend.[7] The disciplinary assemblies followed a strict formula. The president, usually the commander of the house, would give a brief address; and any brother who felt he had committed a breach of the Order's rules would then kneel and confess. Minor matters could be dealt with on the spot: major offences would be reserved for higher judgment. The list of crimes and penalties gives some idea of the strictness of the Order's life and the chief problems

---

6   *The Rule of the Templars: the French text of the Rule of the Order of the Knights Templar* translated by J.M.Upton-Ward, Studies in the History of Medieval Religion IV (Woodbridge and Rochester, N.Y. 1992); see pp.39-72 for the hierarchical statutes.

7   Rule of the Templars, 106-141: 'The holding of ordinary chapters'.

of discipline.[8] Since members of the Order owed no secular allegiance, all the cases covered by the normal communal code fell within the scope of the rule. The severest penalty, expulsion from the Order, was reserved for only one of the usual criminal cases, murder; but eight offences which injured the Order were punished in this way. These included treason and desertion, heresy, purchasing entry into the Order, plotting among the brothers, revelation of the Order's secrets. The most unusual entry is that of 'absence without leave', 'quitting the house other than by the main door', and being away from the house for more than two nights if more than the bare essentials of clothing had been taken. Offenders against these laws were to be sent at once to an even stricter order, preferably Benedictine or Augustine in rule, to expiate their sins. For men trained to fighting and action, the peace of a monastery must have been punishment indeed. Lesser offences, such as disobedience, consorting with women, and attempting to escape from the Order, were punished by the loss of privileges for a year, which meant living with the Order's slaves, deprived of horse, arms and habit. Really serious cases of any of these crimes could lead to imprisonment, sometimes perpetual, in one of the Order's castles.

Some of the knights went to the other extreme, and pursued their religious avocation too far, though this was the exception rather than the rule. Jacques de Vitry, bishop of Acre from 1216, tells of an amusing incident in one of his homilies addressed to the Order. One of the brethren was so assiduous about fasting, being more interested in piety than valour, that when he rode into battle, he was unhorsed by the first blow he received. Another knight, at some risk to his own life, picked him up and put him back on his horse; whereupon he fell off again as soon as he received another blow. As he was remounted for the second time, the knight who had helped him said: 'If you fall off again, Sir Bread-and-Water, it won't be me who picks you up.'[9]

The desired rule was granted at the council of Troyes in 1129, and the increased prestige confirmed by becoming an Order was at once reflected in increased numbers and riches. The first gifts of land to the knights, now known as Templars from their residence near the Temple in Jerusalem, were in France in the autumn of 1127. Hugh de Payens travelled throughout Europe seeking men and money for the Order of which he was now Master. He was well received everywhere, and the order began to develop a formal geographical structure. Provinces of the Order arose in Portugal, Aragon, Castile, England and France. These in turn were divided into preceptories, whose object was to administer the gifts made to the Templars, whether land or money, and to furnish the warriors in Palestine with recruits and financial support. Besides gifts, the Order recruited some notable figures, including Ramon Berenguer III, count of Barcelona, in 1130.

8   *Rule of the Templars*, 142-167.
9   Lecoy de la Marche, *La chaire française*, 399.

The first offensive action in which the Templars took part was the siege of Damascus in 1129, after Hugh de Payens' return to Palestine with some 300 knights whom he had recruited for the campaign. However, it was not until 1147, with the arrival of the Second Crusade, that they saw major operations against the infidel. The intervening years must have seen skirmishes, but nothing that the chroniclers deemed worthy of record; equally, the records of Outremer do not reflect their true prominence in political affairs at this period. A lack of men prevented the Franks from planning offensives in these years; the combined strength of the Temple and such feudal forces as could be raised was overawed by the might of Islam, drawn from a much wider area. As long as the Christians remained on the defensive, these forces were disunited, interested in their own internal squabbles; but an offensive campaign had to reckon with the possibility of a united resistance. That the Templars fought during this period is shown by their use of a battlecry, 'Beauséant', after their black-and-white battle standard. But the decade was primarily one of consolidation, the acquisition of new land, and their gradual acceptance as one of the stable forces in the eminently unstable kingdom. It is only after 1150 that they begin to be given responsibility for the great fortresses of the kingdom; in the 1130s their main castles were a group to the north of Antioch, with just one in Palestine itself.

The great privileges of the Order date from three bulls of Innocent II, beginning with *Omne datum optimum*, probably granted in 1139. For the Order owed no secular allegiance; and this bull, originally designed to provide for the spiritual needs of the Order by giving it its own clergy and churches, freed it from the only immediate rulers it had, the bishops. It could appoint priests and build places of prayer without reference to anyone; and above all it was exempted from tithes, a privilege it shared with the Cistercians alone. Even if this last right was not at once exploited to the full, the Order was exercising it at the end of the twelfth century, and the bishops of Palestine never forgave them for it; their anger still thunders in the pages of William of Tyre and his followers, from whom the history of Palestine must largely be written. Perhaps that is why we hear so much more of Templar treachery than of Templar bravery, a suspicion that is confirmed when we find another conflict with the local clergy between 1198 and 1212: Innocent III had to reprove the latter for their hostility towards the Templars over their right to an annual appeal for alms in every parish.

The efforts of the Templars had not gone unnoticed among the brethren of the Hospital of St John the Baptist, who had long cared for the pilgrims visiting Jerusalem.[10] This establishment, an offshoot of the monastery of St Mary of the Latins,

---

10   On the origins of the Hospitallers see Rudolf Hiestand, 'Die Anfänge der Johanniter' in *Die geistliche Ritterorden* , 31-80.

had come into being after some merchants from Amalfi had been given land in Jerusalem by one of the Egyptian caliphs, which they had used for these pious purposes. The monks had come from Italy and were Benedictines; they had already been caring for visitors to Jerusalem for nearly half a century when Hugh de Payens formed his band of knights. With the coming of Frankish rule, they had benefited greatly from the charity of the foreign knights, and from the new rulers of the Church. They also enjoyed royal patronage, and Baldwin I confirmed their already wide lands in a charter of 1112 witnessed by the new patriarch of Jerusalem, Arnulf.

These newly acquired riches, and donations made to it in Europe, enabled the Hospital, as it was usually known, to set up an international organisation for the care of pilgrims, with hospices strategically sited throughout the pilgrim ports of France and Italy. Under its governor, Gerard, it became an Order in its own right, and this was confirmed in a bull of 1113. Its independence was recognised, and it was taken under papal protection, giving the Master a standing equal to that of a secular prince or an archbishop. The impetus of these early years was maintained under the two succeeding masters, especially in terms of the lands acquired, and the development of the rule. In a document of the 1130s, the Augustinian rule was adopted, with additions emphasising the duty to the poor and the sick, and disciplinary regulations which enjoin that all brothers shall wear the cross, thus identifying them with the crusaders proper.

In all this there is no word of military activity. Both the date and reasons for the change from charity to the sword, and hence the appearance of the Hospitallers as the second of the great military orders, are obscure.[11] The care of pilgrims might easily be extended to include their defence from attack; and parties going on pilgrimage very rarely went without some kind of armament. Likewise, the whole of Frankish Palestine remained throughout its existence to a lesser or greater degree in a state of war, and any gift of property was bound to entail the possibility that it might have to be defended. For both these activities, hired troops may have been used. The first references to the Hospitallers' involvement in warfare all imply the assumption of defensive responsibilities without saying how these were carried out, and even in the 1170s a traveller could write of the Order 'which sustains many persons in its castles, instructed in all arts of war, for the defence of the lands of the Christians against the incursions of the Saracens'.[12]

The gifts received in the early years were free from direct military obligations. The beginnings of the transformation into a military order probably belong to the 1130s; the first recorded acquisition of a castle is in 1136, when Fulk built the key

11   Alan Forey, *The Military Orders from the twelfth to the early fourteenth centuries* (London 1992) 17-19.
12   John of Würzburg quoted in Jonathan Riley-Smith, *The Knights of St John of Jerusalem and Cyprus c.1050-1310* (London 1967) 57.

fortress of Bethgibelin in the south, on the Hospital's land, and then gave it to the Order with the idea that the latter's rich revenues could be made to contribute to the costs of defence. That this arrangement was successful is implied by the gift eight years later of a very much larger responsibility in the north, in the principality of Tripoli, on terms which were entirely in the Hospitallers' hands; and other donations which followed were in the same pattern of great privileges in return for the defence of dangerous and difficult positions. By 1150 these new duties may have been reflected within the Order by the appearance of a small class of knights serving as lay brothers, though the duties of these were probably strictly limited. In the 1160s, the Master, Gilbert d'Assailly used the phrase 'we and our brothers, mingling religious and military duties in defence of the Holy Land', and this probably marks the period when a conscious decision was taken to become a military order like the Templars.[13] But even twenty years later, the Hospital was primarily a charitable order and only incidentally a military force.

Nonetheless, the military side had greatly increased between 1150 and 1180. In 1168 we find it raising fifty knights and a number of native mercenaries at its own expense, for an ill-starred expedition to Egypt. If the venture had succeeded, the Order was to have received lands in return for its expenses, so its motives were not entirely altruistic; and it entered into similar agreements at Antioch, where it was given borderlands which had long since been in Saracen hands. Certainly its knights, whether actual members of the Order, knights holding fiefs from the Hospital, or merely hired troops acting in its name, had acquired a reputation as early as 1157, when a column relieving one of the Hospitaller castles was ambushed, and Nur-ed-Din gave orders for all prisoners to be executed, a measure which was repeated on later occasions when the Order had definitely become a military organisation. That attempts to increase its military element were afoot is shown by the admonishments of Alexander III, in a bull of about 1179, that they should not depart from their original objectives.

It was only after the disaster at Hattin, and the accession of Lucius III, that a change in the papal attitude took place. It seems to have been a recognition of a *de facto* situation rather than active encouragement, but without the approval of the pope as the Order's ultimate ruler, any continued soldiering activity would have been impossible. At all events, the development of the official military institutions of the Hospital was very rapid from this period, and it is hard to see how, in such a war-based state, any other solution would have been possible. Their wealth made them politically influential; and politics were largely concerned with war policies. Besides, the increasing disarray of the secular barons now left the Orders as one of the chief stable forces in

---

13   Rudolf Hiestand, 'Die Anfänge der Johanniter', 73.

the kingdom, and any move to reduce their power would reduce both the chances of internal peace and the strength of Palestine's defences, which had now come to rest largely on the quasi-military gifts to the Hospital and Temple. The burden was such that it had already brought the Hospital near to financial disaster in the 1160s.

Had a strong king emerged in Jerusalem in the latter part of the twelfth century, it is possible that the growth of the Hospital's military power might have been checked, or at least taken a different course; but Guy of Lusignan and his successors were either weak or were thwarted by events beyond their control, and the loss of Jerusalem demoralised the laymen even more than the Orders, who could make fresh appeals for men and money from the West.

Yet the Hospitallers still remained an officially ecclesiastical institution. It was not until 1206, some sixty years after the establishment of the Knights Templar that the statutes were revised to provide for military brethren, at an assembly at the castle of Margat. Until that time only the presence of lay brothers was laid down in the rule and the Statutes of Margat are not an amendment to the original foundation, though they were regarded as almost equally binding. That the brothers of the Hospital themselves had fought the Saracens since the 1140s seems almost certain: but they did so unofficially, even if it was in defence of the Order's estates. The Marshal, who first appears in the 1160s, was probably responsible for the levying of mercenary troops at first, but had become a military commander by the Egyptian expedition of 1168. At Margat, this situation was embodied as part of the Order's institution, and a military force which had grown up haphazardly, partly as a practical measure, partly at the behest of the barons who had wearied of border warfare, and party at least in emulation of the Templars, at last received recognition. The previous existence of the Temple meant that its rules were bound to be based in large measure on theirs; and there were the same restrictions as to entry, that a man must be qualified for secular knighthood before entering the Order. The qualification, however, was not formally set out until 1262, when the test of legitimate noble birth appears. Those who could not join as knights were admitted as sergeants, though they could very occasionally attain knighthood later; and no distinction of dress was made between them and the knights, despite attempts to introduce different garments after the Templar practice.

The military organisation of the Hospital rapidly overtook its charitable counterpart in prestige. By the end of the thirteenth century all the important offices were in the hands of the knights, and the Marshal ranked second only to the Master in authority. He was concerned as much with supply as organisation, and the difficulties of obtaining equipment and especially horses meant that stringent rules had to be laid down. In this the strict discipline of the order was of great assistance, and increased the superiority of the Hospitallers as troops over their secular brethren. We know little about the details of the military discipline imposed, and it is to the rule of the Templars that we must turn for a picture of life within the Orders. For the Hospitallers, only scraps survive to give us a glimpse of what went on; and it does not seem to have differed greatly from the Templar way of life. The address to the candidate who wished to enter the Order shows many of its characteristics:

> Good friend, you desire the company of the House and you are right in this, for many gentlemen earnestly request the reception of their children or their friends and are most joyful when they can place them in this order. And if you are willing to be in so excellent and so honourable a company and in so holy an Order as that of the Hospital, you are right in this. But if it is because you see us well clothed, riding on great chargers and having everything for our comfort, then you are misled, for when you would desire to eat, it will be necessary for you to fast, and when you would wish to fast, you will have to eat. And when you would desire to sleep, it will be necessary for you to keep watch, and when you would like to stand on watch, you will have to sleep. And you will be sent this side of the sea and beyond, into places which will not please you, and you will have to go there. It will be necessary for you therefore to abandon all your desires to fulfil those of another and to endure other hardships in the Order, more than I can describe to you.[14]

The total establishment of the Hospitallers in Palestine remained small despite their great influence. Recent estimates put the figure as low as three hundred in all, since when Hospitaller casualties after a battle were counted these very often included knights serving for pay or feudal service. To lose forty knights, as at Tripoli in 1289, meant that recruits had to be found from the West as a matter of urgency. Hence the exceptional power of the Order stemmed less from its resources of men within its own ranks, than from its military and financial organising ability, and its knowledge of the country. Yet it was not in command of unlimited resources, and many of the hesitations and political errors which mar its record are due to a realisation of the weakness of the Order in relation to the task with which it found itself entrusted. Despite its wide estates in Europe, it was always difficult not only to raise enough surplus cash for Palestine but also to arrange for its safe and rapid transport: the tangible result of an urgent appeal to the prior of the Order in England or Spain would not reach the East for a year or more.

The lesson had to be learnt by experience. For the moment it was war to the death: no Templar was ever ransomed, and Templar and Hospitaller prisoners were often killed by their captors. Losses could be enormous: about four hundred knights were killed in one ambush in 1156. Though this includes mercenary and other troops, it must have

---

14   Riley-Smith, *Knights of St John*, 232; compare the Templar admission ceremony in *Rule of the Templars* 169, on which this is clearly based.

seriously reduced the actual Templar establishment of about five hundred knights. Replacement was slow, since the news took between two and six months to reach Europe, and the recruits had then to be found and equipped. As with financial appeals, it might take a year or more to restore even part of the number.

As the Orders grew more powerful their interests did not always coincide with those of the kingdom of Jerusalem as a whole. The Frankish settlement was small compared with the great powers of the East: it could only hope to survive by presenting a united front and by exploiting the frequent dissensions among the Muslims to the utmost. Instead, the various parties within the kingdom tended to pursue their own ends, and even to bring in Muslim help if they could see a way of doing so. And in addition to the king, the barons, and the Church within the state, the Orders also had to reckon with outside factors, frequent crusades and papal interventions.

The weakness of the royal power in Outremer arose partly from the constitution, which did not provide sufficient authority over unruly barons, but in the main it was the character of the kings themselves that destroyed any hope of leadership from that quarter. The bravest and most able of the rulers, Baldwin IV, was a leper; and none of the succeeding kings was as capable as Baldwin I, the founder of the kingdom. Indeed, it is not difficult to see the history of Outremer as a steady decline from the strength of the state that he ruled. The problem was complicated by a lack of direct descendants, with all the multiplicity of claimants and intrigues for the throne that this entailed. The Orders never played a very respectable part in such affairs. They were too independent to welcome strong rule wholeheartedly: and in any case the Hospitallers were supporters of royal authority, the Templars advocating a strong barony instead, even when they were not each trying to secure the accession of a favoured candidate. As the Orders' power increased, it became more and more difficult for the kings to challenge their authority when they misused it. Even by 1170, the Templars often acted independently of royal officers, and opposed royal foreign policy. They argued fiercely against an Egyptian expedition in 1168, and four years later resisted a royal treaty with the Assassin sect, whose fanatical members were more concerned with the internal politics of Islam than with the Christians. This potentially valuable alliance was prevented when the Templars ambushed and killed the Assassin ambassadors, perhaps because the treaty would have meant the loss of the tribute which the Assassins had paid to the Templars. Nor would the Grand Master surrender the culprits to the king, claiming that he was responsible to the Pope alone.

This independence of action was accentuated by the rivalry between the two Orders. It is rare to find Templars and Hospitallers agreeing on important issues, despite much valuable co-operation at lesser levels, and it sometimes seems as though one Order's approval of a project meant that the other was bound to oppose it. Only in the difficult days after Saladin's invasion and almost complete conquest of the kingdom in 1195 did they work together in the political field: in 1219, on the Fifth Crusade, both Masters opposed the offer of the return of a defenceless Jerusalem as being a military burden which they could not shoulder, and in 1229 they both boycotted Frederick II when he won back Jerusalem, supporting the papal sentence of excommunication which had been pronounced on him for his intolerable delays in setting out on crusade. But these cases were still to prove exceptions.

At worst, the Orders' independence of action became mere rashness and pride in their own power. Although their overall military policy was usually conservative, and prudent, the Templars could be as heedless of consequences as their wilder baronial allies, like Reynald of Chatillon, whose persistent breach of truces became a byword. What Reynald did for gain, men like Gerard of Ridfort did for glory. As early as 1153, Templar indiscipline at the siege of Ascalon had nearly brought about the failure of the entire operation; a fortunate chance (the burning of a siege-machine by the defenders) caused a breach in the section of the wall opposite the Templar encampment. William of Tyre reported that they were so determined to have the glory of the victory that a band of forty men entered the city while others prevented the rest of the army from following. The result, according to William, was a massacre of the knights within the walls which almost caused the abandonment of the siege. The story is somewhat undermined by the fact that the town fell at the next assault a week later. Gerard de Ridfort's activities in 1187 as Grand Master of the Templars were far more serious in their consequences. At a skirmish at the springs of Cresson, he attacked a vastly superior Muslim force, although warned of its size, with a mere handful of knights; only three, including Gerard, survived this disaster. Since the four hundred or so who fell were all members or auxiliaries of the Order, this was a serious blow to its strength; but when Gerard tried to seek revenge in 1189, an overwhelming disaster ensued. Saladin had assembled a vast army, and King Guy was persuaded not to risk battle. Gerard, however, crept to his tent at night, and obtained the order to advance. The defeat at the battle of Hattin that ensued led to the fall of Jerusalem, and indeed of the whole kingdom save only the fortress at Tyre. The lesson was learnt, albeit late, and under the new Grand Master, Robert du Sablé, caution prevailed: we find him, together with the Hospitaller Master, counselling that saddest of all retreats, the withdrawal from Jerusalem in 1191 when Richard Coeur de Lion's generalship had brought the Third Crusade so near its goal. Richard seems to have relied heavily on the Templars, and the eyewitness account of his expedition, the *Journey of the Pilgrims and Deeds of King Richard*, may be the work of an English Templar.

In the following decades, the Templars grew ever more cautious in the eyes of crusaders newly arrived from the west. But their assessment of the situation was a long-term one, while the crusaders wanted instant results. In the first decade of the thirteenth century, for instance, their chief preoccupation was to retrieve the great fortress at Baghras, north of Antioch. When the Fifth Crusade invaded Egypt, the Master of the Temple cautioned Pelagius, the Papal legate in command of the expedition, against the fatal attempt to march on Cairo. But one of the problems was the direct obedience which they owed to the pope, as a result of their exemption form all other ecclesiastical control. Not only did this arouse the hostility of other clergy, but it led to accusations of pride and avarice; it was said that they misused their privileges to offer church burial to excommunicates for a few pence. However, when the greatest of all excommunicates, Frederick II, arrived in Palestine in 1228, letters from the pope to the Masters of both the Orders prevented them from taking the politically wisest course and allying the Orders with the Emperor. As a result, the treaty by which Jerusalem was regained specifically forbade the rearming of the castles of the Hospitallers and Templars. The Templars were accused of plotting to kill the Emperor, and in retaliation Frederick II confiscated their Italian property. Imperial troops under Richard Filangieri remained in Palestine for another decade, and the result was continuing dissension over strategy against the Muslims. After 1240, the two Orders ceased to co-operate politically, the Templars favouring an alliance with the sultan of Damascus, while the Hospitallers argued for a league with Egypt. The Templars won the day, and the alliance with Damascus was confirmed; but the Egyptians invoked the aid of the Turks who lived to the north of Antioch. It was these Khorizmen Turks who seized Jerusalem in 1244, and helped the Egyptians to overwhelm the Frankish army at La Forbie in October of that year, with the loss of most of the knights of both Orders and the Grand Master of the Temple. Five years later, a quarrel between Robert, count of Artois, and the Templars at Mansourah on the Sixth Crusade led to renewed disaster for the Order, with the loss of most of its newly-recruited knights.

The appearance in 1260 on the borders of Palestine of the Mongol hordes who had destroyed or captured the great Moslem cities of the Middle East aroused fears that they would overwhelm the Frankish state as well, despite rumours of their impending conversion to Christianity. Their defeat by an Egyptian army proved a hollow blessing for Outremer, for it was the Egyptians under sultan Baybars who gradually eroded the kingdom from 1265 onward. In the dying days of the kingdom, the fighting spirit of the Orders showed to best advantage, in the series of desperate resistances put up by isolated garrison against the Egyptians' vastly superior forces in the 1270s and 1280s.

Neither of the Orders found it easy to cooperate with crusaders coming from the west. There were good reasons for this. The Orders were deeply involved in the affairs of Outremer, which was their home, and did not welcome the inexpert counsel of eager crusaders, who hoped to solve in a year the problems which the Orders had wrestled with for decades. When the crusaders were safely home, it was they who would be left with the crusade's legacy of untenable fortresses won or patiently earned goodwill squandered. It was such long term views that accounted for their discouraging attitude towards the terms proposed on the Fifth Crusade which would have given them a Jerusalem which they could not defend. Besides this, the inevitable arguments over leadership emerged in the motley armies which set out on campaign: while the Orders were ready to provide generous contingents, they were also reluctant to obey any commanders who were newly arrived from the west. And knights who had crossed the Mediterranean to fight the infidel were usually reluctant to listen to diplomatic arguments; they had come to destroy Islam with the sword, and all too often only bitter experience taught them what the Orders already knew: that Outremer was merely a small, relatively weak, state trying to survive among powerful neighbours, and that diplomacy was frequently the only possible weapon. The Franks had at all costs to prevent the Muslim princes from uniting: and military operations always tended to drive their opponents into alliances. Furthermore, the Orders found difficulty in organising both their defensive garrisons, which were essential to protect the country if a campaign was going badly, and a field army to mount the attack. Even for a small raid in 1187, the Templars had to empty one castle of its entire garrison to find enough troops. They came to rely on knights serving the Order for a fixed term and on turcopoles, lightly armed local troops, who were naturally less reliable under difficult conditions, or on the intermittent presence of crusading armies from the west, and this tendency merely increased their defensive, cautious attitude.

The Orders had begun to develop good relations with the Muslims as early as the 1140s, and cultural interchanges became frequent. The Arab historian Ousama ibn Mounkidh relates that Franks and Saracens used to travel together, telling each other stories to while away the journey. Again, despite the apparent insensitivity of Templar politics at the time, the story of his visit to Jerusalem in 1144 shows that as individuals they respected the Muslims. Ibn Mounkidh made friends with the Templars and was allowed to pray to Allah in a church which had once been a mosque, but now belonged to the Order. One day, as he was in the middle of his prayers, facing south towards Mecca, a Frankish knight seized him and faced him to the east saying 'That's the way you should pray'.[15] The Templars expelled the knight from the church, but he crept in again, and repeated his action. The Templars dealt with him and apologised to ibn Mounkidh, saying that the offender had only just arrived in Palestine and had never seen anyone pray towards Mecca before. Similarly, the friendly exchanges between Richard I and Saladin encouraged an attitude of tolerance, though it was by no means an unquestioning one: the frequency with which the Orders had broken their truces had led Saladin, after the battle of Hattin, to have all the Templar and Hospitaller prisoners

---

15   Usamah ibn-Munqidh, *An Arab-Syrian Gentleman and Warrior in the Period of the Crusades*, tr. Philip K.Hitti (New York 1929) 164.

executed by their Muslim equivalents, the sufis. The better relations between the two religions in the early thirteenth century were also due to the lack of open warfare in Palestine during this period: the crusades centred on Egypt, while the Orders carried out a quiet reconstruction of their strength in Palestine.

By the period of the Sixth Crusade (1248 – 54), Outremer had become a land with little real existence as a secular state. The continuing Muslim successes had fallen heaviest on the feudal lords, who could ill afford to keep their castles on a permanent war footing, and who therefore sold them to the Orders. And the kingdom itself was in no better shape. Dominated by the Orders and their castles, its feudal and economic structure was not capable of sustaining the immense costs of warfare, whether defensive or offensive. The previous decades had seen the great consolidation of Templar and Hospitaller castles. Castle Pilgrim at Athlit was built on the southern frontier of the kingdom to guard the coast road. Safed and Tortosa were rebuilt in the following decades. The style of Templar military architecture is now recognised to be basically that of western Europe, but it was influenced by the requirements of the country and by Byzantine fortresses. A European castle was also a residence: a Templar castle was closer to a barracks, and concessions to gracious living were few and far between. But this is to forget the other side of the coin, the castles as part of a protective network, whether for pilgrims or for those working in the countryside around; their very presence and impregnability were a deterrent in themselves.

However unsubtle such castles were, they were usually very capable of resisting sieges. In 1220 Athlit was under attack for six months, and in 1265 it resisted sultan Baybars; it was only surrendered in 1291 because, as at Tortosa, there were insufficient men to garrison it until help could be sent. The Hospitallers' great edifices at Margat and Crac des Chevaliers rivalled anything that the Templars produced: Crac is the most imposing of the ruins of the castles of the Orders, and its vast mass, built from 1144 onwards in concentric form, was only taken in 1272 when the garrison, once a constant menace to the Muslims of the neighbourhood, was much reduced by lack of money and men.

For as the crusading spirit waned in the West, so the Orders themselves had begun to decline in morale. The endless appeals which grew annually larger as the resources available from Outremer itself diminished, were viewed with increasing hostility by the Templars and Hospitallers in Europe. The Orders' wealth and power had led them to become organisations with very different interests from those originally intended. There was a danger of attracting administrators into the Order, whose skill in financial matters was balanced by a lack of zeal for the Orders' religious and military objectives. Furthermore, it was impossible, even with the immense resources at the Orders' disposal, to supply men and provisions for an entire kingdom from across the Mediterranean; and as the knights were driven back into their garrisons, this was virtually the task that faced the Orders in Palestine in the third quarter of the thirteenth century.

Nor did other circumstances improve the situation. Even as late as 1282, when Egyptian pressure on the kingdom was already intense, the Templars were involved in civil war with Bohemond of Tripoli (a quarrel which only ended when the discontented vassal who had incited the war was captured and buried up to his neck in sand). The crown itself was disputed between Charles of Anjou and Hugh of Lusignan. With the disappearance of Charles' power in 1282 after the 'Sicilian Vespers' and Hugh's death in 1284, the last hope of effective leadership by a strong king vanished. The Muslim respect for the Franks as soldiers had long since been tempered by scorn for their generalship and amazement at their obstinacy in quarrelling among themselves; and the campaigns against Palestine were renewed in earnest until, with the fall of Tripoli in 1289, Acre was the only remaining Frankish city. Two years later, Acre in turn was besieged, and despite an heroic resistance of eight weeks, was taken by a well-equipped Egyptian army. The Egyptians, having once realised their complete military dominance, had decided that there was no need to tolerate the existence of Christian fortresses; and the Orders proved powerless against them.

So ended the kingdom of Jerusalem, a state whose own internal contradictions had almost predetermined its doom. Henceforward both the Orders and the Crusaders were to dream of a glorious return; but the fire of zeal which had inspired the men of the First Crusade to their goal was burning low, and the lustre that had so long surrounded the name of Templar and Hospitaller proved to be much tarnished. The Church, scarcely able to rule its own affairs in Europe, offered precious little hope of being able to rebuild the Eastern kingdom which its fervour had once created. The ideal of a Christian Jerusalem won by the sword endured only as a vision in zealous minds; and the Orders found that a more worldly fate awaited them.

13

The Templars and Hospitallers in Exile

AT THE END of 1306, fifteen years after the loss of Acre, the pope ordered the
Masters of the Temple and the Hospital to produce reports on a proposal for
a union of the two Orders and for a new crusade. The Master of the Hospital, Jacques
de Molay, in a rather naïve reply, opposed the scheme of union; among his reasons
were that the rivalry between the two Orders had been one of the chief spurs to glory,
and that the new Order would be far too powerful! His objections to the new crusade,
which was to be mounted from Armenia and Cyprus, were more sensible; but the pope
does not seem to have been in a mood for such uncooperative answers.

De Molay was probably unaware that the tide of popular feeling was beginning to run
against the Templars. He had been in the east for most of his career, and the criticisms
levelled against the Orders for losing the Holy Land and for lack of action since then may
not have reached him. Since their arrival in Cyprus, the Templars had done little more than
mount some unsuccessful raids on the Syrian and Egyptian coasts. The abuses of Templar
privileges of exemption from royal justice, already a problem when he left for the east, had
grown worse; and those who had envied for many years the Order's vast possessions had
new reasons for attacking it, now that it seemed to have lost its purpose. Counter-proposals
were needed, not refusals, especially since rumours that the Order had secular political
ambitions in the west were circulating.[1]

The Temple was clearly vulnerable in such an atmosphere; but how and why
Philip the Fair of France came to be the leader of the attack on the Order has never
been satisfactorily explained. Greed for the Order's lands and money seems to have
been uppermost; he needed large sums to finance his wars with England and Flanders,
and to pay off debts incurred in the abortive French 'crusade' of 1284-5 against Aragon.
But fear of Templar ambitions within France, dislike of everything combining
ecclesiastical and secular power, his own enthusiasm for a combined Order under his

[1]   The best account of the end of the Order of the Temple is Malcolm Barber, *The Trial of the Templars*
(Cambridge and New York 1978).

leadership, and even genuine belief in the charges against them, have also been advanced as reasons. The financial and political circumstances seem to provide the best explanation, but it is clear that he hoped for some settlement with the pope before the Order was utterly destroyed.

What is certain is that the specific charges were made against the Templars first appear in full in the royal warrants for their arrest in 1307, attributed simply to 'persons worthy in the faith'. The crimes of which the Templars were accused centred round the admission ceremony, which, like all other chapters of the Order, as held in secret. The candidate was said to have to make a triple denial of Christ, spit three times on a crucifix, and give a triple kiss to the officer who admitted him, at the base of the spine, on the stomach, and on the mouth. He was also told that knights must not refuse their bodies to each other; and idols were produced and worshipped at this and other ceremonies. The pope, Clement V, a creature of Philip's but not entirely in the latter's power, was reputedly informed of the charges in 1305, though this seems unlikely. It was not until immediately after de Molay's arrival from the east to discuss the proposed union of the two Orders that the charges were pressed by Philip, in April and May 1307, when he met the pope at Poitiers. Clement saw that something must be done, and on 24 August agreed to hold an inquiry.

Philip had other ideas. Either the Templars had got wind of his intentions, and were preparing to leave France, or the speed at which the pope acted was not swift enough. On 14 September he sent sealed instructions for the seizure of all members of the Order and their property throughout France, to be carried out on 13 October. The coup was carried out with incredible efficiency: only thirteen Templars seem to have escaped. The rest were thrown into prison and charged with the crimes already listed. In the confusion and under the threats of the royal officers all save three admitted them in some degree including de Molay himself, who repeated his admission before the University of Paris on 25 October. The pope remonstrated with Philip for his hasty action; but, because of the admissions and de Molay's letter recommending the other Templars to confess, he could not intervene on the Order's behalf, and on 22 November issued a bull commanding the other Christian princes to arrest the Templars.

If Philip thought he had gained his victory already, he was to be sadly disillusioned. He had made careful preparations, gathering testimony from spies, informers and discontented members of the Order, to ensure that the trial was damning; but he had not reckoned with the resilience of both pope and Order. Philip could not refuse to hand over the prisoners to the papal delegates, and once this was done, de Molay retracted his confession, and advised the other Templars to follow him. The pope realised that Philip's clearcut case was not all that it might seem, and reserved the matter for his own judgment.

This put a very different complexion on the situation. It was most unlikely that more than a reprimand would be issued if Philip allowed the pope to have his way, so the king moved to propaganda. His brilliant publicist, Pierre Dubois, produced pamphlets on de Molay's confession and drafted an appeal from the people of France, which was approved by an assembly in the spring of 1308. Armed with these, negotiations were opened with the pope as to the best method of procedure. Philip gained his point: early in July, Clement delegated the conduct of the trial to the bishop in each diocese, and followed this with the setting up of commissions to investigate the conduct of the Order as a body. The work began in 1309, and the Templars had meanwhile prepared their defence, which rested mainly on two points. All the original evidence had been given by renegades, who could not be trusted, and any confessions made in prison had been extracted under duress. None of the tribunals outside France found sufficient reason for condemnation, but in France, the situation was drastically altered by the presence of Philip's minions. Seeing that the Templars were not going to co-operate, the archbishop of Sens declared all the witnesses who appeared before the tribunal and withdrew their confessions to be relapsed heretics, and had them burnt at the stake.

Under this threat, very few knights were prepared to come forward in the Order's defence, though Aimery de Villiers-le-Duc, the day after he had seen fifty-four of his fellow-knights burnt to death, came before the commissioners in terror of his life, and denied all the charges, saying that the confessions were extracted under torture; 'but he begged and adjured the Commissioners and notaries present not to reveal what he had said to the King's men or his wardens, because he feared a like fate'.[2]

When in June 1311 the commission finished its work in France, it had heard a very small number of witnesses, none openly denying the charges. Yet the Order still had hopes that all was not lost; at the papal council at Vienne in October it was agreed that the knights should be allowed to put forward their defence, and large numbers of Templars gathered for this purpose. It was only by diplomacy that Philip finally gained part of his object in April 1312. The Order was suppressed and its wealth was to go to the Hospitallers. In 1313 the four chief officers of the Temple held at Paris were condemned to perpetual imprisonment; de Molay and another protested, and the King's council sentenced them to the stake.

Such, in its bare outline, was the incredible web of intrigue, double-dealing and mystery that surrounded the end of the great Order. Philip had had a more difficult passage than he might have hoped, but the pope, whether his creature or not, was fully conscious of his position, and of the fact that the Templars, corrupt or otherwise, were

2   Georges Lizerand, *Le dossier de l'affaire des Templiers* (Paris 1923) 188.

a considerable pillar of the Church. Hence Philip had to use pressure to avoid a light sentence and secure the suppression as opposed to admonishment of the Order. He is believed to have dropped his demand for a denunciation of his dead arch-enemy Boniface VIII, who had condemned his high-handed dealings with the Church, in return for the suppression of the Templars, and he certainly had armed followers present during the last stages of the negotiations. Even though Clement V could never have condemned a completely blameless Order, his reasons for the suppression were by his own admission inadequate for a condemnation by the normal course of justice: 'Since we cannot do it by law in the light of the inquisition already held, we have effected it by way of a provision or Apostolic order, a sanction against which there is no appeal and which is perpetually valid.'[3]

The problem of guilt or innocence remains. The confessions can be set aside as inconclusive. They were made after the charges were known, and the torturers asked leading questions. Evidence from countries outside France is totally inconsistent, consisting chiefly of hearsay and rumour. In England, where Edward II had no special love for the Templars, and was delighted to have their estates – the Hospitallers had great difficulty in obtaining anything – it is surprising that only three fugitives from the Order had any accusations to make. All of them spoke of the spitting on the cross and renunciation of Christ. In Italy some confessions were obtained. But where the Order still had work to do, the charges were completely denied. In Cyprus all the brethren defended the Order, and lay witnesses gave evidence of their courage and honesty. In Spain there was armed resistance, and the knights were eventually acquitted at Tarragona in 1312.

The real truth seems to be that the Order was not so much innocent or guilty, but at a low ebb in its fortunes; above all, its morale was low, and it was not especially popular. The loss of the Holy Land had been a shattering blow, and decisive leadership was badly needed. The élite of the Order had been lost; de Molay was not equal to the situation, and never showed any signs of being equal to the responsibilities of the mastership. The brothers were idle; they could not collect funds for an expedition until a new crusade was preached, and the sense of purpose essential to the Order was lacking. Nor did the decline date merely from the fall of Acre; disillusionment with crusading had been evident since the failure of St Louis' crusade in Egypt. The quality of the recruits was lower during the thirteenth century; too many of the members joined it for the security it offered, especially in its richest province, France, with little intention of going to Palestine if they could avoid it. When such men were faced with the terrors of the Inquisition, it is hardly surprising that they failed to put up a united resistance

3   *Magnum bullarium Romanum*, ed. L.Cherubini et. al. (Luxembourg 1727) I, 187.

in the absence of leaders, and union and firm denial were the only hope for the Order against Philip's propagandists.

For propaganda is almost certainly the key to the nature of the charges against the Templars. The renunciation of Christ and spitting on the Cross may have crept into the admission ceremony as symbols of absolute obedience to the Order, but the bulk of the charges were drawn by Philip's chief adviser, Guillaume de Nogaret, and his assistants from the standard cases of heresy of the last two or three centuries. Some of the details can be traced back to the late eleventh century, while the charges made against a group of German heretics in 1233 by pope Gregory IX are very similar to those used against the Templars. De Nogaret used this technique of defamatory propaganda based on heresy against other enemies of his master, and had always been successful. Indeed, the case of the Templars was the only one in which he failed to obtain a final verdict of guilty, because Clement avoided the issue by suppressing the Order. In the face of de Nogaret's record, it would be easy to assume that the Templars were entirely innocent: but it is also possible that the French court had learnt of some real heresy among the Templars and was merely pressing home its advantage by using the accepted descriptions of heretical practice. The final verdict must be that the Order was probably innocent of the main charges, even if there had been occasional irregularities.

That the chief problem in the Order was the knight who had gained admittance purely for the sake of the privileges it offered is borne out by the ceremony of admission. The questions asked of the knight were largely to see that there was no impediment to his joining, such as marriage, debt or chronic illness, illegitimate birth, or membership of the clergy. The greater part of the proceedings were taken up with repeated warnings as to the hardship of life in the Order, and the need for absolute obedience; and the candidate could withdraw after hearing of these discomforts.[4] In addition to the triple vow, he swore to submit to the Rule, to help in the conquest of the Holy Land, never to desert the Order without permission, and never to suffer injustice to be done to a Christian. There was no need to set out the greatness of the Order and the glory of being a member; the emphasis was entirely on the duties and responsibilities, never on the rewards.

For the Order offered many rewards. The Templar was respected and trusted wherever he went; and within its organisation every kind of talent could find a satisfying outlet; the warrior in crusades, the financier in its banking operations, the administrator in the care of its European possessions, the diplomat in its international dealings. The Order offered security in an insecure world; the knights might not know luxury, but

---

4   *Rule of the Templars*, 168-174; compare the Hospitaller admission ritual quoted above.

they would never starve, and, until the last days, they were immune from the whims of secular and ecclesiastical princes alike. As time went on, the laws regarding poverty fell into neglect, and an ambitious knight might hope for rich apparel and costly horses as well; of the other delights of secular knighthood, tournaments and hunting, he would learn little, for tournaments were strictly forbidden to the Orders, and the Templars were only allowed to hunt lions.

The wealth of the Order was the cause of much jealousy. Leaving aside the question of how far the rule of poverty was disregarded by the individual brothers, the size of the Templar estates throughout Europe gave rise to unfavourable comment. They were particularly strong in France and in Aragon; the lands in the latter had come to them in settlement of their claim to the succession to the kingdom in 1141. Their total value and extent has not yet been properly studied; all we know for certain is that the largest single landowner in Europe was the Church, and that the two Orders followed it. Gifts which had once flowed to it for pious reasons began in later years to come for other motives. The secular power of the Temple was considerable, and bribes to obtain its support grew in frequency. We can see the changing position of the Order in its relations with the Plantagenet dynasty. Fulk of Anjou had given the knights at Jerusalem £30 a year as a charitable act towards the new foundation. His grandson, Henry II, also made them large gifts, but in return he obtained the release of two castles which they held in custody as the dowry of his daughter-in-law, and he made extensive use of the services of two leading English Templars, Richard of Hastings and Tostes de Saint-Omer, as diplomats and royal officials. John, fifty years later, attempted to enlist the Order's support in his purely secular struggle with his barons. The Order's treasuries benefited in each case, but its ideals were becoming perverted.

In the disposal of its wealth, the same change of attitude appeared. The object of the great network of Temple preceptories throughout Europe was to provide men and money for the east. As the war against the infidel went from disaster to disaster, many of the Western officers began to regard money sent out to Palestine as a waste of resources better employed in consolidating the power of the Temple in the West, and hence increasing their own standing. The practice of maintaining retinues spread, and the laws about clothing being of a simple nature were increasingly ignored; the resistance to the requests of the Visitors-General, who were the Master's deputies responsible for the transfer of men and money to the east, grew stronger in proportion. Appeals for reinforcements were more and more frequent in the last years of the Frankish rule in Palestine, and complaints about the lack of response equally numerous; the commanders in the field said that they could only raise three hundred knights where they used to send out a thousand. The castle at Tortosa alone had a garrison of 1,700 in normal times, increased to 2,200 in war, and all of them were supported at the Temple's expense. When the initial cost of the building works is added (about twenty times the annual expenses) and the whole figure is multiplied for the dozen major fortresses in Palestine, some idea of the huge costs involved emerges.

A further reason for the reluctance to send out money to the Order in the east was the Order's use of these funds to finance its banking operations.[5] From a very early date, the Order had lent money. Louis VII in 1148 borrowed from them when he ran into difficulties on the Second Crusade. These simple advances developed into a banking network unrivalled in Europe. Sums could be transferred by payment at one Temple preceptory and the issue of a letter authorising withdrawal elsewhere. Although there was a good deal of movement of bullion, and the Order had to send its own money physically to the east, an ordinary pilgrim or crusader could arrange for payments to him during his visit to Palestine by a similar transfer. Nor, despite the theoretical prohibition on the lending of money on usury, did the Temple hesitate to charge interest. The transaction would often consist of the advance purchase of a certain rent for so many years, and such long-term finance, sometimes involving thousands of pounds, made heavy demands even on a treasury as well filled as that of the Templars. It might not merely seem a waste of money to send it to Palestine, where it invariably disappeared like water through a sieve, but it might also cause considerable embarrassment to the financial dealings of the Order.

The Templars specialised in medium-sized loans, up to about £5,000, and could not compete with the Lombard merchants who raised £20,000 for Philip IV's war against England in 1295. Typical Templar transactions are the the three loans totalling just under £3,000 made to king John in 1216.[6] Hence the withdrawal of large amounts to the east was all the more complicated, as it might involve the collection of numerous debts. The Orders were, however, experts in this, since they were on occasion charged with the collection of taxes; with the Hospitallers, they had gathered the 'Saladin tithe' in France and England in 1188 which helped to pay for the Third Crusade, and under Edward I they collected the capitation tax on the Jews, keeping the proceeds as a current account for the king to draw on. In Spain they levied the same type of tax on Jews and Muslims for their own benefit. In France, they actually became the administrators of the royal treasury, whose business was transacted at the Paris Temple itself. And the papacy used the financial and administrative expertise of the Order extensively in the thirteenth century.

If the activities of the Temple in this field are surprising and hardly in accord with the objects for which the Order was founded, they are an indication of the powerful organisation which had sprung from the original band of poor knights. The honesty with which their dealings were conducted does them nothing but credit. Had their

5   On the Templars as financiers, see Malcolm Barber, *The new knighthood*, 266-79.

6   Malcolm Barber, *The new knighthood*, 272.

skill in administration been allowed free rein in Palestine, the result might have been a state as strong as that of the Teutonic Knights in Prussia. But there were too many conflicting interests at work, and at moments the Templars can hardly be blamed for pursuing a self-interested course in the tangled thickets of Palestinian politics. Their real fault was to pursue self-interest too far; when a good leader appeared, they were reluctant to follow him, and when a reasonable truce was made, they were too ready to break it. This was partly the fault of the division of the Order into eastern and Western branches: the Master had to reside in Jerusalem, and tended to be a purely military leader, not a diplomat or statesman.

We no longer value moral zeal in the same way as our forebears of the twelfth and thirteenth centuries, and in conjunction with a delight in war it is gravely suspect to us. So any judgement on the Templars is bound to be coloured; against their failings we can only put qualities which are now devalued. They must stand accused of pride, avarice, and to a lesser degree love of luxury; of an independent pride in spiritual matters; and of misusing their privileges. Pride was the chief of their faults; their efforts in Palestine were largely ruined by it, and it led them to outright treachery at times.

By and large their record in the history of the Kingdom of Jerusalem was politically disastrous, diplomatically inexcusable and militarily incompetent. If they died gallantly for the faith, it was all too often the result of their own foolhardiness. In Europe they were perhaps more successful. They administered well and carefully, and their honesty was beyond doubt; if they were parasites on both Church and state, draining money better used for other ends, it was excused by the universal acceptance of the crusades as a worthy cause.

Yet there was something drastically wrong with an Order which could organise so brilliantly in Europe, and make such mistakes in the east. It was perhaps this: the knights in Palestine were too concerned with the righteousness of their cause, too convinced that one day God would give them the victory, to pursue a steady policy designed at recovering and retaining the Holy Places. They had the sense to recognise the immediate military needs and problems, to build castles and to reject offers they could not maintain, such as those made during the Fifth Crusade of the restoration of an indefensible Jerusalem. Against this, there was no consistency in their policy, no clear plan for uniting the ailing kingdom or dealing with its enemies in diplomacy. As a military Order, the Temple was all too prone to fight at the wrong moments, and all too scornful of peaceful pursuits: the Teutonic Knights were far greater as an organisation.

But here we come to the heart of the matter. The Templars are part of the ideals of chivalry; the Teutonic Knights belong to the history of mediaeval statesmanship and government. The bitter conclusion must be that religious chivalry, an admirable rallying cry in times of stress, was an unsure guide in times of peace; ultimately – as the history of the Templars shows – it was no principle by which to conduct the affairs of this world.

The history of the Hospitallers bears this out: instead of relying on their status as an Order, they imitated the Teutonic knights and became an independent state: and indeed they still enjoy that status, at least in name, today.[7] A year after the taking of Acre, the new headquarters of the Hospitallers was fixed in Cyprus. They had possessed estates there for some time, though these were small; but Cyprus was now the outpost of Christendom in the east. They had also had a fleet of some kind since the early thirteenth century, and a few brothers were in effect sea-captains in charge of a transport fleet. Therefore operations against the infidel could still continue, to harass the enemy while plans for reconquest were drawn up. The proportion of seamen to knights was also far too small, and from the beginning of their stay in Cyprus, knights had to be dissuaded or prevented from coming east, a complete reversal of the position while Palestine was still being defended.

Fortunately, the possibilities of a Hospitaller fleet in the eastern Mediterranean were quickly realised, and the first attempt to organise it was made within months of their arrival in Cyprus. However, the objectives against which it was to be used were far from clear, and no major operations ensued until the spring of 1306. Meanwhile although both the Hospitallers and Templars had both become involved in the internal politics of the island, they were not permitted to increase their holdings of land. King Henry of Cyprus, a descendant of the kings of Jerusalem, remembered the great power which gifts had brought to the Orders in Palestine, and was unwilling to see his own monarchy similarly threatened. Hence their attachment to Cyprus was by no means strong, either in terms of land or influence. The projects for reform which contributed to the downfall of the Templars had a very different effect on the Hospitallers' fortune. The Hospitallers did not make any official reply to the idea of uniting the two Orders, and their memorandum on the possibility of a new crusade, prepared by Fulk de Villaret, was much more detailed and constructive than that of the Templar Master. When a much smaller expedition was finally agreed with the pope at Poitiers in 1307, it was under the command of the Master of the Hospital, and the Hospitallers were never in danger of incurring papal disfavour, despite the fact that some of the charges levelled at the Templars could have applied equally to them. When the Templars were finally suppressed in 1312, the whole of their estates were supposed to fall to the Hospital except in Spain and Portugal, and even though much of the Templar lands and treasure found its way elsewhere, especially in England, an immense amount of wealth came to the Order at a point when, with the loss of Palestine, its resources were seriously depleted. Furthermore, from the papacy's point of view, the condemnation

7   For a survey of the later history of the Hospitallers, see Anthony Luttrell, 'The Hospitallers of Rhodes, Prospectives, Problems, Possibilities' in Fleckenstein, *Die geistliche Ritterorden*, pp .243-266, and Norman Housley, *The Later Crusades* , 214-233.

of the Templars made it imperative that the Hospitallers should succeed. And it was now the single crusading Order in the east, the projected union having in effect come about. Against this, the proceedings against the Templars had brought the whole idea of the military Orders into some disrepute, and the crusade of 1310 was a mere shadow of the grand design set out two years earlier. The Order's survival was no in question, but its power and influence certainly were.

The Hospitallers soon realised that conditions in Cyprus offered very little chance for the recovery of their military strength, due to the suspicion of both king and barons. In 1306, they drew up an agreement with a Genoese corsair for an attack on Rhodes, and energetically pursued the project until the crusade of 1310, albeit a small-scale expedition, enabled the Master, Fulk de Villaret, to complete the conquest and establish Rhodes as the Order's headquarters. From here it could play a part in the affairs of Constantinople, now once more in Greek hands, whose reconquest was usually advocated as the necessary preliminary to any successful crusade; and it would become a sovereign and independent state, like the Teutonic Knights in Prussia, free from the difficulties of domestic politics which had hampered or distracted it since its foundation. It could, and did, become a successful mercantile state, acting as intermediary in the trade between east and west. From here also it could pursue the Muslim corsairs who dominated the seas, and who were from now on its chief enemies. And finally, it could act as a bulwark against Turkish ambitions: for as the crusading ideal faded, the Order was increasingly seen as a defender of Christendom, rather than the protagonist of an aggressive campaign to regain Palestine.

However, freedom from secular sovereignty did not mean that the Order was able to pursue its ends without political problems. Much depended on the character of the Master, who was now more powerful than ever; an autocratic Master tended to arouse enmity within the Order, while a weaker character would be unable to wage war effectively on the Order's enemies. Furthermore, the whole fighting force of the Order was now concentrated in the island, apart from the occasional mainland garrison in Greece or Asia Minor; and while revolt had been difficult in the scattered fortresses of Outremer, here it was only too easy for the dissident knights to band together. As early as 1317, open rebellion had broken out against Fulk de Villaret's rule, and a rival Master was elected. De Villaret, despite his great work for the Order, was forced to resign in 1319.

The ultimate judge of the Order was the pope himself, and John XXII not only played a large part in finding a solution to the difficulties of 1317-19, but also summoned the great chapter-general at Montpellier in 1331 which provided a new framework for the Order. The knights of the various nations from which the Order drew its recruits had habitually grouped themselves by their place of origin; this division into 'langues' was now made official, and certain posts allocated to each langue in order to guarantee the balance of power. Again, Innocent VI played an active part in the Order's affairs, sending a commissioner (Jean Fernandez de Hérédia, later to become one of the Order's greatest masters) to Rhodes in 1354, and holding a reforming assembly at Avignon in 1356. The internal reforms were continued in 1368 and 1370, a sign that the problem of the Order's government was not an easy one. Nor were matters simplified by the Great Schism, which divided the papacy itself from 1378; the defeated party in an internal quarrel could always transfer its allegiance to the anti-pope, though the latter only succeeded in appointing a rival Master in the last years of the schism.

Throughout the later crusades, the Hospitallers largely contributed by sending small contingents of galleys from their island base. They were now a small naval power, aggressive and skilled seamen, who harried the Turkish shipping along the coast of Asia Minor; and all efforts to expand their territories beyond Rhodes had failed, apart from the footholds at Smyrna from 1344-1402, and at Halikarnassos thereafter. Hérédia had dreamt of a Hospitaller base in southern Greece, and the Hospitallers were active in Greek politics for many years. They leased the principality of Achaia from 1376-81, and in 1378 Hérédia himself was captured in an Albanian ambush while campaigning in Greece and had to be ransomed. In 1397, the Order bought Corinth and the Morea, and defended them against the Turks until 1404, when their ruler bought them back again; the Greek population had not taken kindly to Latin rule, though this seems to have been out of sentiment rather than because of any maladministration by the Hospitallers. Meanwhile, difficulties in Europe meant that it was all Hérédia could do to keep the Order intact, during the Great Schism it had been deprived of its revenues in Italy, Bohemia and England, which no longer came to Rhodes. Nonetheless, the Order remained powerful enough to attract the hostile attention of the Egyptian and Ottoman sultans in turn, as the other Christian powers in the east decayed or disappeared.

In 1435 the Sultan of Egypt, Baybars, having reduced Cyprus to the status of a vassal state, turned his attention to the Hospitallers, whose opposition was hindering his projects. The alarm at Rhodes was considerable, and reinforcements of five hundred knights were raised, leaving very few able-bodied men in the West. This energetic reaction gained the nights a breathing-space, but no more than that. The defeat of a squadron of Egyptian galleys in 1440 provoked a furious reaction from Baybars's successor. Four years later a huge Egyptian fleet appeared off Rhodes, and landed a very large Mamluk force. The island was overrun, and the town of Rhodes itself besieged for a month or more; it was only by a daring counter-attack that the Mamluk camp was overrun and the Egyptians put to flight.

When the usual problem of replenishing the treasury from the West arose, a new difficulty presented itself, in that the commanders there had become reluctant to part with the funds which provided them with an easy existence. It was a weakness which had prompted reproofs from the pope in 1343 and 1355, and in 1373 Gregory VII had instituted a census and survey of the Order; it revealed an ageing, largely non-military group in the west, whose ability to provide funds and soldiers for Rhodes was far from great. Had it not been for the vigorous action of de Lastic, the Master, the Order might well have found itself in the same disrepute as the Templars, one of whose chief crimes had been just this luxury. Novices who had taken preliminary vows and then used the order's good name to lead a vagrant life without proceeding further in its ranks had also caused scandal, and had had to be disciplined; and it was only a keen sense of the Order's good name among the council at Rhodes that enabled it to survive in a far from favourable period.

The Hospitallers had now become the chief obsession of the Muslim rulers of the eastern Mediterranean. In the following seventy years they were to prove the truth of Manuel II of Byzantium's praise: 'They are men for whom nothing is more important than what is conducive to good courage, warfare and a noble spirit. To them it is far better to die with glory than to offer their enemies the opportunity of exulting and inflicting wounds on the backs of men who are in retreat.'[8] With the fall of Constantinople in 1453, they were the one defiant outpost of Christianity in the east; and the Ottoman Sultan Muhammad II had demanded tribute from them, only to be met with a curt refusal. After a series of uneasy truces, in 1480 he equipped an even greater force than that of the Egyptians in 1444, under Palaeologos Pasha. Pierre d'Aubusson had spent the preceding years in consolidating the defences of Rhodes, and his prudence was rewarded. Two assaults, preceded by heavy bombardments, were beaten off by the defenders of the fort at the mouth of the harbour, and a third attack, launched against the main town, was thwarted only after a desperate struggle, in which the Hospitallers finally drove back the Turks in disorder and sacked their camp. The arrival of relief ships and the poor state of his troops led Palaeologos to abandon the siege after three months, on 18 August.

D'Aubusson used the experience of the siege to rebuilt the defences even more effectively, and news of the victory enhanced the Hospitallers' standing in the west. Peace treaties with both the Turks and Egypt lasted for more than a decade, and at the beginning of the sixteenth century, the Order's morale and prestige were high. Nonetheless, the Order's days in the east were numbered: fresh triumphs had brought the Turks deeper and deeper into Europe, and it was only their preoccupation in the Balkans that delayed the final settlement. In 1517 they conquered Egypt, removing the one power in the eastern Mediterranean which had rivalled their own. The minor

8   Quoted in Housley, *The Later Crusades*, 233.

successes of the Hospitaller fleet along the coast of Asia Minor only served as an irritant to the Turkish ambitions. The force that sailed for Rhodes in 1522 was the greatest yet mounted against the knights. With all the resources he could muster, Villiers de l'Isle Adam, the Master, had a bare five thousand men, of whom six hundred were members of the Order; nor could he expect help from the west, since Venice had signed a treaty with the Turks in December 1521. The siege was protracted. After the Turks had at first met with strong opposition, doubts about the enterprise began to be felt, and Sulayman the Magnificent himself was summoned to head his army. The undertaking was a formidable one: if the armies were unequal in terms of men, the Hospitallers had made of Rhodes one of the great fortresses of the world. The harbour, with its twin forts at the mouth and heavy ramparts on each side provided good shelter from any besieging army for relief vessels; and the artillery was as fine as any to be found in Europe.

It was on the landward side that the brunt of the attack fell, in particular on the sections of the wall defended by the knights of England and Aragon, where the natural defences were weakest. It nonetheless took two months of bombardment and mining to effect the first breach, which was successfully defended by the English knights on 4 September and again on 17 September. In the general assault on 24 September which followed these two reverses, the Turks were once more repulsed, though the Order's losses were by now heavy and no reinforcements had appeared, despite appeals throughout Europe for men. Sulayman dismissed Mustafa, his general until now, and replaced him by an engineer, Ahmad. A corresponding change in tactics followed. Mustafa, personally brave but not a brilliant strategist, preferred the idea of taking the city by storm. Ahmad changed these plans to a war of attrition, and in this he was helped by the complete failure of all the Order's attempt to break the blockade, despite the supplies which had been gathered at Messina. On 20 December de l'Isle Adam had no alternative but to surrender or face a general assault which he had no hope of resisting, and as Sulayman's terms were magnanimous, he chose to accept. The knights had been in Rhodes for over two centuries when they departed; and with them there disappeared the last impression of the crusading spirit on the eastern Mediterranean.

Once again, the Order was homeless, and it was typical of the changes that had come about since its last exile that its new home was acquired not by force of arms but by diplomacy. Charles V was prevailed upon to allow the knights to settle in Malta, an island whose strategic value he realised, but which his strained resources did not allow him to use properly. The bargain was not an easy one, since the knights were obliged to take on the defence of Tripoli in North Africa as well, a liability in that its position was far from simple to defend; they were almost glad to lose it when it was captured by the Turks in 1551. Besides this they had great difficulty in avoiding more than nominal allegiance to Spain.

With the move to a new theatre of operations, the Knights of Malta, as they were now generally called, were faced with new enemies, the corsairs of the Barbary coast centred on Algeria. These pirates, supported by their fellow-Muslims in the east, had seriously threatened all Mediterranean trade, and carried out daring raids into Italy and Spain in the manner of their predecessors of the tenth century. Once it became apparent that there was no question of reconquering Rhodes, the knights devoted all their energies and experience to turning Malta from a defenceless barren rock into a rich fortress to rival or even surpass their last home, with its splendid castle and the spacious halls of the various tongues. Their position in Europe was not improved by the loss of their English possessions in the wake of the Reformation, which even de l'Isle Adam's diplomatic skill had been unable to prevent, and the German branch, too, was much weakened. It was the French, Spanish and Italian knights who now contributed almost all the Order's members.

The knights had been seaborne for two centuries, but their methods changed to keep pace with the corsair menace. Though they had indeed harried merchant shipping before now, their chief method of attack had been to effect a landing on the mainland and pillage the nearest port. Now the knights formed small raiding fleets, between whom and the corsairs no quarter was asked or given, to attack the shipping of the Levant; and the names of their commanders were as feared in the east as those of the corsair captains in the West.

The measure of their success was a renewed determination on the part of Sulayman to destroy the Order's fortress. By 1565, both sides had made their preparations, Sulayman with a fleet of 180 vessels and perhaps 30,000 men: the Master, Jean de La Valette, with reinforcements from every commandery in Europe and a general appeal to the sovereigns of Europe, which, however, produced no more than a handful of troops from Spain and a papal gift of 10,000 crowns.

The Turkish fleet appeared at the end of May, and began by attacking the fort of St Elmo, guarding the entrance to Grand Harbour, with massive artillery. This quickly reduced its walls, and with the capture of an outpost, the fort became almost untenable. Despite the garrison's insistence that resistance was impossible, La Valette was obstinate that it should be held, and a general assault on 16 June was beaten off. However, the Turks succeeded in isolating the fort completely and took it on 23 June; the garrison was slaughtered, and their mutilated bodies were thrown into the harbour, to be washed ashore below the main fort. From now on, no mercy was shown on either side: in horrible reprisal, the Turkish prisoners in the main fort were executed, and their heads fired by cannon into the enemy camp.

As the Grand Master pointed out, 'poor, weak, insignificant St Elmo was able to withstand his [the Turk's] most powerful efforts for upwards of a month', and the enemy losses had been out of proportion to those of the knights. Yet the Turks now had the upper hand and, on 15 July, were able to deliver a general assault by land and sea, which, though beaten off, came dangerously near to success. A mine dug through solid rock to the north of the fortress resulted in a great breach on 7 August, at which only La Valette's personal courage averted disaster; and the Turks launched two more great assaults on 19 and 23 August, after prolonged bombardments, for the last of which every man capable of moving, even though wounded, had to be employed. The breaches had been repaired, however, and two months' work by the Turkish forces had produced little result. The besiegers in their camp were less at ease in the summer heat than the knights in their beleaguered but spacious quarters. By the time a belated relief force under the viceroy of Sicily appeared on 7 September, there was little spirit left in the Turkish army, and their arrival was the signal for a general retreat. The Order had lost 7,000 men to as many as 20,000 on the Turkish side; but Sulayman had failed to dislodge the knights for a second time.

No enemy as powerful as Sulayman was to reappear in the remaining years of the Order's existence to rouse it to heroic deeds again. Perhaps because of the weakening of Turkish naval power after Lepanto in 1571, and certainly because of the increasing Christian commercial interests in the east, the knights rarely found an opportunity worthy of their prowess. Their alliance with Venice despite the heroic opportunities it gave them in defence of Candia, in Crete, against the Turks in 1666-9, meant that commercial interests now carried great weight in their counsels.

Activity was essential to the morale of the Order; and though after three great sieges in less than a century the mentality that turned Valetta into a monumental impregnable fortress is understandable, this too proved more of a hindrance than a help to a revival in the Order's strength. The only recruits they were likely to attract were soldiers of fortune, eager for action; and instead they were offered a ceremonial, disciplined life of relative ease in a castle that was slowly becoming a palace. Added to this, the Spanish and French political rivalry of the seventeenth century was reflected within the Order, and incessant quarrels distracted the knights. Nor were they effective rulers of Malta or of themselves. The Maltese groaned under heavy taxes, and the knights grew lax in morals,[9] until the island was no more than a despotism in the worst eighteenth-century manner. It was no irony that the seizure of its estates during the French Revolution was to prove its deathblow. Deprived of their resources, divided among themselves, lacking strong leadership, the knights surrendered Malta to Napoleon after a siege lasting only two days. They had become part of the old political hierarchy, unable to find an outlet for their energy in a world which had long forgotten the ideals to which they still subscribed.

9   See Jan Potocki, *The Manuscript found at Saragossa*, tr. Ian Maclean (London 1995) pp.525-533 for a vivid fictional account; Potocki himself had served with the Order in the 1780s.

14

The Teutonic Knights

THE TEMPLARS and Hospitallers had had their roots in Jerusalem. Their life was geared to that of the kingdom of Jerusalem, and when the tide of Muslim conquest flowed back over the ruins of that state, their best hour was past. The Templars never found a new role: lords without dominion, they paid the price of political pride all too quickly. The Hospital became a minor but heroic Mediterranean power, able by skill in war and management to continue to defy the Muslim banners. Both Orders had aimed at great power, and their failure had been sealed by the loss of Jerusalem. The Order which was to achieve that goal was only formed after the Holy City had been finally lost, and was to become the strangest of the many strange governments of Europe: an Order of warrior-monks ruling a commercial empire with a rod of iron.

The beginnings of the story can be briefly told. During the Fourth Crusade, at the siege of Acre in 1190, German citizens had set up a small hospital to tend the wounded and sick. As the eight-month blockade dragged on, what had been a temporary relief became an institution to the crusading army. Towards the year's end, the leader of the German crusaders arranged that it should be subject to the rules of the Hospitallers. It was recognised by the Church as a small independent Order in 1191, and when Acre fell to the crusaders, it was given quarters within the walls. By 1196 it had several branches in the remaining Christian territories in the East, and gained its full status as an Order from Pope Celestine III in that year. It might well have remained a charitable Order but, given the time and place, it was hardly surprising that two years later the assembled leaders of a new German crusade took steps to transform it into an order of knights. This was done early in 1198, under the Templars' auspices; their rule was to be followed by the knights, priests and other brothers, while serving men and lay brothers were to remain under the Hospitallers' ordinances. Heinrich Walpoto, the first Master, was invested with a Templar mantle, and the first brothers were enrolled.

The times might favour the creation of a knightly order, but growth was another matter. The next decade saw steady but scarcely rapid development. Thirteen scattered houses in Palestine, Greece, Italy and Germany were as nothing beside the wealth of Temple and Hospital. Yet the Teutonic Order was fortunate in that its small size made it more flexible than its greater predecessors, and still more fortunate in finding a remarkable leader to guide that flexibility. Hermann von Salza was the greatest of all the Masters of the Orders, of whatever denomination; not in wealth or power, but in statesmanship and foresight. Largely on his own judgment, he shaped the new and fruitful path of the Teutonic knights, whose Master he became in 1210. Throughout Frederick II's quarrels with the Pope he seems to have retained the confidence of both sides; and in St Louis' ill-fated Egyptian crusade he was one of the few leaders to emerge with some credit. During his mastership, from about 1218 onwards, rich gifts began to fall to the Order's portion, and it was soon able to mount its own campaigns.

This was not of itself remarkable, as the older Orders had long been in a position to do this. But at the outset of von Salza's mastership, in 1211, the king of Hungary had sent for the brothers of the Teutonic Order to help him against the heathen of Burzenland. They had fought the campaign largely at their own expense, but when the object was achieved and the reward that they believed they had been promised was not forthcoming, they were not powerful enough to wrest it from him. Their eyes had turned to the pagans of Eastern Europe, however, and other lands could be found, for their leader and others among the brethren had seen here a new objective, fully in accordance with their statutes and likely to offer much richer prizes than the intrigues and disappointments of crusading in Palestine. A new crusade, against the pagans of the north, could justify the Order's existence, and it would win glory by making converts with the sword.

This method of conversion lay at the basis of the Spanish crusade, and was the *raison d'être* of the native Spanish Orders of knights. But in Spain the monarchy held a tight rein on the Orders, and gradually assumed direct control. In Prussia the secular arm had hardly ventured into the field, and the Emperor was in no position to assert his rights. Lip-service was paid to the imperial court when it suited the Order, but the very absence of real imperial control gave the Prussian crusade its peculiar features. The other acknowledged suzerain was the Pope, whose mandate was weak enough in such distant parts, and counted for little more than that of the Emperor. When the project was first mooted both Pope and Emperor hoped to control the impulse of the new crusade and reap the benefits; in the space between their ambition and their real power, the Order created its own state.

Conditions in Prussia and the regions between the Holy Roman Empire and the Orthodox communities of Holy Russia were very different from those in Palestine. The objective of warfare was conversion, not the physical recovery of the holy places, as in the east; and the missionaries and crusaders were backed up by the huge resources of the Christian world in the immediate hinterland. They were the vanguard of western Christendom in expansionist mood, not an outpost separated by half the Mediterranean from the nearest reinforcements. Yet the Church had found conversion by peaceful means well-nigh impossible. Three centuries of missionary activity, as well as a minor crusade in 1147, had preceded the papal bull of 1171, issued by Alexander III, which put fighting the northern pagans on the same footing as a pilgrimage to Jerusalem in terms of spiritual rewards, and effectively turned the ongoing efforts at conversion into a continuous crusade. It was not until the early thirteenth century that two bishops, Albert of Buxtehude and Christian of Prussia, took up the idea of the use of military power as a means of conversion. Albert of Buxtehude had gathered a group of knights to establish a Christian bridgehead in Livonia, the area we now call the Baltic States, which he succeeded in doing at Riga in about 1201. Some of the knights were persuaded to take religious vows, and to form an Order called 'Fratres militiae Christi' to defend the colony. Their cloaks were like those of the Templars, but they bore a red sword and cross on their left shoulder, and hence became known as the Brethren of the Sword. A similar group of knights was founded by bishop Christian; they were based in the fort at Dobrin, and had a star instead of a cross on their cloaks.

In both cases, these were little more than enlarged versions of the kind of confraternity that might be formed to defend a monastery. There were perhaps ten members in the first year, rising to fifty knights and a hundred serving brothers within two years. Most of them came from a small area in central Germany, and the Brethren of the Sword never built up the network of possessions and contacts in Germany and elsewhere that the great Orders relied upon for support in difficulty. Their resources were small, and largely drawn from the land they conquered. A military defeat was liable to mean not only crippling losses in terms of men, but also impoverishment because the source of revenue was lost. Within Livonia, however, they were the greatest power after the bishop, and after 1208 rarely owned less than one-third of the converted lands. The first decade was one of great success: they reached the eastern limits of their conquests, the edge of the Russian territories, very quickly, and their later fighting was largely concerned with the Lithuanians, except for the conquest of the island of Ösel in 1227. Their chief setbacks were the rebellions of 1212 in Latvia and of 1223 in Estonia, when one-third of the Order's members were killed in a concerted rising on 29 January.

Bishop Christian had also directly invoked the protection of crusaders for his converts, in 1217; and it seems that the missionary activities had aroused a heathen reaction. For the Prussians had proved the most obdurate of unbelievers and their resistance increased with each renewed effort to convert them. Recruits were sought in Poland and Germany and the first Prussian crusade took place in 1221. All it produced was a massive retaliation, and by 1224 Duke Conrad of Masovia was in negotiation with the Teutonic knights for help. Hermann von Salza, however, was not going to find himself betrayed again as in Hungary, and it was not until 1230 that the Order was ready to set out. The terms were harsh enough: the duke had to surrender all rights to Kulmerland, including his jurisdiction and patronage. But Hermann had acted wisely, for without a secure and undisputed base the Prussian campaign could not hope to succeed. On the basis of the earlier stages of the negotiations he had already obtained the necessary grant from the Emperor, embodied in the Golden Bull of Rimini of 1226, which made the Order politically independent, owing obedience only to the Emperor himself. In 1234 this was supplemented by a papal privilege which effectively removed the Order from the control of local bishops. The work could now begin.

The first castle on the Elbe had been built by envoys of the knights in 1228, at Vogelsang. This was the base for the first operations: the securing of Kulmerland, and the building of the first great fortresses of Thorn, Kulm and Marienwerder. These and the later strongholds that rose out of the heaths and pine forests on natural and artificial eminences made real the hold of the Order on the land; like islands above the flood, they endured against the tide of the Prussian counter-attacks, as the Orders in Palestine had held the desert from Crac and Banyas; but the latter had been confronted with an enemy equally capable of using fortifications. Remembering their experience in the East, even in the first years of easy success, the knights built well and often, a precaution that paid well in leaner years. The system was well adapted to dealing with an enemy numerically superior but not technically skilled: the knights could retire into their fastnesses and safely watch fire and sword go through the land. As long as their provisions were good, only the remotest and weakest posts fell to the enemy. By 1239, the year of Hermann von Salza's death, the knights had reached the coast, and the key fortress of Elbing between the Baltic and the Drausensee had been built.

Their real problems were internal feuds with the bishops of Riga and external quarrels with the Danes, who had sent missions to Estonia before the arrival of the Germans. It was even more difficult to keep out of secular politics in the northern lands than in Palestine: this was a sphere of influence in which several rulers, lay and ecclesiastic, had well-established claims. The question of the relationship between Bishop Albert and the Brethren of the Sword occupied the energies of both sides for twenty years, and that of their relationship to the papal legates was only settled on their union with the Teutonic Order. These were diplomatic problems, and the Brethren had no men of the stature of Hermann von Salza: indeed, their rivals almost always had the diplomatic advantage. A series of plans for the division of Livonia and the reduction of the Order's standing were only averted by renewed attacks from Russia or the Lithuanians, in which the Brethren showed how indispensable they were. But neither the Brethren nor the bishop could create a unitary state, and the conquered territories were fragmented in the usual feudal way, being held by natives, settlers and monasteries, and only occasionally directly administered by either of the central powers. In a land at peace this would have caused little stress; but where the loyalty of each native and the provision of proper armed service by each settler was vitally important, it increased the problems of defence enormously. Their opponents were reasonably well organised, capable of learning by imitation and copying captured siege-machines and of taking concerted and carefully planned action, as in the Estonian revolt of 1223. This made the division of power a double handicap. Only with the appearance of the papal legate in 1225 did the position begin to favour the Brethren. New bishoprics were created and endowed and the rights of the town of Riga were increased, at the expense of the bishop's position; and when the Brethren made a formal alliance with the townsmen in April 1226, they controlled two-thirds of Livonia.

But prosperity brought corruption. Over-exploitation of their lands and serfs and aggression against their neighbours began to give the Brethren a bad name, and a papal legate, Baldwin of Aulne, was sent to report. He recommended the abolition of the Brethren as an order, and the creation of a papal state instead, but his efforts to establish it by force failed. The Brethren made overtures to the Teutonic Knights for a merger, but a visit by representatives of the latter only led to a report that the Brethren 'were people who followed their own inclination, and did not keep their rule properly, and merely wanted to be given *carte blanche* and not have their conduct looked into unless they agreed to it.'[1]

Baldwin of Aulne, on his recall to Rome, laid a list of complaints before the pope, outlining their malpractices, their power, and in February 1236 the Brethren were tried. The pope found Baldwin partially justified, and condemned the Brethren to surrender two-fifths of their territory. This was a bitter blow to the Brethren, but before it could be implemented worse had befallen. A new crusading army had arrived in Riga in September 1236, and against the advice of Folkwin, the High Master, they and the Brethren had set out on an autumn campaign. Folkwin, knowing the country, had advised the newcomers to wait until winter, an unorthodox procedure in the rest of Europe, where campaigns were usually fought between April and October, but correct enough in the north, where the marshes were only passable in the grip of winter's ice. So when a Lithuanian army trapped the force on a marshy island near Saule in central Latvia, the cavalry could not be used, and about half the Order, including Folkwin, were killed.

The news did not reach the West until spring 1237. Baldwin's papal state had no chance of success in the face of this disaster, and the only practical solution, the

---

1   Eric Christiansen, *The Northern Crusades: the Baltic and the Catholic Frontier 1100-1525* (London 1980) 98

long-mooted union of the Brethren of the Sword with the Teutonic Order, was rapidly completed. The inheritance they brought with them was an equivocal one. On the one hand, there were the loyal lands in Latvia and Estonia, which brought in good revenues and were little trouble; on the other hand, the Teutonic Order was now inevitably faced with a collision with the Lithuanians, whose lands were bordered on three sides by theirs, and inherited old quarrels with the Danes, now firmly established at Reval in Estonia, and the Livonian bishops.

With the implementing of Gregory IX's bull of union of May 1237, the pattern of the Teutonic Order's activities was now set; but two major reverses in 1242 destroyed much of the earlier success and shattered dreams of empire for them. The lesser disaster was the defeat of the Livonian brethren at Lake Peipus in 1242 by the Russian prince Alexander Nevsky, which meant that the larger possibilities of a coastal empire to the north west were ruled out by the Russian preponderance there. All the Livonians' efforts now went into the consolidation of their rule and into joining with their Prussian counterparts by conquering the coast which lay to the south east. However, the knights in Prussia were in no case to make a reciprocal effort, for a greater cataclysm, a major rising of the Prussians, had razed almost all trace of their twelve years' work. Swantepolk of Pomerania, formerly an ally of the Order, had become their enemy in the course of a dispute over an inheritance. He had allied himself with the heathens in Prussia itself, and organised a concerted and general uprising against the Order. Hard-pressed months and years of heroism and rashness followed alternately, and each triumph was liable to have its counterpart in folly. This first uprising took seven years to suppress; and even then the intervention of Rome was needed before peace was made. The treaty which resulted, in 1249, established the legal basis of the state. We shall return to the implications of this later: its immediate effect was to leave the knights free for new campaigns to the east.

The obvious target for attack was now Samland, lying between Eastern Prussia and Livonia, on the coast. A great crusade in 1253 led to the foundation of Königsburg, and a succession of victories, both military and diplomatic, led to the total subjection of the east Baltic coastlands by 1260. But these wide lands were held by a mere handful of men, and a single major defeat in the field could undermine the whole tenuous structure. In a great campaign against the inhabitants of Samland in 1260, a chain of unlucky circumstances led to a massive slaughter of the knights at Durbe. The work of the previous decade soon evaporated. The Lithuanian king, Mindaugas, repudiated his allegiance, and the Prussians rose against their masters again, reducing many of the lesser castles. Only massive efforts from outside saved the Order. Urban IV issued twenty-two bulls calling for crusades between 1261 and 1264, and in 1272 the results began to be evident. By 1290 the last outposts of rebellion had been stilled, and the Order's lords enjoyed peace once more. The years of conquest had come to an end.

The following years were a period of consolidation. One important change came in 1309. The Order, though centred in Prussia, had retained its official headquarters in the East, and the High Masters of the Order as a whole had lived in Acre until the fall of that city in 1291. It was some time before the decision to move the headquarters to Prussia was made, for there was a reluctance to admit that a return to Palestine was unlikely: hence the first choice of Venice in the intervening years, before Marienburg was named as the residence of the High Master. In September 1309 he made his entry into the town. Here a stately gothic castle and church rose in subsequent years – eighteenth-century engravings indicate something of its former magnificence – whose ruins were rebuilt by Hitler and razed again in the fighting of 1945.

The Order was now faced with the problem which had ultimately baffled the Frankish settlers in the East: the administration of its conquest. Palestine had proved too poor a land, and its conquerors too jealous and ambitious, for an adequate army and stable government to be established. Any mediaeval army was directly related to the wealth of the country; troops had to be paid, in cash or in land, and here the Teutonic Knights in Prussia were at an advantage. With proper management the forest could be made to yield an adequate return as cultivated land, and it was never so intensely farmed during their rule as to bring on the evils of dust and drought. The political status of the Order was also much more favourable than that of the Eastern counterparts – the great importance of the imperial bull of 1226 and the ducal deed of gift in 1230 lay in the complete freedom given to the knights. They skilfully played off pope against emperor: owing allegiance to both, they succeeded in obeying neither one nor the other. Sovereigns in their own right, they had no vacillating or overbearing kings to contend with, and turned their energies wholeheartedly to the business of creating order out of chaos. In contrast, in Livonia, where the Order was merely one of the ruling powers, much of its energy was diverted into political intrigue.

The material they had to manage was intractable enough. The Prussians had already shown their independent mettle in the previous fifty years; they were also among the most backward races of northern Europe. Their agriculture was of the most primitive nomadic kind, the year's crop being raised on newly cleared forest land, which was abandoned immediately after harvest. They had few settled centres, and were loath to give up their wandering life. Their paganism, in peacetime relatively harmless, being a nature cult of grove and spring similar to that of the Norse peoples, grew ferocious in war. If their temper was aroused, the captured knights were often sacrificed to propitiate the gods; for the outlying garrisons deep in the forests, battle, despite impossible odds, must have seemed preferable to capture and the risk of torture and death. The efforts of the missionaries had not been successful, and the number of genuine converts was very small; the majority of so-called Christians were liable to revert all too quickly to their fathers' ways. Few of the knights can have spoken their language, and very little is recorded of their beliefs and customs. This lack of communication, in such contrast with relations between Christian and Muslim in the later years of the kingdom of Jerusalem, increased mutual fear and suspicion, and must account for much of the bloodthirstiness of the campaigns.

The kingdom of Lithuania created by Mindaugas was revived by Gediminas about 1310. From now on the leaders of this state were the Order's chief antagonists, for besides being the last heathen remaining in the area they were also pursuing a conflicting course of conquest. From 1300 to 1380 the Order's armies marched against them as many as eight times a year; but the Lithuanians were as stubborn as the Prussians had been, and the fortunes of war remained even. They were skilled riders and daring warriors, moving swiftly across the country, however wild, elusive in retreat and dangerous in victory. Nor were they to be trusted in peacetime. Both skilful and treacherous as diplomats, they outwitted the cleverest minds of the Order on several occasions. By themselves, however, they were not powerful enough to overcome the Order.

Indeed, the Order reached its zenith at this time, under Winrich von Kniprode, a High Master second only in resourcefulness to Hermann von Salza. The achievements of his time were many, but the greatest was undoubtedly the acquisition of Estonia from the Danes, which sufficiently extended the Order's territories in the Baltic provinces to overshadow any remaining local dissidence. He rebuilt many of the Order's castles, and he entertained crusaders lavishly to encourage reinforcements from the west. From the beginning of the fourteenth century, Prussia was just as important as a destination for knights who wanted to go on crusade as the east. The Hospitallers were not in a position to mount frequent expeditions against the infidel, and logistics meant that crusades in the Mediterranean had to be large, well-organised affairs, for which the rulers of Christendom showed little real enthusiasm. By contrast, it was possible to go to Prussia with a handful of companions and to join one of the almost annual winter or summer expeditions against the heathen. The ease with which the journey could be undertaken, and the position of the Teutonic Knights as a state with commercial and political interests in Europe, has led some historians to question the value of these northern crusades, seeing them as either light-hearted or simply military support for a friendly power. But there is no doubt that the journey to Prussia was a highly-regarded enterprise. Many of the great figures of western chivalry went on the *Preussenreise*, the journey to Prussia.[2] Chaucer, in his description of the Knight in *The Canterbury Tales*, that paragon of chivalric perfection, ranks Prussia immediately after

2   See Werner Paravicini, *Die Preussenreisen des europäischen Adels*, I, II, Beihefte der Francia, 17.i, ii, (Sigmaringen 1989, 1995). A further volume is in preparation. For English participation and attitudes to the *Reisen*, see Christopher Tyerman, *England and the Crusades 1095-1588* (Chicago and London 1988) 266-276.

the Alexandria crusade as the chosen destination of many young knights eager to make their reputation.[3] John of Bohemia, renowned as a tourneyer in his youth, and famous for his chivalric death at the battle of Crécy, made three expeditions to Prussia. English noblemen were prominent: Henry IV, as earl of Derby, went in 1390 and 1392, following in the footsteps of his grandfather Henry duke of Lancaster. King Waldemar of Denmark, king Louis of Hungary, Gaston Phoebus, count of Foix, William IV, count of Hainault, Thomas Ufford, earl of Suffolk and Thomas Beauchamp, earl of Warwick are a few of the names that appear in the records, often with two or three journeys to their credit. Two successive counts of Jülich made seven *Preussenreisen* apiece between 1346 and 1400, while Jean le Maingre, sire de Boucicaut, went four times in the 1380s when there was a lull in the fighting between France and England.

If the journey to Prussia was relatively easy – Froissart tells us that it normally took 40 days from Ghent, but that it could be done in as few as 14[4] – the conditions in Prussia itself were also much more secure and civilised than in the east. The visiting crusader would be welcomed at Königsberg, where the army gathered, and would then, if the weather permitted, join one of the summer or winter *Reisen* against the pagans, which might last between two and ten weeks. Most knights would go to Marienburg to pay their respects to the High Master and to obtain formal permission to join the expedition.

During this time, the visitor would have found entertainments of the kind that he would have expected at a western princely court of the period: we hear of dances at Königsberg, and the High Master had his own heralds, minstrels and dwarf in his palace at Marienburg. Leisure hours were whiled away by hunting, playing at dice, or other such diversions; tournaments, however, were forbidden for the knights of the Order, and so were very unusual among the guests; in 1394 such an encounter between French and Polish knights was banned by the High Master.

The high point, however, was the feasts held for the visitors, who would dream of sitting, like Chaucer's knight, 'in the chair of honour, above all nations', as he had done. For this was one of the great celebrations of international chivalry. Marienburg was rebuilt in the last decades of the fourteenth century to cater for such gatherings: the High Master's feasting hall was on a suitably impressive scale, with a vaulted Gothic roof raised on three slender pillars. The ritual of the *Ehrentisch*, the high table or table

---

3   The Knight is not a satirical portrait, as Terry Jones has argued (*Chaucer's Knight*, London 1980); see Maurice Keen, 'Chaucer's Knight' in *English Court Culture in the Later Middle Ages*, ed. V.J.Scattergood and J.W.Sherborne, London 1983, 45-62, and 'Chaucer's Knight Revisited', Harlaxton Medieval Studies, forthcoming, where he argues that the Lollard knights such as Sir John Clanvowe are possible models.

4   Froissart, ed.Lettenhove, X, 243: tr. Johnes, II,2.

of honour, is well-documented, and was held immediately before or after the *Reise*, when the greatest number of visitors were present. 'The criteria by which knights were chosen were neither exceptional feats during the *Reise*, which might not have begun, nor aristocratic birth, nor even wealth, but simply knightly renown as reported by the heralds.'[5] It was a chivalric festival without compare, the ultimate accolade for prowess awarded by the acclaim of those expert in all things knightly. The idea of such a table of honour appears in the statutes of the French Order of the Star and of the Neapolitan Order of the Knot, but neither of these Orders survived for long, and it was only in Prussia that the concept became reality.

The number of knights chosen was small: the sources speak of a dozen or so. They were given a shoulder badge with the words 'Honour conquers all' in golden letters, and their names and shields were recorded in one of the rooms of the castle. We know relatively little about the knights who were thus singled out as paragons of chivalry: for one Schultheiss von Eschweiler, we have an oration by a herald after his death, which tells us that he had been several times to Prussia and Lithuania, and had also been to Asia Minor, Santiago, Jerusalem, Rome, Cyprus, Granada, Byzantium and Scotland. Piety as well as prowess seems to have counted towards qualifying for the table of honour, for three of these are places of pilgrimage rather than campaigns. Furthermore, the emphasis on prowess was such that in 1385, the one surviving official list of participants in an *Ehrentisch* shows that only simple knights were chosen on this occasion, the lords being seated further down the hall.

This was perhaps the ultimate manifestation of chivalry in real life, the nearest to the ideal of the Arthurian round table that was ever achieved. Given that it existed as an institution for little more than half a century, its fame was remarkable: apart from Chaucer, the author of the Catalan romance of *Curial and Guelfa*, written in the 1440s, single out 'the Prussian table' as the outstanding mark of knightly achievement. And when the High Master, Heinrich von Plauen, tried to raise reinforcements in the Order's darkest hour, after Grünwald, he wrote to the rulers of the west to announce a new *Reise*, at which an *Ehrentisch* would be held, as the surest way of securing such support.

The *Ehrentisch* sums up the attraction of the Prussian crusades. Königsberg and Marienburg became place where knights could foregather for chivalric expeditions, on neutral ground; there was a strong religious element, but a relaxed social atmosphere. The fighting itself was not a long-term commitment. In some cases it was laid on almost to order; in 1378, Winrich von Kniprode returned from a winter *Reise* with the duke of Lorraine, to find that the duke of Austria and the count of Cleves were about to

---

5   Paravicini, *Die Preussenreisen*, II, 324.

arrive: a second brief expedition was arranged for them in December. But the magnates were less important to the Order than the constant flow of ordinary knights from Germany and Austria, particularly areas where the Order's presence was strong. This may have been the reason for the institution of the *Ehrentisch*, with its emphasis on knightly deeds rather than rank, assuming that it was a clever and deliberate creation of the Order rather than a spontaneous product of the great knightly gatherings.

Because Prussia was readily accessible and the campaigns were often brief, it is easy to dismiss the crusading warfare as a kind of sport, with the pagans as game to be hunted down by the knights. The reality was very different. The Lithuanians were formidable opponents, capable of inflicting serious reverses on the crusaders, and campaigning conditions were often exceptionally harsh: a really hard spell of weather might lead to the deaths of men and horses through exposure, a sudden thaw might bring the risk of drowning in the fast-flowing rivers swollen by the melting snow, or being cut off in enemy territory. Stories of what might happen if a crusader or knight of the Order was taken alive were horrific: it was said that the heathens bound the knight to his horse and burnt them both alive as a sacrifice to their gods. At all events, there was a steady death-toll among those who ventured to Prussia, and memorials both in the cathedral at Königsberg and as far afield as the little church at Felbrigg in Norfolk testify to the danger of the : Sir Roger Felbrigg's brass records that 'he died in Prussia and is buried there'.

On balance the glamour of crusading in such circumstances outweighed the dangers, and the Order was successful at attracting would-be crusaders from the west; but it had its own problems within Christendom. A papal investigation into the Order was set in motion in 1310, and the Livonian brothers were actually excommunicated in 1312. For a moment it looked as if the Teutonic knights might shared the Templars' fate.[6]

On the other hand, the Order had made diplomatic enemies in the south as its strength and status grew. The most serious of these was Poland, which allied itself with Hungary to keep the knights in check. As the two great Catholic monarchies of Eastern Europe, they regarded the order as intruders, and were jealous of its stable government and accumulating wealth. Hungary was a nominal rather than effective opponent, and the Polish intrigues came to very little until in a black moment for the Order the Grand duke of Lithuania, Jogailo, married the Queen-regnant of Poland, Jadwiga, in 1386, and brought together the Order's two closest rivals. The bitterest blow lay in the conditions of the settlement: Jogailo and his people were to accept Christianity. What

---

6   Christiansen, *The Northern Crusades*, 145.

the Order had failed all these long years to achieve, and what had remained its official *raison d'être* until now, was at one stroke accomplished, and the religious aspect of its wars swept away. Without the clarion call to the crusade, its influence was bound to decline; and the knights found themselves as no more than a secular power struggling for political ends against their fellow-Christians.

That they had legitimate grounds enough for war against the Polish-Lithuanian union in the years that followed cannot be denied, once they had made the initial mistake of meddling in the internal power struggles of the new state. Accustomed to regarding the Lithuanians as their traditional enemy, they could not see that their one hope was to stand aside and let the fragile bonds dissolve of their own accord. They became involved in a quicksand of allegiances, treacheries and double-dealings, in which most of the deceit was on the Lithuanian and Polish side. A series of skirmishes punctuated these manoeuvres, and a major encounter could not be held off for ever. When it finally came, in the summer of 1410, it found the Order apparently as strong as ever. The knights were confident of their own superior skill: and it was a century and a half since their last serious reverse at Durbe. On the other hand, Jogailo was determined to settle matters once and for all; and his mobilisation of perhaps 10,000 troops in a month was a major feat. Once assembled, the army was organised as little as possible, and this very lack of a formal hierarchy and reliance on a central authority was the secret of his success. There were no quarrels as to precedence, no problems of foraging; the only common aim was the destruction of the Teutonic Knights as swiftly as possible. Tartars, Russians and as many other patrons and princes as could be roused formed the larger part of the army: and with this motley array, ranging from the future Khan of the Golden Horde to knights in the strictest European tradition, Jogailo invaded the Order's territory in July. Despite the refusal of the Livonian Master to join in a war begun without his knowledge, the knights were still confident, for the Order's commanders had not been idle.

Pomerania, which had long been coveted by the Poles, was guarded by a small force who could hold off the invader until help came, and the main body of the army was in the centre of the border with Poland. Contact was quickly made and the High Master, Ulrich von Jungingen, decided for immediate action. Although reinforcements were at hand, and he could have delayed until German mercenaries of the Pomeranian army reached him, he chose to strike quickly, relying on his own strength. The strategy used on previous occasions, of withdrawing into the Order's fortresses, no longer seemed profitable: the land was rich and able to support a besieging army well enough, and the Poles were now capable of handling siege-engines successfully. Nevertheless, a retreat into the castles might well have brought in the Livonian branch of the Order, and the vast Polish and Lithuanian army would not have stayed together in a protracted campaign. So there are some grounds for finding von Jungingen's tactics rash: they stem too nearly from the Order's own high opinion of itself. He had little to gain, as defender, from a quick encounter, but on the first intelligence of Jogailo's invasion, he ordered an immediate march toward the enemy.

When, at midday on 15th July the army of the Order halted, after a march of fifteen miles, among the rolling wooded hills round Grünwald,[7] they found Poles and Lithuanians already encamped in the forest. This was the first blow to the Order: the heavy cavalry on which they relied was vastly more effective on open plains than in the forest, and hence their action had to be defensive. Both sides were reluctant to make the first move, and there was some hope of a parley, until the Knights' herald bore two swords to Witold of Lithuania. A general advance ensued, and the shock of the Knights' first attack broke the Lithuanian wing. The centre and Polish left stood firm, however, and the over-eager pursuers on the left were met by Russian squadrons and fresh Polish troops who held them in check. Neither side could make headway, and the High Master was forced to advance with his remaining reserves in a bid to break the Polish line. This decided the battle, but decided it against him. The line held firm, and he and the potentates of the Order were surrounded and killed. The rest of the army tried valiantly to retrieve the lost battle, but when the remnant fled, two hundred of the Order's knights lay dead on the field, and the Order's lands lay open to Jogailo, victor of one of the most spectacular, yet most meaningless, of chivalry's battles.

The truth of the matter was that the Order could not have benefited from a victory. It was neither justified in, nor capable of, conquest of Christian states; relying as it did on a religious impetus, it could not afford to behave like a secular state. Contemporary writers were quick to point out that the Order 'was ordained to defend the faith; and now covetousness leads them to destroy it!'[8] Nor could they rely on rallying crusaders from the rest of Europe to fight against Christian princes; the non-German crusaders had ceased to come in any numbers when the crusade of Nicopolis was launched, and after 1400 the renewal of Anglo-French hostilities had diverted their military ambitions. The last German crusaders came in 1422. As a result, the Order ceased to be an institution with European influence, and retreated into a narrower, merely local existence. The remaining story of its declining years is punctuated by no such dramatic moments as Grünwald; the knights, prudent after the event, avoided a headlong encounter in the second and third northern wars, but were nevertheless forced to conclude disadvantageous peaces both in 1422 and 1435.

Other forces were at work against the outmoded disposition of the Order. The towns and guilds, the small squires and farmers, resented its foreign and exclusive rule, which, while the pagan were still at their doors, they had accepted as a necessary price

---

7   The battle is often called Tannenberg.

8   Christiansen, *The Northern Crusades*, 221.

for protection. Prussians were actually debarred from joining the Order, and the result was not unlike British rule in India in the early twentieth century: an essentially well-meaning administration which grew progressively less able to adapt itself to the realities of political feeling among the people it governed. The situation was aggravated by the Knights' increasing use of mercenaries, and a general raising of the taxes as the treasury grew empty. At a time when the Order needed good administrators above all, the falling off in the standard and number of recruits began. The Order's own standards, too, had fallen from the days when they were 'good monks in the cloister and stern soldiers in the field'.[9]

In the mid-fourteenth century Heinrich der Teichner had complained that knights only went to Prussia to waste money and gain glory, while things went from bad to worse at home; and the Order were accused in 1343 of not converting the conquered heathen because they could tax them more heavily, though Philippe de Mézières, at the end of the same century, surveying Europe from a crusader's point of view, found the Order the embodiment of his ideal of Christian discipline.

Roger Bacon complained that 'the Christian princes who labour for their conversion (i.e. of the heathen), and especially the brothers of the Teutonic Order, desire to reduce them to servitude, as the Dominicans and Franciscans and other good men throughout all Germany and Poland are aware. For this reason they offer opposition: hence they are resisting oppression, not the arguments of a superior religion'.[10] By 1430 the complaints were more general. To oppression was added worldly show, and breach of all three vows; but the Carthusians had been accused in similar terms in 1427, and some of the enormities were magnified by the general growth of anti-monastic feeling. By 1454 the old Prussian League which had been a potential focus for such discontent since its formation in 1240 had become a formidable union of guilds and local nobles, which, supported and financed by Poland, staged a well-timed revolt against the Order. Despite a clever victory at Konitz, where the Order's mercenaries held the Poles and Leaguers at bay until the Marshal overwhelmed them from the rear, the war went against the Order. To pay the mercenaries, it had to give them Prussian towns in pledge, which they then sold to the Poles. By 1466 both the League proper and the Order were exhausted; only the Poles could take advantage of the situation. So, in the Peace of Thorn, Casimir IV accomplished what his forebears had begun to work for before the High Master had even settled in Prussia a century and a half earlier. He took West Prussia for the Polish crown, and forced the High Master to rule the rest as a Polish vassal.

9   Johannes Bühler, *Ordensritter und Kirchenfürsten nach zeitgenossischen Quellen* (Leipzig 1927) 87.

10   Roger Bacon, *Opus maius*, tr. Robert Belle Burke (Philadelphia & London 1928) II, 797

If the Order's star had set, a faint reflection of its old glory lingered in Livonia and elsewhere. The Livonian branch had recovered from the defeat of Vilkomir in 1435 and was in better shape than that in Prussia when faced with new dangers, this time from Russia. Its independent standing had saved it from inclusion in the humiliation at Thorn. In Walter von Plettenberg, it produced the last great statesman of the Order, and in the victory at Pskow in 1502, the last great hour of the Order. Within twenty years the Reformation had undermined the remnants of the Prussian Order, and in 1525 Albrecht of Brandenburg converted it into a secular duchy as a Polish vassal. The Livonian branch survived until 1591, when a similar fate befell it.

What remained was a postscript, though the tradition died hard. The Order very nearly revived, like the Hospitallers, to fight the Turk. In the Peloponnese they had resisted Turkish attacks in the late fifteenth century; and in Austria, where the Order remained strong after its decline in Germany proper, the knights found themselves matched against the infidel from 1529 onwards. The attacks of Sulayman the Magnificent, and a century later those which culminated in the siege of Vienna in 1683, found in the Order a mainstay of the defenders. Their part was admittedly not to lead, as in Prussia and Livonia, but they could provide a full regiment. In any case the majority of their lands were in the troubled borderlands, and had to be defended. The last major field action involving the Order took place in 1697 at Zenta; and it is only with the passing of the menace of Islam from Europe – a menace which was already 400 years old when the Order was born – that its part in military affairs finally became a thing of the past. The Order survived into the world of the Renaissance but this was a world where diplomacy counted for more than zeal, and treaties for more than an Order's vows and aims. The Order counted for no more than the sum of the individual prowess of its members.

The historical reputation of the Order has suffered no less from its zealous supporters than from its enemies; German and Slav historians respectively have seen in it the apotheosis of knighthood, and the nadir of piracy in the name of idealism. To the Prussian Treitschke they were 'conquerors, endowed with the triple pride of Christians, Knights and Germans';[11] to Latvian and Lithuanian historians, the murderers of the infant national spirit of their peoples. But their heritage cannot be evaluated in terms of nineteenth-century nationalism nor in the context of a controversy on the ethics of religious war. On its own terms the Order's achievement was remarkable. Its tradition of diplomacy, from the days of Hermann von Salza, would alone assure its reputation. Of Hermann's own skill as diplomat there is no greater proof than his position of trust

---

11   G. Treitschke, *The Origins of Prussianism*, tr. E. and C. Paul (London 1942) 39.

as the only acceptable intermediary between the excommunicate Frederick II and Gregory IX. He alone of the Masters of the Orders stood at Frederick's side on the forbidden crusade to Jerusalem in 1228; and yet he retained the pope's confidence. Both Emperor and Pope encouraged his Prussian schemes, and gave him practical support at a time when their feud was at its height. He brought about the union with the Brethren of the Sword, despite their embattled position. Here, for once, Hermann cut the Gordian knot to achieve his end: he agreed to yield over a dispute with Denmark which the Brethren of the Sword obstinately refused to do, and to accept the remaining lands. Having arranged this, he then had the two negotiators from the other Order brought to Gregory IX, where they were told that the union had been agreed, and given cloaks of the Teutonic Order to put on. Only afterwards were the terms of the union revealed, and they could no longer argue with von Salza, to whom they now owed obedience.

Hermann's successors maintained this skill, though perhaps without earning the same degree of respect. The Order became a byword for cunning, and a German proverb ran: 'If you're so clever go and deceive the lords of Prussia.'[12] The lords of Prussia succeeded in securing the support of the dominant side in the conflict of Pope and Emperor, changing their real allegiance as necessary. They maintained a system of diplomacy as far afield as England, Sicily and Hungary to gain support for their ends, and such efforts repaid the Order many times over in periods of stress; after Tannenberg, it was support from their old enemy Hungary that helped them to recover, and diplomatic skill meant that the Peace of Thorn was far from unfavourable, considering that a bare handful of castles was all that had been left. It was this, rather than the old fighting spirit, that enabled the Order to survive in some form until the end of the fifteenth century; military reverses were followed by diplomatic recoveries. On the other hand, no amount of diplomacy could resolve the rival aims of the order and her neighbour Poland, once the latter became Christian and the Order's role became secular.

The internal structure of the Order was supremely important to its success. While the other great Orders were assailed on grounds of immorality and luxury, the Teutonic Knights largely avoided such complaints until the very end of their time. Recruitment was limited to sons of knightly parents of German origin, born within the Empire. This avoided the clashes that occurred between the various *langues* of the Hospitallers, drawn from different nations; and it prevented the Order from becoming the pawn of local knights, since no one from the Order's lands could be admitted. On the other hand this led to an aloofness from local pressures that proved dangerous in the last

---

12   Bühler, *Ordensritter*, 119.

years; without a local assembly co-operation was difficult to obtain, and grievances were liable to go unheard.

As in other Orders, the individual knight was subject to his local priory; the priories were in turn administered by the bailiwicks or *Balleien*; and these were answerable to the central administration of the Order, at first in Acre, later in Venice, and finally in Marienburg. Prussia and Livonia were far from being the exclusive habitat of the knights; as with the Templars and Hospitallers, the establishments of the Order ranged from Cyprus, Greece and Calabria through the Tirol to the Rhine, Saxony and the Netherlands. The extreme outposts of the Order's activities were the Holy Land, Spain, Flanders, Gotland, Estonia and Hungary, a circle round the edges of Christendom. But the great reserves of the Order lay in its possessions and ties in Germany. It was the strength of its basis in Germany that prevented it from succumbing to the almost mortal reverses it met with in the course of its crusades, as the Brethren of the Sword had almost succumbed after the battle of Saule.

The higher administration consisted of a general chapter of representatives from each bailiwick, the five great officers, and the High Master himself. The High Master and the great officers decided the day-to-day policy of the Order, but were answerable to the general chapter for their actions; and the High Master, as in the case of von Plauen, in 1413, could be deposed by the general chapter. The election of the High Master was carried out by an electoral college, which was formed by the nomination of one knight as 'election leader'. He would then name another knight to join him, and the two would then choose a third, and so on until thirteen knights were chosen and approved by the Marienburg knights and officers. These thirteen had to be as widely representative of the Order as possible: and their choices were, on the whole, remarkably farsighted, even in the darkest years. Even von Plauen's election was undoubtedly the right choice, while his subsequent deposition has been much debated.

On this administrative system the Order's success depended. It was outstandingly successful, and probably unrivalled by any other mediaeval state. Cases of malpractice were almost unknown, and detailed financial organisation went hand-in-hand with frugal habits for many years. The main aim of the financial machinery was to provide for the expenses of the campaigns; a year rarely passed without a major expedition setting out, and while this constant drain remained, there was little money to spare for misuse on personal comfort. Since the campaigns were undertaken to protect lands which were a major source of revenue, there was no temptation to withhold funds, as with the Templars. Only towards the end of the fourteenth century do signs of heavy expenditure on luxuries appear, and some of this was certainly due to entertainment of secular visitors, for as a secular prince the High Master had to show these outward signs of power by which men of the time distinguished a great prince from a lesser one. The nature of their estates made the knights into men of commerce, trading in

313

corn, hides and wood; and their relations with the north German towns of the Hanse were dictated by both policy and trade. At its height, the Prussian trade carried on by the Order and the merchants of the towns included not only the staple products of the land but a flourishing market in wares brought overland from the Levant and Rumania.

The growth of this trade and the great wealth of Prussia were not only due to financial skill. Since its earliest days, the Order had pursued a deliberate policy of development and colonisation. In this it was fortunately placed, for the great weakness of Frankish Palestine had been its lack of settlers and of manpower, partly due to the distance and climate, but mostly to lack of any concept of colonisation. The Order was near to Germany and the land was favourable; but without encouragement, the colonists would never have come, and the all-important substructure of the state would have depended on the unreliable descendants of the old pagan races. The settlers were given wide privileges, equivalent to the most liberal prevailing in the German towns; and these privileges were codified within three years of the Order's acquisition of Kulmerland in the *Kulmischer Handfest* of 1233. In return for a large measure of freedom in their own affairs, the settlers had to acknowledge the Order's lordship and basic rights and the Order was careful never to grant large estates to individuals; but the Order also waived its rights to many kinds of taxation and made the military service required as light as possible. Trade was made easier by the adoption of a standard coin, replaced over ten years at a set rate of exchange, and the absence of tolls. Nor did the Order's work stop here. Regulations as to the building and layout of houses were laid down, so that there was as little danger as possible of overcrowding or fire, and the best defensive arrangements could be made. A minimum area for each building site was laid down, as well as the basic ground plan for each town; and brick was preferred to wood, tiles to straw.[13]

The Order could only carry out farsighted schemes such as this in Prussia, where it was undisputed master. No bishops could contend with it there, though they were technically masters of nearly a quarter of the land; and the local nobility, despite the Polish-inspired Prussian League of 1240, feared the pagans more than the Order. Most of the disaffected nobles were either killed or deprived of their rank during the rebellion of 1260. Furthermore, the Order actively pursued a policy of buying out their lands and granting them in smaller lots to peasants. In Livonia the Order inherited the quarrels of the Brethren of the Sword with the bishops and the Danish kings, though the terms of union had poured some oil on these troubled waters. Fortunately the

13   Bühler, *Ordensritter*, 77-82.

pressure of external politics alleviated the risk of internal troubles, but Livonia never prospered in the same way as the older territories.

The Teutonic Order was chivalry at its most practical. The Order's faults were the faults of chivalry in real life; its virtues, however, were curiously un-chivalric, the virtues of practical wisdom carefully applied. They cannot be claimed as being of the essence of chivalry, but belonged rather to the science of good government. Behind the skilled diplomats, administrators and warriors, the driving force nevertheless remained that of religious chivalry: the defence and furtherance of the faith by discipline and the sword. This ideal never became irrelevant to the Order's existence; indeed, its downfall came when, in attacking Christian states, it betrayed that ideal, and showed the inherent danger of building a secular state on active idealism: for its purpose had gone and only the outward trappings were left. In its declining days the Teutonic Order did not refuse to fight the infidel, but it made no effort to do so when the infidel was no longer to be found on its doorstep and went on trying to fight the Christians who had once been its pagan enemies. The temper of the fifteenth century was very different from that of the thirteenth; once the crusading ideal had died, conversion into a secular state was inevitable, for chivalry had never envisaged itself as a means of ruling the world; far rather, as a means to right the wrongs perpetrated by the world's rulers. While chivalry made the secular achievements of the Teutonic Order possible by providing the internal discipline and driving force, it had very little impact on the nature of those achievements.

Hand-in-hand with this idealism went a practical machinery which enabled it to continue in its work long after the former had died away. Yet the basis of the Order was not very different from that of the Templars. Indeed, from 1198 to 1245 the Order followed the Templar rules, but following a dispensation in a papal bull of 1244 to change the rules in any details which needed alteration, a revision was undertaken in the light of fifty years' experience. The statutes have come down to us in this later form. The fall into three parts: rules, laws and customs. The rules were the kernel of the Order's life and their first commands were: 'eternal chastity; renunciation of one's own wishes, that is, obedience unto death; and the third is a vow of poverty...'[14] Not even the Master could exempt a member from these rules. All poverty had to be held in the name of the Order, and brethren were not even allowed separate places, such as chests, in which private belongings of any kind might be kept. The habit of the Order was specified in detail: all brothers wore the black cross on their over-tunics, which were always white from 1244 onwards. No brother could possess more than the

14   Bühler, *Ordensritter*, 14.

stipulated number of clothes, and any divergence in favour of worldly splendour was strictly forbidden.

The laws laid strong emphasis on the role of the Order as Christ's warriors, and especially on the need for Christian conduct towards their fellow Christians. They also prescribe the ways in which the brothers had to avoid temptation, especially where women were concerned; and anyone guilty of homosexual practice was to be ejected from the Order at once. Possession of money and the exchange of anything issued to the brothers for personal use were not allowed. Penalties for infringements ranged from three days' penance to what was in effect a year's hard labour, working with the servants and deprived of the insignia of the Order. A second year's sentence or even perpetual imprisonment might follow serious offences. Since the Order was exempt from all royal judges and bishops' courts, it had to have powers of punishment adequate for the most serious crime; and in extreme cases, such as that of the Prussian Master who burnt two rebellious brothers alive, the Order appealed to the pope for sentence.

This discipline was equally adapted for both fighting men and a governing élite. The Order was – and this is one of the most remarkable things about it – very small by our standards: in 1400 there were no more than 1,600 members. Hence its greatest asset was a strong corporate spirit, and this feeling of exclusiveness contributed greatly to its internal stability and the high degree of discipline. Its solidarity was further strengthened by the recruitment of brothers from four or five specific areas in Germany, with very few exceptions, and by the activities of the Order's historians, who wrote epic histories in the vernacular, recording the Order's campaigns and other victories and attributing them to the protection of the Virgin Mary. The cult of the Virgin Mary current among poets and knights elsewhere reached the Teutonic Order too: she was patron saint of the Order, and its castles were named in her honour: three Marienburgs, two Marienwerders, Frauenburg and Marienhausen. The *Officium Marianum* was to be said daily, besides the usual church services; the longest and one of the most important of the rare works of literature produced by the Order, *The Passional*, begins with a life of the Virgin, and contains anecdotes of the Virgin's miracles; from 1309, every member of the Order was supposed to recite hourly either a *Salve Regina* or an *Ave*, and on the Church of the great castle of the Order, named Marienburg in her honour, there stood a twenty-foot high golden mosaic in half-relief of her.

The moral decline of the Order only began to become a serious subject for complaint after the disaster of Grünwald. The crimes complained of seem to imply a feeling of fatalism, that the Order's days were numbered, but the same complaints were echoed elsewhere against knights both secular and religious, and Orders both military and monastic: dicing, drinking, impiety and breach of the three vows. The special charges against the Order were those of worldly show, levelled against the Templars a century earlier, and, most particularly, of oppression. We have considered the Order's government in Prussia already. If there was oppression, it was mild compared with that of other European rulers, and the real cause of irritation was the alien birth of the knights. The ambitious merchants of Danzig could justifiably protest against their exclusion from power; ambition and half-forgotten episodes from the days of conquest, when a civil war was raged by both sides, led to a picture of the knights as sadistic tyrants which lingers in nationalist histories today. In fact, they misused their power very little; their real sin was to be a reactionary institution with little ground for continued existence in times which were increasingly critical of the *status quo*. They had not entirely maintained their early standards: their hospitals had been reduced in number, mercenaries were used from about 1300 onwards, and the criticisms of pomp and pleasure were sometimes more than justified. Yet if the Order's faults were those of other institutions of chivalry as well, its achievements were entirely its own.

15

The Spanish Orders

THE THIRD CORNER of Christendom at which believer and pagan met on the battlefield was Spain. Here the heathen had been established much longer, since the Muslim invasion at the beginning of the eighth century, but they had replaced a Visigothic kingdom which had had strong Roman traditions. Its scattered heirs remembered the days when all Spain had been Christian, and regarded the infidel as an intruder. In the north, the Teutonic knights were the invaders, and the Eastern crusaders lacked the clearly defined territorial aims of the Spanish knights, who were in any case fighting a war of reconversion. The *reconquista* in Spain, which began in earnest under Sancho I of León in the tenth century, was the only fully successful military operation in the holy wars of Christendom, and to some extent this gave it a special character. On the other hand, the military Orders appeared on the scene relatively late, after the first triumphs of the *reconquista* were past, and their part was less than in the East and in Prussia: the war was between two groups of feudal kingdoms in alliance, and the Orders became a component of the Christian feudal host. The Spanish Orders belong less to the history of chivalry than to the internal history of Spain; but their institutions and career illustrate the relation of chivalry to the practical politics of feudalism.

The *reconquista* had begun as a largely political movement, stemming from the growth in power and influence of the Christian kingdoms of northern Spain as the Umayyad caliphate of Cordoba, which ruled half the Muslim world, fell into decline. It was exemplified in its early stages by the Cid, whose heroic reputation was an inspiration to later Christian warriors; yet even he was either in revolt against his lord or actually in infidel service for much of his career. Moor and Christian had lived side by side for too long for religious differences to count for much, and there were no holy places as the goal of the struggle. It was only with the increasing intervention of the Church in secular affairs that the war became a question of beliefs, and mutual intolerance, a necessary prelude to a holy war, appeared.

The papal expedition which produced the triumph and disaster at Barbastro in 1063-5 had been followed by a succession of smaller forays from France, largely organised by Gascons, whose lords had strong political ties with the kingdoms beyond the Pyrenees. But the response to recruiting for these expeditions had been inspired less by the call to a sacred task than by ties of alliance or even friendship, and the hope of booty from the wealthy Moorish kingdoms, whose riches were exaggerated to fantastic proportions. Even the successes in Palestine did not discourage the Spanish expeditions; indeed, they seem to have added new impetus. However, the stout resistance of the southern kingdoms made the struggle a protracted one. The first crusade to be preached as such in Spain was that which led up to the great battle against the Almohades at Las Navas de Tolosa in 1212 (if we discount the crusading absolution given to the Portuguese in 1197 to fight a Christian monarch, Alfonso X of León). However, the success of this expedition was not due to the foreign crusaders, who quarrelled with the Spanish and departed before the battle, leaving the latter to win a victory which halted the last great Moorish offensive against the north. In 1215 Innocent III cancelled the absolutions offered for fighting in Spain on the grounds that the Holy Land required the attention of all available knights. Indeed the crusading idea in Spain was largely local, royal and unofficial. The great thirteenth-century conquests in Aragon and Portugal, which completed the Portuguese *reconquista*, were partly fought with the banners of a papal crusade, and the crusading ideal lingered on in Iberia longer than anywhere else in Europe: the last campaign of the Catholic kings in 1492 and even Sebastian of Portugal's suicidal African raid of 1578 were widely regarded as crusades. But the form of these crusades differed from those in the East in that they were really politically inspired, and the papal blessing was not essential to their success. If it was not forthcoming, there were no drastic consequences such as befell Frederick II in Palestine.

Yet there was enough religious inspiration in the *reconquista* for the Templars and Hospitallers to be eagerly welcomed as a possible source of assistance. By 1134, their fame was such that Alfonso the Warrior tried to leave the kingdom of Aragon to them on his death, to carry on the great succession of victories which had created his realm. 'No king of Aragon was inflamed with a spirit so authentically religious and crusading'[1]; yet the scheme was obviously unworkable, and was rejected, his younger brother, Ramiro, being called from a monastery to assume the throne. The Hospitallers acquired their first real foothold in Catalonia in 1143; the Templars, who had been given their first castle in 1128, were named in the same year as the superiors of a new order to be established by the count of Barcelona, 'a militia ... on the model of the militia of the Temple of

[1] J.M. Lacarra, quoted in T.N.Bisson, *The Medieval Crown of Aragon* (Oxford 1986) 16.

Solomon in Jerusalem'.[2] But though they held some of the frontier forts, their greater preoccupations lay elsewhere. They were more interested in acquiring possessions outside the Holy Land which supported their endeavours there by providing revenue rather than involving an extra drain on their resources.

The rise of the native Orders is mainly due to the reluctance of those from Palestine to commit themselves fully to Spanish adventures. Later nationalist historians found precursors of purely Spanish origin but dubious authenticity, and the idea of the Orders as being at once military and religious is undoubtedly derived from the Templars and Hospitallers. On the other hand, local defence associations, *hermandades* or confraternities, associated with the protection of churches or monasteries, or simply invoking for themselves the protection of a patron saint, may well have played a part. On the Muslim side, similar associations were known as *ribats*; these small frontier stations were found throughout Islam, and to build one was accounted a good work, as was the manning of it; both furthered the cause of the *djihad* or holy war. However, the defenders were not members of any organisation, but citizens who spent limited periods in prayer and fighting in these quasi-religious retreats.

The atmosphere of the Spanish wars did not encourage the zeal with which the Templars and Hospitallers fought in the East. Conditions in the two halves of Spain were too similar and contacts with Moorish civilisation too frequent. Both sides suffered from a proliferation of kingdoms and interminable quarrels among themselves. The advantage, to a much greater degree than in Palestine, went to whichever side was temporarily at one with itself. The humane element of Moorish civilisation had influenced the Christians as well, and the wars were conducted with considerable humanity, slaughter of prisoners being generally frowned upon, even if the terms of imprisonment were harsh. There was surprisingly little attempt at conversion or at religious repression in conquered territories. The worst excesses of the Palestine crusades do not appear; relations between Moor and Christian show the respect bred by familiarity which was so often disturbed in Palestine by new recruits from Western Europe, for whom an infidel was beneath contempt.

The oldest and greatest of the Spanish orders was that of Calatrava.[3] Its foundation came in a period of frustration after the great successes of the Cid and of Alfonso VI, and was partly due to a failure on the part of the Palestinian orders to devote enough energy to the *reconquista*. The Templars had been given the royal fortress of Calatrava in 1147, on what was then the frontier with Islam, which protected the city of Toledo, some sixty miles to the north. This dangerous outpost was no sinecure; and when the

2   Quoted in Forey, *Military Orders*, 24.
3   See Joseph F. O'Callaghan, *The Spanish Military Order of Calatrava and its Affiliates* (London 1975) 'The Affiliation of the Order of Calatrava with the Order of Cîteaux', 180-3.

next major Moorish counter-attack was mounted, they resigned it to Sancho of Castile, on the grounds that it was untenable. The abandonment of such a castle was not cowardice, but a recognition that they could not undertake another major front in their war against the infidel. In desperation Sancho offered it to anyone who was prepared to hold it, with sufficient territory to maintain the costs of defence. The story goes that the heralds offered it three times, and received no reply, whereupon a Cistercian monk, Fray Diego Velazquez, who was at the royal court in attendance on his abbot, Raymond of Fitero, persuaded the latter that this was Christ's cause and the castle could not be abandoned. Diego, an old soldier, must have known the perils of the enterprise; he may also have realised that in Raymond, a brilliant organiser but inexperienced in war, he had found the right man. Within the year, by the end of 1158, Raymond was in Calatrava as Captain-General of a group of knights and monks; Diego had cleared the area of raiders; and the surrounding fields were being cultivated again.

The immediate problem that arose was the status of this new enterprise. Later historians claimed that Fitero's mother-house, the abbey of Escaledieu, was opposed to the whole scheme, because Fitero had been emptied of its able-bodied monks and its abbot. The king is said to have intervened just as Raymond seemed liable to be disciplined, pacifying the abbot of Escaledieu. What is certain is that Calatrava was established as a new house, obeying the Cistercian rule but with special provisos in view of its military role. Under this dispensation, the knights were able to place colonies in nearby strongholds to form a system of defence for the region by the middle of the following decade. But relations within the monastery were not easy: for on the death of the abbot Raymond, a dual election took place, the monks favouring one candidate who would have acted as abbot, the knights another who would have been master. The monks returned to Fitero, which left the knights as a purely military group. This was not what they had wanted, and it was decided to admit priest-brothers, and to apply for a special rule to govern their conventual life, on the lines of those given to the existing orders. So, by a bull of Alexander III at Sens in 1161, the order of Calatrava was formally created, affiliated to Morimond, a daughter house of Cîteaux itself. But by 1200 the Order was directly dependent on Cîteaux; it had suffered badly in the last decade of the century, losing many knights at the disaster at Alarcos in 1195: Calatrava itself fell in the same year.

In its final form, Calatrava owed its first allegiance to kingdom and knighthood, to crusading and Cistercians only when these qualities did not conflict with politics and war. As long as pressure from the Moors was strong, all the forces within the Order worked magnificently together; when internal dissensions divided the Spanish kingdoms, the Order too was divided. Until 1240 the Order's energy, if not rewarded by unbroken successes, was at least directed to the right ends. After Calatrava fell, a new home was only found at Salvatierra after dissensions with the Aragonese members, again on the frontier. This, too, fell in 1211; and it was not until after the great crusade of 1212, when the revenge for Alarcos was exacted in the triumph of Las Navas de Tolosa that the Order was again in possession of Calatrava. Its next home was Calatrava la Nueva, near Salvatierra, chosen because the original fortress was in too unhealthy a site and too far from the frontier. Later a great palace-fortress was built nearby at Almagro.

The idea of 'brotherhoods' of knights, operating together against the Muslims and choosing their own leader, was not uncommon in Spain, but most such companionships were temporary.[4] On the frontier of León, one such brotherhood emerged in the mid-1170s to become in 1176 the Order of San Julian de Pereyro or of Trujillo, and in 1183 the first master was recognised by Pope Lucius III. But such a small body as San Julian seems to have needed support from a more powerful organisation in order to survive, and soon afterwards San Julian placed itself under Calatrava's protection, eventually becoming little more than a minor branch of the latter. It was generally known in later years as the Order of Alcántara, from the fortress which became its headquarters in 1217. Likewise, the Portuguese Order of Evora, founded in the 1160s, came under Calatrava's jurisdiction, and after the reverses of the early thirteenth century was refounded as the Order of Aviz. Aviz became independent of Calatrava after 1238 and flourished where Evora had failed: it eventually provided Portugal with its ruling dynasty when the Master, João, gained the throne in 1384. On the suppression of the Templars, another Portuguese order was founded, that of the Knights of Christ. Under the leadership of their Master, Henry the Navigator, they fitted out expeditions to the Azores and to Africa, beginning with the siege and capture of the Moorish stronghold of Ceuta in 1414. Despite the early successes of the adventurers in the caravels with the red cross on their sails, the exploration never developed into a new missionary crusade. The orders themselves had become part of the past, and merchants, not crusaders, opened up Africa for Europe.

The most important of the Spanish orders, the Order of Santiago, has its own version of its foundation in its statutes. At a time when the Moorish peril was at its height, and the kings of Spain persisted in fighting each other instead of uniting against the common enemy, thirteen knights adopted the badge of a sword with a cross at the hilt, and swore never to injure a Christian, but, renouncing earthly vanities and ordering their life according to Holy Writ, vowed to fight no one but the heathen. Later tradition placed these events as early as the eleventh century, but the accepted date of formation is that of the first evidence of the Order in 1170, when a knightly confraternity was established by Ferdinand II of León after the conquest of Caceres. The following year,

4   Derek W.Lomax, 'Las milicias cistercienses en el reino de León', *Hispania* 23, 1963, 29-42; O'Callaghan, *The Spanish Military Order of Calatrava* , 'The Foundation of the Order of Alcántara'.

the archbishop of Santiago de Compostela admitted the master of the Order as a canon of the cathedral, and he and his successors became brothers of the Order.[5] It was reinforced by a union with a confraternity at Avila, who in 1172 sought to join Santiago's rule. In the deed of union confirming the arrangement, the military ambitions of the infant order were set out: 'if, as may happen, the Saracens are driven out of Spain on this side of the sea, the Master and Chapter propose to go to Morocco, and the brothers will support them. They will also do so, if necessary, in Jerusalem.'[6] In 1175, a bull of Alexander III confirmed the Order's statutes.[7] The ethos behind the traditional version of the early days is borne out by the bull; for the Knights of Santiago were the most unorthodox of the religious orders. Their rule stems from a secular warrior fraternity and from the early influence of the Augustinian canons. Perhaps because some of the founders were married, the original rule allowed brothers to have wives, quoting St Paul ('it is better to marry than to burn'). At a time when the papacy was intent on establishing priestly celibacy as an unyielding principle, it is perhaps surprising that the Pope approved the rule. They were, strictly speaking, not a monastic order, for although most knights lived in community in their castles, the married brothers had their own houses and possessions, though they were expected to join the community during periods of religious fast: their wives were to go to a convent. However, on the death of a knight his family was cared for by the Order, which inherited all his wealth; and there were restrictions on the knight's power to act as a private individual. Marriage of knights was not always regarded favourably; the Order of Montjoie was founded by a knight of Santiago who desired a stricter rule. The similarity to a charitable association was increased by the Order's activities in redeeming prisoners. By 1180 a *casa de merced* had been established at Toledo for the exchange of captives, and this good work continued throughout its history. On the other hand, the rules made the Order wealthy and discipline difficult, and in 1310 a chapter-general at Merida revised them lest the Order should suffer the Templars' fate, which had largely come about from excessive riches and inattention to their true purpose.

For the primary object of the Order was military, despite these other activities; as early as 1177 the knights helped to capture Cuenca and Santiago's services were as valuable as those of Calatrava. The Orders formed the core of most expeditions against the infidel, and even if they were usually greatly outnumbered by the secular levies, they could be mobilised much more quickly, and would serve without time limit.

5   J.L.Martin, *Origenes de la Orden Militar de Santiago*, Anuario de Estudios Medievales, Anejo 6, (Barcelona 1974) 213 ff.
6   Martin, *Origenes de la Orden de Santiago*, 227; see also Bernd Schwenk, 'Aus der Frühzeit der geistlichen Ritterordem Spaniens' in Fleckenstein, *Die geistliche Ritterorden.*
7   Martin, *Origenes*, 248-54/

The two Orders were not competitive in the way that the Templars and Hospitallers were, and there were a series of agreements between them designed to encourage collaboration in the fifty years following 1200, the most important being the *hermandad* or fraternity agreement of 1221.[8] The knights were prominent at Las Navas de Tolosa in 1212, where the Master was standard-bearer, and they kept up an unceasing frontier war in the Order's early years, disregarding royal truces with the Moors, which they did not regard as binding. By mid-century its fame was such that in 1246 Baldwin of Constantinople invited the knights to assist the Latin Empire, promising wide lands in Asia Minor; but the knights were too few in number for such an extensive undertaking, and the scheme came to nothing. Santiago, with its married knights and hence stronger domestic ties, was in any case a purely Spanish institution, while Calatrava, which resembled the international orders very closely, might have mounted such an expedition with less difficulty. There were plans for Calatrava to establish a branch in the East in the early thirteenth century, and the Order had a convent in Prussia in 1229, but its effective field of action never expanded beyond the confines of Spain.

Like the other Orders, in particular Calatrava, the knights of Santiago were also landowners on a vast scale, controlling the settlement and farming of great tracts of land on the frontier. Since they were responsible for the safety of the frontier, they evolved a pattern of life which not only ensured that land newly won from the Moors continued to be farmed, but also that any Moorish raids could be beaten off without too much damage. Settlements therefore consisted of tightly grouped villages dominated by defensive walls and often quarters for a small garrison, an a wide area would be cultivated from each of these, in contrast to the more loosely knit communities elsewhere in Spain. Gradually a pattern of ranch-style farming emerged, which was to have considerable influence on the shape of later agriculture, both in Spain and in the New World. The Order of Santiago became one of the largest wool-traders in Spain in the fifteenth century, rather as the English monks had at times dominated the wool-trade in England. This involvement with farming also meant that the Order never relied simply on castles for its defensive system, but rather on fortified towns and castles integrated with villages, in contrast to the desert strongholds of the Palestinian Orders.

Just as the Orders in Palestine had failed to establish a satisfactory relationship with the secular authorities, so a similar weakness soon appeared in the Spanish Orders. Being more open to secular influence, this took the form of internal quarrels over elections and discipline. In 1175, a former knight of Santiago had founded the Order of

---

8   O'Callaghan, *The Spanish Military Order of Alcántara*, 'The Castilian Reconquest', V, 611-6.

Montjoie in protest against the admission of married knights to Santiago, but it foundered for lack of support, and was merged into the Templars after 1196. More serious than the problem of discipline was that of obedience, particularly over elections. A dissident section of the Order of Montjoie resisted the union of 1196 until well into the thirteenth century, and disputed elections were becoming all too frequent in the other Orders. In terms of external policy, they acted at the behest of the king, and there were none of the examples of a conflicting independent diplomatic policy found in the East. On the other hand they did often continue to fight after royal truces with the Moslems had been established: in 1193 and 1225 they were specifically ordered to do so by the Pope.

Relations with the crown became increasingly a question of royal domination of the orders, and by 1240, the king of Castile was able to intervene in the choice of a new Master of Calatrava. The Spanish Orders lacked the international prestige which had saved the Templars and Hospitallers from local interference: Calatrava was primarily Castilian, and one of the most wealthy and powerful bodies within that kingdom, as well as its only form of standing army. By 1318 Calatrava included not only Alcántara, but also the newly formed Order of Montesa, among its dependents, Montesa having been endowed with the confiscated Templar lands. In 1280, 'the great majority of the brothers of the Order of Santiago' were killed at Moclín, near Granada, and as a result Alfonso X of Castile merged the Order with the newly-formed Order of Santa Maria de España, which appears to have been created as a naval defence force; but the name of the older order was retained.

By 1259 Santiago was insisting on noble birth for anyone wishing to become a knight, and quarrels over rank and points of privilege increased. Calatrava introduced a similar condition soon afterwards, and with this insistence on noble birth the connection with the royal court, and hence the possibilities for royal interference, increased. From 1254 the king expected to have a say in elections, and the arguments grew more and more frequent. In 1326 the Master was deposed for retreating in face of the enemy; the abbot of Morimond, which had been Calatrava's mother-house since 1275, reinstated him, only to find that a new royal candidate had taken power meanwhile: the situation was complicated by a schism with the Alcañiz branch of the Order. No sooner was the last breach healed than a new royal outrage created worse storms. In 1342 the king's gift of the mastership of Santiago to Don Fadrique, his seven-year-old bastard, led to protests from the Master of Calatrava. When challenged to appear at court he shut himself up in his castle, and was beheaded when royal troops took it by storm. In 1353 the Master of Calatrava fell to the assassins of Pedro the Cruel for plotting against his favourite, Doña Maria de Padilla; and Don Fadrique met a similar fate at Seville for suspected treason. The masters were by now almost entirely secular figures: in 1451, the Master of Alcántara left considerable wealth to his fourteen bastards, obtaining a papal bull authorising him to do so.

Yet the old spark remained as long as the Orders' objective and *raison d'être*, the Moorish kingdoms established in Andalucia, remained undisturbed. Even when there was little enthusiasm for the war against the Moslems in Castile, the Master of Alcántara set out to attack the Moors in 1394, but his zeal was greater than his judgement – a chronicler said that 'he believed whatever he chose' – and he and his men were overwhelmed. The last flowering of the *reconquista* in the fifteenth century finds the two sides of their character in evidence at once. Alvaro de Luna, as constable of Santiago, won a great victory at Higuera in 1431; but, elected as Juan II's favourite, he fell in a palace revolution in 1453. Enrique IV's illegitimate son, Rodriguez Tellez-Giron, was appointed Master at the age of eight, and supported Queen Isabella's rival in the dispute for the throne; yet he was the last great heroic figure of the Order, serving the Catholic kings well after his reconciliation with Isabella, and dying before Loja during its siege in 1482. Under the leadership of the Catholic kings the last embers flickered into flame again at the taking of Granada, the emotional climax of Spain's medieval history: the acting master of Calatrava, Diego Garcia de Castilo, hoisted the Spanish flag over the Alhambra on the morning of 2 January 1492, marking the end of the efforts of five centuries to dislodge the Moors from Spain.

The Catholic kings had already seen the danger of a rich and idle Order brawling among themselves for want of better work, and in 1485 they had declared their intention of reserving the mastership to the Crown. In 1493, the Order of Santiago was placed under royal administration; and in 1523 the three main orders were permanently incorporated into the Spanish crown.

Of the two Orders, Calatrava's constitution was more liable to lead to dissent over elections, and its real influence was less despite greater fame. Santiago, as the single example of an Order where members could marry, has its place in the history of chivalry, if only to prove that marriage seemed to be no deterrent to deeds of arms. Nonetheless, it was usual for the Master to remain unmarried, a custom which was not broken until 1350, in order to avoid the danger of the mastership becoming hereditary (though nephews of previous masters were twice chosen). The religious element was never very strong, and the Order of Santiago in its later years is best seen as a kind of defensive organisation combined with a standing army. Individuals might pursue the war against the heathen wholeheartedly, but the knights as a body grew content to leave the initiative to others.

The Spanish Orders were from the start hampered by too close a relationship with the secular state. While the Orders in Palestine were a mainstay of the Frankish kingdom in the absence of an adequate feudal army, it is tempting to wonder how different the Spanish *reconquista* would have been without the Orders. Drawn largely from the knightly class they supplemented, their contribution was more one of spiritual than of physical reinforcement. Once their spiritual nature became openly subordinated to political pressures the only remaining advantage was that of their special constitution as a kind of standing army, unpaid yet always on the watch. Their value is shown by their survival until the end of the *reconquista*, although fighting was irregular and occasional for the last forty years. They remain no more than a large footnote to the pages of Spanish history, a kind of symbol of the spirit of Spain during those years: high aims and chivalry corrupted by petty ambitions and pride, yet in the end victorious.

PART FIVE

Chivalry and the State

16

The Prince and Chivalry

JUST AS THE CHURCH had viewed the rise of chivalry with a dubious eye, and had only reluctantly accepted the possibility of turning it to religious ends, so monarchs were doubtful of the new spirit abroad among their knights. The knights were, after all, their army, or the most effective part of it, and to have them always hankering after adventures abroad, whether in the lists or on crusade, meant that the kingdom's military resources were depleted. William I remarked of one of his subjects that he would be a much better knight if only he was not always going off on pilgrimage; and by 'a much better knight' he meant a knight more useful to himself. The insistence on individual honour set chivalry and good discipline in the field at loggerheads, as we have seen; the tournament could be both a graveyard of good fighters and a meeting-place for rebels; and the right to make knights could be used to conjure up an armed force. Hence royal opposition to chivalry in its early stages is scarcely surprising: tournaments were banned or restricted by royal command in England and France, and throughout Europe there was an attempt to make the conferring of knighthood a ceremony hedged round by strict regulations.

For many knights were also barons, and as such ranked immediately below the king in the social hierarchy. The royal interest demanded that such men should be taught obedience and discipline before the code of individual heroics which chivalry preached. As long as the game of power politics was played between the barons and the king, chivalry was a subversive force, for it reflected the barons' aspirations of independence. As soon as other forces, the townsmen and merchants, threatened the hegemony of the lords, chivalry became a bond between king and lords against the upstarts. Hence the edicts against tournaments gradually disappeared and were replaced by the attitude of the German *Turniergesellschaften*, whose determination to exclude all those not properly qualified was encouraged by the various princes of the Empire, including the Emperor himself. Royal decrees on knighting became less concerned, as in Frederick Barbarossa's laws, with the possibility that a peasant rabble might be given knightly arms, than with the social aspirations of the bourgeois families.

Yet from the beginning the king or prince had also been a knight, as we have seen. The earliest records we have related to knighting ceremonies of any kind involve Charlemagne's descendants, and it had always been of the utmost importance in primitive warrior societies that the chieftain should be seen as a warrior *par excellence*. Frederick Barbarossa, Richard Coeur de Lion and St Louis set examples of the king as crusading knight, an ideal which touched the sceptical Frederick II as well, and which almost every monarch of the later Middle Ages aspired to but could never find opportunity to accomplish. The king as secular knight was another matter. Crusading vows could be a useful way to find favour with the Church, and no one dared criticise a Christian king for such an undertaking. Secular chivalry, on the other hand, was all too liable to scathing attacks from the Church or from popular poets: the chivalry and generosity of John the Good at Poitiers and afterwards nearly ruined France. Yet even if policy dictated a course unfavourable to the aspirations of knighthood, the king as an individual could share those aspirations at the same time, being a knight himself and brought up in knightly society.

The image of the ruler as warrior is reflected in their official emblems; princes had traditionally been depicted with sword and sceptre, as symbols of their political authority, and kings continued to appear thus on the face of their seals, but by the mid-twelfth century, Geoffrey of Anjou is portrayed on his commemorative enamel in Le Mans cathedral armed with sword and shield. Royal and princely seals provide ample evidence of the ruler in the guise of warrior: from the eleventh century onwards, the typical princely seal has an equestrian portrait of its owner on the reverse, in full armour, idealised not as a ruler, but as a knight. William I of England appears thus on his great seal, and as time goes on the images become more elaborate: Henry the Lion of Saxony appears with a flowing pennon on his lance,[1] and a century later Ottokar of Bohemia is depicted in full jousting accoutrements, with a magnificent helm and horse-trapper.[2] In another context, princes are shown as knights in their funeral effigies. When a new tomb was made for Robert Curthose at Gloucester Cathedral in the 1250s, he became a figure in contemporary armour, one hand ready to draw his sword and leap into action. The ultimate images of the chivalric ruler are the tomb of Edward the Black Prince at Canterbury, and the figure of king Arthur on Maximilian I's tomb in the Hofkirche at Innsbruck. That these images related to the personal status of the king or prince concerned is borne out by their absence from the coinage of medieval Europe. The only example of a medieval king shown as a warrior on his coins that

1 *Die Zeit der Staufer: Geschichte - Kunst - Kultur*, ed. Reiner Haussherr (Stuttgart 1977) II, 28.
2 *Die Zeit der Staufer*, II 39

comes to mind is John the Good; contemporary critics certainly felt that he confused chivalry and government once too often.

For political and social reasons, the knighting of a prince had to be attended by suitable pomp, and such occasions became festivals of chivalry. The imperial feast for the knighting of Frederick Barbarossa's sons at Mainz in 1184 was the first major example of royal or imperial ceremonial in chivalric guise, and from 1250 onwards there are few such investitures for which the chroniclers do not record that two or three days of jousting ensued, and that the great chivalric virtue of largesse was suitably honoured. By 1313 Philip the Fair was prepared to employ his publicist, Pierre Dubois, to write a treatise setting out the virtues of tournaments, in order to persuade Clement V, who had just condemned that very sport in the bull *Passiones miserabiles,* to lift his ban for three days at the knighting of the royal princes. In it Dubois makes the point that any royal edicts against tournaments had been instigated by clerks in the king's entourage, rather than by earlier monarchs themselves, who had enjoyed tournaments.

Edward I was an excellent example of this contradiction. He himself was a great participant in and patron of tournaments: at his knighting there had been a tournament, and he went abroad in 1260 to tourney in France, where he lost horses and armour, was badly beaten and injured, and still remained an enthusiast. Yet during his reign at least twenty-eight bans on tournaments are to be found in public records. And the paradox increases when we find the end of the campaigning in Wales in 1284 being celebrated by a great tournament, a tournament at Winchester in 1290 (for which the round table now in Winchester Castle may have been made)[3], a round table tournament at Falkirk during the Scottish campaign of 1302, and an Arthurian festival which may have been a tournament as well at his wedding to Margaret of France in 1299. Tournaments were now treated as something which could be invidious to the national war effort – most of the bans derived from the critical period of the Scottish wars at the end of Edward's reign – but which were a perfectly respectable royal occupation at others. And their appearance during or after campaigns suggests that they were being used as an inducement or reward to knights on active service, while the events at Edward's marriage were designed to recall his achievements in the field.

That some of this stemmed from Edward's own enthusiasm is shown by the lack of other examples of royal tournaments associated with campaigns. On the other hand, most of the increasingly elaborate tournaments of the fourteenth and fifteenth centuries occurred at either knightings, marriages or, more rarely, triumphal entries. Royal pageantry, designed to impress the subject with the awe of kingly pomp, adopted the tournament as one means of doing this; but it had a second, subtler, design as well: the

---

3   Martin Biddle, *King Arthur's Round Table* (Woodbridge 1996, forthcoming).

strengthening of the links between the lords and the crown through their vocation of knighthood. This is in essence the one object of royal concern with chivalry. The mass knightings, such as that at Edward II's knighting in 1306, were another way of producing links between the sovereign and his knights; these had been practised from as early as 1125, when Adalbert of Austria is said to have had more than a hundred companions. Now the chivalric vows and the idea of knighthood as an order were used to reinforce the feeling of brotherhood. The later knighting ceremonies contain a prayer that the new knight may use his weapons faithfully in the service of the kingdom of France, or England, or Castile, as the case may be; so the international ideal is not emphasised, and the brotherhood is first and foremost composed of the knights of one nation under their ruler.

Hence the king became the chief patron of chivalry. In the twelfth century even such a model of chivalry as Richard Coeur de Lion had not pretended to this position, but left such frivolous matters to lesser princes such as the counts of Hainault, and no chronicler ever saw their fondness for tournaments as anything other than youthful folly. On the other hand, the Angevin court under that most practical of monarchs, Henry II, had become a centre for the literature of chivalry, and no monarch felt offended by the dedication of a poem or romance. And from the king as a patron of chivalric literature to becoming the patron of chivalry itself was but a short step. Much of Edward I's enthusiasm seems to have been for the kind of chivalry which based itself on literature, and in the fourteenth and fifteenth centuries the same literary basis underlay most of the royal pageantry.

The prince's court, if the prince was so inclined, could be deliberately transformed into a centre of chivalry. René d'Anjou and Maximilian I in the fifteenth century were enthusiasts for tournaments, but the subtlest and most successful interplay of court, politics and chivalry was at the court of Edward III of England. [4] Married to Philippa of Hainault, whose family had long been patrons of chivalric festivals in the Low Countries, he encouraged not only the spectacles of chivalry, but also used its ethos to weld his inner circle of courtiers into a close-knit brotherhood-in-arms, invaluable in war and politics as well as in the lists. The underlying influence was that of literature: Edward's mother Isabella had had a considerable collection of romances, and Philippa was one of Froissart's first patrons; the king himself owned a number of volumes on Arthurian subjects. [5] And the romance of *Perceforest*, an elaborate and voluminous

---

4   Vale, *Edward III and Chivalry*, 42-94.

5   In 1335 he paid the exceptional sum of £66 13s 4d for a book of romances; the seller was a nun at Amesbury, and it is possible that it was a book owned by his great-grandmother, Eleanor of Provence, who had become a nun there in 1287. See Frederick Devon, *The Issue Roll of Thomas Brantingham* ... (London 1837) 144.

account of the history of Britain before Arthur's times, was probably written in Edward's honour. We have already looked at the tournaments of his reign, and we shall return to his most notable chivalric institution, the Order of the Garter. Yet however skilfully Edward used chivalry as a weapon of policy, his personal enthusiasm was also a major factor. Froissart claimed that he fought incognito at the siege of Calais under Sir Walter Manny, and he did the same in tournaments, becoming the equal of his fellow-knights rather than their sovereign lord. The same mixture of personal and political affairs pervades the history of chivalry at the Burgundian court, though none of the dukes could match the tourneying expertise of Edward III.

During the fourteenth century, we see the princely enthusiasm for chivalry being formalised, as secular chivalry developed into an institution which could be turned to political and diplomatic ends. Thereafter, chivalry largely survived in this courtly context. At the tournaments at the great diplomatic meetings in 1520 between Henry VIII and Francis I, known as the Field of Cloth of Gold, the sporting side of this event was as carefully arranged as the actual political discussions.[6] Unusually, the defendants were the two kings jointly with seven of their knights each. The tournament was proclaimed in France, England and the Low Countries, but the only challengers were in fact other English and French knights. The exact details of the tiltyard survive, and the regulations for the combats themselves were also very precisely laid down; even the type of armour was specified, and various 'pieces of advantage' were forbidden. Rules were also laid down for scoring.

The challengers arrived in 14 'bands', averaging ten in each. The two kings fought intermittently in the tournament; Henry, as was his wont, seems to have been over-eager: on one day, 'he ran so freshly and so many courses that one of his best coursers was dead that night'. Francis appeared in a series of superb costumes whose mottoes combined over a space of three days to spell out a chivalric theme: 'heart fastened in pain endless/when she/delivereth me not of bonds', in contrast to Henry's use of patriotic motifs. In all, more than 327 spears were broken in the jousting. The tournaments followed: these were not full tournaments in the traditional sense, but combats of two against two. These were followed by combats on foot between pairs of knights, with blunted spears, swords, and (in the English fashion) two-handed swords. The two kings were naturally at the head of the list of prize-winners, though both acquitted themselves well, heading the scoring in the jousts on some days.

The jousts at the Field of Cloth of Gold served no political purpose other than to cement Anglo-French friendships: in this, they were only temporarily successful, for France and England were at war within two years. Chivalry – as always – took second

6   Joycelyne G. Russell, *The Field of Cloth of Gold* (London 1969) 105-141.

place to politics. For an example of a Renaissance tournament with an overtly political message, we need to turn to the festival at Binche in 1549.[7] In the middle of a lavish festival given by the mother of the emperor Charles V, Mary of Hungary, a theatrical tournament was presented, in the manner of the prologues to the fifteenth century *pas d'armes* but acting out the dramatic narrative which had previously only appeared in literary form. The prelude, in the form of two successive petitions to the emperor, set out the plot, which was a carefully devised version of the usual romantic 'story line'. The evil enchanter Norabroch held various knights prisoner in the invisible Castle of Darkness; to counter his magic, the good queen Fadade had placed three great columns on the neighbouring Fortunate Isle, one of jasper and two others with a sword held fast in it, inscribed with a prophecy, which foretold that the knight who drew the sword would overcome Norabroch's magic and release the prisoners. To reach the Fortunate Isle, three knights had to be overcome in single combat, and those who were defeated by them joined Norabroch's prisoners.

The tournament was fought in the usual way, but with suitable scenery and theatrical effects; the challengers all adopted disguises, and the jousts were interrupted by sudden storms or doleful cries from the prison. One knight succeeded in defeating the three knights and drawing the sword, but found that the prophecy decreed that only a prince could succeed in the quest. At the end of the second day of jousting, a knight named Beltenebros appeared, vanquished the defending knights and drew the sword. Having identified himself as a prince, the Castle of Darkness became visible; with the magic sword, he overcame the magician's knights and broke a mysterious flask by which the spell was maintained. As soon as the prisoners were freed, he identified himself as Philip, Charles V's heir.

Because the outcome of the festival at Binche could have only one result, we must assume that in Philip's case the three combats were stage-managed. It was possible for other knights to reach the Fortunate Isle, but the prophecy was designed to eliminate them. On the other hand, Philip had to succeed in the jousts in order to get to the final stages, and under ordinary circumstances, this could not be guaranteed. Although there are many instances of kings or princes winning tournament prizes, the Binche scenario is most unusual in relying on a pre-arranged victory, particularly as Philip was a competent but not outstanding fighter, who came second in a foot challenge at Whitehall five years later.

After 1550, it became increasingly unusual for monarchs and princes to take part in serious jousts, and one unlucky accident was in itself enough to put an end to the tradition of royal participation. On 30 June 1559, Henri II of France took part in a

---

7   Roy Strong, *Art and Power* (Woodbridge and Los Angeles 1984) 91-4.

tournament at Paris to celebrate his daughter's wedding to Philip of Spain. He jousted against Montgomery, the constable of France, and both spears were shattered; but Montgomery failed to lower his broken end quickly enough. It caught Henri on the face; a splinter went through his visor and pierced his temple, causing the wound from which he died ten days later.

But the danger of tournaments was nothing new, and the death of Henri II would have had little long-term effect if there had not been other factors working against the tournament. The changing techniques of warfare led to a decline in the tournament as a sport, though it is easy to overlook the continuing role of the cavalry charge with couched lance: it was still part of the training of British regiments in the early twentieth century. The technique of lance combat was not abandoned suddenly: it merely declined in status, from a central place in late medieval strategy to a very minor role in seventeenth century warfare. And the late medieval foot combats introduced the latest techniques into the world of the tournament, particularly fighting with pikes, which the Swiss infantry perfected in the late fifteenth century.

The tournament continued in its other role, as a triumphal occasion, until the end of the sixteenth century. However, it was no more than one ingredient in a complex mixture of parade, theatre and 'magnificence', and quickly became a merely formal part of the proceedings. For instance, in the famous festival given at Bayonne in 1565 by Catherine de' Medici, the 'tournaments' do not seem to have involved much real fighting, but rather a display of horsemanship. In Italy, the Este court at Ferrara saw a series of thematic tournaments on the lines of the festival at Binche, where the fighting was merely an episode in a dramatic scenario, with a specific title. *Il Tempio d'Amore* of 1565 was probably outlined by the great poet Torquato Tasso, and was played out in an arena with a series of elaborate entries for each new group of participants. The Italian and French tournaments become by the early seventeenth century *carrousels*, not unlike the games on horseback which we saw presented before Charles the Bald eight hundred years earlier.

It was only in England that a semblance of the old tradition flourished, in the Accession Day tilts held under Elizabeth I.[8] There were jousts to celebrate Elizabeth's coronation in January 1559, and three further jousts around London that same year, so it looks as though such activities were actively encouraged by the queen from the beginning of her reign. The first accession day festival was ten or eleven years later, but the celebrations were sporadic until 1580; from then until the end of her reign we have records of an Accession Day joust in every year except 1582 and 1592: the series continued throughout James I's reign. Under Elizabeth, the tilts were part of the ritual

---

8   Roy Strong, 'Popular celebration of the Accession Day of Queen Elizabeth I' in *Tudor and Stuart Monarchy* (Woodbridge 1995), II, 116-38.

surrounding the cult of the Virgin Queen, and the dramatic element was provided by the individual knights. Perhaps the best example of this is the triumph devised for the ambassadors of the duke of Alençon in 1581, when the French prince was seeking Elizabeth's hand in marriage. As at Binche, the allegorical setting was appropriate to the occasion, and all the proceedings, including the fighting, were scripted to achieve a single outcome. Sir Philip Sidney and three other knights, calling themselves the 'four foster children of desire', attacked a fortress of 'perfect beauty', defended by twenty-two knights. Each of the four challengers jousted six courses against the defenders of the fortress, then fought with swords and finally at the barriers. The four then made a speech to the queen declaring their submission, and she in turn presented them with an olive branch 'in token of her triumphant peace and of their peaceable servitude'.

The tradition of *imprese* or complicated mottoes, similar to that used by Francis I at the Field of the Cloth of Gold, grew to such an extent that printed sheets were produced to explain the appearance of the knights and the meaning of their inscriptions; Sir Henry Wotton, in James I's reign, commented that 'some were so dark that their meaning is not yet understood, unless perchance that were their meaning, not to be understood'. The main theme, under Elizabeth, was a romantic cult in her honour. In James's reign, the themes were less focussed, and there were mutterings of dissent: Francis Bacon, at the end of the reign, saw such occasions as mere vanity:

> For jousts and tourneys and barriers, the glories of them are chiefly in the chariots, wherein the challengers make their entry, especially if they be drawn with strange beasts, as lions, bears, camels and the like; or in the devices of their entrance; or in the bravery of their liveries; or in the goodly furniture of their horses, and armour. But enough of these toys.[9]

Bacon might disdain the tournament, but they were highly popular with spectators, and with many of the participants. Sir Henry Lee, Elizabeth's Master of the Armoury, was the driving force behind the tilts of her reign, and the personal enthusiasm of Prince Henry, James I's eldest son, gave an added impetus to what had become a rather formal occasion, to the extent that he aroused his father's suspicions – no very difficult task in James I's case, but an interesting comment on the potential of the tournaments as a political weapon. A contemporary writer noted that Henry 'put forth himself in a more Heroick manner than was usual with Princes of his Time, by Tiltings, Barriers and other exercises on horseback . . . . which caught the peoples eyes. '[10] Henry died at the

---

9   Quoted from the *Essays* in D.J.Bland, 'The Barriers', *Guildhall Miscellany*, no.6, 1956, 7.
10   Arthur Wilson, *The History of Great Britain*, 1653, quoted in Roy Strong, *Henry, Prince of Wales* (London 1986) 153.

age of eighteen in 1612, and although princes continued to appear in dramatic tournaments, the 'heroic' manner had vanished. The shadows of warfare gave way to the illusions of theatre, and the tournament as a contest of skill between fighting men expert in arms was no more.

By the seventeenth century chivalry had been kept alive in too artificial a world for too long. It had had no place on the battlefield for almost a century, and its magic was beginning to grow weak. The ideals of knighthood had no place in royal courts where Castiglione and Machiavelli were admired, and where gentlemen and diplomats took precedence over mere rude soldiers. So royal patronage of chivalry disappears, and new means of propaganda are sought in an increasingly literate age. The taste for the spectacular abates; and only at the end of the century does it reappear at Versailles. Between the last Renaissance festival and the first of the Sun King, classicism has beaten down the old romantic literature. Arthur is back among the Breton fables, a classical restraint is the order of the day, not fantasy; and the pageantry of the tournament has been transmuted into theatrical spectacles, ballet and opera. Only in the secular orders of knighthood does a trace of chivalry's glory remain.

The Secular Orders

Until the fourteenth century, the idea of knighthood both as a universal order of society and as specialised groups within that order had been the monopoly of the Church. But the trial and downfall of the Templars and the failure of the Church to relieve the Holy Land by a crusade, combined with the crisis within the ranks of the Hospitallers had led to disaffection among secular knights with the ideals set up by the religious Orders. They turned from the crusading epics to the romances, and the Arthurian court became increasingly the focus for their dreams. Here the institution of the Round Table represented a kind of secular Order, an equal fellowship of knights chosen for their merit. And the author of a romance outside the Arthurian cycle envisaged an Order for knights who had shed their vices, especially the vice of pride. The idea of a group of knights bound by oaths of loyalty was as attractive to secular monarchs as it had been to the Church; and as the star of the religious orders waned, so a new phenomenon, the secular orders of knighthood, arose.[11]

The earliest of such secular orders is more in the nature of a fraternity of knights, the kind of mutual association which may also lie at the root of the military religious orders. The order in question was founded by Charles I of Hungary, and the chance

11   D'A.J.D. Boulton, *The Knights of the Crown* (Woodbridge and New York 1987).

survival of its statutes is the only record of its existence. It was probably established in 1325, and was dedicated to St George: the surviving statutes record amendments to the original regulations, and were drawn up on St George's day in 1326. The king was not head of the new institution, was was described as a fraternal union, whose purpose was the defence of the kingdom. It seems to have been part of Charles's strategy of reducing the power of the older baronial houses by creating a new class of royal vassals centered round a resplendent court. In addition to its general purpose, the society undertook charitable works, but its members also promised to report anything they heard which might harm the king or his realm. They were also 'to follow the king in all pastimes and knightly games', which implies a connection with tournaments. But in the absence of any further appearances of the brotherhood in history, we can only conjecture as to how long the society survived, or how far it achieved its purposes.

We know far more about the Order of the Sash or Banda, which is the first secular order on record to be headed by a monarch. The difficulty in writing its history lies in assessing the reliability of the sources, which, as so often in mediaeval Castile, are unsupported by any archival evidence in the form of official records. In the *Chronicle of Alfonso XI*, under the year 1330 we read:[12]

> The king being at Vitoria, because in times past the men of his kingdoms of Castile and León had always practised chivalry, and he had been told that they did not do so in his day, in order that they might be more eager to practise it, he commanded that some knights and squires of his household should wear a sash on their clothes, and he, the king, would do likewise. And being at Vitoria he sent orders to those knights and squires whom he had chosen for the purpose to wear clothes with, on them, the sash which he had given them. And he also put on clothes with a sash: the first clothes made for the purpose were white, and the sash dark. And from then on he gave each of these knights similar clothing with sashes each year. And the sash was as broad as a man's hand, and was worn over cloaks and other garments from the left shoulder to the waist (i.e. diagonally): and they were called the knights of the Sash (*de la Banda*) and had statutes among themselves on many good matters, all of which were knightly deeds. And when a knight was given the sash, he was made to swear and promise to keep all the things that were written in that book of statutes .... And it happened afterwards that if a knight or squire did some feat of arms against the king's enemies, or tried to perform such a feat, the king gave him a sash and did him high honour, so that all the others wished to do good knightly deeds to gain that honour and the goodwill of the king...

The knights of the Sash reappear on two further occasions in the *Chronicle*: before Alfonso's coronation at Burgos in 1332, when jousts were held at which the knights

12   *Cronicas de los Reyes de Castilla*, 231-2.

held the lists against all comers, and in 1333 at Valladolid in a tournament at which they fought together against the challengers, the king doing great deeds on their side.

The *Chronicle of Alfonso XI*, in the absence of other sources, is generally held to be reliable, though it does seem to have been edited at some point. The most recent opinion is that a very full version, of which traces remain in two MSS of the Chronicle and in a sixteenth-century Portuguese historian's work, was the original, written about 1344. This was then condensed in about 1360-70, by order of Pedro the Cruel, Alfonso's son, to fit into the series of official chronicles, the *Cronicas de los Reyes de Castilla*. A rhymed version, the *Poema de Alfonso el Onceno*, was made during the same period: but neither the poem nor its presumed source throw any additional light on the passage.

The only supporting documents are sixteenth-century copies of the statutes. The language and style point to a direct copy of an almost contemporary manuscript, and the prologue claims that the rules which follow were laid down by Alfonso XI at the foundation of the order in the year of his coronation, which does not agree with the *Chronicle*, though the discrepancy is only a minor one. The statutes proper begin with the reasons for founding the order

> 'because chivalry should be greatly honoured and advanced, and because that thing in all the world which most appertains to a knight is truth and loyalty, and which is most rewarded by God, for that reason (the king) ordered this book to be made f the order of the Sash, which is founded on two principles: chivalry and loyalty...'[13]

There follow the twenty-two headings of the rules, as follows:

> How the knights of the sash should try to hear Mass each morning
> What the knights of the sash should have in the way of arms and equipment
> How the knights of the Sash should avoid playing dice, especially on campaigns
> The speech and clothing to be adopted by the knights of the Sash
> How the knights of the sash should behave when eating and drinking
> How a knight should be invested with the sash
> How a knight of the Sash should act if another knight wishes to challenge him for the sash
> How a knight should act if challenged for the sash outside the Royal court
> The penalty for striking or drawing a sword against another knight of the Sash
> How a knight of the Sash who has a grievance against the king should proceed
> What the knights of the Sash should do if any knight repudiates his homage to the king or to the king's son

13   Lorenzo Tadeo Villanueva, 'Memorial sobre la orden de Caballeria de la Banda de Castilla', *Boletin de la real academia de la historia*, lxxii, 1918, 436-65, 552-74.

How a knight of the Sash should proceed if another knight of the order is found guilty
of a capital crime
The knights of the sash to form one squadron in the royal army on campaign
Chapters of the Order to be held at least three times a year
How the knights of the Sash are to behave in jousts
What should be done if two knights of the Sash quarrel
Procedure at a knight's marriage
Procedure at a knight's death
Procedure at a tournament
How the knights of the Sash are to observe everything in this book
The organisation of tournaments
The organisation of jousts [14]

It is clear from this outline that jousts played as large a part in the order's affairs
as did the conduct of war. In many ways, the statutes are reminiscent of the tournament
rules which were increasingly common throughout Europe at this period, whether in
the early 'round table' meetings with their pacts to use certain types of weapons, or in
the later fourteenth-century oath to keep the peace enforced at major tournaments.
But this element is probably accounted for by Alfonso's personal prowess as a jouster,
if we may believe the chronicle on that score. More important are the provisions for
loyalty to the king and avoidance of quarrels, as well as those for behaviour. All these
statutes seem to aim at a distinctive *corps d'élite*, set apart both by their way of life as the
most polished of courtiers and by their special oaths of loyalty, as well as their function
as the royal bodyguard in war. This is borne out by the terms of the oath administered
to the knights when they joined the order. The king and at least six knights were to
be present

and the knight to whom the sash is to be given shall come fully armed: and they shall
ask him whether he wishes to take the sash and be a member of the knights of the Sash.
And if he says yes, they shall say: 'You have to swear two oaths. The first is that you will
serve the king all your life or will always be a vassal of the king or of one of his sons:
but if it befalls that you leave the king's service or that of his sons, you shall return the
sash to the king ... And the second oath that you have to swear is that you will love the
knights of the Sash as your brothers, and that you will never challenge a knight of the
Sash unless it is to help your father or brother. And if two knights of the Sash quarrel
or fight, you shall do everything to part them, and if you cannot part them, you shall
not help either of them.'[15]

14   Villanueva, 'Memorial sobre la orden', 554 ff.
15   Georges Daumet, 'L'ordre castillan de l'écharpe', *Bulletin hispanique*, xxv, 1923, 12-13.

Alfonso had particular reason to value loyalty to his person and peace among his knights. He had come to the throne before he was two, and a troubled regency of thirteen years had followed. Continual revolts and intrigues had seriously weakened the kingdom, and much territory was lost to the Moors. Though Alfonso's first campaigns in 1327 and 1330 regained some of this, his domestic troubles continued. He had one of the former regents assassinated in 1326: but another former regent was still rebellious in 1332, and became a vassal of the king of Aragon at about this time. Nor were matters improved by Alfonso's rejection of his Portuguese queen in favour of his mistress Leonor de Guzman, whose bastard son later brought about civil war after their father's death. Furthermore, Alfonso's relations with the military orders of Santiago, Alcántara and Calatrava were poor, though they had not yet deteriorated to the nadir of the 1340s when Alcántara was in open revolt. So the Order of the Sash may have been an attempt to bind the nobles to personal loyalty to himself, improve the royal army for campaigns against the Moors, and provide an alternative to the existing military orders.

The later history of the Order of the Sash did not bear out these hopes. It scarcely appears in the history of Alfonso's own reign, experienced a brief revival under Pedro the Cruel, when buildings in Seville were decorated with the arms of the knights. It is mentioned in the *Victorial* of Don Pero Niño, the 'unconquered knight', early in the fifteenth century, and in 1457 a visiting German nobleman recorded that he was given the order of 'la banda de Kastylla' as a personal honour from the king. It was revived in the sixteenth century but even then only survived for a few years. If it arose out of a period of political turbulence, it needed a degree of political stability to survive: and Castile at this period could not offer that stability.

Fourteen years after the foundation of the Banda, two other monarchs showed an interest in the idea of a secular order. Edward III, at a great feast and tournament at Windsor in January 1344, put forward the idea of an Order of the Round Table. On the day after the tournament, the king dramatically announced his vow to found an Order with that name which was to have 300 members, and commissioned a building to house its assemblies. We have what may be an eye-witness account of the occasion, in which the writer emphasises that it was to be a re-foundation of the Round Table, 'in the same form and state as it was left by king Arthur', a phrase which rings true in the light of Edward's Arthurian enthusiasms. In the event, it was not England but France which saw the first practical steps towards a new royal order: John, duke of Normandy and heir to the French throne, submitted a proposal to the Pope, which Clement VI approved in six bulls dated 5 June 1344. This 'Order of the Star' was to consist of 200 knights and a college of canons, under the patronage of the Virgin and St George, on whose feast days the knights were to assemble for a religious ceremony, jousting being specifically excluded. However, the disaster at Crécy two years later delayed the execution of the scheme, and it was not until 1352, soon after John became king, that the Order was actually inaugurated.

When Edward III returned to the idea of an order of knighthood after the siege of Calais in 1347, he had evidently changed his mind about the idea of a Round Table on a grand scale. What finally emerged was much closer to the Order of the Sash, and it is possible that it was indeed modelled on the Spanish order to some extent. A marriage treaty with the son of Alfonso XI, later to be known as Pedro the Cruel, had been agreed in March 1346, following a embassy by Henry earl of Derby and William earl of Salisbury three years earlier, during which they had fought under Alfonso's banner at the siege of Algeciras. Both earls had been involved in the plans for the Round Table order in 1344, and were named as the first two magnates to take the oath in support of the venture.[16] The more modest order of 26 knights which emerged in 1348 bears two other similarities to the Order of the Sash: both orders use an item of clothing which can be fastened *outside* armour as their insignia, and both have a strong connection with tournaments. The resulting Order of the Garter does seem to have been closely connected both with Edward III's military activities and with his enthusiasm for jousting. Twenty-two of the founder members had been at the battle of Crécy, and of the remaining four two had been fighting in Gascony. Furthermore, because of the arrangement of St George's chapel, with its traditional facing pews, the knights were divided into two 'sides', and those on the prince's side had all been in the vanguard at Crécy, which he had commanded. It has indeed been argued that the first use of the Garter emblem recorded in the royal accounts is during, rather than after, the Crécy campaign. Equally, the founder-members were prominent in Edward III's tournaments both before and after the campaign, and formed the centre of a close-knit group around the king. The Order, whatever its real origins, served to strengthen the king's relationship with his leading nobles, a crucial factor in the success or failure of any medieval monarch.

The actual occasion of the decision to found the Order, and the reason for the choice of the garter as its symbol remain obscure. The earliest surviving version of the statutes, dating from 1415, gives no clue, and it was only in the mid-fifteenth century that stories to account for the garter emblem are recorded. The earliest version is that of Joanot Martorell in his romance *Tirant lo Blanc*: when the hero is admitted to the Order, the following story is told about its foundation:

> This order's inspiration ... came from an incident one day when we were dancing... by chance one damsel named Honeysuckle drew near the king. As she whirled, her left garter, which was trimmed with silk, fell off. Those nearest His Majesty beheld it on the

16   Boulton, *Knights of the Crown*, 109.

floor, and do not imagine, my lord, that she was fairer or more genteel than the others...
One of the knights near the king said: 'Honeysuckle, you have lost your leg armor. You
must have a bad page who failed to fasten it well.' She blushed slightly and stooped to
pick it up, but another knight rushed over and grabbed it. The king then summoned the
knight and said: 'Fasten it to my left stocking below the knee.' The king wore this garter
for more than four months.[17]

Eventually, so Martorell continues, an old servant told him that the queen and his
courtiers were amazed that he continued to honour 'such an insignificant damsel' in
this way, to which the king replied: 'So the queen is disgruntled and my guests are
displeased', and he said in French, 'Puni soit qui mal y pense'. 'Now I swear before
God that I shall found a new knightly order upon this incident..'

Martorell was certainly in England in 1438-9 and died in 1468, so the story must
have been current not later than the 1460s. We have corroborating evidence from
Mondonus Belvaleti, an Italian Benedictine who wrote a treatise on the Order in 1463,
in which he says that 'many assert that this Order took its beginning from the feminine
sex, from a lewd and forbidden affection'. But the suggestion made in the seventeenth
century by Elias Ashmole in his history of the Order, that the motto refers to Edward's
claim to the French throne, and that the colours of gold and blue are the French royal
colours, is still the most plausible.[18]

The foundation of the Order of the Garter is a skilful interweaving of politics and
chivalry, and the brilliant success of the idea is largely due to the presence of elements
which appealed to the knights, especially the Order's association with tournaments,
and a diplomatic usefulness which gave the sovereign an interest in keeping it alive,
whether to reward his military commanders or honour his allies.

The terms of the foundation, which were strictly adhered to and are the basis of
the modern order, were that the Order should consist of the sovereign and twenty-five
knights. This was a very small group, and the order owed much of its reputation to the
fact that the temptation to increase the number was resisted until the seventeenth
century. Associated with these knightly members was an equal number of priests, and
twenty-six poor knights maintained at the Order's expense. So, like the mediaeval
guilds, it combined with its main purpose, the furtherance of chivalry, those of religion
and charity. The nature of the chivalric obligations involved shows it to have had a
strongly practical military aspect. Knights were not to bear arms against one another

17   Joanot Martorell and Martí Joan de Galba, *Tirant lo Blanc*, tr. David H.Rosenthal (London 1984)
      pp. 121-22.
18   See Richard Barber, *Edward Prince of Wales and Aquitaine* (London and New York 1978) 86-7 for
      a fuller discussion and for the problem of the word 'garter'.

unless in obedience to different liege lords or in settlement of just quarrels, and they were to form a military élite, whom the sovereign was to 'prefer' in any warlike expedition. The numbers were to be chosen 'among those most profitable to the crown and Kingdom'.[19]

The membership of the Order continued to be a group of lords and knights closely associated with the sovereign up to the Civil War, with one important change. Of the knights elected to replace deceased or (very rarely) degraded members up to 1600 only six are foreigners of no more than knightly standing. However in the same period fifty-one foreign sovereign princes were offered or accepted the order. The diplomatic purpose behind this is clear. By associating them with an English order, it was hoped that they would prove favourable to the English interest, and such elections are particularly noticeable during Henry IV's diplomatic manoeuvres after his usurpation of the throne in 1399. Philip the Good, though friendly to England, refused the Order apparently for this very reason, that he was not prepared to enter into such a commitment, when offered it in 1422. Apart from this, the bulk of the knights of the Garter were military officers of the English crown. Military distinction was the only qualification for the admission of an English subject not of royal blood, until with the rise of the Tudor civil service Thomas Cromwell became the first purely secular member. Two of the three original reasons for which a knight could be degraded were military: treason and flight in battle (heresy being the third), though wasteful living was later added. There are several examples of degradation during this period, though it is unlikely that any of the Garter knights suffered a ceremonial as elaborate as the degradation from ordinary knighthood inflicted on Sir Ralph Grey in 1464. The latter was convicted of treason, and sentenced to have his spurs hacked off, his coat of arms torn from his body, another surcoat bearing his arms reversed put on, and his armour broken up, a sentence which, with the exception of the reversing of the arms which the king excused, was duly carried out.

The Order of the Garter's six hundred years of continuous existence is in sharp contrast to almost all other chivalric orders. Its French counterpart, the Knights of Our Lady of the Noble House, usually known as the Order of the Star,[20] finally saw the light in 1351-2. It was a much larger institution; the original 200 knights proposed in 1344 had been increased to 500. Other alterations had been made in view of the Garter's existence: St George was no longer a patron, and Our Lady was the Order's sole protector. There is no hint of frivolity about the enterprise: its emblem, a star, bears the motto *Monstrant regibus astra viam*, 'The stars show kings the way '. Its objectives

19   Yves Renouard, 'L'ordre de la Jarretière et l'Ordre de l'Etoile', *Le Moyen Age*, 55, 1949, 281-300 (p.292).

20   Boulton, *Knights of the Crown*, 167-210.

were more idealistic than those of the Garter, the furtherance of chivalry and the increase of honour, though an ordinance of 1352 adds a military purpose: it is to further the unity and accord of the knights of the realm and animate their prowess in order to ensure its security and peace. All deeds related at the *Table d'Honneur* were to be deeds of war, and no member could hold another order, a regulation aimed at those knights who might aspire to the Garter as well, and which shows the nationalist character of both Orders.

While the Garter's prestige was enhanced by the English victories, the Order of the Star was virtually annihilated in Brittany in August 1352, at the battle of Mauron, having held only one general chapter early in 1352, and having reached a strength of only 140 knights out of a possible 500. Jean le Bel attributes this to a vow taken by the knights never to retreat more than a quarter of a mile in battle, and says that eighty-nine knights of the Order were killed because of this; but even if the vow is true, his figure would seem to be exaggerated. With the capture of John the Good at Poitiers only four years after its foundation, the Order of the Star never really became active, and the gift of its house at St-Ouen to the dauphin Charles in 1374 marked the end of all possibility of revival.

If the Garter and the Star belonged to the sphere of international politics, the rivalries within France and England gave rise to a series of lesser orders. The royal ducal houses of Bourbon, Orléans and Brittany each had their own badge and Order. Louis II of Bourbon's Escu d'or (Golden Shield) was short lived, but the Porc-Epic (Porcupine) of Orléans was widely distributed in the decade following 1430, and the Hermine (Ermine) of John IV of Brittany was still in use in 1532. All of them, however, showed the inherent difficulty of any secular Order, that it relied for its glory entirely on the prestige of its leader, and on the patronage, both political and financial, that he could offer, though the intention was the reverse, that the Order should enhance its patron's standing.

'By 1380, a monarchical order had been founded in every major court of Latin Christendom';[21] the range and variety of these orders was remarkable, from a direct imitation of the Garter (the Order of the Buckle in Germany) to orders which had more than a passing resemblance to crusading institutions, such as the Order of the Collar founded by Amadeus of Savoy in connection with his planned expedition to the East. The Order of the Golden Fleece belongs to the same group but was by the far most successful of the new foundations. Most of the late fourteenth century orders barely survived the death of the king who founded them. It was the wealth and energy, as well as political acumen, of the Valois dukes of Burgundy and their Imperial and

---

21   Boulton, *The Knights of the Crown*, 289.

Spanish heirs, that made this the greatest Order in Europe. Founded by Philip the Good on the occasion of his marriage to Isabella of Portugal in January 1430, it was a project that he had long cherished. it was modelled closely on the Garter, and had a similar number of knights, twenty-four excluding the duke, though this was almost immediately increased to thirty and later to fifty. Its avowed objects, as set out in the foundation charter, were as follows:

> To do reverence to God and to uphold the Christian faith, and to honour and increase the noble order of chivalry; and also for the three following reasons: firstly, to honour older knights whose noble and high deeds are worthy of recognition; secondly that those who are now strong and able-bodied, and exercise deeds appropriate to chivalry every day, may have cause to continue them even better than before; and thirdly, that knights and gentlemen who see this order worn... may be moved to noble deeds themselves and lead such a life that their valiance will earn them great fame, and they will deserve to be chosen to wear the said order: my lord the Duke has undertaken and set up an order called 'La Toison d'Or'.[22]

The motives ascribed to Philip besides those set out in the statutes have been various. At some later date, a romantic legend was invented to explain the choice of the symbol of the Golden Fleece; it was in memory of a lady at Bruges whose golden hair Philip admired, despite the mockery of his courtiers at its unfashionable luxuriance in an age which liked a broad forehead with the hair drawn back on the head. The real reason seems to have been the hoped-for parallel between Jason's heroic endeavour with a small band of companions in classical myth and the deeds which the new order would undertake. Again, its links with crusading projects led contemporary chroniclers to see it as a kind of permanent crusade. Its real purpose was designed to increase the partisans of the House of Burgundy, and to enhance the prestige and independence of the ducal house: in refusing the Order of the Garter, Philip excused himself by saying that he was about to found his own Order. In Philip's diverse territories a unifying force was badly needed, and he attempted to strengthen the bonds between the nobility which had already been established at ducal festivals and tournaments. Louis XI paid tribute to the Order's success when he copied it, even in small details, for his Order of Saint Michael. Even more strongly nationalist than the Garter, it became attached to the sovereignty of Flanders when the Burgundian empire disintegrated, but until then it had drawn for its recruits on all the Valois lands. The original members included six cousins of the duke, and three members of the distinguished knightly family of de Lannoy. No foreigners were included.

---

22   Baron F. A. F. Reiffenberg, *Histoire de l'Ordre de la Toison d'Or depuis son institution jusqu'à la cessation des chapitres* (Brussels 1830) xx; author's translation.

The strictly Burgundian nature of the membership was due to the use of the Order as a kind of advisory council to the duke; and except for emperors, kings or dukes (a clause added later so that the gift of the Order could be used as a diplomatic weapon), no other order might be held. The chapters of 1468 and 1473 in particular aired their grievances to Charles the Bold in no uncertain terms, and reprimanded him for being over-eager to go to war; but the Order never had real political influence and there were frequent complaints that the Order's advice was not sought by the monarch. Yet the members of the Order were still represented on the governing body of the Netherlands as late as the eighteenth century. Besides this, the general chapter held an inquest on the behaviour of the other members, reproving offenders for their faults. One of the de Lalaing family was told that he was too dirty in appearance, while two other knights were accused of being too fastidious; the 1545 chapter, in a puritan mood, produced an exceptional list of sins – adultery, concubinage, drinking and bad temper – and deprived one knight of his insignia for a year. In more serious cases such as criminal offences the chapter claimed to be the only court in which members of the Order could be tried, and a clause to this effect was inserted in the Statutes of 1516. However, when the counts of Egmont and Horn stood accused of treason in 1568 and insisted on trial by the Order instead of by the Spanish authorities, they were overruled on the strength of a case of 1468 in which the court's jurisdiction had been limited to matters of honour, and no full-scale criminal trial ever occurred. The last general chapter took place in 1559, as the lengthening shadows of religious dissension darkened the Low Countries, and Philip II and his successors were loath to summon a meeting of respected figures who might have opposed their policies. Thereafter appointment to the Order remained the gift of the king, but was purely honorific; a revision of the statutes in 1631 confirmed this, and it became part of the Spanish aristocratic world, where status and precedent had come to rank before real honour or worth.

Besides these Orders of openly high intent, there is another group of Orders from the same period whose only *raison d'être* was a chivalric whim on their founders' part.[23] Boucicaut's *Ordre de la dame blanche à l'escu verd* (Order of the White Lady on a Green Shield), to protect defenceless and disinherited ladies, which he founded in 1399 and which lasted about five years was another courtly Order, though with charitable undertones. Varying degrees of organisation for such Orders, down to the mere wearing of a badge appropriate to the fictional theme of a *pas d'armes* led Olivier de la Marche to comment that 'when a prince gives some device to several noblemen without a number and chapters, it should not be called an Order, but only a device'.[24] The Order

---

23 Boulton calls these 'votive' orders, because a vow is the usual reason given for their foundation (*Knights of the Crown*, pp.xix-xx)
24 Lewis, *Later Medieval France*, 177.

of the *Fer de Prisonnier* of John I of Bourbon, and the device of the Dragon of Jean I of Foix were such, not unlike the liveries of English retinues of the mid-fifteenth century applied on a higher level, badges of personal alliance rather than of membership of an Order.

Many of the Orders had in their statutes echoes of the military Orders and of the long awaited crusade which never materialised. One article of the Garter statutes refers to distant expeditions, which are probably crusades; and in 1454, many of the knights of the Order of the Golden Fleece took the crusading vow. In René d'Anjou's Order of the Crescent the Order could only be renounced if the knight became a monk, and in the brotherhood of arms of the 'Tiercelet' those members who had made the journey to Prussia had a special mark on their insignia, one golden spur if they had not actually seen action there, two if they had fought the heathen.

At the other extreme from the purely chivalric Orders are the practical associations, such as the Order of the Falcon or 'Tiercelet' and the Order of the Golden Apple. The object of these was that their members should band together to share the profits and hazards of war, just as brothers-in-arms did. The Tiercelet was founded in Poitou around 1380, and consisted of eighteen local lords, the Viscount of Thouars being the most important. The members of the 'Tiercelet' named one of their number as leader in war, and a deputy if needed; they contributed to each other's ransoms, shared the booty and looked after the dependents of those killed. Their annual service and insignia distinguished them from a mere mutual assurance group, even if they were a 'body' first and an 'Order' second, and there was no attempt to create a permanent institution which would outlast its original members.

The secular Orders finally degenerated into mere honorifics. Of the reasons listed in the statutes of the Golden Fleece one came to dominate the rest; 'to honour older knights whose noble and high deeds are worthy of recognition'. The corporate existence of the Orders instituted after 1450 was minimal, and often there were no limits on the number of knights holding the honour, which was merely at the sovereign's discretion. A brief ceremony and a medal replaced that corporate spirit which briefy appeared in the great Orders, and which was the driving force behind some of the lesser ones. But the knight's idea of glory was too individual and personal for the secular Orders to become more than a series of marginal notes in the history of chivalry. It is by their later incarnation as orders of merit rather than of knighthood that they are remembered, and their greatest age was to be in the nineteenth century, when they proliferated in every petty court of Europe, until only a handful remained that were not mere badges. In the smaller world of chivalry personal valour had needed no medals to distinguish it.

17

The Epic of Chivalry Revived

THE LITERATURE OF CHIVALRY continued to flourish during the fourteenth century, though there were no great innovations on the scale of the cycle of Arthurian romance that had been created during the thirteenth century. Much of what was written reworked existing material; *Sir Gawain and the Green Knight* is a classic example of this, drawing together two existing stories to create a new masterpiece in which the original plots interweave seamlessly. But the anonymous poet's skill was exceptional, and many of the 'new' romances manage nothing more than a warmed-over version of old adventures in the setting of Arthur's or Charlemagne's court. Indeed, the most interesting work is often to be found on the fringes of the chivalric world: *Sir Gawain* itself is written in an archaic form – alliterative verse – and probably for a provincial audience. At the great royal courts where chivalric display flourished, the literature of chivalry was more prosaic and less inspired: the vast romance of *Perceforest*, telling of pre-Arthurian Britain, may have been written for Edward III in the 1340s. Although it draws on a remarkable variety of folklore and other sources, it is almost impenetrable and immensely long. The chronicler Jean Froissart attempted a lengthy Arthurian verse romance, *Meliador*, which he completed in 1388; it lacks the immediacy of his historical writing, and is often little more than the description of one tournament after another.

But the most popular reading seems to have been the various compilations which tried to weld the stories of the main cycle of the Arthurian romances into a more coherent entity. This was particularly true in countries such as Italy and Spain, which came late to the chivalric legends; in the early fourteenth century, Rusticiano da Pisa – who also recorded Marco Polo's account of his travels when they were fellow-prisoners – claimed to have used a book left in Italy by Edward I when he was en route for the crusade as the basis for his romance, which survives in later French versions as *Meliadus* and *Guiron le Courtois*. These retell the Arthurian stories using a new hero as the focal figure. Some twenty-five years later, an unknown writer compiled a more traditional version, the *Tavola Ritonda* or *Round Table*, using different parts of the French romances. The same process of quarrying the original cycle happened in Spain, in the late fourteenth century, when the adventures of Arthur's knights were gathered under the general heading of the quest for the Holy Grail, though this theme in fact scarcely figures in the sprawling book that resulted. Even in France, new compilations of chivalric romance were in demand: a prose version which contained a complete history of Britain up to Arthur's death as told in the romances, was produced for the library of Louis II of Bourbon in 1391. The Charlemagne legends, collected from the degenerate versions of the *chansons de geste* still circulating, were fashioned into a verse cycle in the late thirteenth century, which in turn was the basis for a prose rendering in 1454, and was finally translated into English by Lord Berners as *The Boke of Duke Huon of Bordeux*. Another Arthurian compendium was produced for Jacques d'Armagnac in 1470, and in Germany, Ulrich Fuetrer produced his *Buch der Abenteuer* at the court of Albrecht IV of Bavaria, aiming to present an all-embracing history of Arthurian and Grail chivalry.

The most famous of these types of compilation is that of Sir Thomas Malory. Approaching the material from a very different angle, his eight romances each tell a single story, seven of them carefully extracted from the French prose works, whose tapestry-like interweavings he unravels to present a much clearer and sharper tale. As a group, they cover the whole history of Arthur, and it was this that enabled William Caxton, when he came to print them, to present them as one book, using the title *Le Morte Darthur*. Even if Malory himself did not set out to make 'of this vast assemblage of stories, one story and one book',[1] he deliberately includes all the greatest episodes of the cycle, and covers the whole history of Arthur's rise and fall. Unlike the French scribes, he was not writing for a patron, but for 'jentylmen and jentylwymmen' of his own standing, who were eager for such reading matter. Beside Malory's works, printed for 'many noble and dyvers gentylmen of thys royame of England'[2] who had asked for an English version of the Arthurian legend, Caxton also produced a translation of Raimon Llull's fourteenth-century work as *The Book of the Ordre of Chyvalry* at the request of 'a gentyl and noble esquyer'[3]. Writers such as Gilbert de la Haye and Henry Lovelich were busy with their own versions of the literature of chivalry, writing like Malory as enthusiastic amateurs rather than professional makers of romance.

In the course of his translations, Malory not only unravels the tales, but also makes many subtle alterations of emphasis, by omission and selection, and more rarely by addition. He sees chivalry as a secular institution with moral rather than religious

---

1   G. Saintsbury, *The English Novel* (London 1913) 25.
2   Malory, *Works*, I, cxlii.
3   Llull, *The Book of the Order of Chyvalry*, 121.

associations.[4] Thus Lancelot is his true chivalric knight, rather than the spiritual Galahad; and Arthur, from the shadowy figure of the French romances, becomes the archetype of heroic knighthood. Part of the change in Arthur's character comes from the English romance from which he derives *The Tale of the Noble King Arthur,* where Arthur is portrayed almost in the manner of a *chanson de geste* as a second Charlemagne. This in turn enhances his standing when the tragedy of his involvement with Lancelot and Guinevere reaches its climax; it is from the highest point of the Wheel of Fortune that he falls to his doom. Around Arthur, as the greatest prince of his time, the great knights gather; and they are no longer merely knights, since many of them play a part as Arthur's military commanders in the Roman wars of the second tale, especially Lancelot and Gawain, who only appear in the French romances as knights-errant. This practical view of knighthood reflects the realities of courtly life in the fourteenth and fifteenth centuries, where the great jousters and exponents of chivalry were likewise the king's right-hand men in the field.

Malory also alters the conception of the Round Table, until we would scarcely be surprised to find him inserting its statutes as an Order into the text: he does in fact invent an oath which Arthur makes all the members of the Round Table swear each Pentecost. He imagines it as a secular company with a practical mission in the world, the keeping of order in unruly times, and derives this from the view of knighthood propounded by the Lady of the Lake in the French *Prose Lancelot,* that knights were appointed defenders of the weak and powerless in the days after the Fall when envy and covetousness began to increase. He has a much clearer view of good and evil than appears in the French romances; the wickedness of the 'false traytour knight' Breunys Sanze Pyté (the Merciless) and a Tarquyn stands out sharply. Hence the Round Table becomes a continuation of Boucicaut's Order of the White Lady on a Green Shield and of the Order of the Golden Fleece, and represents the true fulfilment of knight-errantry. Malory selects adventures which have a high moral intent in keeping with his theme, preferring the rescue of damsels and overthrow of wicked knights in single combat to the enchantments and marvels which were one of the chief delights of his original. And such a theme would appeal strongly to his readers in the England of the Wars of the Roses.

Likewise, Malory rejects the now moribund ideal of courtly love. Lancelot is challenged by a damsel whom he has just rescued, who says: 'But one thyng, sir Knyght, methynkes we lak, ye that ar a knyght wyveles, that ye woll not love som mayden other jantylwoman', and repeats the rumour that he loves Guinevere. Lancelot, instead of

---

4   See Beverly Kennedy, *Knighthood in the Morte Darthur,* 2nd edn (Woodbridge & Rochester N. Y. 1994).

protesting his single-minded adoration of his lady, defends himself on quite different grounds:

> For to be a weddyd man, I thynke hit nat, for that I muste couche with hir and leve armys and turnamentis, bartellys and adventures. And as for to sey to take my pleasaunce with peramours, that woll I refuse: in prencipall for drede of God, for knyghtes that bene adventures sholde nat be advoutrers nothir lecherous, for than they be nat happy nothir fortunate unto the werrys; for other they shall be overcom with a sympler knyght than they be hemself, other ellys they shall sle by unhappe and hir cursednesse bettir men than they be hemself. And so who that usyth peramours shall be unhappy, and all thynge unhappy that is about them.[5]

Knighthood is entirely practical, a vocation from which there is no respite. Love has become an obstacle on the knight's road, as Iseult points out when Tristram refuses to go without her to Arthur's court: 'For what shall be sayde of you amonge all knyghtes? "A! se how Sir Trystram huntyth and hawkyth and cowryth within a castell wyth hys lady, and forsakyth us. Alas!" shall som sey "hyt ys pyte that ever he was knyght, or ever he shulde have the love of a lady".'[6] The lady is no longer the inspiration of the knight, fount of all his prowess; instead knighthood itself urges him on. Knighthood can only survive as long as it remains the supreme ideal; the darkness of tragedy begins to descend when the knights put their personal feelings before all else; and that includes Lancelot's love for Guinevere as well as the hatred of Mordred and Gawain's loyalty to his dead brothers.

Nor does Malory require a higher motive for knighthood than good deeds in this world. Finding the Grail adventures to be an essential part of the stories he was translating, he does not abandon it, even though it sets up a greater ideal than that of the Round Table; instead, he excises the numerous diatribes on the depravity of the knights of this world wherever he can. When he comes to deal with the failure of the greatest of the secular knights, Lancelot, to achieve the quest, he emphasises his partial success, in the vision of the Grail at Carbonek. And of the problem of grace and repentance little remains. Malory accuses Lancelot of other failings, saying that he is unstable, but does not specify his sinfulness beyond this. The grave and noble pages which tell of the achievement of the quest belong to a separate world. Galahad and Perceval move beyond secular concerns into the spiritual realms at the supreme moment when the Grail is accomplished; but secular knighthood is nonetheless represented by the nine knights of Gaul, Ireland and Denmark, and by Sir Bors; but as Sir Bors returns to Camelot

---

5   Malory, *Works*, I, 270-I.
6   *Ibid.*, II, 839-40.

from Sarras, bearing Galahad's greeting to the court, we feel that it is the Round Table above all else that has made this achievement possible. Arthur claims it for his knights when at the end of the quest he makes 'grete clerkes to com before hym, for cause they shulde cronycle of the hyghe adventures of the good knyghtes'.[7]

Malory's greatest achievement is to give us a last glimpse of the high purpose that chivalry could inspire, even though he is writing in days when the ideals of knighthood were all too often confused with the pomp and circumstance of court ceremonial. Caxton insists rightly on his moral intent in his preface: 'For herein may be seen noble chyvalrye, curtosye, humanyté, frendlynesse, handynesse, love, frendshyp, cowardyse, murdre, hate, vertue, and synne but t'exersyse and folowe vertu..'[8] It is only because Malory has conveyed this moral sense so powerfully that he is able to depict in his closing pages the full force of the tragedy of Arthur, the dark hour of the destruction of loyalty and knighthood, contrasting the nobility of chivalric intentions with the frailty of the human condition.

The combination of reality and chivalry appears in a much less earnest but highly attractive form in the work of his contemporary, the Catalan writer Joannot Martorell, whose account of the founding of the Order of the Garter has already been quoted. *Tirant lo Blanc* is a splendid mixture of fact and fantasy; the exuberance of the author leads him to plunder a wide range of romances and historical episodes for his hero's adventures. Martorell himself had seen military service and had had a long-running chivalric quarrel with a man who, so he claimed, had seduced his sister by promising to marry her; he repeatedly challenged him to single combat, without success. His book is full of soldierly bravado and forthright opinions, and Tirant's chivalric adventures are modelled on those of contemporary Catalan knights-errants, such as Philip Boyle, who fought a challenge against Sir John Astley in the presence of Henry VI in London in 1442; Boyle had also been challenged by Martorell himself. And Tirant's military adventures, which occupy the second half of the book, are based on the exploits in the eastern Mediterranean of the Catalan adventurers led by Roger de Flor in the early fourteenth century, whose deeds were recorded by one of their number, Ramon Muntaner.

The style of the novel moves equally between the fantastic and the real, with high-flown speeches which come down to earth in a few pithy closing sentences. The book as a whole undergoes a shift in tone as it moves from Tirant's youthful knight-errantry to his deeds in the Emperor's service: towards the end of the book, Tirant consummates his love-affair with the princess Carmesina, which had begun as a model of courtly love, in an entirely realistic scene. He dies before he can marry her,

7   Malory, *Works*, II, 1036.
8   *Ibid.*, I, cxlvi.

and the idealised element returns as the two lovers ascend to heaven, summoned by a 'clarity of angels'.

It is the wide sweep of Martorell's imagination, his wry self-consciousness, his wit and ultimately his acknowledgement of the real world that makes this a romance with a difference, perhaps even as Mario Vargas Llosa says, making him 'the first of that lineage of God-supplanters —Fielding, Balzac, Dickens, Flaubert, Tolstoy, Joyce, Faulkner — who try to create in their novels an "all-encompassing reality".'[9] Martorell certainly bestrides the two worlds of medieval romance and the modern novel; his themes are often taken from medieval romance. The story of William of Warwick which opens the book is a simple adaptation of an earlier tale, and the hermit who expounds chivalry to Tirant is very like the figure who opens Raimon Llull's *Book of the Order of Chivalry*. But thereafter, Martorell's independent spirit takes over, and he creates an entirely new tale, realistic, psychologically acute, often ironic, ranging across every kind of topic and genre. But the old values of chivalry still reign supreme, which, given Martorell's fondness for chivalric quarrels in real life, is exactly what one would expect. The Greek emperor declares that 'no good feat of arms was ever performed in this world unless it was for love'; and before Tirant knows that Carmesina returns his love, his one ambition is to be remembered not as a soldier, but as a lover — his epitaph is to be 'Here lies Tirant, who died because he loved so greatly'. And knightly vows and challenges are commonplaces: during a campaign, Tirant swears that he 'will never sleep in a bed nor wear a shirt until I have killed a king or a prince', and his companions make similarly extravagant promises. As to challenges, Tirant's great enemy is Kyrieleison de Muntalba, to whom he sends bombastic letters of defiance; but unlike Martorell's own *cartas de batalla*, they result in a real combat, with Kyrieleison's gigantic brother Thomas, after Kyrieleison himself has died of rage on learning of Tirant's feats of arms. And even if Tirant's deeds – and the deeds of many of the other knights – represent a kind of wish-fulfilment, the world in which Martorell sets them is often splendidly vivid and detailed, whether he is describing a rich suit of clothes or a meal or a palace intrigue. Martorell's prose has an immediacy which convinces us that these are, if not reality, the genuine daydreams of a fifteenth century knight.

Tirant lo Blanc does not stand quite alone. While Martorell was writing his masterpiece, Antoine de la Sale was creating a similar fictitious story about a knight's career, which he completed in 1455. He chose a historical figure, the Angevin knight Jehan de Saintré, and wove round him an imaginary biography. Saintré is taken up as a penniless squire by a wealthy and beautiful lady, who provides for all his needs and instructs him in the ways of the world, in religion and in chivalry, rather as the Lady

---

9   Mario Vargas Llosa, *Carta de Batalla por Tirant lo Blanc* (Barcelona 1992) II.

of the Lake had once taught Lancelot the code of knighthood. The narrative tells of Saintré's successes in the lists, citing historical characters like Boucicaut as evidence of the truth of the story. He departs on crusade to Prussia, and in his absence his lady consoles herself with a young nobleman who has recently become abbot of a rich monastery. When Saintré discovers he has been deceived, he challenges the abbot, who insists on a wrestling match, in which he twice defeats Saintré; but Saintré then lures him into a combat in armour, with axes, and has his revenge on both him and his lady in the end. It is a kind of extended version of a story by Boccaccio, rather than a work on an epic scale like *Tirant*, but it shows that the old taste for romances was being replaced by a demand for something more up to date and earthy, even if the result was an uneasy mixture of high seriousness and near farce. And there is a ferocity in de la Sale's closing attack on love which seems more than just a literary exercise, a heartfelt cry from one who has suffered in real life:

> Ah, false. wicked and traitorous love, must you be ever like unto Hell, that was never yet surfeited with swallowing-up of souls? Will you likewise never be sated with tormenting and wounding of hearts?... you have taken captive the hearts of some and have dealt full falsely and evilly therewith, and then left them all confounded, so that you are answerable for the loss of their souls and their lives (unless God have mercy upon them). and their honour.[10]

This is no longer the world of the chivalric romances, but a realistic view of misdirected passionate love, which rewards not with an ethereal bliss but with frustration and waste of energy.

By contrast, the Italian romances were to move away from realism into the realms of poetic fantasy. The greatest of all Italian poets had portrayed the romances of chivalry as a snare and a delusion; in the *Inferno*, Dante lays the blame for the fate of Francesca da Rimini and Paolo Malatesta on the tale of Lancelot and Guinevere:

> *One day we read in pastime how in thrall*
> *Lord Lancelot lay to love, who loved the Queen:*
> *We were alone – we thought no harm at all.*
>
> *As we read on, our eyes met now and then,*
> *And to our cheeks the changing colour started,*
> *But just one moment overcame us – when*
> *We read of the smile, desired of lips long-thwarted,*

10   Antoine de la Sale, *Little John of Saintré*, tr. Irvine Gray (London 1931) 314-5

Such smile, by such a lover kissed away.
He that may never more from me be parted
* Trembling all over, kissed my mouth. I say*
The book was Galleot, Galleot the complying
Ribald who wrote; we read no more that day.[11]

Dante censures the frivolous romance as much as he does the behaviour of the lovers: yet the next great epic poems in Italian after his were to draw on that very stuff of courtly legend for their inspiration, as chivalry became the preoccupation of the Italian princes. The new humanism was not necessarily hostile to chivalry. If in scholarly circles the philosophers of classical Greece were preferred as models of behaviour, at the courts of Renaissance Italy the new learning was merged with the older courtly ideal to create a kind of chivalric humanism, drawing on both traditions. It was particularly at Ferrara that the epic was revived, its beginnings being the Charlemagne romances which Barberino had collected under the title *I Reali di Francia* (The peers of France) at the end of the fourteenth century. We are back in the world of the *chansons de geste*: loyalty and treachery loom larger than love and courtesy, and the basic motif is Christianity's struggle against the pagan lords. The more sophisticated Florentine court under the Medici princes found such material apter to parody than to serious ends, and the *Morgante Maggiore* of Pulci (1470) exaggerates the giants and marvels until they seem ridiculous.

However, in Ferrara under Hercules I matters were seen differently. Hercules, a great jouster, was regarded as the type of perfect knighthood, and under his patronage Boiardo wrote his epic *Orlando Innamorato*, in which courtly love and the magical are borrowed from Arthurian legend and attached to the epic of Roland. It is not an entirely serious work, 'plesaunte to rede in' rather than instructive; action and adventures are preferred to any attempts at psychology, and the unexpectedness of its marvels is one of its joys. The poet himself equates the strange and the pleasant: 'I will relate to you the strangest, most delightful and truest thing in the world, if God gives us peace.'[12] Its great success was probably due to just this lack of high intent in an age which often took itself very seriously, and also to its attractive, nostalgic view of the past:

The love that to their ladies fair
* The knights in ancient times once bore,*
* Their famous battles and adventures strange,*
Their deeds in jousts and feats in tournaments

11   Dante, *Inferno*, tr. Dorothy Sayers (London and Baltimore 1949) canto v, 127 ff.
12   Matteo Maria Boiardo, *Orlando innamorato* ed. L. Garbato (Milano 1970) i.i.1.

Are told throughout the world today,
And all of us are eager listeners,
One favours this knight, the next man that,
As if they were alive and with us still.[13]

Boiardo left the *Orlando Innamorato* unfinished, breaking off to lament how reality, in the shape of Charles VIII's invasion of 1494, had disturbed the peace which the writings of romances demanded.

Ludovico Ariosto's poem *Orlando Furioso*, written between 1505 and 1516 and revised in the 1520s, is, in name at least, a continuation of the *Orlando Innamorato*. It is conceived on a much grander scale, a chivalric epic, which is also a courtier's homage to his patron, recreating — or rather creating — the legendary origins of the house of Este. The theme of the poem is boldly stated at the outset, in a frank imitation of the *Aeneid*:

Ladies and knights, arms and lovers,
Courteous deeds and bold I singe.

Its subject matter is ostensibly drawn from the stories about Charlemagne and his peers (the matter of France) as well as those about Arthur (the matter of Britain) and Alexander (the matter of Rome). Ariosto plunders these three great themes of medieval romance wholesale, though the framework remains Charlemagne's wars against the pagans. From the Arthurian romances he borrows chiefly the idea of knight-errantry, the quest for adventure and encounters with magic, while from the Alexander stories come the marvels of the East. He adds to this folktales, episodes from Italian *novelle*, imitations of classical literature, anything, in short, that pleases his fancy. To take just one example, the story of Ginevra, in which a lady is accused of adultery because her maid has impersonated her, comes from *Tirant lo Blanc*; and it was to reappear in Shakespeare's *Much Ado about Nothing*. Ariosto extends the range of chivalric romance enormously, both in subject-matter and in style. The plot and the ideals are indeed borrowed from the world of chivalry, and chivalry is maintained by Ariosto as the proper touchstone for knightly behaviour.

The verse-form of the poem may also have a chivalric forerunner. In the late 1470s, Angelo Poliziano had celebrated Giuliano di Piero di Medici's victory in a tournament at Florence in 1475 in the same eight-line stanzas which Ariosto uses, and his *Stanze per la Giostra*, with their mixture of classical myth and realistic descriptions of the jousting, may well have been one of Ariosto's models.[14] And Poliziano is also treating the same themes of love, war and honour.

---

13   Boiardo, *Orlando innamorato*, II, xxvi, 1.

Superimposed on this is an entirely new attitude to the telling of the tale itself. Ariosto the author plays a prominent and conscious part in the poem: where the old romances – and Malory in their wake – appealed to authority, to their predecessors, real or imaginary, as the source of their story, Ariosto is his own helmsman in the racing tide of his narrative. His favourite device is to switch the focus of the narrative at a crucial point, a forerunner of the modern 'cliffhanger' serial: if his heroine is about to be raped, his hero treacherously enchanted, he gaily turns away to pick up another of the *varie file*, the different threads that his art requires, or simply announces that the present canto has gone on too long and he will stop before the audience gets bored. And just as his tale has many threads, so he is master of a variety of genres: adventures in the old style, realistic descriptions of sieges, sexual frankness, astute character sketches, a page or two of well-turned flattery.

The delight of *Orlando Furioso* is that it multiplies the unexpectedness of the chivalric romances, the uncertainty beloved of the knight seeking adventures, and makes it the principle of the epic itself, extending the range of its mood and mode until everything from low comedy to high tragedy is swept into the scheme of things.

There is also an extraordinary delight in the fantastic. Ippolito d'Este, at whose expense the first edition was published, is said to have to turned to the poet when he looked at his presentation copy and to have remarked, 'And where did you find all this bollocks [*coglionerie*], Messer Ludovico?' One assumes that he was teasing the poet; but Ariosto knew what he was about: the feats of his heroes, bloodthirsty at first sight, become an ironic send-up of the praise of the warrior in the old French epics, an exaggerated versions of the battle scenes of the *chansons de geste*. We cannot take this bloodthirstiness seriously when a war is won with the help of stones which become horses and leaves which become ships. The fantasy distances us from the apparent reality; it has the effect of throwing the characters of the protagonists into relief. On the other hand, it also becomes a private joke between the author and the reader, ridiculous but enjoyable.

Contemporary critics condemned Ariosto for the lack of unity in the *Orlando Furioso*, referring to the classical unity demanded by Aristotle in his *Poetics*. Given that the *Aeneid* and the Latin poets are a very strong influence, they had some cause to mistake Ariosto for simply another of the new humanists. Furthermore, the second part of the poem has long passages on contemporary Italy, praising its poets and (of course) the princes of Ferrara, while bemoaning the political state of the country, and this has nothing to do with chivalry or romance. However, a better image of Ariosto is as the *uomo universale*, closer to Shakespeare in his variety than to his classicising

14   On Poliziano, see Ruggero M.Ruggieri, *L'umanesimo cavalleresco italiano* (Napoli 1977) 149 ff.

fellow-countrymen. His avowed intention is to entertain, even though early commentators were at pains to find allegorical meanings and deep allusions throughout his work. He is skilful enough not to preclude the possibility, and there is an underlying pattern of thought behind his enchantments and delights. It is essentially a humane, tolerant philosophy, smiling tolerantly at man's frailty, with no great regard for religion. In a sense, Ariosto promotes chivalry in the place of religion: the supreme moment of the poem is when Leone recognises Ruggiero's ultimate act of chivalry, and repays him in kind with an equally chivalrous action. Ruggiero is in love with Bradamante, the warrior maiden (modelled perhaps on Camilla in the *Aeneid*[15]), and his love is returned. But Leone has rescued Ruggiero, and in return Ruggiero has agreed to fight, disguised as Leone, against Bradamante: if he is able to vanquish her, she will become the victor's bride - who will, of course, be not Ruggiero but Leone. Ruggiero fights and wins; he rides off, stricken at heart, and Leone, concerned at his sudden disappearance, goes in search of him and learns the truth, at which he surrenders his claim to Bradamante:

> *Such chivalry as this he's never known,*
> *Nor ever heard of in all history,*
> *Nor will it equalled be in future times*
> *In any regions or in any climes.* [16]

In the end, through all the convolutions of the plot, the smiling, half-ironic banter of the narrator, there is a real belief in human worth and in nobility of spirit. Without this inner strength, the poem would be no more than a court masque, an empty show. If Ariosto at first detains us by amusing us, he ends by moving us deeply.

Ariosto's last revisions date from the 1530s, and his work spans the early years of the northern Reformation, and the growing seriousness of the second part may to some extent reflect the changing political scene. His successor in the epic tradition, Torquato Tasso, writing in the years around 1570, inhabited a different, more earnest world altogether, that of the Counter-Reformation, which had begun at the Council of Trent in 1548. For him, like Milton, the epic was an entirely serious occupation, and he found his theme in the stories of the First Crusade. Here chivalry's purposes and accomplishments were both at their highest; and here was a theme worthy of the darker days of the Counter-Reformation which nonetheless retained the chivalric framework beloved of the court at which he worked. He had already completed a simple chivalric

---

15   Examples of female warriors are very rare in the medieval romances; the best instance is Heldris de Cornouailles' *Le Roman de Silence*. Another possible model is Orable-Guiborc in the *chansons de geste*.

16   Ludovico Ariosto, *Orlando Furioso*, tr. Barbara Reynolds (Harmondsworth & New York 1973) XLVI, 38, 5-8.

romance, *Rinaldo*, in which his moral earnestness and his love of the idyllic, at its purest in his lyric poems, had appeared. His reading of poetic textbooks, such as Aristotle's *Poetics* and study of classical examples before he embarked on the *Gerusalemme Liberata* (Jerusalem Freed), as well as his researches into the history of the First Crusade, showed the seriousness with which he approached the task. This was to be a work which would educate first and entertain afterwards.

In fusing the heroic epic and chivalrous romance as Ariosto had done before him, he blends an attempted realism in his descriptions of war and of love (which he sees as an eminently human and fallible force) with a supernatural machinery deriving from classical poetry. The unity of action of classic epic and the adventures in the style of medieval romances were of course at loggerheads. If he retains Ariosto's diversity, his seriousness is sometimes disquieting amid such improbable material; he is less approachable for a modern reader, though perfectly intelligible to his own contemporaries. From the outset it is clear that he is the more ambitious poet. The opening lines half-echo Ariosto:

> The sacred armies and the godly knight
> That the great sepulchre of Christ did free.
> I sing; ...[17]

but at once declare that the emphasis will be on godliness as central to chivalry. Rinaldo, after his escapade with the temptress Armida, must first repent his sins before he can once more work valiant deeds; and Tasso makes much of the historical episode of the Mass and procession before Jerusalem's walls during the siege. In contrast, the pagans find little tolerance for their ways as they 'to idols false for succour call', and only conversion redeems them.

Love, for Tasso, is a snare and entanglement. Both Rinaldo and Tancredi fall in love with pagans, Rinaldo with the beautiful but evil Armida, Tancredi with the warrior Clorinda who disdains love. Yet Rinaldo's sojourn in the enchanted garden and Tancredi's grief for his killing of Clorinda bring them to salvation in the end. There is nothing particularly courtly about their passion: Rinaldo falls above all to Armida's physical charms:

> As when the sunbeams dive through Tagus' wave
> To spy the storehouse of his springing gold,
> Love-piercing thought so through her mantle drave.
> And in her gentle bosom wander'd bold:

17 Torquato Tasso, *Gerusalemme Liberata* i.i.1; tr. (as *Jerusalem Delivered*) Edward Fairfax (London 1600).

It view'd the wondrous beauty virgins have,
And all to fond desire with vantage told.[18]

And it is only at the last when he has her at his mercy that a nobler love, destined to end in marriage, springs up between them. Tancredi's love for Clorinda is indeed unassuaged, but only because her Amazon ways allow no room for such feelings, and even at her death she has no fond word for him other than gratitude for his baptism of her.

Chivalry is therefore a martial and religious virtue; which is not entirely unexpected in a poem on this theme. It extends further than the crusaders, however, for Suleiman, the sultan who defends Jerusalem against them, is chivalrous in his way, and Tasso paints him as a noble, stout-hearted warrior, and others among the Saracen army are similarly courageous. Yet, lacking the Christian belief, they cannot prevail. The fulfilment of the ideal in Tancredi and Rinaldo combines the virtues of the courtier, consideration, gentleness and good manners, with bravery and vigour and a spiritual maturity. It owes little to knightly ideals, far more to the teachings of Castiglione overlaid with the new religious seriousness of the Counter-Reformation. And Tasso regards his heroes less as examples of chivalry than as representatives of physical and spiritual perfection to whom chivalry is a natural and incidental virtue, inherited from their forebears but no longer the greatest of their guiding lights, just as it was to their counterparts in real life.

The last of the great chivalric epics, avowedly modelled on Tasso, might seem to be Edmund Spenser's *The Faerie Queene*. The question is whether this is in essence a chivalric work, or whether it is merely decked out in the trappings of knighthood, like Elizabeth's knights at the Accession Day tilts. It is easily answered: this is allegory, not heroic epic, with an underlying Protestant ethic hostile to some of the fundamental elements of chivalry. For instance, physical love is generally condemned, as exemplified by the episode where Sir Guyon binds the enchantress Acrasie. What we have here is a key to the new age, as Spenser declares in the preface addressed to Sir Walter Raleigh:

> The generall end therefore of this book is to fashion a gentleman or noble person in vertuous and gentle discipline: Which for that I conceived should be most plausible and pleasing, being coloured with an historicall fiction, the which the most part of men delight to read, rather for variety of matter, then for profite of the ensample ... I labour to portraict in Arthure, before he was King, the image of a brave knight, perfected in the twelve private morall vertues, as Aristotle hath devised.[19]

18   Tasso, *Jerusalem Delivered*, IV, xxxii.
19   Edmund Spenser, *The Faerie Queene* (Cambridge 1909) I, 526-7.

Chivalry is only a part of his overall scheme, and we stand on the threshold of the reign of the knight's successor, the gentleman.

With the coming of the printing press, the romances were at once in far greater demand that before. The *Orlando Furioso* was immensely and deservedly popular, being translated into every major European language by the end of the sixteenth century; but less likely romances also gained a new lease of life. *Amadis de Gaula*, a work which scarcely survives in manuscript form, but may have been written as early as the beginning of the fourteenth century, was printed in 1508, and went through nine editions in the next twenty-five years; whereupon a torrent of romantic prose flooded the Spanish market, to be eagerly swallowed by all and sundry. The original four books of *Amadis*, a neat enough romance in the late Arthurian manner, with a well-organised plot, and rendered in noble Spanish prose, were not enough for a voracious and indiscriminating public. The adventures in *Amadis* revolve around the lives and loves of Amadis and Oriana whose passion is tested by a series of enchantments and adventures; the characters and the story are not wholly unconnected, and the two lovers have an ideal quality worthy of Tasso. What matters is that Amadis,

> shall be the flower of knighthood in his time; he shall cause the strongest to stoop, he shall enterprize and finish with honour that wherein others have failed, and such deeds shall he do as none would think could be begun nor ended by body of man. He shall humble the proud, and cruel of heart shall he be against those who deserve it, and he shall be the knight in the world who most loyally maintains his love, and he shall love one answerable to the high prowess.[20]

Compared with the French romances of the thirteenth and fourteenth centuries, there is a lack of logic about the adventures, which are often episodes inserted at random; and, more curiously, there is a streak of wanton cruelty which is surprising: 'In the gate-way Galaor found the first knight whom he had smote down, who was yet breathing and struggling; he trampled him under his horse's feet and then rode away.'[21] Amadis, too, can be as cruel as his brother; and violence is apparently relished purely for its own sake, not as a necessary byproduct of skill in arms.

This, however, like all the romances, is 'literature of escape'; and the demand for such relief from the tedium of everyday life was far greater than the literary skill available. Continuations of *Amadis*, in all another eight books, and their successors, concentrate on adventure; they emphasise their remoteness by high flown and archaic

---

20   Vasco Lobeira, *Amadis of Gaul*, tr. Robert Southey (London 1872) 17-18.
21   *Ibid.*, I, 100-1.

language, or by a new 'elegance' of style which is more euphuistic than anything the Elizabethans ever dreamt up. Here is a sunrise:

> With difficulty the rubicund father of the untutored youth Phaethon, revealing himself in the northern tropic of the lower hemisphere, advanced on swift Phlegonian chariot to clear the golden and profulgent path of the twelfth zodiac, sending from his fourth sphere to the circumference of the immovable earth most certain harbingers of his approach.[22]

Each romance becomes, not an intricate tapestry of themes as in the French cycles, but an overloaded cart of words, the wheels of whose plot creak along under the burden. And yet, in an age of widening education and new leisure, the fashion caught on. Between 1508 and 1535, twenty-eight new romances (including some sequels) appeared, and numerous reprints made. It was to a new audience that they were addressed, for while the rich French or Flemish bourgeois might have run to the luxury of an occasional manuscript, books were within the reach of much humbler pockets. They aroused fanatical belief, and St Teresa of Avila is said 'to have devoted herself passionately to these books',[23] and even to have written one in her youth. Apocryphal stories of their effect abound. There is the tale of a man who returned home to find the household in a state of mourning, all weeping together, and when he asked if a son or relative had died, they answered, 'No'. 'Why then do you weep' he enquired, perplexed. 'Sir,' they said, 'Amadis is dead.'[24] And one Simon de Silveira is said to have sworn on the Gospels that every word in *Amadis* was true; but then he was the man who, having won a lady after a lengthy courtship, took his revenge on their wedding night by asking for a candle when they retired, and reading *Palmerin of England* for so long that the lady, taking it amiss, said to him: 'Sir, is that what you married for?' Whereupon he replied: 'And who told you, Madam, that marriage was anything else?'[25]

The vogue for such works continued throughout the century, despite attacks from critics and from the Inquisition. Amadis and Palmerin and their respective clans were the leaders, and a host of lesser figures tagged along behind. Italy, France and Germany each took up the vogue. In France, the various books of *Amadis* were printed 117 times —an average of eight times for each book — between 1540 and 1577, and it was still well known in 1666, when La Fontaine referred to it; in Italy, there were several dozen printings between 1546 and 1615; only England, with a strong literary activity of its

---

22   Henry Thomas, *Spanish and Portuguese Romances of Chivalry* (Cambridge 1920) 140-1.
23   *Ibid,* 150.
24   *Ibid.,* 80
25   *Ibid.,* 117-8.

own and few links with popular culture on the Continent, remained relatively aloof. In all this, little of the old ideals was left. *Amadis de Gaula* was at least reasonably respectful of chivalry, and more moral than many of its predecessors in that all its liaisons end in marriage. Later works dwelt only on the theatrical and melodramatic side of the adventures, until the once noble knights are no more than performers going through their tricks to amuse a clamouring crowd, stripped f all ideals and growing ever more fantastic in their feats. The tables are turned: chivalry has become the people's plaything.

Yet there was one more masterpiece to come, perhaps the most astonishing work in all the literature of chivalry, comic, satirical and yet deeply concerned with the values of chivalry. If the romances were already at a low ebb in 1600, Byron's famous phrase about Cervantes and his *Don Quixote*, that he 'smiled Spain's chivalry away', has some truth in it. Like all great comedy, Cervantes keeps his comedy near to reality, and the fundamental absurdity from which his humour springs is the close juxtaposition of real life and romance.

    Don Quixote seems to have derived from an anonymous play of about 1590, in which one Bartolo, bereft of his wits by reading too many chivalric ballads, sets out in Quixotic style: but Bartolo is swiftly brought to his senses after only one adventure. Given the idea, the story seems to have shaped slowly in Cervantes's mind. The first seven chapters, before Sancho Panza appears, are little more than an expanded version of Bartolo's mishap. Once the inquisition on the books of chivalry has taken place, and Sancho Panza's native wit has been brought to salt the Don's dry and elegant discourses. the theme and counterpoint of the work are complete. The object stated in the Prologue now comes to the fore: 'this book of yours is at no more than destroying the authority and influence which books of chivalry have in the world and among the common people',[26] and remains as a guiding thread through the book. The theme reappears in the canon of Toledo's diatribe:

> I have never seen a book of chivalry with a whole body for a plot, with all its limbs complete, so that the middle corresponds to the beginning, and the end to the beginning and middle; for they are generally made up of so many limbs that they seem intended rather to form a chimaera or monster than a well-proportioned figure. What is more, their style is hard, their adventures are incredible, their love-affairs lewd, their compliments absurd, their battles long-winded, their speeches stupid, their travels

26   Miguel de Cervantes Saavedra, *The Adventures of Don Quixote*, tr J.M.Cohen (London & Baltimore 1950) 80

preposterous and, lastly, they are devoid of all art and sense, and therefore deserve to be banished from a Christian commonwealth, as a useless tribe.[27]

And the last sentence of the second part repeats the author's avowal of his intention:

For my sole object has been to arouse men's contempt for all fabulous and absurd stories of knight-errantry, whose credit this tale of my genuine Don Quixote has already shaken, and which will, without a doubt, soon tumble to the ground. Farewell.[28]

Don Quixote is nonetheless a romance of chivalry in all its outward appearances. It consists of a series of adventures with the obligatory diversions and inserted stories; it uses the conventional language of the romances (something which no translation can ever convey); and in many ways it conforms to the ideal romance of which the canon of Toledo speaks, which under the guise of the popular formula will give the author an opportunity to display his versatility in 'the epic, the lyric, the tragic and the comic, and all the qualities contained in the most sweet and pleasing sciences of poetry and rhetoric'. It has, too, 'an ingenious plot, as close as possible to the truth', and it achieves 'the excellent purpose of such works, which is, as I have said, to instruct and delight at the same time'.[29]

In fact, *Don Quixote* owes a good deal to Ariosto's *Orlando Furioso*, and shares many attitudes with *Tirant lo Blanc*. These two books escape the fate of most of the volumes in the priest's great burning of Don Quixote's books. Ariosto in translation is no use to the priest: 'but if he speaks in his own tongue, I will wear him next my heart'. As for *Tirant lo Blanc*, for its style it is the best book in the world. Here the knights eat and sleep and die in their beds, and make their wills before they die, and other things as well that are left out of all other books of that kind'.[30] Cervantes inherits from Ariosto the idea for some of his scenes and episodes, but above all they share an enthusiasm for variety and flights of fancy. *Tirant* is less of an immediate influence, because the vein of down to earth common sense which earns Cervantes' approval is cast in a very different form in the Catalan novel: it sets off and emphasises the special nature of knighthood, rather than deflating its pretentiousness.

It is by their heroes, however, that books of chivalry stand or fall. Cervantes has seen this; he accepts the formula, and attacks chivalry at its central point. If the hero becomes a comic figure, he seems to say, all your elaborate trappings are so much glittering tawdry; and my hero is only a little more comic than yours. Don Quixote, 'verging on

---

27   Cervantes, *Don Quixote*, 425.
28   *Ibid.*, 940.
29   *Ibid.*, 426.
30   *Ibid.*, 426

fifty, of tough constitution, lean-bodied, thin-faced, a great early riser and lover of hunting',[31] is not so different from Lancelot when he sets out on the quest for the Grail, except that the romances know nothing of age, and toughness and early rising are equally unromantic. His habits are exactly those of the knight-errant: he is careful to regulate his sleeping hours by the approved rules; each time he sleeps beneath the open sky 'it seemed to him that he was confirming his title to knighthood by a new act of possession',[32] and he is careful to do his duty as a lover: 'He spent the rest of the night in thoughts of his lady Dulcinea.'[33] All that divides Don Quixote's actions from those of the real knights-errant of romance is his awareness of correct behaviour: he always feels that this or that ought to happen to him, and makes certain that it does, while in the romances from which he draws his inspiration it goes without saying that the adventures appear of their own accord, and the knights are really sleepless for love.

This perpetual self-consciousness is sharply contrasted with Sancho Panza's natural earthiness. Don Quixote lies in self-imposed wakefulness, 'while Sancho Panza's sleep, as he settled down between Rosinante and his ass was not that of a rejected lover, but of a soundly kicked human being'.[34] Cervantes subtly underlines the unnatural life of the romances, which is one of his chief objections to them, and whenever Quixote threatens to become too fantastic, Sancho is there at hand to bring him back to earth – or at least to somewhere near it.

Sancho, being unaffected by Don Quixote's madness, sees windmills as windmills and sheep as sheep, but if he believes his own eyes, he believes his master's interpretation of what he sees. And Don Quixote lives in a world which is almost permanently under the enchanter's spell. Windmills become giants, sheep opposing armies, a barber's basin Mambrino's helmet. But such a device palls quickly enough, and Cervantes is prepared for this. Having made his initial point about the absurdity of the romantic setting, he turns the enchantments into the key to his hero's development. In this, again, he is offering an unfavourable contrast to the romances, where a perfect knight is always a perfect knight, and like some comic-strip hero, always emerges victorious and unchanged in the end. Life is not like that; Don Quixote is a more subtle and resilient character than we at first suspect. True, he remains steadfastly convinced of the reality of knight-errantry as he imagines it; but he manages to reconcile the everyday world and his own vision to a remarkable extent. When in the second part enchantments are contrived by Samson Carrasco and by the Duke and Duchess, who have read of his adventures of the first part in print, he overcomes their ingenious attempts to mock

31   Cervantes, *Don Quixote*, 84
32   *Ibid.*, 95.
33   *Ibid.*, 95.
34   *Ibid.*, 60.

him by a high idealism which no amount of ridicule can touch. Even when Sancho deliberately deceives him for reasons of his own, and presents 'three peasant girls... riding on three young asses or fillies' as Dulcinea and her attendants, and seems to have the upper hand over his master, Don Quixote goes surely on his way: and in the episode of his dream in the Cave of Montesinos he makes such an enchantment a commonplace and natural event which troubles him not one whit. He says that one of the peasant girls borrowed money of him, and by ways of thanks 'leaps two yards, by measure, into the air'; at which Sancho breaks in to demand: 'Are such things possible in the world? Can there be enchanters and enchantments so strong as to have changed my master's sound wits into this raving madness?'[35] Yet despite the author's pretended doubts as to the authenticity of this episode, it is all of a piece with Don Quixote's way of thought; and as the knight resists all attempts to shake his belief, we begin to wonder if he is not a lone sane voice in a world gone mad.

For from the enchantments, his own logic produces greater truths. When he defends himself before the Duke and Duchess, he speaks of these enchanters, and especially of Dulcinea's transformation, which is the cruellest blow of all, 'for to rob a knight-errant of his lady is to rob him of the eyes with which he sees, of the sun by which he is lighted, and of the prop by which he is sustained'. The Duchess objects 'that your worship never saw the lady Dulcinea, and that this same lady does not exist on earth, but is a fantastic mistress, whom your worship engendered and bore in your mind, and painted with every grace and perfection you desired'. '"There is much to say on that score," replies Don Quixote. "God knows whether Dulcinea exists on earth or no, or whether she is fantastic or not fantastic. These are not matters whose verification can be carried out to the full. I neither engendered or bore my lady, though I contemplate her in ideal form"...'[36] Cervantes sums up the place of the lady in chivalry perfectly.

But Cervantes also moves far outside the world of chivalric romances. Don Quixote starts out as a symbolic figure of folly with human traits added, and ends stripped of his symbolism as an entirely living character, vindicated in his apparent folly. Sancho grows in stature as his native wit takes him safely through situations beyond his experience. For Cervantes has lived up to the versatility to be found in the ideal chivalric novel of the canon of Toledo; and he has made of it something quite new as a result. If he began by satirising the mere formulae of chivalry, he ends by hinting at alternative views of life, based on his experience and reading.

He had been scholar, soldier, official, playwright and author in his day; when he wrote the last pages of *Don Quixote* he was famous without the rewards of fame. He had read the books of the Erasmian thinkers and of the Counter-Reformation, as well

35   Cervantes, *Don Quixote*, 624.
36   *Ibid.*, 680.

as Italian epics and literary theory; in short, he was a man of far wider horizons than his predecessors as writers of romance, and romance did not allow of any wider vision than its own narrow conventions. Like Ariosto, he is very much present, as the author, in his own work; he inserts autobiographical episodes of his captivity in Moorish hands; he throws in fashionable pastoral scenes and lyrics (being particularly proud of the latter). And he can create the character of Sancho, who holds as much of our attention as Quixote himself. At a higher level, he takes the patent unreality of books of chivalry as a starting point for a subtle exploration of the nature of reality, disguising this schematic reasoning behind the vital and spontaneous surface of the book.

Like his hero, Cervantes still continued to keep some affection for and belief in the romances; the enchantment lingered on. At the end of the prologue to part two he says: 'I forgot to tell you that you may look out for *Persiles*, which I am just finishing, and the second part of *Galatea*.'[37] Of these two projects, only Persiles was completed: and it proved to be a romance of chivalry in which the author not only fulfils the canon of Toledo's rules as to variety, but also obeys its regulations as to the central figures, giving them 'all those attributes which constitute the perfect hero, sometimes placing them in one single man, at other times dividing them amongst many'. Classical romances as well as mediaeval and modern are laid under contribution; the geography is at once realistic and fantastic; and the whole work was the apple of its author's eye. Yet it was Don Quixote, the fallible hero, who proved immortal, like Malory's Lancelot; we are readier to sympathise with their humanity than to marvel at the gilded perfection of a Perceval or Persiles.

Don Quixote had an immediate success; a spurious second part was published before Cervantes provided his own, and translations were quickly made. It is the last major work to be inspired by the ideals of chivalry, partly because its satire was all too effective, and even the most traditional courtier could hardly take his disguise in a tournament seriously after reading it, and partly because the age of chivalry was near its close. In any case, the Spanish romances had been a very late and unreal flowering. But in Cervantes' pages there is more true insight into chivalry's real meanings than in many far more serious works; and for all his comic ways, the lean and lonely figure of the Knight of the Sad Countenance on the dusty Spanish roads is no unworthy tailpiece to the procession of knighthood.

---

37   Cervantes, *Don Quixote*, 470.

18

Critics of Chivalry and Advocates of Reform

CHIVALRY WAS AN IDEAL which aimed to soften the rough ways of the soldier, and substitute a controlled and disciplined way of life for the old heroic frenzy. Its critics from the very earliest days accused it of failing to find the golden mean of an effective but civilised knighthood; and if the criticism of the over-warlike barons of Germany in the eleventh century already quoted is one side of the picture, the other is represented in the mid-twelfth century by Peter of Blois, who complains that not only does military discipline no longer exist, but that soldiers going to war 'take wine instead of swords, cheeses instead of lances; bottles instead of blades, spits instead of spurs'. The newly made knights at once go off to break their vows, 'oppressing the poor subjects of Christ, and miserably and unmercifully afflicting the wretched, in order to sate their illicit lusts and extraordinary desires in the sorrows of others'.[1] He compares these so-called Christian knights unfavourably with the soldiers of ancient Rome, brave and virtuous despite their paganism. The preamble to the Rule of the Templars, written about 1130, says of the early members of the order of knighthood in general that 'they despised the love of justice, which belonged to their duties, and did not do as they ought, that is defend poor men, widows, orphans and the Church: but instead they competed to rape, despoil, and murder.' And Urban II, launching the First Crusade, was reported to have made similar criticisms, saying that knighthood (militia) was now falsehood (malitia). Other writers accuse thirteenth-century knights of going to war 'all dressed up like a knight going to the Round Table' or of going 'to war dressed for a wedding'.[2]

Throughout the twelfth century, writers attacked knights as violent, greedy, disorderly, luxury-loving and proud. The same catalogue of vices recurs in the poems which deplore the present state of the world, a popular genre with clerics of the period. To some extent, they are simply repeating a conventional portrait of the knight, embellished to taste, as in the punning lines of Bernard de Morval:

1   For Germany see p.243 above; Peter of Blois, *Epistolae*, xciv, in Migne, *PL*, 216, 293-7.
2   Lecoy de la Marche, *La chaire française*, 392.

Miles atrox rapit, angit, agit, capit, urget egentes,
Quos premit opprimit, omnibus imprimit undique dentes.

At the end of the century, another poet declared that 'knights are the worst because of their pride, the way they covet horses and rich clothing, living wastefully and dissipating their goods, glorying in vile deeds. . . if they see anything they want, they carry it off, seize it or take it by force.'

John of Salisbury, in book VI of his *Policraticus*, is chiefly concerned with soldiers, but the portrait he paints of knights who love chivalric display is sharply satirical:

> If they break any lances, which their artful laziness has contrived to have mad as fragile as hemp, if the gold leaf or red-lead or other coloring matter has been knocked off their shields by some chance blow or other accident, their garrulous tongue, if they find any to listen, will make the incident memorable from century to century.[3]

In times of peace knighting was neglected, and became purely honorific. In war it became a matter of military standing, and was more easily acquired by knighting on the battlefield. In times of anarchy the knights reappeared; but instead of being defenders, they became aggressors. If they had not always been a sure defence in times of trouble before, they proved a far worse menace now that they acknowledged no responsibilities. In Germany the 'robber knights' were partly excused by the needs of poverty: the economic decline after 1300 demoralised the *ministeriales*.[4] The Westphalian lords of the mid-fifteenth century had 'fields so unfruitful that they lie as desert, uncultivated. . . you could not watch without tears the way in which these fine knights had to fight, day in, day out, for their food and clothing, and risked the gallows or the wheel in order to avoid hunger and want'.[5] On the other hand, there was a strong and stubborn tradition of independence of authority, aggravated by the persistence of the idea of private war as a legal right. Even the Golden Bull of Charles IV in 1356, attempting to impose order on the riven Empire, confirmed that, provided due notice of three days were given, private war remained the subject's inalienable right. In the early sixteenth century this right degenerated into little more than a system of legalised highway robbery in the hands of men such as Götz von Berlichingen, Franz von Sickingen and their associates, who declared war on Mainz, Nuremberg and other towns in turn, and were thus licensed to plunder their merchants at will. 'Knight' in such cases had come to mean merely an armed horseman; the wheel had come full circle.

3   John of Salisbury, *The Statesman's Book*, tr. John Dickinson (New York 1927) 185.
4   Arnold, *German Knighthood*, , 247.
5   Adolf Waas, *Der Mensch im deutschen Mittelalter* (Graz-Köln 1965) 132.

Likewise, whenever ordered government broke down, as in France in the Hundred Years' War, and particularly at the end of the fourteenth and beginning of the fifteenth century, the old instincts for plunder and rapine re-emerged among the knights. Bertran de Born sang the glories of war, war for no matter what cause; and he at least had wrested a castle of his own from his brother. A knight of the 'free companies' which ravaged France under the guise of greater political ends would have echoed his words cheerfully, but pleaded the same need as his German counterpart. Often unpaid and unprovisioned, whether living as garrison of a fortress or as a raider in enemy territory, he was forced to forage, and when foraging failed, to extort a living from the neighbouring peasants. This he did by the system known as *appatis;* at best this was a kind of local taxation, properly administered and accounted for, but when the same people had to pay it to as many as ten garrisons or companies, small wonder that they fled to the towns or eked out a living in the forests. The security which the knight's presence had once implied was now sold in the form of safe-conducts through the territory he controlled, and such documents were not cheap: 12s 6d for a month's safe conduct for a good ploughman who earned £3 in a year was no small sum. The sword had become a means of making one's future, and those who did not perish by it in the process might amass great wealth. Ransoms among the knights themselves were one matter, but to extort money from the common folk was another. Unfortunately, the latter was often easier; and it is not surprising that the knights as a class fell into disrepute during the fifteenth century.

By this time, however, the majority of so-called knights had no claim to the title: the few remaining knights who had adhered to the old practice and who had been ceremonially knighted, were a very small part of the class of armed warriors now termed knights. And the world of the lawless brigands who went under the once proud title was nearer to reality than that of the genuine knights, with their nostalgia for imagined glories of the past.

If the knight's behaviour in warfare was open to attack, his life of supposed luxury and vainglory in peacetime was equally a subject for adverse comment. The most obvious targets for such criticism were tournaments, officially execrated by the Church as 'detestable fairs'. All sensible men recognised them as folly, so ran one line of argument, despite their value as military training, because of the excesses which they brought in their train: thus Humbert des Romans in the thirteenth century, speaking of the 'insensate prodigality of the nobles' in pursuit of glory, of the use made by some 'who take advantage of tournaments in order to settle private feuds',[6] and of the debauchery to which they are exposed. If only knights would use them as occasions

---

6   Lecoy de la Marche, *La chaire française,* 394.

for the practice of arms and nothing more, tournaments might be tolerable. Jacques de Vitry, bishop of Acre, writing before 1240, was one of the first to point out that tourneyers committed all the seven deadly sins: pride, because of their desire for praise; envy, because they resented greater praise for other tourneyers; anger, because they struck out when tempers became frayed in the sport; avarice, because they desired other knights' horses and equipment and even sometimes refused to ransom each other; gluttony, because of the attendant feasting; sloth, because of the reaction to defeat in combat; and lust, because of the desire to please wanton women by wearing their favours in the lists. Most dramatic of all, however, are the legends woven around real episodes and designed to put fear of God into the erring knights. The tournament at Neuss, where the soberest authorities give a figure of forty-two dead , became the basis of Thomas of Cantimpré's lurid warning in his book of miracles:

> Hear what happened in our time, as all Germany knows. In the year of our Lord 1243 near the noble town of Neuss on the Rhine, many nobles, dukes, counts, barons and knights gathered for a tournament. A certain brother Bernard of the order of Preachers arrived with a companion, and pleaded with them, almost in tears, to spare each other and desist from their foolish plan, and to have pity on Christianity and the Church in her affliction, which was being ravaged even then in Hungary, Slovakia and Poland by the Tartars. When many would have willingly desisted as he asked them, a certain count of Castris mocked the friar, and those who agreed with him: and when the squadrons of knights assembled, the miserable man began that wicked tournament. Early in the morning of the same day, so many said, a great cloud appeared like a clod of earth with birds like crows croaking, and hovering around it. And I am convinced that these were demons which foreshadowed coming ills. And soon, when the tournament was in progress, both knights and their attendants fell in such heaps and in such numbers, some dead, some driven mad, some permanently disabled, that no one would doubt that this seemed to be the sport not so much of men, but, by divine vengeance, of demons. The total of dead was reckoned at 367. Among whom the first to die was said to be the Count of Castris who had obstinately opposed the friar. On the night after this had happened, demons in the shape of armed men were seen to gather near Isscha in Brabant, as the priest of that village says: and I believe that they were rejoicing over such evil deeds.[7]

Thomas goes on to relate the horrifying torments that await those killed in tournaments, including armour covered with spikes on the inside (in the manner of an Iron Maiden), baths of flames, beds of red-hot iron, and the embraces of a huge and horrible toad, the latter punishments because the knight in question had been wont to

7   Thomas of Cantimpré, *Thomae Cantipratani . . . miraculorum, et exemplorum memorabilium suit temporis libri duo*, ed. Georgius Colvenerius (Douai 1605).

take a bath after a tournament and then have himself put in bed with a young girl, to whom he would make love. Similar terrors were in store for those who killed knights in tournaments: their victims' ghosts might appear and warn them of their approaching fate. As Caesarius of Heisterbach says in another book of miracles, 'As to these who die in tournaments, there is no doubt that they go to hell, unless they are helped by repentance,'[8] unlike those who die in a just war, to whom no blame is attached.

The theme of the seven deadly sins would be invoked time after time by preachers and poets, perhaps most memorably by Robert de Brunne in his *Handlyng Synne*, but other side-effects of tourneying were also considered. Thomas of Chartres complained in one sermon that tournaments were a great cause of debt and that they encouraged violence; he quoted the example of peasants coming to watch the sport armed with great sticks only to find themselves disarmed and beaten up by the tourneyers.

One of the most damning indictments of tourneying came from the pen of the Dominican, John Bromyard, who saw the darker side of the sport. Tournaments were governed by no law (except the law of destruction) and were lawless. The young lord was drawn into tourneying and other chivalric sports which quickly emptied his pockets so that, on the advice of his counsellors, he turned to his lands to raise money and imposed heavy dues and exactions on his tenants. The poor were also his victims on the way to and from tournaments, because the lord purchased food and equipment from them, but only paid with tally sticks which he failed to honour and which proved worthless. All this expense, which ruined his lands and his already impoverished tenants, was purely for vainglory.

It is worth quoting in full one of Bromyard's more bitter passages, which is clearly an accurate reflection of the harsh realities of such occasions. When nobles went to tournaments it was, according to Bromyard, only to show off their wealth:

> Who has been heard to praise, or could praise any of them for strenuous battling with the enemy, or for their defence of country and church, as Charlemagne, Roland, Oliver and the other knights of antiquity are commended and praised? But rather for this—that they have a helmet of gold worth forty pounds, aillettes and other external insignia of the same style and even greater price; that so-and-so carried into the lists a huge square lance such as no-one else carried, or could carry, or that he flung horse and rider to the ground; and that he rode so well and wielded that lance of his so nimbly, as if it were of the lightest: or again, that so-and-so came to Parliament or to the tournament with so many horse.

This vignette of knightly conversation is followed by a diatribe against the tourneyers:

8   Caesarius of Heisterbach, *Dialogus miraculorum* ed. Joseph Strange (Cologne, Bonn & Brussels 1851) II, 327.

And what, after all, is praise of that kind but praise of the impious, of wretches and of the timid? . . . For they expose themselves in places and times of peace and not of war; and to their friends, not to their enemies. Of what value are arms adorned with gold, then, that only make the enemy bolder . . . which too, when in flight from their foes, they fling away, so that they may flee the faster—as happened of late? What praise is it to bear a most mighty lance against a man of peace, and to fling horse and rider to the ground, and not touch the enemy with any lance whatever, because one does not want to approach him near enough to let him touch one with the largest kind of weapon? Or what praise is it that such a man rode so well and wielded his lance with such ease, that he conducted himself so nimbly against his friend and neighbour and fled so nimbly from the enemy of the realm? What praise is it that such are glorious and seek praise in prohibited deeds of arms, as in tournaments and the like, while in deeds of virtue, such as in just wars and in defence of their own country, they are timorous, cowardly and fugitive, allowing the enemy to devastate the land, to plunder and to pillage, to burn the towns, destroy the castles and carry off captives?[9]

Though written in the fourteenth century, Bromyard's work was a compilation of thirteenth century sources, which would have served as the raw material for sermons; his criticisms would therefore have reached a large audience.

But this is propaganda rather than criticism, propaganda based on the Church's inflexible opposition to tournaments. As that opposition begins to weaken, so does the attack: and later detractors of chivalry turned to more general themes. Though complaints such as Jacques de Vitry's that knights did nothing but pillage and rob are not unusual in the twelfth and thirteenth centuries, it is only with the succession of French defeats in the Hundred Years' War that serious attacks are made on the ideal of chivalry as a whole. Here was a court acknowledged to contain the flower of Europe's knights and to be unsurpassed in matters of chivalric taste, defeated twice in ten years, and the bitter years of disorder that followed showed that the knights did not practise what they preached but were just as eager to make their fortune from booty as the rest of the men-at-arms. Froissart records frequent changes of loyalty without a qualm; and he hardly troubles to distinguish between *routiers* and true knights. Eustace d'Aubrecicourt, of whom he makes much, had lived off the land with an armed band in Champagne for many years; and yet Froissart says at the end, 'God has his soul, for he was a very valiant knight in his day.'[10] It is only correct behaviour towards other members of the knightly class that counts; the sufferings of the common people go unnoticed.

9   G.R.Owst, *Literature and Pulpit in Medieval England,* (Oxford 1961) 332-336.
10   Froissart, *Chroniques,* ed. Lettenhove, VIII, 103; tr. Johnes, I,458. He may have been the son or brother of Sanchet d'Aubrecicourt, one of the founding knights of the Order of the Garter.

It is from the people that the complaints against knighthood are most serious. In England an anonymous poet had written a biting satire directed against the renewal of the war in France in 1337, based on the so-called *Vows of the Heron*. It was a custom of the time that knightly vows should be made on the bird which was the centre of the feast. Edward I had vowed by the swans to conquer Robert Bruce in 1306, and Philip of Burgundy was to take the crusading 'vow of the pheasant' in 1454. The poet, however, exaggerates the vows until they become ridiculous or brutal, and makes the whole episode a grim, almost humourless satire on enthusiasm for war and the custom which epitomised it. Other English clerics complained that knighthood was in decline in the late fourteenth century, perhaps thinking of the luxury of Richard II's court: 'Today many knights are given up to wantonness and ease, to dicing and fowling. Many of them spend more time upon the ornamentation of their clothing than on the exercise of arms, the business of wars, and the endurance of labours.' The writer goes on to bewail the vanished days when 'there were many strenuous knights in this land, alike of the Round Table and of the *gartir*.' In the end, his topic is the familiar one of nostalgia for a lost (but imaginary) golden age.

In France Eustace Deschamps, writing at the same time as Froissart, uses the common theme of the contrast between the knights of old and the knights of today in his *Lay de Vaillance.*:

> Once knights used to be properly trained, spending eight or ten years in the profession of arms before they were actually knighted. They were courteous, godly, restrained in speech, not miserly, and 'their hearts were not stolen away by soft beds'. Nowadays the knights sleep until the sun is high in the sky, and when they wake up their first thought is where to find some good wine. They are lazy wastrels, fond of dressing up in fine clothes; but what can be expected of men who have been knights since they were ten or twelve years old, and were never properly trained?[11]

Yet for all this Deschamps sees chivalry as something of value, worth rescuing from its present pass. His remedy is sometimes austere: the nobles should disdain wealth, refrain from marrying too soon, if at all; but sometimes it is not entirely unattractive to the knights, as when he advocates more jousts and tournaments as a means of training for them. And some of the blame attaches to their commanders, who failed to maintain discipline and to plan adequately.

Alain Chartier, writing after Agincourt, is not so convinced of the value of chivalry itself. He sees it as a decoration for tournaments and feasts, best left to heralds and

---

11   Eustace Deschamps, *Oeuvres complètes*, ed. De Queux de Saint-Hilaire and G. Raynaud, Société des anciens textes françaises (Paris 1878-1903).

masters of ceremonies, and when in the *Livre des quatre dames* he attacks the French knights it is for their lack of martial virtues, a theme which he takes up again in the *Quadrilogue invectif* of 1422. He sees love of luxury as the chief reason for the defeat of French knighthood, an accusation already made by Honoré Bonet in his *Tree of Battles*. Not only did the knights lead a life of ease, but they regarded war as a means of obtaining wealth, in which robbery and pillage were more important than fighting the enemy, and their mercenary nature is underlined. Besides this, he has no time for the international aspects of chivalry: a knight's job is to fight his country's foes, not fraternise with them, and patriotism is one of his greatest virtues. He sums up by blaming lack of loyalty, inadequate spending on military matters and lack of good counsel as the causes of the disaster.

The same ideas are the basis of Jean de Bueil's manual of knighthood in the mid-fifteenth century, *Le jouvencel*. The knight is to be a professional soldier above all else; de Bueil's own experience has taught him this. Training is all-important, and the greater a man's rank, the greater his pride in his profession should be, and the less he should object to being put under a skilled captain despite the latter's inferior social standing. Even though he allows the value of an almost chivalric comradeship-in-arms, the hard school of the camp is the only way to make a good soldier. He would not have approved of Monsieur de Croy encamped before Neuss sighing for 'the ladies to entertain us, to admonish us to bear ourselves well, to give us tokens, devices, veils or wimples'. War is much too practical a matter for such courtesies, though ransoming is a good commercial proposition. De Bueil is much more interested in cannon and siege-machines in strategy and tactics, than in honour and glory. And for this reason he is flatly opposed to jousting, which is not only a waste of time but all too often of men as well:

> First, those who do it wish to take someone else's property, namely their honour, in order to gain a vainglory of little worth: and in doing so, he does service to no one, spends his money, risks his body to take life or honour from his opponent, and little profit comes his way; while he is occupied thus, he abandons war, the king's service, and the general good; and no one should risk his life except in worthwhile activities.[12]

De Bueil expounds a completely modern view of warfare, where the efficiency of the soldier ranks above all other considerations; and though the veneer of chivalry survived into Francis I's Italian campaigns, the realities of warfare were on de Bueil's side. The knight could only justify his presence in the warfare of the following century by his skill as a commander.

12   Otto Cartellieri, *The Court of Burgundy* (London and New York 1929) 87.

The decline of chivalry became a stock theme with writers; Malory sees the world reflected in the romances he is translating as a golden age, and bemoans the fact that love is not what it used to be, while he exhorts all true Englishmen to remember the ideals of the Round Table and to cease their civil wars. Caxton paints a more orthodox view in his epilogue to his translation of Raimon Lull's *Book of the Order of Chivalry*:

> O ye knights of England, where is the custom and usage of noble chivalry that was used in those days? What do ye now but go to the baths and play at dice? And some, not well advised, use not honest and good rule, against all the order of knighthood. Leave this, leave it and read the noble volumes of *Saint Graal*, of Lancelot, of Galahad, of Tristram, of Perceforest, of Percival, of Gawain and many more. There shall ye see manhood, courtesy and gentleness. . . . Alas, what do ye but sleep and take ease, and are all disgraced from chivalry. I will demand a question, if I should not displease: how many knights are there now in England that have the use and exercise of a knight, that is to say, that he knows his horse, and his horse him; that is to say, he is ready at once and has everything that belongs to a knight, a horse that is compliant and broken to his hand, his armours and harness suitable and fitting, and so forth. I suppose that if a due search were made, there would be many found that are lacking, the more's the pity. [13]

Other writers had reached the conclusion that chivalry had had its day on the battlefield without being able to make such practical suggestions for the new mode of warfare as de Bueil. Philippe de Mézières, enthusiast for the crusading ideal, saw that ideal come to grief in the disaster at Nicopolis, and found his worst fears as to chivalry's military value confirmed. From his participation in the crusade of 1346, he had realised that the Turks were a formidable and capable enemy, and that chivalry, instead of being an advantage to the Christian army, had become a positive hindrance. In his scheme for a new and disciplined Order of religious knighthood, the Order of the Passion of our Lord Jesus Christ, he attacks crusaders who followed only one of 'the great ladies of this world', vainglory, in such expeditions. But chivalry itself is not at fault; it is only that knights forget that obedience is also a knightly virtue. His Order is to be a secular revival of the old military Orders, designed to set out as a single great crusade of 21,000 men, under strict discipline; and the details of transport and organisation are carefully set out. Mézières's insistence on the practical aspects of warfare shows that he had realised some of the faults of the earlier attempts at crusades, yet the idealists who might have been attracted by his project would prob ably have brushed all this aside: the contradiction at the heart of his scheme remains. Even so practical a man as Jean Gerson failed to see that chivalry called for self-discipline according to its ideals, and

13   Llull, *The Book of the Ordre of Chyualry*, 121-4.

offered in return a reward in terms of personal glory, while warfare needed corporate discipline imposed in order to gain a corporate end.

Other aspects of chivalry besides its military failings came in for criticism in the fifteenth and sixteenth centuries. Its pomp and pageantry were not the only targets for attacks by the Puritans. Roger Ascham found its literature as well to be subversive, 'as one for example, *Morte Arthure:* the whole pleasure of which booke standeth in two speciall poyntes, in open mans slaughter, and bold bawdrye: In which booke these be counted the noblest Knightes, that do kill most men without any quarell, and commit fowlest aduoulteries by sutlest shiftes.'[14] And the main impetus of that literature, courtly love, had long ago been a target for criticism. The reaction begins not with the preachers, one of whom even agrees that 'a knight is only brave if he is in love', but with secular writers who champion the woman's cause and see it as a mere masculine deception. The Chevalier de la Tour Landry, instructing his daughters in about 1371, tells a story of Marshal Boucicaut's father. Three ladies discovered that he had sworn true love to them all within the past year, and when challenged, he merely replied that he had been sincere on each occasion. And when he advocates 'love paramours', saying 'For in certayne me semeth that in good love an trewe maye be but welthe and honour, and also the lover is better therefore, and more gay and holy; and also the more encouraged to exercyse hym selfe more ofte in armes, and taketh therefore better maner in al estates, forto please unto his lady or love,' a classic statement of chivalric love, his wife gives him short shrift: 'These wordes are but sport and esbatement of ordes and felawes in a language much comyn.'[15] Christine de Pisan, writing in fifteenth-century Burgundy, likewise distrusts the flattering intentions of the knight, whose supposed chivalry she would prefer to see replaced by real military ardour.

In the love poems of the fourteenth and fifteenth centuries a similar change takes place. Realism is the hallmark of the criticism of chivalry here: courtly love bears no relation to what actually goes on. The *Cent Ballades* of Jean le Seneschal reflect this neatly. When the author has finished his description of 'the code of the perfect knight and perfect lover, able to resist the seduction of passing love, and desirous of giving himself solely to his lady',[16] he asks for opinions on whether fidelity is better than change in love. Of thirteen replies some prefer constancy, some prefer change, some are evasive: but the bastard de Coucy sums it up nicely:

Most honoured lady, your splendour fair

14   Roger Ascham, *English Works*, ed. William Aldis Wright (Cambridge 1904) 231.
15   Geoffroy de La Tour Landry, *The Book of the Knight of La Tour-Landry*, ed. Thomas Wright, EETS. OS 33 (London 1868) 171-2.
16   Jean Le Seneschal, *Les Cent Ballades*, ed. Gaston Raynaud, Société des anciens textes françaises (Paris, 1905) i.

Has overwhelmed me, and I am yours.
I shall not waver, I yield me quite:
Thus say they all; and yet it's never so.[17]

And the Duc de Berry advocates this kind of behaviour quite openly: swear constancy, seek change.

By the end of the fifteenth century there was little enough real substance in chivalry for moralists to regard it seriously. The spate of romances in the early sixteenth century provided a new and much easier target for their attacks. Here were the peacock feathers of knighthood, its vain adventures, with no possible claim to moral worth. Juan Luis Vives, like Ascham an educationalist, attacked them in 1529 as being 'written and made by such as were ydle and knew nothinge. These bokes do hurt both man and woman, for they make them wylye and craftye, they kyndle and styr up covetousnes, inflame angre, and all beastly and filthy desyre.'[18]

Yet the Inquisition, which might have been expected to take a very dim view of such trifles, never placed a single chivalric romance on the *Index Expurgatorius*. Indeed, the humanist critics may be suspected of trying to divert attention from their favourite classical and philosophical reading, which was often seen as much more subtle and dangerous. There were bans on the import of romances into the Spanish colonies in the New World in 1531 and 1553, on the grounds that they might hinder the spread of Christianity there, though shipments continued nonetheless. In Spain the story of a priest who believed all the romances to be true because they bore on the title-pages the state's licence to print them aroused bitter comment; but there was no real effort to take measurements against the books of chivalry, which might corrupt morals but preached no heresies.

So the inheritance of chivalry was divided: the knight at war became the professional soldier, the knight in love either a poet whose delicate conceits were the sum of his longings or an honest married man, and the knight of romance a scarecrow mocked by all and sundry. And so the knight at court became something else as well, the courtier and gentleman. The new men of the Renaissance were by no means a sudden phenomenon: the duties of a knight had become more and more complex as each successive moralist or teacher of manners added his views. From the simple restraints on the misuse of a warrior's power, the duties enjoined on a knight had come to include all the social graces. He was expected, if he was to be thought fully chivalrous, to be

17   *Ibid.*, 227.
18   Thomas, *Spanish and Portuguese Romances*, 162-3.

With the advent of printing and the great increase in secular education that followed in its wake, the old chivalric habits, which had done well enough for the fifteenth century, became outmoded. Della Casa's *Galatea*, with its insistence on the outward forms of behaviour, good manners, points the way. New ideas and fashions, new entertainments and arguments, could be spread quickly; where there had been one manuscript, there were twenty books for each man to read and form his own opinion. The intellectual ferment that resulted was almost entirely artistic and secular. What marks off the gentleman from the knight is above all his critical appreciative attitude towards both politics and art, an attitude which permeates Castiglione's study of the new man, *The Courtier*. In these dialogues ascribed to his fellow-courtiers at Urbino, the new ideals are set out for the first time – if one can call them ideals: qualities would be a more appropriate word. The courtier is opportunist where the knight was loyal; he is more concerned with cutting a good figure than with real skill in war or tournament; he will admire chaste women, and yet take his *amours* as he finds them; and above all he will seek his own fortune. But against this he will value learning and appreciate the painter's and sculptor's work, and will at least be gracious and well-mannered. Castiglione tells an anecdote against those who have only one purpose in life. A lady asked a man to dance with her, and was told

> that such frivolities were not his business. And when at length the lady asked what his business was, he answered with a scowl: 'Fighting...' 'well then,' the lady retorted, 'I should think that since you aren't at war at the moment and you are not engaged in fighting, it would be a good thing if you were to have yourself well greased and stowed away in a cupboard with your fighting equipment, so that you avoid getting rustier than you are already.'[19]

At first sight, Castiglione's motto seems to be moderation in all things; but we find it is a purposeful moderation. Affectation in dress draws unfavourable comment, as does boasting or drunkenness; and it is not the principle of moderation, but other men's opinions that are important. The courtier at war should accomplish the bold and notable exploits he has to perform in as small a company as possible and in view of all the noblest and most eminent men of the army, and, above all, in the presence, or if possible under the very eyes, of the prince he is serving. For it is certainly right to exploit the things one does well.[20]

This is a world of career-seeking which contrasts sharply with the idle glory of chivalry; and if it is more practical, it is scarcely an attractive ideal. And the condition

19 Baldassare Castiglione, *The Book of the Courtier*, tr. George Bull (London & Baltimore 1967) 58.
20 Castiglione, *The Book of the Courtier*, 115.

and connoisseurship of the courtier is, we feel, bent to the same end: to shine in his prince's eyes by finding the right words to praise the latest masque or painting. It is a more polished world, but its daggers are polished too, and the competition for favour is as intense as the financial rewards are necessary to the courtiers' existence.

Nonetheless, the love of art is genuine, and love itself is taken seriously. Castiglione's discourse on love is full of noble ideas, and its philosophical heights are explored enthusiastically by his audience. When he equates goodness and beauty he expresses the new hedonism perfectly, and if the courtier-gentleman has to know how to make his way into the prince's favour, he will also know how to enjoy his reward.

Castiglione's influence was wide. Published in 1528, *The Book of the Courtier* met with wide approval, from England to Spain, and became the model for many later works on the education of a gentleman. More important, it coloured the thought and manners of Europe in a way that the previous courtesy books, with their insistence on form and behaviour without giving thought to the inward attitude of mind, could never have succeeded in doing. It came at a moment when the organisation of the state was assuming increasing importance, and when a career in the state's service was as high a calling as arms had once been. The old paths to renown on the battlefield and in the lists were no longer open; Castiglione showed the new way of intellectual and physical grace.

Epilogue

The ideals of chivalry appeal to the emotions, and they flourish best in a gothic and romantic climate; neoclassicism appeals to reason and to the sense of order. When the seeds sown by the Renaissance humanists became the classical movement of seventeeth-century France, chivalry was driven from the land which had for so long been its chief refuge. In England its last flourish coincided with Inigo Jones' revival of the Gothic; but puritanism was as ardently on the side of order and restraint as the advocates of neoclassicism. Milton, seeking for a noble theme for his epic aspirations, rejected the Arthurian tales as too fantastic. When fantasy returned, the Restoration court preferred to follow continental fashions.

It was only when antiquarian interest turned towards the mediaeval period in the eighteenth century that chivalry was once again studied; and just as it had gone out with a dying gothic movement, so it reappeared in the revival of the gothic, and was soon in literary favour once more in England and Germany. Hurd's *Letters on Chivalry and Romance* of 1762 were the beginnings of a flood of reprintings of old texts, studies of the trappings of chivalry, and recreations in fiction of the Middle Ages. The fruits of antiquarian researches such as those of La Curne de Ste Palaye in France were popularised by books like Kenelm Digby's *Broad Stone of Honour* and a dozen other general outlines of chivalry, including Sir Walter Scott's *Essay on Chivalry*. The Waverley Novels aroused the enthusiasm of readers everywhere, and the baronial gothic which succeeded the lighter, more imaginative style of the eighteeth century was in large part inspired by them.

The literary inheritance of the Middle Ages was so rich that English writers were able to explore it for nearly a century before it palled. But it was only in the stability of Victorian England that the cult could survive so long, and could produce such strange manifestations as the great tournament at Eglinton in 1839, where the enthusiasm of a few noblemen led them to spend a fortune in recreating a fifteenth-century joust. Even in England such nostalgia for the past had its political overtones. The Eglinton tournament arose out of the reduction in pageantry at the coronation of William IV, and the radical press had a field day at the participants' expense. Nor, despite the gentle golden glow of Tennyson's verse and of Pre-Raphaelite interpretations of chivalry in art, was the ideal itself without its critical opponents. Thomas Arnold saw it in the blackest of lights: 'If I were called upon to name what spirit of evil predominantly deserved the name of Anti-Christ, I should name the spirit of chivalry – the more detestable for the very guise of 'Archangel ruined' which has made it so seductive to he most generous minds.'

But the champions of the new order, whether Arnold and his militant Christianity or the evangelists of radical politics on the Continent, were hardly to be expected to approve an ideal so reactionary in the enthusiasm it aroused and so individualistic in its search for perfection. Chivalry had been used for far too long as a mere escape from reality for its ideals to have any relevance to the problems of society; the themes which had once had very concrete implications for the world in which they had been developed had lost all but the remotest link with everyday life; the word itself had acquired a new meaning, that of the very courtesy and politeness which had replaced chivalry proper. All that remained of the old high dreams and visions was an empty shell, a pretty relic of the past, fit to while away an idle moment.

Bibliography

Abbreviations

CDS   Chroniken der deutschen Städte
EETS   Early English Text Society
EHR   *English Historical Review*
Foedera   Rymer Thomas *[et al.] Foedera* (London 1816-69)
MGH   *Monumenta Germaniae Historiae*
NS   New Series
OS   Old Series
PL   *Patrologia Latina*
RS   Rolls Series
RHGF   Bouquet, Martin *Recueil des historiens de Gaule et de la France* (Paris 1738-1904)
SHF   Société de l'Histoire de France
SS   Scriptores

Select Bibliography

The bibliography which follows does not aim to be comprehensive, but to offer a guide to the major works on each topic, giving preference to recent studies. Sources of quotations are given in the notes.

Bibliographies

On courtly culture in general, see Joachim Bumke, 'Höfische Kultur: Versuch einer kritischen Bestandsaufnahme' *Beiträge zur Geschichte der deutschen Sprache und Literatur* 114, 1992, 414-492

Extensive bibliographies can also be found in the following works cited under *General Studies* below:
Borst   *Das Rittertum im Mittelalter*
Cardini   *Alle radice della Cavalleria*
Keen   *Chivalry*

Specifically on courtly love, there is useful information up to 1976 in:
   Boase   *Origin and Meaning of Courtly Love.*
For Arthurian romance and related topics, see:
   Bibliographical Bulletin of the International Arthurian Society, 1949-

B. General works

The earliest works are usually mainly concerned with the knightly orders and their origins, such as:

Sansovino, Francesco   *Origine de'cavalieri* (Venezia 1566)

Segar, William   *Honor, Military and Civill* (London 1602)

Favyn, André   *Le théatre d'honneur et de chevalerie ou l'histoire des ordres militaires* (Paris 1620)

La Colombière, Marc de Vulson, sieur de   *Le vray théatre d'honneur ou le miroir héroïque de la noblesse* (Paris 1648)

Ménestrier, Claude-François   *De la chevalerie ancienne et moderne* (Paris 1683)

Sainte-Marie, Honoré de   *Dissertations historiques et critiques sur la chevalerie ancienne et moderne, séculière et régulière* (Paris 1718)

More general studies appear from the eighteenth century onwards:

La Curne de Sainte-Palaye, Jean-Baptiste de   *Mémoires sur l'ancienne chevalerie* (Paris 1759-81)

Hurd, Richard   *Letters on Chivalry and Romance* (London 1762)

Gassier-St. Amand, J.M.   *Histoire de la chevalerie française ou recherches historiques sur la chevalerie* (Paris 1814)

Scott, Sir Walter   *An Essay on Chivalry* [originally for the fifth edition of the Encyclopedia Britannica] (London 1816)

Digby, Kenelm Henry   *The Broad Stone of Honour, or rules for the gentleman of England* (London 1822)

Büsching, Johann Gustav   *Ritterzeit und Ritterwesen* (Leipzig 1823)

Mills, Charles   *The History of Chivalry, or Knighthood and its Times* (London 1825)

James, G.P.R.   *The History of Chivalry* (London 1830)

Kottenkamp, Franz Justus   *Der Rittersaal: eine Geschichte des Rittertums* (Stuttgart 1842); tr. as *History of Chivalry* (London 1857)

Gautier, Léon   *La chevalerie* (Paris 1884); tr as *Chivalry* (London 1949)

Henne am Rhyn, Otto   *Geschichte des Rittertums* (Leipzig 1893)

Cornish, F.W.   *Chivalry* (London & New York 1901)

Pivano, Silvio 'Lineamenti storici e giuridici della cavalleria medioevale' in *Memorie della Accademia Reale delle Scienze di Torino*, 2nd series, 55, 1905, 255-336

von Gleichen-Russwurm, A. *Der Ritterspiegel: Geschichte der vornehmen Welt im Romanischen Mittelalter*, Geschichte der europäischen Gesellschaft II (Stuttgart 1918)

Meller, Walter Clifford *A Knight's Life in the Days of Chivalry* (London 1924)

The most important modern studies are

Prestage, Edgar (ed.) *Chivalry* (London 1928)

Painter, Sidney *French Chivalry: chivalric ideas and practices in mediaeval France* (Baltimore 1940)

Borst, Arno 'Das Rittertum im Hochmittelalter, Idee und Wirklichkeit', *Saeculum* 10, 1959, 213-31

Mor, Carlo Guido 'La cavalleria' (1964, rptd in Borst, *Rittertum im Mittelalter*)

Borst, Arno (ed.) *Das Rittertum im Mittelalter*, Wege der Forschung 349 (Darmstadt 1976)

Keen, Maurice *Chivalry* (London 1984)

Chickering, Howell and Seiler, Thomas H. (eds.) *The study of Chivalry: resources and approaches* (Kalamazoo, MI, 1988)

Harper-Bill, Christopher, and Harvey, Ruth (eds.) *The Ideals and Practice of Medieval Knighthood: Papers from the first and second Strawberry Hill conferences* (Woodbridge & Dover, N.H., 1986; *II: Papers from the third Strawberry Hill conference* (Woodbridge & Wolfeboro, N.H., 1988); *III: Papers from the fourth Strawberry Hill conference* (Woodbridge & Rochester, N.Y., 1990). Continued as *Medieval Knighthood IV: Papers from the fifth Strawberry Hill conference* (Woodbridge & Rochester, N.Y., 1992); *Medieval Knighthood V: Papers from the fifth Strawberry Hill conference* (Woodbridge & Rochester, N.Y., 1995)

Flori, Jean *Chevaliers et chevalerie au moyen âge* (Paris 1998)

C. The origins of knighthood and the early history of medieval cavalry

Arnold, Benjamin *German Knighthood 1050-1300* (Oxford 1985)

Bloch, Marc *La société féodale* (Paris 1939-40); tr. as *Feudal Society* (2nd. edn., London 1962)

Boutruche, Robert *Seigneurie et féodalité: I. Le premier âge des liens de l'homme a l'homme* (Paris 1959)

Bumke, Joachim *The Concept of Knighthood in the Middle Ages* (New York 1982)

Cardini, Franco *Alle radice della cavalleria medievale* (Firenze 1981)

Coss, Peter *The Knight in Medieval England 1000-1400* (Far Thrupp & Dover, N.H., 1993)

Davis, R.H.C. *The Medieval Warhorse: origin, development and redevelopment* (London 1989)

Duby, Georges *La société aux xie et xiie siècles dans la région maconnaise* (Paris 1953)

Duby, Georges *The Chivalrous Society* (London 1979)

Fenske, Lutz, Rösener, Werner, Zotz, Thomas (eds.) *Institutionen, Kultur und Gesellschaft im Mittelalter: Festschrift für Josef Fleckenstein zu seinem 65. Geburtstag* (Sigmaringen 1964)

Fleckenstein, Josef *Ordnungen und formende Kräfte des Mittelalters: ausgewählte Beitrage* (Göttingen 1989)

Ganshof, F.L. *Feudalism* (London 1952, 3rd edn. 1964)

Genicot, L. 'Noblesse, ministerialité et chevalerie en Gueldre et Zutphen', *Le moyen âge* 71, 1965, 1-22.

Hyland, Ann *The Medieval Warhorse from Byzantium to the Crusades* (Far Thrupp & Dover, N.H., 1994)

Morris, Colin, '*Equestris ordo*: chivalry as a vocation in the twelfth century' in *Religious Motivation: Biographical and Sociological Problems for the Church Histoiran*, ed. Derek Baker (Oxford 1978) 87-96.

Ordinamenti militari in occidente nell'alto medioevo, Settimane di studio del centro italiano di studi sull'alto medioevo (Spoleto 1968)

Otto, Eberhard F. 'Zur Abschliessung des Ritterstandes', *Historische Zeitschrift*, 162, 1940, 19-39.

Parisse, Michel *Noblesse et chevalerie en Lorraine médiévale: les familles nobles du xie au xiiie siècle* (Nancy 1982)

Tabacco, Giovanni 'Su nobiltà e cavalleria nel medioevo. Un ritorno a Marc Bloch?', *Rivista storica italiana*, 91, 1979, 5-25.

Verriest, Leo *Noblesse. Chevalerie. Lignages.* (Brussels 1960)

D. Knighthood and its ceremonial

Ackermann, Robert W. 'The knighting ceremonies is the middle English romances', *Speculum* 19, 1944, 285-313.

Erben, Wilhelm 'Schwertleite und Ritterschlag: Beiträge zu einer Rechtsgeschichte der Waffen', *Zeitschrift für historische Waffenkunde*, 8, 1918, 1920, 105-67

Flori, Jean *L'idéologie du glaive: préhistoire de la chevalerie*, Travaux d'histoire éthico-politique 33 (Genève 1983)

Flori, Jean *L'essor de la chevalerie: xie - xiie siècles*, Travaux d'histoire éthico-politique 46 (Genève 1986)

Flori, Jean 'Les origines de l'adoubement chevaleresque: étude des remises d'armes et du vocabulaire qui les exprime dans les sources historiques laines jusquau début du xiie siècle', *Traditio*, 35, 1979, 209-272

Houdenc, Raoul de *Le roman des eles* and the anonymous *Ordène de chevalerie*, ed.Keith Busby (Amsterdam & Philadelphia 1983)

Pietzner, Fritz *Schwertleite und Ritterschlag* (Bottrop i.W. 1934)

Winter, Johanna Maria van 'Cingulum militiae: schwertleite en *miles*-terminologie als spiegel van veranderend menselijk gedrag', *Tijdschrift voor Rechtsgeschiednis* 44, 1976, 1-91.

E. Chivalry, the court and literature

1. Courtly origins, the troubadours and minnesinger

Bezzola, Reto R.   *Les origines et la formation de la littérature courtoise en Occident (500-1200)*, Bibliothèque de l'Ecole des Hautes Etudes (Paris 1944-63)

Boase, Roger *The Origin and Meaning of Courtly Love: a critical survey of European scholarship* (Manchester and Totowa, N.J. 1977)

Brinkmann, Hennig *Entstehungsgeschichte des Minnesangs* Deutsche Vierteljahresschrift für Literaturwissenschaft und Geistesgeschichte Buchreihe 8 (Halle 1926)

Bumke, Joachim   *Courtly Culture* tr. Thomas Dunlap (Berkeley, Los Angeles, Oxford 1991)

Burgess, Glyn 'Chivalric activity in the anonymous lays' in Angeli, Giovanni & Formisano, Luciano (eds.) *L'imaginaire courtois et son double* (Salerno 1992)

Chanson de geste und höfischer Roman: Heidelberger Kolloquium 30. Januar 1961, Studia Romanica 4 (Heidelberg 1963)

Crosland, Jessie *The old French epic* (Oxford 1951)

Denomy, Alexander J.   *The Heresy of Courtly Love* (New York 1947)

Dronke, Peter   *Medieval Latin Poetry and the Rise of the European Love-Lyric* (Oxford 1965)

Dronke, Peter *Poetic Individuality in the Middle Ages: New Departures in Poetry 1000-1150* (Oxford 1970)

Faral, Edmond *La chanson de Roland: étude et analyse* (Paris 1934)

Fleckenstein, Joseph (ed.)   *Curialitas: Studien zu Grundfragen der höfisch-ritterlichen Kultur*, Veröffentlichungen des Max-Planck-Instituts für Geschichte 100 (Göttingen 1990)

Fletcher, Richard   *The Quest for El Cid* (London 1989)

Frappier, Jean 'Sur un procès fait à l'amour courtois', *Romania* 93, 1972, 145-193

Frings, Theodor   *Minnesinger und Troubadours* Deutsche Akademie der Wissenschaften zu Berlin Vorträge und Schriften 34 (Berlin 1949)

Hill, Raymond & Bergin, Thomas Goddard (eds.)   *Anthology of the Provençal Troubadours* Yale Romanic Studies 17 (New Haven, CT, & London 1941)

Jackson, W.H. (ed.)   *Knighthood in Medieval Literature* (Woodbridge 1982)

Jaeger, C. Stephen   *The Origins of Courtliness: Civilizing Trends and the Formation of Courtly Ideals 939-1210* (Philadelphia 1955)

Kuhn, Hugo   *Minnesangs Wende* Hermaea: Germanistische Forschungen. Neue Folge 1 (Tübingen 1952)

Lazar, Moshé   *Amour courtois et "fin'amors" dans la littérature du xii⁰ siècle*, Bibliothèque française et romane série C: études littéraires 8 (Paris 1964)

Nagel, Bert   *Staufische Klassik: Deutsche Dichtung um 1200* (Heidelberg 1977)

Nelli, René & Lavaud, René   *Les Troubadours* (Bruges 1966)

Paterson, Linda M.   *The World of the Troubadours: Medieval Occitan society c.1100-c.1300* (Cambridge & New York 1993)

Sayce, Olive   *Poets of the Minnesang* (Oxford 1967)

Schnell, Rüdiger   *Causae amoris: Liebeskonzeption und Liebesdarstellung in der mittelalterlichen Literatur*, Bibliotheca germanica 27 (Bern & München 1985)

Schnell, Rüdiger   'Die 'höfische' Liebe als 'höfischer' Diskurs über die Liebe' in Fleckenstein, *Curialitas*, 231-301

Taylor, R.J.   *The Art of the Minnesinger* (Cardiff 1969)

Uttley, Francis L.   'Must we abandon the concept of courtly love?' [Review article] *Medievalia et Humanistica* 3, 1972, 299-324

2. The Romances of Chivalry

Archibald, Elizabeth and Edwards, Tony (eds.) *A Companion to Malory* (Cambridge & Rochester, N.Y. 1995)

Barber, Richard   *King Arthur: Hero and Legend* (Woodbridge and New York 1986)

Brewer, Derek (ed.) *A Companion to the Gawain Poet* (Cambridge & Rochester, N.Y. 1996)

Chrétien de Troyes   *Arthurian Romances* tr. D.D.R. Owen (London 1987)

Frappier, Jean   *Chrétien de Troyes: l'homme et l'oeuvre* (Paris 1957)

Frappier, Jean   *Etude sur La Mort le Roi Artu: roman du xiii⁰ siècle, dernière partie du Lancelot en prose* (Paris 1936)

Gottfried von Strassburg   *Tristan* tr. A.T. Hatto (London & New York 1960)

Köhler, Erich   *Ideal und Wirklichkeit in der höfischen Epik: Studien zur Form der frühen Artus- und Graldichtung* Beihefte zur Zeitschrift für Romanische Philologie 97 (Tübingen 1956)

Lacy, Norris J. (ed.) *The New Arthurian Encyclopedia* (Chicago & London 1991)

[*Perlesvaus*] *The High Book of The Grail* tr. Nigel Bryant (Cambridge 1978)

[*Prose Lancelot*] *Lancelot of the Lake* tr. Corin Corley (Oxford 1989)

[*Vulgate Cycle*] *Lancelot - Grail: the Old French Arthurian Vulgate and post-Vulgate in Translation* ed. Norris J.Lacy (New York & London 1993-)

Wolfram von Eschenbach *Parzival* tr. A.T.Hatto (Harmondsworth & New York 1980)

3. Chivalric Biographies and Handbooks

Boucicaut, Jean le Maingre dit *Le livre des faicts du bon messire Jean le Maingre, dit Boucicaut* in Michaud et Poujoulat, *Nouvelle collection des mémoires pour servir à l'histoire de France* (Paris 1854) II, 205-332

Chandos Herald, 'The Life of the Black Prince' in Richard Barber, *Life and Campaigns of the Black Prince* (London and New York 1986) 84-139

Chastellain, Georges 'Le Livre des Faits de Jacques de Lalaing' in *Oeuvres* ed. Kervyn de Lettenhove (Brussels 1866) VIII, 188-246.

Crouch, David *William Marshal: Court, Career and Chivalry in the Angevin Empire 1147-1219* (London & New York 1990)

Cuvelier *Chronique de Bertrand du Guesclin* ed. E.Charrière (Paris 1839)

de Gamez, Gutierrez Diaz *The Unconquered Knight: a chronicle of the deeds of Don Pero Niño* tr. Joan Evans (London 1928)

Gaucher, Elisabeth *La Biographie Chevaleresque: typologie d'un genre xiiie -xve siècle* Nouvelle Bibliothèque du moyen âge 29 (Paris 1994)

Kaeuper, Richard W., and Kennedy, Elspeth *The Book of Chivalry of Geoffroi de Charny: Text, Context, and Translation* (Philadelphia 1996)

La Marche, Olivier de la *Mémoires* ed. Henri Beaune & J. d'Arbaumont, SHF (Paris 1883)

Llull, Raimon *The Book of the Ordre of Chyvalry*, tr. William Caxton, ed. A. T. P. Byles, EETS OS 168, 1926

Mailles, Jacques de *The right joyous and pleasant history of the feats, gests and prowesses of the chevalier Bayart* tr. Sara Coleridge (London 1906)

[Ulrich von Liechtenstein] Thomas, J.W. (ed. & tr.) *Ulrich von Liechtenstein's* Service of Ladies, University of North Carolina Studies in the Germanic Languages and Literatures 63 (Chapel Hill, N.C., 1969)

William Marshal *L'histoire de Guillaume le Maréchal, comte de Striguil et Pembroke* ed.Paul Meyer, SHF (Paris 1891-1901)

F. Tournaments

Barber, Richard & Barker, Juliet *Tournaments: Jousts, Chivalry and Pageants in the Middle Ages* (Woodbridge and New York 1989)

Barker, Juliet *The Tournament in England 1100-1400* (Woodbridge & Wolfeboro, N.H., 1986)

Cripps-Day, F.H. *The History of the Tournament in England and France* (London 1918)

Fleckenstein, Josef *Das ritterliche Turnier im Mittelalter: Beiträge zu einer vergleichenden Formen- und Verhaltensgeschichte des Rittertums* Veröffentlichungen des Max-Planck-Instituts für Geschichte 80 (Göttingen 1985)

La Civiltà del Torneo (sec.XII-XVII); Giostre e Tornei tra medioevo ed età moderna Atti del VII convegno di studio, Centro Studi Storici, Narni (Narni 1990)

de Lena, Pero Rodriguez *El passo honroso de Suero de Quiñoñes* ed. Amancio Labandeira Fernandez (Madrid 1977)

René d'Anjou *Oeuvres complètes du Roi René* ed. Comte de Quatrebarbes (Angers 1845)

Truffi, Riccardo *Giostre e cantori di giostre* (Rocca S.Casciano 1911)

Vale, Juliet *Edward III and Chivalry* (Woodbridge 1982)

Van de Neste, Evelyne *Tournois, joutes, pas d'armes dans les villes de Flandre à la fin du moyen âge (1300-1486)* Mémoires et documents de l'Ecole des Chartes 47 (Paris 1996)

G. Warfare

Bonet, Honoré *The Tree of Battles* ed. & tr. G.W.Coopland (Liverpool 1949)

Bradbury, Jim *The Medieval Siege* (Woodbridge & Rochester, N.Y. 1992)

Contamine, Philippe, Giry-Deloison, Charles, & Keen, Maurice H. (eds) *Guerre et Société en France, en Angleterre et en Bourgogne XIVe -XVe siècle* (Lille 1991)

Curry, Anne & Hughes, Michael (eds.) *Arms, Armies and Fortifications in the Hundred Years War* (Woodbridge & Rochester, N.Y. 1994)

Duby, Georges *The Legend of Bouvines: War, Religion and Culture in the Middle Ages* (Oxford and Los Angeles 1990)

Contamine, Philippe *War in the Middle Ages* (Oxford 1985)

Hewitt, H.J. *The Organisation of War under Edward III* (Manchester 1966)

Kaeuper, Richard *War, Justice and Public Order: England and France in the Later Middle Ages* (Oxford & New York 1988)

Keen, Maurice 'War, Peace and Chivalry' in Brian Patrick McGuire, ed. *War and Peace in the Middle Ages* (Copenhagen 1987) 94-117.

Morillo, Stephen *Warfare under the Anglo-Norman Kings* (Woodbridge & Rochester, NY, 1994)

Smail, R.C. *Crusading Warfare* (2nd edn. Cambridge 1994)

Strickland, Matthew *War and Chivalry: The Conduct and Perception of War in England and Normandy, 1066-1217* (Cambridge & New York 1996)

Verbruggen, J.F. *The Art of War in the Middle Ages* (Woodbridge & Rochester, NY, 1996; originally published as *De Krijgskunst in West-Europa in de Middeleeuwen, IXe tot begin XIVe eeuw* Verhandelingen van de Koninklijke Vlaamse Academie voor Wetenschapen, Letteren en Schone Kunsten van België, Klasse der Letteren 20 (Brussels 1954).

H. The Crusades

Christiansen, Eric *The Northern Crusades: the Baltic and the Catholic Frontier 1100-1525* (London & New York 1980)

Dubois, Pierre *The Recovery of the Holy Land* tr. Walther I.Brandt (New York 1956)

Erdmann, Carl *Die Entstehung des Kreuzzugsgedankens* Forschungen zur Kirchen-und Geistesgeschichte 6 (Stuttgart 1935)

Flori, Jean *Pierre l'Ermite et la première Croisade* (Paris 1999)

Housley, Norman *The Later Crusades: from Lyons to Alcazar 1274-1580* (Oxford & New York 1992)

Iorga, Nicolai *Philippe de Mézières 1327-1405 et la croisade au xive siècle* Bibliothèque de l'école des hautes études 110 (Paris 1896)

Mayer, Eberhard *Geschichte der Kreuzzüge* 6th edn 1965

Mézières, Philippe de *Le songe du vieil Pelerin* ed.G.W.Coopland (Cambridge 1969)

Riley-Smith, Jonathan *The First Crusade and the Idea of Crusading* (London 1986)

Riley-Smith, Louise and Jonathan *The Crusade: Idea and Reality* (London 1986)

Riley-Smith, Jonathan *The First Crusaders 1095-1131* (Cambridge & New York 1996)

Runciman, Steven *A History of the Crusades* (Cambridge 1951)

Setton, K.M. (ed.) *A History of the Crusades* (Madison, WI & London 1955-1989)

Tyerman, Christopher *England and the Crusades 1095-1588* (Chicago & London 1988)

I. The Military Orders

Barber, Malcolm (ed.) *The Military Orders: Fighting for the Faith and Caring for the Sick* (Aldershot & Brookfield, VT, 1994)

Fleckenstein, Josef, and Hellmann, Manfred (eds.) *Die geistlichen Ritterorden Europas* Vorträge und Forschungen 26 (Sigmaringen 1980)

Forey, Alan *The Military Orders from the twelfth to the early fourteenth centuries* (London 1992)

1. The Templars

Barber, Malcolm *The New Knighthood; a history of the Order of the Temple* (Cambridge & New York 1994)

Barber, Malcolm *The Trial of the Templars* (Cambridge & New York 1978)

Bernard of Clairvaux, 'De laude novae militiae' in Migne, *PL*, 182, 922-39.

The Rule of the Templars: the French text of the Rule of the Order of the Knights Templar tr. J.M.Upton-Ward (Woodbridge & Rochester, N.Y. 1992)

2. The Hospitallers

Delaville Le Roulx, J. *Les Hospitaliers en Terre Sainte et à Chypre (1100-1310)* (Paris 1904)

Delaville Le Roulx, J. *Les Hospitaliers à Rhodes jusqu'à la mort de Philibert de Naillac (1310-1421)* (Paris 1913)

Riley-Smith, Jonathan *The Knights of St John of Jerusalem in Jerusalem and Cyprus c.1050-1310* (London 1967)

3. The Teutonic Knights

Benninghoven, Friedrich *Der Orden der Schwertbrüder: Fratres Milicie Christi de Livonia* (Graz & Köln 1965)

Bühler, Johannes *Ordensritter und Kirchenfürsten nach zeitgenossischen Quellen* (Leipzig 1927)

Paravicini, Werner *Die Preussenreisen des europäischen Adels* Beihefte der Francia 17 (Sigmaringen 1989, 1995; in progress)

Tumler, P. Marian *Der deutsche Orden im Werden , Wachsen und Wirken bis 1400 . . .* (Wien 1955)

4. The Spanish Orders

Guitton, Francis *L'ordre de Calatrave* Commission d'histoire de l'ordre de Cîteaux 4 (Paris 1965)

Lomax, Derek *La orden de Santiago* Consejo superior de investigaciones cientificas, escuela de estudios medievales 38 (Madrid 1965)

J. The Prince and Chivalry; the Secular Orders

Anglo, Sydney (ed.) *Chivalry in the Renaissance* (Woodbridge & Rochester, NY, 1990)

Anglo, Sydney *Spectacle, Pageantry and Early Tudor Policy* (Oxford 1959)

Ashmole, Elias *The Institution, Laws and Ceremonies of the Most Noble Order of the Garter* (London 1672)

Beltz, George Frederick *Memorials of the Most Noble Order of the Garter* (London 1841)

Benson, Larry D., & Leyerle, John *Chivalric Literature: Essays on relations between literature & life in the later middle ages* Studies in Medieval Culture XIV (Kalamazoo 1980)

Boulton, D'A.J.D. *The Knights of the Crown: The Monarchical Orders of Knighthood in Later Medieval Europe 1325-1520* (Woodbridge and New York 1987; rev. ed 2000)

Cartellieri, Otto *The Court of Burgundy* (London & New York 1929)

Courteault, Henri *Gaston IV, comte de Foix* (Toulouse 1895)

Huizinga, Jean *The Waning of the Middle Ages* (London & Baltimore 1949)

Jacquot, Jean (ed.) *Les Fêtes de la Renaissance* (Paris 1956-60)

Kruse, Holger, Paravicini, Werner & Ranft, Andreas (eds) *Ritterorden und Adelsgesellschaften in spätmittelalterlichen Deutschland: ein systematisches Verzeichnis* (Frankfurt & New York 1991)

Leschitzer, Simon ed. 'Der Theuerdank . . . nach der ersten Auflage vom Jahre 1517' *Jahrbuch der Kunsthistorischen Sammlungen* 8 (Wien 1888)

Lettenhove, Kervyn de *La Toison d'Or* (Bruxelles 1907)

Loomis, Roger Sherman 'Edward I, Arthurian enthusiast' *Speculum* 28, 1953, 114-27

Scaglione, Aldo *Knights at Court: Courtliness, Chivalry and Courtesy from Ottonian Germany to the Italian Renaissance* (Berkeley, Los Angeles & Oxford 1991)

Vale, Malcolm *War and Chivalry: Warfare and Aristocratic Culture in England, France and Burgundy at the End of the Middle Ages* (London 1981)

K. Late chivalric literature

Ariosto, Ludovico *Orlando Furioso* tr. Barbara Reynolds (Harmondsworth & New York 1975)

Cervantes Saavedra, Miguel de *The Adventures of Don Quixote* tr. J.M. Cohen (Harmondsworth & Baltimore 1950)

Lobeira, Vasco [?Joham de] *Amadis of Gaul* tr. Robert Southey (London 1872)

Malory, Sir Thomas *The Works* ed. Eugène Vinaver, rev. P.J.C. Field (3rd edn, Oxford 1990)

Tasso, Torquato *Godfrey of Bulloigne, or, the Recovery of Jerusalem [Gerusalemme Liberata]* tr. Edward Fairfax (London 1851)

Thomas, Henry *Spanish and Portuguese Romances of Chivalry* (Cambridge 1920)

L. Critics of chivalry and advocates of reform

Castiglione, Baldassare *The Book of the Courtier* tr. George Bull (Harmondsworth & Baltimore 1967)

Kilgour, Raymond French *The Decline of Chivalry as shown in the French Literature of the Late Middle Ages* (Cambridge, Mass., & London 1937)

La Sale, Antoine de *Little John of Saintré* tr. Irvine Gray (London 1931)

La Tour Landry, Geoffroy de *The Book of the Knight of La Tour-Landry* ed. Thomas Wright, EETS OS 33 (London 1868)

Lecoy de la Marche, A.   *La chaire française au moyen âge* (Paris 1886)

Owst, G.R.   *Literature and Pulpit in Medieval England* (Cambridge 1933)

Whiting, B.J. 'The vows of the heron', *Speculum* 20, 1945, 261-78

Index